P9-DVV-355

FROM THE RESEARCH LIBRARY OF

RICHARD M. FIELDER

PIONEERING AND AWARD WINNING

WRITER AND PRODUCER OF

TELEVISION AND SCREEN

1925 – 2020

HIS WORKS ARE ARCHIVED AT

THE AMERICAN HERITAGE CENTER

WWW.UWYO.EDU/AHC

FILMOGRAPHY AT WWW.IMDB.COM

Also by Geoffrey Cowan

SEE NO EVIL

THE PEOPLE V. CLARENCE DARROW

THE
PEOPLE
v.
CLARENCE
DARROW

The Bribery Trial of America's
Greatest Lawyer

GEOFFREY COWAN

For Richard —
A wonderful historian + writer
who brings the American past to life for
millions —
with great respect.

July, 1993

TIMES T BOOKS

RANDOM HOUSE

Copyright © 1993 by Geoffrey Cowan

All rights reserved under International and Pan-American Copyright
Conventions. Published in the United States by Times Books, a division of
Random House, Inc., New York, and simultaneously in Canada by Random
House of Canada Limited, Toronto.

Grateful acknowledgment is made to the following for permission to reprint
previously published material:
COLUMBIA UNIVERSITY: Excerpts from the Lincoln Steffens Papers housed in the
Rare Book and Manuscript Library, Columbia University. Used by permission;
THE HUNTINGTON LIBRARY: Excerpts from the C.E.S. Wood Collection housed at the
Huntington Library, San Marino, California. Reprinted by permission of the
Huntington Library, San Marino, California; THE NEW YORK PUBLIC LIBRARY:
Excerpts from items in the National Civic Federation Records from the National
Civic Federation Records, Rare Books and Manuscripts Division, the New York
Public Library, Astor, Lenox, and Tilden Foundations. Reprinted by permission;
OHIO UNIVERSITY LIBRARY: Excerpts from the E. W. Scripps Papers housed in the
Archives and Special Collections Department at the Ohio University Library.
Used by permission; SOUTHERN CALIFORNIA LIBRARY FOR SOCIAL STUDIES AND RESEARCH:
Excerpts from the Leo Gallagher Papers housed at the Southern California
Library for Social Studies and Research. Used by permission.

Library of Congress Cataloging-in-Publication Data
Cowan, Geoffrey.
    The People v. Clarence Darrow: the bribery trial of America's
greatest lawyer / Geoffrey Cowan.
        p. cm.
    Includes index.
    ISBN 0-8129-2179-8
    1. Darrow, Clarence, 1857–1938—Trials, litigation, etc.
2. Trials (Bribery)—California—Los Angeles. 3. Lawyers—United
States—Biography. I. Title. II. Title: People v. Clarence Darrow.
KF224.D28C68 1993
345.794'94'02323—dc20
[347.9494052323]   92-56471

Manufactured in the United States of America

9 8 7 6 5 4 3 2

First Edition

DESIGN BY GLEN M. EDELSTEIN

FRONTISPIECE: Darrow in 1912 (courtesy of the *Los Angeles Times* Archives)
JACKET COVER: Darrow in 1907 (courtesy of the Bettmann Archive)

For Aileen

And in memory of

Paul Cowan
(1940–1988)

Clarence Darrow has finally come to trial. . . . The clerk, a white haired man, arose. His voice clicked as he read in mechanical tones, "The People against Clarence Darrow . . .

"The People, the State, against Clarence Darrow."

That phrase rang and rang through my brain like the monotonous beat of a gong. . . . I wondered if that was the form of the indictment in the case of other famous men who broke Society's laws.

Did Pilate read in the judgment halls, "The case of the State against the Carpenter of Nazareth?"

Was it written in the documents, "The State against Socrates?"

The State against Clarence Darrow!

Suddenly the empty mechanical phrase became to me luminous and real. The State is against him. The wording of his indictment is exact. In the eyes of the State, Clarence S. Darrow has long been an outlaw. . . .

The State was against him in the great railroad strikes. . . .

The State was against Clarence Darrow in the anthracite coal strike. . . .

The State was against Darrow when he espoused the cause of the outraged miners of Idaho. . . .

That is why today there is rejoicing in stock markets, in business offices, in financial circles, in wealthy clubs . . . because men of property, the Lumber Trust, the railroads, the Merchants and Manufacturers and now the Steel Trust have indicted Clarence Darrow.

Mary Field
Organized Labor
May 25, 1912

CONTENTS

ACKNOWLEDGMENTS

The inspiration for this book came from my friend David Rintels, author of *Clarence Darrow,* the one-man play that starred Henry Fonda. In the mid-1970s, while writing *Darrow,* David became intrigued by the unusual and explosive relationship between Darrow and Earl Rogers, the great lawyer who represented Darrow in his bribery trial. David suggested that I explore that story in a play of my own.

Like many lawyers of my generation, I had always admired Darrow; his career was one reason that I went to law school, one reason that I believed that lawyers could be a force for constructive social change, one reason that I helped to start the first general service public interest law firm. I admired Darrow so much that I—along with David Rintels, Stanley Sheinbaum, and my wife, Aileen Adams—established the Clarence Darrow Foundation, an organization that funded public interest law and gave awards to men and women whose work furthered Darrow's ideals. I was captivated by the notion of writing about Darrow but did little about it for more than a decade.

Then, in 1987, I returned to the story as a possible book. My agent, Peter Matson, embraced the project at once, and we quickly sold the idea to Peter Osnos at Random House. Throughout six years of exhausting work, Peter Osnos was an indefatigable source of encouragement, criticism, and creativity, and his superb editorial talents were wonderfully complemented by those of Ken Gellman, who matured from assistant to editor during the years of our association.

As soon as I signed a contract with Random House, I wrote to Irving Stone, whose *Clarence Darrow for the Defense* continues to inspire readers around the world. He invited me to his lovely hillside home in Beverly Hills, where he took me into his private study and offered me as much coffee and advice as I could absorb. In two lengthy meetings, Mr. Stone treated me as a young protégé. He gave me access to his papers at UCLA and offered dozens of insights into the process of researching and writing a biography, including the assurance that "everything is findable." Unfortunately, he died in 1989. Though my findings and conclusions differ sharply from his, I am eternally indebted to him for his support and inspiration.

My adventure began in earnest in the summer of 1987 when Peter Blodgett of the Huntington Library suggested that I read the remarkable papers of two of Darrow's close friends, Colonel Charles Erskine Scott Wood and Sara Bard Field. Thanks to Edwin Bingham, I soon learned that the heirs of Colonel Wood and Ms. Field had donated a complementary and almost equally interesting set of papers to the Bancroft Library at Berkeley. The Huntington and Bancroft collections offer the full story of Colonel Wood and Sara Field, who was his girlfriend and, much later, his wife. They also provide a wealth of material about Sara's sister, Mary Field.

As the book explains, Mary was Clarence Darrow's girlfriend and publicist. Sara lived with Mary in Los Angeles during the McNamara trial, and her daily love letters to Colonel Wood were filled with gossipy details about Darrow and his community of friends. Wood also kept up a regular and intimate correspondence with two other men in Los Angeles who were involved with Darrow's work: W. W. Catlin, an anarchist banker, and Larry Sullivan, a shadowy gumshoe who worked for the McNamara defense team.

The Wood papers offered an entirely fresh view of Darrow—a perspective that, once understood, was corroborated by literally dozens of credible sources. I began to understand Darrow's flaws and his failings, as well as his strengths and his triumphs.

I soon learned that, thanks to Arthur and Lila Weinberg, Mary Field's heirs had given a cache of Darrow's letters to the Newberry Library. They had deposited her other papers—including hours of interviews taped by her daughter, Margaret Parton—at the University of Oregon Library, where my work was aided by Hilary Cummings, James Fox, and a graduate student named Susan Rochester.

I found other important aspects of the radical and labor sides of the story in a number of collections. I am particularly grateful to Robert Mathes, secretary and treasurer of the Edward W. Scripps Trust, for donating Scripps's papers to the University of Ohio, and to Seth Lerner, the original Scripps archivist, who helped us wade through the new treasure trove of material. Other important manuscript collections include the AFL Papers, which are available on microfilm; the papers of Frank Morrison at Duke University, where Betty Krimminger provided invaluable research services; the McNamara Papers, which were copied for me by Anne Gilliland of the University of Cincinnati; and the papers of Fremont Older, the San Francisco Labor Council, Lincoln Steffens, and Brand Whitlock. The best collection of Darrow papers is at the Library of Congress.

The participants on the other side of the story seem to have destroyed most of their papers, but fortunately Tom Powers and Professor Dallas Jones of the University of Michigan agreed to change the rules in order to provide me with access to the purged but still extremely valuable papers of Walter Drew, commissioner of the National Erectors' Association. Other revealing information is in the papers of William Howard Taft at the Library of Congress, the papers of Moses Sherman and Otto Brant at the Sherman Library, and the Justice Department files at the National Archives, where Loel Solomon did yeoman research work. Unfortunately, neither Harrison Gray Otis nor Harry Chandler appears to have left any helpful papers, but the newspaper that they built does offer great assistance to historians through the Los Angeles Times History Center, where first Carolyn Strickler and then Craig St. Clair were unfailingly helpful. I am particularly grateful for Mr. St. Clair's assistance in procuring a score of wonderful photographs of the drama.

Throughout this project, I have been blessed with a succession of resourceful research assistants, notably Melissa Lane and Dan Johnson; they both spent months traveling around the country visiting archives and poring through mountains of material. In later years, I was also aided by the efforts of a number of UCLA undergraduates, including Laureen Lazarovici, Christina Nicolosi, Lisa Pondrom, Valerie Goo, Laura Spanjian, and Steve Loh.

Though almost everyone with firsthand knowledge of the events has long since passed away, I do want to give heartfelt thanks to Sara Field's daughter, Katherine Caldwell, for sharing childhood memories of Darrow, as well as of her mother, stepfather, and aunt. I also spent a delightful afternoon with the late Judge Lester Roth, then in his mid-nineties and still on the bench, who as a young man attended the Darrow trials and delivered newspapers to Earl Rogers. Though they were born long after the trial, Moira Ford shared memories of her father, Joseph Ford, and Oscar Lawler, Jr., described his father. I also appreciated time spent with one of Darrow's few surviving colleagues, Elmer Gertz of Chicago.

A number of descendants of the participants kindly tried to help me with my research. The list includes descendants of William Burns, including Bruce Burns; of Bert Franklin, particularly John, Michael, and Terry Franklin; of John Fredericks, including Doris Dohn, John and Debra Fort, Mrs. William Hilker, and Jim and Carol Toney; of Earl Rogers, including Kathy Sloane, who tracked down a wonderful picture of her great-grandfather; of Olaf Tvietmoe, including Owen Tvietmoe. John Fort remembered his grandmother sitting by a huge fire in her Bel Air home one August day shortly after John Frederick's death. He asked her why she was throwing papers into the fire on such a hot afternoon. "I'm burning your grandfather's papers," she told him. "If they come to light it will destroy half the people in this town."

On one exceptionally sad occasion, I was too late to find what I was looking for. In 1932, Margaret Johannsen wrote a letter to her close friend Mary Field stating that she had kept all of Mary's wonderful letters, starting with those written during the Darrow trial. She urged Mary to have them published. After several weeks, I finally tracked down Anton and Margaret Johannsen's granddaughter, Marion Despard. "I had those letters when I came from Florida to California a few years ago," Mrs. Despard said, "but I haven't been able to find them since. They must have been lost in the move."

Among others who helped with my research were Len Small and Don des Lauriers, who found records of Darrow in Kankakee, Illinois; John Van de Kamp, who, while attorney general of California, granted access to the files of former California attorney general U. S. Webb; Ira Reiner, who, while district attorney of Los Angeles, aided my efforts to find files going back some eighty years; Randy Tietjen, who shared research he is compiling for a book of Darrow's letters; John Miller, who introduced me to Katherine Caldwell; Henry Christian, for comments on Louis Adamic and his papers; Leo Cherne, who tried to find some old files; Professor Jacqueline K. Parker, for discussing her oral interview with Helen Valeska Bary; Mort Levine, Elaine Levine, Donna Harris, and Lisa Christenson, for their efforts to find a 1912 diary kept by Cora Older; Bruce Paisner, for assistance in tracking down old files of William Randolph Hearst; Professors Gary Fink and James Goodrich, for attempts to locate information about former Missouri governor Fred Gardner; labor editor Roger Sheldon, for research on the Carpenters Union; Lou Castrini, for his efforts to dig into the old files of the Merchants and Manufacturers Association; Ed Mosk, who had a lifetime fascination with this episode in Darrow's life and the life of Los Angeles; and archivists Vickie Booth, E. Cheryl Schnirring, Ralph Pugh, Katharine Vogel, William Selm, Robert Glass, Ken Craven, Peter Hoefer, Gisela S. Terrell, Norma Ortiz-Karp, John Schwoerke, Philip Cronewett, Susan Boone, and John Hoffman.

Though the Federal Bureau of Investigation was not formed until a decade after the end of this story, I made countless requests for files under the Freedom of Information Act, hoping that some gem would turn up. Ultimately, I obtained several pounds of materials, but nothing of use. Nevertheless, I want to thank the FBI's hardworking staff and, in particular, FBI historian Susan Rosenfeld Falb.

Several friends and colleagues read drafts of the book, offering invaluable advice and insights. I am particularly grateful to Lucy

Eisenberg, who read early chapters; David Rintels and Leroy Aarons, who each read two drafts of the book; and Max Byrd, William Deverell, Roger Lowenstein, Kevin O'Connell, Ron Olson, Jim Rosenau, Phil Ryan, Rose Styron, Henry Weinstein, and my sister, Holly Cowan Shulman. Katherine Caldwell and Elmer Gertz also read the manuscript and offered helpful comments.

So much changes during the years it takes to write a serious biography. One of my children, Gabriel, grew from childhood to manhood; the other, Mandy, from kindergarden to, as she says, "double digits." They were a source of constant inspiration, support, and understanding as I snuck upstairs at night and on weekends to the loft office where I lived with Darrow's ghost.

During those same years, my best friend and best editor—Paul Cowan—fought a heroic, losing battle with leukemia. This book is dedicated to his memory.

And it is dedicated to the woman who above all others believed in this project and in me. Turning from her work as counsel to victims of rape, child abuse, and incest, Aileen read countless drafts, offered unfailingly wise counsel, and listened cheerfully to accounts of the romantic intrigues and legal and political battles of women and men who died long before either of us was born. Aileen managed to help me love both the past and the present and to find special meaning in both.

CAST OF CHARACTERS

IN 1911

CLARENCE DARROW—Perhaps the greatest lawyer in American history, Darrow represented a range of clients, including labor leaders such as Eugene Debs and corporate leaders such as William Randolph Hearst. His powerful pleas on the behalf of poor coal workers in the anthracite coal arbitration of 1903 had electrified the nation. His novels, philosophical essays, and speeches, as well as his celebrated cases, had won a wide audience of passionate admirers. But by 1911, many close friends felt that he had betrayed his earlier principles, that he had come to love money and fame too much, that his brilliant mind was now serving the rich more than the poor. What's more, at fifty-four years of age he was feeling tired and old. He had achieved a great triumph in 1907, winning an acquittal for Big Bill Haywood and other labor leaders accused of murdering former Idaho governor Frank Steunenberg. But that victory had taken a terrible physical and financial toll. Never again did he intend to take on a grueling case in a city far from his comfortable Chicago home. When James and John McNamara were charged with committing the "Crime of the Century," bombing the *Los Angeles Times* and killing twenty men, he resisted taking the case—until the pleas of his friends in labor forced him back into active duty.

DARROW'S COMMUNITY OF FRIENDS

Darrow had an incredibly wide range of friends throughout the United States. For purposes of this story, however, a few people stand out.

R U B Y   D A R R O W — A vivacious young society reporter, she married Darrow in 1903, when he was forty-six and she was thirty-four. Four years later, after the Haywood trial, she nursed Darrow back to health and made him promise never again to take on such an all-consuming case. Having established a comfortable and prosperous life with Darrow in Chicago, Ruby resented his decision to move to Los Angeles to represent the McNamaras.

M A R Y   F I E L D — Darrow's protégée and girlfriend, she made the transition from social worker to radical journalist after meeting Darrow in 1908. Against Darrow's wishes, she came to Los Angeles to cover the trial—and to resume their relationship.

S A R A   F I E L D   E H R G O T T — Mary's younger sister was trapped in a loveless marriage with a Baptist minister. When they moved to Portland, Oregon, in 1910, Darrow introduced her to his friend Colonel Charles Erskine Scott Wood, with whom she soon had a torrid affair.

C O L O N E L   C H A R L E S   E R S K I N E   S C O T T   W O O D — He was so successful as a corporate lawyer that Portland society accepted his eccentricities, his devotion to poetry, and his friendship with anarchist leader Emma Goldman. Admiring Wood's legal skills and his poetry, Darrow asked him to sign on as cocounsel in the McNamara case. Wood refused, partly because he distrusted Darrow's legal methods. But he encouraged Sara to go to Los Angeles to cover the trial, live with Mary, and send him intimate reports.

L I N C O L N   S T E F F E N S — The famous muckraking journalist who uncovered stories of bribery and corruption, many of which were collected in his book *Shame of the Cities.* He covered the San Francisco graft trials of 1907–1908, where he became friends with detective William J. Burns and journalist Fremont Older. In 1911, he came to Los Angeles to report on *why* the McNamaras had bombed the *Times,* not whether they had. He soon set out to try to settle the case.

FREMONT OLDER—A crusading San Francisco editor who helped to uncover graft and corruption, Older became disillusioned when minor participants were jailed and several major corporate leaders went free. He and Steffens were confidants of Darrow, but they also maintained close ties to the prosecution's chief detective, William J. Burns.

E. W. SCRIPPS—An outspoken friend of the worker, Scripps owned the United Press and a series of labor-oriented papers, including the Los Angeles *Record.* Semiretired in La Jolla, south of Los Angeles, he followed radical politics with intense interest and did not hesitate to pepper Darrow with advice.

EUGENE DEBS—Darrow's first great client, Debs organized the railroad workers' union and then the Socialist Party, becoming its presidential candidate in five elections, starting in 1900. By 1911, Debs had become disillusioned with Darrow, claiming that he "loved money too much." Nevertheless, he helped organize a national campaign to build public pressure to help Darrow free the McNamaras.

W. W. CATLIN—An old Darrow friend from Chicago, Catlin had moved to Los Angeles before the trials. Along with Debs, Wood, and many others, Catlin felt Darrow had lost his moral center and only cared about personal glory and financial gain.

DARROW'S CHICAGO WORLD

JOHN PETER ALTGELD—A radical judge and governor who was almost a father figure to Darrow, Altgeld's career ended, in part, because he courageously followed Darrow's advice and pardoned the so-called Haymarket Anarchists in 1893. As Altgeld's world crumbled, Darrow offered him a place in his law firm, staying loyal to the last. He died in 1902.

EDGAR LEE MASTERS—Later a great poet best known for the *Spoon River Anthology,* he was Darrow's law partner in 1911. Though he resented Darrow's decision to take the McNamara case, he spent hundreds of uncompensated hours helping Darrow prepare his own defense.

KEY FIGURES IN THE MCNAMARA CASE

THE DEFENDANTS

JOHN JOSEPH (J. J.) MCNAMARA—The treasurer of the Bridge and Structural Iron Workers' Union, McNamara was a beefily handsome, courageous, and respected labor leader. A self-made lawyer and a devout Catholic, he quickly became a hero to the working masses.

JAMES BARNABAS (JIM) MCNAMARA, AKA JAMES BRICE—An anemic, foul-mouthed apprentice printer, Jim was constantly in trouble and seemed eclipsed by his older brother—until his brother gave him the chance to start planting explosives.

MATTHEW SCHMIDT—A radical labor organizer who followed Anton Johannsen from Chicago to San Francisco, Schmidt helped Jim McNamara plan the *Times* bombing and was named in the criminal indictments. Schmidt managed to evade the police and detectives for several years.

DAVID CAPLAN—A San Francisco grocer and anarchist, he also helped plan the bombing, was named in the criminal indictments, and managed to hide out underground.

DARROW'S DEFENSE TEAM
IN THE MCNAMARA CASE

JOB HARRIMAN—A tubercular one-time Socialist Party vice-presidential candidate (1900), Harriman moved to Los Angeles for his health and quickly became a major force in both labor and socialist circles. He was the McNamaras' chief lawyer until Darrow arrived on the scene, and was the odds-on candidate to become the first Socialist mayor of Los Angeles.

LECOMPTE DAVIS—A noted Los Angeles criminal lawyer.

JOSEPH SCOTT—A powerful Irish orator and business-oriented lawyer, Scott served as the elected head of the Los Angeles school board.

CYRUS MCNUTT—A retired Indiana judge.

FRED MOORE—A radical lawyer who specialized in representing anarchists and Wobblies, Moore worked on the McNamara case as a member of LeCompte Davis's law firm, but quickly shifted to other matters. His later cases included the San Diego free-speech fight and the famous 1912 textile strike in Lawrence, Massachusetts, where he represented the IWW strikers.

JOHN HARRINGTON—The first employee in the McNamara defense, Harrington was, according to Darrow, "the best evidence gatherer I have ever seen." The men had worked together in Chicago, where Harrington was an investigative lawyer for various companies. The unfortunate similarity between the names of John Harrington, the lawyer-detective, and Job Harriman, the Socialist lawyer, often caused confusion, though the men had little else in common.

BERT FRANKLIN—A former detective on the staff of the county sheriff and then the U.S. Marshal, Franklin actively sought employment with Darrow. He was hired as chief jury investigator, reporting directly to Darrow.

LARRY SULLIVAN—A colorful and controversial former prize-fighter, bar owner, banker, and anarchist sympathizer, Sullivan was hired by Darrow at Colonel Wood's suggestion.

BERT HAMMERSTROM—Ruby Darrow's younger brother, Hammerstrom spent the summer of 1911 doing undercover work for the defense.

FRANK WOLFE—A Socialist journalist and former editor of the Los Angeles *Herald,* Wolfe became a publicist for the McNamara defense team while also running as a Socialist candidate for the city council.

THE DETECTIVES

WILLIAM J. BURNS—The most celebrated (and self-promoting) detective in American history, Burns wrote magazine features promoting himself as the American equivalent of Sherlock Holmes. Having secured the evidence in the famous San Francisco graft trials four years earlier, he had devoted friends (Steffens and Older) and intense enemies (Harrison Gray Otis and Earl Rogers) in surprising places. He was hired by the city to find the men who had blown up the *Times.* He also hoped to collect about $100,000 in reward money that had been promised to whoever found the guilty parties.

GUY BIDDINGER—A former Chicago police officer, Biddinger was Burns's right-hand man.

SAMUEL BROWNE—The chief detective for the district attorney's office, Browne felt that he—not Burns—was entitled to the $100,000 reward for capturing the McNamaras.

JAMES BADORF—A private detective, Badorf was on the payroll of Walter Drew and the National Erectors' Association (NEA).

ROBERT FOSTER—A former New York police officer, Foster was on the payroll of the NEA.

THE PROSECUTORS

CAPTAIN JOHN FREDERICKS — The tall, lean, righteous district attorney of Los Angeles, Fredericks was a hero to the antiliquor forces, who hoped that a celebrated victory would carry him into the governor's mansion.

JOSEPH FORD — A young, recently widowed Irish intellectual, Ford had a combative style that was a liability as well as an asset. Though on the public payroll, Ford also represented Detective Burns in his effort to collect the reward money for capturing the McNamaras.

THE JUDGE

WALTER BORDWELL — An establishment lawyer and potential candidate for high office, Bordwell lived at the city's exclusive California Club.

THE BRIBED JURORS

ROBERT BAIN — A Civil War veteran, now in his seventies, Bain had suffered financial reversals and was working as a carpenter to make payments on a new house.

GEORGE LOCKWOOD — Another Civil War veteran and a former county employee, Lockwood had retired to an alfalfa ranch in Covina.

WITNESSES

ORTIE MCMANIGAL — The star witness for the prosecution, McManigal claimed to be Jim McNamara's cohort in a national dynamite conspiracy organized by the International Association of Bridge and Structural Iron Workers.

EMMA MCMANIGAL — The state hoped that Ortie's wife would be another star witness, but Darrow hoped that she would help the defense, instead, by talking her husband out of testifying.

GEORGE PHILLIPS—An employee of the Giant Powder Works in San Francisco, Phillips said he could identify the men who bought the explosives.

KURT DIEKELMAN—A Los Angeles hotel employee, Diekelman talked with Jim McNamara on the evening of the *Times* bombing.

FRANK ECKHOFF—A longtime McNamara friend from Cincinnati, Eckhoff decided to cooperate with the prosecution.

LABOR LEADERS

SAMUEL GOMPERS—A former cigar maker, Gompers did as much as anyone to build the American Federation of Labor into a nationally credible and generally conservative union—only to have his union and his career threatened by the sensational charges against the McNamaras. After forcing Darrow to take the case, Gompers quickly emerged as point man for the national defense.

FRANK MORRISON—The secretary-treasurer of the AFL, Morrison had exclusive control over the collection and distribution of money for the McNamara Defense Fund.

ED NOCKLES—A Chicago labor leader, Nockles was a close friend of Darrow's.

OLAF TVIETMOE—Called "the Viking" because of his Norwegian birth, icy temperament, and powerful bearing, some considered Tvietmoe the most important labor leader on the West Coast. He was secretary-treasurer of the California Building Trades Union, editor of its publication, *Organized Labor,* and head of the racist but popular Asiatic Exclusion League. As a leader of the effort to organize workers in Los Angeles, he (along with his ally, Anton Johannsen) was widely believed to have arranged for the *Times* bombing.

ANTON JOHANNSEN—Built like a fire hydrant, with an anarchist's temperament, and with a boisterous laugh that earned him the label "the Laugh of Labor," Johannsen was as warm as Tvietmoe was cold. He and his artistic wife won the friendship of all of the radicals, particularly Mary Field. Johannsen worked as state organizer for the California Building Trades Union.

FRANK RYAN—President of the Bridge and Structural Iron Workers' union, Ryan claimed to know nothing of the *Times* bombing, but later was charged as a ringleader in a series of seventy bombings around the country.

EUGENE CLANCY—The West Coast head of the Iron Workers, Clancy brought Jim McNamara to the Coast.

BUSINESS AND COMMUNITY LEADERS

HARRISON GRAY OTIS—The outspoken and opinionated owner of the *Los Angeles Times,* Otis drove around town in a car with a cannon on the hood and used the paper as a cudgel in his crusade for industrial freedom. The dynamiters placed a bomb at his home, as well as at his paper. Though he hated the murders at the *Times,* he was at least equally concerned about his real estate ventures in the San Fernando Valley, which would be jeopardized by a Socialist victory at the polls, and his one-million-acre ranch in Mexico, which was threatened by the Mexican Revolution.

HARRY CHANDLER—Otis's polished and financially astute son-in-law and real estate partner, Chandler was Otis's heir apparent.

FELIX J. ZEEHANDELAAR—Secretary of the Merchants and Manufacturers Association, and a key Otis ally and retainer, Zeehandelaar's home was also targeted by the dynamiters.

WALTER DREW—As commissioner of the National Erectors' Association, Drew was responsible for tracking down the men who had been placing bombs at construction sites around the country. He was based in New York, but spent much of his time in Indianapolis arranging for a national dynamite conspiracy trial that he and his clients considered far more important than the McNamara case.

OSCAR LAWLER—Having recently returned to Los Angeles from a job in the Taft administration, Lawler took charge of the West Coast effort to prosecute the labor leaders who had been involved in the national dynamite conspiracy.

MEYER LISSNER—Sometimes called the leading reformer in Los Angeles, Lissner helped elect Hiram Johnson as governor and then became his clearinghouse for patronage. Though he hated General Otis for his reactionary and anti-Semitic views, Lissner was even more troubled by the Socialist Party and the threat posed by Job Harriman's campaign for mayor.

THOMAS E. GIBBON—A leader in municipal affairs, Gibbon was friendly with the reformers and with General Otis.

OTTO F. BRANT—Head of the Title and Trust Company, Brant occasionally served as a front man for Otis and Chandler when they wanted to keep their participation secret.

DARROW'S DEFENSE TEAM IN HIS OWN TRIAL

EARL ROGERS—As general counsel of the Merchants and Manufacturers Association, and the author of the city's notorious antipicketing ordinance, Rogers was known, to use Debs's phrase, as the "most notorious capitalist retainer" in Los Angeles. But he was also the city's most brilliant, if unorthodox, criminal lawyer—the triumphant defender of the corporate defendants in the San Francisco graft trials and the one man who seemed capable of preserving Darrow's freedom.

HORACE APPEL—A brilliant, fiery Mexican-Jewish lawyer, Appel tended to compete with his famous cocounsel for the public's attention.

JERRY GEISLER—In his first case as a bag-carrier and researcher for Darrow and Rogers, Geisler grew to admire both men. He later became one of the most celebrated criminal lawyers in Los Angeles. To his dying day, he kept pictures of Darrow and Rogers on his desk.

CYRUS MCNUTT—The only member of the McNamara team to serve on the Darrow defense, McNutt died before the trial began and was replaced by Horace Appel.

THE JUDGE IN DARROW'S TRIAL

GEORGE HUTTON—Kindly and conciliatory, Hutton was an inexperienced criminal court judge and no match for the powerful lawyers arrayed on both sides of the case.

****

****

PROLOGUE

O N A RAINY NIGHT in late December, 1911, Clarence Darrow sadly walked along the dark and almost deserted Los Angeles boulevards to a tiny side street that he had visited countless times during the past six months. The warm rain washed away the faint smell of horse manure that still gave some of the city's streets a pungent odor. A few cars passed him, and then a horse and buggy, a remnant of an era that was fast fading into history.

Slouched in an oversized raincoat brought months earlier from his lovely home in Chicago, Darrow was a weary and lonely figure as he climbed the steps of 1110 Ingraham Street, a block south of Wilshire Boulevard near downtown Los Angeles. He felt as deserted as the night. Almost all of his friends had abandoned him.

A month earlier he had been a national icon, brought to Los Angeles by popular demand to represent the McNamara brothers in a trial hailed as the greatest labor case, the greatest murder case, the greatest political trial in the country's history. He had come West as the leader of a massive band of radicals, intellectuals, workers, and reporters, who were prepared to follow him anywhere.

Now they felt betrayed—and he was alone. His wife, Ruby, was still on his side, but he had never been able to talk freely with her about his cases or his problems. For the most part, she knew only what she read in the papers. Throughout his life, he had always found companionship outside the home. On this night of desperation, he felt the need for his girlfriend, not his wife.

****

When Mary Field heard the knock at the door, her heavy long brown hair was unfastened for the night; it hung down past her waist. She quickly put on a loose-fitting thrift-shop bathrobe and opened the door. For almost four years, Mary had been Darrow's admirer, protégée, ally, and lover—the other woman, who knew his soul intimately.

Darrow was standing in the corridor, soaking wet, his thin brown hair in disarray, his weathered skin more wrinkled than ever, his sad blue eyes swollen from sleepless nights and tearful days. He looked even more slovenly than usual, his raincoat weighted down at the pockets.

He asked if he could come in, and Mary said he could, of course.

Mary's tiny flat was almost barren, her few belongings already packed for the voyage north. Tired of being an afterthought in her lover's life, treated as "a hot water bag," she planned to leave for San Francisco in the morning. Darrow slumped down in a wooden chair at the kitchen table, under a bare overhead light hanging on a cord. He surprised Mary by pulling a bottle of whiskey out of a coat pocket and putting it on the table. Darrow usually didn't drink. She brought him two glasses and he poured a shot in each.

"Molly," he said. "I'm going to kill myself." He pulled a revolver out of his other trench coat pocket and put it on the table, beside the bottle of whiskey.

"They're going to indict me for bribing the McNamara jury," he said. "I can't stand the disgrace." And he started to cry.

Her heart breaking for him, Mary smoked an endless chain of cigarettes as she used all of the arguments that she knew to talk him out of suicide. She spoke to him of religion, reflecting her own strict Baptist background. But Darrow didn't put much stock in God. Then she said it would be wrong to kill himself, that people would always think the worst and his legacy would be destroyed. The only way to save his reputation was to stand and fight, to be bold and courageous.

And so it went, on into the early hours of the morning.

Finally he gave in. "Well, Molly," he said at last, "maybe you're right."

He got up slowly and put the half-empty bottle in one pocket and the revolver in the other. Then he walked sadly out into the rain.

Less than a month later, Clarence Darrow was indicted for bribery.

❊ ❊ ❊ ❊

Some eighty years after his trial and fifty-five years after his death, Clarence Darrow enjoys a remarkable reputation as a man of courage and conscience, an inspiration to thousands of American lawyers. To the public, he is best known for his defense of John Thomas Scopes's right to teach Darwin's theory of evolution, brilliantly dramatized in the play and movie *Inherit the Wind;* and for his plea for clemency on behalf of Nathan Leopold and Richard Loeb, the teenagers from suburban Chicago whose grisly effort to commit the perfect murder was told in the novel and film *Compulsion.* More broadly, he is known as the century's greatest champion of labor and the poor, the "attorney for the damned."

But the public knows little, if anything, about Darrow's most dramatic and traumatic case—the trial of Clarence Darrow. What is known about Darrow's own trial is an incomplete and, in important respects, misleading version of events that has effectively served for half a century to protect his reputation against charges that he was an adulterer and a corruptor of American justice. Sugarcoated accounts of this seminal period in Darrow's life appear in two magnificent books that have defined Darrow for posterity: his autobiography, published in 1932, and Irving Stone's *Clarence Darrow for the Defense,* published nine years later. Both books inspired thousands of committed young women and men to become lawyers; they deserve a special place on any shelf of popular literature about the law. But in fundamental respects, they should not be viewed any more uncritically than Parson Weems's inventive portrait of George

Washington as the boy who couldn't lie to his father after chopping down a cherry tree.

There is, of course, nothing unusual about an autobiography that mists over some troubling facts in the course of remembering a life well lived. Irving Stone's decision to skim over some hard truths, however, deserves more comment. Just after writing *Lust for Life,* he entered into an agreement with Clarence Darrow's widow, Ruby, to purchase and use her late husband's papers, and to cooperate in the writing of a major biography. From Ruby's perspective, at least, they were engaged in a collaborative venture, "a memorium to our beloved and worthy C.D."

"Aren't we a pair of honest-to-goodness friends of Clarence Darrow?" she asked, "trying to do him justice, and honor, and make the history of his life and career as dignified and decent, yet truthful as possible?" For the Los Angeles chapters, she begged Stone to treat Darrow charitably—"You cannot possibly doubt that Mr. D. was framed," she insisted in one letter—and she beseeched him to ignore Darrow's affair with Mary Field Parton. "I shudder at the indecency of Mary Field Parton, for it is nothing less than that that she should force herself upon you and try to force herself into the biography," Ruby wrote. In the end, Stone glossed over some difficult and unpleasant aspects of the Los Angeles story, exonerating Darrow of bribery and only indirectly mentioning "a clever and talented woman" who "caused Ruby hours of anguish" in Los Angeles.

Faced directly, however, the story of Darrow's trial defines the man and the age in which he lived, offering a far more complex account that can help us understand our own troubled times.

❋ ❋ ❋

The trial took place in 1912, in an age of industrial violence, a second Civil War, where the forces of government and industry often conspired to keep workers, immigrants, and revolutionaries in their place. Throughout America, and particularly in Los Angeles, industrialists generally controlled the press and the office of the local prosecutor. Businessmen hired teams of private detectives to do their bidding.

Their power was reinforced, not held in check, by the courts. After all, as Darrow quipped, "You can't get a judge unless he's a lawyer and served the rich—or hopes to serve the rich." Judges regularly invalidated progressive legislation that would assure safe working conditions or limit the exploitation of child labor. Speaking for reformers everywhere, Theodore Roosevelt railed against decisions made by judges who "exert their power in protecting those who least need protection and hardly use their power at all in the interest of those who most need protection." His Progressive Party made court reform—including the popular election and recall of judges—a centerpiece of its 1912 presidential campaign.

Even juries couldn't be trusted, since they generally were limited to property holders, who tended to side with the rich against the poor.

With the deck so heavily stacked in favor of big business, some radicals were tempted to palm a few cards of their own. In a sense, their attitude was the inevitable result of a system that seemed inherently unfair. Their tactics might not be nice or ethical—or even legal—but they were designed to produce a kind of rough justice.

Clarence Darrow took that philosophy to its logical extreme. Reared as a committed if somewhat lonely idealist in rural Ohio, he launched his career in Chicago during an era that called for principled radicals. But during a quarter of a century of personal and national transformation, he was corrupted by what one friend called "the awful compulsion of the age, to make money" and by personal tragedies and experiences that led him to conclude that efforts at economic reform—and, indeed, life itself—were essentially futile. By 1911, he had become, in the words of one friendly journalist, a "moral cynic." A bit unfairly, old friends commented on his bitterness, his hopelessness, and the absence of any remaining ideals or convictions. In fact, Darrow did have some ideals—but he had lost his moral compass. He had also lost the respect of most of his one-time admirers, for most men and women who shared his contempt for the system were not prepared to abuse or abandon it. For them, Darrow's indictment for jury bribery only offered further cause to disdain or, worse, dismiss their wayward friend.

Against the backdrop of a legal and industrial system that was seeking to find its own moorings, Darrow's trial offered him a unique chance to seek something more than an acquittal. He asked the jury—and his friends—for understanding, acceptance, redemption, and forgiveness. This is a deeply personal story, but it also offers lessons from which we all can learn, in an era when society itself seems again to have lost its moorings—where the gap between races and classes has grown once again; where immigrants are again blamed for the ills of society; where many leaders of business and government are again being compromised by the promise of easy and quick financial gain; and where the courts are, once again, generally on the side of the rich and the powerful.

The trial of Clarence Darrow offers a chance to reflect again on the meaning of justice in America.

Part I

THE EDUCATION OF
CLARENCE DARROW

Chapter One

GROWING UP

C LARENCE SEWARD DARROW WAS born in Farmdale, Ohio, on April 18, 1857, and grew up in the nearby hamlet of Kinsman. He hated his first name. He called it "inane," an embarrassment, a "cross" he had to bear—and he never forgave his parents for choosing it.

He had other reasons to resent his parents. Though they were freethinkers politically, Amirus and Emily Darrow retained the cold Puritan bearing of their Connecticut forebears. He described them in his autobiography and, even more revealingly, in *Farmington,* a haunting account of his childhood in rural America. Probably neither story is precisely true, but each is as accurate as Darrow's sensibilities would allow. Though styled as a novel, Darrow called *Farmington,* which he wrote in his mid-forties, "an expurgated story of a life," "neither fact nor fiction." The names of the characters and locations are changed, but virtually all of the other verifiable details and observations are accurate.

Amirus and Emily Darrow were so undemonstrative, Clarence wrote, that "I cannot recall that my mother ever gave me a kiss or a caress. . . . I have no feeling of a time when either my father or my mother took me, or any other member of our family, in their arms."

To demonstrate affection would have seemed a sign of weakness, not love.

Darrow knew that something was missing. "As I look back," he said, "I do not have the feeling of closeness that should unite the parent and the child." The house was filled with rigid rules that were enforced with the threat of a whipping. He often "went to bed to toss and turn of the promised punishment, and in the morning, however bright the sunshine, the world was wrapped in gloom." His agnostic parents forced their children to go to church and Sunday school, but never allowed them to believe in Santa Claus.

On the last day of school one June, Amirus Darrow came to hear his son and several of his son's classmates deliver prepared speeches. That night, Clarence's father lavished praise on a young red-haired speaker, predicting that he would be a great orator and make a mark in the world. "I would have given everything I possessed if only my father had said that about me," Darrow recalled. "But my father said not a single word."

Instead, Amirus Darrow hounded Clarence about the need to study Latin and Greek, and after a time the barbs became exceedingly painful. Young Clarence dreamed of becoming an author, but his father always told him that he "could never write a book" unless he mastered Latin and Greek. For Clarence, who had no aptitude for ancient languages, it was a constant, painful battle. His father repeatedly pointed out that Darrow's older brother had managed to learn languages. What was wrong with *him*? Why couldn't he be like his brother? Then Amirus would launch into his lecture about John Stuart Mill.

"At a very early age I was told again and again that John Stuart Mill began studying Greek when he was only three years old," Darrow recalled. "I thought then, as I do today, that he must have had a very cruel father."

❋ ❋ ❋ ❋

Darrow's mother died in 1872, after a long illness. Clarence had just turned fifteen. Trying to remember her thirty years later, Darrow was certain that she must have been kind, but he could not recall "any great affection that I had for her." He admired her industry and the way that she held a poor family together and still found time to keep abreast of current affairs. But he did not remember loving her—or ever telling her that he did. Those unspoken words were a permanent source of guilt. He felt "endless regret" that he had done nothing to "lighten the burdens of her life" by telling her that he loved her.

Though he was the fifth child in a family of seven, he was not much closer to his sisters and brothers than to his parents. "We never said anything about our love for each other, and our nearness seemed to bring about our antagonism more than our love," he reported. They would, of course, come to each other's aid when necessary, but they spent as little time together as possible.

Instead, young Clarence found endless joy with friends in a magical Tom Sawyer world where, as he remembered it, he loved swimming in the river, ice skating, sledding, nutting, and blackberrying. His fondest memories were of baseball, his "one unalloyed joy in life." The boys played during the lunch hour at school, on summer evenings, and on Saturday afternoons. For all of his successes in court, for all of his fame, Darrow would write when he was seventy-five that "never has life held anything quite so entrancing as baseball."

As he grew older, Darrow romanticized the happier moments of his youth, and he tried to mask the pain. But the dichotomy between the joyous world of play and his bitter life at home undoubtedly affected the relations that he developed with his own family as he grew older. "In great trouble or in a crisis of life we seem to cling to our kindred, and stand by them, and expect them to stand by us," he observed; "and yet, in the little things, day by day, we look for our companionship and affection somewhere else."

So, too, would the adult Clarence Darrow seek companionship and affection outside the home.

❊ ❊ ❊ ❊

Emotionally distant as they were, Darrow's parents offered much to admire and emulate. From them, he learned to love books, political independence, and grand ideals and ideas. He did appreciate his mother's hard work and how she had kept the family together in financially austere times, and her commitment to the rights of women and blacks. But his father was his chief inspiration. "More than anything else," he said, "my father influenced the course of my life and its thought and activities. Above all things else his deep convictions and his devotion to ideals as he conceived them did the most to keep alive a certain sense of duty to what seemed to me the good and the true."

Amirus Darrow was reared as a Methodist and attended Allegheny College, a Methodist institution in Meadville, Pennsylvania. In his senior year he was charged, perhaps unfairly, with misusing the key to the debating society hall, and he was expelled from the school. Insisting that he was innocent, Amirus appealed to the board of trustees. Ultimately the board offered to reinstate him—not because he was innocent, but because the expulsion had violated the school's charter. In order to return, they ruled he would have to acknowledge misconduct, accept a reprimand from the college president, and promise to obey the school's rules in the future. It was not a satisfactory result. Deeply stung by the episode, Amirus decided to complete his studies at the city's more liberal Unitarian seminary, earning a degree in theology.

Before long, Amirus found that even Unitarianism was too rigid for his beliefs. He was too much of a skeptic to preach religion to others, so he left the church and tried to develop a theology of his own. It wasn't easy. Once he abandoned the Unitarian Church, as his son later observed, Amirus found himself "out on the open sea without a rudder or a compass, and with no port in sight."

Instead of saving souls, Amirus Darrow wound up burying bodies as a simple undertaker and wood craftsman in Kinsman, Ohio, a small town located about twenty miles west of Meadville, Pennsylvania. He didn't have a head for business and always lived at the margin, but his devotion to reading, study, and debate earned him a reputation as the most learned man in Kinsman. Not everyone in town considered that to be a compliment. "The old parson and the doctor were the only neighbors who seemed able to understand the language he spoke," Clarence recalled.

The Darrows lived in the God-fearing, Christian agricultural heart-land, where men were expected to work and believe, not to read and doubt, and Amirus suffered for his eccentricities. Almost unconsciously, Clarence "learned to understand the tragedy of [his father's] obscure and hidden life, and the long and bitter contest he had waged within the narrow shadow of the stubborn little town." He was called an "atheist" and deemed "the village infidel." However alienated they may have felt from their father and from each other, the Darrow children did have a certain enforced bond. They had to fend for themselves intellectually, to learn and debate, to feel like "strangers in a more or less hostile land," and to find solace in the knowledge that there were other infidels elsewhere in America.

Their home became known as a safe house for itinerant philosophers making their way across America and as a stop on the Underground Railway, offering succor to slaves on their way to freedom. When he was a small child, his parents told Clarence stories of "Frederick Douglass, Parker Pillsbury, Sojourner Truth, Wendell Phillips, and the rest of that advance army of reformers, black and white, who went up and down the land arousing the dulled conscience of the people to a sense of justice to the slave. They used to make my father's home their stopping place, and any sort of vacant room was the forum where they told of the black man's wrongs." Late at night, Clarence would lie in his bed, listening to their philosophical discussions. His parents were such passionate abolitionists that they named their son for William Henry Seward, the outspoken abolitionist who later served as Abraham Lincoln's secretary of state. No matter how much he resented the name Clarence, the boy could take a certain pride in his middle name.

"I could never be thankful enough that my father was honest and simple, and that his love of truth and justice had grown into his being as naturally as the oaks were rooted to the earth along the little stream," Darrow wrote. And those qualities became rooted to Clarence Seward Darrow as well.

❋ ❋ ❋ ❋

Fortunately, there were those in Trumbull County who considered a Friday or Saturday night debate to be as exciting as a high school basketball game is considered today. As the leading town dissenters, one or more of the Darrows was often invited to participate. Clarence soon found that he excelled at debate as well as at baseball. Week after week, as he got older, he would appear for the unpopular side, speaking to a crowd of churchgoing farmers and small businessmen, seeking a way to persuade them that everything that they had long held sacred could somehow be squared with views that they found abhorrent.

Honing his skills in front of that audience, Darrow found that he could win the minds of his listeners with a homespun blend of warmth, humor, and simple phrasing—and a well-placed and biting attack on his opponent's inevitable intellectual inconsistencies. It was that skill—his brilliant gift of oratory, orneriness, and originality—that prepared Darrow to become America's greatest lawyer.

He also had another unusual talent—or affliction. Whether inherited or acquired, Darrow had an exceptional ability to feel what others felt, to sense their pain and adopt it as his own. It was almost a sixth sense, like the ability of someone with arthritis to feel a change in the weather, or a psychic's ability to hold an article of clothing and visualize the last person to wear it. Darrow felt the pain of those who were starving in poverty, of children forced to work in coal mines, of men sitting on death row waiting to die. "Not only could I put myself in the other person's place, but I could not avoid doing so," he wrote. "My sympathies always went out to the weak, the suffering and the poor." To an extraordinary degree, Darrow felt their anguish—and, with his uncommon gift of language, he had the ability to communicate their grief to any audience that would listen to his evocative words.

❄ ❄ ❄ ❄

If Clarence was inspired by his father's idealism, he was also motivated by Amirus's professional failures, and goaded by his parental scoldings. He was determined to achieve economic security, make a name for himself, write a book—and maybe even deliver a memorable speech or two—all without having mastered either grammar or Greek.

At first, his chances seemed no more promising than his father's. In 1873, about a year after his mother's death, Darrow left home for Allegheny College, but, like Amirus, he didn't earn a degree there.

In fact, he only lasted a year. When Amirus Darrow sank perilously close to economic ruin in the financial panic that seized the nation that fall, Clarence dropped out of college and found a job teaching school.

Three years later, with the family more secure, he followed in his father's footsteps again. This time it was to the law school at the University of Michigan. His father had spent a year studying law at Michigan during the last year of the Civil War, in 1864–65, when Clarence was seven. But after the war ended he had dropped out and gone back to making funeral caskets. Like his father, Clarence only lasted for a year in law school—but this time he decided to see the enterprise through to completion. In those days it was common to study for the bar through apprenticeship in a law firm, and Darrow, who didn't much like formal education—or formal anything, for that matter—found work with a small law office in Youngstown, Ohio.

A year later, just after his twenty-first birthday, he persuaded a committee of examiners to let him join the bar.

For the next nine years, Darrow had a rather pedestrian law practice in Ashtabula, Ohio, settling disputes between farmers, playing poker in the evenings, winning the office of city solicitor. During those years he also married his childhood sweetheart, Jessie Ohl, and they had a son, born on December 10, 1883, whom they named Paul.

In one sense, Darrow must have felt like a success. He had become a skilled lawyer, exceeding his father's professional achievements and earning a place of respect in the community. But as he neared thirty, he had not written a book, not given a great speech, and not yet made a mark on the world.

❋ ❋ ❋

In early 1887, Darrow decided to move to Chicago. With a gentle smile, he later claimed that he was motivated by a woman who refused to sell him a house in Ashtubula because she doubted that he could make the payments. Out of spite, he said, he told the woman that he didn't want the house anyway, that he was planning to move to Chicago. The story was typically Darrow's—wry, self-deprecating, and suffused with the moral that our lives are ruled by fate, that even the most important decisions are the result of small events we can never predict or control.

There may have been some truth in the story about the house, but there were other, far more important reasons for moving to Chicago, reasons that were to chart the course of Darrow's career. America in 1887 was in the midst of a revolution that had been spawned in the years following the Civil War. Thanks in large measure to the extraordinary growth of railroads, which were built at a furious pace in the decades after the war, the entire economic and social life of the country began to change, and change rapidly. A golden spike driven into the tracks at Promontory Point, Utah, in 1869, marked the creation of a railroad that could cross the nation; fourteen years later, a second national line was finished. *The New York Times* crowed that "a wilderness is now open to civilization, and one which is adequate to support in comfort the surplus population of all of Europe . . . which will within a few years work economic and social changes of which what has already happened in Great Britain affords but a faint far-off hint."

The European masses did begin to flood to America, but not to live in comfort. They came to chop down trees in the magnificent timber forests of the West and to ship the lumber to market; they came to haul coal in the deep fields of Pennsylvania, to dig and ship the ore that fueled the great new engines of progress; they came to do the heavy lifting in the sweltering mills that produced huge quantities of iron and steel for railroad tracks and for huge new buildings in cities where the engines took them; they came to lay the train tracks and to build skyscrapers and bridges, climbing out on dangerous scaffolding thousands of feet above land or water; they came to slaughter cattle in the Chicago stockyards where trains brought thousands of head of cattle to be butchered and shipped off to other markets; and they came to work in hundreds of new industries made possible by the railroads and by the harnessing of electricity, by the invention of steel and skyscrapers and the telegraph and the telephone, and by the thousands of new uses for oil.

An age of industrial capitalism was born, in which each industry produced its own tycoons or barons—or, as journalist and historian

Matthew Josephson called them, "robber barons"; men of staggering wealth who dominated markets and ultimately dominated men. With unforgivable arrogance, the men who ruled the railroads and steel and coal and oil swept over their competitors and then set about bending their workers to their will. Huge new impersonal companies, where workers were fungible and spoke languages that were unintelligible, replaced the crafts and small farms where employers knew their apprentices and workers. On the average, laborers worked a six-day week, ten hours a day. Many worked as many as ninety or one hundred hours a week, all for meager wages. They lived in squalid conditions, frequently in houses owned and rented out by the companies; often as many as six people lived in a single room and five hundred people shared the same privy. Working conditions were foul and dangerous. In many industries the annual death rate for workers was at least one man per thousand; the accident rate was far higher.

When one group of laborers held out for higher wages or shorter hours or better conditions, the barons hired others to take their place, often pitting one group of immigrants against another, threatening the English with the Irish and the Irish with the Germans, keeping up what one journalist called "a constant war of races." When men tried to form unions, and the unions went on strike, and the strikers tried to block a fresh trainload of immigrants from taking their jobs, the barons called in the police or the Pinkertons, a new breed of private detectives who carried guns and clubs and were prepared to do whatever was necessary, to spill whatever blood it took, to keep the plants open. As Jay Gould reportedly remarked when one of his railroads was threatened with a strike, "I can hire one half the working class to kill the other half." When the men still fought back, and whenever the nature of the work would allow, the barons hired women and children and paid them even lower wages than their husbands and fathers.

Millions of Americans, witnessing a fresh and brutal form of poverty, tried to understand the new economic order and to find ways to change it. Working feverishly on a fresh theory, in 1879 Henry George produced an enormously influential book called *Progress and Poverty* that argued that population growth and economic progress were making land scarce and expensive, allowing idle landowners to reap unjustified returns. As a solution, he proposed a single tax on land to replace all other taxes. The revenues, he claimed, would be large enough to finance a glorious age of public ownership and public works. To some it seemed a utopian formula. Within a few years, Single Tax clubs sprang up all over the country and George's disciples numbered in the hundreds of thousands. Taking a different approach, political leaders began to call for the breakup of large concentrations of industrial power, introducing and finally passing legislation to outlaw trusts and combinations that caused the restraint of trade and production.

Other theories were more radical. Coming from Germany and Russia and Ireland, the new immigrants brought with them revolutionary theories as disparate as Karl Marx's communism and Mikhail Bakunin's anarchism. Putting an American face on those theories, hundreds of thousands of people were attracted to some form of socialism or public ownership of industry, while others called for an individualistic or philosophical form of anarchism.

Meanwhile, workers were fighting back. Haltingly at first, they formed unions and went on strike. The first major strikes swept the nation in the summer of 1877, as Darrow was preparing to become a lawyer. In the decade that followed, as he worked in his small town law practice, representing clients in disputes over "horse trades, boundary lines, fraudulent representations" and criminal complaints involving "the sale of liquor or watering of milk before it was sent to the factory," workers across America were becoming increasingly aggressive. In 1881, there were 471 strikes affecting 2,928 companies and 129,521 employees; by 1886, there were more than three times as many strikes, affecting three times as many companies and workers. About half of the strikes could claim some measure of success.

＊ ＊ ＊ ＊

Though living in rural Ohio, Darrow began to believe that America was living through its second great civil war. The Civil War of the 1860s had been the defining experience in his parents' life and the clearest battle of his own youth, as abolitionists, and finally the nation as a whole, fought to free the slaves. It seemed at first that the war had been successful. But now, with the nation's economy expanding at a furious rate, there was a new form of slavery. In the language of the day, workers had become "wage slaves," and a "war" was on between "Capital" and "Labor." In the last war, his parents had been passionate but passive observers. With a new war brewing, Darrow decided to sign up for combat duty.

"I lived in a small town," he explained to a friend a few years later, and "these modern thoughts about the rights and wrongs of labor, and the wrongs of the world, had just taken possession of me. . . . I came to Chicago. I determined to take my chances with the rest, to get what I could out of the system and to use it to *destroy* the system." Or at least to destroy the system's economic injustices.

❋❋❋❋

Like people the world over, Darrow's eyes had been fixed on Chicago since May 4, 1886—the day that the famous Haymarket Affair began. At ten-thirty that night, during a rally in Chicago's Haymarket Square, someone threw a bomb that killed seven police officers. The press and the police immediately blamed leaders of the city's powerful anarchist movement.

Following the story closely, first in Ashtabula and then in Chicago, Darrow became convinced that the facts did not add up. The rally had been called by the city's labor leaders as part of a national crusade to create an eight-hour work day. About three thousand people had been in attendance earlier in the evening, but by ten-twenty the event was all but over, ended by a light rainfall. Mayor Carter Harrison had left a few minutes earlier and had stopped by a police station to confirm that everything was peaceful. Only about two hundred people remained, listening to the final speaker. Then, for no apparent reason, 180 policemen appeared and ordered the meeting to end. The speaker complied, and started to get off the wagon on which he had been standing. As he did so, someone threw a dynamite bomb. It exploded near the first line of police. In reaction, the police started shooting and charged toward the crowd, swinging their clubs. Within minutes, seventy officers and fifty civilians were injured, and seven police officers and one civilian were fatally wounded. In less than two months, eight anarchists were charged with the murders and put on trial.

It seemed clear to Darrow that the men were not being tried for anything that they had done, but instead for holding beliefs that were unacceptable to the robber barons. Yet for the industrialists who were working their laborers for ten to twelve hours a day, there was no need to prove any direct connection to the violence; anarchistic views and support for a major strike were cause enough to judge them guilty.

The barons had made their views about Albert Parsons and August Spies, the most famous of the accused, clear in a newspaper editorial written three days before the policemen were killed. "There are two dangerous ruffians at large in this city; two sneaking cowards who are trying to create trouble. One of them is named Parsons; the other is named Spies," said the *Chicago Mail.* "Mark them for today. Keep them in view. Hold them personally responsible for any trouble that occurs. Make an example of them if trouble does occur."

At the anarchists' trial, the judge employed some highly unorthodox tactics. Instead of choosing the jury by lot, the judge appointed a special bailiff and gave him personal power to choose prospective jurors. He allowed one juror to serve despite the fact that he was a relative of one of the dead police officers. He forced the eight men to be tried together for conspiracy, though the prosecutors never sought to prove that they had ever conspired together.

The sensational trial lasted all summer. All eight were convicted. Seven were to be hanged, one to receive a fifteen year sentence. Before condemning the men to death, the judge allowed each to make a personal statement to the court. Their words had a powerful effect on the world's conscience—and on Darrow. His great speeches in years to come often echoed their sentiments.

"I saw that the bakers in this city were treated like dogs," Oscar Neebe said. "I helped organize them. That is a great crime. The men are now working ten hours a day instead of fourteen and sixteen hours. . . . That is another crime. And I committed a greater crime than that. I saw in the morning when I drove away with my team that the beer brewers of the city of Chicago went to work at four o'clock in the morning. They came home at seven or eight o'clock at night.

They never saw their families or their children by daylight. . . . I went to work to organize them. . . . That is a great crime."

Like four of his codefendants, August Spies had been born in Germany. With his still thick German accent, he spoke for hours, ending with the promise that the legacy of the condemned men would endure. "If you think that by hanging us you can stamp out the labor movement," he said, "then hang us! Here you will tread upon a spark, but there and there, behind you, in front of you, and everywhere, flames blaze up. It is a subterranean fire. You cannot put it out."

During the months that followed, voices around the world rallied to the anachists' side. At a mass meeting in London, George Bernard Shaw spoke to a huge rally, as over sixteen thousand workers joined in protesting the verdict. In France, the chamber of deputies asked the governor of Illinois for clemency. In America, *Atlantic Monthly* editor William Dean Howells rallied intellectuals to the side of the condemned men. When the executions went ahead as planned, August Spies made one final statement from beneath his hood, on his way to the gallows. "There will come a time," he predicted, "when our silence will be more powerful than the voices you strangle today." His prediction has come true. In the words of Page Smith, "The Haymarket Affair, in all of its ramifications, was one of those events that leave an unmistakable mark on history."

It also left an indelible mark upon Clarence Darrow.

❊ ❊ ❊ ❊

It was no accident that the Haymarket Affair occurred in Chicago rather than in some other city. It was a teeming metropolis in the midst of political and economic turmoil. In the aftermath of the Civil War, it had become the transportation hub of America, with railroad lines running to every major city and every section of the country. It had become a center of manufacturing, a focus of nearly all parts of the U.S. economy, and hog butcher to the world. Its population had exploded—from 30,000 in 1850 to 500,000 in 1880 and, with the aid of some newly annexed suburbs, 1,100,000 in 1890. In 1889, it passed Philadelphia as the nation's second largest city. A year later it outbid New York, Philadelphia, and Washington, D.C., for the right to present the 1893 World's Columbian Exposition, celebrating the four-hundredth anniversary of Europe's discovery of America.

Some of the new arrivals were American-born hayseeds from farming communities in Ohio and Nebraska, but most were immigrants, pouring in from Europe to work in the stockyards and the rail yards, the garment shops and print shops. Soon the city was dominated by men and women who spoke German and Russian and Polish and Yiddish, or spoke English with an Irish brogue. More than three quarters of the population were foreign-born or the children of foreign-born.

While the poor workers struggled in the sweatshops and factories, a fabulously rich class of millionaires appeared—the Swifts and Armours, who made their fortunes selling meat; the Pullmans, who made palatial cars for railroad travel; the McCormicks, whose machines were harvesting the nation's wheat; and merchandising magnates like the Fields and Rosenwalds. They built spectacular homes along Lake Michigan, in the area soon known as the Gold Coast, and were envied and hated by their workers.

Labor organizers and radical leaders found the city to be remarkably fertile ground. Around the nation in 1886, 190,000 workers went on strike in support of the eight-hour day. More than 80,000 of the strikers were in Chicago. Partly due to the huge base of new immigrants, the more radical movements of the era found more fertile soil in Chicago than in any other city, including New York. Albert Parsons and August Spies were part of the International Working People's Association, an anarchist group that called on its members to arm themselves and to "spread the idea of revolution and the spirit of revolt by deeds." Over half of the International's members lived in Chicago, and five of its eight official organs were published there: four in German, one in English.

✳ ✳ ✳ ✳

For all of its poverty and political ferment, there was something magical about Chicago in 1887. Arriving in the city that same summer, novelist Theodore Dreiser likened it to "a scene in a play," with a "double row of gas lamps flaring in the dusk, Madison street horsecars, yellow in color, jingling to and fro, their horses' feet plop-plopping as they came and went." The city was filled with country bumpkins like Darrow and Dreiser, "life-hungry natives of a hundred thousand farming areas, of small cities and towns," filled with "bumptiousness," ambition, self-assurance, and courage. "The spirit of Chicago flowed into me and made me ecstatic," Dreiser wrote. "Its personality was different from anything I had ever known; it was a compound of hope and joy in existence, intense hope and intense joy. Cities, like individuals, can flare up with a great flare of hope."

In the big city for the first time in his life, Darrow basked in the urban glow. "Chicago had that wonderful power which clings to it still," he wrote, "that power of inspiring everyone who touches it with absolute confidence in its greatness and strength." It was a city that inspired new movements in architecture, politics, and poetry, not to mention new heights of political corruption. Using the capacities of structural steel, the city gave birth to the world's first steel-frame skyscraper in 1885, helping spawn a school of great architects that included Louis Sullivan and Frank Lloyd Wright. To cope with the flood of new arrivals, reformers like Jane Addams opened settlement houses, creating pioneering experiments in social work. City politics were dominated by corrupt ward heelers with colorful nicknames like "Hinky Dink" Michael Kenna and "Bathhouse" John Coughlin. Intellectuals, creating what came to be called the Chicago literary renaissance, organized clubs, met in restaurants and saloons, and started poetry magazines like *The Dial*.

❈ ❈ ❈ ❈

At first the city seemed overpowering, leaving Darrow feeling discouraged, lonely, and so hopelessly homesick that he considered returning to Ashtabula. He and Jessie rented a modest apartment and he took a desk in a law office and waited for clients to appear. No one came. During his first year in the city he earned less than three hundred dollars. Walking down the great city streets, he studied each face, desperately hoping to find someone that he might have known in Ohio. He would stop at the city's busiest corner, at Michigan and State Street, looking closely at everyone who passed, but he recognized no one.

Hoping to make some friends, he decided to join one of city's countless clubs. In Ashtabula (which Darrow soon jokingly referred to as "Asstabula"), Darrow had been impressed by Henry George's notion of a single tax on property as a way of achieving economic justice. He became a member of the Henry George Single Tax Club, which gave him an opportunity to speak for the Democratic party several times during the 1888 election campaign. But he was invariably last on a long list of speakers, and no one noticed.

"I was in gloom amounting almost to despair," he recalled. "If it had been possible, I would have gone back to Ohio." But it wasn't possible. He had too much pride, too much to prove to his father, too much faith in himself and in his future. Surely his time would come.

It did. On February 20, 1889, a few months before Darrow's thirty-second birthday, at a huge meeting of the Tariff Reform Convention, the delegates engaged in a bitter and spirited debate over protectionist legislation. The Central Music Hall was filled to overflowing. Henry George was the guest attraction that evening, and he gave a splendid speech in favor of free trade. Then it was Darrow's turn. Having heard the major speaker, the audience started to get up to leave. Darrow knew that he would have to capture his audience's attention at once. His first words, carefully chosen, were so arresting that a few people started to resume listening, then a few more. Finally the whole hall was attentive as Darrow discussed the impact that a tariff would have on workers. Tariff backers claimed that protectionism would allow manufacturers to pay higher wages. That might be true in theory, Darrow said, but manufacturers would never pass the benefits on to their employees. He called free trade "a step toward the emancipation of industrial slaves." He finished to great applause.

"I have talked from platforms countless times since then," he wrote forty years later, "but never again have I felt that exquisite thrill of triumph after a speech."

The next morning he was again up at an early hour to get the papers. "This time my name was all over the front page," he wrote. Well, not quite. It was in a paragraph at the end of articles on the third page of the *Chicago Tribune, Chicago Times,* and *Daily Inter-*

Ocean. It took up a bit more space on the second page of the *Chicago Herald.* One commentator called it "rather dull, plodding." No matter. At last Darrow was in the press—and he felt that his career was launched.

❋ ❋ ❋ ❋

When Darrow described himself as lonely and friendless during his first year in Chicago, he was not counting his relationship with John Peter Altgeld, the man destined to become the successful father figure that Darrow had never enjoyed.

Darrow had heard of Altgeld before moving to Chicago. In 1884, Altgeld wrote *Our Penal Machinery and Its Victims,* a powerful plea for society to focus its energies on eliminating the causes of crime rather than on punishing wrongdoers. During the next few years, he mailed some ten thousand copies of the book to people who might have some impact on the criminal justice system. One copy went to a judge in Ashtabula who passed it along to Darrow. It was filled with sentiments that rang true, combining science, legal theory, and logic. "Only recently have we begun to recognize the fact that every man is to a great extent what his heredity and environment have made him," Altgeld wrote. The thought hit Darrow like an express train. It was, he said, "a revelation." He had already rejected any religious explanation for man's behavior. Now he also became convinced that man is not entirely responsible for his own acts. People commit crimes, rather, because of poverty or injustice, or because nature drives them to it. Nor do jails deter or prevent crime, Altgeld argued. By warehousing the poor, and turning first-time offenders into hardened criminals, jails are, in reality, an essential part of the problem.

Darrow read the book with hungry fascination. Everything it said echoed in his mind, and its sentiments formed the basis of a philosophy that served him for the rest of his life. "This book and the author came to have a marked influence on me and my future," he later wrote.

Almost as soon as he arrived in Chicago, Darrow went to see Altgeld, who had just been elected to the superior court. There, sitting behind an odd little walnut desk, was a small man with a close-cropped beard that covered a harelip and a countenance that cartoonists would ultimately use for bitter partisanship, making him appear ugly and sinister. But to admirers it was a face of compassion, "sad with all the utter woe of humanity." Like so many others in Illinois, Altgeld was an immigrant, and he still spoke with a trace of a German accent. In some respects he was very different from Darrow. Ten years Darrow's senior, he was Jewish, had accumulated a fortune in real estate (though one of his investments would ultimately bring him to financial ruin), and had already mastered the world of Illinois politics. But the two had much in common. Almost overnight, they became close friends.

❊ ❊ ❊

Darrow joined Altgeld as a member of the Sunset Club, a collegial meeting place for mainstream politicians, radicals, literati, and business leaders who gathered together twice a month at fine restaurants. For a man who was largely self-taught, with only one year of college and one year of law school, the Sunset Club offered the greatest education of his life. As Kevin Tierney observed, its members became in a sense, Darrow's teachers, his friends, and his fraternity brothers.

Among the topics that absorbed their circle of friends in the fall of 1887 was the fate of the Haymarket anarchists. Like liberals around the world, they could hardly contain their anger when the state supreme court upheld the guilty verdict and the governor of Illinois, in a ruling that clearly represented a political compromise, granted clemency to some, but allowed four of the men to be hanged that November. They called it "judicial murder."

Following the hanging, Darrow made a comment that stuck with some of his friends. "What ought to be done now," he said, "is take a man like Judge Altgeld, first elect him mayor of Chicago, then governor of Illinois." At the time it sounded like a naïve remark from a bright, eager, and well-meaning country bumpkin.

Altgeld did not try to become mayor, but in 1889, shortly after Darrow's Music Hall speech, he did manage to put his own man in office. It was an episode that must have taught Darrow volumes about how financial interests, personal pique, and high-stakes politics worked in the big city. While serving on the bench, Altgeld had continued his work as a real estate developer, purchasing an eight-story building on the Chicago River. The city, however, built a bridge over the river, near his building, forcing Altgeld to spend $60,000 in alterations. He asked the city to help pay for his costs. The city attorney agreed to pay Altgeld $24,000, but at the last moment the plan was vetoed by the mayor, John A. Roche. Altgeld was determined to get even.

In the election of 1889, Mayor Roche was backed by the Good Government movement, as well as by most of the city's labor leaders. He was the overwhelming favorite to beat his opponent, De Witt Cregier. But Altgeld engineered and financed an ingenious political maneuver. Using five thousand dollars of his own money, he printed ballots for a special bipartisan "Anti-Machine Ticket" headed by Cregier. By attracting thousands of Good Government voters to its reformist-sounding cause, the device put Cregier's candidacy over the top. In an admiring story, the *Chicago Times* called it a "swift, noiseless weapon . . . fatally effective" that had "originated with a calm, resourceful man of indomitable industry."

Altgeld did not want much in return. After all, his purpose had been personal revenge, not political advantage. But he did ask Cregier for one favor. He asked him to offer his young protégé a legal plum by naming him as special assessment attorney for the City of Chicago. Within a year, Darrow had graduated to the lofty post of Acting Corporation Counsel for the City of Chicago.

The episode taught Darrow a profound lesson. Through his independent wealth, Altgeld was able to buck the system. He could fight for radical changes in the penal system by distributing free copies of his book to thousands of people who would never have heard of it, much less have bought it, otherwise. And now those resources had made it possible for one man to change the outcome of an election, even when he wasn't running. There were, he concluded, noble reasons to become rich.

Darrow was also learning something from Altgeld about means and ends. "He would do whatever would serve his purpose when he was right," Darrow told an interviewer years later. "He'd use all the tools of the other side—stop at nothing—but always with an end in view—to do good for the poor man. He was perfectly un-scrupulous in getting ends, but absolutely *honest* in those ends."

❋❋❋❋

When Mayor Cregier was unseated in 1891, Altgeld again came to Darrow's rescue, helping him land a job in the law department of the Chicago and North Western Railway. Perhaps surprisingly, Darrow's most heroic early moments occurred while in that corporate post. He quickly signed on as the unofficial manager of Altgeld's cam-paign to become the first Democratic governor of Illinois since the Civil War—and the first Jewish governor ever. To the delight of progressives everywhere, Altgeld was elected in 1892.

Many of Altgeld's friends, including Darrow, expected him to pardon the surviving Haymarket anarchists as soon as he became governor. He didn't, and many of his supporters quickly became restless. In early March, 1893, Darrow took the train to Springfield to deliver a painful message. He told Altgeld that his friends were "growing doubtful and restless and disappointed, and that it should be done at once." He told him that "everyone expected it" and that neither Darrow nor any of his other friends could see any excuse for waiting.

"Go tell your friends that when I am ready I will act," Altgeld said a bit tartly. "I don't know how I will act, but I will do what I think is right." He paused for a moment, lost in thought, and then con-tinued. "We have been friends for a long time. You seem impatient; of course I know how you feel. I don't want to offend you or lose your friendship, but the responsibility is mine. I have not yet exam-ined the record. I have no opinion about it. It is a big job. When I do examine it I will do what I believe to be right, no matter what that is."

Darrow was furious. The issue seemed so clear to him. "If that's your attitude, I'm through with you," he shouted. "I want nothing more to do with you until you do something about those anarchists. It's plainly the proper and popular thing to do."

"Don't deceive yourself," Altgeld told his emotional young pro-tégé, his face betraying his deep inner turmoil. Then he added these prescient words. "If I conclude to pardon these men, it will not meet with the approval that you expect. From that day on, I will be a dead man."

A few weeks later, Altgeld acted. He followed Darrow's advice and pardoned the men—though he made the serious mistake of issuing a detailed, legalistic, and some thought sophistic explanation for his decision. The result was as he had predicted. "Immediately throughout the world, a flood of vituperation and gall was poured upon Altgeld's head," Darrow wrote in his autobiography. "Governor Altgeld was in the way of the forces that control the world, and he must be destroyed." He had to be destroyed, of course, because of a decision that Darrow had implored him to make.

The press and public began to claim that Altgeld was an anarchist himself; that he looked like an anarchist (and he did, in cartoon caricatures); that he hated policemen, especially Irish policemen; and that he had pardoned the men for political reasons, as a part of a deal with his supporters or in hopes of winning a seat in the U.S. Senate. The charges were unfair, but they stuck. And they hurt.

Darrow went to the state capitol as often as he could after the pardon was granted. "The great building," he wrote, "seemed lonely and abandoned. The governor's suite of rooms were barren and deserted. He was almost always alone." Darrow would go to the governor's quarters and "sit and look at him in silence, just to be with him." He tried to share the pain, but there was little that he could do to lighten the burden.

It took the better part of a decade for Darrow to fully understand how a fickle and thoughtless public could combine with the vindictive leaders of industry to crush a once great spirit. But before it was over, Altgeld was dead, and so was Darrow's belief in the goodness of man and the inevitability of human progress.

❊ ❊ ❊ ❊

While Altgeld remained in office, vilified and caricatured throughout the land, Darrow's own importance grew. He began to age noticeably, but still exuded country charm with his rich, slow drawl and simple, colorful phrasing. He was in constant demand as a lecturer, speaking at the Chicago World's Fair, to the freethinkers and radicals at Robert Ingersoll's Secular Union, to his friends at the Sunset Club, and to the attractive young social workers at Hull House, which had recently been founded by Jane Addams and Ellen Gates Starr. They all loved and admired him. But his wife and child, who also loved him, started to notice that he was seldom at home. Following the pattern that he had learned as a child, he had begun to seek companionship and affection elsewhere.

Darrow's first notable case began on October 28, 1893, when a religious zealot named Patrick Eugene Prendergast marched into the office of Mayor Carter Harrison and claimed that he was entitled to a political appointment in return for his campaign work. As soon as Mayor Harrison turned him down, Prendergast pulled out a gun and assassinated him.

Prendergast became Darrow's client. Though the man was clearly guilty, Darrow tried to save his life by representing him at a sanity hearing in the spring of 1894. When that failed, Darrow took the train down to Springfield to plead with Governor Altgeld for clemency. There he met Altgeld's young assistant, Brand Whitlock, who later became a famous novelist and the mayor of Toledo, Ohio.

To Darrow's surprise, Whitlock said that he, too, was against capital punishment. Whitlock later described the scene. Suddenly, on Darrow's face, "tired, with the expression of world-weariness life gives to the countenance behind which there has been too much serious contemplation of life, a face that seemed prematurely wrinkled, there suddenly appeared a smile as winning as a woman's, and he said in a voice that had the timbre of human sympathy and the humor of a particular drawl: 'Well, you're all right then.' "

Retiring to Altgeld's antechamber, the men soon moved from a discussion of politics to a discussion of literature. Both admired writers who were realists, and they talked about Tolstoy, Thomas Hardy, and Darrow's friend William Dean Howells, the great novelist and critic. Darrow made a compelling case for the virtues of realism, rather than puritan platitudes, in literature and art. Before long it was clear that both men were more interested in literature than the law.

The episode led to a close friendship between two remarkable sensibilities, but it did not help to spare Prendergast's life. Feeling that he had pardoned enough radicals for one term in office, Altgeld allowed the punishment to stand.

✿ ✿ ✿ ✿

Although Darrow did not manage to win a pardon for Eugene Prendergast, his efforts did win the admiration of Eugene Debs, whose newly formed American Railway Union had just gone on strike against the Pullman Palace Car Company, manufacturer of most of the country's passenger railroad cars. Built by George Pullman, one of Chicago's great entrepreneurs, the company dominated every phase of its workers' lives. Pullman built a town that was something like a feudal manor, with George Pullman as the absolute monarch. He owned all of the land, all of the houses, even the churches and libraries. As one worker put it, "We are born in a Pullman house, fed from the Pullman shop, taught in the Pullman school, catechized in the Pullman church, and when we die we shall be buried in the Pullman cemetery and go to the Pullman hell."

Life for the Pullman workers was hard enough before the recession of 1893, but in that year, when tens of thousands of businesses were facing bankruptcy, the Pullman Company decided to preserve its enormous profits by cutting wages by twenty-five percent. To make matters worse, the company did not reduce rent on the Pullman town's houses—which were already at least twenty-five percent more costly than comparable houses in Chicago. Stories of hardship were rampant. One skilled mechanic earned a paycheck of seven cents after working ten hours a day for twelve days. His actual wages were $9.07, but the company had deducted nine dollars, the rent that he owed for his company house. A seamstress in the town said that after her father died, she had been forced to pay sixty dollars in back rent that he owed the company after thirty years of faithful service. A minister reported that the residents of Pullman were on the brink of starvation.

In May 1894, the Pullman company workers went on strike. It was clear that they were not strong enough to win on their own, but they had a fighting chance if they could gain the backing of Debs's railway workers. After the company rejected proposals for arbitration, the American Railway Union ordered a full-scale strike, cutting all sleeping cars from trains around America. By late June, 125,000 men had joined the strike, stopping traffic on twenty railroads.

The railroads promptly counterattacked. The General Managers Association, representing all twenty-four railroads terminating or centered in Chicago, asked the federal government to intervene. Conveniently, the attorney general was an owner and former director of several major railroads. Relying in part on the Sherman Anti-Trust Act, which ironically had been adopted in 1890 to prevent the monopolistic practices of corporations, the government charged Debs's union with a conspiracy to restrain trade. Within days, a court issued an injunction banning the strike. If the strike continued, Debs could be sent to jail for contempt. Nevertheless, Debs refused to yield.

Recognizing the importance of talent as well as symbolism, Debs asked Clarence Darrow to represent him. In his work for Prendergast and the Haymarket anarchists, as well as in his speeches, Darrow had demonstrated that he was no ordinary corporate attorney. Now Debs wanted him to go a step further. The Chicago and North Western Railway had allowed Darrow to work on those other cases. Indeed the company's president, Marvin Hughitt, had even supported Darrow's plea on behalf of the anarchists. But they could not allow him to represent the railway union against the railroads. Darrow would have to defect.

Courageously, Darrow switched sides. The core of his defense was an attack on the concept of criminal conspiracy, a concept he had grown to hate while watching it used against the Haymarket anarchists. In a tactic that he would use again and again, Darrow turned the charge upside down. He converted the railroads and the prosecutor into the defendants, charging that they were the real conspirators, that they had conspired to destroy the lives of the nation's most valuable workers.

"This is a historic case which will count much for liberty or against liberty," he began, speaking in his low, musical drawl. "Conspiracy, from the days of tyranny in England down to the day the General Managers' Association used it as a club, has been the favorite weapon of every tyrant. It is an effort to punish the crime of thought."

In a brilliant stroke of courtroom genius, Darrow announced that he intended to call George Pullman and the leaders of the General Managers Association as his witnesses. "If the government does not, we shall try to get the General Managers here to tell you what they know about conspiracy," he declared. "These defendants . . . are brought into court by an organization which uses the government as a cloak to conceal its infamous purposes." Pullman suddenly disappeared, and the tide began to turn. As the generally antilabor *Chicago Tribune* noted, "It is not strange that he should not be willing to go on the stand and be questioned by Mr. Darrow." Darrow had hoped for a confrontation with Pullman. Then, to his chagrin, one of the jurors fell ill and could not be replaced. Nevertheless, he won a great victory when the prosecution was dropped.

Or it seemed that he had won a victory. Still learning the ropes of practice in the big time, Darrow had not reckoned on another arrow in the prosecution's quiver. As soon as the government abandoned the conspiracy case, it charged Debs with contempt of court. It was a hard charge to fight. The injunction might have been improperly issued, but Debs still had an obligation to obey the court's order. In a battle that ultimately went all the way to the United States Supreme Court, Debs was convicted and sent to jail for six months.

Darrow had argued his position with exceptional logic and eloquence, winning himself countless friends and a national reputation. But his client had been sent to jail—and Darrow had learned a bitter and enduring lesson in political science. With the exception of a few rare men like John Peter Altgeld, the government was, in the final analysis, on the side of corporate interests. And with even fewer exceptions, the courts would rule for capital. Indeed, it didn't even help much to have legislatures pass laws that were designed to protect consumers or workers, since in the end the courts would twist those laws as they saw fit, turning them 180 degrees, using them to help capital and not labor. That was what they had done with the antitrust laws. That was, no doubt, what they would do whenever they had the chance.

❋ ❋ ❋ ❋

More and more, Darrow was in demand as a lecturer, and his words contained a lasting power that led them to be frequently published and widely discussed. Often he sounded a radical theme, laced with compassion and hope. He delivered one of his most important speeches in November 1895, arguing for the right of revolution and claiming that the times were ripe for such a conflagration. He argued that if it happened, injustice would be to blame, not the men and women who carried the message or fired the weapons. He recalled the story from *Les Misérables* in which a priest upbraids a revolutionist for the cruelty of the revolution and the man answers: "A storm had been gathering for fifteen hundred years; it bursts; you blame the thunderbolt."

"With the land and possessions of America rapidly passing into the hands of a favored few," Darrow told his audience, "with great corporations taking the place of individual effort; with the small shops going down before the great factories and department stores; with thousands of men and women in idleness and want; with wages constantly tending to a lower level; with the number of women and children rapidly increasing in factory and store; with the sight of thousands of children forced into involuntary slavery at the tender age that should find them at home or in the school; with courts sending men to jail without trial for daring to refuse to work; with bribery and corruption openly charged, constantly reiterated in the press, and universally believed; and above all and more than all, with the knowledge that the servants of the people, elected to correct abuses, are bought and sold in legislative halls at the bidding of corporations and individuals; with all these notorious evils sapping the foundation of popular government and destroying personal liberty, some rude awakening must come.

"If it shall come in the lightning and tornado of civil war, the same as forty years ago," he pleaded, "when you then look over the ruin and desolation, remember the long years in which the storm was rising; and do not blame the thunderbolt."

❊ ❊ ❊ ❊

Though he sometimes talked like a revolutionary, Darrow had not given up on elected government. He was determined to do what he could to make it better. So in 1896, he threw his energies into electoral politics. He managed Altgeld's reelection campaign, joined Altgeld in leading the Illinois delegation to the Democratic national convention that nominated William Jennings Bryan, and ran for congress himself.

The election was a fiasco. All of his candidates lost. They were defeated, he was convinced, because of a corrupt system.

"In the last days of the campaign," he later explained, "an enormous fund was raised and spent in the centers of population, including Chicago. Within two days, many of the Democratic leaders were reached and the whole organization disrupted. As a consequence . . . the whole ticket was defeated." That included Bryan and Altgeld—and Darrow, who lost by 590 votes.

He was particularly distressed about the defeat of Altgeld, who was attacked viciously for the pardons. Running for vice-president, Theodore Roosevelt marched into Illinois and charged that Altgeld "would connive at wholesale murder and would justify it by elaborate and cunning sophistry for reasons known only to his own tortuous soul."

On election night, Darrow came to the governor's luxurious suite at the Palmer House hotel, wanting to be at Altgeld's side. He knew that Altgeld was certain to lose, but his heart ached at the prospect and he tried to sound hopeful. In an effort to lift Altgeld's spirits, Darrow joked that the governor would have to put on a special attachment of police officers to handle the huge demonstration when he won. Finally one of their coworkers arrived in the room carrying a batch of telegrams.

"We are hopelessly lost," the man reported.

"I feel the same way," said Altgeld with a smile, "but Darrow here thinks we are going to win. He thinks I had better be guarded because there will be a terrible commotion over our victory."

But there was no commotion. Only tears.

The final humiliation for Altgeld as governor occurred at his successor's inaugural. It was the custom in Illinois for the outgoing governor to say a few words in parting, and Altgeld had prepared a short address. But Altgeld's successor, casting aside both custom and courtesy, refused to let him speak.

Darrow would support candidates again, and even run for office again. But he would never again fully believe in the courts, the electorate, or the government. Like some decaying fruit, his idealism had begun to putrefy.

Chapter Two

DO NOT BLAME THE THUNDERBOLT

IN EARLY 1897, DARROW'S life was in turmoil. He had lost faith in electoral politics; his friend John Peter Altgeld was out of office, humiliated; and his marriage was on the rocks. In March, Jessie filed for the divorce. The terms were amicable, but the process was painful. Apparently they parted by mutual consent, without recriminations. But Darrow must have missed Jessie, his son, Paul, and the security of home. A year later he asked her for a reconciliation. But it was not to be.

Darrow moved into the Langdon apartments, near Jane Addams's Hull House, and for the first time in his life began to live as a freewheeling bachelor. He spent even more time at the Sunset Club, joining its steering committee; he wrote essays on literature and gave lectures to young social workers—sometimes at Hull House, sometimes in his apartment, where he loved to debate philosophy and to read poetry and literature to friends. He professed disdain for marriage and, surrounded by adoring young women, he preached the case for free love. To some of the new circle of devotees he was a sort of "household God," as one visiting student wrote. But to others, he soon became a fallen angel.

After the electoral defeats of 1896, Darrow became, with a few major exceptions, a conventional corporate lawyer, turning his attention, as he later wrote, "exclusively to the law. For the next few years I was constantly in court, trying all sorts of cases that fall to the general practitioner." A general practitioner, of course, uses his contacts to buiid a client base, and Darrow naturally exploited his expertise in municipal law and his relationships with government officials. He represented pretty well anyone who could afford his fees. As he told one friend in 1897, after leaving the railroad, "I have sold my professional services to every corporation or individual who cared to buy. The only exception is that I have never given them to oppress the weak, or convict the innocent."

Darrow continued to give great lectures and to write stirring essays. His admirers might not have minded, or even noticed, the trend that his law practice was taking if he had not agreed to represent Commonwealth Edison in its effort to secure an exclusive franchise for the distribution of electricity in Chicago. It took more than a spoonful of sugar for his friends to swallow that particular client. Darrow had long argued that utilities should be publicly owned, believing that municipal ownership would assure the public of lower rates. Worse, he and his friends were pretty well convinced that Commonwealth Edison had bribed the city council to win the franchise. In Darrow's phrase, they had secured it "for boodle." Nevertheless, Darrow, with his expertise in municipal law and his contacts in city government, joined Commonwealth Edison's legal team in an effort to override a veto by Mayor Carter Harrison II. Not surprisingly, as soon as Commonwealth Edison won the franchise, Darrow's clients turned around and sold it to another private company at a huge profit.

Many of his friends, including the community of adoring young social workers, were stunned and hurt. Ellen Gates Starr, cofounder of Hull House, wrote a pained letter expressing the disillusionment that she and others felt. Darrow took her letter to heart and expressed genuine concern that "so many of my good friends feel hurt (almost personally) in reference the matter of which you wrote." He admitted that "judged by the higher law, in which we both believe, I am practically a thief. I am taking money that I did not earn, which comes to me from men who did not earn it, but got it because they had the chance to get it." But Darrow argued that it was necessary for him to represent clients such as Commonwealth Edison in order to finance his more radical work. It was a lesson that he had learned by watching Altgeld a decade earlier use his money to distribute his books and to win elections against great odds.

"I believe that *society is organized injustice,*"—Darrow under-lined the phrase—"that business is a legal fraud, that a land owner is a pirate." He told her about his friend Swift, a man who had decided to live a pure but ineffective life. Darrow explained his decision to take a different course of action in order to fight for radical or even revolutionary change.

"I determined to give my energies and ability to help change the system under which all of us are compelled to live," he said. But it would cost money, which meant that he would have to represent a few pirates. After all, he noted, "Society provides no fund out of which such people can live while preaching heresy."

❋ ❋ ❋ ❋

At the turn of the century, Darrow became an increasingly important critic—or heretical preacher—on the subject of industrial injustice. His views were generally presented in powerful lectures and essays, but sometimes he found a client with a case that offered him the chance to present his philosophy in court. One such client was Thomas I. Kidd, general secretary of the Amalgamated Woodwork-ers Union.

The Kidd case took Darrow out of Chicago for the first time in his career, out into the hinterlands, to Oshkosh, Wisconsin, as the peripatetic defender of labor in a case with national overtones. In some respects, the trial was a replay of the Debs case. George Pullman, of the Pullman Palace Car Company, had cut his workers' wages; George Paine, of the Paine Lumber Company, had fired the men who worked in his factories and replaced them with women and children—often the wives and daughters of the men who were fired—at lower wages. Debs had been charged with a conspiracy for organizing railway workers in support of the Pullman employees; Kidd was charged with conspiracy for leading the lumber company workers in a strike against unfair wages.

As in the Debs case, Darrow turned the tables on the prosecutors, putting them on trial, arguing that the real conspiracy was between the lumber company and the government. He asked the jury to ignore the facts that had been introduced against his client and to focus instead on the cruelty of rich corporations like the Paine Lumber Company. His powerful, hypnotic rhetoric carried his rapt audience along with him.

"You have heard a great deal of evidence as to whether Thomas I. Kidd provoked this strike," Darrow said. "I don't care whether he did or not. . . . It is impossible to present the case to you without a broad survey of the great questions that are agitating the world today. For whatever its form, this is not really a criminal case. It is but an episode in the great battle for human liberty, a battle which was commenced when the tyranny and oppression of man first caused him to impose upon his fellows and which will not end so long as the children of one father shall be compelled to toil to support the children of another in luxury and ease.

"The Paine Company may hire its lawyers and import its leprous detectives into your peaceful community; it may send these defendants to jail; but so long as injustice and inhumanity exist, so long as employers grow fat and rich and powerful through their robbery and greed, so long as they build their palaces from the unpaid labor of their serfs, so long as they rob childhood of its life and sunshine and joy, you will find other conspirators, thank God, that will take the place of these as fast as the doors of the jail shall close upon them.

"This is not a criminal case, and every actor concerned in this drama understands it well. . . . Deep in the mind of every man who thinks, is the certain knowledge that this drama in which you play such an important part is but a phase of the great social question that moves the world. . . . [The strike] was but an incident in a great struggle which commenced so many centuries ago and which will and must continue until human liberty is secured and equality has come to dwell upon the earth. . . ."

Darrow's magnificent defense produced a double victory. Thomas Kidd was acquitted, and Darrow's closing argument was published in a pamphlet that William Dean Howells called "as interesting as a novel."

❋ ❋ ❋ ❋

A few years later, Darrow represented striking anthracite coal workers in a sensational proceeding that offered an even better chance for
him to use his great rhetorical skills to educate the country about the
injustice of the industrial system. Coal mining had become a vital but
hazardous industry, where workers, many of them children, were
badly exploited, earning about $250 a year. Each year, five out of
every thousand laborers were killed on the job; thousands more
were maimed, disfigured, or injured. Finally, the United Mine Workers organized a strike that immobilized the industry. In early 1902,
147,000 miners walked off the job.

By fall, the strike had paralyzed the nation. It was clear that during
the winter thousands of people would freeze from lack of heat.
President Theodore Roosevelt forced the contending forces to agree
to arbitration, and he named a special seven-member commission to
hear testimony. Darrow represented the workers.

For months, the arbitration was headline news. The coal operators
tried to put the miners on trial, listing episodes of criminality and
violence that had occurred during the strike, but Darrow brought
forth scores of witnesses who earned sympathy for the miners with
compelling stories of children who were forced to work in horrid,
dangerous conditions for meager wages.

In December, Darrow wrote "The Breaker Boy," a deeply affecting short story that captured the essence of the testimony. In the
style of the realist writers he so admired, he described Johnny
McCaffery. His father died in the mine when Johnny was just eleven.
His mother hoped that Johnny would become a scholar, but when
her husband died she had no choice but to send the lad to work,
pretending that he was twelve. He started off at the coal chute, or
"breaker," picking slate from the coal as it slid down the chute. For
forty years he worked in the mine, at a succession of jobs, until his
health was broken. "His face was scarred and one ear was missing. . . . One arm was crippled from a fallen rock and his right hip
was never free from pain. . . ." But his real problem was asthma. "He
wheezed instead of breathing, and he could only walk a very little
way and could stand upon his feet only a few minutes at a time." He

should have retired, but he needed to earn money for his family. "The mine boss was really not unkind," Darrow wrote with bitter irony, "so when John told him that he could not go down the shaft again, he promised him an easier job." He sent John McCaffery back to the breaker, where he had begun his dismal career some forty years earlier.

The following spring, Darrow hammered away at the same themes in eight hours of closing arguments to the arbitration commission, putting the industrial world on trial.

"I have heard my clients—147,000 workingmen who toil while other men grow rich, men who go down into the earth and face greater dangers than men who go out upon the sea or out upon the land in battle, men who have little to hope for, little to think of excepting work—I have heard these men characterized as assassins, as brutes, as criminals. . . . I shall apologize for none of their mistakes and excuse none of their misdeeds. But I will say it does not come well from their accusers to call them criminals, and I cannot refrain in speaking of a long series of causes which brought about these dire results. . . .

"When they refuse to raise our wages, suppose I say: 'No, Mr. Operators; you are criminals.' I say that legislative body after legislative body, court after court, investigating committee after investigating committee, have pronounced you criminals and outlaws. . . . I say you are carrying on your business in conflict with the spirit of the letter of the Constitution of the great commonwealth in which you live. . . .

"When I think of the cripples, of the orphans, of the widows, of the maimed, who are dragging their lives out on account of this business, who, if they were mules or horses would be cared for, but who are left and neglected, it seems to me this is the greatest indictment of this business that can possibly be made. . . .

"They are fighting for slavery, while we are fighting for freedom. They are fighting for the rule of man over man, for despotism, for darkness, for the past. We are striving to build up man. We are working for democracy, for humanity, for the future, for the day that will come too late for us to see it or know it or receive its benefits, but which will come, and will remember our struggle, our triumphs, our defeats, and the words which we spake. . . .

"This contest is one of the important contests that has marked the progress of human liberty since the world began. . . . It has come to these poor miners to bear this cross, not for themselves—not that, but that the human race may be lifted up to a higher plane than it has ever known before."

One newspaper called Darrow's speech "brilliant," a summary of "all the philosophy, all of the hopes and pleas and demands of the anthracite coal workers and, in a measure, of trade unionists everywhere." When the commission issued its report in March 1903, the miners were awarded back pay and a wage increase. Samuel Gompers, president of the American Federation of Labor, called it "the most important single incident in the labor movement in the United States."

❊ ❊ ❊ ❊

Although his public pronouncements were winning ever-wider audiences of admirers, Darrow's private views were becoming increasingly cynical and bleak. There were many reasons for Darrow's change of mood: the growing gap between rich and poor, the injustices of the police and criminal courts, the corruption that riddled Chicago's industrial and political life. But none affected him more profoundly than his personal experience in watching the continuing destruction and humiliation of the man he most admired.

Before becoming governor, John Peter Altgeld built the Unity Building, a magnificent sixteen-story skyscraper, on a prime piece of real estate in downtown Chicago. The building was a great source of pride, but some financial miscalculations forced Altgeld to put all of his assets into it, an amount that Darrow estimated at six or seven hundred thousand dollars, and he encumbered it with a two-million-dollar mortgage. For the first few years the Unity Building prospered, boasting several major corporate tenants, but when Altgeld pardoned the Haymarket anarchists, many of the best tenants left. They were replaced, as Darrow reported, by "young lawyers, radicals and idealists, many of whom could not pay their rent."

When Altgeld returned to Chicago after the election of 1896, Darrow found him "dazed and lifeless." He told his young friend that he was too old to begin a new career, that "he would be content to crawl under a sidewalk and die." He despised the law, convinced that the best attorneys sold their services to the highest bidder in order to ruin people and to intensify the gap between rich and poor. But at least he had the Unity Building.

For two years, the former governor went to the Unity Building and "sat in his office, day after day, receiving visits from the poor, the dreamers, the unadjusted and unadjustable . . . pathetic idealists, with their haunted and faraway gaze." Darrow continually tried to lift Altgeld's spirits, but to no avail. Finally, in 1899, Darrow helped persuade the former governor to run for mayor, hoping that he would win, convinced that the campaign would bring him back to life. The race was a fiasco. While still admired by radicals and intellectuals, Altgeld finished third.

Though he loved his old friend, Darrow was determined not to be so naïve. "Altgeld was too ethereal-minded to know that 'the people' are also a myth, the figment of an illusion, a special cohort that only eyes of faith can see," Darrow sadly explained. A month after he lost the election, the banks foreclosed on the Unity Building, eliminating his only remaining source of revenue and prestige. He couldn't bear to remain in the building as a tenant.

Again Darrow came to the aid of the man who had meant so much to him. He persuaded Altgeld to join his successful law firm, respectfully changing the name to Altgeld, Darrow, and Thompson. It was a selfless act of love. Altgeld "had never been a good lawyer," according to Darrow, and he brought in few, if any, clients. He used to fall asleep at his desk. On law firm stationary, he sent out letters announcing that "I have gone to work and am trying to make an honest (?) living—although I have a deep conviction that a reformer ought not to have to work." But at least he had somewhere to go.

At a few minutes past midnight on March 12, 1902, Darrow received a long-distance call from Joliet, Illinois. Altgeld had collapsed while giving a speech on the Boer War, pleading for the underdogs, deploring the treatment of the Boers by the British. Darrow caught a train to Joliet early the next morning, but it was too late. Altgeld had died at four A.M. of a cerebral hemorrhage. He was fifty-four years old. Darrow brought Altgeld back in a casket and made all of the arrangements for a splendid funeral.

Darrow's speech at Altgeld's funeral was one of the most poignant of his life. Calling him "one of the rarest souls who ever lived and died," he paid homage to "the most devoted lover, the most abject slave, the fondest, wildest, dreamiest victim that ever gave his life to liberty's immortal cause. . . . The fierce bitterness and hatred that sought to destroy this great grand soul had but one cause—the fact that he really loved his fellow man."

Throughout his life, Darrow remembered how Altgeld had lived—and how he had been destroyed. His funeral tribute was the only speech that Darrow included in his own autobiography. His spiritual father was dead, and Darrow could not help forming a deep and permanent resentment of the forces that had brought him down.

❋ ❋ ❋ ❋

After his mentor's death, Darrow began to change. He replaced Altgeld in his firm with a younger partner, an aspiring poet and tireless worker named Edgar Lee Masters. But he couldn't replace Altgeld in his life. Darrow seemed rudderless. He was still capable of writing powerful essays and giving great speeches, but his private comments were increasingly bitter and cynical, and he began to represent rich corporate clients in cases that victimized laborers and the poor. The change seemed to accelerate after the summer of 1903, when he married Ruby Hammerstrom, a society reporter from Galesburg, Illinois.

When they met, Ruby was a handsome brunette with piercing brown eyes and a light complexion who dressed beautifully in the Gibson Girl fashion of the era. In his mid-forties, Darrow was a tall, hulking former farm boy with blue eyes, hair like straw, skin like leather, and clothes that seemed to have been bought at a thrift shop. Ruby was twelve years his junior, and people often commented on the difference in age. She wasn't like the social workers and political reporters that he generally dated, the idealistic, adoring but combative radicals who loved to talk politics but insisted on holding him to the high ideals that he set forth in his speeches.

Darrow married Ruby on the rebound from Katherine Leckie, an ardent feminist and passionate supporter of organized labor who was a top reporter for Hearst's *Chicago American*. In his biography of Darrow, Irving Stone calls Leckie "Miss X" and describes her as a high-spirited Irish woman with blue eyes, a magnificent figure, and "the inimitable Irish genius for repartee. She kept Clarence chuckling, kept his imagination jumping apace, kept his blood tingling . . . and constantly delighted by outsmarting him, by thinking swifter and deeper than his fumbling male mind could carry him." Darrow and Leckie were inseparable, perfectly matched, planning to be married. Then suddenly their affair flew apart, and Darrow turned to Ruby.

Unlike Leckie, Ruby was no fire-breathing activist. When introduced to Darrow, she was engaged to a stockbroker. No doubt she found Darrow's idealism appealing, but the man she agreed to marry was a successful Chicago attorney, not a knight on a glorious steed. His radical girlfriends fed his ego, but Ruby made him feel secure. His father had lived on the financial margin, and his spiritual mentor, John Peter Altgeld, was almost penniless at the time of his death. In Ruby, he found someone much like his own mother, a woman who could take care of his personal needs and manage his finances, a woman who offered more security and certainty than fun and stimulation, though she offered some of both. He deliberately married a woman who expected him to become a prosperous and solid citizen, not a marginal dreamer like his father had been or the almost destitute kind of idealist that Altgeld had become.

Darrow's wedding to Ruby managed to capture all that his friends were to find most troubling about the new man and his new wife. After returning triumphantly from the anthracite coal hearings in the spring of 1903, he earned fresh acclaim and headlines as the lawyer for nine hundred men and women who were on strike against the Kellogg Switchboard Company. A court issued an injunction against picketing, and judges started to send strikers to jail by the carload. Darrow eloquently told the court that if all of the union workers were sent to jail for picketing, he would walk the picket line himself.

Nevertheless, the judge fined the strikers and the battle escalated. By the end of June, violence was a daily occurrence, the plant was in a state of siege, and the city was gripped by the largest riot since the Pullman strike.

Here is how Altgeld's biographer described what happened next. "Clarence Darrow, on this day of carnage and devastation, astonished his friends by getting married to a vivacious journalist only half his age. The ceremony was performed by his favorite ally on the Cook County bench, Judge Edward Dunne. After a champagne breakfast at the home of the wealthy inventor of shorthand, John R. Gregg, the couple secretly boarded a train for Montreal [and from there they headed off for Europe]. Strike or no strike, Darrow and his bride spent three sybaritic months on the Continent. His departure left the defense of the strikers in the hands of his partner, Edgar Lee Masters . . . [who] attacked the contempt cases with passion."

It was a symbolic start to Darrow's new life with Ruby.

❋ ❋ ❋ ❋

After they returned from Europe that fall, Ruby set out to dress her husband properly, to purchase clothes that would combat his rumpled, small-town image. She bought him silk shirts, tailored suits, oversized monogrammed handkerchiefs, and black satin ties made to order by Marshall Field. She felt that Darrow's head was too large for his frame and that he tended to wear hats that "left him looking too small, suggesting a squatty head and shoulders." Wanting her famous husband to look as though he had "the same proportions as other men," she ordered specially designed hats from the Knox Company in the East. She even tried to do something about his hygiene. Before their marriage, Darrow had gained a reputation for having dirty fingernails. Now, on special occasions, Ruby would send her husband off for a manicure and pedicure.

They moved out of the rooms at the Langdon and into a luxurious apartment on the city's affluent North Side.

❋ ❋ ❋ ❋

During the next three years, Darrow still delivered passionate speeches and wrote stirring essays; he occasionally undertook the visible defense of an underdog; he published a poignant autobiographical novel and a stinging novelized attack on criminal punishment. His deepest wish was to give up the law entirely, to spend all of his time writing and giving lectures. He would have loved to edit a magazine. But the only way to finance his life-style—and, perhaps, save enough money to become a man of letters—was to handle a certain number of cases that seemed contrary to his professed principles. He became the kind of lawyer he had once attacked, the kind of lawyer that Altgeld warned him against becoming. In the process, he became more and more bitter; his conversations became dark and often vicious. He was caught up in a cycle where his philosophy justified the handling of cases in which his clients had victimized the poor; and his choice of cases required that he become increasingly cynical.

On December 30, 1903, the nation was shocked by the Iroquois Theater fire. The theatergoers, mostly children, had been watching a matinee performance of *Mr. Bluebeard,* starring Eddie Foy. At a few moments past three, a red velvet curtain caught fire, lit by one of the floodlights. As the blaze spread, the audience ran for the exits, but twenty-nine of the thirty exit doors were locked. People raced for the windows, trampling over everyone and everything that was in their way. It was the greatest disaster in the city's history, with more than twice the fatalities of the great citywide fire of 1873. Bodies were carried out in bushel baskets. For days, relatives searched emergency rooms for the remains of loved ones. When everyone was accounted for, 596 people, most of them children, were dead.

In the weeks that followed, the *Chicago American* led a crusade to prosecute those responsible for the carnage: theater owners who had ignored city laws; fire inspectors who had failed to inspect; the mayor, who was responsible for the chief fire inspector. In the end, a large number of people were dragged in front of a grand jury, and most of the responsible men were indicted. But while others wanted justice for the dead, Darrow came to the aid of some of the defendants, working behind the scenes to have their cases dismissed. "It is not just," he said, "to lay the sins of a generation on the shoulders of a few." In the end, no one was sent to prison.

One of Darrow's most important clients was William Randolph Hearst, the newspaper magnate with political ambitions who had started publishing the *Chicago American* in 1900. At the Democratic convention of 1904, Darrow seconded Hearst's nomination for president of the United States. Later that year, he defended Hearst and the *Chicago American* against a tort claim brought by Mary E. Spiss, a pedestrian who was badly injured when hit by a one-ton advertising sign that contained nearly three thousand electric lights and was hung over State Street in downtown Chicago. It was illegal to hang signs over the sidewalk in Chicago, but Hearst had persuaded the government to make an exception in his case. When Miss Spiss won an eight-thousand-dollar jury verdict, Darrow appealed. Representing Hearst, he argued that the verdict was excessive. The court, however, noting the "nature and effect of the injuries," concluded that the award "cannot be regarded as excessive."

Another case that troubled Darrow's friends involved Union Traction, a streetcar company formed by Charles Yerkes, the high-handed and highly controversial entrepreneur who served as the model for the protagonist in Theodore Dreiser's novel *The Titan*. People were regularly crippled in streetcar accidents, but when they sued, juries tended to find for the defendant, or to award exceptionally small amounts. The explanation soon came to light. Lawyers for Union Traction had been bribing the jurors. The government proceeded to indict seven men, including the company's attorney, Cyrus Simon. Following instructions from Simon, one of the attorneys had bribed the constable who was to choose the jurors, as well as the jurors themselves. All seven defendants were convicted, though several of the decisions were reversed on appeal. Darrow was the chief trial attorney for three of the lawyers.

Some of Darrow's friends in labor were furious. One of Debs's top aides in the Pullman strike attacked Darrow for "defending men who had bribed juries in cases where crippled children were asking for justice from the traction companies which had injured them." Darrow's explanation was far from satisfactory. He said that he had simply been serving as a lawyer. Then, in a move that inspired further dismay, Darrow promptly hired Cyrus Simon to work in his office.

Darrow always had some glib explanation for taking these cases, but after a while his friends, who were turning into his critics, began to conclude that he had simply become greedy, that he would handle any case for a fee, no matter who was hurt. They were troubled by cases that went beyond a quest for financial security and seemed to be based on avarice. But it was the cynicism, more than the avarice, that so offended longtime admirers. He defended his work and his increasingly iconoclastic political views by resorting to arguments that were, to put it mildly, sophistic. He was a fatalist, he said. No one was really responsible for his actions. There wasn't much that one could do to make the world better—the forces of capital were too strong, the impoverished masses were too ignorant and fickle.

He seemed distrustful of everything—of the courts, which he regarded as instruments of capitalist tyranny; of reformers, who often seemed more interested in closing saloons than in improving the life of the poor; of women's suffrage, which he feared would only produce more intolerant voters; of socialism, which he feared would do away with personal liberty; of anarchism, which seemed unrelated to the realities of life. While like-minded men such as Louis Brandeis were advocating antimonopoly laws to break up huge corporations such as U.S. Steel, Darrow felt, reluctantly, that such conglomerations of industrial power were "in harmony with the deeper laws of industrial life—laws which in the end control; and all legislative efforts to hamper this growth by civil and criminal law are worse than futile—they are mischievous and meddlesome in the extreme." He didn't even believe in strikes. Although closely allied with labor, which generally found it impossible to make progress without going on strike, Darrow publicly argued that labor union strikes "were not advisable and would prove a detriment to unionization." When men strike for higher wages, he explained, employers increase prices, thus leading the consuming public to blame and oppose unions. Perhaps most tellingly, Darrow had no confidence in the public to act in its own interest, either as voters or as workers.

In retrospect, many of Darrow's viewpoints have proved to have merit. But rather than using his sharp mind to refine proposals advanced by his friends, to blink a yellow warning light, Darrow found a way of denouncing everything, of putting a red stoplight at every turn in the road. Whatever their merits, Darrow's caustic arguments were particularly offensive to men and women who were living in an era of belief, when almost everyone was either an anarchist, a socialist, a progressive, or a capitalist. Almost everyone believed in something. Everyone but Darrow.

※ ※ ※ ※

Darrow's friends continually spoke of his weaknesses. They still loved his sense of humor and his brilliant oratory, but many, perhaps most, found his outlook too bleak, his comments too caustic, and some turned from him in disgust. On January 8, 1907, shortly after moving from the North Side into an even more spacious apartment on the South Side, near the newly built University of Chicago, the Darrows invited Hamlin Garland, the famous novelist of the Midwest, over to dinner. Later that night, Garland recorded his reactions in his journal. "He is humorous, but he is also tragic in the hopelessness of his outlook," Garland wrote. "I found him more grave and even more bitter than his writing indicated. He talks with much of the same acrid humor. . . . His aggressive cynicism makes him repellent to many—hence he is to me a lonely figure. . . . We began our careers on a common ground, but he has gone . . . on into a dark and tangled forest land. He may be right, but at present he seems to me a destructive force merely."

An anarchist friend from the Sunset Club, Austin Willard Wright, reached a similar conclusion. "Darrow has no principles whatever," he said. "He knows nothing of principles—he's 'up in the air' resting nowhere and upon nothing. . . . He has a few fine sentiments, that's all. . . . He professes to hold feelings of utmost contempt for millionaires, while his acts emphasize greed for money equal to that of the most insatiable of millionaires. . . . I once had a fondness approaching affection for Darrow, but the withering blight of his moral bankruptcy fell upon everything of that kind, and so shriveled them up that they died."

Frederick C. Howe, a leading reformer from Cleveland, who later became famous as the U.S. immigration commissioner, described an episode with Darrow that typified his dominant mood. Howe worked with Cleveland mayor Tom Johnson, the great reformer, who was widely considered the best mayor in America. "Clarence Darrow was a frequent visitor in Cleveland," Howe wrote. "Personally, I never knew whether I admired or disliked him most. . . . He was an extraordinary personality—cynic and pessimist about politics and society. Society could not be saved, he said, and it wasn't worth saving anyhow."

When the famous muckraking reporter Lincoln Steffens came to interview him in his Chicago law offices, Darrow took his card and studied it for a moment trying to remember how he knew the name. Then he threw back his head, looked at Steffens's face, and started to laugh.

"Oh, I know," Darrow sputtered. "You are the man that believes in honesty!"

Steffens later described the scene. "Darrow laughed and laughed and laughed. He took and he shook my hand, but he laughed till tears came into his eyes. And he did not invite me into his office; he did not answer my questions. They only amused him the more, and I—well, I ran away."

❀ ❀ ❀

By the early years of the century, Darrow had a national following as a result of his writing, his lectures, and a few major cases. What made him truly famous, a national celebrity, was a series of murder cases in Idaho in 1907, the Haywood-Moyer-Pettibone cases, which, in his words, provided "a vivid picture of industrial warfare," pitting the Mine Owners' Association against the leaders of the Western Federation of Miners, the radical union that represented their workers.

For fifteen years the men who drilled the hills of Colorado, Montana, and Idaho, blasting the earth in search of gold, silver, copper, and lead, had been pitted in trench warfare against those forces that denied them a decent wage or even the right to strike. When owners brought in nonunion labor to operate the mines during a strike, the miners twice blew up mines and mills in the rich Coeur d'Alene mining region of northern Idaho. Between 1902 and 1904, forty-two men were killed and more than one hundred injured in the industrial warfare in Colorado.

In late 1903, the Mine Owners' Association made it clear that they would only hire workers who renounced the Western Federation of Miners. As the battle intensified, the tactics became more violent. On June 6, 1904, agents of the mine workers blew up a railway depot, killing thirteen men and wounding a number of others.

Then, on December 30, 1905, former Idaho governor Frank Steunenberg was killed by a bomb that exploded as he opened the gate to his home in Caldwell, Idaho. The murder of Governor Steunenberg, a sworn enemy of the union, seemed to be a clear part of that struggle.

Usually it was impossible to pin such crimes on any union leader, but this time the government located a powerful witness named Harry Orchard, whose name soon became infamous. Orchard, who was a new arrival in the small town of Caldwell, Idaho, claimed to be a sheep buyer, but he had made no noticeable effort to buy any sheep. On New Year's Day, 1906, Orchard was arrested and charged with the murder.

For ten days he maintained his innocence. Then the case was taken over by James McParland, a master detective who worked for the Pinkerton Detective Agency and had long been a representative of the mine owners in their battles with the union. McParland moved Orchard from the Caldwell jail, where he had been treated as an ordinary prisoner, to the Idaho state penitentiary, where he was placed in a dark cell on "murderers' row." Two weeks later, McParland visited Orchard in his cell. According to McParland's contemporaneous report, he told Orchard that the state had enough evidence to convict and execute him, but that "the hanging of him would be very little satisfaction" compared with the conviction of the men in the "Inner Circle" of the Western Federation of Miners. The detective promised to take care of Orchard "if he would come up and make a full confession of all that he knew in this case." McParland assured Orchard that if he implicated the union leaders he would "not be hung"; if not, "you will be hung in very quick order."

Orchard immediately confessed to a long series of crimes, including at least eighteen murders and a string of dynamitings. More important, he said that he had been hired by three leaders of the so-called Inner Circle: mine worker union president Charles Moyer, executive board member George Pettibone, and union secretary-treasurer William "Big Bill" Haywood. The outspoken, one-eyed Haywood was an especially attractive catch for the authorities since, just a year earlier, he had presided at the founding convention of the Industrial Workers of the World—a left-wing alternative to the American Federation of Labor.

The governor of Idaho, Frank Gooding, immediately asked for the extradition of the labor leaders from Colorado, where the union had its headquarters. Local authorities, acting under the supervision of the Pinkerton Detective Agency, arrested them in Denver on a Saturday evening. At eight P.M., the detectives found Moyer at the Denver railroad depot as he was about to leave for the mining camps in the Black Hills. An hour later, they arrested Haywood in the company of a woman—reportedly his sister-in-law—in what was then called a house of assignation. Pettibone was arrested at his home shortly before midnight. Although the men were entitled to a full hearing under Colorado law, they were denied a chance to meet with lawyers or friends or to make any objection to their arrest in court. Early the next morning, the detectives placed the three handcuffed prisoners on a specially chartered train to Boise, Idaho.

The case became a national sensation. It was widely felt that Orchard's confession had been procured by means of torture, or "the third degree," and that the men had been kidnapped. An effort to appeal to the U.S. Supreme Court to return the men to Colorado failed. In a ringing dissent, Justice Joseph McKenna said that the men had been kidnapped, that "kidnapping is a crime, pure and simple," and is even worse "when the law becomes the kidnapper." But the rest of the court voted to deny jurisdiction in the case.

Labor leaders around the country knew that the best man to handle the case was Clarence Darrow, famous for his defense of labor leaders Debs and Kidd. For Darrow, there was the prospect of enormous national attention and a fee that could finally allow him to retire from the practice of law. Also, despite his apparent cynicism, he believed deeply in the cause. He may have believed that Haywood was innocent; he certainly believed that in a just society citizens should not be kidnapped to stand trial; and that, even if the accused were guilty, such violence was part of the "thunderbolt" produced by years of industrial injustice.

At dinner with Darrow on the eve of his departure for Idaho, Hamlin Garland gained the distinct impression that he was more interested in attacking the industrial system than in saving his clients. "He is in sharp demand by the incarcerated labor leaders," Garland wrote in his diary, "but I was not entirely convinced that his action was dictated solely by a sense of justice. He takes a savage literary joy in striking at society over the shoulders of crime. I feel power, but not high purpose in his program." In all likelihood Darrow relished both prospects: the chance to defend three heroes of labor and the opportunity to put the industrial system itself on trial and expose its abuses to the world.

✳ ✳ ✳ ✳

To prove its case, the prosecution would need more than the uncorroborated testimony of a man who admitted to being a coconspirator. But the prosecutors were confident of victory. They claimed that Harry Orchard's testimony would be backed by two other powerful witnesses: Jack Simpkins, a member of the union's executive committee, who allegedly helped Orchard arrange for Steunenberg's murder; and Steve Adams, who had signed a confession admitting that he had collaborated with Orchard in a series of related dynamitings.

The defense team, coheaded by Darrow and Edmund Richardson of Denver, immediately managed to put the prosecution on trial. Day after day, the papers were filled with fresh stories about the improper kidnapping of the defendants, taken to Idaho without so much as a court proceeding in Colorado; about the abuses of the mine owners and the lengths to which they and their Pinkerton Detectives would go to control the system of justice, to manufacture evidence, to maintain a system of economic slavery.

Meanwhile, Jack Simpkins, one of the state's star witnesses, mysteriously disappeared. He had sent a telegram to Moyer in early 1906, while trying to arrange a lawyer for Orchard prior to his confession.

He was never heard from again, although he was renominated and reelected to the union's board. Reports placed him in such disparate places as British Columbia and Mexico. The Thiel Detective Agency claimed that Simpkins met Clarence Darrow in Spokane, Washington, in October, 1906. Whatever the explanation, he was not available at the time of the trial.

But the testimony of Steve Adams could still be damaging. He and Orchard claimed to have worked together closely on a number of dynamite jobs, including the bombing of a train depot in June, 1904, which killed thirteen nonunion laborers. Adams had also confessed to the murder of a woodsman named Fred Tyler.

Convinced that the Pinkerton detectives had frightened Adams into a confession by threatening to convict him of murder if he did not cooperate, Darrow hoped that he could persuade Adams to repudiate the confession by promising to defend him in any criminal proceeding. Adams was being held in the penitentiary, and the only way to communicate with him was through his relatives, who would be entitled to see the prisoner. Darrow tracked down James Lillard, an uncle of Adams's who lived in Baker, Oregon, and persuaded him to visit Adams in jail. The strategy worked. After talking with his uncle, Adams repudiated his confession. In return, Darrow agreed to defend Adams when he came to trial for the murder of Fred Tyler.

Darrow's remaining task was to challenge the credibility of Harry Orchard—which was relatively easy since it was generally believed that Orchard's confession had been improperly procured, and since he, by his own admission, was responsible for killing at least eighteen men.

In February, 1907, Big Bill Haywood went on trial for murder. His trial was front-page news for six months. The prosecution had every resource at its command, including the Pinkerton Detective Service and a team of lawyers headed by William E. Borah, who had just been elected to the U.S. Senate. It also had the support of President Theodore Roosevelt, who created a sensation when he said that Haywood, Moyer, and Socialist leader Eugene Debs, were "undesirable citizens."

But Haywood had some advantages of his own. Besides the fact that the most important corroborating witnesses against him had either recanted their testimony or disappeared, he had the powerful, daily courtroom work of a team of lawyers headed by Edmund Richardson and Clarence Darrow. At fifty years of age, Darrow was in top form. He used all of the tactics hewed in the Debs and Kidd cases, and he added one more: true venom. The dark, acrid qualities that had become troubling to so many of his friends became a feature of his courtroom persona. As Haywood recalled it twenty years later, "Darrow, in this case, as in others that he has defended, picked out a 'goat' among the prosecution lawyers. In this instance it was Jim Hawley upon whom he concentrated his sarcasm. He was at times so venomous that Hawley's son threatened to kill him with personal violence."

On a sweltering summer day, Darrow rose to make his final summation. Once again, he captivated the jury with an overwhelming, hypnotic argument, painting a picture that placed his client in the long line of heroes who had been sacrificed on the altar of greed. Once again it was *Les Misérables,* as Darrow told the jury not to blame the thunderbolt—for even if they killed Haywood, his truth would carry on. His eight-hour argument combined the themes used in the Debs and Kidd cases, even using some of the same phrases, but it went farther than ever before in endorsing violence.

"You are asked to take his life because down in Colorado and up in the Coeur d'Alene, he has been against the Mine Owners' Association, and because he has been organizing the weak, the poor, the toilers; has been welding together in one great brotherhood those men; has been calling them to fight under one banner for a common cause—for that reason he has raised up against him the power of this body of men, you are asked to kill Bill Haywood.

"To kill him, gentlemen! I want to speak to you plainly. Mr. Haywood is not my greatest concern. Other men have died before him. Other men have been martyrs to a holy cause since the world began. Wherever men have looked upward and onward, forgotten their selfishness, struggled for humanity, worked for the poor and the weak, they have been sacrificed. They have been sacrificed in the prison, on the scaffold, in the flame. They have met their death, and he can meet his, if you twelve say he must. But, gentlemen"—Darrow turned to face the prosecutors—"you shortsighted men of the prosecution, you men of the Mine Owners' Association, you people who would cure hatred with hate, you who think you can crush out the feeling and hopes and the aspirations of men by tying a noose around his neck, you who are seeking to kill him, not because he is Haywood, but because he represents a class. Don't be so blind. . . ." Now he was speaking again to the jurors. "If at the behest of this mob you should kill Bill Haywood, he is mortal, he will die, but I want to say that a million men will grab up the banner of labor at the open grave where Haywood lays it down, and in spite of prisons or scaffolds or fire, in spite of prosecution or jury or courts, these men of willing hands will carry it on to victory in the end."

Those powerful words, though, were mingled with a new sentiment that many found deeply offensive. "I don't care how many wrongs they committed," Darrow announced. "I don't care how many crimes these weak, rough, rugged, unlettered men who often know no other power but the brute force of their strong right arm, who find themselves bound and confined and impaired whichever way they turn, who look up and worship the god of might as the only god they know—I don't care how often they fail, how many brutalities they are guilty of. I know their cause is just."

❊ ❊ ❊ ❊

Haywood was acquitted on July 28, 1907. Some of Haywood's radical friends sent a telegram to President Roosevelt. UNDESIRABLE CITIZENS VICTORIOUS, it said. REJOICE. Nationally, Darrow was a hero, having won a case that many considered the greatest legal battle in American history.

People close to the case, and close to Darrow, were far less enthusiastic. They resented Darrow's words endorsing violence. The victory, they felt, had more to do with the lack of corroborating witnesses, with the judge's jury instructions, and with Richardson's conduct of the case, than with Darrow's argument. After the acquittal, Richardson condemned Darrow's speech as "rank. It was enough to hang any man regardless of his innocence or guilt." One juryman said: "Haywood was not shown to be guilty. If the defense had not put in any evidence after the state closed its case, the verdict would have been the same."

Whatever its impact on the jury, Darrow's speech said a good deal about the man and how he had changed. Somehow, some dangerous poisons had merged into his gentle soul in the years since Altgeld's death. On reading the speech, various friends exchanged letters speculating about how and why Darrow had changed. Writing just a week after the acquittal, an old friend from the Sunset Club in Chicago captured the sentiment felt by many. "I think we should take and enjoy the good he has given us, and overlook his personal weaknesses," he said. "He is a strange mixture of craft and courage, generosity and penuriousness, consideration and despotism, honesty and deviousness; and yet he has a big brain and a kind heart at base. So I have concluded that the only way is to enjoy his writings and avoid the man."

Rumors also started to spread about Darrow's trial tactics. Some people were convinced that he had kidnapped or paid off key witnesses to prevent them from testifying. Others hinted at jury tampering. The court bailiff was accused of taking six thousand dollars to let the jury be bribed. Back in Chicago, Darrow's law partner, Edgar Lee Masters, heard the stories. "The newspaper grape vine is that Darrow bribed the Steunenberg jury," he later confided.

❋ ❋ ❋ ❋

The Haywood case took more out of Darrow than he had anticipated. After months of grueling work, he was exhausted, but there was an overwhelming amount of work left to do. The state still intended to prosecute Moyer and Pettibone, and Darrow had agreed to represent Steve Adams as well. During the late summer and fall, he developed a serious flu and, far worse, a violent infection in his left ear. None of the doctors in Boise could find a cure, nor could Darrow find help anywhere in the surrounding area.

When the pain became unbearable, as it often did, Ruby would use a hypodermic needle to inject him with codeine. The opiate soothed him, but it also caused him to doze off, dreaming fitfully of "Red Wing, weeping her heart away," a song about an Indian maiden whose lover had gone away and never returned, a tune played by the owner of the home in which they were staying. As he became used to the codeine, Ruby had to inject him with larger and larger doses to give him relief or put him to sleep.

Finally he was in too much pain to continue with the trial. In January 1908, after making the opening statement on Pettibone's behalf, Darrow went to Los Angeles in search of medical treatment. After a week in the California Hospital, Clarence and Ruby moved into a small apartment in downtown Los Angeles where they were visited by a succession of physicians, each trying to find a way to cure the infection. Finally, more than five months after the pain had first appeared, an operation cured what was discovered to be a freak case of mastoiditis, which could well have killed him.

Though Darrow survived, he was physically weakened and financially drained by the ordeal. While the Darrows were in Los Angeles, a stock market crash wiped out their savings. Ruby, fearing injury to his health, did not tell Darrow that documents needed to be signed to release him from speculative investments that were rapidly losing their value. When he learned, too late, that he had lost everything, he was furious.

"Do you realize what you've done to me?" he shouted at Ruby. "You've thrown away my life savings, my dream of retiring. Now I'll have to begin all over again—be a slave to that irksome law work. We'll never be able to travel the world, write all those books! I'll never forgive you for this—never, never!"

❋ ❋ ❋

Back in Chicago, Darrow felt old and frail, alienated from Ruby, depressed by the prospect of returning to the practice of law. He promised Ruby that he would only take relatively easy cases that could be handled within close range of home. He would leave the long, exhausting work to younger men. Occasionally he would take up some lost cause if it could be done with minimal effort, but he agreed to devote most of his time to major clients such as the Chicago Title and Trust Company, or to serving as an arbitrator in labor disputes.

As one friend put it, Darrow began to act "as though life were a mere mechanical going on for him." He was ready for a release, ready for someone who was not, like Ruby, a part of the painful ordeal he had just endured; he was ready to find someone who admired and adored him, who made him laugh, who shared his love of good literature, and who did not expect him to dress like a banker and behave like a proper lawyer.

When he met her, Mary Field was a petite settlement-house worker who had been radicalized by seven years of experience with immigrants. She was thirty years old, with a salty smile and dark brown hair that was long enough for her to sit on. Raised in Detroit under the thumb of a tyrannical Baptist father and a gentle Quaker mother, she had come to Chicago to help immigrants find a better life in America. Before long, she was living and working at Jane Addams's Maxwell Street settlement, which specialized in helping Jewish immigrants, most of whom had recently fled from persecution in Russia. Living with immigrants, Mary quickly learned to admire their strength and to hate their oppressors. She grew increasingly radical until March 1908, when she became slightly notorious by coming to the defense of Lazar Averbuch, a Russian Jewish immigrant who was charged with stabbing Chicago's chief of police.

Clarence Darrow and Mary Field were first introduced that spring, at a meeting to gain support for another Russian revolutionist, a man named Christian Rudovitz. Darrow was serving as Rudovitz's lawyer, organizing public support and drafting petitions to the government to prevent the extradition of a man who would face certain death if forced to return home. As she watched Darrow speak at the rally, Mary Field fell in love. Tall and hulking, with a deep rich voice and a face lined with wrinkles earned over his fifty years, he seemed a romantic and powerful figure. He understood the plight of such men as Averbuch and Rudovitz, of the refugees she worked with every day, who seemed so alien to most Americans, yet were the political descendants of our revolutionary forefathers. When he spoke there was no one like him.

Unlike some of Darrow's more critical friends, Mary Field considered him one of the greatest men in history. It did not occur to her that he had become cynical or had betrayed his ideals. On the contrary, she put him in the company of Jesus and Tolstoy, of "those who have loved and served their fellow men with sincerity and singleness of heart." For a man with a certain amount of vanity, who was beginning to doubt his continuing importance and vitality, she was a hard woman to resist.

Mary and Darrow were fellow champions of the romantic cause of the Russian revolutionary, and she was a stimulating conversationalist who amused him as much as he amused her. "Mary could say the funniest things . . . that would make the hardest man laugh," one friend recalled. She tried to tease him into writing his autobiography, offering to help him in any way she could. He called her Molly. Like all of his friends, she just called him Darrow.

Mary became Darrow's assistant and protégée as well as his companion. One day, after seeing his friend Mother Jones, the aging labor leader, who was in town to raise money for the mine workers, he called Mary on the phone. "Molly," he said, "I kind of noticed that Mother Jones's coat looked horrid. Of course she's kind of old. I don't 'spect she could probably catch a fella."

Though he was generally quite tight with money, Darrow asked Mary to buy a coat for Mother Jones at Marshall Field's department store. It should be good and warm, he said, "but it doesn't have to be so purdy" (which was how he pronounced pretty).

Mary found Mother Jones to be "an ageless character dressed in black with a little bonnet covered with pansies." When Mary described her mission, Mother Jones was pleased. "Sure, I would like to have a coat, and I could use some nice wool pants and woolen stockings," she said. "You might as well outfit me."

Darrow, of course, then had to pay for her winter wardrobe. "I don't know how much money you'll need," he told Mary, "but I've got some on me." He reached down into his pockets and removed a big wad of bills, in a ball, all crumpled and moist.

"Darrow," Mary said, "that looks as if you've used it for a pocket handkerchief."

"It is kind of messy, isn't it," Darrow answered. "But I guess it will buy something."

Mary became increasingly drawn to what seemed his infinite compassion and tenderness, his understanding of defeat and of sorrow.

He seemed almost cursed by his unique ability to feel, to physically experience, the suffering of others. On one occasion she joined him in jail, where he was representing a female labor leader who had just been arrested. Darrow had tears coming down his cheeks at the thought of people being jailed for demanding decent wages. She found his sympathy for pain to be so deep that he felt others' agony himself, as if he had a toothache.

❈ ❈ ❈ ❈

Although he enjoyed speaking at large meetings and was constantly in demand, Darrow liked nothing better than a sociable evening reading poetry or short stories aloud, or talking about Tolstoy. Mary went with him on outings in a remote suburb where they talked philosophy, politics, poetry, and love.

Close as they were, marriage seemed out of the question. After the stock market failure of 1907, Darrow needed security more than ever. Even if she did not offer such challenging and invigorating company, Ruby did offer loyalty and stability; she, not Mary, could offer the kind of solid, stable environment that his mother had provided for his father. After a while, Darrow gave Mary the money to go to New York City, where they could have a less secretive relationship and where she could pursue a career as a writer.

While she was in New York, Darrow remained Mary's friend and benefactor, sending her money and advancing her career. With his help, Mary quickly began to make a reputation for herself. Darrow introduced her to his friend Theodore Dreiser, whose *Sister Carrie* had been officially published in 1900 but, because of its supposed immorality, was still not generally available to readers. Dreiser was editor of *The Delineator,* a popular magazine that specialized in publishing dress patterns along with fiction that was of special interest to women. He shared Darrow's enthusiasm for Mary's writing talent and promised, as she put it, "to make me literarely." Dreiser gave her enough assignments to keep her going, and her article in the September 1910 *Delineator* quickly became a succès d'estime.

"That piece of yours in *The Delineator* was a beautiful thing" wrote John S. Phillips, the editor of *America Magazine.* "I wish that we could have it for *America Magazine*—and I may tell you that it is only now and then that I feel envious of what I see in other magazines." Within weeks, Mary was writing for *America* as well.

Meanwhile, Mary was making her own friends in New York. She moved into an apartment with Ida Rauh, a founder of the Provincetown Players, who was soon to marry Max Eastman, the poet, philosopher, and founding editor of *The Masses*. Their circle included writers such as Dreiser, actors and actresses such as Maude Adams, artists such as the sculptor Jo Davidson, and activists such as the reformer Frederick Howe.

Darrow was delighted, and a bit tantalized, by the literary and social success of his petite protégée. "You have gone so far I can't see you any more," he wrote. "You never were very large. We will have to stop praising you pretty soon, or you will lose your head— poor little Miss Field—when will you write your autobiography? D--n if I wouldn't like to see you Molly, dear."

He did manage to visit her from time to time in New York. One Friday when he was visiting the city, Darrow took Mary, along with a pretty actress and a young man who was a descendant of William Cullen Bryant, on an outing in the country. While the actress grandly kept on her gloves and watched the scene, the others took off their shoes and stockings and ran through the fields filled with violets and trillium, but they didn't pick any of the flowers because Darrow argued that it was a shame to break up their little love affairs.

Back in Chicago, Darrow found that he missed Mary more and more. He told her that he was planning to move to New York soon, where he would be near to her. "I miss you all the time," he wrote. "No one else is so bright and clear and sympathetic to say nothing of sweet and dear. Am tired and hungry and wish you were here to eat and drink with me and talk to me with your low, sweet, kind sympathetic voice."

They were brought together more quickly and with more intensity than either of them could have imagined. But it was in Los Angeles, not New York. Two brothers had been charged with bombing the *Los Angeles Times* and killing twenty men. When the leaders of labor and the American left begged him to take the case, the invitation proved irresistible. But it sucked Darrow down into a whirlpool of events that exposed his greatest weaknesses and strained his internal contradictions to the breaking point.

Part II

THE McNAMARA CASE

The McNamara case came like a thunderclap upon the world. What was it? A building had been destroyed and twenty lives had been lost. It shocked the world. Whether it was destroyed by accident or by violence no one knew, and yet everyone had an opinion. Everybody who sympathized with the corporations believed it was dynamite; everyone who sympathized with the workingman believed something else. Society was in open rupture; the weak and the poor and the workers whom I had served were rallying to the defense of the unions and to the defense of their homes. They called on me. I did not want to go. I urged them to take someone else. But I had to lie down my own preferences and take the case. There was a direct cleavage in society. Those who hated unions, and those who loved them. The fight was growing fiercer and bitterer day by day. It was a class struggle, filled with all the venom and bitterness born of a class struggle. These two great contending armies were meeting in almost mortal combat. No one could see the end.

Clarence Darrow
Summation to Jury
The People v. Clarence Darrow
August 15, 1912

Chapter Three

THE CRIME OF THE CENTURY

W HEN THE CALLS FOR help started to arrive in late April, 1911, Darrow was in Kankakee, Illinois, working on a case that was fairly typical of his new, less demanding practice. It was the case of Charles Myerhoff against the board of directors of the Kankakee Manufacturing Company.

Myerhoff was an elderly Civil War veteran who, four years earlier, had invested most of his life savings in the company. Along with scores of other farmers and small businessmen, he did so in response to a series of deceptively promising advertising brochures and letters that made false claims about the company's property, assets, and revenues. When he lost his entire investment, he sued the company's directors for fraud.

That Clarence Darrow was involved in such a case would not have surprised his thousands of admirers around America. What would have surprised those who did not know him—and would have further contributed to the bitter disillusionment of his one-time friends—was that Darrow was counsel to the directors of the Kankakee Manufacturing Company.

Darrow did not contend that the advertisements and representations were accurate. As he studied the facts, he learned that they plainly were not. Instead, he offered a purely legal argument. No matter what the company claimed in its advertisements and letters, Darrow said, the investor had a legal responsibility to check all of the facts for himself. He argued that the court's responsibility was to apply the law—not the Golden Rule.

As Darrow was presenting these arguments in court, wearily building up once again a nest egg that he could use to retire from the law, an event occurred that stunned the nation. On April 22, John Joseph "J. J." McNamara was arrested in Indianapolis. As secretary of the International Association of Bridge and Structural Iron Workers, J.J. was one of the most impressive young labor leaders in America. Along with his younger brother, Jim, who was arrested in Detroit, J.J. was charged with murder—not a murder in Indianapolis, but a murder in Los Angeles. The brothers were charged with blowing up the *Los Angeles Times* building and killing twenty men.

Within hours, Darrow began to receive telegrams, letters, phone calls, and visits from labor leaders around America pleading with him to take charge of the case and protect labor's good name.

❉ ❉ ❉ ❉

The destruction of the offices of the *Los Angeles Times* had occurred more than six months earlier, in the middle of the night, on October 1, 1910. Twenty men had been killed in the most sensational act of industrial violence in the country's history, which newspapers across the nation quickly called the Crime of the Century. The bombing was the deadliest salvo in a fierce battle that had engulfed the city for years, a fight in what one commentator called "the bloodiest arena in the Western World for Capital and Labor."

Los Angeles in 1910 was a boomtown that fed primarily on its own growth. Aggressive promotional campaigns urged people from other states, particularly those from colder climates, to move to the beautiful West Coast, where one could bask in the sun, eat oranges from the backyard for breakfast, and make money effortlessly by investing in real estate. For those with an ailment, the warm climate and salt sea air were guaranteed to provide a cure. People flooded to Southern California: people from small, cold towns in the Midwest; those who were older, ailing, or financially independent; and those who hoped to find work in a booming economy. Before long,

Los Angeles was growing exponentially, multiplying six-fold between 1890 and 1910. The city was moving like an express train, and the fuel that fed the economic engine was construction.

Los Angeles should have been a construction worker's paradise, with plenty of good work for everyone, but it wasn't—thanks in large measure to the two-fisted union-busting efforts of Harrison Gray Otis, the tough-talking, walrus-mustached, seventy-three-year-old owner and publisher of the *Los Angeles Times.*

Otis had not always been anti-union. Early in life, he had joined the International Typographical Union (a gesture he later dismissed as "a folly of youth") and had quit a job as editor of the *Rock Island Courier* when the paper's owner refused to sign a union shop agreement. But any lingering sympathy for labor evaporated in 1882, when he took over as editor and part owner of the *Times.*

He resented it when the International Typographical Union insisted that he give preferential treatment to union members; within a few years, push and shove came to ball and chain as Otis and the printers launched an all-out war. When the city's economy tumbled in 1890, Otis asked his printers to accept a 20 percent cut in wages. The ITU declared that its members would walk off the job if their wages were cut.

"Go ahead," Otis thundered, "walk! I will get it out myself. I haven't forgotten how to set type."

But he didn't have to go that far. When the union went on strike, Otis told the printers to go to hell. He locked them out and brought in a team of strikebreakers from Kansas City.

To retaliate, the unions tried to persuade advertisers and subscribers to boycott the paper. The ITU paid for five thousand lapel buttons proclaiming I DON'T READ THE TIMES and fined its own members five dollars for refusing to wear them.

Otis wasn't fazed in the least.

"But you will!" he roared, when he saw the union buttons.

As Otis gained fame as a foe of union organizers, the American Federation of Labor mobilized a national boycott of companies that advertised in the *Times.* Somehow their efforts generally seemed to misfire. Six hundred female members of the Ladies' Garment Workers' Union sent letters objecting to advertising by the maker of

Bishop's Pills. Unfortunately, the product was for use by "men only"—and all of the letters were misaddressed "Bishop, Salt Lake City, Utah," where they wound up in the hands of the bishop of the Mormon Church.

Most of the city's businesses continued to advertise in the paper, which had a daily circulation of 55,000 and a Sunday circulation of 85,000. In 1910, Otis made an annual net profit of $463,000 on gross earnings of $1,552,000.

Otis loved the fight with the unions. He had a preference for hot wars—twice wounded in the Civil War, he reenlisted during the Spanish-American War in 1898 and the Filipino Insurrection in 1899— but during peacetime he devoted his military acumen to the war against labor. He called his home on Wilshire Boulevard "the Bivouac"; he labeled his employees at the paper "the Phalanx"; and he preferred to be called "General Otis." With his stern gaze, walrus mustache, and white goatee, the "General" drove around town in a car that was specially outfitted with a cannon on the hood. He was "like gunpowder," one employee observed, "a dictator who accepted no opposition."

When a young reporter named James Pope failed to show up for a meeting of the Phalanx, he was chewed out and ordered to report to General Otis's office. After a few minutes, Otis's secretary announced that the General was ready to see him.

Pope entered the room and saw the aged leader sitting behind his desk, a grave look on his face. Pope saluted and clicked his heels. "Pope reporting for service, sir." He promised never again to miss a meeting of the Phalanx.

Otis began to smile. "Return to duty," he said crisply, returning the salute. Pope turned about-face and marched out of the office in full military form.

Inspired by battlefield rhetoric, Otis called organized labor "a tyranny—one of the most monstrous tyrannies that the world has ever seen." He elevated his venom to a creed, treating "Industrial Freedom" as a sacred right, "vital to private and public liberty, vital to the prosperity and progress of the citizen and of the country, vital to the good of the industrial world, vital to the best interests of the

Republic and all its citizens." He was determined to drive every vestige of union labor from the city.

To carry out his campaign against unions, Otis played a key role in organizing and mobilizing some 85 percent of the city's businesses into the powerful and highly disciplined Merchants and Manufacturers Association. Like Otis, the M&M's leaders were convinced that the city's economic success had as much to do with industrial freedom as with orange groves. They hated unions almost as much as they worshipped growth. As the San Francisco *Bulletin* explained, "the Merchants and Manufacturers Association has one confession of faith, one creed: 'We will employ no union man.' The M&M also has one command: 'You shall employ no union man.' The penalty for disobedience to this command is financial coercion, boycott, and ruin. 'You hire union men and we'll put you out of business,' says the M&M, and the employer knows that the oracle speaks. 'You declare an eight-hour day, and we'll stop your credit at the banks,' and the M&M does what it says."

The M&M's tactics were hugely successful. The city became known as Otistown of the Open Shop, and "the most unfair, unscrupulous and malignant enemy of organized labor in America."

✳ ✳ ✳ ✳

By sharp contrast, San Francisco had become a labor organizer's paradise. As one observer noted, after 1908 "not a hammer was lifted, or a brick laid, or a pipe fitted, or wall plastered or painted or papered without the sanction of the unions."

While many people gave Otis the principal blame—or credit—for this difference between the cities, larger questions of electoral politics played an important role as well. Thanks in part to the large population of politically conservative retired men and women from the Midwest, Los Angeles labor leaders were never able to take control of the city government. But at the turn of the century, labor leaders in San Francisco were winning a series of startling political victories.

In 1901, the San Francisco Employers Association seemed on the verge of crushing union labor. But workers quickly organized the

Union Labor Party and won the mayoral election that year. With their friends in control of city spending and the police force, the San Francisco unions won a series of major concessions, and the Employers Association was disbanded. In short order, San Francisco became the first and only closed-shop city in America, where only union members were allowed to work.

By 1910, the discrepancies between working conditions in California's two largest cities had begun to produce serious consequences, particularly in the metal trades. As labor historian Grace Stimson explains: "The contracts between the San Francisco Metal Trades Council and the California Metal Trades Association, due to expire on June 1, 1910, specified the eight-hour day. Northern employers, however, who had long suffered from the competition of manufacturers in Los Angeles and other coastal cities, where labor costs were lower and the working day longer, declared against renewal of those contracts unless San Francisco unions equalized wages and working conditions up and down the coast." Unless they wanted their own hours increased and their wages lowered, the San Francisco unions would have to turn Los Angeles into a union city.

The San Francisco contracts were extended until August 1, 1910, to allow adequate time for the test. "The ultimatum," as Stimson noted, "was a powerful incentive for a supreme effort to organize Los Angeles."

Feeling the pressure, the San Francisco unions proceeded to mobilize a full-scale attempt to organize the Los Angeles building trades, and particularly the metal trades. In February, the San Francisco leaders promised that they would provide full support for the effort. On May 18, they joined with an official of the Los Angeles Metal Trades Council in sending a letter to employers demanding an eight-hour day and a minimum daily wage of four dollars. The unions said that they would call a general strike of the metal trades unions if they did not receive a favorable reply by June 1.

A week later, the *Los Angeles Times* announced that the employers had thrown the letter in the trash basket. As promised, on June 1 the metal trades unions of Los Angeles began a walkout.

❋ ❋ ❋

Two days later, Eugene Clancy of the Bridge and Structural Iron Workers sent a letter from Los Angeles to his union's handsome, devoutly Catholic secretary-treasurer, John J. McNamara, in Indianapolis. As the leader of the Structural Iron Workers' Union in San Francisco, and a member of the union's national board, Clancy was the leading Structural Iron Workers official on the West Coast.

"I have been here five days now and they have started here the greatest strike any part of the country has had in a long time," Clancy crowed. "All the shop men of the Union Iron Works and Bakers Iron Works and Llewellyn Iron Works are quitting."

Clancy asked J. J. McNamara to send one of his top men to help with the situation. "Send Hockin at once," he wrote. "He will make his salary—if not in money, in goodwill for the Iron Workers." But Herbert Hockin was not available. So J.J. sent his younger brother, Jim, instead.

❋ ❋ ❋ ❋

As Clancy knew, Hockin and the McNamara brothers were part of a last-ditch campaign to use the tools of industrial terror to assure economic survival. The campaign had begun five years earlier, after the steel industry set up the National Erectors' Association in an effort to destroy their union. In 1905, the construction industry began to bypass union contracts by subcontracting work to non-union companies. Union complaints were to no avail.

Even in an era of mean-spirited corporate conduct, the effort to reduce wages for bridge and structural iron workers seemed especially dastardly. They were the men who risked their lives every day by crawling out on long scaffolds, atop bridges and buildings, with no life net to save them from a fall to the cement or rushing rivers hundreds of feet below. It was a dangerous and nomadic life that appealed to adventurous daredevils, most of them with little or no education. At least one hundred structural iron workers were killed on the job each year—or about one in every hundred. "We work with a man one week and the next we read of his falling to his death," McNamara once explained. "We become so accustomed to it that I never realized what it meant until I sat by my own brother's deathbed last year." Nevertheless, iron workers only earned about

$2.50 a day—and the industry thought even that salary was too high.

When normal negotiating tactics failed, J. J. McNamara and his colleagues found an effective alternative: dynamite. From February 1908 to April 1911, the union planted explosives at some seventy job sites of companies that refused to be organized by the Structural Iron Workers. Significantly, no one had been killed in any of the explosions; the average loss to property was about one thousand dollars.

The violence worked. Despite the concentrated opposition of the United States Steel Corporation, which had destroyed most of the other unions in the field, the Bridge and Structural Iron Workers made major gains. A government report noted that they quickly moved from being the lowest paid building trade to one of the highest.

The successful campaign was organized by J. J. McNamara. McNamara's top lieutenant was Herbert Hockin, a labor organizer and dynamite expert from Detroit. And his most effective field men, the people who actually went around the country setting off explosions, were Ortie McManigal and Jim McNamara, J.J.'s younger brother.

The two brothers were as different as the children of the same parents can be. The older brother by six years, J. J. McNamara was the shining light of one of the most important unions in America. Intensely religious, athletically built, he had a choirboy face and winning smile that would soon become nationally famous. As the oldest child, he had left school in his early teens to help support his family. With agility and strength, he had been willing to take the risks associated with structural iron work, climbing out on the high and narrow scaffolding of skyscrapers and bridges with nothing between him and certain death far below. He became popular with his fellow workers, was elected a delegate to the union's convention, and became the full-time secretary-treasurer at the age of twenty-eight.

Shortly after his election to that post, J.J. began a process of self-education, starting with a night course in business, followed by two years of night school at the Indiana School of Law, where he earned a degree in 1909. He also served as editor of the union's publication, *Bridgeman's Magazine,* where he published articles on sociology and economics, and even some poetry. At thirty-four, he was unmarried, supported his mother, and went to visit her in Cincinnati every weekend.

By contrast with his handsome, self-made, devoutly religious brother, Jim McNamara was an anemic, chain-smoking ne'er-do-well. He hated the Church, loved liquor and gambling, and spent most of his time with married women or prostitutes. Between 1901 and 1907 he had at least four affairs with older women. Three of them were married, and the other was a widow.

Jim spent some time working as a printer, but due to his independent attitude and loud mouth, he always managed to get himself fired—and once was even run out of town. He lost his last printing job in 1907 when he called the foreman—who had threatened to fire him if he didn't work overtime—an "old gray-haired son-of-a-bitch."

"You old bastard," Jim said. "You can take your old job and stick it up your ass."

J.J. came to the rescue. He loved his younger brother and may even have admired his independent orneriness. In any case, he needed someone whom he could trust to blow up buildings around the country. For several months, Herbert Hockin taught Jim how to buy, transport, and detonate dynamite and nitroglycerine. Together, they bought electrical fuses and detonating caps and dry cell batteries that would cause the material to explode. They practiced lighting fuses with the butt of their cigars. Hockin demonstrated how two men, hundreds of feet apart, could communicate with each other by a gesture or a puff of a lighted cigar. He taught Jim how to make use of the time it took for a long fuse to burn its way to the bomb, how to establish an alibi by stopping in a saloon or meeting a railroad conductor before the bomb went off.

Jim's first job was in Cincinnati on May 9, 1909. The Cincinnati Southern Pacific railroad was building a new bridge over the Ohio river, and the steel girders were being placed by a large erecting firm from Pittsburgh that, despite Hockin's pleas, had refused to employ union labor. The explosion was a success. It caused minimal damage and no casualties. But the company was forced to hire six additional security guards. There was a fresh incentive to enter into a contract with the union.

By the time he was asked to go to the West Coast a year later, Jim McNamara was a professional at his trade, more dynamiter than printer and certainly more dynamiter than iron worker. He felt ready to act on his own.

❉ ❉ ❉ ❉

Clancy seemed satisfied with the choice and wanted Jim to head West at once. By mid-June, fifteen hundred workers had quit their jobs and the San Francisco labor leadership had set up the General Strike Committee in Los Angeles, led by Olaf Tvietmoe.

Tvietmoe, the secretary-treasurer of the state's Building Trades Union, was known to some as "the Viking" and to others as the "Old Man" of the San Francisco labor world. At six feet, he weighed over three hundred pounds, walked with a limp, and carried a large, heavy cane. He was an imposing figure, a powerful force with slate blue eyes, dark hair, and wire-rimmed glasses that hinted that he was an intellectual as well as a fierce leader of the masses. He had immigrated to America from Norway in 1882 at the age of seventeen, and he remained proud of his Scandinavian roots. He loved to quote Norwegian works and had translated one of Bjornstjerne Bjornson's plays into English. He played the violin, read Greek, and, serving as editor of a weekly publication called *Organized Labor,* wrote prose faster than most people could read.

Tvietmoe's political power was reinforced by his role as head of the Asiatic Exclusion League—an openly racist group that sent out virulent propaganda attacking Chinese, Japanese, and Koreans—and by his close association with Building Trades Council president P. H. McCarthy, who was also the mayor of San Francisco. Tvietmoe associated with mainstream politicians and hoped to make a fortune through his role as an investor and officer of the Sunset National Oil company. Yet when it came to union organizing he was a militant combatant who believed that the fight between capital and labor was truly a war. One old friend described him as "a man of power. I think he could tear people apart with his hands if he tried." There was, people felt, "something rather gigantic about Tvietmoe."

Tvietmoe's top deputy was a former woodworker and carpenter named Anton Johannsen. While Tvietmoe was generally considered the most powerful labor leader on the coast, Johannssen had some-thing of a national reputation, thanks to a book by Hutchins Hap-good, the radical journalist. A few years earlier, Hapgood had set out to find the prototypical working man, someone to use as the protag-onist of a book on American labor. He found his man when he saw the short, stocky, German-born organizer drinking beer and holding forth at the bar of the Briggs House in Chicago. He had "the power-ful body of a young mechanic; short and thick-set with stubbed and horny hands; his head is a bullet, his brow broad, his eyes large, deep and kind." They talked about Tolstoy, labor, and life. Hapgood was captivated by Johannsen's "intellectual vigor, his free, anarchis-tic habit of mind, and the rough sweet health of his personality." Above all, Hapgood was struck by Johannsen's remarkable laugh.

"He laughed like the Olympians," Hapgood wrote, "huge volumes of enjoyable sound; all higher and lower enjoyments were in this wonderful laughter, which years afterward, when he became notorious if not famous (which in his case was the same thing) thrilled into a tradition." Inadvertently, Hapgood's book gave Jo-hannsen his nickname. He called his book *The Spirit of Labor.* In no time, Johannsen was joyfully known as "the Laugh of Labor."

But Johannsen was exceptionally serious about his work. He considered himself a practical anarchist. He loved the anarchists' belief in individualism, and their powerful emotions. He cared too much about individual liberty to be a Socialist, and he was too radical for the national leadership of organized labor, symbolized by AFL president Samuel Gompers, whom he considered too diplo-matic. It would be better for the labor movement, he said, "if there were more emotion in the American Federation of Labor." Shortly after *The Spirit of Labor* appeared, Johannsen had a chance to join a less diplomatic and more emotional group of men: he moved to California with his wife and small children, found a small home in Corte Madera, near San Francisco, and began to organize in earnest.

❋ ❋ ❋ ❋

Under the leadership of Tvietmoe and Johanssen, the General Strike Committee paid Los Angeles strikers a stipend of seven dollars a week and provided low-cost food through a grocery store at the

Labor Temple that was stocked with food that had been brought in at cost from San Francisco. Strikers were organized into squads of ten; to earn their strike benefits, they were required to perform picket duty.

But the Los Angeles business community, lead by the Merchants and Manufacturers Association and the Founders Association and cheered on by General Harrison Gray Otis and his *Los Angeles Times*, fought back. At their request, the M&M's general counsel, Earl Rogers, drafted an ordinance, allegedly designed to prevent labor violence, that outlawed picketing in Los Angeles. Though the unions challenged Rogers to cite a single example of labor violence, and turned in a petition, signed by thousands of citizens, that asked that the ordinance be put to a popular vote, the Los Angeles city council unanimously adopted the ordinance on July 16.

Clancy knew the situation had to be addressed soon. "Has Jim left for here?" he wired J.J. on July 12. "If not, have him come at once."

✻✻✻✻

When Jim arrived in San Francisco, he went to see Clancy as well as Tvietmoe and Anton Johannsen who, in turn, introduced him to two anarchists who had some experience with explosives. One was David Caplan, a short, dark-haired Jewish immigrant from Russia who ran a small grocery store with his wife, Flora. The other was Matthew Schmidt, or "Schmidty," a one-eyed carpenter who was Johannsen's best friend.

Schmidty soon became Jim McNamara's best friend in San Francisco. They spent time almost every day together, talking, going to shows or to dinner at the Bohemian Café with Schmidty's friend Belle Lavin, dropping by Tvietmoe's office at the Asiatic Exclusion League, spending Sundays in Corte Madera, playing cards at Presenti's Hotel, or enjoying lunch at the Johanssens' warm and unpretentious home. Not wanting to remain in any location for too long, Jim spent a few days at the Winchester Hotel, stayed for almost two weeks at Lena Ingersoll's boardinghouse, and then moved into the Hotel Argonaut, where Schmidty checked in as his roommate.

Meanwhile, Jim was carrying out various projects under the supervision of Eugene Clancy, the Iron Workers official who had brought him to the coast. On August 20, Jim dynamited the Pacific Coast Lumber Company in Oakland, California. A week later, at Joe's suggestion, Clancy sent Jim to Seattle, where he blew up the Stone and Webster office building.

In mid-September, Jim was instructed to make arrangements to use his professional expertise in Los Angeles. Using the name James Brice, he worked with Caplan and Schmidt to buy dynamite in San Francisco and transport it to the City of Angels—which the Iron Workers called "the scabbiest town in the United States."

❋❋❋❋

Los Angeles was boiling over with labor excitement in the summer of 1910. After the city council passed its antipicketing order on July 16, workers representing all of the striking unions held a meeting at their headquarters, a building called the Labor Temple. By secret ballot, the workers voted overwhelmingly to defy the ordinance, to continue picket duty, and to go to jail if necessary. Early the next morning, Anton Johannsen took a group of labor organizers to Sixth and Spring Street, where the Llewellyn Iron Works was erecting the eleven-story Los Angeles Trust and Savings Building. As Johannsen was talking to some of the nonunion men, trying to get them off the job, Mr. Llewellyn, accompanied by a police officer, ordered them to leave. Johannsen and his colleagues retreated to the sidewalk and held their ground. Moments later, a team of police officers arrived and placed the organizers under arrest. By the end of the day, twenty-seven men were in jail.

On the next day, a Saturday, eighty-five men were arrested. More were arrested the following Monday, and that evening the strikers held a huge rally. Though one hundred police officers told them to disperse, some three thousand people gathered along Main Street, stretching from First to Fifth and from Main to Wall, listening to speeches, singing "La Marseillaise," and cheering on the strikers.

Soon, whether by accident or design, strikebreakers started to die. The first man killed was a nephew of James J. Jeffries, the famous boxer who had retired six years earlier as heavyweight champion of the world. In mid-August, a derrick at the Alexandria Hotel Annex construction site fell, killing Jeffries and injuring two of his fellow nonunion workers. The derrick fell again the next day, killing one man and injuring two others. Labor organizers claimed "the scabs [were] killing each other through their own incompetency." Others suspected darker reasons. In any case, nonunion workers began to get the message: it was dangerous to be a nonunion laborer.

Reporting to the Iron Workers convention in Rochester in late September, Eugene Clancy captured the excitement of the moment. "Los Angeles has at last woken up," he told the delegates. "The union spirit has taken possession of that town in a remarkable degree. For years it has been known as the scabbiest town on the continent. No one could get a job except through the secretary of one of the bosses' associations, and if a man desired to quit his job, he would have to have the consent of the same secretary, or he would not work in Los Angeles any more. The so-called 'open shops' were closed to union men.

"Today there is such a militant spirit that six hundred and ninety-seven men, on a secret ballot, voted to go to jail rather than abide by the outrageous antipicketing ordinance passed by the so-called Good Government city council. Men are flocking to the unions, eager to assist those on strike. To protect them from the spies of the bosses, they are being initiated secretly in their own homes."

Clancy ended his report with the hope that "our brothers in the East will appreciate the peculiar conditions that exist in the West, and realize that we have been able to combat these conditions only by utilizing every weapon at our command."

※ ※ ※ ※

Schmidty, Caplan, and McNamara had their work cut out for them. They had to find and buy a sufficient quantity of dynamite and arrange a way to transport it to Los Angeles. They began by arranging to buy the powder from the Giant Powder Company, a manufacturer of high explosives, explaining that they needed to use it to blow up some stumps. They said they needed five hundred pounds of 80 percent gelatine, which was to be wrapped in stick form and loaded in boxes. Schmidty, acting for the group, paid $82.10 to the shipping clerk in San Francisco, but said that he wanted to pick it up by launch at the company's Oakland warehouse. The shipping clerk agreed, and gave Schmidty a receipt.

The group had decided to bring the dynamite to Los Angeles by water, but to do so they needed to rent a boat. On September 17, Schmidty took out advertisements in the *San Francisco Call* and the *San Francisco Examiner.* They said: "Wanted by a party of men 16–24 foot launch for ten day's cruise around bay and tributaries. Best of references." Two days later, Schmidty and Jim went down to the docks in East Oakland looking for a launch. Finally they found a twenty-three-foot cabin cruiser called *Pastime* that belonged to E. H. Baxter and Allen Burrowes.

After agreeing to pay $30 for a week's use of the boat and leaving a $250 deposit, the men took the boat to Sausalito, where they stayed at the Miramar Café, changed the boat's name to *Peerless,* and waited for Caplan to join them.

On September 23, the three men took the launch to the Giant Powder Company's Oakland facility. Schmidty, who was wearing a blue jumper with a flowery stripe, got out of the launch at the Powder Company's wharf. A few moments later he was approached by George Phillips, the company's assistant superintendent.

"Are you looking for anybody?" Phillips asked.

"I am after some powder," Schmidty said.

"Have you got an order?"

"Yes," Schmidty said, taking an order from his pocket.

A Portuguese employee went to get three or four boxes of explosives, which the group loaded onto the ship. At one point Schmidty called Caplan by name. "Hey!" Jim shouted at him. "Get wise on names."

The launch then took off for Los Angeles with its cargo. It was returned to its owners on September 28. Later that afternoon, Jim and Schmidty checked out of the Argonaut Hotel, where they had remained registered while on the boat. On their way out, Schmidty asked the bellman to get a suit of clothes that he had sent to the tailor shop to be pressed. Schmidty then returned to Belle Lavin's home, and Jim left for the railroad depot to catch a train to Los Angeles.

The next morning, Jim McNamara registered at the Baltimore

Hotel on Fifth Street in downtown Los Angeles, identifying himself as J. B. Brice from Chicago. The desk clerk, Kurt Diekelman, was also from Chicago. When he saw the registry, Diekelman spent a few minutes chatting with the new guest about his hometown. Jim then went to his room, where he spent the next day assembling the materials for three time bombs, each consisting of a clock and a battery connected by wire to a ten-quart can of nitroglycerin. Late the following morning, after noticing a sign that required guests to check out by three o'clock, he went down to the lobby to find Diekelman. Jim explained that he planned to catch the late evening Lark train for San Francisco, and asked if it would be all right to stay in the room until six or seven o'clock. Diekelman said that would be fine.

Jim left the hotel at five-thirty—to plant a bomb in the alleyway next to the *Los Angeles Times.*

❀ ❀ ❀

If workers considered Los Angeles "the scabbiest city" in America, they considered the *Los Angeles Times* the country's scabbiest paper by far—a natural target for an attack on the city's antilabor forces. The battle in the summer of 1910 was precisely General Otis's cup of poison. There was plenty of room for bias, invective, caricature, editorial opinions—and even some good solid reporting.

On August 24, the paper printed an article contending that the San Francisco bosses had come to town to instigate violence. The headline alone told the story. BRUTAL, it said. BREAK HEADS IS THE ORDER. NOT ENOUGH BLOODSHED HERE FOR LABOR BOSSES. TVIETMOE AND GANG ARRIVE ON MISCHIEF BENT. CLIMAX OF ATTEMPT TO FASTEN YOKE ON CITY.

Using their power base in San Francisco, the labor leaders fought back. Two weeks later, when Otis and his son-in-law, Harry Chandler, were in San Francisco, Tvietmoe and his allies sued the *Times* and its top executives for criminal libel. A police court judge immediately ordered the arrest of the *Times* executives, but Otis and Chandler were promptly released on bail.

Otis was a hornets' nest—mess with him and he stung back. On the morning of September 30, the paper carried a typical Otis-inspired diatribe. It accused labor of "the dastardly attack on a corpse and its bearers at the Hotel Alexandria Annex," which was being built with nonunion labor; of "an attempt to blow up the Hall of Records in order to wreak vengeance on the open shop contractor and in the hope of killing some of the nonunion workers who might be about the premises;" and of "the assault on Edward C. Hoffman, a free workman employed in a disunionized iron works."

All of the charges were denied and denounced by the unions. But they added to Jim McNamara's anger and sense of mission as he headed for the *Times.*

❀❀❀❀

At five forty-five P.M., as night fell on the city, Jim McNamara planted a suitcase containing sixteen sticks of 80 percent dynamite in the alleyway behind the *Times.* He set the timer to go off at one A.M. Then he placed time bombs at "the Bivouac," General Otis's residence on Wilshire Boulevard, and at the home of Felix Zeehandelaar, the powerful secretary of the Merchants and Manufacturers Association.

His work completed, McNamara began the job of establishing an alibi. He went back to his hotel and checked out at seven o'clock. Then he headed for the train depot and caught the late night train back to San Francisco.

As he left the city, Jim McNamara did not know that the alleyway behind the *Times* was also known as Ink Alley. Nor had he taken a close look at the barrels that were stored only a few feet from his suitcase. Had he done so, he would have seen that the barrels were filled with printer's ink that was certain to ignite as soon as the bomb went off.

❀❀❀❀

That same evening, Harvey Elder, the paper's new assistant city editor, had a light dinner with a young colleague at Tony's Spanish Kitchen, a popular theatrical hangout on North Broadway that was run by a man named Ismael Ramirez. Since the gringos couldn't quite master Ismael, they called him Tony. He returned to the paper just after sundown, but before he could settle down at his desk, Elder was paid a surprise visit by his young mother, who wanted to see him at his new post.

"Their half-ashamed pleasure together that evening over his new position inside the rail was touching and gentle to see," the *Times* later reported, in an account that was, perhaps forgivably, a bit romantic. "As she left the office that night, Elder followed her to the door and both their faces were glowing with pleasure."

❋ ❋ ❋ ❋

Cy Sawyer was a thirty-four-year-old hunchback with a wife and two children who were used to having him work the night shift. He was also one of the city's most talented telegraph operators, skillful at rapidly translating the dot-and-dash Morse code into alphanumeric characters as dispatches came in from around the country. That night he had been assigned to transcribe reports from Nassau County, New York, the scene of the 278-mile Vanderbilt Cup, the greatest motor-race in America. At twelve-thirty A.M., acting on his editor's instructions, Sawyer sent a message to a reporter in New York. It was three-thirty in Mineola, Long Island, and spectators were already beginning to arrive for the race. "Send us a good account of the race," Sawyer's message said. "At the crack of the pistol, begin sending the actual scenes on the track." With a hunger for disaster that seemed more tragic than ironic only a few moments later, the message added, "describe in detail any accidents as they occur."

At one A.M. PST, Sawyer tapped in some final instructions for the transmittal. Moments later, as he was decoding Sawyer's message, the wireless operator in New York heard a faint click on the line. The circuit had gone dead.

"Wire open," the New York operator shouted to a nearby editor as he attempted to repair the link. He repeatedly tried to reestablish contact with Sawyer, tapping out the dots and dashes that signified *TS*, the code for the *Los Angeles Times*. There was no response. Instead, as he was typing *TS* for the fourth or fifth time, a message came across the wires from the chief of the main Western Union office in Los Angeles. "Poor old Sawyer will answer no more calls," it said. There had been an explosion, he explained, and the city was on fire.

❋ ❋ ❋ ❋

By a few minutes after one A.M., the *Los Angeles Times* building was a torch, ablaze with the largest fire that the city had ever seen. It was doubtful that anyone would survive.

❋ ❋ ❋ ❋

When the blast occurred, Harvey Elder was in the city room. Finding the stairs blocked by flames, he ran to the third floor windows on the First Street side of the building. He climbed outside and hung onto the ledge until he heard a shout from two firemen and a policeman who were holding a life net down below. They had already saved several editors and pressmen who had no other exit. They urged him to jump.

But Elder missed the net. At seven-thirty A.M., he died at Clara Barton Hospital of burns and of the injuries sustained in his fall.

❋ ❋ ❋ ❋

When the explosion hit, the newspaper's engravers were at work on the sixth floor. They tried to escape down the staircase, but were met with a wall of flames on the floor below. The men then climbed up to the roof and worked their way through the thick smoke to the edge of the building, which was separated from a rooming house by a narrow alleyway.

Someone down below heard the engravers' cries for help and rushed to the top of the rooming house carrying a ladder. When the ladder proved too short, the men put one end on the extreme edge of the roof, and held the other end with their hands, carefully crawling to safety. One engraver, Huber Bruce, became separated from the others. Finally, finding a telegraph cable that spanned the alleyway, he climbed across it, hand over hand, to the roof on the other side.

❋ ❋ ❋ ❋

The first police officer on the scene was Eddie King. He and a partner had been searching the Boyle Heights district for a holdup man who had been conducting a series of robberies in women's clothing. The robber walked the streets and approached single men, pretending to be a prostitute. Then he would bring out a gun and ask for their money.

King and his partner were crossing Spring Street on their way back to the First Street police station when they felt the blast. It shattered the ground and broke glass windows all around them. As they approached the *Times* building, they saw workers leaping out of the upper floors of the structure, which was a tower of flames. King and his partner ran to the side of the building and started to collect the injured and carry them across the street to wait for ambulances to arrive.

❋ ❋ ❋ ❋

Moments later, Harry Chandler arrived, tears streaming down his cheeks. General Otis was in Mexico, where he had been sent by President William Howard Taft as America's representative at the Centennial of Mexican Independence. As president of the *Times,* and Otis's son-in-law, Chandler was in charge. He had left the building just minutes before the explosion, but his secretary, who stayed on, had been killed in the blast.

Chandler addressed the survivors. He announced that General Otis, ready for any contingency, had set up an emergency printing plant on College Street and that the owners of the Los Angeles *Herald* had offered to do anything they could to help. The *Times*'s editors had two hours to put out a newspaper.

All employees who were able to walk assembled at the offices of the *Herald* where, joined by other reporters who had heard the news at home, they started to write, interviewing each other, looking at what notes they had instinctively scribbled, gathering in reports from the receiving hospital, counting the missing and the dead. Twenty of their colleagues, they learned, had been killed.

Finally, using the *Herald*'s presses, they printed a one-page edition of the *Times.*

UNION BOMB WRECKS THE TIMES, said the headline. "They can kill our men and wreck our buildings," the editorial boldly proclaimed, "but, by the God above! they cannot kill the *Times.*"

❋ ❋ ❋ ❋

When the bombing occurred, most of Jim McNamara's friends from San Francisco were out of the state. Johannsen was in Des Moines, Iowa, and Clancy, who had gone east in late September for the Iron Workers convention in Rochester, New York, was in Boston, where he and Mike Young, a fellow executive board member, were about to go on a three-day yacht trip.

Getting off the *Lark* train in San Francisco, Jim felt in danger and alone. The news of the deaths was a shock to him. He had had no intention of causing such wholesale slaughter. With Clancy and Johannsen out of town, he didn't know where to turn. He looked for Schmidty at Belle Lavin's, but W. H. Brown, a fellow boarder who answered the door, told Jim that Schmidt had left that morning.

Finding himself practically friendless in San Francisco, Jim left for Seattle, but he felt hunted there as well. A few days later, he boarded a train for Chicago, but it seemed that everyone was talking about the murders. He felt that all of the passengers were looking at him. He didn't feel safe anywhere.

To elude any possible detectives, he switched trains and headed for Salt Lake City, where he hoped to stay with J. F. Munsey, one of his brother's colleagues on the Iron Workers' executive board.

Once he reached Munsey's home, McNamara finally felt secure, particularly when Munsey assured him that Clancy was on his way there from Indianapolis. Munsey sent a telegram to J.J. in Indianapolis. "Everything is OK," Munsey reported on October 10. "Glad C [Clancy] is coming. Patient [Jim McNamara] is out of danger and will get well. He is improving right along. You can depend on me to handle matters carefully. Will wire you if there is any change."

❋ ❋ ❋ ❋

J. J. McNamara had a sense that his brother was not only frightened but might even be suicidal. He needed to find some additional way to take care of him. He told Jim to go to Ballagh, Nebraska, where he could hide out with their sister, Alice, and her husband, Howard McKnab. He arranged for their mother to be there as well, telling her only that Jim was in some kind of union trouble.

Then J.J. called Frank Eckhoff in Cincinnati. Eckhoff had grown up next to the McNamaras, knew the whole family, and was one of Jim's best friends. He was one of the few people whom they had taken into their confidence about the dynamite jobs. J.J. asked Eckhoff to meet him in Indianapolis.

Eckhoff had an idea what had happened. "I guess you read about it," J.J. said when they met on October 21. "I am afraid we are in bad." He told Eckhoff that he wanted him to find his brother in Ballagh, Nebraska. Eckhoff was to tell Jim to go to Sioux City to find work, any kind of work. J.J. would send money to tide him over.

When he arrived at Ballagh by wagon the next day, Eckhoff was met by the members of the McNamara family. "He is in there," Howard McKnab said, pointing to a nearby sitting room. Jim McNamara was wearing a brown suit, tan shoes, and a gray alpine hat. In an effort to disguise his appearance, he had the beginnings of a beard and was wearing gold-rimmed spectacles.

Jim was surprised to see Eckhoff. He was expecting to see his brother.

"Let's take a walk," Jim suggested. As the two men went through the fields toward a stable, Eckhoff explained his mission.

"I guess you know all about it, don't you," Jim said. "I guess you read all about it."

Eckhoff said he had.

Despondent, Jim said he had never meant to kill anybody. Now he was thinking of killing himself. He asked Eckhoff to go hunting with him the next day, and to shoot him when he wasn't looking. It was no use trying to persuade him to move to Sioux City. Eckhoff had his hands full just trying to persuade Jim to remain alive and to go back East with him.

They left for Chicago early the next morning.

❋ ❋ ❋ ❋

J.J. continued to be as worried about his brother's mental health as about his physical safety. He went to Chicago, where Ortie McManigal was about to go off with some friends on a hunting trip in the Wisconsin woods. J.J. asked Ortie to take his brother with him.

"Jim has changed so much his own sister didn't know him," J.J.

explained. "I want you and Jim to stay up there until the close of the hunting season no matter what the others do. Jim has dropped the name Brice. He now calls himself Frank Sullivan so try to call him 'Frank' or 'Sullie' and for heaven's sake don't make a slip on his name."

Jim met the hunting party on November 6 in Kenosha, Wisconsin. Ortie had heard rumors that Jim had become mentally unbalanced, and he observed that his friend was drinking heavily. He struck Ortie as "a nervous wreck, almost insane." On their first day in the woods, Ortie heard a pistol shot and the whisper of a bullet zipping by his ear. The ground was covered with snow, and there were no animal tracks to be seen. Mounting a stump, Ortie saw Jim a hundred yards down the hillside. He ran down the hill and accused his friend of purposely shooting at him, perhaps in the hope that Ortie would kill him in self-defense.

Jim admitted that he had been trying to scare him.

The two men sat down on a log in the snow. They were silent for some time. Finally, Jim spoke.

"I never expected to kill so many people," he said. "If they ever catch me, they'll take me back to Los Angeles and hang me without a trial."

It took Jim several weeks to gain control of himself, to get enough composure and self-confidence to return to the world outside the woods. But by the time the hunting season ended on December 3, he had emerged from his depression. He had even made friends with a group of hunters who had a nearby campsite. On the day before leaving the woods, he posed with them for a picture.

❋ ❋ ❋ ❋

By December, Jim was well enough to resume his work. Back in Chicago he dropped in on the McManigal family for dinner one night, bringing a bucket of sauerkraut. When he left, he took with him a piece of venison that they had saved for J.J. from their hunting trip.

A couple of days later, he met with his brother and Ortie at the Iron Workers headquarters in Indianapolis to discuss the possibility of planting another bomb in Los Angeles. J.J. said that he had seen

Tvietmoe in St. Louis and that Tvietmoe wanted a "Christmas present." J.J. had promised to give one to him. They concluded that Ortie should go to the West Coast and plant bombs at the Llewellyn and Baker iron works and at the *Times* auxiliary plant.

Jim helped Ortie get the explosives, told him how to find the targeted bomb sites in Los Angeles, and saw him off on a train for the coast. But the union's present to Tvietmoe was a disappointment. The explosion at the Llewellyn Iron Works early Christmas morning injured a night watchman and caused twenty-five thousand dollars in damage. But Ortie didn't put any bombs at the Baker Iron Works or at the *Times* auxiliary plant.

When Ortie got back to town in January, J.J. wanted to know "why in Hell" Ortie hadn't placed bombs at the other locations.

Ortie had a relatively simple answer. It was just too dangerous. "Los Angeles looks like a bad town," he explained when they met for breakfast at the train depot. "Every man you look at looks like a deputy sheriff or officer of some kind."

❈ ❈ ❈ ❈

During the first months of 1911, Ortie and Jim began to regain their self-confidence as they planted bombs at job sites in the East and Midwest. In March alone, the union planted bombs in Springfield, Illinois; Milwaukee, Wisconsin; French Lick, Indiana; Omaha, Nebraska; and Columbus, Indiana.

As they traveled from city to city, they didn't notice that something was different: A team of men from the Burns Detective Agency was watching their every move.

Chapter Four

THE ARREST OF J. J. McNAMARA

ITHIN HOURS OF THE explosion, the city of Los Angeles began a full scale manhunt to find the men who had blown up the *Times*. Accompanied by enormous national fanfare, the city's investigation was conducted by William J. Burns, the most famous detective in America. As Jim McNamara rambled across the country, Burns and his men began a relentless search for those who had destroyed the *Times*.

Nearing his fiftieth birthday, William J. Burns was one of America's most celebrated—and controversial—men. His bushy mustache and squat, bulging figure were instantly recognizable—if not from newspaper photos, then from the comic pages. His foes on William Randolph Hearst's *San Francisco Examiner* made him the butt of what they called the Mutt cartoons, which regularly burlesqued his work in the guise of someone lampooned as Detective Tabasco.

To his manifold enemies, he was a fraud, a publicity-seeking charlatan who was capable of planting evidence to manufacture his cases and feed his huge ego. But to his admirers, and they were legion, he was an American Sherlock Holmes, the greatest detective in history. Most reporters treated him with awe. "William Burns is without doubt the most resourceful and brilliant detective in the United States, and the whole world might be included," one reporter wrote. "The great police system of Paris and that of Scotland Yard have not produced in all their long history a man to match him in ability to think out the snarled problems of mystery and crime."

Burns first generated national headlines in 1905, when the secretary of the interior asked the Secret Service to assign its best man to help investigate allegations of land and timber frauds in Oregon. Working with special prosecutor Francis J. Heney, Burns uncovered a vast scheme of corruption involving some of the most powerful men in the Northwest. He proved that private corporations had been stealing huge tracts of land from the federal forest service by submitting counterfeit homestead claims. When the arrangement drew the attention of federal land agents, land speculators like S.A.D. Puter put the agents on their private payroll; when there was a logjam in Washington, Puter and his colleagues made large cash payments to Senator John H. Mitchell, the patriarch of the state's Republican party. Burns's impressive detective work led to criminal indictments, a close alliance with President Theodore Roosevelt, and a series of adulatory stories by famed muckraker Lincoln Steffens.

Following a string of successful prosecutions in Oregon, both Burns and Heney were asked to come to San Francisco, where the city's crusading newspaper editor, Fremont Older, was calling for a major investigation of political graft. They took Steffens with them, the muckraker later explained, as "a sort of prophet and jester." Working in secret, Burns, Heney, Older, Steffens, and a handful of other leaders, including President Teddy Roosevelt, tracked their prey. When the case became public, Burns generated two years of headlines and hatred as he helped to expose a system of corruption that involved payoffs and bribes to almost all of San Francisco's leaders by interests ranging from prize-fight promoters and prostitutes to officials of the Pacific Gas and Electric Company and the Southern Pacific Railroad.

Trapped by the evidence, the city's political boss, Abraham Ruef, confessed to taking bribes. His testimony led to the conviction of Mayor Eugene Schmitz and, most important, the indictment of the president of the United Railroad, Patrick Calhoun, whose company had been granted a highly controversial overhead-trolley franchise by the city's Board of Supervisors. Calhoun was the stuff of legend:

the strikingly regal grandson of South Carolina senator John C. Calhoun, the great states' rights champion, he had come within one vote of being elected to the U.S. Senate from Georgia. He was the big corporate fish that the reformers wanted to capture.

But Calhoun outwitted the reformers by hiring Earl Rogers, the cleverest and most resourceful criminal lawyer in the West. With Rogers at his side, Calhoun quickly concluded that he could generate political support during the trial if he could force labor leaders to declare a strike against his street railway company and then save the city by breaking the strike. It was a Machiavellian strategy—and it worked. Calhoun imported twelve hundred strikebreakers, demolished the strike, and won accolades from thousands of longtime enemies. "I believe him guilty and I would vote to acquit him," one of the city's business leaders announced, "simply on account of his heroic stand on the street car strike."

Calhoun became an overnight hero to the state's anti-union forces. One of his strongest champions was the state's leading foe of unionism, "General" Harrison Gray Otis. During the strike, Otis flooded San Francisco with special editions of the *Times* that were filled with attacks on the strikers. When Burns found out that Calhoun had paid the *Times* fifteen thousand dollars, he charged that the publisher was selling his news columns to Calhoun. Otis called the allegations "ridiculous," but they were reprinted around the world.

The cases became so inflamed that prosecutor Heney—a western cowboy who had once killed a man in self-defense—was shot; the bullet went through his lower face, deafening an ear and just missing his tongue. He was replaced as special prosecutor by an equally zealous assistant named Hiram Johnson, who soon parlayed his new fame into a successful reform-oriented campaign for governor.

Heney wasn't the only target. Hated because of his crusading editorials, San Francisco *Bulletin* editor Fremont Older heard dozens of stories about assassins who were out to kill him. Then in late September 1907, he was kidnapped at gunpoint and placed on a train heading south.

"Make an attempt to escape," his seatmate announced, "and I'll shoot you."

By a stroke of luck, one of the other passengers on the train recognized Older. He also recognized his captor as one of Earl Rogers's henchmen. He got off of the train at Salinas and alerted the press and the authorities. When the train stopped at Santa Barbara, it was surrounded by the police and several hundred spectators. The entire train crew was placed under arrest until Older was safely in the hands of his friends. Even in the wildish West, those antics were hard to forgive.

The explosive relationships forged in the San Francisco graft trials were still smoldering when the *Times* was bombed in 1910. Burns's work in the cases had helped to make him internationally famous, thanks in part to Steffens's ceaseless drumbeat. But it had left him with a group of powerful enemies in Los Angeles, including General Otis and attorney Earl Rogers.

❋ ❋ ❋

Though his headquarters was in Chicago, Burns arrived by train in Los Angeles on the morning of the bombing. His appearance in the city was a coincidence. He was scheduled to address the convention of a major client, the American Bankers Association. When he got off the train he was greeted by E. R. Mills, the head of his local office, who showed him the day's astonishing headlines.

Almost as soon as Burns arrived in his room at the luxurious Alexandria Hotel in downtown Los Angeles, his telephone rang. The operator announced that Mayor George B. Alexander was in the lobby and would like to meet with him. A Scottish immigrant in his early seventies, who had spent years living in Iowa before moving to Los Angeles, Alexander had been elected mayor as the result of a recall campaign staged by the city's Good Government Organization. He was a centrist reformer, opposed on the left by the city's strong socialist-labor coalition and on the right by the *Los Angeles Times* and the forces of capital.

When the mayor reached Burns's room, he grasped the detective's hand. With his extremely long white goatee, Alexander looked like Uncle Sam. "This certainly is a stroke of fortune," Alexander began, "you being right in the city at a time like this. I wired all over the country in an effort to find you, only to learn that you were due here in Los Angeles this morning. It seems like fate." After describing what was known about the bombing, Mayor Alexander asked Burns to find the dynamiters "no matter what the cost and no matter who they are."

Burns had reason to suspect that J. J. McNamara and the Structural Iron Workers' Union were involved. For months, his agency had been working for McClintic, Marshall and Company, a contractor that had been a victim of a similar explosion, in which two huge bridge girders had been destroyed by dynamite. After a brief investigation, Burns had concluded that the explosion was caused by a time bomb consisting of a clock and a battery connected by wires to a ten-quart can of nitroglycerin. Looking for a possible culprit, Burns quickly began to suspect the Structural Iron Workers, who, after all, had a motive.

"This may surprise you," he told Mayor Alexander, "but I already have a very good idea who is responsible for this outrage."

Nevertheless, there was sure to be a problem if Burns took on an assignment for the city. As a result of the San Francisco graft trial, Otis would surely object to any investigation conducted by Burns.

"Mayor Alexander," he said, "I have certain very influential enemies here in Los Angeles owing to some investigations I have made in the past. They will try to thwart me at every turn if they find out what I am doing. So I accept the responsibility of this investigation on the condition that I will be obliged to report to no one—not even you—until the job has been brought to a successful conclusion."

Alexander immediately agreed to Burns's terms. During the next few days the offer was sweetened as a variety of entities—including the Los Angeles County Board of Supervisors, the Merchants and Manufacturers Association, and at least one labor union—offered rewards that, at least on paper, added up to $100,000. And the job became even more intriguing three months later, on Christmas Day, 1910, when Ortie McManigal's bomb caused $25,000 worth of damage at the anti-union Llewellyn Iron Works in Los Angeles.

But as Burns had anticipated, not everyone approved of Mayor Alexander's decision to hire him. The choice was denounced by General Otis, and by the Merchants and Manufacturers Association, which announced that it was going to hire its own investigator—

none other than Burns's nemesis, Earl Rogers, the famous criminal defense lawyer, successful defender of Patrick Calhoun, and the author of Los Angeles's notorious antipicketing ordinance.

✳✳✳✳

Within the city, there were many opinions as to who was to blame for the explosion. The *Times,* of course, promptly placed the blame at the door of organized labor. The banner headline on their special one-page edition on the morning of October 1 had proclaimed that UNIONIST BOMB WRECKS THE TIMES. Within a week that announcement was backed by a committee of community leaders, who said that the explosion had been caused by dynamite. During the days that followed, the *Times* printed a series of stories asserting that certain labor leaders were under investigation.

But the unions also wasted no time in getting their story across. The California State Federation of Labor named a prestigious panel to investigate the cause of the explosion. On October 26, the panel issued a report that flatly contradicted virtually everything that had been printed in the *Times.* Based on several sources of evidence, the report concluded that the fire was caused by gas, not dynamite, and said that the gas was the result of leaks caused by Otis's own negligence. As for the bombs found at the homes of Otis and Zeehandelaar, the report suggested that they had been planted there by a detective named Tom Rico—the same man who found them.

The report did not accuse Otis of causing the fire himself, but it did accuse him of attempting to fasten the guilt on labor in order to avoid being prosecuted for criminal negligence, to collect more than $500,000 in insurance money, and to strike a blow at unionism in the court of public opinion. "No union man blew up the *Times,*" the report concluded. "There is no sane union man who could not have predicted that the dynamiting would be used as an excuse for a general and indiscriminate persecution of union men and women."

Some friends of labor went even further in denouncing Otis and his allies. On October 15, 1910, Socialist Party leader Eugene V. Debs, who had won 420,820 votes in the last presidential election, claimed that "union haters" blew up the *Times* as part of their anti-union activity. While that claim may have seemed farfetched, many Angelenos began to conclude that the explosion had simply been a terrible accident.

As the months wore on, Burns seemed to disappear. Fed by stories in the *Los Angeles Times,* the people of Los Angeles began to suspect that Alexander had been duped. By March, Alexander, who was about to enter a hotly contested reelection campaign, stopped paying the famous detective.

Then Burns pulled off a coup that electrified and polarized America. He organized a team of detectives from Los Angeles and Indianapolis that arrested J. J. McNamara.

❅ ❅ ❅ ❅

On Saturday afternoon, April 22, 1911, four detectives arrived at the union's Indianapolis office, on the fourth floor of the American Central Life building. Inside, the union's executive board was holding a special session.

Down on the street, a light afternoon drizzle fell gently into an open-topped car where a driver waited with the motor running. Burns himself was at the Indianapolis police station, waiting for his prey to arrive.

One of the detectives knocked at the glass pane of the door marked HEADQUARTERS—INTERNATIONAL ASS'N OF BRIDGE AND STRUCTURAL IRON WORKERS.

A moment later, a handsome, clean-shaven man in his middle thirties opened the door.

"We are looking for Mr. McNamara," one of the detectives said.

"I'm McNamara," the man at the door answered. His tone was strong and confident.

"Well, Mr. McNamara, the chief of police wants to see you at the station."

McNamara was stunned. The union had gotten away with its illegal acts for several years, and J.J. had begun to feel invulnerable. He turned around, looking for guidance from union president Frank Ryan and the six other members of the executive committee, who were sitting at a large and beautiful mahogany conference table.

"You better go ahead with them," Ryan said.

"I'll get my hat," McNamara told the detective, regaining his composure. While crossing the room, he paused to close the union's safe and to toss some keys on the table. "I'll be back in time to make the motion for adjournment," he joked to his colleagues. Then McNamara neatly adjusted his hat and amiably left the room with two detectives who hurried him downstairs to the waiting automobile.

After McNamara's departure for police headquarters, two Indianapolis police detectives remained in the Iron Workers' boardroom. President Ryan asked them why McNamara was being taken to the police station. The detectives said they were not authorized to answer that question. Ryan then asked them to leave the room so that he could resume the meeting. They refused and announced that the members of the board would not be allowed to leave the room either. The union's entire executive board was, without explanation, being held prisoner.

Ryan tried to reach the union's attorney, Leo Rappaport, by telephone. But it was after hours on a Saturday, and there was no answer. Ryan didn't know who else to call. He was from Chicago and the other board members were from other parts of the country—Mike Young from Boston, John T. Butler from Buffalo, Henry W. Legleitner from Pittsburgh, Herbert Hockin from Detroit, and Gene Clancy from San Francisco. They were all strangers in town.

❊ ❊ ❊ ❊

While the executive board members desperately tried to find some way to help him, McNamara was rushed down to the police station and arraigned in front of police court judge James A. Collins. With Burns looking on, the judge read from a document that had been handed to him by Los Angeles deputy district attorney Joseph Ford. McNamara paled visibly. The papers, which were signed by the governors of California and Indiana, asked the court to send John J. McNamara to California to stand trial for dynamiting the *Los Angeles Times* and the Llewellyn Iron Works. He was, in short, wanted for murder.

The judge announced that he intended to honor the extradition papers and allow McNamara to be taken to California at once.

McNamara scrutinized the judge in silence. Finally, he cleared his throat with an effort and he pleaded for time.

"Judge," he said, "I do not see how a man can be jerked up from his business when he is committing no wrong and ordered out of the state on five minutes' notice. Are you going to let them take me without giving me a chance to defend myself? I have no attorney and no one to defend me."

Indiana law required courts to "give the defendant an opportunity and time to employ counsel, if he so desires." But Judge Collins was not impressed. He interrupted McNamara in mid-argument and asked whether he was the man named in the documents. McNamara admitted that he was. Judge Collins then asked James Hosick, a detective from Los Angeles, whether he could identify McNamara as the man named in the extradition papers. Hosick said that he could. The judge declared the proceeding closed and ordered McNamara taken from the courtroom.

At six forty-five P.M., McNamara left the police station, handcuffed to Detective Hosick and accompanied by a detective from Chicago named Guy Biddinger. The detectives rushed McNamara into a waiting car to take him out of Indianapolis—and out of the state.

❊ ❊ ❊ ❊

As soon as McNamara was safely on the road, Burns left police headquarters and, trailed by police, government officials, and the press, joined the detectives who were holding the union's leadership captive.

Watching the crowd of men searching the room, union president Ryan tried to protest, but to no avail. Police superintendent Martin J. Hyland proceeded to read them a search warrant, and announced that McNamara had been arrested for the *Times* and Llewellyn bombings.

The union leaders gasped in astonishment and said it couldn't be true. They said their lawyers would get McNamara released from jail at once. Then they were told, for the first time, that he was already on his way to California.

Ryan angrily resumed his objection to the presence of so many police in the union's offices. "How many men does it take to search these three rooms?" he asked.

"You look here," Hyland countered, "we will have just as many men to search these offices as we think we need."

Then Ryan noticed Burns. The detective was sitting at McNamara's rolltop desk, with the top up, examining a pile of papers.

"Why this—what is this?" Ryan demanded of Hyland, pointing to Burns. "What's he doing? You have taken Mr. McNamara away, and he is not here to protect his belongings."

Hyland didn't answer.

Outraged, Ryan turned to the man at the desk. "Who are you, that you have a right to come in these offices and search these apartments?" he demanded.

"Burns," the man answered, still rifling through papers.

A reporter described the scene: "For an instant, intense silence reigned in the room. Two pairs of eyes blazed into each other. Then Ryan observed, simply and expressively, 'Ah, and who is *Burns?*' "

Ryan knew who Burns was, of course, but he asked for identification. In response, the detective gave the union president "the meanest look he ever experienced. Burns looked at Ryan from head to foot, and then met the Iron Workers' president's eyes directly and invited him to start trouble."

Trying to avoid a confrontation, Superintendent Hyland explained that Burns was a private detective and that the police had given him the right to join them in searching the premises.

A moment later, one of Ryan's colleagues announced that there was a man in the next room looking at the union's checkbook, examining duplicate copies of checks that McNamara had issued during the past year.

Going into the other room, Ryan recognized the man instantly. He was prosperous and stocky, with a smooth oblong face and hidden eyes that led enemies to joke that he looked like an overgrown potato. It was Walter Drew, "Commissioner" of the National Erectors' Association, the organization that had been trying to break the ironworkers for five years. Ryan was furious. The last thing he wanted was to allow Drew to gain access to the union's private files.

All of the union's leaders felt invaded, violated. But their anger grew to fear during the next few hours as Burns conducted his investigation while they remained helpless.

First, Burns attempted to open the union's safe, but when no key would fit he sent for a drill. Leaving one of his operatives to wait for the locksmith to arrive, Burns led his entourage, including a large number of admiring newspaper reporters, to a barn just outside of town. The barn, west of Big Eagle Creek, belonged to a man named W. D. Jones, who said he had rented it to McNamara to store letter files for the Iron Workers. The ground outside the barn was muddy after a day of light rain. Inside, Burns and his men found two quart cans of nitroglycerin and fifteen sticks of dynamite packed in sawdust inside a piano box.

Burns then took his colleagues and camp followers back to the American Central Life building where, acting on a tip, they went to the basement. There they located a small vault that allegedly had been used by J. J. McNamara to store materials. Not finding keys for the vault's heavy door, they forced it open. Inside, the detectives found a room filled with dynamite. On the shelves were seven packages of dynamite, weighing perhaps two hundred pounds, as well as a box of percussion caps and yards of fuse. Most important, perhaps, the detectives emerged carrying a box containing a dozen small alarm clocks that closely resembled one found next to General Otis's house in Los Angeles that had not detonated.

Finally, at about two A.M., Burns returned to the union's offices, where the locksmith and drill had arrived, as had Leo Rappaport, the union's attorney. It seemed that no one wanted to drill the safe since there was a risk that it contained explosives that might detonate on contact. Viewing the stalemate, Burns asked the Iron Workers' leaders to give him the combination. But they refused.

"McNamara is the only man who knows it," Ryan said, "and you've carried him off, God knows where."

"Well, the safe's got to come open," Burns said, looking for help. "I guess I'll have to tackle it myself." He found the proper spot to drill, got down on his knees in front of the safe, and took up the drill as the other onlookers retreated to relative safety.

"I protest," Rappaport shouted, as the diamond drill bit into the steel over the tumblers of the safe. "Are we living in darkest Russia?"

Burns looked up for a moment, bit his black mustache, and returned to work. Finally the tumblers fell back, and Burns opened the door, exposing a pile of union books. As detectives pulled the books from the shelves, Rappaport protested again. "Have we no rights?" he angrily demanded.

"Not under the circumstances," Burns answered.

"You'll hear from us for this outrage," Rappaport continued.

"Shut up," ordered the chief of police. "You'll hear from me if you're not careful."

After the books were removed, the detectives found a series of inner lockers and drawers that were also locked. When one of the union leaders said that only McNamara had the keyes, Walter Drew handed a set of keys to one of the police officers. They were the keys that McNamara had thrown on the table earlier that evening.

The keys worked. As an officer opened the locks, Drew tried to lean over Rappaport's shoulder to see what was going on. Rappaport angrily told him to stand back, but Drew shouted that he did not plan to take orders from the union's attorney. Rappaport pushed the NEA lawyer, and the two men started a fight that ended only when a couple of detectives pulled them apart. Meanwhile, the remaining contents of the safe were removed and sent off to police headquarters for further inspection.

At three-thirty A.M., the search was completed, and the union's executive board was finally permitted to leave the building.

❋ ❋ ❋ ❋

Unquestionably, Burns had collected an imposing array of evidence. He claimed that for the past three years, McNamara had been arranging for a group of operatives to plant dynamite at anti-union buildings—including the *Los Angeles Times* building and the Llewellyn Iron Works. Three people had been involved in the *Times* bombing, he said, and their leader was a man who went by the pseudonym of James Brice.

It was a powerful story, but to millions of Americans, who learned about Burns's work in the papers the next morning, the case seemed just a little too pat. In the words of President Ryan, it seemed that "an arrangement had been made to place" incriminating evidence with the union, and the entire enterprise appeared to be "a prearranged plan to discredit our organization and its officials and organized labor generally. Everything connected with this outrage had the appearance of being especially staged for its spectacular effect."

Walter Drew, after all, was the avowed enemy of the Iron Workers' Union, and Burns had a powerful financial incentive to make his case appear as strong as possible. After Mayor Alexander stopped paying his bills, Burns had continued to pursue the case, running up a significant debt. "Being hard pressed for money at this time," he later wrote, "I was compelled to go to friends and borrow ten thousand dollars." He knew that he could lose it all unless he could solve the *Times* bombing case and collect the hundred thousand dollars reward. According to his detractors, Burns was fully capable of manufacturing evidence in order to earn that reward.

If the evidence was really so strong, critics wondered, why had it been necessary to send McNamara out of the state in such haste, without even the most rudimentary hearing?

❋❋❋❋

During the days that followed, the press became fascinated with the whereabouts of J. J. McNamara as he crossed the United States on his way to California. But Burns was afraid that the union and its friends would succeed in springing McNamara free, either through a highjacking or through a friendly judge in one of the jurisdictions along the way, so he arranged a blind route to fool the press as well as any possible foe.

As he left the police station in Indianapolis at six forty-five P.M., McNamara was placed in a seven-passenger Owen Motor car, a fifty-horsepower automobile with a top and side curtains that was capable of traveling at least seventy-five miles an hour. Detectives Hosick and Biddinger, assigned to travel with him, were equipped with an arsenal that included a Winchester rifle, several large-caliber revolvers, and at least two hundred rounds of ammunition. Burns instructed the driver, Frank P. Fox, to drive the car as fast as possible. If necessary, he was to drive it through any obstacles that McNamara's friends might place in its path—regardless of damage to the automobile or danger to the lives of its occupants.

Averaging more than forty miles an hour, the car reached Terre Haute in the early morning, driving through mud that reached up to the hubs of the wheels. "We were exceedingly lucky to go so far at the rate of forty miles an hour without a puncture," Fox reported a few days later.

At one-forty A.M., they boarded the *Pennsylvania Flyer* for St. Louis. To confuse reporters, the group had a very public breakfast in St. Louis and ostentatiously purchased tickets to Pueblo, Colorado, on the *Missouri Pacific* line. Then they quietly climbed back on the *Pennsylvania Flyer,* staying on it through Kansas City, to Holsington, Kansas. They got off the train at Holsington, took a waiting auto to Great Bend, Kansas—"over the wildest country imaginable," one of the detectives recalled later—and caught a local train to Dodge City. At Dodge City they checked into a hotel where they waited for the Santa Fe line's *California Limited* to arrive.

❊ ❊ ❊ ❊

Early the next morning, they boarded the famous *California Limited*—the fastest train through to Los Angeles. When it began its Chicago to Los Angeles route in November, 1896, the *California Limited* was described as one of the world's wonders. Limited to seven through cars, it was brilliantly lighted by electricity and evenly heated throughout. A brochure boasted that it has "a car for nearly every travel need—sightseeing, sleeping, dining, reading, writing, smoking and social gatherings." It even had a barber shop.

Unknown to J. J. McNamara, there were two other prisoners heading for California on the same train. Though J.J. was kept in the dark for two more days, by Tuesday morning the rest of the country knew that one of the other men on the train was J.J.'s brother, Jim. They were being held prisoner in adjoining cars. Burns announced to the press that James Barnabas McNamara was the man known as James Brice—the suspect accused of placing the bomb in the alleyway at the *Los Angeles Times.*

❊ ❊ ❊ ❊

In total secrecy, Burns's operatives had apprehended Jim McNamara and his companion, Ortie McManigal, ten days earlier in Detroit.

When arrested, the men were carrying a suitcase full of explosives; at the least, they could be held for illegal possession. To keep the arrests secret and to avoid the risk of unfavorable court proceedings, Burns arranged for the men to be taken to Chicago and held prisoner at the suburban home of a Chicago police detective named William Reed.

Shortly after arriving at Reed's home, Ortie McManigal agreed to cooperate with the investigation. In a confession dictated to Burns while Jim McNamara was held in a separate room, McManigal said that he and Jim had worked directly for J.J., planting dynamite at dozens of anti-union work sites around the country. McManigal said that he had bombed the Llewellyn Iron Works in Los Angeles, and that Jim, working with two anarchist colleagues, had bombed the *Los Angeles Times*. McManigal said that Jim McNamara used the pseudonym James Brice, and he identified the two anarchists as David Caplan and Matthew Schmidt. Both men were still at large.

Later, when Ortie's confession became public, critics claimed that it was filled with lies, that he had been subjected to "the third degree" and had been tortured into making a confession. But Burns answered by saying that he had won McManigal over by appealing to his love of his wife and children. Burns had promised that the court in Los Angeles would go easy on him if he agreed to cooperate.

However it was obtained, Burns and McManigal agreed not to tell Jim about the confession until J.J. was arrested. For ten days Burns also kept it secret from the press, while using it to persuade the authorities in California, Illinois, and Indiana to order that McManigal and the McNamaras be extradited to Los Angeles to stand trial.

❈ ❈ ❈ ❈

On Sunday morning, the story of J. J. McNamara's arrest was on front pages everywhere. By Tuesday, the arrest of Jim McNamara and Ortie McManigal was in the headlines. Everyone in America, except the brothers McNamara, knew that Ortie McManigal had confessed. But Caplan and Schmidt were still on the loose.

Burns said he was convinced that an attempt would be made to kill McManigal and free the McNamaras, and press reports about Jim

McNamara's blunt statements seemed to confirm that fear. At Lexington Junction, Missouri, Jim told a Kansas City reporter that "this train will either be wrecked or blown up before we reach Los Angeles. I have eluded my captors enough to get word to my friends to see that we do not get to the Coast alive."

The detectives were prepared for the worst. At the very first sign of danger, they announced that "the prisoners will be surrounded with a cordon of men armed to the teeth and entrenched in a steel Pullman car."

Jim McNamara and McManigal were kept locked in a special car that was added to the *California Limited* at nine P.M. on Saturday night, when the train stopped in Joliet, Illinois. Their hands and feet were manacled, and they were guarded by four detectives. Fearing possible misuse of a razor, they did not allow Jim to shave. Besides their revolvers and automatic pistols, the detectives were armed with two additional heavy Winchester rifles.

To some, Jim McNamara's bold and threatening statements provided evidence of his guilt. To others, they weren't his statements at all; they were part of a gigantic scheme of disinformation, designed to destroy the cause of labor in America.

❋ ❋ ❋

Traveling across America's West by train, the brothers seemed a study in contrasts.

On Tuesday afternoon, three days into the trip, J.J. was still fastidious. He was clean-shaven, wore a black derby, a brown suit, black shoes, white wing collar, and an immaculate light shirt. Detective Guy Biddinger said "he was a model prisoner and it would have been hard to find a better companion. Throughout the trip he was always gentlemanly in demeanor. He talked on many subjects, and his conversation was interesting at all times."

"Frankly, he does not look like a man who would plot a crime," John Alexander Gray reported as the train passed through Arizona. Gray, who wrote for Hearst's *Los Angeles Examiner,* was the only reporter allowed to accompany the prisoners on the train. "This man," he said, "may be the most amazing criminal of the age, or a just and unjustly accused man. He has a splendid, upright physique and a clarity of complexion that indicate perfect health and habits that know no excess."

J.J. enjoyed comfortable banter with Gray as well as with the other reporters who seized a moment with him as the train stopped in stations along the way. "There's one pleasant thing to be said about this trip," Gray observed as they sat in J.J.'s compartment. "You are going to an ideal country and your fare is paid by someone else."

"I'll be going back under different circumstances soon," McNamara replied, looking up from a magazine. "I'd much rather pay my own way."

After interviewing J.J., Gray arranged to talk to Jim McNamara, having promised the detectives that he would not tell either man that the other was on the train. He found Jim "a difficult proposition for an interviewer."

During the half hour that Gray spent in his compartment, Jim rolled at least a dozen yellow paper cigarettes. The ends of his fingers, Gray observed, were as discolored as those of a cigarette fiend. He was much smaller than his brother. He weighed less than one hundred and fifty pounds and was about five feet eight inches tall. To Gray, he appeared gaunt, almost anemic, with a shock of brown hair plastered down his head, a long thin nose, a wide forehead like his brother's, and eyes that alternately seemed blue and yellow as they continually shifted, holding "a light of amusement, mixed with insolence." Though only twenty-nine years old, Jim McNamara looked about ten years older. Gray found him "the reverse of neat, both as to features and his clothes." Throughout the interview, McNamara lay stretched out on the seat.

Noticing a deck of cards nearby, Gray asked Jim if he had been playing cards.

"Yes," Jim answered. "Solitaire."

"Can you beat it?"

"No," Jim said, "it's been my experience that you can't beat any game in this life." To Gray, the remark summarized Jim McNamara's attitude—indifferent and cynical. That observation was no doubt shaped by the detectives, who told Gray that Jim McNamara was an anarchist and possibly insane.

He had a rough and distinctive manner of speech. When told that a reporter wanted to interview him, Jim admonished one of the detectives: "If you do," he said, "I'll cut his gas jet off" (rough translation: "I'll cut his throat"). He was plainly a heavy drinker, downing a dozen small bottles of whiskey on Tuesday, each of which held about two ordinary-sized drinks. He said the liquor was for stomach trouble.

But throughout the train trip he also displayed ingenuity and a mischievous sense of humor. There was an electric fan in each compartment. After studying the fan for a while, Jim converted it into a roulette wheel. He numbered each of the blades and each of the screen sections and then placed bets on the wheel. He put the odds at eight to one and asked one of the detectives to bet eighty cents to his ten that he could not call the number of the blade that would stop in a certain division of the screen protector.

In talking to his captors, he had a favorite remark. "We will never reach California," he said again and again with bravado. "I know we are going into a ditch." Was he conceding his guilt? Or was he displaying an offbeat personality with a sense of gallows humor?

❋ ❋ ❋

By Wednesday morning, when the train crossed the Colorado River into California, it had become clear that the prisoners would reach their destination. Jim began to abandon his bravado and decided to "doll up a bit," putting on a clean shirt and black overcoat. He agreed to be shaved by the detectives, who wanted him to look just as he had on October 1, 1910, when the *Times* was bombed.

As the train passed through smaller California towns such as Needles, Coffs, Cadiz, Ludlow, and Daggett, crowds gathered around the train to catch a glimpse of the world-famous prisoners. But at each station the men drew down the curtains.

Finally the train reached Barstow, where for the first time, the detectives allowed a crowd of reporters and photographers to climb on board. Momentarily it seemed that Jim would at last start to relax. But then one of the reporters told him the bad news. He explained that McManigal had confessed and had charged him and his brother with bombing the *Times*. The news broke down the stoic reserve he had shown since his arrest in Detroit.

The train was scheduled to arrive in Los Angeles at three P.M., but Burns, fearing a last-minute escape, had arranged to have some of the passengers disembark in Pasadena an hour earlier. Burns had another motive as well. There was a witness who claimed to be able to identify Jim McNamara as the man known as James Brice.

* * * *

The witness was Lena Ingersoll. She told police that a man using the name James Brice had stayed at her San Francisco boardinghouse the previous September. One afternoon, she said, she had listened to a conversation through his keyhole and had heard him discussing plans to dynamite buildings in Los Angeles.

Los Angeles district attorney John Fredericks summoned Mrs. Ingersoll. On the evening before the McNamaras' train was scheduled to arrive, she caught the eight o'clock overnight train to Los Angeles. But to Fredericks's alarm, one of the other passengers was another target of the district attorney's investigation, labor union leader Anton Johannsen, known to be a close friend of Matt Schmidt. And, traveling with Johannsen was Job Harriman, a leading Los Angeles labor attorney, who had been in San Francisco consulting with that city's labor leaders about the defense of the McNamara brothers.

When the train arrived at the depot the next morning, Harriman gave Mrs. Ingersoll a ride to the Hotel Chapman. District Attorney Fredericks wanted to keep her as distant as possible from men such as Harriman and Johannsen. An hour after her arrival at the Hotel Chapman, Fredericks insisted that she give up her hotel room and stay with one of his friends instead. And he quickly arranged to have Jim McNamara removed from the train in Pasadena, instead of Los Angeles.

At 1:55 P.M., the Los Angeles sheriff, William Hammel, drove up to the front of the Hotel Green, directly across from the Pasadena train station. Almost at once, another sheriff's car, carrying a heavily veiled woman, drove up next to Sheriff Hammel. Moments later, a half-dozen police officers arrived at the station along with a few reporters who had been tipped off to the change of plans. They walked over to the train tracks, where they mingled with twenty or thirty civilians who were planning to meet relatives on the train.

The *California Limited* pulled in almost exactly on time, at 2:05 P.M. Before the press could mount the train, two Burns detectives, accompanied by McManigal, jumped from the coach and started to run toward a waiting automobile. An instant later, two more Burns detectives got off the train with J. B. McNamara.

Watching from her car, the veiled woman pointed at the prisoner. "That's Brice!" she shouted.

McNamara turned toward the shouting woman. He glanced at her for a moment, then quickly shielded his face with his hands and headed for the car that was to take him to the Los Angeles county jail.

※ ※ ※ ※

The authorities did not want J. J. McNamara to get off the train with his brother. They distracted his attention during the stop in Pasadena and kept him on the train until the next stop. Then, at the Raymond station, they led him off the train, treating him almost as a dignitary, rather than a prisoner.

Reporter John Gray found the scene astonishing. "His manner was so dignified and impressive," Gray recounted, "that the officers were at pains to assure him that the exigencies of the situation compelled the sort of treatment they were giving him. Nothing more strange, more amazing has ever been know since there was law and the ability of the law to conjure force to execute its dictates, for here, practically unguarded and treated with all courtesy, was the man accused of having told his brother to bomb the *Los Angeles Times*."

J.J.'s composure lasted until he reached the Los Angeles jail. There, entering the office, he saw his brother for the first time. He was plainly shocked. His face paled perceptibly, and he asked for a chair with a gesture of his hands. After that first glance, J.J. did not look toward his brother. Twenty minutes later, Jim left the room with the Los Angeles jailer, and J.J. was alone again.

But he would not remain entirely alone. It had taken the detectives four days to shuttle J. J. McNamara from Indianapolis to Los Angeles. The labor movement put those same four days to good use. They used the time to persuade Clarence Darrow to return to active duty.

Chapter   Five

CLARENCE DARROW
TAKES THE CASE

WHEN WORD OF J.J.'s arrest reached the public, a single recent memory dominated the thoughts of the American left. For socialists, anarchists, intellectuals, and members of organized labor, the McNamara case quickly became a replay of the sensational Haywood-Moyer-Pettibone murder trial that had dominated the news some four years earlier. In that case, Pinkerton detectives had apprehended the labor leaders in Colorado, hauled them into Idaho at gunpoint, and forced them to stand trial for the murder of former governor Frank Steunenberg. All of the power of the mine owners, the Pinkerton agency, and the government had been thrown into the effort to convict them. Yet they had been acquitted, thanks to the combined forces of labor, the socialist press, and an outstanding team of lawyers.

When the McNamaras were arrested, many felt that this was simply a repeat of an outrage that they had already witnessed. The brothers were, in effect, innocent by analogy. The president of the Indiana Federation of Labor, for example, immediately announced that "the capitalistic interests are behind this, just as they were behind the fight on Haywood, Moyer and Pettibone." A group of labor leaders issued a statement noting that "when we recall that the detectives were as cocksure of the conviction of Haywood, Moyer and Pettibone as Burns now is of convicting the three men he has arrested, we have a right to doubt their guilt." Haywood quickly penned an article of his own. Reading about the arrests, he said, "is like reading a brief chapter of my own life."

For millions, the Haywood-Moyer-Pettibone case proved that the money interests were capable of concocting a phony case against the leaders of militant unions such as the Mine Workers and the Structural Iron Workers. More important, it showed that the forces of labor and socialism could win against amazing odds. Or at least that they could win if they had Clarence Darrow as their chief attorney.

The leaders of labor knew at once that they had to persuade Darrow to represent the McNamaras, both because of his unique skills and because of the obvious similarity to the Idaho cases. Indeed, the parallel to those trials quickly became a part of the national vocabulary. Such comparisons, of course, are often misleading, but there is an inevitable tendency to build analogies around the experiences of the last war, and the last war between capital and labor had been fought in Idaho and it had been won by Clarence Darrow. Because of the symbolism, and because of his talents, it was essential for labor to persuade him to serve as the commanding general in Los Angeles as well.

But Darrow was, in effect, retired from active combat.

* * * *

The calls to Darrow started coming as soon as people learned that J. J. McNamara had been arrested. No one cared much about his younger brother, Jim, who wasn't closely connected with the union movement. No one of any consequence had heard of him. But J.J., that was something else. As the secretary-treasurer of a major union, a part of the American Federation of Labor, his case was of intense concern.

On Monday, April 24, the leaders of all of the unions headquartered in Indianapolis organized a conference to support their colleague. The Barbers were there, as were the Bricklayers, the Carpenters, the Machinists, and the Mine Workers. They knew J. J. McNamara. He was a self-made, hard-working, temperate, God-fearing Catholic. He would never have been part of such a scheme. And why would he have anything to do with bombing a newspaper all the way out in Los Angeles? Clearly the charges against him had been manufactured—perhaps by General Otis or Detective Burns or NEA commissioner Walter Drew, or maybe by all of them acting together. There was no limit to the villainy of the capitalist ogre. They were determined to find J. J. McNamara the best lawyer in America. They sent for Clarence Darrow.

✳ ✳ ✳ ✳

When he got the call from Indianapolis, Darrow was in Kankakee, Illinois, defending his corporate clients in the case of *Charles Myerhoff* v. *The Kankakee Manufacturing Company.* The trial would last for two or three weeks. When it was over, if he succeeded, his clients on the board of directors would still be rich, and Charles Myerhoff would still be destitute. It was the kind of case that financed his lifestyle, made Ruby happy, involved miminal physical or mental strain, and could be justified by the age-old explanation that every client deserves a lawyer. It was not, however, the sort of proceeding that Darrow wanted memorialized on his tombstone.

But the kidnapping of the McNamaras—there was a great case, a battle worthy of Clarence Darrow, an event that would enable him to break out of his mood of irrelevancy, to educate the nation again about the great issues of industrial injustice, to represent men whose lives were in jeopardy, to climb back into the headlines, to return to the center of the national stage, and to add a further claim to his place in history. It would remind the world, and himself, that he was still alive.

Before undertaking such a case, though, there would be serious problems to overcome. The McNamara trial was sure to last for months, possibly years. It would be taxing, and Darrow was feeling frail. Moreover, the trial would take place in a city controlled by the forces of capital. Though he had a few friends in Los Angeles, he also had nightmares, haunting memories of his illness only three years earlier. And then there was his pledge to Ruby, the promise to become a noncombatant. All those problems made him resist. But in the end, he needed this case as much as it needed him.

On Tuesday morning, April 25, Darrow took an early train to Indianapolis. Meeting with the committee of union presidents, he got quickly to the point. It would be a hard fight and would only be winnable if the defense had the full and unequivocal support of organized labor. This would have to become a crusade, not just for the Iron Workers, but for the American Federation of Labor, which would have to back it with every bit of energy, money, and influence that it could command. Darrow said he would have to spend a day or two deciding whether to take the case. Most important, he would have to talk to Sam Gompers and the national leadership of the AFL.

Before leaving town that afternoon, Darrow gave the union leaders a lesson in the nexus between propaganda and law. To make it a crusade, he told them, the focus would have to shift. The public would have to stop thinking about the twenty men who had died. As long as those men were on the public's mind, there would be a cry for revenge and McNamara would be sucked down by the demand for blood. McNamara's friends would have to make J.J. the victim and make the forces of capital the villains. Labor and its allies would have to focus the nation's attention on the illegal way in which he had been yanked out of the state and dragged across the country. If they could show that the McNamaras were like Moyer, Haywood, and Pettibone, that Burns was like the Pinkertons, and that Ortie McManigal was another Harry Orchard, then the nation would know that these men had been framed. That they were innocent by analogy.

To make his point, Darrow dictated a quick statement for the press. Since J.J. was not in California at the time of the bombing, he could not properly be extradited. "He was," Darrow stated, "clearly kidnapped." It was a brilliant stroke that demonstrated Darrow's skill as a legal propagandist. Within days, all of labor and their allies in the press had adopted the theme. J. J. McNamara had not simply been arrested. He had been *kidnapped.*

❋ ❋ ❋ ❋

After Darrow hurried off to catch a 3:10 P.M. train, the labor leaders unanimously voted to offer him the job. As he had asked, they immediately sent word to Sam Gompers urging the AFL to take full responsibility for J. J. McNamara's defense.

In 1911, Samuel Gompers *was* the AFL, just as Eugene Debs was the Socialist Party. A Jew who was born in London of Dutch parents, he was thirteen when his family immigrated to the United States in 1863, while the Civil War was at its apex. He grew up in relative poverty on the East Side of New York, living in a tenement, breathing the sickening stench produced by a slaughterhouse on one side and a brewery on the other, sitting with his father at a table in his family's kitchen–living room, rolling cigars, covering the apartment with tobacco dust.

Though he studied debate and history and language, there was never much doubt that he would follow his father into the cigar trade. Cigar makers in America, as in England, were skilled craftsmen who tended to be fundamentally conservative, focused on better wages and working conditions for their own craft, rather than for workers in general. But Gompers quickly became immersed in the internecine warfare of radical politics. Many cigars, in that era, were manufactured in tenement houses where there was no concern for industrial hygiene or occupational health. Disguising himself as a book salesman, Gompers went door to door pretending to sell sets of Dickens novels, but actually looking for Dickensian working conditions. Most of the workers he found were immigrants from Bohemia, "little children with old-young faces and work-weary figures," whose circumstances he described in a series of exposés published by the *New Yorker Volks-Zeitung* beginning in October, 1881.

With the support of the Amalgamated Trades and Labor Union and the New York Health Department, the cigar makers pressed for tenement-house legislation. Their supporters ranged from Theodore Roosevelt, the Republican Party reformer from Manhattan's silk-stocking district, to Senator Thomas Grady, a leader of the Tammany Hall Democrats. But their original sponsor was Edward Grosse, a lawyer and member of the Typographical Union. To Gompers's astonishment, the Socialist faction of the cigar makers' union disrupted meetings at which Grosse spoke. It seemed to Gompers that the Socialists were prepared to defeat Grosse at the polls, even though it would jeopardize the tenement-house legislation. "They preferred to see evils continue," he explained, "rather than see remedies from any other agencies than those prescribed in Socialism."

Five years later, Gompers helped to found the American Federation of Labor. Although he aligned the union with radicals and even Socialists where it seemed necessary—he joined with Darrow in supporting the cause of the Haymarket Anarchists and in working with Debs on the Pullman Strike of 1894—Gompers became increasingly pragmatic. He was convinced that confrontation should only be used when conciliation would not work; he was mindful of the greater power of capital, and committed to the cause of free enterprise, which fueled the corporations that gave work to his constituents.

Over the years, Gompers also became increasingly critical of radical union organizing tactics although, as a federation, the AFL necessarily had to accept diverse approaches on the part of its constituent member unions. While keeping the union out of most electoral campaigns, he became an outspoken critic of socialism and the Socialist Party. "I want to tell you Socialists," he said in 1903, "that I am entirely at variance with your philosophy. . . . Economically, you are unsound; socially, you are wrong; industrially, you are an impossibility." The Socialists were equally contemptuous of Gompers, whom they attacked for his friendships and life-style as well as for his philosophy.

At bottom, Gompers was a realist who, when it was necessary, could and did work with leading capitalists, with Republicans, with Democrats, or with Socialists, in the interest of building his union. But Gompers could fight with anyone, too. In an age of toughness—when rough brawlers such as Theodore Roosevelt and General Otis took pride in mortal combat—Gompers could mix it up with the best of them, left or right, tall or short. At five feet four inches, he was squat but sturdy. He claimed that his short legs were an advantage; "My legs are so short I can never run away from a fight," he would joke. By 1911, his head of jet black hair had begun to lighten and thin, he had shaved his full dark mustache, and he wore wire-rimmed spectacles. But with his powerful build, square chin, and determined demeanor, he seemed as pugnacious as ever.

And he was not about to let the forces of capital run roughshod over the leadership of the Structural Iron Workers' Union.

❀ ❀ ❀ ❀

By the time he received the telegram from the labor leaders in Indianapolis, Gompers had already decided that it was essential to hire Darrow to represent the McNamaras. He had been enraged by the first reports of their arrest. He had never heard of Jim McNamara, but he knew J.J. and knew of his intense loyalty to union labor. He was certain that he had been framed. Of even more concern, he saw the arrest as the start of an attack on all of union labor. He immediately sent a telegram to union president Frank Ryan. "Feel confident Secretary McNamara is innocent," he said. "Is it not possible to secure legal counsel?"

Gompers had known Darrow for twenty years. He knew his strengths as well as his weaknesses. He was prepared to use both to persuade him to take on this case. On Wednesday, the United Press sent out a story definitively reporting that Darrow planned to turn the unions down. But Gompers refused to accept that answer. He knew that Darrow could be reached by flattery, impressed by money, and touched by sentiment. If all else failed, he could also be moved by fear.

After reading the United Press story, Gompers sent a telegram to Darrow in Chicago. "There is no other advocate in the whole United States who holds such a commanding post before the people and in whom labor has such entire confidence," he said. "You owe it to yourself and to the cause of labor to appear as the advocate of these men so unjustly accused."

Gompers followed up by placing a long-distance telephone call to Darrow. In 1911, such calls were still a rare and expensive occurrence and only used for essential matters. Gompers promised that the AFL would back the defense to the hilt. He pleaded with him to take the case, arguing that no one else could save the reputation of organized labor and save the lives of the McNamaras.

Finally, when Darrow still resisted, Gompers made a not-too-subtle threat. "You will go down in history as a traitor to the great cause of labor if now, in our greatest hour of need, you refuse to take charge of the McNamara case."

There was little Darrow could do. If he agreed to take the case, he would be a hero, back at center stage, fighting for the principles he believed in, helping working men to avoid the hangman's noose. Equally important, if he could clear fifty thousand dollars for handling the case, he would have a total pot of a hundred thousand dollars—a large enough nest egg to leave the law, to write, and possibly, to start some kind of magazine.

But if he refused, the consequences could be unbearable. He would lose his most important client, undermine his ability to serve as a management-labor mediator, be deemed a traitor by his most loyal friends, and if Gompers could be believed, damage rather than enhance his place in history.

Darrow finally said he would take the case if the AFL would meet certain conditions. He insisted that they agree to let him control its direction and chose his own cocounsel; turn the case into a national crusade; and guarantee him a fund of at least $200,000, of which $50,000—after expenses—would be his fee. The price seemed exceptionally high to some members of the AFL executive board, but they needed him, and Gompers agreed to meet Darrow's terms.

After arranging to sever ties with his law partners, and getting Ruby's reluctant permission to break his promise never again to undertake such a taxing case, Darrow made his announcement. When they heard the news, the world of the American left was overjoyed—the world of labor, the Socialists, the anarchists, the intellectuals, the men and women who worked with their hands, who built the tall buildings, who risked their lives high on bridge scaffolds, the children who worked in locked-in sweatshops making garments for the rich, the church-going faithful who hated kidnappers and believed in the innocence of a young Irish lad who didn't drink or smoke, or who hated the detectives who were known to use the third degree to obtain untrue confessions and to plant evidence to make their cases foolproof—they all rejoiced. For Clarence Darrow, the man who had beaten the Pinkertons and saved Big

Bill Haywood, Clarence Darrow, defender of labor and the poor, was at the helm.

❄ ❄ ❄ ❄

But Darrow was worried, not joyous. In part, he was still feeling weak and insecure. "I would have much preferred that a younger and stronger man had been chosen," he told reporters. "I dread the long railroad journeys, the sleepless nights, the heavy mental work inseparable from the defense of these men. I nearly died of exhaustion following the strenuous work I did in the Moyer-Haywood-Pettibone cases."

Unfortunately, Darrow had another serious problem. He was certain that his clients were guilty. Worse, he was convinced they would be hanged. After he agreed to take the case, Darrow couldn't ethically share that concern with anyone: not with Gompers, not even with Ruby. But before he agreed to take it, during the one day when he planned to decline, he shared his concern with at least one friend.

Speaking in total secrecy, he explained how he felt to Ernest Stout of the United Press. While labor was still wooing him, Darrow told Stout that he had decided not to take the case because he was convinced that the brothers were guilty. Stout's UP dispatch that Wednesday reported that Darrow had decided to turn the job down. The news report did not mention all of Darrow's concerns, but Stout did report the conversation to his superior, Roy Howard. In a special memo, Howard then notified other top UP managers that Darrow had said that he "would not defend the McNamaras or McManigal because Burns had absolute proof of their guilt, and because he [Darrow] was sure they were going to be hung, and he didn't care to take the case which he felt he had no chance of winning."

Once he agreed to take the case, Darrow grappled with his own insecurities as well as with the fact that Burns had an exceptionally strong case against his clients. "I go at it with fear and foreboding," he wrote to his longtime friend Brand Whitlock. "I dread the fight and am in the dark. If I could avoid it I would, but how can I? They are my friends and in trouble and have an insane faith in me and I don't see how I can disappoint them much as I tremble at the plunge."

Then, in a comment that displayed remarkable prescience, he confessed, "I feel like one going away on a long and dangerous voyage."

* * * *

If the voyage seemed dangerous at the outset, however, Darrow's spirits were quickly lifted by a brief, triumphant trip to California. It was precisely the tonic that his tired spirit needed. Everywhere he went, Darrow found friends and supporters. On May 23, he arrived in San Francisco, a city controlled by the leaders of labor. During the next two days, the press followed him everywhere, describing his appearance, quoting his observations, singing his praises.

Darrow spent an evening with a group of radical and literary friends at the home of Fremont Older, the crusading editor of the San Francisco *Bulletin*. At dinner, the topic quickly turned to women's suffrage, a hot subject in California since the state was about to vote on a constitutional amendment that would give its women the right to vote. Virtually all of the men in the rather large assemblage were opposed to suffrage, partly because they expected women to vote for more conservative candidates.

"The things they said were funny," one of the men present reported a few days later, "and yet, at the same time, almost scandalous. They showed such a deep-seated contempt for women." Darrow was the mildest of them all, but he, too, "acknowledged that he was not really in sympathy with [women's suffrage]."

After another strenuous day of meetings with labor leaders, Darrow went to the train station to catch the night train for Los Angeles. But before he could board, a bevy of reporters surrounded him, forcing him to hold an impromptu news conference to discuss how he felt about participating in what some people were calling the greatest criminal case in American history.

"I did not want to take this case," Darrow said. "I hesitated and argued against it, but I did not feel that I could decline after the way in which it was put up to me. I could not desert the cause in which I have labored all my life, even for health's considerations."

One reporter asked a particularly difficult question. What if Darrow knew that they were guilty? he inquired. Would he still defend them?

"It is a lawyer's business," he said, "to take a case whether his client be guilty or innocent."

As events would soon prove, the McNamara case was somewhat more complex than Darrow's statement would suggest. The right to counsel is at the core of the American system of criminal justice, and even guilty defendants are fundamentally entitled to legal representation. But guilty defendants are not necessarily entitled to the nickels and dimes of working men and women who are led to believe in their innocence as a matter of religious faith.

* * * *

Darrow arrived in Los Angeles at nine-fifteen the next morning. With the effervescent Anton Johannsen at his side, he went directly to the county jail to meet his famous clients. As always, the McNamara brothers were a study in contrasts.

Despite a month in jail, J. J. McNamara, labor leader and now national martyr, was as imposing as ever. He came into the corridor from his cell wearing a steel gray suit, with his shirt open at the throat. During the past few months his brown hair had turned to gray, offering a strange contrast with his young face. Otherwise, there was no sign that he had changed. He seemed like a high-minded man with a clear conscience. But Jim McNamara, the younger brother, was as anemic and foul-mouthed as ever.

Darrow did not ask them if they were guilty.

After leaving the prisoners, Darrow went to the Higgins Building, where Job Harriman had rented a suite of offices for the defense team. Then, at last, he went to his suite at the lovely Alexandria Hotel. Darrow had been working for twelve straight hours. To his surprise, he was loving it.

In excellent humor, he held a series of interviews with friendly reporters. He told them that he felt better than he had for years. Being back at the center of attention in a great case for labor had started to revive his spirits.

Darrow started to play with his new acquaintances from the press.

He asked for their advice about how to handle the case and whether to move it to another city. A Hearst reporter described what he called Darrow's "Li Hung-chang act of interviewing the interviewer, with a pertinacity that deserved better results." When a photographer from the left-leaning Los Angeles *Record* arrived and asked him to pose, Darrow gave his interviewer a quip designed for his particular audience. "I will think about socialism," joked Darrow, who tended to think like a Socialist and vote as a Democrat, "and then I will be sure to look pleasant."

Continuing in the same jovial vein, Darrow commented that he had spent a lot of time with pressmen since arriving in California. "They have snapped me and sketched me," he said. "They have got about everything from me except my thumbprints. I kicked at that."

His good humor continued the next morning, when he succeeded in surprising and impressing the community by his choice of co-counsel. In addition to Job Harriman, the labor lawyer and Socialist leader, Darrow announced the hiring of Joseph Scott, president of the Los Angeles school board, a mainstream, business-oriented lawyer who was one of the city's leading Catholics; of former Indiana judge Cyrus McNutt; and of the well-known criminal lawyer Le-Compte Davis. Davis was perhaps best known for his successful defense of Burr Harris, a black man who had been charged with sending poisoned candy to his white "benefactress." Davis's work in that case, which he handled for free, was regarded by many lawyers as the most brilliant defense ever presented in a Los Angeles courtroom.

Darrow made his first court appearance on Saturday morning. He was joined by his cocounsel, and by the McNamara brothers, who were both clean-shaven and in an apparently happy frame of mind. At Darrow's request, the court agreed to give the defense an extension of time so that Darrow could return to Chicago to wind up his affairs.

Before leaving town, Darrow was again asked that nagging question. "Do you believe the men you will defend are innocent?" asked Otheman Stevens of the *Examiner*.

Darrow gave Stevens one of his famous, wry smiles. "I always believe in the innocence of the men I defend," he said.

❈ ❈ ❈

As in Idaho, the defense strategy started with public relations. Darrow told one labor leader that "the public is all we have to rely on in this case." With the support of the Socialists, labor, and some friendly journalists and opinion leaders, Darrow hoped to build a powerful public base of support for his clients and their cause—and, at the same time, promote widespread suspicion of those who were trying to convict them.

The campaign for public opinion began at once—and made an immediate impact. "I am very deeply interested in the tremendous fight that confronts Clarence Darrow in the Los Angeles situation," one of Darrow's key journalistic allies explained. "We must endeavor to break into the solid wall of black prejudice that exists in this country against the toiler." The Socialist Party and the AFL provided the battering ram to break down that wall.

The Socialists' strongest instrument was *Appeal to Reason,* the party's weekly organ, which had built up a circulation base of over 400,000. In capital letters, Eugene Debs told the *Appeal's* audience that the *Times* was to blame for the deaths. "THE TIMES AND ITS CROWD OF UNION-HATERS ARE THEMSELVES THE INSTIGATORS IF NOT THE ACTUAL PERPETRATORS OF THAT CRIME AND THE MURDERERS OF THE TWENTY HUMAN BEINGS WHO PERISHED AS ITS VICTIMS," he said. Debs promised readers that the party would "throw this paper and all its resources into the fight for the Iron Workers arrested on the palpably trumped-up charges of dynamiting the *Times* Building." He called the McNamara case "The Last Big Fight."

Starting in May, the newspaper sent its top investigative reporter, George Shoaf, to Los Angeles, and began to distribute forty thousand copies a week to local residents. Shoaf, who had been the paper's "war correspondent" at the Idaho trial four years earlier, quickly endorsed the theory that the explosion had been caused by gas, not dynamite. The McNamaras, he announced, are "as innocent as newborn babes." The Socialists mailed that message into every home in the county.

❈ ❈ ❈

AFL president Samuel Gompers quickly emerged as an exceedingly effective critic of Burns and guarantor of the McNamaras' innocence. He did not, of course, know much about the younger brother, Jim, but he truly believed that J.J. had been framed. Gompers was impressed by J.J.'s wire promising his mother that "we are absolutely innocent" and by his telegram to the leaders of labor, asserting that "I am innocent of any infraction of the law in word or act." Privately, Gompers was told by a close friend that "I have known John J. McNamara personally for a number of years and it is impossible for me to connect him with the serious acts." His friends in San Francisco labor provided similar assurances. Burns had forced McManigal to "confess," they said, by threatening to have him prosecuted for a murder that he had committed in Ohio.

Having satisfied himself that the brothers had been framed, Gompers sent a telegram to J.J. in prison. "We all feel confident of your and your brother's innocence," he said, "and will do everything lawful within our power to help in its establishment before the courts." He sent a copy of the telegram to Iron Workers president Frank Ryan, along with his personal assurance that he believed in the brothers' innocence. He sent similar private messages to his own executive board and to Olaf Tvietmoe in San Francisco.

Darrow knew of these communications. But he did nothing to warn Gompers that his assurances were excessive. He made coy, lawyerlike statements of his own, continuing to say that "I always believe in the innocence of the men I defend." But he allowed Gompers to go dangerously far out on a limb.

Gompers became the point man in a bitter war of phrases with William J. Burns. In a nasty opening shot, Gompers charged that "these men have been arrested on charges that are absolutely false. I have investigated the whole case, and Burns has lied." He said that Burns "is well known to have no hesitancy or scruples in manufacturing evidence and charges against others. A detective agency such as this is itself accused before the bar of public opinion."

Burns was furious. Feeling that his case was foolproof and self-evident, he could not imagine how Gompers could insist that the men were innocent. Nor did he appreciate the attacks on his methods and his character.

"What has become of Gompers's conscience?" Burns asked. "Hasn't he got any? Does he want to class himself with the McNamaras and McManigal? Is he of the same breed as they? Does he want the country to think that he is? We've got the goods on the prisoners, and Gompers knows so better than anyone else."

He was convinced that Gompers would hang himself with his own rhetoric. "The day will come," Burns promised, "when Gompers will have to admit the guilt of the McNamaras and McManigal, not only for dynamiting the *Los Angeles Times* building, but for numerous outrages that have shocked the country. Before the trial ends, Gompers will be proved not only a liar, but a fool."

Finally, the war of words had drawn blood. The defense was winning the early rounds. But there was a risk. Through his very public defense of the McNamaras, Gompers had also put himself, and the credibility of American labor, on trial in Los Angeles.

❊ ❊ ❊ ❊

To Darrow's delight, the public relations strategy was working. The AFL printed up tens of thousands of buttons and stamps with handsome pictures of J. J. McNamara. All of them carried the same slogan: KIDNAPPED. It was a theme that quickly took hold. No one thought or said much about the younger brother. The focus was on J.J., the upstanding labor leader, and the claim that he had been framed and abducted.

The public was increasingly inclined to think that the case was a setup. One of the first to see the trend was Harry Chandler, publisher of the *Los Angeles Times* and son-in-law of Harrison Gray Otis. On May 30, 1911, Chandler sent a long and slightly panicky letter to Otis, who was in Washington on business. "They are doing the most that the active use of money and devilish scheming can do to change public sentiment their way here," Chandler reported. "They are sending a copy of the 'Appeal to Reason' to every resident of Southern California and claim they are going to continue until after the trial of the dynamiters is concluded."

Chandler felt that there was good reason to believe that those efforts were succeeding. "Our solicitors going through East Los Angeles and Boyle Heights find that from thirty to fifty percent of the apparently intelligent people whom they call upon are filled up with the socialistic and anarchistic idea that these men are innocent and that Burns and the corporations have 'framed up' a case on them."

It was proving relatively easy to win the war of public opinion. But Darrow soon found that he would have a devil of a time trying to undermine the facts of the case itself.

Chapter Six

"A TOUGH GAME"

F ROM THE OUTSET, DARROW knew that Burns had a rock solid case against his clients, particularly against the younger brother. There was so much evidence. There were witnesses from San Francisco and Los Angeles who could identify Jim McNamara as James Brice, the man who arranged for the bombing. There was Lena Ingersoll, the San Francisco boardinghouse proprietor who had recognized Jim as he left the train in Pasadena. There were hotel clerks and train conductors; there were men who had sold him dynamite or had transported the dynamite from San Francisco to Los Angeles. There was the physical and documentary evidence that had been seized at the union's headquarters in Indianapolis. Above all, there was Ortie McManigal.

This was not the first time that Darrow had faced overwhelming odds. He had overcome an exceedingly powerful case in Idaho by converting a key witness to his side and, according to those in a position to know, by eliminating some key prosecution evidence and manufacturing some evidence of his own. He hoped to use the same tactics in Los Angeles. But Darrow soon learned that Los Angeles was not like any other town he had ever seen. The forces of capital, backed by Burns and the police and the courts, were everywhere.

❋ ❋ ❋ ❋

Darrow's strategy and philosophy during the months that followed are described in rich detail in the remarkably complete correspondence of Colonel Charles Erskine Scott Wood, his close friend from Portland, Oregon. Darrow had asked Wood to be his cocounsel in the McNamara case, but Wood had refused, largely because of what he knew about Darrow's character and methods. The correspondence is particularly interesting because Wood accurately predicts and condemns the tactics that Darrow would eventually use in preparing for the McNamara trial. Based on reports of what Darrow had done in Idaho, Wood was convinced that Darrow would use any device to win—including bribery and perjury. Wood considered these tactics to be wrong as a matter of political philosophy, legal ethics, and trial strategy. He was also certain that they would come to light.

Darrow considered Wood one of the great men of the era. He was a West Point graduate and military hero who—while maintaining his military title—quit the service after winning the bloody battle against the Nez Percé Indians and witnessing the army's mistreatment of Chief Joseph and his tribe. He became an outstanding corporate and admiralty lawyer in Portland, Oregon, but his passionate concerns were poetry and social justice. He spent his spare hours working for radical friends such as Emma Goldman and the leaders of the Industrial Workers of the World. Though married to a Catholic woman, and the father of several children, he also developed an intense relationship with President Theodore Roosevelt's sister, Corinne Robinson, who shared his love for poetry.

Darrow and Wood had much in common. They were outstanding lawyers who preferred literature to law and wanted to spend the rest of their lives as writers. They earned a good living representing the rich, but had a much greater sympathy for the poor. When the case arose, they were working together on behalf of a rich bank executive who had been accused of fraud. Not incidentally, they also happened to be brothers-in-law in sin.

❋ ❋ ❋ ❋

Thanks to Darrow, Erskine Wood had just begun a torrid love affair with Mary Field's younger sister, Sara Field Ehrgott. Like Mary, Sara was petite and rebellious, but instead of leaving her family for college and then for settlement work, as Mary had done, Sara had escaped from her oppressive father by marrying Albert Ehrgott, a politically liberal but socially conservative minister.

Mary introduced Darrow to Sara in the summer of 1908. The three spent several days together at a resort outside of Chicago, talking about social welfare, philosophy, politics, and poetry. After that, Darrow occasionally visited Sara at her home in Cleveland, where her husband was a minister. But when he saw her there in the spring of 1910, Darrow found Sara in tears. She had just learned that the church deemed her husband too radical for the pulpit in Cleveland, which at the time was one of the most progressive cities in America, and planned to send him to Portland, Oregon.

"Here I have lived in this wonderful atmosphere of progress and brave endeavor," she sobbed, "and I've got to go to that desolate country."

Darrow tried to console her. While agreeing that Portland was not so advanced as San Francisco or even Seattle, he said that "there is one man out there that I think you will like, and you will surely meet him." Doubting that one man was enough to save a city, Sara ignored his assurances and continued to cry.

Then one day in the middle of October, 1910, while she was outside working in the garden of her new house in Portland, a taxi drove up through the mud of the unpaved street, and out stepped Clarence Darrow. He was in town to deliver a lecture denouncing prohibition. "I want you and your husband to come to dinner," he announced, "and to meet my friend Colonel Wood."

"Oh, Darrow," she said, "I haven't got any decent clothes, and I'm all mud."

"Don't worry," Darrow quickly reassured her. "We're going to dine in a very bohemian place. You can wear any old thing at all." Then, giving her one of his wry smiles, he added: "You know I have never been a fellow that dressed up very much."

So Sara agreed to join Darrow for dinner.

Persuading Wood to join him was a bit more difficult, since Wood and his wife already had dinner plans.

"Why don't you just lie to her," Darrow suggested. "I find that's the easiest way."

"Well I don't," Wood said, in a comment that highlighted a fundamental difference between the two men. "It's not my method." But Wood agreed to arrange for his brother to take his wife to dinner in his place.

"Who is this person, anyway?" Wood asked.

"Her name is Mrs. Ehrgott. She's a minister's wife."

"What?" said Colonel Wood, incredulous. "What would I have in common with a minister's wife?"

Darrow leaned over toward his companion. "Listen," he said in a conspiratorial tone. "She's one of us."

❋ ❋ ❋ ❋

As promised, Darrow chose a bohemian Portland restaurant called the Hofbrau as the spot to introduce Sara Field Ehrgott to Colonel Wood.

Sara was struck at once by the colonel's appearance. He had a stunning full gray beard, long, curly gray hair, a beautiful complexion, and the keenest and kindest eagle blue-gray eyes that she had ever seen. He was so handsome and striking that people turned to look at him wherever he went. In Europe he was constantly taken for a great composer.

Colonel Wood was accompanied by two young women. One was his secretary, Katherine Seaman, who, though Sara had no way of knowing it at the time, was also his mistress.

Darrow arranged to seat Wood next to Sara, and the two immediately started to talk about modern literature. Sara asked him if he was reading H. G. Wells, who had just written *Ann Veronica, a Modern Love Story,* in which Wells urged greater freedom for women.

"No, I've heard of it," Wood answered, a bit sadly. "I get very little time for outside reading, and I'm very sorry, because I remember what Bacon said, that 'much reading maketh a full man,' and I know I should read more. But I'm always caught up in some very important case on which I have to read a great deal to get all the back-

ground, and the result is that if I do pick up a book it's usually"—
and here he smiled—"a book of poetry."

"Oh, yes," Sara said happily, "I remember that Mr. Darrow told me
that you are a poet."

"I am, but I wish I had more time to write."

Later Darrow brought the conversation around to Galsworthy,
whose new play, *Justice*, provided a realistic portrayal of prison life
that roused so much feeling that it led to a series of reforms. Galsworthy had also just published a book of short stories. "If Wood will
let us go over to his private office afterwards," Darrow said, turning
to the Colonel, "I'll read one of the stories to you."

Sara's husband had a meeting to attend, but everyone else was
delighted, so after dinner the merry crew, absent Reverend Ehrgott,
went to Colonel Wood's office in the chamber of commerce building. Sara was not prepared for what she saw. Room 419 of Portland
Commerce—which soon became an important part of her life—was
the most beautiful study she had ever seen. It had Oriental rugs, a
fine piece of English furniture for a desk, and objects of art all
around. The room was Wood's aesthetic self; it was to his law offices
as poetry is to a legal brief.

Darrow loved to read aloud, both poetry and prose, and he did
it beautifully. As Sara sat there listening to Darrow and taking in the
room, she watched Colonel Wood and noticed how he fitted into
these surroundings, listening attentively and appreciatively to Darrow, the two men together in an element that suited them and
pleased them much better than a court of law.

As she was leaving the office, at the end of an evening that she
would remember forever, Wood drew her aside. "Darrow tells me
that you do some writing, and that you have written some poetry,"
he said.

"Well, I sat in on a course of criticism one year at Yale," she
answered, "but I doubt that I've written anything of importance."

"You took a course of criticism?"

"Yes."

"Well," Wood persisted, "I need some help on criticism. I've
written some sonnets. I wish you would look at them and tell me if
they are worth anything."

So Sara flew home with the sonnets, and Darrow left the evening with the warm glow that comes from making two friends happy—and, as he may have guessed, making a match.

❋ ❋ ❋

With their mutual love of literature and the Field sisters, Darrow and Wood could have had a marvelous time working together on the McNamara case. But Erskine politely turned Clarence down. He was reluctant to leave his family and his law practice, but just as important, he was convinced that Darrow would wind up using unethical tactics. "It would be fun if I had accepted the offer to work with Darrow," he told Sara, "but I knew it would be these tactics because I know what was done at the Moyer-Pettibone-Haywood trial at Boise."

In a series of letters, Wood spelled out the approaches that he expected Darrow to use. He was certain that Darrow would manufacture and eliminate evidence. "The jurors in Boise openly say they did not believe the testimony for the defense," he told a friend. "Little by little, through injudicious people on the inside, it has leaked out in braggadocio that the defense was manufactured."

He was certain that Darrow would eliminate and create evidence in Los Angeles, too. More than that, he predicted, Darrow "will use bribery where safe, perjury where safe. He will manipulate and marshal labor all over the United States at psychological moments to appear in masses and utter threats, arousing a bitterness, a reckless-ness meant to intimidate a jury in Los Angeles, but thereby arousing a sentiment of clan against persons and individuals more dangerous than dynamite, for it will prevent discussion and understanding—and precipitate a warfare of force."

"The more I have thought of this matter," he continued, "the more I think a tremendous tactical mistake is being made; that the enthusi-asm in action, the personal vanities of the actors, the desire to succeed, are leading backward and will ruin the very cause they profess to serve"

"Depend on it," he predicted. "No one will be deceived."

❋ ❋ ❋

Darrow's first and most important task was one of the least troubling from an ethical standpoint. There were lots of ways that the state could corroborate Ortie McManigal, but there was no way to replace him. The defense would be well on the way to victory if it could persuade Ortie to repudiate his confession.

In trying to convert McManigal, Darrow employed a tactic that he had used to great effect in Idaho. The state's principal witness in Idaho was Harry Orchard, but there were two men who might have been able to corroborate his tale. One, Jack Simpkins, conveniently and mysteriously disappeared. The other, Steve Adams, agreed to repudiate his own confession after Darrow tracked down an uncle in a cabin in the mountains of Oregon, sent the uncle in to talk with Adams, and promised to represent Adams in any cases brought against him by the government.

In similar fashion, Darrow hoped to use Ortie's relatives to convert him. The effort began exceptionally well. During the first weeks of June, while back in Chicago, Darrow and some of his labor union allies persuaded Ortie's wife to help the defense. That in itself was important, since Burns had publicly called Emma McManigal "one of the most important witnesses against J. J. McNamara." It would be nice to embarrass Burns and to have Emma on J.J.'s side.

More important, Emma agreed to use her charms on her husband, and to help Darrow enlist the aid of Ortie's uncle, George Behm. Behm was Ortie's closest relative and closest friend. An old railroad engineer, Behm was like a father to Ortie, having brought the boy up after the death of his mother. Between his wife and his uncle, Ortie would be surrounded.

With Darrow's encouragement, Emma sent a telegram asking Uncle George to meet her in Chicago on Sunday, June 18. The old man cheerfully agreed to come.

That Sunday, as it happened, was Darrow's last day in Chicago. He and Ruby were scheduled to catch an afternoon train for the Coast. As he planned for his departure, Darrow no longer was filled with fear. His mood was as sunny as the Chicago summer day. No longer the old and tired crusader, he had already been intoxicated by the glory and power that came from handling what was shaping up as the most celebrated trial in American history. He felt young again.

His name was on the lips of audiences and speakers at a series of huge events being organized in every major city to promote his work and the cause of his clients. Leaders of the Socialist Party and the AFL were planning what they called a Monster Rally, to be held in New York's Carnegie Hall the next weekend. And as if to give the great lawyer a fitting send-off, a giant parade and demonstration was scheduled to be held later that same afternoon in Chicago. Some eighty thousand supporters were expected to attend.

At a few minutes past eleven A.M.—as crowds were beginning to gather for the parade—Emma McManigal and one of Darrow's associates picked Behm up at the train station and brought him to the Darrows' apartment. Darrow's greeting was warm and friendly, the coded language used to receive a fellow believer in the cause of organized labor. He showed the old railroad engineer into his spacious, sun-filled living room and introduced him to a group of labor leaders who were assembled for one final strategy session. Before long, they were old friends. Behm would be only too happy, he said, to go to Los Angeles to help persuade Ortie to see the light. He would head for the Coast as soon as he could put his personal affairs in order.

Late that afternoon, as the crowds were returning home from the demonstration at Riverside Park, Clarence and Ruby Darrow took a cab to the Chicago and Northwestern station, where they boarded the train for Los Angeles. Ruby left with "a heavy heart," but Clarence was euphoric, buoyed by a stimulating blend of excitement and apprehension.

It was not, however, a euphoria that would last for long.

❋ ❋ ❋ ❋

The Los Angeles that greeted the Darrows that June was a city in transition, changing so fast that some one hundred thousand people had moved there since Clarence Darrow had left, with his mastoiditis cured, just four years earlier. That was a third of the city's current population, as many people as had lived in the entire community in 1900.

Only a generation earlier, Los Angeles had been a pleasant and permissive land of Padres and Dons, a playground for miners and cattlemen who came west from Nevada, Arizona, and the interior regions of California to taste the city's color and glamour, to bet on horse races that pitted the magnificent silver-maned dun horses from the haciendas of Monterey against the superb steeds of the southern Dons, to play poker and get drunk in the city's hundred saloons, and to visit the high-priced prostitutes in the sumptuous parlor houses of Commercial, New High, or Merchessault streets, or the less pricey ladies in their cramped rooms or "cribs" on Alameda Street.

During the years between 1821 and 1848, all of California was part of Mexico. The Treaty of Guadalupe Hidalgo divided the state in half, giving the United States control of Upper, or Alta California, and Mexico control of Lower, or Baja California. In 1849, as some of the old timers could recall, the dividing line was established a few miles south of San Diego. California (actually, Upper California) officially became a state the following year.

People in their sixties remembered the years just after statehood, when much of the land was still owned by a few hundred great Dons, many of them friends or former military aides of the Mexican governors, who had been given huge rancheros that they expected to own forever, men such as Juan Bandini, who, after coming to California from Peru in the early 1820s, acquired a ranchero that stretched from Baja California to the San Bernadino mountains. Bandini's family, like many of the Dons, married into American families. One daughter, Ysidora, married a cousin of Ulysses S. Grant; another, Arcadia, married Abel Stearns, who became a Mexican citizen after moving from Massachusetts to California.

The Bandinis created legendary festivals, "fandangos and fiestas," as author Kevin Starr described them, "that went on for days at a time, often ending with the *cascaron,* eggshells filled with confetti and cologne, which the men and women broke flirtatiously on one another's heads." But in a remarkably short time, most of the Dons lost their land to the new laws and new economic realities that statehood brought with it. Juan Bandini had lost all of his holdings by the time he died in 1859. Not even his Yankee-born son-in-law, Abel Stearns, who was for a brief time the largest owner of land and cattle in Southern California, could hold on to the rancheros. The drought years of 1863–64 drove Stearns deeply into debt, and by

1868 he was forced to sell all of his holdings, totaling some 177,000 acres. Most of them were subdivided into small tracts for the great new California industry: residential real estate.

The end of the era of the Dons was hastened by the advent of transcontinental railroads, which first reached Los Angeles in 1876. Prior to the arrival of the railroads, travelers could go north on the Coast Line Stage Company, which took four hazardous days to reach San Francisco, or go east by coach, stopping for a time at an old Mormon settlement at the foot of Cajon Pass, and then continuing on a weekly four-horse "mud wagon" headed for the still wild Arizona Territory. There was also the Butterfield Overland stage-coach, which ran from St. Louis to San Francisco via El Paso and Los Angeles. The trip from St. Louis could take twenty days, and passengers were advised to carry blankets, extra food, and water for the desert crossing, and a revolver to assist in the coach's defense. It was not an inviting trip for travelers who wanted to visit, or leave, Southern California.

All that was changed by the railroads. For a decade, the Southern Pacific held a monopoly on transcontinental traffic, but the Santa Fe arrived on its own track in 1887, triggering a rate war that briefly drove cross-country ticket prices down to one dollar. Thousands of families started to migrate from the Midwest to Southern California, attracted by the lure of lovely weather and cheap housing. The immigrants couldn't even pronounce the name of their new home (a leading writer called it "America's one unpronounceable city"), but the population of Los Angeles, which stood at about forty thousand in 1890, began to double every seven years.

It was a heady time dominated by a spirit of boosterism and growth that was fueled by the wealth of Southern California agriculture and real estate, orchestrated by the railroads and the chamber of commerce, and fanned by General Otis's *Los Angeles Times*. By 1905, the Southern Pacific Railroad and the California Fruit Growers' Exchange were promoting the region along with its produce as the route to a happy life. The Southern California citrus industry, with its prize-winning seedless oranges, was especially appealing. Billboards in Iowa promised "Oranges for Health—California for wealth" as part of a campaign that increased orange consumption by

50 percent. In 1908, they took the campaign national, advertising orange juice as a health cure and even inventing the Orange Blossom Cocktail. Nationwide consumption of oranges jumped six-fold. By 1910, California was exporting some forty thousand refrigerated boxcars of fruit each year.

Combining the dreams of fantasy, fruit, and religion, the railroads described Los Angeles as a Garden of Eden for God-fearing Midwestern farmers. The immigrants were welcomed by the new city fathers, who hacked down beautiful groves of oranges, lemons, and pears to make room for the new settlers, and tore down vineyards to build the city's new streets. The number of building permits continued to grow each year, from 7,373 in 1908 to 12,408 in 1911 and 16,453 in 1912. By 1911, the city was building at least fifty-four miles of new dwellings per year. One day in 1911, someone put a notice in the *Times* saying that former Iowans would hold a picnic at Westlake Park the following Thursday. More than 35,000 people showed up.

As the Midwestern invasion continued, those with Mexican blood began to move into Sonora Town, a separate section of the city. By 1911, the names of Junipero Serra, Juan Bautista de Anza, Portola, Ortega, were unknown to Los Angeles school children. "The Iowa invasion had completely wiped out the Spanish atmosphere," one transplanted Hoosier recalled. "The Iowans made hash of the romance of our pueblo. A fandango just didn't make any sense to them. Not even the Normans, over-running England, or the Spanish conquest of Mexico, made a more profound change in the psychology of an invaded land than did the Iowans in Los Angeles.

"They plastered the town with Protestant churches where only Catholic bells had tolled," he said. "They yanked out picturesque Spanish names by the roots; had Wednesday night prayer-meetings; voted the Republican ticket; wore ankle-length under-drawers and frowned upon Demon Rum.

"But they made a sleepy little Mexican pueblo over into a great city."

❊ ❊ ❊ ❊

Thanks to the most miraculous public transportation system in America, in 1911 you could live in a area that remained rural and still work in downtown Los Angeles. One evening, a visiting journalist went to the Mason Theater and sat next to an Iowa native who had come downtown to the theater with his family. While waiting for the show to start, the reporter asked why the family had decided to move to Los Angeles.

"I insist upon living in the woods," the ex-Iowan began, "but I'm a shoe-merchant and I have to keep my store in the city. You see, I like to go to sleep with the mockingbird singing to me, and at the same time I want to be able to go to the theater two nights a week. I couldn't do all these seemingly inconsistent things anywhere else in America."

"You can do all of them here?" the journalist asked, somewhat incredulous.

"Easily! I live in an orange grove in a meadow twelve miles from this theater, and I'll be in my bed out under my favorite tree forty-five minutes after the final curtain falls."

The explanation, he said, was not the automobile, which had just started to be purchased in large numbers but was not yet used as a general means of conveyance. Rather, it was the city's fabled "red car," which covered twice as much territory as any other electric interurban system in America. The system's six hundred passenger cars seemed to go everywhere in the region, carrying 225,000 people per day.

To demonstrate the miracle of the red car, the transplanted Iowan described his activities that day. "I got out of my outdoor bed at six," he said, "thrust my feet into slippers and went in my pajamas to get the morning paper that was caught in the rose tree by the front gate. . . . At seven-thirty I got up from the breakfast table and left home for business. At eight my eldest daughter left to come in to town to the art institute. At eight-thirty the two kids departed for their grammar school three miles away. . . . When I got home from the store the whole family was on the tennis court and we had a lively hour before dinner. Tonight we all came in to the show."

He pointed to the group next to him. "This is my little flock beside me," he boasted. "Healthy bunch, eh?"

That story, not surprisingly, was promptly printed in *Sunset* magazine, encouraging thousands more to come to sunny, civilized, prosperous, healthy, Southern California.

Small wonder, then, that Los Angeles had begun to look like paradise. "In the mind of the average Way Down Easterner," one observer noted, "Los Angeles life is an uninterrupted revel of orange blossoms and sweet bird music, a twelve-months' siesta in shirtsleeves upon the bungalow's sunny porch, a continuous round of sightseeing and pleasure for those who have the price and strength to enjoy the multitude of diversions.

"This vision of the chillbrained Easterner" he wrote, "is substantially correct."

❊ ❊ ❊ ❊

All of the prosperity, however, had been purchased at a cost: The Spanish culture had been virtually obliterated; capital and labor were in a state of virtual warfare; and the city government was heavily influenced by a handful of men, including the leaders of the Southern Pacific Railroad and the owner of the *Los Angeles Times.* Ironically, the forces that had done most to bring newcomers to Los Angeles—the General and the railroad—soon became the targets of the new immigrants and of the values that they brought with them to Southern California.

Up through the late nineteenth and even the early years of the twentieth century, Los Angeles had been known—and loved—for its wild and colorful nightlife, for such women as Madam Van, a regal, middle-aged courtesan, whose establishment on Alameda Street was marked by two bronze lions at the front gate. When a new woman joined her harem, Madam Van would announce her availability by dressing her up in the height of fashion and driving her in an elegant carriage through the streets of the city. There were several burlesque houses in the heart of town, including Pop Fisher's on Spring Street and, perhaps most famous, Pearl Morton's, an adobe house that was flush with the street and had iron railings and little balconies like those in New Orleans. The city was also fabled as the home of championship prize fights, which were held in Vernon or in stifling upstairs rooms that were called "athletic clubs" to avoid problems with the police, and saloons were everywhere.

But the newcomers were overwhelmingly Christian and moralistic, determined to recreate the world of small-town middle America; indeed, as is so often true of immigrants, they were determined to create a world that might even be more austere than what existed, because the image that they carried in their minds was inevitably less complex than the reality of the world that they had left; and so the newcomers launched a frenzied effort to impose an acceptable level of Christian morality on their new home. That meant doing away with the prostitution, the gambling, the political corruption, and the booze—the very qualities that had given zest to the city's reputation in the century just passed.

The frivolity and gaiety were anathema to the city's new majority. Led by Edwin T. Earl, they launched a crusade to clean up the city. Earl, inventor of the refrigerated railroad car, became rich as the largest packer and shipper of fruit in Southern California. After selling his firm to Armour and Company in 1900, Earl bought the Los Angeles *Evening Express* and in no time became the bitter rival of his neighbor and one-time friend, Harrison Gray Otis. As the men vied for power in the city, each paper looked for stories to expose and crusades to champion, and whatever one supported, it seemed, the other opposed.

While Otis was allied with the old guard, conservative, Taft wing of the Republican Party, Earl was an early champion of the progressive wing of the Republican Party reform forces led nationally by Theodore Roosevelt, and soon to be led in California by Hiram Johnson. The editor of the *Express* was a young man named Edward Dickson who, though barely thirty, had joined forces with three other reform-minded, business-oriented Los Angeles Republicans, including Meyer Lissner, a lawyer and real estate investor who some years earlier had been a pawnbroker and jeweler in San Francisco. The four friends formed a political reform group called the Non-Partisan Committee of One Hundred. Later they created a statewide organization called the League of Lincoln-Roosevelt Clubs.

Vowing to wrest control of Los Angeles politics from the grasp of the Southern Pacific Railroad, the reformers fielded their own slate of candidates for city office in 1907. In a stunning race, their candidates won seventeen of twenty-three contested offices, and only narrowly failed to beat Arthur Harper, the Democratic Party's candidate for mayor, who was backed by the *Los Angeles Times*. Earl then hit upon a method of seizing control of power in the city by stressing an issue that would ignite local passions, sell papers, upstage Otis, and bring the forces of reform to power. It also happened to be an issue that he held dear: the fight to clean up Los Angeles.

Earl had received evidence that some top city officials were extorting payoffs from whorehouses, gambling parlors, and saloons. Before long, the reform forces uncovered a pattern of payments by vice bosses to leaders of the city administration, including Mayor Harper. As it happened, the reformers had recently persuaded the city to adopt an ordinance that enabled citizens to recall an elected official. A recall campaign was launched against Mayor Harper, and in 1909, as it gathered steam, Harper decided to resign, the first victim in America of such a campaign.

In the mayoral election that followed, the forces of reform, the Good Government crowd known popularly as Goo-Goos, backed a benign elderly Iowa native named George Alexander. A favorite of the city's Anti-Saloon League, Alexander had been unseated as a county supervisor by the Southern Pacific machine a year earlier. Wearing outfits that highlighted his uncanny resemblance to posters of Uncle Sam, he campaigned for office as "Honest Uncle George," striking a theme that appealed to the city's new moralistic majority, as well as to progressives who opposed the power and corruption symbolized by the Southern Pacific Railroad. Since Harper had withdrawn from the race, Alexander's strongest opponent was Socialist candidate Fred Wheeler, a leading labor union leader. Alexander won, edging out Wheeler by sixteen hundred votes.

The government immediately started to padlock parlor houses and cribs, driving most prostitutes and gamblers out of business. The reformers censored theaters, closed dance halls, restaurants, race tracks, and roulette tables, challenged the propriety of boxing matches, read the riot act to men who earned money by racing blind pigs, and imposed a midnight curfew. It was a city consumed with efforts to put proper attire on bathers, to chase lovers from the beaches and public parks, to arrest "mashers" who winked or spoke to women on the street. The government even made it a crime for an unmarried man and woman to be alone together in an apartment. Before long, Los Angeles became the subject of Eastern parody. A famous *Smart Set* article called it "Los Angeles—the Chemically Pure."

Elated by their political success, some reformers began to talk privately about destroying the *Times.* In late 1909, Meyer Lissner told Senator Robert LaFollette that "if we follow up on our advantage and handle the situation properly it is only a question of time when we can put it absolutely out of business."

A few months later, Lissner and the other reform leaders nominated one of their own to become the new, progressive Republican governor of California. As their candidate, they chose Hiram Johnson, the crusading lawyer who had gained national fame as prosecutor of the San Francisco graft cases. Short, stocky, and serious, with a round and somewhat florid face, Johnson was a fiery reformer. Ironically, his father, Grove Johnson, was a former spear-carrier for the Southern Pacific's interests, and had been defeated for reelection for congress when his support of the railroad alienated his constituency. Relations between the two men cooled when Hiram refused to manage his father's reelection campaign, but the son retained a certain familial loyalty to his father, if not to his father's politics.

Although the Republican primary was not scheduled to be held until August, the reformers nominated Johnson in the early spring of 1910, leaving him with four months to campaign against a fragmented field of three party regulars. The campaign against him was filled with invective, led by poisonous phrases from the pens of the men at the *Los Angeles Times.* As the summer wore on, the paper, unfairly, began to attack him as a clone of his father. In late July, a *Times* cartoon depicted Grove and Hiram Johnson as tools of the Southern Pacific. The cartoon was captioned "Like Father, Like Son." In the days that followed, the paper claimed that Hiram had been on the pay of the Southern Pacific until he found greener pastures elsewhere.

Finally, Hiram Johnson had had all he could take. On August 5, 1910, he skewered Otis with a bitter and lengthy invective that soon became a part of California lore. Responding to a question about Otis, asked by someone, probably a plant, in the audience of one of his speeches in Los Angeles, Johnson said: "In our city [of San Francisco] we have drunk the dregs of the cup of infamy; we have been betrayed by public officials; we have been disgraced before the world by crimes unspeakable; but with all the criminals who have disgraced us, we have never had anything so degraded, so disreputable, and so vile as Harrison Gray Otis and the *Los Angeles Times.* The one blot on the fame of Southern California, and the one bar sinister on the escutcheon of Los Angeles, is Harrison Gray Otis, a creature who is vile, infamous, degraded, and putrescent. Here he sits in senile dementia, with gangrened heart and rotting brain, grimacing at every reform and chattering in impotent rage against decency and morality, while he is going down to his grave in snarling infamy."

The message hit its mark. When the *Times* building was dynamited less than two months later, General Otis blamed one person outside of organized labor, suggesting that the bombing had been provoked by Hiram Johnson's powerful invective. But Johnson won the race for governor, placing one of General Otis's most bitter enemies at the head of the government of the state of California.

✳ ✳ ✳ ✳

While the city's reputation and politics were dominated by middle-class Midwestern transplants, there was also a seething underclass. Unlike Chicago, where those of foreign birth were the overwhelming majority, less than 25 percent of the Los Angeles population had been born outside the country. But as historian Dan Johnson found in examining the city's 1910 census data, Los Angeles had a distinct working-class population whose life-style never found its way into railway company propaganda or *Sunset* magazine portraits. Residing in the eastern and southern parts of the city, near the railroad yards and harbor, they lived in another Los Angeles, in a world of rotting boardinghouses and cramped apartments. When urban reformer Jacob Riis visited the city at the turn of the century, he found some slums that were as bad as those in Manhattan, or worse. Ironically, the industrial monolith represented by General Otis and the Merchants and Manufacturers Association helped fuel a working-class backlash. Cheered on by the *Times*, the city's corporate leaders quickly built the greatest open-shop organization the country had ever known. But starting in 1907, labor fought back with every device at its command. As one radical newspaper observed, "from the workers' standpoint, Otis is really a good capitalist. His heartless, brutal attacks on Labor are helping the cause of social revolution."

To some, the concerns of the progressives and the working class seemed to merge in a common hatred of the Southern Pacific Railroad and the *Los Angeles Times*. But the groups had totally different agendas and interests. As George Mowry noted, "the progressives' bias against labor was always greater than against the large corporation." In office, the reformers excluded the labor movement from the corridors of government. Then, in the summer of 1910, when labor unions started to organize the city in earnest, the progressive reformers showed their true allegiance. Without debate, Mayor Alexander and his colleagues on the City Council voted for the infamous antipicketing ordinance drafted by the Merchants and Manufacturers Association. That vote offered one more powerful reason for Socialists and labor leaders to back a movement of their own.

Almost overnight, the Los Angeles left became a vibrant political force. Perhaps the change was best described by Emma Goldman, the radical leader, who visited Los Angeles each May as part of a nationwide speaking tour designed to spread the gospel of anarchism. "Two years ago," she wrote, "Los Angeles was a health resort for parasites and cranks, a city that consisted almost entirely of tourists, without any personality of its own." But now a fundamental change had come over the land. "The eternal spirit of revolution and the solidarity of labor have transformed the sickly hot-house flower into a rugged wild plant with its branches reaching out for more light and freedom."

✳ ✳ ✳ ✳

If there was a single leader of the Los Angeles revolution, it was Job Harriman. An orator of exceptional eloquence, he was a magnetic figure, with a thin, swarthy face, flashing steel-blue eyes, a shock of jet black hair, and long slender hands. Even his critics found him "fascinating and handsome" as he approached his fiftieth birthday. A decade earlier, he had run for vice-president of the United States on Eugene Debs's Socialist Party ticket. He moved to Los Angeles in 1905, seeking a cure for tuberculosis. Like many of his contemporaries, he invested in get-rich-quick schemes—a seedless apple, and real estate along the route from Los Angeles to the new port—but devoted most of his time to his new law practice, quickly becoming the city's leading labor lawyer.

Unlike most Socialist Party leaders, he was firmly convinced that the party should put itself at the service of organized labor. He was certain that labor and the Socialists could form a majority if they worked together, but his views were highly controversial, so controversial in fact that he was denied admission to the Socialist Party of Los Angeles for almost four years. Finally the party relented, allowing him to sign up in late 1908, but his views remained as firm as ever. "My position is and always has been that we should support any labor movement, whether local or general, and the more I see of our movement the greater the necessity of this course appears," he told his close friend Morris Hillquit, who was an important Socialist Party leader in New York. Later he added his view that "whenever there is a labor movement in the field we should support it. If it is a strike, we should support it and our men should be subject to the orders given by the men at the head of the strike. If there is a political party in the same locality with a bona fide Labor ticket, we should not put a ticket in the field but should support them."

A number of local leaders remained "bitterly opposed" to Harriman's views, convinced that he was "intriguing" with the San Francisco labor leaders "to turn the Socialist state and local organization over to them." In fact, the San Francisco leaders were powerful allies, particularly after they sent Anton Johannsen to Los Angeles to organize the striking workers. With Johannsen's invaluable assistance, Harriman quickly gained control of the party's machinery. He remained determined to carry out his dream of a marriage between socialism and labor.

When the city began to throw strikers in jail right and left, Harriman told Hillquit that "we will have to use war measures" and urged the National Socialist Party not to "take too close notice of it." If allowed to follow their own plan of action, Harriman promised, "we will have a great movement here in the city of Los Angeles before another year rolls by."

Harriman had served as the McNamaras' first lawyer, and he remained as a cocounsel after Darrow arrived. In late May, the Socialist Party nominated him for mayor. The primary was scheduled for October 31 and the run-off for December 5, 1911. If he won, the impact would be profound; he could help to make Los Angeles vastly more supportive of organized labor and, not incidentally, create a climate that was deeply sympathetic to the McNamaras. Two years earlier the Socialists had come within sixteen hundred votes of capturing city hall. Now there was a real shot at victory—with a charismatic candidate, the backing of the San Francisco labor leaders, and the battle cry that the McNamaras had been framed. By the summer of 1911, the McNamara cases had become a central part of the "great movement" for control of the city by the forces of socialism and labor.

❀ ❀ ❀ ❀

As Emma McManigal stepped off the train in Los Angeles in late June, Job Harriman was there to welcome her. At the request of Darrow, who had arrived in Los Angeles a few days earlier, Harriman had arranged for Emma to stay at his rooming house. She was accompanied by her two young children, Evelyn, age seven, and Walter, age five. Since she was physically weak, a longtime victim of nervous prostration, Emma's traveling party included her close friend Sadie McGuire.

Emma was also greeted, less warmly, by two Burns detectives who followed her every move.

Harriman promptly took Emma to the county jail, where she was allowed to have a brief visit with her husband while three Burns detectives looked on. Harriman was pointedly excluded from the encounter.

As soon as he was brought into the reception room, Ortie rushed over to embrace his wife. He had not been told that she was in Los Angeles. Emma kissed him affectionately, but quickly made it clear that she was not just there to see him. She was a woman with a mission.

"I only have fifteen minutes to stay with you," she said as he held her to him. "I want you to sign a note from Clarence Darrow. Place yourself in the hands of the union's attorneys. As soon as you do, Darrow will arrange to get you out on bond." She promised Ortie that Darrow and his friends would take him back to Chicago and get him any job he wanted.

Ortie tried to explain his side of the story. He told her why he had confessed, why he felt that his was the best course for their family, why he wanted her to support him. He even asked one of the Burns detectives to explain things to her. But she put her fingers in her ears and told them to shut up. She said Ortie would never see her again if he didn't sign the note from Darrow.

In tears, Ortie agreed to sign.

❋ ❋ ❋ ❋

For a moment, Darrow seemed to have won a major victory. But he had not reckoned on the combined power of Burns, the prosecutors, and the Otis-dominated business leadership of Los Angeles. Knowing how persuasive Darrow could be, they were determined not to let him meet their prize witness. The ever-present Burns detectives went with Ortie to his jail cell and quickly convinced him to write a second note repudiating the first. In it, he refused ever to see Clarence Darrow.

That was only the beginning of the prosecution's show of power. Within the next two days, they showed Emma—and Darrow—what it meant to take on the forces of capital in Los Angeles.

While Emma and Ortie were at the county jail, Emma's trunk arrived at the train station. Job Harriman arranged to have his fourteen-year-old son, Gray, pick it up at the depot. But when the young man arrived, he was told that two Burns men accompanied by a Los Angeles police detective had already taken the trunk to the county garage, where it had been impounded and was being held as evidence.

When told that the trunk had been seized, Darrow was furious.

He stormed down to the garage and angrily lectured a young deputy district attorney on elemental notions of privacy and criminal procedure. Impressed and outclassed, the young prosecutor finally agreed to instruct the detectives to open the trunk and inspect it on the spot. It contained nothing more than family clothing. The police were forced to allow Darrow to return the trunk to Mrs. McManigal.

❋ ❋ ❋ ❋

The government's efforts were orchestrated by District Attorney John Fredericks, an ambitious, self-righteous prosecutor who was almost as close to the leaders of the *Los Angeles Times* as Harriman was to the leaders of labor.

The son of a Methodist minister, Fredericks had been educated at a private academy near Pittsburgh, and had the erect bearing of his German ancestors. Tall and thin, with short, neatly combed dark hair, a long neck, and wire-rimmed spectacles, he had a homely, wedge-shaped patrician visage. Seeking to turn a liability into an asset, admirers compared his appearance to Abraham Lincoln. He was an excellent horseman who had commanded a cavalry troop during the Spanish-American war, earning the rank—and title—of captain. But his military service also demonstrated a weakness that would come back to haunt him. He was a man of enormous rectitude and pride, incapable of admitting error or accepting criticism. "One thing his troop was famous for," an admirer wrote. "They always made the best time on the march, yet their horses were always the freshest at the end of the journey." He was not accustomed to failure.

Fredericks was a hero to the California Anti-Saloon League, which proclaimed that his law enforcement record "reads like a romance." When he took office, there were at least seventy social clubs in the county that sold liquor, a league pamphlet explained. Within a few months, only two or three were still in business. Friendly newspapers hailed his personal investigation of a house that raced blind pigs; they showed pictures of him with 945 poker chips captured on gambling raids; a headline announced that, due to his efforts, the city's GUTTERS RUN RED WITH RUM. But despite their mutual hatred of sin, the Good Government reformers were not Fredericks's major allies. When the Republican Party split in two, he declared for the conservative faction, the backers of President William Howard Taft and General Otis, not the insurgent followers of Teddy Roosevelt and Hiram Johnson. With so many top state and local offices in the hands of reformers, Fredericks became the political darling of the old line business community, the last best hope for General Otis and the *Los Angeles Times,* the prohibitive favorite to win their backing for governor in 1914. The best way to win statewide acclaim, as everyone knew, was to prove that the McNamaras were guilty. Anything less would be a political disaster.

So Captain Fredericks put all of the government's considerable resources to work.

❈ ❈ ❈ ❈

Not in the least embarrassed by the episode with the trunk, Fredericks kept up the pressure on Emma McManigal. That same Sunday afternoon, as another welcome-to–Los Angeles gesture, the district attorney sent Emma McManigal a subpoena, ordering her to appear before the grand jury the next morning. He wanted to question her about her relationship with J. J. McNamara, including reports that J.J. gave her fifty dollars and told her to make sure Ortie "keeps his mouth shut." The story, if true, would corroborate some of Ortie's claims.

Emma went to Darrow for advice. He told her not to answer any questions at all. He also explained that she would have to go through the ordeal alone, since no one is allowed to accompany a witness at a grand jury proceeding. Following the instructions dutifully, Emma refused to answer any questions when she appeared in court on Monday morning. The district attorney gave her a warning. If she did not cooperate, he would ask presiding judge Walter Bordwell to hold her in contempt. When she insisted on remaining silent, Judge Bordwell scheduled a contempt proceeding to be held the following Saturday.

As she exited the grand jury room, frightened and upset by what had just occurred, Emma passed through an anteroom, where she had a chance encounter with her husband. Ortie pleaded with her, begging her to side with him and with the prosecutors, rather than with Darrow. As they spoke, with tears streaming down their cheeks, Emma fainted. When she recovered, she asked to be taken to "Darrow, my friend."

❋ ❋ ❋ ❋

Darrow still hoped that George Behm could turn Ortie around. Behm arrived in Los Angeles the next afternoon and promptly arranged to visit his nephew in jail. Ortie was happy to see his favorite relative, but he was as obstinate with his uncle as he had been with his wife.

Behm returned to Darrow's office totally discouraged. He told Darrow that McManigal was not the man he used to know, that he had been bought or hypnotized or had lost his mind; that he would like to have Ortie in front of his engine when he was traveling down the track at a high rate of speed; that the boy took after his father, not his mother; that there wasn't a drop of Behm's blood in him.

It was a long shot, but Darrow told Behm to keep going back to visit Ortie in the hopes that he would weaken or change his mind. Behm visited his nephew again on July 10, 14, and 15. The reaction was always the same.

To no avail, Behm even tried some psychological warfare. One day he took Ortie's five-year-old son with him to the post office. As they passed the courthouse, Behm heard a voice calling to him from the jail.

"Hey!"

Behm looked up at the jail window and saw his nephew.

"Hey," Ortie shouted again. "Uncle George. Bring over the boy and let me see him."

Behm didn't answer. He took the boy to the post office, and then back to Darrow's office, where he told Darrow what had happened.

"I didn't take the boy over," Behm explained. "I didn't pay any attention to the hollering."

"That's right, goddammit," Darrow said. "Tease him and then he will come across."

❋ ❋ ❋ ❋

Meanwhile, Mrs. McManigal was feeling intense pressure from Captain Fredericks and his allies. To her great relief, the court did not hold her in contempt. Judge Walter Bordwell ruled that the confidential relationship between husband and wife gave her the right to remain silent. But the Burns detectives continued to follow Emma everywhere, making life impossible for her and for her children. Whenever she left the house, they trailed behind her in an automobile. Once, while driving without lights, they ran into her seven-year-old daughter, Evelyn, causing what the Socialist press called "serious injuries."

The pressure on Emma became increasingly unbearable. Finally, in mid-July, she collapsed and was admitted to Pacific Hospital. The hospital issued a bulletin saying that Mrs. McManigal probably would lose the use of her legs and might be permanently paralyzed. Her lawyer, John F. Tyrell, blamed her condition on Burns. "Everywhere she turned," he said, "a Burns man followed. Detectives appeared at the doors of her home disguised as book agents, salesmen, and what not. Two Burns detectives even followed the ambulance that took Mrs. McManigal to the hospital."

Emma's illness offered a public relations coup for the defense. The National Socialist Press News Service reported that "public sympathy took such a decided swing in favor of the defense after the facts became public of the torture of Mrs. McManigal that prosecutors became alarmed."

❊ ❊ ❊ ❊

Throughout the summer, the prosecutors continued to make effective use of the grand jury. Hoping to prevent any further efforts to influence government witnesses, the district attorney's office asked the grand jury to examine whether the McNamara defense team was attempting to intimidate or corrupt the state's witnesses. They subpoenaed George Behm to appear in court on Monday, July 31. Since he could not accompany Behm at the grand jury hearing, Darrow, aided by cocounsel LeCompte Davis, met with him on Sunday night at his Higgins Building office. The lawyers instructed the old railroad engineer to refuse to answer anything of substance.

George Behm's testimony the next morning was as amusing as it was consistent, as he tried to follow Darrow's instructions:

Q: Where do you live in Los Angeles?
A: That don't concern the case.
Q: Do you know Ortie McManigal?
A: That don't concern the case.
Q: What relation are you, if any, to Ortie E. McManigal?
A: That don't concern the case.
Q: Were you instructed before coming before this grand jury to make that answer to every question?
A: That don't concern the case.

And so it went for more than twenty minutes, until the members of the grand jury were no longer amused and the patience of the prosecutors gave out. Finally the grand jury's foreman decided to ask Superior Court judge Walter Bordwell to issue an order requiring Behm to testify. The judge complied and a hearing was set for August 3, 1911.

With careful coaching by Darrow and Davis, Behm managed to avoid answering questions in an incriminating way when he faced the grand jury again on August 3. But by then he was more than anxious to leave Los Angeles. A week later, he and Emma caught a train back home.

Darrow's efforts to convert McManigal had obviously failed. Now he needed to make certain that no one corroborated Ortie's testimony.

❊ ❊ ❊ ❊

As the summer progressed, it became increasingly clear that the government's case against Jim McNamara was exceptionally strong, even stronger than Darrow had expected. It seemed likely that McManigal's confession would be corroborated by documentary evidence, as well as by several eyewitnesses, including at least one man who had sold dynamite to Jim in San Francisco and another who could prove that Jim was in Los Angeles on the day of the bombing.

The government's case against J.J. for the *Times* bombing was far less compelling. He had sent his brother to the Coast with the knowledge that Jim would be used as an instrument of destruction, but he had no prior knowledge of the plan to place bombs at the *Times* or at the homes of General Otis and Felix Zeehandelaar. The district attorney could probably prove that J.J. was directly responsible for the bombing of the Llewellyn Iron Works, but at least J.J. could not be hanged for that crime, since no one was killed by the blast.

Gradually Darrow became convinced that it would be impossible to win either case without engaging in tactics that would be costly—and of questionable legality. He sent a series of letters to Samuel Gompers that demonstrated his growing anxiety. "We are having a fierce time," he wrote on July 8, after Behm had paid his third unsuccessful visit to Ortie. "All the town seems to be bent on getting blood and it is a fearful fight." Everything costs money, he explained. The detectives and the dynamite experts had to be paid, and "then the McManigal matter has cost and is costing money. It goes every way and I am as careful as can be." Without more money, though, he just didn't see how he could manage the campaign on all fronts. "I want to win if there is a way and must leave nothing undone and still cannot make promises I can't keep."

In response, Gompers explained that the AFL operation was just moving into high gear. Every union had been asked to raise an average of twenty-five cents from each of its members. "You may count upon our doing our level best," he promised.

But it was fast becoming clear that the union's level best might not be good enough. "There is no way to try this case with a chance of winning without a great deal of money," Darrow complained to Gompers a week later. "The other side is spending it in every direction. Then they have all the organized channels of society, the state's attorney, grand jury, police force, mayor, manufacturers association. Everyone is afraid of the line-up and there is little light anywhere.

"Burns's whole force, utterly regardless of personal rights, is everywhere in evidence, intimidating, hounding, and bulldozing, the grand jury kept constantly in session to awe every one who comes as our witness. No one will do anything without money. It is a tough game and I want you to understand it."

And the tough game was going to require some unusual and unsportsmanlike tactics.

❋ ❋ ❋ ❋

From the first, Erskine Wood had expected Darrow to use unorthodox tactics. His fears were confirmed in early July, when Darrow sent one of his associates up to Portland to ask some troubling questions about a detective named Larry Sullivan—a man that Darrow had hired, based on Wood's recommendation.

Wood had known Larry Sullivan for years. A clever gumshoe with a colorful past, Sullivan spent the early years of the century running Sailor's Retreat, a saloon, casino, and boardinghouse in Portland's rough waterfront district. When his partner was convicted of murder, Sullivan closed Sailor's Retreat and became a celebrated exhibition prizefighter, gaining particular notoriety by lasting out a ninety-two-round bout with Tommy Ward on a river barge. He dabbled in politics, earned enough money to buy a lovely home, and married the daughter of a Portland police lieutenant. Ever the adventurer, Sullivan moved to the gold rush boomtown of Goldfield, Nevada, where he opened a mine, started a securities firm called the Sullivan Trust Company, and made, and then lost, a fortune.

Despite Sullivan's erratic reputation, Wood considered him trustworthy, if properly handled. Sullivan had done some detective work for Wood in Portland, and the men shared an infatuation with anarchism, Emma Goldman, and the radical Industrial Workers of the World. Sullivan also had a natural emotional sympathy for the McNamara brothers. His father had been a miner, he had always believed in labor, and as a fellow Irish Catholic, he had a strong feeling of kinship with the men who had been arrested. As he wrote to Wood, "I believe those McNamara men are getting jobbed." For what it was worth, he also had excellent access to the district attorney, having worked as a supervisor in a mining operation that was largely owned by District Attorney Fredericks.

In the spring of 1911, Larry Sullivan was living in Los Angeles and looking for work. Darrow wanted to hire investigators that were every bit as aggressive and resourceful as those working for Burns and the district attorney; he even hoped to find a few men who had worked for the D.A. and could spy on the prosecutors as successfully as the prosecutors were spying on him. Wood recommended Sullivan, but he took pains to warn Darrow that his friend had "a certain unscrupulous temperament where his enthusiasm is enlisted and might, because of a reckless unscrupulousness, injure the side he is working for. But he will never do so intentionally, and will never betray partners he has started to work with."

* * *

In early July, a lawyer named Fred H. Moore appeared at Wood's office in Portland. Wood had known Moore slightly over the years as a mutual friend of anarchists and Wobblies. That spring, Moore was in Los Angeles, working in the offices of Darrow's chief cocounsel, LeCompte Davis. Moore said that he had been sent up to Oregon from Los Angeles to pose a question of great urgency and considerable secrecy.

Precisely how far, he asked, could Larry Sullivan be trusted?

Wood repeated what he had told Darrow: His friend was loyal but perhaps capable of going beyond the bounds of normal propriety. Then Wood asked Moore why he wanted to know.

Moore's answer confirmed Wood's fears about the direction in which Darrow and his employees were headed. He said that the defense team wanted to ask Sullivan to help destroy evidence that could convict the brothers, and to help manufacture evidence that could help acquit them. As Wood later put it, the defense wanted Sullivan "to frame up or carry out a plan looking to the defense and acquittal of the accused men regardless of the facts."

Politely but firmly, Wood tried to show Moore the folly of such an approach to the trial, explaining at length that he considered Darrow's win-at-all-costs strategy wrong both as a matter of political philosophy and of legal tactics. But when the lawyer left, Wood was certain that his comments would fall on deaf ears. After all, Moore was only an errand boy. Wood was convinced that Darrow would use Sullivan for some improper purpose—and that Sullivan would believe that he was doing so with Wood's support.

Wood was so troubled by what he heard that he wanted to go on record with his reactions immediately. He promptly sent a lengthy letter to W. W. Catlin, a jolly former banker and fellow anarchist who had known both Wood and Darrow for years and was now living in Los Angeles. He asked Catlin to serve as "a permanent repository of my personal position in what I regard as an important matter." More important, he asked Catlin to show the letter to Sullivan to make certain that Sullivan understood just how totally he disapproved of any such tactics.

Though he doubted that his concerns would have much impact on his friend's actions, Wood told Catlin to "show this letter to Darrow if you choose."

In any case, by the time Wood's letter arrived, it was too late. The defense had already begun its efforts to manufacture and destroy evidence.

※ ※ ※ ※

Larry Sullivan spent most of July in San Francisco, where he stayed at the Manx hotel and operated under the orders of Darrow's chief of investigation, John Harrington. His mission was to track down possible prosecution witnesses, and to try to persuade them not to testify.

The defense was particularly interested in George Phillips of the Giant Powder Works, one of the men who had sold the explosives to Jim McNamara and his associates. Phillips had told the prosecutors that he could positively identify Jim. He would be a powerful witness.

Operating under the pseudonym of Mr. Kelly, and armed with a letter from a priest, Sullivan arranged a meeting with a clerk at the offices of the Giant Powder Works. The clerk's name was Michael Gilmore, and he was, of course, well acquainted with George Phillips.

"My dear Michael," the priest's letter began. "I wish you would assist this man in the information which he will need. Help him in every way you can. Mr. L. M. Kelly will explain when he sees you."

When they met, Sullivan (as Kelly) told Gilmore that he was a relative of the McNamaras and was convinced that the case was a frame-up. He asked Gilmore to help persuade Phillips to change his testimony and to say that the man who bought the powder had been missing a finger on one hand.

If he went along, Phillips would be well rewarded. "Phillips can name his own price and the money will be handed to him by you," Sullivan told Gilmore. But if Phillips persisted in testifying against McNamara in Los Angeles, Sullivan said, "he will not die a natural death."

✳ ✳ ✳ ✳

While Sullivan was busy threatening possible prosecution witnesses, other employees and friends of the defense were engaged in efforts to spirit possible witnesses out of the state. For example, the defense was concerned about the testimony of Lena Ingersoll, the boarding-house proprietress who had identified Jim McNamara as James Brice. Darrow therefore sent one of his top investigators off to meet with Lena's husband, Mr. D. H. Ingersoll, at a San Francisco hotel. Darrow's investigator offered to pay five thousand dollars to the Ingersolls if the couple could arrange to be out of the state during the trial.

Darrow even got Ruby's brother into the act. One of the most troubling potential witnesses was Kurt Diekelman, the Los Angeles hotel clerk who remembered talking with Jim McNamara on two crucial occasions: first, when he registered at the Hotel Baltimore as J. B. Brice; and later, on September 30, 1910, when Jim asked for permission to stay at the hotel past the normal three P.M. checkout time so that he could catch the late-night train to San Francisco. Diekelman had the ability to knock a gaping hole in Jim's alibi.

Early that summer, Diekelman had moved to Albuquerque, New Mexico, where he got a job as the headwaiter at the Fashion Café. But he kept the district attorney apprised of his movements, promising to return to Los Angeles as a witness whenever needed. He did not know that while in Albuquerque he was being kept under close surveillance by a Burns agent named Bert Damon; nor did he know that he was being sought by representatives of the defense.

At eleven o'clock on the morning of September 16, 1911, a man walked into the Fashion Café and introduced himself to Diekelman as Bert Higgins, a member of the McNamara defense team. "We've been looking all over the country for you," "Higgins" started, "but we finally tracked you down through your mother up in San Francisco. I understand from your folks that you intend going to Chicago very soon."

Diekelman said that he did hope to go to Chicago, but that he was waiting to be called as a witness in a trial in Los Angeles. Higgins offered to arrange for him to go to Chicago and be paid for working, or even for not working. After thinking it over, Diekelman agreed to go, taking a hundred dollars for expenses and a free ticket on the *Santa Fe Limited* headed for Chicago.

Once in town, Diekelman headed for Darrow's law office, where he met Higgins and Chicago labor leader Ed Nockles. Higgins started by announcing that he had been using an assumed name. "My name is not Higgins," he said, "I want to set you right on that. My name is Hammerstrom. I am Mr. Darrow's brother-in-law." As they were leaving the building, Hammerstrom took his guest down the hall to the office of former mayor Ed Dunne, the man who had presided at the Darrows' wedding ceremony, and Dunne vouched for Hammerstrom's identity.

But Darrow's efforts to remove Diekelman from Burns's clutches didn't succeed for long. A couple of days later, while Diekelman was enjoying himself in Chicago, Guy Biddinger of the Burns agency tracked him down and told him he was needed back in Los Angeles. This time the Burns agents proved more persuasive. Diekelman returned to Albuquerque, where he was again available to testify in the trial.

✳ ✳ ✳

As it happened, Detective Biddinger was himself a target of Darrow's campaign. A Burns detective assigned to the McNamara case, Guy Biddinger had arrested Jim McNamara and Ortie McManigal on April 14 in Detroit. During the next two weeks, he had obtained Ortie's confession, gone off to Indianapolis to help arrest J. J. McNamara, and then taken (or kidnapped) J.J. across the country to Los Angeles. He was probably Burns's most trusted agent.

Darrow first met Biddinger in early June, just after returning from his triumphant trip to the Coast. To some, it might have seemed reckless to try to enlist a Burns detective as a double agent; but Darrow had located useful inside sources before and he had found them to be reliable when offered enough money. The introduction was made by William Turner, a Chicago detective who had worked for Darrow in Idaho. Turner told Biddinger that Darrow had paid as much as fifteen thousand dollars to some double agents in the Haywood case and that Biddinger could make a fortune by supplying information from the Burns camp. Darrow's own proposal to Biddinger was a bit more modest. He offered to pay up to five thousand dollars for important information. Biddinger said that under the right circumstances he would be interested in selling information to the defense team.

For the next two months, Darrow stayed in touch with Biddinger through Turner, often asking whether there was anything that they should discuss. Finally, in mid-August, Biddinger called Darrow to say that he had something to report. They met twice during the next two days. At the first meeting, Biddinger told Darrow about several important documents that would implicate J.J. in the bombings. As the meeting ended, Darrow suggested that they meet again eight A.M. the following morning in the bar of the Alexandria Hotel.

When Darrow arrived at the hotel, Biddinger was already in the saloon, sitting alone in a booth. A *Times* reporter named William Porter was at the bar when Darrow entered. "Here's a funny coincidence," Porter called out, as Darrow approached Biddinger. "Here is Darrow, the McNamara lawyer, and a Burns detective and a *Times* reporter. Let's all have a little drink."

"No thanks," Biddinger replied, getting up from the booth. "I'm not drinking anything." He went down the hall to a washroom. When he returned, Darrow was alone.

"I have got that money for you," Darrow said.

"I don't want to take it here," Biddinger responded. "We may be watched."

"Do it here, open and above board. If anyone asks, just say we know each other from Chicago. We have a right to meet and talk and have a drink."

"No," Biddinger said. "I won't do it here. You go up to the mezzanine floor. I will meet you there."

As they walked into the elevator, Darrow handed Biddinger a roll of bills. It was only five hundred dollars. "I thought you were going to bring a thousand," Biddinger protested.

"We are a little bit short this morning," Darrow explained. "Money isn't rolling in as fast as we expected. So far we have only got eighty thousand dollars and everybody is after it. Give me a little time and I will take care of you. Don't worry.

"There's something that really concerns us," Darrow said. "There is some man in the Iron Workers' organization who is tipping everything off to Burns. I would like to find out who it is."

Biddinger looked at Darrow for a moment. Then he offered the name of Gene Clancy, the most important Iron Worker official on the West Coast.

"I am under the impression he is the one that is tipping the stuff off to Burns," Biddinger said. "I think I can prove it to you. I am going to be in San Francisco next week, and I know that Burns has an appointment with him. I will try to arrange to let you see them together."

Back at the Higgins Building, Darrow penned a hasty note to his friend Fremont Older, the crusading editor of the San Francisco *Bulletin.* Older was close to the city's top labor leaders, but he had also been friendly with Burns for years, since their work together on the San Francisco graft trials. Not even Older could be trusted with information about Biddinger's secret role, but he might be able to shed some light on the Burns-Clancy relationship.

"Burns made a strange remark about Clancy," Darrow wrote, "which has set me thinking and made me suspicious—I hate to be suspicious. I thought I had better find out if you know Clancy and get your opinion. Mr. Burns today said he was going up to San Francisco tomorrow and would see you. . . . You might get something out of B. Still, you might not."

A few days later, in response to a wire from Biddinger, Darrow took a train to San Francisco and met the detective at the Palace Hotel. Biddinger reported that Clancy and Burns were scheduled to meet that afternoon.

Darrow said that he had an appointment to go out automobile riding with Fremont Older and that he would leave word at the hotel where he could be reached if the men should have a rendezvous.

By the way, Darrow asked, do you have any idea where the meeting is to take place?

Yes, Biddinger announced. "I understand the meeting is to take place in Mr. Older's office."

Darrow was stunned. It just didn't seem possible. Older was his close friend, one of the most liberal editors in America. Darrow couldn't believe that Older would have arranged a meeting between Burns and Clancy. And yet, these were strange times, and Older had known Burns well and fondly for many years.

"The chances are," Biddinger said, "that this has been going on for a long time with Mr. Older's knowledge." Biddinger promised to let Darrow know as soon as he saw the men together.

Biddinger had been expecting a large reward for the information. He was surprised when Darrow only handed him two hundred dollars. "It is an awful difference between two hundred dollars and five thousand dollars, isn't it?" Biddinger remarked, somewhat bitterly. But he took the money anyway.

In the end there was no meeting between Burns and Clancy. The labor leader became ill and was admitted to the German Hospital later that afternoon.

It took almost a year for Darrow to find out that Biddinger had been acting as a double—or, more accurately, triple—agent. Whenever Darrow paid him, Biddinger turned the money over to Burns and the prosecutors. Moreover, he was lying about Clancy and Older. Both men were loyal to Darrow. But Biddinger thought that he could unnerve his opponents by sowing some fresh distrust in their camp.

❋ ❋ ❋ ❋

By September 1, Darrow had another reason for intense concern. The defense fund's bank account was running on empty, and angry creditors were pounding at the door. Yet on that date Darrow did something most peculiar. He gave Olaf Tvietmoe a check for ten thousand dollars. The reasons for that payment, and the route taken by the check, became a central mystery in the months ahead.

When they agreed to take responsibility for funding the case, Sam Gompers and the AFL insisted on having full control of all of the money that came in—and on a full accounting of all of the money that was paid out. Like Erskine Wood, Gompers had undoubtedly heard rumors about the improper use of money in some of Darrow's previous cases. He insisted on scrupulous record keeping. He would not even allow anyone else to give money to Darrow and his team. When Olaf Tvietmoe offered to send money to Darrow from San Francisco, Gompers turned him down cold. All money had to be sent to Darrow through the AFL, with checks signed by Frank Morrison, the union's longtime secretary.

But by late August, the checks had almost stopped coming. Between July 8 and August 3, Morrison forwarded sixty-five thousand dollars, which to Darrow seemed little enough; but in the weeks that followed, the flow of money had dropped to a trickle. On August 18, Morrison sent a check for ten thousand dollars; three days later, on August 21, he sent another check for the same amount. But that was all.

As of September 1, the defense was effectively bankrupt. As Darrow told Biddinger, the money wasn't rolling in as quickly as he had hoped, and everyone wanted to be paid. Darrow sent a letter to Morrison on September 1, calling it absolutely essential that a substantial amount of money be forwarded to him at once.

Notwithstanding his financial problems, however, Darrow did not deposit the ten-thousand-dollar check dated August 21. After sending his urgent appeal to Morrison on Friday, September 1, Darrow caught the train for San Francisco, where he was scheduled to spend the Labor Day weekend. He took the uncashed check along with him.

As always, Darrow's movements in San Francisco were monitored by detectives working for the prosecution. They watched him the next morning when he went to Tvietmoe's office at the Asiatic Exclusion League, and as he and Ruby departed on a two-day vacation trip to Santa Cruz in the company of Mr. and Mrs. LeCompte Davis.

But the detectives kept an eye on Tvietmoe. Later that same Saturday morning, they watched as Tvietmoe went to the Anglo and

London-Paris National Bank on the corner of Sansome and Sutter streets. Tvietmoe was accompanied by Cleveland Dam, a prominent lawyer who represented Mayor P. H. McCarthy as well as the State Building Trades Council.

The lobby of the bank was crowded, but the detectives were able to observe Dam as he went up to a railing and spoke to a bank vice-president named Charles Hunt. Dam handed Hunt a check, but the vice-president immediately returned it to him. Dam then walked across the lobby where he found Tvietmoe, who signed the back of the check. Then, with Tvietmoe at his side, Dam returned to the railing and gave the freshly endorsed check to the vice-president. He then took a check of his own and executed it in the presence of Mr. Hunt.

Leaving Dam at his desk, Mr. Hunt next escorted Tvietmoe across the lobby to the window of a teller named Alfred Ledeme. The teller took the check and promptly disappeared into the recesses of the bank's vault. As the detectives watched the scene, Tvietmoe went back across the lobby and sat down in a chair near Hunt's desk. Moments later, Ledeme emerged from the vault with a two-inch stack of large bills, which he carried across the lobby and gave to Tvietmoe.

The detectives had no way of knowing what to make of the transaction. They had no way of knowing that Tvietmoe had just deposited Darrow's ten thousand dollar check in the State Building Trades Council's Defense Fund, and that Tvietmoe had converted the payment into cash. But that transaction would later be a matter of considerable importance.

When he was so strapped for money himself, why did Darrow give ten thousand dollars to Olaf Tvietmoe—and what did Tvietmoe do with it?

❋ ❋ ❋ ❋

McNamara Day had arrived. On the first Monday in September, all across America labor unionists celebrated more than just Labor Day. As a rallying cry as well as fund-raising device, Samuel Gompers had asked union leaders to make September 4, 1911, McNamara Day, a special event, "a day of protest against the outrage, and as an evidence of our confidence in the innocence of our men, it is suggested that . . . labor men and friends, whether in parade or along the line, in picnic ground, meeting or elsewhere, wear a button appropriate to the occasion."

The parade in Los Angeles featured some 35,000 marchers, many wearing specially minted buttons with a smiling picture of J.J. surrounded by the word KIDNAPPED; some supporters of Socialist mayoral candidate and McNamara cocounsel Job Harriman also carried flags inscribed UNITED WE STAND, UNITED WE VOTE; suffragists carried the familiar yellow and black banner with the slogan VOTES FOR WOMEN; and a division at the end of the parade carried signs in Spanish proclaiming support for the Mexican revolution. More than two hours and three miles long, the parade circled through downtown, past the jail at Temple Street, where the marchers took off their hats to the McNamara brothers and the band struck up "La Marseillaise." Then it wound its way to a huge barbecue in Luna Park, where children rode the whirling tub, the merry-go-round, and the miniature railway, visited the House of Mirth, fed peanuts to monkeys, listened to a roaring lion and a laughing hyena, and feasted on ice cream, red-hot sandwiches, and soda water. Some of the more serious-minded celebrants delighted to a stem-winding political speech by candidate Harriman, who urged voters to support the Socialist slate since "whether it's water for the people, or telephones, or electricity, or gas, or a clothing factory, or a supply house, or a bank, it is the old, old fight made by the few to extract a living from the labor of the many."

An equally festive mood buoyed the laboring men and women of San Francisco, who were treated to a tub-thumping speech by none other than Samuel Gompers, in the labor capital of California to celebrate McNamara Day. Flanked by union leaders Olaf Tvietmoe and P. H. McCarthy, the Grand Old Man of Labor was forced to climb onto a table draped with an American flag to make himself heard by the thousands of McNamara-button-wearing partisans who had come to cheer. "We know J. J. McNamara," Gompers shouted to the crowd. "We know him as an intelligent, serious, and thinking man, full of human sympathy and kindness." He paused to let the crowd shout its approval. "We are not only going to continue to believe that the McNamaras are innocent of the crime charged against them—at least until the jury has decided otherwise—but we propose to continue to do everything in our power to see that they are properly defended when the day of the trial comes." Applause. "And not only that—we are tired of this procedure of man-stealing." Applause. "They do not steal the Rockefellers." Applause. "They do not steal the Astors or the Vanderbilts." Applause. "But they don't mind stealing the men of labor." The men and women with their KIDNAPPED buttons roared their support.

Caught up in the excitement of the California political movement, Gompers took a steamship to Los Angeles, where he arrived on September 10, just in time to praise the McNamaras, urge laborites to vote for women's suffrage, and give his political support to Job Harriman in a rousing speech to a crowd of five thousand supporters at the Shrine Auditorium. Such support for a Socialist candidate was highly unusual, if not unheard of, for the normally cautious and mainstream leader of the AFL. "Let your watchword be 'Harriman and Labor,'" Gompers told the wildly cheering crowd. "When you say good morning to your neighbor, shout 'Harriman and Labor'; when you kiss your sweetheart goodnight, whisper 'Harriman and Labor'; when you meet a friend on the street, say 'Harriman and Labor'; make it your cry and keep it up until the last ballot shall be counted and Job Harriman elected triumphant."

The next day, after huddling with Darrow about the trial and the need to raise far more money, Gompers went to the jail to meet with the two men whose innocence had become a matter of religious faith. Accompanied by Darrow and a group of local labor leaders, Gompers greeted the brothers on the second floor of the jail, in a hallway near a tier of cells. Reporters watched and photographers took pictures as Gompers cordially shook hands and then posed with the two prisoners. J.J. gave his visitor a coaster that he had made by pasting cancelled stamps and bits of cigar bands on the bottom of a glass plate. Then Gompers met with the men alone for about an hour.

Three months later, when the political situation had changed dramatically, Gompers was to repeat again and again the substance of the interview. "I went to see Big John," Gompers explained. "He's a big, tall fellow. Taking me by the hand he said, 'Sam, tell the boys I am innocent. Give them this message from me and tell them how grateful I am for their assistance.

"He looked at me frankly and openly," Gompers insisted. "And I believed what he said."

"After talking to them," Gompers told supporters a few days later, "I am convinced that they are the victims of the most diabolical plot ever hatched in our country."

Darrow did not tell Gompers that the case was looking hopeless. Nor did he tell him about the ten-thousand-dollar check that he had given to Olaf Tvietmoe.

Chapter Seven

THE TRIAL OF THE CENTURY BEGINS

A S THE CASE BECAME more hopeless, Darrow's professional and personal behavior became more risky, erratic, and self-destructive. Nowhere, on a personal level, was it more fraught with danger than in his relationship with Mary Field. He had sent Mary off to New York two years earlier, partly so that their relationship would not disrupt his marriage. He saw her there, introduced her to friends, and delighted in her success. But he did not expect her to move back into the center of his life.

When the McNamaras were arrested, several publications, including *American Magazine,* asked Mary Field to cover the trial for them. She wrote to Darrow, telling of the offers, expecting him to rejoice at their chance to be together at a great moment in history. But Darrow asked her not to come. No doubt he feared that their affair would humiliate Ruby. He may have expected her to ask for money, either from him or from the defense fund. But most important, their relationship would certainly engage the interest of the prosecution and its allies. Darrow sent letters warning Mary—accurately—that he was being watched by detectives, that she would "expose or divert" him, and that *"any,* even purely friendly intercourse of a formal nature would be out of the question."

But the trial seemed certain to be *the* political event of the era, more important than the Haywood trial and in a far more appealing venue. Though his letters wounded and infuriated her, Mary came anyway. She was an independent woman, a talented reporter. She had as much right as anyone to cover the trial. If necessary, she would stay clear of him, abide by his wishes, and spend her time with other friends, including other reporters, some friendly labor leaders, a college chum—and her younger sister, Sara.

Sara had arranged to cover the trial for *The Pacific Monthly* and the *Portland Oregonian.* Nearing her thirtieth birthday, she too wanted to be present at the great showdown between capital and labor. And, like Mary, she had personal reasons for coming. Her life with Rev. Albert Ehrgott had become intolerable, but divorce was out of the question, and it was becoming impossible to arrange secret rendezvous in Oregon with her new great love, Erskine Wood. Since it was only natural for Erskine to spend some time in Los Angeles, visiting Darrow and attending the trial, the city became a logical place for romantic trysts. So Sara and Mary made plans to live and work together in Los Angeles.

❋ ❋ ❋ ❋

When Sara coasted into the San Pedro harbor on the *Rose City* steamer, Mary was there to greet her at the dock. It was the morning of Tuesday, October 10, 1911, the day before the scheduled start of the trial. Mary had arrived in town a few weeks earlier and had found a charming apartment for them to share.

The sisters took an electric train into the city. As they passed through fields of freshly planted orange groves, Mary announced that she and Darrow were together once again. Sara was stunned. What about Darrow's letters warning about the detectives and insisting that they stay clear of each other?

All that was in the past, Mary said. Darrow had called on her as soon as she arrived in town. He told her to ignore all of the warnings in his letters. He was delighted that she had come. Indeed, Mary announced, Darrow wanted Mary and Sara to join him for dinner that very evening.

And what an evening it was! Statewide, it was election day, perhaps the most important election day in California history, with a remarkable ballot featuring the most significant reforms ever presented to the state's electorate. The new governor, Hiram Johnson, in office for less than ten months, had put much of the Progressive movement's political agenda up for a vote—including proposals for women's suffrage and for the initiative, referendum, and recall. It was an historic day for California voters—and it was the night before Darrow was to start his defense in the most celebrated case in the history of the American West.

Wrinkled but tanned by his months in the California sun, Darrow met the sisters at a hotel. Before dinner, he whisked them off to a crowded downtown streetcorner, where they watched as the early election returns were posted outside a large building.

Sara, an ardent suffragist, was somewhat distressed to find that Darrow did not support the right of women to vote, arguing—or teasing—his case on "biological grounds," calling it "ladies' suffrage" and insisting that women were certain to vote for stricter restrictions on social conduct. Most of the early returns opposed suffrage, and Darrow infuriated Sara by applauding every time a new "no" vote was recorded. It was not easy to accept the gentle joshing of a man who had humiliated her sister so recently—though Sara had the last laugh on women's suffrage a day or two later, when final returns from around the state produced a razor-thin victory.

Then Darrow took them off to dinner in a pretty restaurant filled with lights and music, where they talked for hours. Sara noticed that her sister was drinking and smoking too much, but Mary seemed to have forgotten or forgiven Darrow's rejection. Darrow "seemed tickled to death to have Mary there and she, poor little dear, forgot all the past and soaked in the present." Darrow couldn't help crowing over Mary's newfound literary successes—her story entitled "The Wine Press of Poverty" in Theodore Dreiser's *Delineator* and an intimate account of a clothing workers strike that she had written for the *American Magazine.*

"Did you see Mary's article in the *American?*" he asked Sara. "Isn't it a dandy? You know the *American* has one of the largest circulations in the country."

Darrow seemed to feel that he had "made" Mary and, in a sense, Sara had to agree that he had.

Darrow's recklessness continued after leaving the restaurant. In a city known for its prudishness, its laws against "mashers" who so much as flirted with a woman on the street, and where he was almost certainly being watched by Burns detectives or city police, he expansively put his arms around both women as he started to walk them home. Sara was offended by the gesture and deliberately dropped her handkerchief so that she could gracefully move away to a respectable distance. Darrow kept his arm around Mary as the threesome made their way to the tiny two-room apartment at 1110 Ingraham Street that the women were renting for thirty-five dollars a month.

※ ※ ※ ※

A woman's apartment could be a dangerous meeting place in a city where it was a crime to be alone with a woman, other than one's wife, in a room with a bed. Yet the two rooms quickly became a hideaway for Darrow, a second home where he could retreat from the office and from his life with Ruby. As Sara described the place, "everything disappears—the bed walks into the wall and becomes more panelling; the coffee pot goes up the chimney; the couch slides out the window." In the weeks that followed, Darrow often came there for dinner. Sara acted as chaperon and then slipped away to a friend's apartment so that Darrow and Mary could be alone.

But Darrow did not confine his advances to Mary. A few days after arriving in Los Angeles, Sara came home to her apartment from a meeting and found that Darrow, who had been visiting Mary earlier in the day, was still there. She retreated to the kitchen to prepare dinner "when out came C.D. and in a moment he was hugging me like an old grizzly to my unspeakable discomfort. I told him I was 'not eligible' "—after all, she was married to Albert Ehrgott, the minister, and was having an affair with Erskine Wood, the lawyer-poet—at which point Darrow "made the rather strange remark that if I were out of funds I should come and see him anytime." Nor was that the last time that Darrow made advances toward Sara. A few days later, when she was interviewing one of the men in his office, Darrow asked Sara to come into his private room. He then locked the door and, in Sara's phrase, "proceeded to *make love* to me in high style." But Sara rejected his advances, unlocked the door, and said "Good afternoon, Mr. D., I'll interview you some other time." Darrow was furious, but Sara just walked away.

Darrow's nocturnal absences were exceedingly painful to Ruby, who had been forced to uproot their household and to move to Los Angeles where, but for a few old close friends, she was a stranger. Ruby naturally learned about Mary. It was a wound that remained raw for the rest of her life.

❋ ❋ ❋ ❋

One can only speculate about the connection, if any, between Darrow's reckless personal actions and the conduct of his professional life, but it was not easy to plan a defense when with each passing day his case looked more hopeless.

Jim's case, in particular, was becoming desperate: nothing was going right. Darrow promised to prove that the explosion that killed the *Times*'s employees was caused by gas, not dynamite, and that the gas came from a leak produced by General Otis's own negligence. But the gas theory was falling apart. In a dramatic gesture, Darrow announced that he intended to present a spectacular courtroom demonstration of an explosion on "a miniature business block, complete to the most minute detail, featuring a model of the *Los Angeles Times* building, with one side cut away to show a tiny printing press, linotype machines, desks, and all the machinery of a great newspaper office." The defense committee spent thousands of dollars on the construction of a miniature, which Darrow's employees blew up over and over again in an effort to show that gas, not dynamite, must have been responsible for the fire. Unfortunately, the simulation proved just the opposite. It showed that dynamite could—and probably did—cause the explosion.

Nor did the alibi defense hold much promise, particularly after the first week of October, when Burns and his men found Kurt Diekelman, the hotel clerk, in Chicago, and persuaded him to return west. With witnesses like Diekelman to place Jim in Los Angeles at the time the bomb was set, how could Darrow possibly persuade the jury that the younger brother had been in San Francisco on the night of September 30, 1910?

Disregarding his ethical obligation of confidentiality, Darrow started to tell a few friends, including Mary, that Jim was "guilty as hell" and didn't have "a shadow of a chance to win."

※※※※

Hearing Darrow's complaints, everyone was prepared to offer suggestions for different lines of defense. Perhaps the most intriguing was that proposed by those radicals who urged Darrow to admit that Jim *had* planted the dynamite—but to mount a defense based on the theory that his act was necessary and justified. It was an argument that newspaper publisher E. W. Scripps advanced in a "disquisition" that he sent to his colleagues and employees at the United Press and at the newspapers that he owned around the country. There was a war between capital and labor; capital was using all of the tools of power at its disposal, fortified by the force of the state, enslaving, impoverishing and even murdering workers, including women and children; working men and women, under the circumstances, were justified in taking any action that could earn them decent working conditions and a decent wage. John Brown, after all, had been an outlaw and a criminal before he became a savior and a hero. The same defense could be mounted for Jim McNamara. Properly presented, it could place the entire unjust industrial world on trial. It might not win him his freedom, but—with the eyes of the world watching, and with Clarence Darrow as his spokesman—it could be a hell of a trial.

There were, unfortunately, some serious practical problems with such a defense. Today it would be called a defense of necessity. While it seldom succeeds, the defense occasionally offers political activists a chance to turn their own trial into a political forum. But Darrow was certain that the judge would refuse to recognize such an argument, leaving Jim with no defense at all.

Darrow did briefly flirt with the idea of bringing in the evidence through a slightly different approach. He considered arguing that Jim had been insane, or had been swept up by a fanaticism that amounted to a form of madness—and that his insanity was the product of the industrial system. That approach might have allowed Darrow to present evidence of societal abuses—but it would, by definition, have had to be based on the premise that Jim was not so much a hero as he was deranged. It was not the sort of stuff that legends are made from.

A few Darrow allies such as Erskine Wood advocated another alternative. Plead them guilty and admit that their action was wrong. Make them villains rather than heroes, or at least hold them up as men whose actions, no matter how understandable, were badly misguided and ultimately destructive. Wood, of course, thought Darrow had made a mistake by winning freedom for Big Bill Haywood by "crooked methods." "I myself think it would have been a thousand times better had Moyer and Haywood been imprisoned for life or hung," he wrote Catlin. Wood was convinced that Darrow's victory in the Haywood case had encouraged some radicals to use force in the belief "that they will occupy the limelight on a world's stage and then be saved at all hazards by the use of millions of money and the moral support of the entire working class. The whole thing, to my mind, is vicious and corrupting and instead of saving such a person at the further sacrifice of the cause by false and corrupting methods I would feel more like shooting him with my own hands as the empty-headed and traitorous weakling who had put back the wheels of Progress."

There was, in any event, an overwhelming practical reason why Darrow could not abandon the McNamaras, plead them guilty, or use the kind of defense that the radicals wanted. His real client was the AFL, or at least the AFL was paying his bills. The AFL, under Gompers's leadership, was an avowedly conservative enterprise that had expressly, vehemently, and repeatedly renounced the use of force as a means of achieving social justice. That fundamental tactical position set them apart from some leaders of the Socialist Party, and from the Industrial Workers of the World, which felt that violence was a necessary and inevitable part of the struggle between capital and labor. Furthermore, Gompers and his colleagues had raised money for the defense fund by assuring the nation that the boys were innocent. With the AFL writing the checks, there was no way that Darrow could admit that either McNamara was guilty—or could argue that the deed was justified.

****

Darrow soon became tired of hearing criticism from those who wanted to second-guess his trial tactics, particularly those with radical credentials. His strategy was to develop the best case possible and secure the most favorable jury available, while creating a climate that put labor into a sympathetic light, that mobilized the community behind the notion that the McNamaras must be innocent, and that focused so much attention on the abuses of capital and the state that people didn't really examine the facts of the case.

From around the country he invited reporters and commentators with a larger vision to come to Los Angeles, men such as Lincoln Steffens, the muckraking journalist; Brand Whitlock, the radical novelist and Toledo, Ohio, mayor; and Charles Edward Russell, the columnist and Socialist candidate for governor of New York. They could help to put the case into perspective.

Perhaps his strongest ally in the endeavor to shape the press reports was Fremont Older, the editor of the San Francisco *Bulletin.* Older, however, was having a hard time persuading the public that this was a labor-capital struggle rather than a murder trial. Too many agreed with Theodore Roosevelt's simple aphorism that "Murder is Murder." Perhaps the public was sympathetic to the McNamaras in the late spring, but by fall, as the case came to trial and more evidence came to public light, the mood had shifted.

"It is difficult for me to convince any large number of people here that any trial of McNamara that does not bring the great background into the case is not a fair trial," Older brooded. "In the *Bulletin,* I am giving the sympathetic note, endeavoring to break down the frightful prejudice there is here against them, but am not succeeding fully."

Most important, perhaps, Darrow planned to delay the start of the trial while helping to build support for the campaign of his cocounsel, Job Harriman, who had a chance of becoming the first Socialist mayor in Los Angeles history. If Harriman were elected it would change the mood of the city—and it could change the balance of power as well. The mayor could name the chief of police, and Harriman seemed likely to name as the new chief one of Darrow's closest friends and allies, Chicago labor leader Ed Nockles. With Harriman as mayor, and Nockles as chief of police, there might even be reason to hope that the charges against J. J. McNamara would be dropped.

❋ ❋ ❋ ❋

Above all, though, Darrow needed to procure a friendly jury, a jury composed of men who were sympathetic to labor, or who would at least be impressed by the arguments that Darrow intended to advance. Jury selection is one of the most important skills of a criminal defense attorney, requiring intelligence and astute insights about the attitudes of prospective jurors. But, given the composition of the jury lists, it was certain to be difficult to find a neutral jury, much less a friendly one.

Jurors for trials in Los Angeles were drawn from a jury wheel that in the fall of 1911 contained slips of paper with the names of about sixteen hundred talesmen, or potential jurors. At the start of a trial, the court clerk would reach into the wheel and take out the names of the men who would compose the first venire, or panel, to be considered for jury duty. The names of the men in the venire were then placed in a tin box on the judge's desk. It was the clerk's responsibility to shake the box, reach into it, and draw out the name of each juror to be examined. The list of jurors inevitably reflected a class bias, since it only included property-holding voters, thus excluding all women and many working-class citizens.

"The old venire contains a long list of names that looks as though the prosecution selected from the tax list the wealthiest and most prominent capitalists of the county," one critic noted. Of 840 names, there were 213 ranchers, 111 real estate men, 93 retired merchants, 49 contractors or builders, and 23 bankers. The list included Harry Chandler of the *Los Angeles Times* and two members of the Llewellyn Iron Works family.

❋ ❋ ❋ ❋

To coordinate his investigation of possible jurors, Darrow chose Bert Franklin. A short, stocky, dapper man with a neatly trimmed mustache and a well-developed taste for alcohol, Franklin was a forty-three-year-old native of Iowa. He had decided to open his own detective agency after spending three years as head of criminal investigations for the Los Angeles County sheriff's office and five years as chief deputy U.S. marshal. In June, just before leaving his job with the U.S. marshal, he had asked three of Darrow's cocounsel—LeCompte Davis, Job Harriman, and Joe Scott—to recommend him for a job with Darrow. They had put in a few good words with Darrow, as had Aloysius McCormack, the U.S. attorney for the Los Angeles region.

Darrow told Franklin to develop background information about those in the jury pool. Working with a small army of his own investigators, Franklin was to find out what he could about their age, nationality, financial standing, feelings about the causes of the explosion and the possible innocence or guilt of the McNamaras. He was to learn about their jobs (were they affiliated with a labor union or with a company that was antilabor?); their reading habits (did they read the *Los Angeles Times* or *Appeal to Reason*?); their religion (were they Catholic, or did they have anti-Catholic feelings?); their friends, their feelings about capital punishment, their attitude toward capital and labor.

But Franklin did not confine himself to developing information that could help Darrow determine which potential jurors might be sympathetic to labor. He went a step further. He attempted to make sure that at least one or two of the jurors would be on Darrow's side.

❊❊❊❊

On Friday, September 29, court clerk George Monroe turned the wheel and removed the names of 125 men—the initial pool of potential jurors. The veniremen were instructed to appear in court during the following week. The judge quickly eliminated those whose health, hearing, or type of employment would make it impractical for them to serve on the jury for a trial that could last at least three months. By Friday, the judge had pared the list down to forty-three men to be examined for possible jury service.

Franklin obtained the list of names from the county clerk and immediately went to work. On Friday afternoon, October 6, he went to the home of Robert Bain, a seventy-year-old Civil War veteran who proudly wore the Grand Army of the Republic's bronze badge of honor in his lapel and had a certain local notoriety as the owner of an old Civil War drum that he carried each year in the city's Memorial Day parade. Bain was a handsome, square-faced, gray-haired man of few words. Having made some bad real estate investments, he was struggling along on a small salary as a carpenter.

With his wide acquaintance among older Angelenos, Franklin had known Bain for a number of years. Bain was out working on a carpentry job, so when Franklin rang the doorbell that afternoon, Dora Bain was at home alone. She was not fully dressed, but at the sound of the bell she slipped into a kimono. While she was changing, Franklin came around to the back of the house and knocked at the window.

Though she recognized him as an acquaintance of her husband, she did not invite him in at once, preferring instead to talk with him through the window. As they were chatting, she described her efforts to earn some money for a blind friend by selling subscriptions to the *Los Angeles Examiner.* A worthy cause, said Franklin, who offered to buy a year's subscription for nine dollars. Despite her attire, Dora then agreed to let him in the house, so that she could give him a receipt.

Franklin complimented her on the house, which was newly purchased, and she said that she had not been so happy since she and Bob were married.

"What do you owe on it?" he asked.

She said it was none of his business. But when he said that he might be in a position to help out, she began to talk more freely. She explained that the house had cost eighteen hundred dollars, that they were paying it off at the rate of fifteen dollars a month, and that the happiest day of her life would be the day that she could hand her husband the deed and say, "Bob, this is our home." That was the opening Franklin was looking for.

"Mrs. Bain," he said, "I think I can very soon place you in the position that you can do that." Franklin said he could help her realize her dream and provide the financial protection that she and her husband would need now that they were nearing the end of their working years. All he wanted in return was for Robert Bain to do what he would no doubt be predisposed to do anyway: serve as a member of the McNamara jury, and vote to acquit the young men who had been framed and were now about to be unfairly convicted.

"The prosecution are buying witnesses and jurors," he told her, "and we have got to use the same tactics that they do to keep even. It is a question of capital against labor. These boys, Mrs. Bain, are as innocent of that crime as you are."

After promising that neither she nor her husband would ever mention the matter to the district attorney, Mrs. Bain agreed to ask her husband to accept Franklin's offer of five hundred dollars for agreeing to go on the jury and another thirty-five hundred dollars when he voted for acquittal.

❈ ❈ ❈ ❈

That evening, after supper, Dora Bain broached the subject with her husband. He resisted, she later recalled, but "I flung myself on the floor and with my arms clasped around his knees, I begged piteously. He finally yielded, but when he did he pushed me from him. He never looked into my eyes again."

Later that night, while Dora was at a lodge meeting, Franklin dropped by to see the Civil War veteran. After talking for a few minutes, Franklin gave him four hundred dollars in twenty-dollar bills. He explained that he was a few dollars short, but would pay Bain the remaining thirty-six hundred dollars when he voted to acquit.

When Dora came home later that evening, Bain took the money from on top of the dresser and handed it to her. "Here is the money," he said coldly. "I do not want it. I never want to see it. After seventy years in which I have served my country, my honor is gone."

Three days later, Bain went off to the courthouse. As one of the forty-three candidates who survived the judge's first cut he, along with the other jurors, was required to remain in confinement in a special hotel reserved for the jurors and was not allowed to return home. To Dora, the decision to accept the bribe was the most painful experience of her life. "I have never had a happy moment since then," she confided two months later.

It was not a pleasant transaction. But Franklin could be certain that if Bain were chosen for the jury there would be at least one vote for acquittal.

❀❀❀❀

Early on Wednesday morning, October 11, a crowd of more than one thousand spectators gathered outside the county jail, hoping to catch a glimpse of the defendants as they left for what was being billed as "the greatest trial of the century" and "the greatest trial in the history of the West." Another several hundred men and women jammed the steps in front of the new Hall of Records building, where the trial was scheduled to start at ten A.M. Inside, packed elevators carried passengers to the eighth floor, where Department Nine, a large and ornate courtroom, had been outfitted with fresh carpeting to prevent the slightest sound from disrupting the proceedings.

The room (decorated in "mild café au lait"), normally accommodated about 150 visitors, but it had been cut in half for the great trial, with a special section reserved for desks to be occupied by some sixty-four journalists from around the world who had been granted credentials. Besides blotters, stationery, pencils and pens, which were available at each table, some of the desks were outfitted with soundless telegraph instruments for the use of the wire service reporters.

The only women correspondents from out of town were Mary Field, representing *American Magazine,* and Sara Ehrgott, whose credentials were from *The Pacific Monthly.* Shortly before court began, Mary and Sara fought their way through the throng in front of the courthouse and managed to squeeze their way onto an elevator with an officious operator, down a corridor lined by inquiring deputy sheriffs, across a bridge, and then into a side entrance to the courtroom that had been reserved for the prisoners, the lawyers, the detectives, certain celebrities, and the press. Finally, after presenting their credentials, they were allowed into the press section, where they were assigned seats between young Earl Harding, of Joseph Pulitzer's New York *World,* and Edward Hamilton, the seasoned and cynical star reporter from Hearst's *San Francisco Examiner.*

They spent a few minutes looking around the remarkable room, watching the lawyers in front, sitting at the great table, waiting for the prisoners and the judge to arrive. There was Darrow, the center of attention, their dinner partner of the night before, neatly dressed in a gray tailor-made suit that would soon look rumpled, wearing a long black tie that drooped from a careless bowknot, fingering the gold-bowed spectacles that he wore only when reading. He was sitting in front with his cocounsel: with Job Harriman, who would use the trial as an instrument in his campaign for mayor; with Joe Scott, the imposing Catholic orator and lawyer, former Chamber of Commerce president, and present elected head of the school board, who lent centrist legitimacy to the defense; with LeCompte Davis, "ruddy and Oregon apple-like," the experienced lawyer who knew far more about the practice of California criminal law than anyone else on the defense team; and with Judge Cyrus McNutt, the sweet old radical who had a useful specialty in Indiana law, where he had served for years as a state court judge—and sitting with them, at the front table, just behind Darrow, was Ruby, the only woman allowed to sit up front of the courtroom railing, dressed to the nines in a tailored suit from Chicago, her waist neatly shaped by a girdle, her print blouse choked up stylishly around her neck, her hair beautifully coiffed under a broad-brimmed hat, posing for photographs and gossiping gaily with a friend from back home. To Mary, sitting a few rows back, in her loose-fitting thrift-shop dress, the scene was at once exhilarating and painful.

After looking around the room for a few minutes, Sara turned to Hamilton and, caught up with her own ideological zeal, asked him what she quickly realized must have seemed a rather naïve question. "How many see in this trial a vast historical and sociological significance?" she inquired. "How many realize that the wheels of revolution move a little faster today?"

The hardened journalist took a close look at Sara and Mary before giving his answer. "About two," he said.

Of course Mary and Sara were more focused on the political issues than on the question of guilt or innocence partly because they, unlike other members of the press, had been told by Darrow that the men were "guilty as hell."

Presently the two prisoners, escorted by sixteen police officers, stepped off the elevator and entered the courtroom. John, "a big, rosy cheeked, good looking man with a shock of iron-gray hair visible under the brim of his derby hat," with a quick gait, was joined by shackles to his younger brother, Jim, "a puny, pale-faced little man, who wore a dark mustache, which made his pallor all the more noticeable." At the entrance to the courtroom, the police removed the prisoners' handcuffs, but Jim continued to cling to his older brother and, once seated, leaned on John's strong shoulder during a good portion of the morning session.

The press lauded J.J. as "self-educated and strong looking," saying that he had the most "distinguished personal appearance" of anyone in court, but the papers couldn't find enough nasty things to say about his brother. Hearst's *Los Angeles Examiner* called Jim a "snarling, bitter, obscene-speaking printer." Pointing to his "shifting eyes, his weak and scraggling mustache, his weak chin and his hang-dog expression," the paper said there was "nothing about him to admire." One headline proclaimed:

THE MCNAMARAS——A CHARACTER STUDY:

J.J. STRONG, VITAL——J.B. A WEAKLING

Indeed the descriptions of Jim were so unfriendly that J.J. felt compelled to come to his brother's defense. In a statement issued the next day, J.J. asked the press and public not to judge the guilt or innocence of his brother "Jimmie" by his facial characteristics or by the set of his chin.

But if the press was there to watch J.J., the matinee idol whose face was on the fund-raising stamps and on the buttons worn by thousands of workers around the nation, they were soon to be disappointed. The first order of business in the courtroom that morning was to decide whether to try the cases together or separately. Clarence Darrow quickly announced that he wanted to have the cases tried separately. It was a strategy that was certain to help J.J., since there was less evidence against him than against his younger brother. In fact, since the prosecutors' case against J.J. was still largely circumstantial, they declared that they intended to try Jim first.

J.J. was sent back to his jail cell, to start a wait that some thought could last for as long as a year before his case would come to trial. Some experts predicted that jury selection alone would take at least three to six months. It was not, as advertised, to be the case of the government against J.J., or the government against the McNamara brothers. Instead, this great American trial was to be the case of the People against lowly James B. McNamara.

❋ ❋ ❋

Jury selection offered Darrow a chance to pursue a strategy that was carefully planned. Besides using it to choose a panel of sympathetic men, he intended to use the selection process, which was public, as a way to underline the political context of the case: to explain to the jurors and the nation that this was, at bottom, about the war between capital and labor. If it took a year to get a proper panel, so much the better: the political climate could only improve.

Darrow quickly entered the fray with an intensity that delighted the packed chamber. "Clarence Darrow, whose slightest act or play of feature is noted with keen interest by every man in the courtroom, displayed for the first time some of the qualities which have given him fame, which dominate men and convince judges and sway juries," wrote one correspondent.

While in the courtroom, Darrow was constantly in motion, displaying "the activity of a steam jumpingjack," twitching his shoulders, beating his fist on his palm or on the table, drumming the desk with the end of his pencil. Much of his time was spent nervously walking back and forth in front of the railing, pacing the floor like a caged lion, sparring with opposing counsel or with the judge. Even when holding a casebook and arguing a point of law, he would thrust his head forward and beat the law book with his free hand, speaking energetically and eloquently of the injustice to his clients.

He relished the chance to test wits with the veniremen, to ask a difficult and perhaps unfair question, to allow it to be excluded by the judge, to befriend the potential juror by asking an unrelated series of questions, and then, at some unexpected moment, to find a hidden disguise for the question that had earlier been forbidden. "He drills with the ruthlessness of the dentist down into the nerve cavities," Mary Field observed. "A juror's attitude to Labor, his attitude toward religion, his wife's father's business, his bed-time, his conversation with the corner grocer, his conduct back in Kansas, his attitude toward crime, the books and newspapers he read, what he said to his wife Monday morning, how often he drove into town, where he bought his socks, did he or didn't he, why he did or didn't, in, in, in, he bores."

Darrow's style was also remarkably engaging, adding bits of humor and flashes of satire to the otherwise often dull routine of jury selection. He enjoyed chatting with old socialists and sparring with young capitalists. He welcomed the chance to argue points of law and to advance points of philosophy. Friendly reporters commented on "the magic of his personality," his "forceful or whimsical expression as suits his mood," and his "remarkably mobile face."

His wit was particularly inspired by discussions of the veniremen's financial condition. "You know, every man is a capitalist in Los Angeles who doesn't sleep in a disappearing bed or eat at a cafeteria," he quipped one afternoon. On another occasion, a venireman disqualified himself because his property was in his wife's name. "Most workingmen's property is in their employer's name," Darrow dryly commented.

Most of the time, Darrow's lined face offered a warm glow—but when provoked, he was a tiger. "The smile that is as winning as a child's is seldom absent from Darrow's face,"one reporter noted. So "the contrast when his mouth tightens and his blue eyes gleam with anger make those rare moments more electric in their effect of arousing interest." Darrow used anger to great effect. At times he was genuinely provoked by the prosecutors or the judge, but his comments were always also intended to play to a different audience: the public, whose support both he and his client badly needed.

"I presume you have heard of the bitter war that is going on in this country between labor and capital?" he asked the first juror on the stand.

"I have read of it," answered Z. T. Nelson, sixty-four, who had been a farmer, a grocer, a piano dealer, and a real estate agent before retiring.

"You know that most men have taken sides in that war," Darrow continued.

"Yes," Nelson replied cautiously.

"On which side is your sympathy?" Darrow inquired.

Before he could answer, the prosecutors were on their feet, objecting that the question was irrelevant. Little matter: Darrow had made his point. This was not simply the People against J. B. McNamara. This was the case of capital against labor—and everyone had better understand it.

❋ ❋ ❋ ❋

As jury selection continued, much of Darrow's ire and frustration was aimed at Judge Walter Bordwell, who seemed unnecessarily hostile. The defense distrusted him from the start, even asking him at one point to step down from the case. He was a well-groomed, Taft-oriented Republican who carried a walking stick and lived at the exclusive California Club. Darrow had been particularly offended by Bordwell's role in presiding over the grand jury investigation that had been used to indict the defendants and, as the McNamara brothers saw it, to intimidate supporters such as Emma McManigal.

Bordwell's rulings during the jury selection process were particularly important. Since each side was only entitled to exclude a certain number of men without cause, both the defense and the prosecution wanted to persuade the judge to do the work for them, using his unlimited power to ban jurors whose bias made them ineligible to serve. But all of Bordwell's rulings seemed to favor the prosecution.

One intense clash involved the eligibility of two veniremen named A. C. Winter and Walter Frampton. Both men quickly admitted their belief that the *Times* had been blown up by dynamite, rather than by gas; they had thus prejudged a crucial issue of the case. They also were convinced that if a man were indicted he should be presumed to be guilty—although the American system of justice is based on precisely the opposite presumption.

Darrow vehemently argued that the judge should exclude both men from serving on the jury. Judge Bordwell took several days to reach a decision, while Darrow grew increasingly impatient, particularly since the men were allowed to continue sitting, eating, and living with the other jurors in their isolated quarters, where their prejudices might rub off on others.

Finally, Darrow announced that the defense "will refuse to go on with this case" until the judge makes a ruling.

"Now Mr. Darrow, there is no occasion for a remark like that," Judge Bordwell replied testily, peering down at Darrow. "I am going to take time to examine this record."

Darrow, "red as a flame," spit his words back at the judge. "Then we refuse to go on." But Darrow's gesture proved futile, since the judge was able to force the trial to continue.

The next day, Bordwell ruled that both Winter and Frampton were qualified to serve.

Furious, Darrow rose, requesting permission to ask Winter another question or two.

"The application is denied," answered Bordwell. "The court is of the opinion that he will give both sides a fair and impartial trial."

"I would like to be heard on it, Your Honor," pleaded Darrow.

Bordwell refused. "The matter may be considered closed," he said.

Even Edward Hamilton, who had no particular use for the defense, thought that the judge had been unfair. "In all the years that I have reported court proceedings," he told Sara later that day, "I have never heard such biased rulings."

❋ ❋ ❋ ❋

Although the bitter fight over the selection of a jury was to last for almost two months, the first group of potentially acceptable jurors was identified less than a week after the case began. The man whose name topped the list was Robert F. Bain.

During questioning, Bain offered a little something for everyone. For Darrow, he noted that he had originated the first labor union in Los Angeles—"old Fifty-six," as he called it. Asked whether he thought that the *Times*'s attitude toward labor justified unusual tactics by unions, he said, "Yes, to hold their own." Furthermore, he said that his wife would not permit him to subscribe to the *Times*.

Judge Bordwell jotted down a series of notes on the juror. Many sounded favorable to the defense, but some indicated that Bain would be inclined to give a fair hearing to the prosecution's case. "On Christmas he avoided discussion with his brother-in-law and nephews because it was a distressing subject—so many killed. One nephew is a nonunion electrician. No feeling against D.A. Juries are chosen to bring verdicts, not to disagree."

Captain Fredericks was no doubt heartened by these comments, and by the discovery that Bain was not only a patriot but had attended Grand Army of the Republic post meetings with General Harrison Gray Otis and had, on one occasion, gone out with his G.A.R. drum corps in support of Fredericks's campaign.

Darrow passed over that admission with a shrug.

"That is, you would drum for anybody?" Darrow inquired with a touch of irony.

"Yes," said Bain, "if we were paid."

Bain became the first juror accepted by both the prosecution and the defense. Now there was at least one sure vote for acquittal.

＊＊＊＊

Every day, it seemed, the courtroom was filled with spectators who gave special meaning to the proceedings. Toward the front of the room were some of the great men and women of California and the West, celebrities that Edward Hamilton, the seasoned old wit from the *San Francisco Examiner,* engagingly pointed out to Sara and Mary. The visitors included Romualdo Francisco de Valle, one of the last of the Dons, small and dark, a former state senator and assemblyman of polish and culture and exquisite diction; Don Miguel Estudillo, a state senator from Riverside County, who carried with him "the atmosphere of the last bit of romance left in this storied country;" and Senator Thomas Gore of Oklahoma, the famous blind U.S. senator, friend of Darrow, who was in town on a lecture trip.

Further back in the courtroom were the men and women who were paying for the defense with their hard-earned dimes and quarters, the workers who believed in the McNamaras and in Darrow and in the cause of industrial justice, wearing trade union labels and the Socialist Party's bright red button. Fremont Older's reporter described them as a "detachment of society's outcasts who listen to the proceedings with an interest that never flags. In their eyes blazes the fire of fanaticism. Their faces are scarred and seamed by a heritage of bad food, bad blood, exposure and hardship. Their grimy clothing smells and the air of the courtroom is tainted with their breaths. Any one of a dozen of these men would fit into the picture that Carylyle or Dickens has drawn of the French Revolution."

❄ ❄ ❄ ❄

Joining these observers in the room was a procession of visitors who were part of an unusual strategy organized by the prosecution, a strategy that the county's chief detective, Samuel Browne, called "the silent third degree." Every day Detective Browne brought witnesses into the room, seated them close to the front, and allowed them to stare at Jim McNamara. The first such visitor was a tall man with a black mustache, a teamster who had been employed in the stock room of the *Times* at the time of the explosion. He had told the grand jury that he had seen a man loitering about the alley where the explosion occurred. On the second day of the trial, with jury selection just beginning, Assistant District Attorney Joe Ford entered the room with the witness and seated the tall man with the mustache just a dozen feet from the prisoner.

Jim McNamara, as always, was chewing gum, wearily watching the proceedings, with his chin resting on his hand. As soon as he saw the man with the mustache sit down, Jim nudged the bailiff and asked him to get the attention of Darrow, who was pacing near the railing.

"They've brought that fellow here to identify me," Jim whispered to his lawyer.

Darrow simply smiled his deep, wrinkled smile.

"I never saw him before," Jim said.

Darrow told him not to worry. But Jim knew that the man with the mustache could place him at the scene of the crime on the night of the explosion. If credible, it would be extremely damaging.

As the day wore on, observers thought that Jim McNamara, who was already pale, grew paler under the strain, and that his eyes seemed even more deeply sunken than they had before.

During the weeks that followed, the prosecution brought some twenty-eight different people into the room to identify Jim McNamara, including, allegedly, a woman for whom he had bought an imitation sealskin sack and who pointed to the sack when she caught his eye; a musician from the Bohemian Café in San Francisco to whom McNamara, in a mood of drunken sentimentality, had given a ten-dollar gold piece for playing the "Traumerei"; and a bartender who had sold him a drink a few minutes before he planted the bomb behind the *Times* in Ink Alley. There were women he had known, men he had gotten drunk with, drivers who had taken him around San Francisco and Los Angeles, the general delivery clerk who had handed him his mail as J. B. Brice.

It was, as Detective Browne later explained, "a story that I was telling him without saying anything to him. He would tell Darrow and then Darrow would whisper to LeCompte Davis and Davis would come to me and say: 'Who's this fellow you had in court to identify Jim?' And I would say, 'Forget it.' Then the next day I would produce a couple of more witnesses from different sections."

❋❋❋❋

Both sides were capable of such psychological warfare. Darrow's strategy was to build popular support—even adoration—for his clients, or at least for J.J., while vilifying the state and developing a mood of popular discontent that would make a successful prosecution politically and socially untenable. One Sunday, Erskine Wood was a featured speaker at a McNamara rally in Oregon. It was, he noted, "a demonstration ordered by Darrow to bully the jury and obstruct the course of justice by intimidation." Though he spoke "against the policy," Wood immediately regretted participating in an event designed to interfere with the natural course of justice. It is doubtful that his qualms were shared, or understood, by most of those whom Darrow called on to help.

All around America, workers wore pins and buttons with J.J.'s face and the words MCNAMARA BROTHERS NOT GUILTY, and JUSTICE FOR THE MCNAMARAS—KIDNAPPED—AFL; sympathizers affixed stamps with J.J.'s picture to their letters. J.J.'s handsome face was everywhere. None of the buttons or stamps featured a picture of his anemic younger brother.

In early October, in time to coincide with the start of the trial, J.J.'s supporters released a short movie called *A Martyr to His Cause,* a propaganda version of J.J.'s famous kidnapping, which was watched by an estimated fifty thousand supporters during its week-long premier run in Cincinnati. As Frank Morrison of the AFL noted in a letter to Darrow, the movie was a political statement rather than a factual recitation. "The scenario has been favorably passed upon," he observed, "but the story of the picture, as it is ready for exhibition, and the story from which it is taken, very often differ materially. " That was to be expected, of course, since the movie, and, indeed, the entire campaign to free the McNamara brothers, was far less concerned with accuracy than with the need to engage the emotions of the working classes on behalf of a cause that was, for all of its faults, just.

The movie's script presented the case as J.J.'s supporters wanted it to be known. Though Jim was on trial, he was never mentioned.

❈ ❈ ❈ ❈

The rallies, buttons, stamps, and film were only one small part of the campaign. They helped to raise money for the case and to make J.J. a hero. But Darrow had a far more profound strategy in mind. As Wood noted, Darrow wanted to raise a climate of public anger about the case that would make it impossible for the prosecution to continue.

In late October, the purpose of the campaign was candidly set forth by Eugene Debs at a Carnegie Hall rally that was packed with angry men and women waving red flags and Socialist banners. The conviction of the McNamaras, Debs warned, would produce the greatest anticapitalist demonstration in American history.

"Behind this trial there is the mighty Steel Trust," Debs shouted. "After kidnapping the McNamara brothers, they are now trying to convict them by equally unfair means. Who got the evidence in this case? The detectives, yes, the detectives. The detectives say they have unpublished and inevitable proof of the guilt of the McNamaras. . . . I know by my own experience there is no crime that [the detectives] will not commit. They can always find the dynamite, for they put it there themselves.

"But look out for great developments. The workingmen cleared Moyer, Haywood, and Pettibone. They made it impossible for President Taft to sentence [Socialist editor] Fred Warren. And now they have another great chance to come to the front. I appeal to each one of you to be on the alert for the right time to act, and if these men are railroaded to injustice, then we'll give them such an exhibition of the united forces of the working class that they won't soon forget it.

"I believe that we can make our protest so emphatic that Wall Street will become so alarmed that in less time almost than it takes to tell it, a message will be made to flit across the continent which will entirely change the program of action. And the accused men will walk free without a blemish upon the record of their manhood."

The message was brought even closer to home by dispatches from journalist friends of the defense. "To the dispossessed in the rear of the courtroom," Fremont Older's San Francisco *Bulletin* declared, "McNamara is a persecuted man, a martyr; Darrow is a hero; the District Attorney a very devil, the judge a monster. Among them are many potential bomb throwers. If McNamara's life goes out on the scaffold at San Quentin, a white flare of hate will sweep over the land. It will burn hottest where society's outcasts gather in squalid rooms and make bombs, dreaming meanwhile of revolution. Perhaps even the judge wonders if there isn't a better way."

❋ ❋ ❋ ❋

Although he seemed bold in the courtroom, Darrow was given to violent mood swings, rotating from regular fits of anger and irritation to moments of intense pleasure. "He would have faith in the morning and be despairing in the evening," Johannsen recalled. His volatility was, at least in part, produced by the sharp changes in his feelings about the case: what would happen to Jim, would he be hanged?; what would happen to J.J., would he be tried and convicted?; and what would happen to him, to his reputation and his finances? Some days he was elated by a good ruling from the court, a piece of information about one of the jurors, a powerful rally by his allies, or news about a witness or a piece of evidence that could be kept away from the government. Other days he was infuriated by Judge Bordwell, by a new witness against his client, by the deteriorating finances of the defense team.

Darrow "was so horrid tonight, I couldn't stand him," Sara wrote to Erskine one Wednesday evening in October. "Mary and I cooked a dandy dinner but he arrived all out of sorts and nothing was decent. He sat on his chair like a spoiled baby and expected us to *amuse* him, shake our rattles, dangle our bright balls, etc.—not me! Me for out doors fast as I could go. . . . Poor Mary! I left him in the dumps with her. . . . He reflects the state of the case—and just now it's been going against the defense."

Just two days later, on a lovely Friday afternoon, Darrow was back again at the Field sisters' apartment. A changed man, he was as upbeat and cheerful as he had been glum and sullen. He came by their house with an auto and took the two women, along with young Earl Harding, the New York *World* reporter who was falling in love with Sara, on what Sara described as a "glorious spin. We went over the hills and through Elysian Park to Pasadena, arriving there after dark. Then we had a horrid dinner at a lovely Spanish Inn where our eyes were pleased if not our palates (the awful messes they served were all Spanish!) and then home through the dark and through a light rain that splashed in my face with daring, stingy slaps—Oh! but it was glorious."

❊ ❊ ❊ ❊

Some of Darrow's most serious problems were financial. The unions were assessing members for at least a day's wages, but for all of their efforts, they did not seem capable of raising money as fast as he and his colleagues needed to spend it. His funding problems were so severe that Darrow, in his more hopeless moods, wanted to drop the case. But how could he? Who could understand it? If he couldn't drop the case, he would have to find some other way to cut it back or end it.

In desperation Darrow sent his old friend Ed Nockles to San Francisco to try to coax some more money out of Olaf Tvietmoe. "Ed will explain something about financial matters," Darrow wrote to Tvietmoe in mid-October. "I am not going to bore you any more, but I am going to have [to have] assurance of the money that is needed or finish up Jim's case without putting any more money in it and then quit the game. I am simply not going to kill myself with this case and then worry over money and not know what to do."

But Tvietmoe was not allowed to send money directly to Darrow even if he wanted to. Gompers had insisted on having full control of the funds from the start. He may, in fact, have been concerned about the ways in which the money would be used if the collections and expenditures were not all centralized. As early as May, he had told Tvietmoe and Darrow that no money could be used for the case unless it came through the AFL's special account. Now he felt obliged to restate his policy. "I know that there is some talk of transmitting directly from San Francisco and vicinity to Mr. Darrow the funds which may be needed," Gompers told Tvietmoe. "Such a course" is out of the question. It would be "harmful, impractical, and sure to lead to confusion."

※ ※ ※ ※

Darrow was trapped. When Darrow acted "spoiled," "horrid," and "down in the dumps," as Sara observed, he had good reason. His clients were guilty as hell; the combined forces of capital and the government were arrayed against him; his expenses were mounting daily; he had no money to pay his employees or his creditors. And he was still only in the jury selection stage of the proceeding. Yet much as he may have wanted to quit, he was blocked by the same forces that had compelled him to take the case in the first instance. In April, organized labor had insisted that he take the case; now, five months later, organized labor would never understand and never forgive him if he tried to drop it.

Caught in the center of the country's greatest trial, in the beauty of Southern California, in a losing case that he couldn't escape, and in between two women who loved him, Darrow could perhaps be forgiven if he experienced wild mood swings.

※ ※ ※ ※

With the noose tightening around Jim's neck, there was, for a while, still hope for J. J. McNamara. As long as he could be spared, Darrow could have some kind of victory. But thanks to the intervention of President William Howard Taft, the government was assembling a strong case against J.J. for his role in the bombing of the Llewellyn Iron Works, if not for his part in bombing the *Times*.

When Jim's trial began on October 11, the evidence that could send J.J. to jail was still in Indianapolis, in the hands of the local prosecutors, men who were friendly to labor. Darrow had good reason to believe that it would never be used against his clients.

Much of the evidence had been seized from the files of the Iron Workers' union at the time of J.J.'s arrest, taken from the union's secret vault by William Burns and by Walter Drew of the National Erectors' Association. Burns wanted to use the evidence in Los Angeles, but Walter Drew and the NEA had a different goal. They wanted to use it as the centerpiece of a case against the union's top officials for the seventy or eighty bombings around the country. That prosecution would be brought in Indianapolis.

The Los Angeles prosecutors knew that the evidence seized from the union would make the case against J.J. overwhelming. While it would not connect him to the bombing directly, it would help to prove that he had ordered Ortie McManigal to bomb the Llewellyn Iron Works. In the words of NEA Commissioner Walter Drew, the evidence in Indianapolis was so strong that it would "bury J.J.M." With good reason, the Iron Workers' leadership did not want the evidence to get into the prosecutors' hands. They knew that the information could convict J.J.; equally important, they knew that it could be used to send the entire executive board to jail. They were determined to destroy the evidence as quickly as possible. As Walter Drew noted, "About the only hope that the other side has in these cases, is to get enough advance knowledge of the evidence to enable them to explain, evade, destroy or make away with the proof in some manner."

Drew was convinced that the Iron Workers and their allies were capable of doing just that. He was being trailed by seven men in Indianapolis. James Badorf, the NEA's man in Los Angeles, was being followed by eight union representatives. "There is no coup that they would not undertake to get these papers once they know how important they are," Drew warned.

As the Los Angeles trial date grew near, Drew began to receive warnings that he and his operatives might be in physical danger. One of the warnings came from Burns, who sent Drew a telegram warning him of a "scheme maturing to slug you and Badorf." Burns's agents kept a watch on Drew's house in New York. But Badorf was in Los Angeles, where the danger was even more acute.

"Take care of yourself personally," Drew cautioned Badorf in early October. "Don't get into any dangerous or out of the way places that you can't avoid. It would also do no harm to change your boarding place once or twice a week."

* * * *

While looking out for their own safety, Drew and his men were having a difficult time insuring the safety of the documents. The materials were in the custody of the local Indianapolis prosecutors, but unions were powerful in Indianapolis, and the prosecutors were quietly returning some of the key documents to representatives of the Iron Workers. Drew's agents became convinced that the Indianapolis courthouse was "dangerous for evidence." They watched helplessly as the prosecutor, Frank Baker, gave postcards, expense accounts, checkbooks, letters, and telephone bills to union lawyers. Drew became convinced that the unions owned Baker "Body and Soul."

Drew finally gave up any hope that the Indiana authorities would prosecute the union's executive board or protect the evidence. He was certain, too, that they would never send any important files to the prosecutors in California. But he had one last card to play—he could try to get the federal government to take over the case.

In 1911, the federal government's powers were relatively limited. The bombing of construction sites was a violation of state—but not federal—law. Undaunted, Drew found another basis for federal intervention; he identified a statute that made it a federal crime to carry dynamite on interstate railroads. Armed with that law, he wrote to attorneys in the U.S. Department of Justice asking them to take control of the evidence and to file federal charges against the union's leaders. If they did so, they would also be able to share the evidence with the Los Angeles district attorney's office.

"The need for federal action in Indianapolis is emphasized by the fact that the Prosecuting Attorney of Marion County is not only taking no steps to prosecute under State Laws," he wrote to U.S. Attorney General George Wickersham, "but has publicly announced that he intends to turn over to attorneys for J. J. McNamara and the Executive Board of the Iron Workers Union the greater part of the evidence seized in the secret vault in the basement. The return of this evidence means, of course, its absolute loss to any prosecution, Federal or State."

For several crucial weeks in the early fall, however, attorneys in the Justice Department resisted Drew's appeals. In part they were concerned about the limited reach of federal law, but to a large extent their motives were political. It seemed likely that President Taft would be challenged in the 1912 Republican primaries by a representative of the party's progressive wing, most likely Robert LaFollette or former president Theodore Roosevelt. In the general election, he would face a major challenge from the Democrats as well as from Eugene Debs's Socialist Party. Under the circumstances, he would need all the friends he could find.

At the Justice Department, it seemed, Darrow's public relations campaign was having an effect. "In view of the public feeling that has been excited over the proceedings against the alleged dynamiters," a Justice Department official noted, it seemed unwise to let Drew and his associates "use the Federal Government for the purpose of pulling their chestnuts out of the fire."

❋ ❋ ❋ ❋

Walter Drew knew that his best hope of getting support from the Justice Department was to make a direct appeal to President Taft himself, who would soon be in the area on a barnstorming campaign across the country, a "swing around the circle," visiting old friends and trying to make new ones in an effort to bolster his chances of reelection.

General Otis was a fierce Taft loyalist. Indeed, when the explosion at the *Times* occurred, Otis was in Mexico as a presidential representative. A few days before the president's scheduled arrival in Los Angeles, Otis wrote a personal letter to the president, offering proof that "the explosion of the *Times* building was only an incident in the carrying out of the general purpose to establish a reign of wholesale terrorism and intimidation." Otis asked for an opportunity "to clearly present the evidence to you" so that Taft would instruct the attorney general "that his usual prompt and energetic action is vitally necessary in this case." Taft suggested that they meet at the home of his sister, Mrs. William Edwards, where he would be staying while in Los Angeles.

The district attorney arranged for a third man, Oscar Lawler, to join the meeting. Lawler knew the facts of the case and enjoyed the president's confidence. He was a young lawyer and Taft protégé who had served in the Justice Department, leaving with a letter in which Taft called him "a first class man" and a very competent attorney. Now Lawler was back in Los Angeles, where he was helping the Merchants and Manufacturers Association prepare the government's case against the McNamaras.

The three men met at the Edwardses' home, late in the evening of October 17, after guests had departed from a dinner in the president's honor. They went out into the Edwardses' garden, where the three-hundred-pound president sat in a chair that had been specially designed for him. General Otis began the discussion by describing the many unsuccessful efforts to get help from the Justice Department. He explained that they needed Taft's help, but didn't want to hurt him politically.

"Mr. President," General Otis said, "this is a very serious matter. You're in the midst of a campaign for reelection, and we wouldn't want anything that would injure or interfere with your campaign."

After Otis had finished, the president got up from his seat and walked over to Lawler, who had remained standing. He placed his hand on the young man's shoulder.

"Lawler," he said, "you have been examining the facts in this matter for a long time. Have I your assurance as one lawyer to another that there have been violations of federal law?"

"Yes, Mr. President," Lawler said. "Just scores of them."

Taft then turned to Otis. "General," he said, "I appreciate very much your personal consideration but you know that one of the duties prescribed by the Constitution for the Executive is to see that the laws are faithfully executed. As between that and any consideration of my campaign, there can be no choice."

Before ending the meeting, he assured Lawler that he would hear directly from Attorney General George Wickersham before noon the next day.

Taft was true to his word. The next morning, Wickersham wired Lawler that the federal government would become involved in the case. In less than two weeks, Charles W. Miller, the U.S. attorney in Indianapolis, initiated a federal criminal grand jury investigation of the Iron Workers' Union, charging them with an unlawful conspiracy to transport dynamite across state lines. The new proceeding gave the federal government the power to seize the evidence. Once they had it in their own hands, the Justice Department's lawyers immediately sent the evidence off to Los Angeles.

❄❄❄❄

A curious episode that may have effected the president's thinking has been the subject of some historical debate. Early on the morning of October 16, 1911, just hours before the train carrying President Taft from San Francisco to Los Angeles passed over the El Capitan Bridge near Santa Barbara, a watchman for the Southern Pacific railroad discovered thirty-nine sticks of dynamite affixed to the bridge. Press reports the next day speculated that the dynamite had been planted by anarchists who wanted to kill the president, or by striking railroad workers attempting to disrupt the Southern Pacific. Others have since theorized that the dynamite may have been planted by opponents of labor who were hoping to gain the president's support.

Interestingly, the episode did not particularly disturb the Secret Service agents traveling with the president. "Everything fine," one agent wired back to Secret Service headquarters in Washington. "Today A.P. will carry story of an attempt to dynamite train last night. As far as I can learn there is absolutely no truth in it." Taft himself was not even informed of the episode until he was at the dinner party at his sister's house, at least twenty hours after it was discovered. Nevertheless, the attempted dynamiting was quickly used to support the call for federal action, and it may well have made Taft and the Justice Department more receptive to the request for aid. Drew highlighted the incident in a letter that he wrote the next day to the assistant attorney general, who had resisted taking decisive action. "The recent attempt to dynamite a bridge over which a train carrying the President of the United States was soon to pass," he argued, "must be an evidence that this dynamiting business is a national problem and that no particular State or group of employers should be left to try to cope with it alone. It seems to me that this last occurrence makes prompt and energetic Federal action so natural a sequence, that if it fails to materialize, it would be occasion for comment."

❋❋❋❋

Darrow immediately denounced the federal action as a "clever trick." Leo Rappaport, his cocounsel in Indianapolis, fought valiantly to find some legal pretext to prevent the federal government from gaining control of the evidence and sending it to Los Angeles. But they faced a decidedly uphill battle.

On November 7, Darrow learned that the government had gained control of an exceptionally dangerous witness. Frank Eckhoff had been taken into custody, or, as Darrow's allies saw it, he had been "kidnapped." Eckhoff could be particularly effective against J.J. A lifelong friend from Cincinnati, he had been involved in several of J.J.'s dynamiting projects and, at J.J.'s request, had helped to advise and shelter Jim in the days following the *Times*'s bombing. Darrow had hoped that Eckhoff would refuse to talk and would resist any effort to send him to Los Angeles. But on Monday night, November 6, Eckhoff left Cincinnati for Los Angeles in the custody of Burns's agent Guy Biddinger.

J. J. McNamara was told that his friend had been kidnapped and Eckhoff's wife said that "the manner in which the detectives worked was just like kidnapping." But the press reported that he had accompanied Biddinger willingly. In Cincinnati, the McNamara family, convinced that the brothers were innocent, could only conclude that Eckhoff "knows nothing of the case, but is pretending to in order to receive money for his services."

To Burns, the cooperation of Eckhoff was a turning point. Calling him "the best witness" we have, Burns said that labor organizations went "up in the air" when they learned that Eckhoff had left town in the company of his detectives.

❋❋❋❋

About the only good news for the defense that fall was the election results on October 31. But that was very good news indeed, for in a remarkable feat, Job Harriman won the primary election for mayor of Los Angeles.

Harriman's campaign for mayor was a centerpiece of Darrow's strategy. If Harriman won, the city would be filled with a new political climate—and city hall, as well as the police department, would be filled with new leaders. Darrow hoped that the community at large, and its business and government leaders in particular, would be more sympathetic to his clients and perhaps even willing to settle the case.

There was a widespread belief that the McNamara Defense Fund had financed Harriman's campaign, and that Darrow was the campaign's organizing genius. "The Socialists were equipped with a machinery of powerful propaganda," a star reporter for *Collier's* magazine said shortly after the election. "Their headquarters were run on a huge scale, with large forces of clerks. Their speaking campaign required the renting of large halls every night. They passed around the collection plate at these public meetings, but the funds thus derived could not have constituted more than a mere drop toward the heavy expenses of their campaign.

"The impression current in Los Angeles is that a share of the McNamara defense fund had been diverted to financing the Socialist campaign. If an accounting is ever made of the funds turned over to Darrow, it will probably be shown that the Socialist campaign was part of his stage setting for the case. He had done such things before. It is conceivable that he built up the Socialist sentiment to terrorize capital and so create a basis for a trade later should an an emergency develop. . . . There was money and there was directing genius behind it. Never in its history had Los Angeles been seized with such a panic of fear."

Going into the last weeks of the campaign, experts were beginning to doubt that Job Harriman would even make it into a runoff. The betting odds were 1 to 3 that George Alexander would get more than half the votes. Harriman was considered to be in a dead heat for second place. One expert predicted that Alexander would get eighteen thousand votes, W. C. Mushet nine thousand, and Harriman seven thousand. But when the vote was held on Halloween—watched excitedly by Sara and Mary, who rushed downtown to get the election returns after celebrating at a party with dark lanterns and cider and apples and pumpkin pie—the Socialist was far in the lead.

Harriman polled more than 20,183 votes, while Alexander won only 16,790. There would, of course, be a runoff election between Harriman and the mayor. That election would be held five weeks later, on December 5, 1911. Much could happen during those five weeks, and there was the imponderable effect of women voters who, thanks to the passage of suffrage on the October 11 statewide ballot, would be eligible to vote in Los Angeles for the first time. But for the moment, Harriman was the front-runner.

It was a great victory for Socialism and organized labor: the promise of success in the antilabor citadel of America; a moment, supporters felt, to be savored by all who cared for mankind. "My Socialist blood is running high," wrote Sara on the night of the election. "It's simply wonderful to see the enthusiasm of the people! Their poverty and misery is drowned in this great onward march they are making. Oh! the divinity of the revolt—the holiness of rebellion!" At last the Darrow camp had cause to cheer.

Even the judge's rulings seemed a bit more balanced. A few days after the election, Sara leaned over to Edward Hamilton, the crusty old reporter for the *San Francisco Examiner,* and asked whether he had "noticed a disposition to milder rulings on the part of the judge since the election."

Hamilton looked at Sara for a moment, then burst into laughter. "Why you queer little woman," he said. "I was thinking that very thing myself."

❋ ❋ ❋ ❋

For a few days, Harriman's victory lifted Darrow's spirits immensely. Shortly after the primary, he visited the Field sisters' apartment in a splendid mood, anxious to read some of his favorite poetry. He asked Sara if she had any of Erskine Wood's poetry and she brought out a copy of his sonnets. Darrow began to read them out loud with great feeling and understanding, always adding, "Now there's a great man for you!"

Then he read in Heinrich Heine's *Reisebilder,* and Sara listened happily to the language and the irony and the lyric reading until the tiny hand on her watch told her that it was time for her to leave the apartment, to let Darrow and Mary enjoy a few hours alone, much as she would have liked to be with Erskine Wood, her great man.

❋ ❋ ❋ ❋

Watching all of these events from his nest in Oregon, Erskine Wood the poet would have savored his friend's taste in sonnets. But Erskine Wood the philosopher-lawyer, whom Darrow had unsuccessfully tried to enlist as a member of his defense team, was becoming increasingly critical of his old friend's personal behavior and professional tactics.

Wood's entertaining letters to Sara, punctuated primarily by dashes, were no doubt influenced by a certain jealousy and anger prompted by Darrow's sexual overtures to Sara and callous treatment of Mary; but they provide a heartfelt critique of the man and his methods. They were also something more than the comments of a distant observer, since Wood was planning a trip to Los Angeles in mid-November, where he would join Darrow and the sisters who were the objects of their extramarital affairs.

Some of Wood's comments dealt with Darrow's relationship with Mary; others examined his ethics and performance as a lawyer. To Wood, there was a direct link between the way that Darrow would treat Mary and the way that he would handle the case. Both would be determined and impaired by certain fundamental character flaws.

"If you get a key to a person's nature and it is the universal pass key," he wrote, "you know in advance what they are going to do. Darrow is above all things Selfish—with a not necessary adjunct to selfishness, vanity, and a side development—avarice."

Wood began his analysis with an examination of Darrow's treatment of Mary—from early summer, when he had asked her not to come to Los Angeles ("he feared she would compromise him with the world and he is in such matters a coward"), to the fall, when he was spending so much of his leisure time with her ("he is glad she has come, has a spasmodic return of physical passion which makes him even gay and adoring.") But, Wood predicted, "when he is sated he will treat her like a sucked orange. When his personal fears are aroused he will run from her—and if necessary deny her thrice before the cock crows. When she and her work pay tribute to his vanity he will use her to that end. [But if she ever criticizes him] he will turn her off like a dog—as he will in the end anyway. . . ."

Wood was convinced that Darrow's approach to the case would fall victim to the same traits of character that would ultimately victimize Mary. His letters to Sara underlined the same concerns that he had spelled out in July in the letter that he had asked W. W. Catlin to share with Darrow. "Darrow is not making this fight for the cause of labor—nor for the McNamaras—but for C. Darrow. And in this he is like most of us lawyers. We prate of our fight for justice. We are fighting for our own glory and profit. Darrow's glory and Darrow's profit is what he is fighting for. Of course these can only be served by the McNamara defense and indeed acquittal. That is why he is unscrupulous to win—he knows as well as I do that true devotion to the great cause would be to lend his great influence to teach labor that only by a repudiation of such methods can it ever hope to win. He knows and sees as clearly as I do that he is sowing the wind and the poor generations to come will reap the whirlwind—he is undermining not building up—he is setting up false idols, not leaning away a veil. He knows it. He does not expect to lose. He's only telling you that to enhance the glory of C. Darrow when the victory comes."

✳ ✳ ✳ ✳

At the core of Wood's concern was his love of truth—or at least of truth as he defined it. "Truth," he was convinced, "is inseparable from the cause." The cause of freedom, the cause of justice, the cause of philosophical anarchism. Wood believed that if acquittal were secured through corrupt means—through intimidation, bribery, or perjury—the McNamara case would send out a false message: that violence works, that its perpetrators have the support of the leaders of socialism and labor, and that those who are caught can escape from the law.

Darrow, however, had a different vision of the rule of law and of the place of the law in society. While his strongest emotions were reserved for J.J., he believed in Jim's cause as well. He was convinced that Jim's trial could play a central role in educating the public about the issues at stake in the battle between capital and labor—as the Debs, Kidd, and Haywood cases had done. He viewed Jim McNamara as a pawn who, though perhaps technically guilty of blowing up the *Times,* was innocent of any evil intent. Certainly he did not intend to kill anyone. He was simply the thunderbolt. If his intent was criminal at all, it was based on the belief that it would do some good for the toiling masses; it was the result of forces in the society that were far more evil than he.

If Jim McNamara were found guilty, Darrow believed, it would send a dishonest message to the world—a message that labor unions were the instruments of violence and that the leaders and agents of capital were the victims, rather than the victimizers, in the world's great struggle. Since the evidence against him had been secured through force, through the work of union-busting detectives, and he had been illegally kidnapped and brought to California to stand trial in a proceeding filled with witnesses who had been coerced and cajoled by the government, an aggressive posture by the defense was more than warranted in the interest of true justice.

It was the kind of argument that stimulated Darrow, combining history and philosophy with an understanding of human nature and the law. One night in early November, soon after the mayoral primary—and just before the capture of Frank Eckhoff—Darrow came to the Field sisters' apartment in a buoyant mood and made a proposition. He announced that he intended to engage Wood in a debate on the topic "What is Truth?" with Sara and Mary as their audience and judge.

But before they had a chance to engage in their great debate, a man arrived in Los Angeles whose idiosyncratic notions of truth and justice would quickly have a profound impact on the trial.

Chapter Eight

LINCOLN STEFFENS

THE TRIAL ATTRACTED A community of America's intellectual elite, including the great muckraker Lincoln Steffens. He came as a reporter—but he soon became a protagonist in a high-stakes political adventure that quickly got out of control. By 1911, Steffens had earned an international reputation for his pioneering articles exposing municipal corruption—many of them collected in his landmark book, *The Shame of the Cities.* Short, dapper, and eccentric, Steffens was a fastidious dresser given to wearing high collars and three-piece suits, and sported a handsome dark mustache and a well-trimmed goatee. "He was a delicately built little man," his friend Mabel Dodge remembered, "with a rapier keen mind. His brown hair came down on his forehead in a little bang, and he had sparkling steel-blue eyes shining through gold-rimmed spectacles, and a sudden lovely smile."

Max Eastman, editor of the radical *Masses,* dismissed Steffens as an intellectual lightweight. "Steffens learned to be happy without hard thinking by developing a kittenish delight in paradox," Eastman said. "If he could find a pause in which to remark that 'the good men are worse than the bad,' or 'enough organization will disorganize anything,' or some such sly jab at rationality, he would feel that he had arrived at the end and summit of the life of reason."

Eastman's colorful description was not entirely fair. Unlike Darrow, who was, if anything, a fatalist, and was content to debunk all ideologies, Steffens desperately wanted to find some solution to the world's problems. When he couldn't decide which formula worked, he acted as a scientist ("a true political scientist," as he called himself), using the world as a laboratory in which to conduct and examine a series of experiments. "My observation was that none of the creed-bound radicals, whether socialists, anarchists, or single taxers, were thinking and seeing," he wrote in his *Autobiography*, yet he "did not want to miss the show. I was afraid to join anything. I proposed to play with all of them and work with some, as I did, experimentally."

Steffens had changed considerably in the decade since his one previous encounter with Darrow, the meeting in the lawyer's Chicago office where Darrow had laughed at the muckraker's naïve view of government and society. While he still had an intense interest in reform, he had grown wary of reformers. Too often he found them puritanical, unrealistic, self-righteous, hypocritical, and ultimately ineffective. People assumed that he was a Good Government reformer, but in fact he had grown to prefer the "bad men," the corporate, political, and labor bosses, who were tough, direct, and effective. For Steffens, who loved nothing so much as the humor of the human condition, this insight was perfectly suited to the well-developed sense of irony that was at the core of his own incessant banter and wit. What was needed, he sometimes said, were "honest crooks."

When he arrived in a town to start exploring a story, he made it his practice to go directly to the big men who ran things—who were the real decision-makers in any community. He had once believed in democracy, arguing that "the people are a jury that can't be fixed, and you only need a majority of them to get the chance to do justice." But his belief in the public's good judgment had been badly shattered by the defeat of most of his friends in the election of 1909. By 1911 he was pretty well convinced that change was more likely to be brought about by "strong men" who really knew how the society worked rather than by weak idealists who had a misguided belief in the virtues of the electorate.

Remarkably, even those who might have had the most to hide from a crusading reporter almost invariably found themselves confiding in him. He was a delightful, nonjudgmental listener. Steffens knew that he had one quality in common with such people: his own weaknesses. He knew that he, like everyone else, was capable of immoral acts; that he, too, could be bribed. In this respect, at least, he had no self-delusions. Or so he thought. In fact, his naïve belief in the honesty of strong men, in the power of a good idea, in the validity of conducting experiments in social reform, and in his own ability to "help bring about an essential change in the American mind," was shortly to prove the greatest self-delusion of all.

❋ ❋ ❋ ❋

When Steffens arrived in Los Angeles on November 6, 1911, he was, in a sense, coming home. He had grown up in Sacramento, where most of his close-knit family still lived, and he dreamed of retiring to California with a stable of old reformers, to "a little heaven for friends." But his plans for the coverage of the McNamara case were not exactly designed to please the friends that he hoped to gather around him in his old age.

Steffens was not, as the defense expected, prepared to advance the line that the McNamaras had been framed. On the contrary, he was convinced that they were guilty—and he intended to reveal his conclusions to the world. While in Paris in July, he had dined with William J. Burns, his old friend from the Oregon timber fraud and San Francisco graft cases. Steffens wanted to hear all about the case in Los Angeles, and Burns tried to persuade Steffens of the McNamaras' guilt. The news probably did not come as a shock to him, since he had long heard rumors that the Structural Iron Workers had been blowing up buildings and bridges as a part of their war with the steel companies.

In London a few weeks later, after a visit to the House of Commons, Steffens took a walk on the Thames river with James Kier Hardie, a staunch Labor member of Parliament. Kier Hardie took it for granted that organized labor was responsible for the *Times* bombing. He suggested that Steffens cover the trial.

"Why don't you as a journalist study out the causes of the rage that is so strong that it makes a union blow up the steel structures they build?" Hardie asked. "See if you can't make your inquiry more interesting than the question whether the dynamiters are guilty of murder. We have got somehow to consider the causes of strikes and crimes and wars—not only the right and wrong of them."

According to his own account, Steffens then sailed for home with the intention of reporting the McNamara trial for a syndicate of newspapers. "Not the trial itself," he explained to his father, "but the cause, consequences, and the significance thereof." He knew that it would be a delicate job. His radical friends in New York all thought that the McNamaras were innocent, believed it as an article of faith, and Darrow, who had summoned him to Los Angeles, wanted Steffens to write stories that would reinforce the case for their acquittal. But Steffens couldn't bring himself to contribute to the sham. It seemed fundamentally wrong to make the rank and file of labor believe what he knew to be a lie, whereas he felt that there was much to be gained by using the case to educate the public about the reasons why some labor leaders were prepared to resort to violence.

"It's a delicate job," Steffens wrote before departing for the coast, "somewhat like handling dynamite. But somebody has to tackle it hard; why shouldn't I be the McNamara of my profession?"

****

On the morning of his arrival in Los Angeles, Steffens went directly from his hotel to the courtroom, where he greeted Darrow, met the gum-chewing Jim McNamara, and observed the trial, which was still in the jury selection stage. A young assistant district attorney named Ray Horton was firing a series of questions at an elderly venireman named George Morton and then claiming that he was hard of hearing and too weak to survive a long trial. The defense was convinced that Morton's only offense was the fact that he subscribed to the Los Angeles *Record* and *Appeal to Reason*. Finally, Darrow rose in anger.

"Old men are not the only garrulous ones," Darrow began, looking straight at the young prosecutor. "Nor will a green old age look so green to my young friend in a few years. This man is challenged simply because he read the *Appeal to Reason,* and yet in that box nearly every man has imbibed the doctrine and faith of the *Los*

Angeles Times on the question of union labor. Morton is the one man here who plainly appears not to be prejudiced against us. But the state wants to get rid of him in order that they may fill the box with men who favor their side. That any man should be discharged because his political views do not suit the district attorney is a denial of the right of fair trial to the defendant."

It was a speech aimed at the public, the press, and perhaps directly at Steffens, summarizing the politics of the trial. It was not, however, either designed for, or likely to be persuasive to, Judge Bordwell. Shortly before the court recessed for the day, the judge announced his decision. He told Darrow that the man's opinions were not at issue.

"Mr. Morton's mental grasp isn't what it once was," the judge said. "He may be excused."

✳ ✳ ✳ ✳

As was his normal reportorial style, Steffens went straight to the city's leaders, the men who knew what was really going on in Los Angeles and could make things happen. He met with business leaders, including Meyer Lissner, the progressive Republican powerhouse who was Governor Hiram Johnson's most important local ally; he met with everyone involved in the prosecution and defense; and he met with the tough labor leaders who, Steffens believed, had probably been responsible for the bombing. The labor leaders might be the hardest to persuade, since his stories could put their lives and their organizations in danger.

The most important labor leader, for Steffens's purposes, was the top representative of the San Francisco unions, tree-trunk-shaped Anton Johannsen, the man widely assumed to have brought Jim McNamara to the Coast. Johannsen had just returned from a two-week trip to the Midwest, where he had been raising funds for the McNamara Defense Committee. Steffens took him out for dinner to discuss his journalistic plan, his intention to write a series of syndicated articles that would tell the truth about labor's role in the dynamitings in order to get the country to face up to the injustices in industrial America.

During the course of a drunken evening, the muckraker "discussed everything and nothing," Johannsen later recalled in amusement, "and came to the same conclusion on both." After a while, Johannsen started holding forth on the problems that working people had faced throughout history, regaling Steffens with stories about the plight of the common laborer. All of a sudden Steffens interrupted with what seemed a bizarre suggestion.

"Jo," he announced, "I wish you would be indicted for murder."

"What the hell for?" asked Johannsen, flabbergasted. He knew perfectly well that the district attorney still wanted to indict him for the *Times* bombing. But Steffens was making a polemical point, not a threat.

"Well, if you were indicted for murder and permitted me to advise the defense, I would engage for your defense one of the best criminal lawyers in the country—not a philosopher or a poet, but a real criminal lawyer. You would plead not guilty, and we would arrange to have the attorneys defend you on the grounds of emotional insanity. Of course, I know you are crazy, but everybody doesn't, and of course you are insane on the labor question. Under that theory, the defense would be permitted to introduce any testimony that would be considered as contributory to your insanity, and in the course of the trial every injustice that labor has suffered under the present social and economic system could be introduced as testimony on the grounds that it had contributed to your insanity. You'd get up there and tell the world how the workers have been mistreated throughout history—about the poor Egyptian slaves that built the pyramids for the goddamn pharaohs. You'd tell about the galley slaves in Rome that were chained to the boats and died young. And you'd tell about the serfs in the Middle Ages who worked for the nobility in Prussia and Russia and the British Isles. You'd tell the world about the blacks who were dragged over here and abused as slaves for hundreds of years—and then you'd talk about the workers who were killed by the steel barons and the police in Pennsylvania at the Homestead Mines and in the Cherry Mine disaster and the Triangle Shirt Factory fire—and Jo, the world couldn't stand it.

"Of course you might get hung," Steffens concluded, laughing with his rigid smile. "But it would make a hell of a fine story."

Given those circumstances, Johannsen had to agree that it would be better to have the reasons for the bombing come out through the press than through his own losing trial.

❋❋❋❋

Gradually, Steffens gained support for his journalistic approach. On Friday, November 17, he wrote a letter to his sister summarizing the results to date. "I want to assume that organized labor has committed the dynamiting and other crimes charged against it, and raise the question: Why? Why should human beings, as they are, feel so hateful that they want to kill? I have been working [to get] the consent of the big labor leaders to my making this assumption in print, and then expressing their defense of crime. They are for it. Darrow, McNutt, Fox, Irwin, Harriman are all for it.

"Today I put it up to J. J. McNamara. His eyes flashed; he is willing, but I told him not to consent till he had thought it over. It might put his life in jeopardy, for I include the *Times* building explosion in my list."

Meanwhile, Steffens made plans to take Darrow away for the weekend to E. W. Scripps's huge ranch, where they could relax and discuss literature, philosophy, journalism, and the trial with a wise old observer whom they both respected and loved. That trip began the most fateful two weeks in Darrow's life.

Sunday, November 19, 1911

From his two-thousand-acre ranch just north of San Diego, curmudgeonly newspaper publisher E. W. Scripps had been watching the trial with more than casual interest. He had been fairly certain from the outset that the McNamaras were guilty—or, to use a judgment-free phrase, were responsible for the bombing. After all, his ace reporter in Chicago had informed him that Darrow himself thought the men were guilty and would be hanged. But like Steffens, Scripps tended to believe that the act was justified and should be publicly admitted and debated.

Not quite in retirement, Scripps spent his days at Miramar, a ranch in the foothills of La Jolla, living in a modern Spanish house built around a large patio. He read widely, sponsored pioneering scientific research at a nearby biological station, and shot off tough-minded, radical, and often eccentric letters to the field lieutenants who were running his wire service, the United Press, as well his powerful chain of working-class newspapers, including the Los Angeles *Record*. He kept in touch with events through the papers, his correspondents, the long-distance telephone, and a succession of visitors who made the easy pilgrimage to his ranch.

His visitors on Sunday, November 19, were the "rather odd" duo of Darrow and Steffens, down for a day of relaxation and serious talk with the wise "old crank." Scripps greeted them at the Linda Vista station as they got off the Santa Fe train. Tall, lanky, blotchy-faced, with a cast in one eye and a full copper-colored beard that was slowly turning to gray, he was, as usual, wearing a woolen vest, a pair of soiled trousers that were stuffed loosely into his big black leather boots, and a sporty cap designed to prevent him from catching cold. Driving his big Packard too fast along the winding, sage-brush-lined trail, he took his guests back to his estate, where they spent the day racing cars on the publisher's private speedway, visiting Professor W. E. Ritter at the biological laboratory that Scripps was building, and sitting in his study, discussing everything from socialism to anarchism, as Scripps smoked an endless chain of mild, made-to-order Key West cigars, letting the ashes fall carelessly on his vest.

Observing his guests closely, Scripps found it "rather odd to see the big, hulky, rough lawyer, and the dapper little litterateur, together in the same room, and discussing the same subjects. Steffens can't help but be finicky; alike in his ideas and his person," whereas Darrow "is a great big brute of a man, with every fiber coarse, but sturdy. Even his sentiment is elephantine." Darrow was genuinely well read, intellectually curious, clear thinking, and a man of "physical and moral courage." "Everything about Darrow suggests a cynic," Scripps observed. "Everything but one thing, and that is—an entire lack of real cynicism."

Sitting in Scripps's spacious study, the men talked about starting a weekly magazine with Darrow as co-owner and editor; they discussed the upcoming Los Angeles election, which they all expected Job Harriman to win; they took a vote and unanimously decided that they were not Socialists, but would all like to see Socialist candidates elected at all levels. At last, after hours of talk, they turned to the McNamara trial.

Sadly, Darrow began to muse about the hopelessness of both cases. J.J. still had a chance, but things were beginning to look bleak now that the prosecution had its hands on Frank Eckhoff and on the evidence seized in Indianapolis. Worse, Darrow said, the case against Jim is a "dead cinch." He felt like a doctor who has finally decided that his patient's disease is incurable—and fatal. Those interested in Jim's case, Darrow concluded, should proceed on the assumption that "the boy will be hanged."

At least he needn't die in vain, Steffens offered. His case could be used to educate the public about the causes of the war between capital and labor and about the need to find some better solution, a nonviolent common ground.

That wasn't much solace to Darrow. "I can't stand to have a man I'm defending be hanged," Darrow said. The boy didn't intend to kill anyone. It never occurred to him that the dynamite would ignite those cans of ink in the alleyway. "I just can't stand it," he repeated.

Scripps, who usually dominated the discussions in his study, had been waiting for the right moment to tell Darrow about his theory of belligerent rights. He was, he said, pretty well convinced that the men should be treated as wartime prisoners, combatants in the war between capital and labor. If somehow that war could be settled, then the two brothers could be set free—pardoned or given amnesty—with the rights of belligerents.

Scripps had written something that he wanted to share with them. Brushing the ashes off of his vest, he got up from his swivel chair and walked over to an alcove where he removed a manuscript from a locked black steel box. It was his disquisition on "Belligerent Rights." Scripps asked Darrow to read it out loud.

For the next fifteen minutes the group sat enraptured as the words were brought to life. "Most of us who have even the most general knowledge of ordinary events have a pretty well defined idea of what the rights of belligerents are, though it may be difficult for others as it is for myself to define the meaning of the term." With his deep, warm reading voice, Darrow brought out the texture and passion in Scripps's words. "A belligerent is a man who is carrying on any sort of warfare against any other man or number of men, whether he is acting alone, as a member of a small band, or in the unit of a great national army. . . . There have been cases where the United States government has recognized revolution and the belligerent rights of revolutionists. . . .

"Today in nearly all civilized countries there is going on to a greater or lesser extent a revolutionary warfare between the classes. In the United States this warfare has already proceeded to such an extent that the insurgent revolutionists are known to have destroyed the lives of many individuals and to have destroyed many millions of dollars worth of property. Let us take the case of McNamara, secretary of the Structural Iron Workers' Union. For the purpose of this disquisition, let us admit that he is guilty—that he did plan the explosion and directed it, and paid for it. This explosion caused the death of twenty or more innocent men. These men that were killed should be considered what they really were—soldiers enlisted under a capitalist employer whose main purpose in life was warfare against the unions.

"If belligerent rights were accorded to the two parties in this war, then McNamara was guilty of no greater offense than would be the officer of any band, large or small, of soldiers who ordered his men to fire upon an enemy and killed a great number of them. . . . Is he a martyr or a patriot? . . .

"It is customary even for the most liberal of newspapers, clergy, unions and private citizens to publicly deprecate all sorts of violence in labor troubles. . . . [But] if the leading citizenry should adopt another course and consider that in the main the employers and capitalists fully merit all that they suffer as a result of their acts of oppression and warfare against labor, it is highly probable that the government would soon take notice of such public opinion, and that . . . capitalists and employers generally would seek for, and find, ways of peaceful cooperation with the men who are or should be their partners—the workingmen under their direction. . . ."

For all of his world-weariness, Darrow was moved. "It's a very sensible article," Darrow said after finishing. "I just wish that the people of Los Angeles would see it that way."

"What do you mean?" Steffens asked.

"I just wish that they would see that it's in the best interest of the community to settle this case without shedding any human blood," Darrow said. "But they never will."

Despite Darrow's skepticism, the discussion exhilarated Steffens. Rather than simply educating the public by writing a story, perhaps he could do so by bringing the parties together to settle their differences in the context of one of the greatest capital-labor battles in history.

Monday, November 20, 1911

After riding the midnight train back to Los Angeles, Steffens and Darrow grabbed an early breakfast at a hotel near the train depot. They sat for a while in silence, cold, tired, and uncomfortable from the long night in a sleeping car. Finally Steffens spoke.

"Darrow, you were talking yesterday about a settlement of the case," Steffens began, lighting up a cigarette. "Did you really mean it?"

"Yes. I'd like to settle it," Darrow replied vaguely, "but it's impossible, of course."

"But why not try it?" Steffens persisted.

To Darrow, Steffens must have seemed the same woolly headed reformer that he had laughed at in Chicago a decade earlier and had ridiculed as "the man who believes in honesty." Still emotional, still feeling the pain of a likely hanging for his client, he tried to explain the facts of life without being patronizing. The idea of a settlement was premised on the notion that J.J. would be set free. Any other solution, any agreement that called for a guilty plea by J.J., would be rejected by the forces of labor who had so much invested in his innocence. They might, of course, agree to let Jim take the rap if J.J. could be released, since they had never much cared about Jim. But Fredericks, the straight-laced district attorney, was not likely to let J.J. off the hook; nor would such a compromise sit well with the businessmen of Los Angeles or the members of the National Erectors' Association.

But Steffens wouldn't let go. Exhausted by his friend's persistence,

Darrow at last consented to let him try to arrange a settlement that would result in all charges being dropped against J. J. McNamara. But he added several caveats. First, he would not agree to let Jim be hanged. Second, the proposition would have to be endorsed by the owners of the *Times,* since it was their building that had been destroyed. Finally, Steffens would have to make it clear that he was acting as an independent agent and that the settlement proposal did not come from anybody connected with the defense. Otherwise, people might think that Darrow was admitting his clients' guilt. Indeed, they would not even tell the McNamara brothers about Steffens's initiative.

According to his account of the breakfast, Steffens took that suggestion one step farther. He told Darrow to repudiate him, even denounce him, if Steffens's efforts proved an embarrassment.

Would Steffens stand for that? Darrow asked. He'd have to do it pretty fiercely.

No problem, Steffens said. He would be willing to lie in order to protect Darrow and his clients. If asked, he would steadfastly deny that the matter had ever been discussed with the defense.

※ ※ ※ ※

When Darrow arrived in court from the train station that morning, a friendly new face was in the room. Erskine Wood had arrived in town to observe, to help Darrow, and to spend a romantic week with Sara. Despite their philosophical differences, the two old lawyer-philosophers were happy to be together. Darrow suggested that he, Wood, and the Field sisters dine with Lincoln Steffens the following night, and Wood cheerfully agreed. When Wood expressed an interest in meeting his famous client, Darrow scribbled a warm note to J.J., giving Wood access to the prison.

"Dear Joe," he wrote on a long yellow sheet. "This will introduce Mr. CES Wood of Portland, Oregon. Mr. Wood is an old friend of mine and friend of yours and friend of everybody's. You can talk with him in perfect confidence."

After moving around the room, chatting with the other lawyers and a few reporters, Wood joined Sara and Mary in the press section. With green pen in hand, he drew a quick sketch of one of the jurors to send off to Sara's small children in Portland. The man he chose to draw had a classic face of sturdy character and experience. It was the old carpenter, Robert Bain. The first man approved for the jury. The first man bribed by the defense.

As Wood drew his sketch, Sara studied Bain, too. She decided that he had "the only face in the jury box that would appeal to a sculptor, seamed with expressive lines, strong and rugged with a firmness that tends just a bit to hardness." While studying the old carpenter, she noticed something unusual. She saw him throw a kiss to his wife, who that morning had sent him a buttonhole bouquet. And she saw Dora Bain throw a little kiss back.

"Romance in a murder trial," Sara jotted in her notebook—not suspecting just how much a part of the trial's intrigue the Bains had become.

❋ ❋ ❋

That same morning, Steffens went to see his best business-world contact, Meyer Lissner, a sometime entrepreneur, sometime lawyer, whom Steffens called "a sort of political boss of the reformers." As one of the organizers of the Good Government movement in California, Lissner gained statewide power in 1910 when the progressives took control of the California Republican Party and installed him as chairman of the party's State Central Committee. With Hiram Johnson's stunning victory in the fall gubernatorial election, Lissner became the governor's principal clearinghouse for political appointments.

During the fall of 1911, Lissner's major preoccupation was the defeat of Job Harriman. Originally, he had planned to stay out of the mayoral election, but Harriman's showing on October 31 changed all that. Like the rest of the city's business elite, Lissner was desperately concerned that a Harriman victory would turn Los Angeles into a San Francisco–like closed-shop town. The result, he felt, would be devastating for business. Indeed, he told Governor Johnson that he was ready to let the entire reform movement go down the drain "rather than let Los Angeles be thrown under the sort of tyrannical domination of labor unionism that exists in San Francisco." Coaxed on by a broad coalition that ranged from Governor Johnson to

General Otis, Lissner agreed to take charge of the anti-Harriman forces during the five-week runoff. So Lissner had his own agenda when he received Lincoln Steffens at his office on that lovely mid-November morning.

Steffens began by reminding Lissner that the San Francisco graft trials had left deep class wounds that continued to haunt the city; he described the conditions he had witnessed in Europe, where class struggle had become the central fact of political life. A bitter trial, he said, would have the same effect in Los Angeles. The business leaders might think that they wanted blood, but in the end the brutal fight would damage them even more than it would hurt labor.

"Anyway," Steffens said, "labor is licked here. What are you going to do about it. Keep fighting? What you need in Los Angeles is peace, a peaceful climate in which to get on with your lives and with your work. And the only way you will get peace will come from the Golden Rule, and that applies to the McNamara case." Steffens then proposed that the "big men" of the city could start with an act of generosity toward labor, by agreeing to set J.J. free and offering to start meeting with labor leaders to solve the city's problems. In return, Jim would plead guilty, accepting any punishment other than death.

Lissner paid close attention. No doubt Steffens's words appealed to the idealist in him, but it had far more effect on the pragmatic politician. To a man whose first priority was to win the upcoming election, a guilty plea must have sounded like political manna from heaven. If a deal could be concluded before the December 5 runoff, it would humiliate Job Harriman and ensure victory for George Alexander. Lissner agreed to help.

Then, remembering Darrow's instruction, Steffens said that it was essential to get the owners of the *Times* to back any settlement. Lissner thought it over for a moment and concluded that the best man to talk with *Times* president Harry Chandler would be their mutual friend Tom Gibbon. A prominent lawyer, Harbor Commission member, and former newspaper editor, Thomas E. Gibbon was one of the few men who moved comfortably between the world of the reformers and the world of the Otises and Chandlers.

Gibbon came over to Lissner's office at about noon. After expressing some initial opposition, he saw the benefits of a quick guilty plea. He agreed to take the proposition to Harry Chandler, but said that he would have to understand exactly what kind of settlement they intended to propose. Steffens prepared the following memo, which Lissner's secretary then typed in triplicate.

"Party on trial"—that is, James B. McNamara—"to plead guilty and receive such sentence as the court might administer (except capital punishment) all other prosecutions in connection with the affair to be dropped."

Later that afternoon, Gibbon reported that Chandler was willing to support the proposed settlement. For Steffens, who wanted to try out his theory of Christian mercy on a grand scale, it was a dream come true. The big men of the community seemed to understand that they could help to bring about a better, more harmonious day. Evidently it did not occur to him that some of the players might also have another reason for cooperating.

※ ※ ※ ※

Lissner and Steffens were under the impression that Harry Chandler intended to call the district attorney directly. They were wrong. Like Darrow, Harry Chandler wanted plausible deniability. He wanted the settlement effort to succeed, but he did not want to put his fingerprints on the plan.

Instead of calling District Attorney Fredericks, Harry Chandler called his friend Otto F. Brant. Brant was another of the city's big men, the general manager and principal owner of the Title Insurance and Trust Company. This was not the first time that the owners of the *Times* had asked Brant to serve in a confidential capacity. Seven years earlier, he had acted as the front man for General Otis's secret purchase of the Los Angeles *Herald.*

Harry Chandler, General Otis, and Otto Brant all had a huge financial stake in the outcome of the election. They were major investors in the Los Angeles Suburban Home Company, which had recently gained control of some 47,500 acres of land in the arid San Fernando Valley, just north of the city of Los Angeles. On March 14, 1911, the company filed a subdivision map of their plan to build the largest land development in Los Angeles history.

Opposition to the Home Company's proposal was a centerpiece of Job Harriman's heated campaign for mayor. The land was virtually worthless so long as the area remained arid, but it would become enormously valuable if supplied with water, particularly if the water was inexpensive. The Suburban Home Company was expecting to gain cheap and plentiful water from the Los Angeles Aqueduct, a 230-mile, $23-million project nearing completion, which would carry huge amounts of water to Los Angeles from the Owens Valley. The aqueduct, financed with public funds, was certain to produce more water than the city needed. The issue was: Who would be allowed to use the surplus water?

The Socialists charged that the aqueduct had been built with public funds to provide surplus water for private projects—and that such water would be sold to Chandler, Otis, Brant, et al, at a sharply reduced price. In a major campaign flyer called "The Aqueduct Conspiracy," Harriman hurled a direct challenge at Mayor Alexander. "Mr. Alexander," Harriman asked, "is it not a fact that secret plans for handing the aqueduct water over to the land barons were proposed and agreed on by your officials in April 1911 at a private luncheon at the ranch-house of the Mission Land Company?" Harriman promised that a Socialist administration would revoke such private deals. He would insist on charging fair commercial prices for publicly financed water, or he would ask that it be used exclusively for public purposes.

In an effort to rebut charges of a secret deal, Mayor Alexander repeatedly stated that "not a drop of aqueduct water can be alienated by the city without a two-thirds vote of the people." That assertion was powerfully and effectively backed by the Public Service Commission. On November 18, 1911, the commission told the *Times* that any decisions of the city "must be submitted to a vote of the people." That statement was a setback for the Socialists.

When Harry Chandler called him on November 21, Otto Brant was very much concerned about the outcome of the election. The financial interests at stake were underlined in a message that Brant received that same day from Moses Sherman, one of the other investors in the Suburban Home Company. In a note riddled with quotation marks and parenthetical phrases, Sherman boasted that the Public Service Commission's statement "will take the stuffing out of the 'enemy' (no more 'talk' that General Otis 'owns the valley' and the twenty three millions of Aqueduct money was spent, especially for him.) Now, if we can beat this Socialist (Labor Union) 'gang' on December 5th, I hope we can do some business (make headway)."

Brant was delighted to make the call to District Attorney Fredericks. If they could arrange for Jim McNamara to plead guilty, they could be certain of beating the "Socialist (Labor Union) 'gang' " in the election and be assured of doing some business (making headway). But they had to work quickly. To influence the electorate, the settlement would have to be announced within ten days—by Friday, December 1, at the latest.

❋ ❋ ❋ ❋

It is unclear whether Steffens fully understood the political implications of the deal that he was seeking, but Darrow did. Darrow knew that the driving concern for the business leaders was the need to defeat Harriman at the polls. As he explained later, "I was aware that one of the strongest motives that would appeal to those concerned with the prosecution was the contest for Mayor then going on in Los Angeles. . . . Any one could easily see that a plea of guilty would lessen the popularity of the Socialist ticket and make sure the election of the regular Republican."

It was clear, he added, that "if they did not plead before the election we could never get the district attorney to accept the plea."

Absent a guilty plea, the mayor's race was too close to call. Some Progressive Republican leaders were confident of victory, sharing the view of Hiram Johnson, who was telling friends with absolute certainty that "Alexander is going to win in December." But Job Harriman was equally confident, privately claiming that "I do not think it is possible for them to defeat us at the polls." J. J. McNamara was receiving similar encouraging reports, as was Fremont Older. Over the weekend, Scripps, Steffens, and Darrow all had expressed confidence that Harriman would prevail. Too much was at stake for Chandler and Brant to leave the results to chance.

Aware that time was of the essence, Brant immediately called Fredericks and arranged to meet him the following day.

Wednesday, November 22, 1911

On Wednesday, Fredericks came to Brant's office at the Title Insurance and Trust Company. Without mentioning Chandler by name, Brant explained that some leading citizens had asked him to present the arguments for ending the McNamara cases, promising that Jim would plead guilty if the state would agree to release his older brother. Captain Fredericks asked which leading citizens he was representing, but as Chandler had requested, Brant said that he would rather not say.

Had Brant discussed the proposal with Darrow? Fredericks asked.

No, said Brant. In fact, his contact was at least three persons removed.

Well, if you want to pursue it further, Fredericks suggested, come back to me with a written statement saying precisely what Darrow is prepared to do.

❀ ❀ ❀ ❀

Oblivious to events in Los Angeles, William J. Burns raised the temperature of the dispute with a speech in New Orleans that evening. Always a self-promoter, he was acting as a free-lancer now, throwing his own personal jabs; but as the man who had tracked down the defendants, his words were highly publicized. In a bitter attack on Samuel Gompers and Eugene Debs, Burns claimed that the defense had collected more than one million dollars, much of which would be used for illegal purposes. "I tell you they have the money and they have endeavored to buy our witnesses. They have offered some of the prosecution witnesses their own price. And when these witnesses refused to accept the offers, they have been threatened with death. We have found it necessary, in fact, to hide some of our witnesses."

From Atlanta, where he was presiding at the AFL's annual meeting, Gompers shot back an equally spirited response. The union, he said, refuses to believe evidence "furnished by liars, perjurers, kidnappers, thieves and conspirators" like Burns and his employees.

Thursday, November 23, 1911

Darrow desperately wanted the ear of someone wise and close to labor, someone whom he and Steffens could trust to be discreet and supportive; someone like Fremont Older, the compassionate and radical editor of the San Francisco *Bulletin*. On Wednesday morning, Darrow and Steffens sent an urgent wire to Older in San Francisco.

"Can you get to an important conference at Hotel Alexandria here tomorrow?" they asked.

Older took the night train to Los Angeles, where he met Steffens at the Alexandria Hotel early Thursday morning. The two journalists—who had been close friends since their work together on the San Francisco graft trials—spent the morning together at the hotel. Then they walked five blocks to the defense committee's offices in the Higgins Building, where they waited for Darrow to return from court.

In his usual excited and fast-paced manner, Steffens provided Older with an elaborate and euphoric description of his grand scheme and recounted his meetings with the leaders of the business community. He proudly announced that everyone seemed to be agreed on a plan that would call for J.J. to be released in return for a guilty plea by Jim. The younger brother would be sentenced to life in prison, but would not be hanged. Sitting in Darrow's office, he showed Older the typed statement that he and Lissner had agreed upon, and told Older that Darrow had signed off on it as well. Now they wanted Older to help them decide how to explain the plan to labor.

Obviously there would be deep resentment by working men who had put their faith in Jim's innocence, Older said. But his paper would do its best to educate its readers.

As they were meeting that morning, however, a hitch was developing down at the courthouse. During a break in the trial, Fredericks approached Darrow.

"What is this gink Steffens trying to do?" he asked.

"I guess you know as much about it as I do," Darrow answered with a smile. "This fellow would plead guilty, if the other fellow could be turned loose," he said, pointing to Jim McNamara. Fredericks was neither amused nor interested. He told Darrow that he would never agree to a plan that did not include some punishment for J.J. as well.

When Darrow returned to his office he was out of sorts. He was happy to see Older, but had lost any hope of achieving a settlement. Over lunch at Levy's restaurant, the men decided that Steffens should place another call to Lissner to try to get matters back on track.

That afternoon, while Darrow was in court, Steffens met with Lissner, Gibbon, and Chandler. They all seemed to feel that Chandler was the key. As the most aggrieved party, as well as a staunch Fredericks supporter, he might be able to persuade the district attorney to go along with the agreement. Chandler agreed to make another overture to Fredericks that afternoon to try to persuade him to drop all charges against the older brother. Once again, however, he failed to inform Steffens that all contacts with Fredericks would be handled by Brant, without using his name. As a result, Brant's efforts were certain to carry less weight with the district attorney.

Understandably, Steffens brimmed over with enthusiasm that evening when he made his report to Darrow and Older at an early dinner. But his enthusiasm was misplaced.

✻✻✻✻

In a set of negotiations being conducted through intermediaries—some of whom are three steps removed from the principals—misunderstandings are sure to occur. Perhaps it was such a misunderstanding that led the businessmen to believe that there were two ways to make the deal acceptable: either J.J. could be given some jail time, or Jim could be hanged. With the understanding that the defense would never agree to let J.J. be punished, Brant offered a new proposal to Fredericks when the two men met late that afternoon.

As requested by Fredericks in their first meeting, Brant gave Fredericks a document that, he said, Darrow had agreed to support. It was the typewritten note prepared by Steffens in Lissner's office. It stated, "The party on trial to plead guilty and receive such sentence as the court may administer (except capital punishment). All other prosecutions in connection with the affair to be dropped." But the words had been edited. A pencil line had been drawn through the words "except capital punishment." The deletion had been made with the agreement of the defense, Brant claimed, because Fredericks had said that he would not agree to the earlier offer.

Fredericks was indignant. He didn't care about hanging Jim. What he cared about was convicting both men. He told Brant that he would never allow J.J. to escape without punishment.

Brant said that he would relay that message to his intermediaries, but he was certain that the negotiations were at an end. It was his understanding that Darrow absolutely insisted on securing J.J.'s freedom as part of any settlement.

That evening, Chandler told Steffens—and Steffens told Darrow—that Fredericks would not agree to any settlement that did not include jail time for J.J.

❀ ❀ ❀ ❀

The negotiations were becoming too delicate for Darrow to handle alone. It had been helpful to talk with Older, but any settlement would have an impact on all of organized labor. Somehow, he would have to get their blessing.

Unfortunately, there was no one in California to speak for labor. The major leaders—including Johannsen, Tvietmoe, and George Gunrey of the International Molders' Union—had all gone to Atlanta for the AFL's annual meeting. One of the major topics at the meeting was the McNamara trials—the need for labor to remain solid, the threat that Burns and the government represented, the need to find new ways to finance the huge defense fund. Echoing the words used by Gompers a day earlier, the convention adopted a resolution calling for an enlarged defense fund to protect the McNamaras from evidence "furnished by liars, perjurers, kidnappers, thieves and conspirators."

That night Darrow sent a wire to Sam Gompers in Atlanta. "Have Tvietmoe, Nockles, Fitzpatrick or Johannsen come first train. Bring Gunrey if possible. Wire train route."

Gompers paid little attention to the wire. Overwhelmed by the work of the convention, and immunized to the consistently panicky tone of his lawyer's messages, Gompers simply gave the telegram to Tvietmoe and asked him to handle it. Since the wire had mentioned Nockles, who was in Chicago, Tvietmoe contacted Nockles and asked him to catch a train to the West Coast. The men in Atlanta thought no more about it.

Friday, November 24, 1911

Captain Fredericks felt obliged to do some checking of his own. Since some of the investigation had been financed by the National Erectors' Association, and it was their members who had been the target of the McNamaras' major dynamiting efforts, he sent a telegram to NEA commissioner Walter Drew. He reported that Jim "is willing to plead guilty and take the limit if action is dismissed against J.J." Fredericks said that he was "personally opposed to the proposition" since he had strong cases against both men.

Interestingly, Drew was more conciliatory. He didn't care if J.J. spent any time in jail, or even pleaded guilty. He did, however, think it essential that J.J. admit some guilt and agree to help convict the other members of the union's executive board.

"I hardly believe that J.J. intended to kill twenty-one people," he said. "I would personally be willing to see the murder case dismissed on condition of full confession and on condition of J.J.'s turning state's evidence in connection with the regular dynamiting cases."

Drew, however, doubted that Darrow would go along with any such arrangement, even one that released J.J. without making him serve any jail time. Darrow's only real concern, he believed, was in protecting the Iron Workers and the AFL. "I believe that attorneys for the defense are more dominated by the suggestion and the interest of certain Labor Organizations than they are by the interest or lives of the individual defendants, and that either or both of these men will be sacrificed if it can be done in a way to protect these Organizations."

✻ ✻ ✻ ✻

Fredericks also had some information that he was holding close to the vest. He knew about the bribery of Robert Bain. With Bain holding out for an acquittal, there would be a hung jury and the case would have to be tried again.

Fredericks had a plan. It was possible, under California law, to have as many as fourteen jurors accepted for service; the extra men would serve as alternates in case one or two of the regular jurors were somehow incapacitated during or prior to trial. No prosecutor, however, had ever taken advantage of that law.

On Friday, Fredericks announced that he would ask the court to impanel the extra jurors. The defense objected, arguing that such a move would violate the federal constitution. But Judge Bordwell indicated that he would rule favorably on the motion. After that, Fredericks thought he would only have to sit and wait until all fourteen men had been accepted by both sides. Then he would reveal that Bain had accepted a bribe.

The defense would be stunned, the publicity would be devastating for labor, and the district attorney would be left with at least twelve reliable jurors.

❋ ❋ ❋ ❋

Fredericks had one other bit of information that would prove to be even more important and dangerous for Darrow. He knew that the defense team, through Bert Franklin, had approached a second potential juror by the name of George Lockwood. The approach had been made by Bert Franklin.

This time, Franklin chose the wrong man. Now semiretired and living on a small alfalfa ranch near Covina, George Lockwood had worked with Franklin in the Los Angeles County sheriff's office. Though he had known Franklin for years, he was outraged and insulted by the suggestion that he take a bribe. On November 14, unknown to Franklin, he reported the conversation to Fredericks.

The district attorney told Lockwood to sit tight. Sooner or later, his name would be drawn from the wheel. When it was, Bert Franklin was certain to come calling again. And the district attorney would be prepared with a devastating trap.

Saturday, November 25, 1911

The court session on Saturday morning was cut short at a few minutes past nine because of the death of the brother of one of the jurors. LeCompte Davis took the opportunity to hurry to the side of his partner, Jud Rush, who had been stricken with apoplexy in the course of another trial. It seemed that the case was jinxed.

"I hope nothing happens to James B. McNamara," Darrow commented dryly when he arrived in court and learned of the illnesses. In fact, Jim was not looking at all well. The *Times* claimed that several physicians were predicting that he would collapse.

The clerk was scheduled to draw a new venire of fifty additional men later that morning. Though he was suffering from a cold himself, Darrow remained in the courthouse throughout the first part of the day, waiting to see what names were on the new list. To pass the time, Darrow chatted with some of his favorite reporters. Shortly before noon, the clerk entered the courtroom and went through the elaborate ritual of shaking the jury box and withdrawing fifty slips of paper—the names of the men who would be on the next venire.

One of the names he drew was George Lockwood.

Sunday–Monday, November 26–27, 1911

As District Attorney Fredericks had predicted, Bert Franklin did not wait long to visit Lockwood. He went out to his ranch early on Sunday afternoon. Lockwood met his visitor on the front lawn and walked him around the house, out to the barn. There was a hot, fierce Santa Ana wind.

"Have you been served yet?" Franklin asked.

No, he hadn't.

"Well, your name was drawn yesterday and you will be served between now and tomorrow morning. George, there is four thousand dollars in it for you, and I want you to have it." He said that he would give Lockwood five hundred dollars for entering into the arrangement and another thirty-five hundred if he was chosen for the jury and voted for acquittal.

Lockwood shouted, trying to make himself heard above the wind. "If I go into this, I don't want no mistake about the money. I want to be sure of it."

"There isn't a shadow of a doubt but what you'll get it," Franklin assured him. He suggested that they step into the barn where they would be more comfortable.

"The five hundred dollar proposition seems straight enough," Lockwood said once they were inside. "But this thirty-five hundred dollars. I can't see how I could be at all sure that it would be paid over after the matter was accomplished." This was the strategy that had been proposed by Detective Sam Browne of the district attorney's office. It seemed to be working perfectly.

"I'll tell you what I'll do," Franklin said. "I'll give the money to Captain White who will hold it for us until the case is over." Captain White was a mutual friend who had been the county jailer during the years when Franklin and Lockwood worked for the county sheriff. Lockwood agreed that White was a perfect man to hold the balance of the funds.

They made an arrangement to meet at the ranch the following evening. Franklin said he would bring "the Big One" with him. He was referring to Captain White, but Lockwood thought he meant Darrow himself. When Franklin appeared at the ranch on Monday evening, neither man was with him, nor did he have the money. He said that it would take him another day to get the cash.

Since Lockwood was scheduled to appear in court the next morning at nine-thirty A.M., they agreed to meet in downtown Los Angeles. The rendezvous was scheduled for nine A.M. Tuesday at the corner of Third and Los Angeles streets.

On Sunday afternoon, while Bert Franklin was meeting with George Lockwood at the ranch, Clarence Darrow was holding separate meetings with his clients at the city jail. While waiting for the labor leaders to arrive from Atlanta, he wanted to find out just how far he could go in trying to negotiate a plea bargain.

The meetings took place in a small room at the end of a dimly lit corridor. The room had a window, chairs, a table covered by a white towel, and a bouquet of flowers that had been sent to J.J. by an admirer. With Darrow was Cyrus McNutt, the elderly former Indiana judge.

First they met with Jim—pale, nervous, gum-chewing, but, in his own way, heroic. His first preference, Jim said, was to go forward with the trial. Even if the lawyers couldn't prove his innocence, he felt that the trial would serve an important purpose by dramatizing the issues in the great battle between capital and labor. No doubt his views had been influenced by the meetings with Steffens. While proving that he had never intended to kill anyone, Jim was confident that Darrow could demonstrate that his acts had been justified and that they paled by comparison with the daily cruelty of the leaders of industry. He was prepared, even anxious, to die a martyr. But Jim said that he would plead guilty—and agree to take a life sentence— if by doing so he could be of greater use to labor and if his guilty plea would gain freedom for his brother and the others who were accused as his associates and accomplices.

On one point, however, he was adamant. He would not plead guilty unless his brother was set free as part of the bargain. It was the first of several statements by Jim that showed the depth of his convictions and the strength of his personal and political loyalties.

Then the lawyers met with J.J.—strong, fresh, and bright as the day he was arrested, dressed in gray prison garb that dramatically highlighted the premature gray of his hair. His sentiments were as noble as his brother's. He, too, was prepared to plead guilty, he said, and to accept a term of up to ten years in prison, if it would save his brother's life. Though it might ruin his career as a labor leader, and he would be condemned by some of his colleagues, his brother's life was worth the sacrifice.

It was the gift of the Magi. Each brother was willing to give up something dear to him in order to help the other. But the gifts were irreconcilable, since Jim would never plead guilty unless his brother was released.

Never, that is, until the defense was irretrievably shattered by events on the following Tuesday morning.

Chapter Nine

THE STREETCORNER
BRIBE

Tuesday, November 28, 1911

K NOWING NOTHING OF THE efforts to settle the case, Bert Franklin continued with his attempt to find additional jurors who would promise to vote for acquittal. On Tuesday morning, George Lockwood took a streetcar into town and got off at the Fifth Street stop. Since he was a bit early—it was only eight-thirty and the rendezvous was set for nine—Lockwood bought a few items in the Owl Drugstore, then walked aimlessly for a quarter of an hour, killing time. At about nine, he arrived at the busy intersection of Los Angeles and Third Street. There was no sign of Franklin, who had gone into a nearby saloon to have a shot of whisky and use the men's room. But Lockwood immediately saw Captain White, the man designated to hold the bribe money, waiting on the street corner.

"Good morning, Cap, What's new?" Lockwood asked.

"Nothing," said the 250-pound former jailer, who now operated a jewelry store on North Broadway. "Except a mutual friend of ours entrusted me with some money to be paid to you on certain conditions." White showed him a small roll of bills. "Are you ready to receive it?"

Although the traffic made them relatively inconspicuous, Lockwood knew that there were as many as six city detectives watching the scene. Some were from the police department, others from the district attorney's office. He also knew that he had to delay the transaction until Franklin arrived. "How much money," he inquired, "and what are the conditions?"

"I am to hand you five hundred dollars, and to hold three thousand for you until the jury renders a verdict of not guilty or the jury is hung in the McNamara case."

"It don't go," Lockwood protested. "There was to be thirty-five hundred held, not three thousand." He looked up and down the street. "Where's Franklin?"

"He just went away from here," White said.

Lockwood had to continue to delay. "Well it don't go at all. There was to be four thousand dollars in this roll." He tapped on the bills that White was holding in his hand.

"Well maybe there is," White said. "I haven't examined it very carefully. I'll just walk up the street a bit and have a look." He walked a few steps away and took a closer look at the bills that he had been given by Franklin. There were six yellow $500 bills and one $1,000 bill. He came back a minute later and announced that there was, in fact, $4,000 in the roll.

Lockwood took a $500 bill from Captain White. Still trying to buy time until Franklin arrived, he protested that the bill was too large to dispose of quietly. "It should have been in twos and fives," he said.

As Lockwood was talking, a man on a motorcycle pulled up next to the curb, near where they were standing. Lockwood recognized him as a detective named Allison.

A moment later, Franklin emerged from the saloon and walked toward them. "Bert, I'm afraid something is wrong," Lockwood said when Franklin reached them. "After you left last night, my wife and I both thought we heard somebody out there at the place."

"Are you giving me the straight goods?" Franklin asked. He took a quick look up and down the street. At the far end of the block, near Los Angeles Street, he saw Detective George Home of the Los Angeles police department. "Don't look around; don't look around,"

Franklin shouted at Lockwood. "The sons of bitches. Let's get out of here." They started walking north on Third Street, away from Detective Home.

As they approached the corner of Third and Main they saw someone crossing the busy intersection in their direction, hurrying past the pedestrians, automobiles, and teams of buggies, horses, and wagons on the congested street.

It was Clarence Darrow.

What was Darrow doing there? Why had he come to the scene of the bribe? It was a question that would linger for eighty years.

Seeing his employer approach, Franklin stopped dead in his tracks. "Wait a minute," he said to Lockwood. "I want to speak to this man."

But before Franklin and Darrow could exchange a word, Detective Sam Browne, who had been watching the scene from a perch in the hallway of a nearby building, rushed to where the men were standing, put his hands between them, and placed Bert Franklin under arrest.

✳ ✳ ✳ ✳

The arrest was front-page news across the country. JURY BRIBERY IS CHARGED IN MCNAMARA TRIAL. A somewhat sensational account in *The New York Times* began with a statement alleged to have been made by Franklin: "I have fixed two members of the permanent jury in this trial and I am going to get a couple more before I am through."

Most of the story quoted Detective Sam Browne who said that "it was hard to arrest Bert Franklin since he has been a personal friend of mine for years and my daughter was soon to have attended his daughter's wedding." Nevertheless, in language that sounded like it came from the *National Police Gazette,* Browne related that after watching the bribe take place, Detective Home "thrust his automatic pistol against the body of Franklin, and I did the same with White. 'Keep your hands in your pockets,' I ordered them and marched them that way to the office of Mr. Fredericks," where White and Lockwood were promptly released with the understanding that they would testify against Franklin.

Significantly, none of the stories that next day mentioned that Darrow had also been at the scene. The San Francisco *Bulletin* reported that he had learned of the arrest while in court listening to the preliminary examination of a venireman.

Franklin's arrest immediately became Darrow's top concern. Working with LeCompte Davis, his cocounsel, Darrow promptly arranged to pay Franklin's ten-thousand-dollar bail. Darrow also secured the services of one of the state's most prominent defense attorneys, former governor Henry Gage, to represent his chief jury investigator. He paid Gage's ten-thousand-dollar cash retainer by draining the meager resources of the McNamara defense fund.

To pay for these unexpected expenditures Darrow sent an urgent wire to Frank Morrison at the AFL headquarters. "Can't you send us draft at once," he pleaded.

During the day, Darrow deflected all questions. At six P.M., he called reporters to his office to release a brief statement. "We have had only about five minutes with Franklin and we have not gone far enough into the matter to be able to make much of a statement. About all we can say is that there is nothing to it. Certainly we gave him no such sum of money for any such purpose. Franklin has been in our employ, in charge of the investigation of talesmen. His reputation was first class, both privately and as deputy United States marshal. United States attorney McCormack speaks well of him; so does United States marshal Youngworth. We have his assurance that he is innocent of the charge.

"I have no theory as to how this thing occurred," Darrow said. "It is a mystery to me. I do not understand it."

❋ ❋ ❋ ❋

Steffens learned of the arrest in the early afternoon. While passing through the lobby of the Alexandria Hotel, he saw the headlines in the "Extra" edition of the Los Angeles *Evening Express*. Worried about the impact on the negotiations, he arranged an immediate meeting with Lissner and Gibbon that turned into what Steffens called a "rattling conversation." The business leaders wanted to know what Steffens knew about Franklin and what the arrest would mean for the defense. After some discussion, they decided to continue with the efforts to settle the case as though nothing had happened. They called a meeting of the city's most important business leaders, to be held at Lissner's office the next evening.

Then Steffens went to find Darrow in his Higgins Building office. Showing him the Extra, Steffens asked what impact the arrest would have on the negotiations.

"None whatsoever," said Darrow, pacing back and forth in his usual restless fashion. Then he stopped, turned around for a moment, and added: "Not as far as I'm concerned. It may make a difference with your crowd." Darrow had taken to calling the business leaders "your crowd" with a tone of irony that had echoes of his old disdain for Steffens.

Steffens told Darrow that he had just seen some of the members of what Darrow called his "crowd" and that they were going ahead with their efforts.

A large banquet was held that night in Steffens's honor, organized by some of the city's leading journalists. According to an article in *Collier's* magazine, it was arranged hastily as a forum for Darrow to make an announcement. Steffens invited Mary and Sara to come as his guests—the only women in a room with 150 men.

Calling his address "Our Job," Steffens spoke on what the press could do to improve the relations between capital and labor. Then it was Darrow's turn. To the surprise of some in the audience, he made no announcement. Even more surprising, the great orator's talk was "wretched."

❀ ❀ ❀ ❀

Now back in Oregon, Erskine Wood read about the arrest in the Portland newspapers. It seemed to confirm his prediction that Darrow would try to bribe the jury, and that he would get caught.

"I have read of the Franklin bribery," he wrote Sara as soon as he read the news. "It looks real to me, knowing what I know. Why, even the old Greeks had discovered that as a *policy* honesty and truth were best." He asked her to give a message to his friend Larry Sullivan, the overzealous detective whom he had warned against unethical tactics. He wanted Sara to teach Sullivan the moral that bribery was wrong. "I fear his own moral would be: 'what a damned clumsy cuss. He ought to be caught.' "

＊＊＊＊

Franklin's arrest added urgency to Darrow's efforts to persuade the McNamara brothers to plead guilty. With Friday as the effective deadline, time was exceedingly short. To make matters worse, Thursday was Thanksgiving, a holiday in which it might be hard to reach all of the parties.

He had to think, too, of the risk that he would be implicated in the bribery. So far the district attorney had concealed from the press the fact that Darrow was at the scene when the arrest took place. The San Francisco *Bulletin* reported that "Fredericks admits that no more arrests can be made, and thus far there has been not a scrap of evidence uncovered to show that any of the defense attorneys knew of the alleged bribery scheme." But Darrow was not so confident. There was no reason to trust Fredericks or his associates to keep his presence a secret. Other papers were reporting that there would probably be further arrests and that "names of lawyers for the defense are mentioned freely, but so far no official has made any statement." At a minimum, exposure would damage his reputation. At a maximum, he might be charged with bribery—particularly if Franklin turned against him.

For Darrow, the need to settle the case became more urgent than ever. The arrest of Franklin, and the discovery that at least one juror had been bribed, was certain to make the case far more difficult to win. The political and judicial climate would be more hostile to his clients than ever. There might even be more sentiment for hanging Jim McNamara. Darrow had always hated capital punishment. "The only way out that I could see was through a plea of guilty," he later wrote.

Darrow also knew that a settlement would be in his own self-interest. Darrow knew that Fredericks must have some motive of his own for not disclosing that he had been at the scene. One day it was sure to become public, and when it did, the consequences were certain to be devastating. While it would alienate his friends at the

AFL and the Socialist Party, a settlement would help to insulate him from a bribery charge.

The master criminal-defense attorney knew that a settlement could offer him a perfect alibi if he were criminally charged. After all, why would he bribe a juror when he knew that the case was about to be settled?

Wednesday, November 29, 1911

The pressure was taking a terrible toll. Even the arrival of Ed Nockles on Tuesday morning did not do much to lift Darrow's spirits. Steffens observed that "you could see him age from day to day." One reporter said that he seemed to have grown twenty years older.

He was in a foul mood on Wednesday morning, and his comments to the press and potential jurors were more testy than ever. "Any statement that I or any man connected with me would have any thing to do with bribery is a lie," he told *The New York Times.* "All we want is a fair jury."

In apparent pursuit of such a jury, Darrow spent most of the day in court, cross-examining potential jurors, including a farmer named A. W. Stewart who said that he spent much of his time working as a member of the Los Angeles Elections Board.

"That isn't much of an occupation, is it?" inquired Darrow skeptically.

"Well, it is in this town," Stewart answered.

Though Darrow seemed suspicious of him, and asked a number of other hostile questions, he finally agreed to let Stewart serve as the tenth member of the jury. As the day drew to a close, Stewart took his seat in the box.

❋ ❋ ❋ ❋

The pressure on Darrow was also intensified by another court proceeding that morning: the arraignment of Bert Franklin. Over the protests of former governor Gage, Franklin's attorney, who said that he needed time to clear his calendar and to become familiar with the case, the court scheduled the preliminary hearing for the following Monday, December 4.

The prosecutors made it clear that they expected to use the case against Franklin to create further legal problems and embarrassment for the defense. As the *Los Angeles Examiner* reported, "Presumably the District Attorney will endeavor to put into evidence at the Franklin hearing Monday testimony that will show wide ramifications of the alleged attempts to bribe prospective jurors in the McNamara case and will drag others further into the shadow of suspicion." Darrow was well aware that he was one of those whose name was likely to surface quickly and prominently.

Deputies from the district attorney's office spent the remainder of the day conspicuously rushing around the city in automobiles, summoning witnesses for the Monday hearing.

* * * *

As planned, the meeting of business leaders took place in Lissner's office on Wednesday evening. For Lissner, it offered a chance to buttress his position with the support of other members of the city's financial establishment. For Steffens, it offered one more chance to press for J.J.'s full release—and to lead Los Angeles toward a new era in the relationship between capital and labor.

After Lissner said a few words of introduction, Steffens launched into his now well-rehearsed pitch, appealing to their idealism, as well as to their self-interest in the advantages of a city where there was industrial peace. He told them that they had "licked labor over and over again" in Los Angeles, that if they needed to prove that labor was to blame they couldn't have a better case study than Jim McNamara who, once he confessed, would be "a symbol of the guilt of organized labor," and that the city therefore had "a better chance than any city in the United States to turn around and be handsome." He pleaded with them not to take two victims, to persuade the district attorney to settle for the younger brother, and then to turn their attention to working for labor-capital harmony.

The toughest questions came from Fred Baker, whose Iron Works had been the target of fierce organizing. His resentment was intense, but as the session progressed, he finally agreed that it was worth trying to find a new day, free from class hatred and violence. The group staunchly refused to interfere with the district attorney, or to attempt to pressure him into allowing J.J. to go free without punishment. But they adopted a resolution, proposed by Fred Baker, agreeing to back the D.A., whatever his decision might be. What's more, if a settlement was reached, they decided, they would join in the effort to set up a conference with labor on the labor situation in Los Angeles.

With only two days remaining to secure a settlement, it was clear that both brothers would have to plead guilty to win Fredericks's support. So before the end of the day on Wednesday, LeCompte Davis went to see Fredericks again. For the first time, he indicated that the defense might be willing to have J.J.—as well as Jim—plead guilty.

"You know I've been against you all the time on this," Davis told the district attorney. "I've stood out for the dismissal of all charges against J.J. But if you are still of the same mind, I'll see if I can get the consent of J.J. to plead guilty to the Llewellyn Iron Works charge if you will not oppose our efforts to obtain clemency for him."

Fredericks said that he would even go a step further. He would advise the court, in setting the sentence, that he felt a certain amount of consideration was due the defendants who had pleaded guilty.

Davis asked where he would be able to find Fredericks the next day, Thanksgiving.

"I'll be playing golf in the morning," the district attorney said, "but I should be home by three P.M."

Davis said that he would give him a call on Thursday afternoon to let him know whether both men would agree to plead guilty.

They had less than forty-eight hours to arrange a settlement by the Friday deadline.

Chapter Ten

THE CONFESSIONS

Thanksgiving Day. Thursday, November 30, 1911

THE AIR WAS WARM and the flowers in bloom for Thanksgiving in Los Angeles. One of the prosecutors, Ray Horton, spent the day at a croquet championship, while his boss was off on the golf links. The ten jurors, still being kept in relative isolation, were treated to automobile rides and to a big dinner in the jury dining room of the New Broadway Hotel, prepared by their special cook, "Mammy" Minnie Martin. The meal featured a suckling pig that had been on the fire since five A.M. In the evening they attended a party at the Belasco Theater where, from specially reserved box seats, they watched *The Rose of the Rancho.* Lincoln Steffens had hoped to spend the holiday in Northern California with his sister, Dot, but felt obliged to stay in Los Angeles instead, "to spend the day here on the job." While Mary and Sara celebrated Thanksgiving dinner with a small group of friends at the Van Nuys Hotel, up in Oregon Erskine Wood played host to Sara's husband and small children.

Clarence Darrow spent the day in the county jail, trying to persuade his clients to plead guilty.

At precisely one P.M., in the trustees room of the county jail, the McNamara brothers and some of their fellow prisoners sat down to a special banquet. Hosted and arranged by the prisoners themselves, the event was held in honor of the county's sheriff, cook, and jailers. The improvised banquet tables, decorated with dinner cards and a profusion of flowers sent from labor union admirers, featured a menu consisting of ripe olives, celery, mushroom cocktail, oxtail soup, roast turkey, giblet gravy, cranberry sauce, Macaroni Italienne, green peas, candied sweet potatoes, hot mince pie, ice cream, café noir, assorted nuts, and raisins. Besides the famous brothers, the band of prisoners included General Rhys Pryce and Captain Jack Mosby, leaders of the Mexican Rebellion; Dr. J. W. Jones, confessed briber of a city police officer, just sentenced to serve a year in San Quentin; R. R. Herbert, alleged to have taken bribes from two women; A. C. Garber, a former post office auditor who had been convicted of being short on his accounts with the government; recently sentenced convicts J. M. Graybill and J. H. Sliger; and George S. Loudon, wanted by the post office officials in Kansas City.

After a delightful meal, with decorum that one newspaper called "as strict as at the Alexandria Hotel," the prisoners thanked the sheriff, jailer, and cook for their fine treatment. Then they asked J. J. McNamara to make a few remarks. Wearing a dark suit with a cutaway jacket, J.J. rose to speak. On his lapel was a button that bore his likeness, one of the thousands that had been spread across the land.

"Gentlemen," he began, "I have always felt that my lot has been cast among the common people. I have worked with them, and today am glad to be with you, to eat with you and to feel the spirit of Thanksgiving. In many ways we have much to give thanks for— for the treatment we have received while here and to be where men and officials are humane."

Shortly after two P.M., just before the celebration ended, the two brothers offered toasts to their fellow prisoners in water-filled glasses. Then they drank a toast to each other and clasped hands in a warm embrace.

"I'll go the limit for you, Joe," the younger brother promised, with touching emotion.

"Altogether," the *Los Angeles Times* reported, "the prisoners spent the best day since their incarceration." From outward appearances, one would never have known that when they toasted each other at that Thanksgiving luncheon, the McNamara brothers were in the midst of a debate over a decision that would affect them for the rest of their lives.

※ ※ ※ ※

What the press did not know was that J.J. and Jim had just come from separate meetings with Darrow, Steffens, and several of the other defense attorneys including LeCompte Davis and Joe Scott. The lawyers had explained that due to a series of new developments, both cases were now hopeless. The arrest of Bert Franklin on Tuesday had created a climate that was certain to affect the judge and jury; on Wednesday night, the defense team had blown up a miniature model of the *Times* Building, effectively proving that the explosion had been caused by dynamite; and, by using new technologies in ways that are now familiar, the prosecution had been spying on the defendants. Friends of the defense had found a wire dangling from the window of an unoccupied third-floor cell where the prisoners had held some of their most private conversations with friends and attorneys. The lawyers speculated that it was part of a dictograph arrangement that allowed government detectives, sitting in a cell on the second floor, to listen to what was said.

Darrow's message was clear. Both brothers would have to plead guilty. If they did not make a decision that afternoon, Jim would almost certainly hang. J.J. could postpone his fate, to be sure, but he, too, would be convicted and sent to jail. If he were not found guilty of bombing the *Times* building, he would certainly be nailed for ordering the bombing of the Llewellyn Iron Works. The brothers could forestall their fate; they could not avoid it.

With Thanksgiving lunch about to start, everyone agreed to postpone the painful session until later in the afternoon.

After lunch, the attorneys talked to the brothers together for the first time. Jim began by restating the position that he had tried to make clear to his lawyers earlier in the week. He was anxious to plead guilty—so much so that some of his lawyers feared that he would call out in court proclaiming his guilt. Even the National Erectors' Association, with its secret sources, had become convinced that "J.B. is weakening and intends to confess anyhow," and that "J.B. desires to 'die as a martyr.' " But he would only plead guilty if the state agreed to release J.J.

For the first time, Jim spoke directly to his older brother. "I am willing to plead guilty. I am willing to do anything to save you, Joe." Then, turning to the lawyers, he repeated his position again. "If it will save Joe," he said, "I am willing to plead guilty to murder." But he would only plead guilty if Joe—that is, J.J.—were set free.

"I won't stand for that at all," J.J. answered angrily. He was not willing to let his younger brother take the rap all by himself, not if it cost him his life. Besides, Darrow was almost certain that J.J. would be convicted of complicity in the Christmas Eve dynamiting of the Llewellyn Iron Works, in which property was damaged but no lives were lost. Why not plead guilty to the Llewellyn dynamiting now, if by doing so he could save his brother's life? "I am going to plead guilty to conspiracy in the Llewellyn job," J.J. announced.

Jim was stunned. It was the first time that he had heard that his brother intended to plead guilty in order to save his life. "I'll never stand for that," Jim protested. He turned to his lawyers. "I don't think you fellows have a right to put it to him that way," he said.

Joe Scott, the Irish Catholic attorney who had developed an especially close relationship with the brothers, tried to intervene. "What of it, Jim," he asked, with his hint of an Irish brogue. "What do you mean?"

"Just this," Jim said. "I am willing to go before the court and take the blame. I will plead guilty. I have worried about this thing until I can stand it no longer. I do not fear for myself, but I cannot sit here day after day and see Joe placed in danger. I dream of that and that only, night and day. I have reached my limit, and I am going to do something, and do it now. I am willing to save my brother, for he knew nothing of this, and is as guiltless as you are." He went on to explain that a confession by Joe was unacceptable because it would be unfair to his brother, painful to his mother, and devastating to organized labor.

After all, J.J. was a labor leader and he was not. J.J.'s was the face on the buttons and the stamps. J.J. was the hero of the movie. J.J. was the man that laborers all over America believed in. "I am ready to plead guilty because I am only a scrub printer and labor will not suffer if a scrub like me is found guilty," he said. "But Joe is an outstanding leader throughout the country. It would be a big body blow to labor if he pleads guilty."

Scott was incredulous. "But when J.J. pleads guilty, it may save you from the gallows," he said.

"What of it?" asked Jim.

"You would make a pretty picture up there."

"I would show good principle and do it for a principle," Jim said confidently.

Scott couldn't help admiring the man who would die for his cause. "Shades of Robert Emmet," he said to himself, thinking of the leader of an abortive Irish nationalist uprising who became a romantic hero of Irish lost causes after he was hanged for treason in 1803. What a man you are, he thought to himself.

There was an impasse. It was still the gift of the Magi.

❊ ❊ ❊ ❊

The lawyers decided to take a short recess for a conference in Darrow's office. When they left the room, Scott told Darrow that he thought that the jail chaplain, Father Edward Brady, might be able to talk some sense into the young man. After all, despite his rebellious views, Jim had been brought up in the Church, and Father Brady could emphasize what a hanging would do to his mother, and to his soul. Besides, Jim and Father Brady had developed a close relationship.

"Get him by all means," Darrow said.

Scott went over to the cathedral, where he had attended services earlier that morning. Father Brady, he learned, was attending a Thanksgiving dinner in Azusa. Scott reached him by telephone and explained the situation in total confidence. Father Brady agreed to come to the jail posthaste.

❊ ❊ ❊ ❊

As soon as the lawyers left the jail, LeCompte Davis called Captain Fredericks, who had just returned home from his game of golf. It was shortly after three P.M. Davis explained that they had not been able to get the consent of "the big man" yet and asked if it might be all right to call back at nine o'clock.

"All right, if you get the consent of both men," Fredericks said. "If you do not, don't call me up. It is useless to waste time under any other circumstances."

❋ ❋ ❋ ❋

When they returned to the jail, Darrow and Davis found that Jim was more receptive to their arguments. His visit with Father Brady had made an impact.

The lawyers said that they admired Jim's loyalty to his mother, his brother, and organized labor. But all of those interests would be best served by a guilty plea. If Jim were hanged, his brother and his mother would suffer for the rest of their days, and in the end, J.J. would be convicted for his role in the dynamiting of the Llewellyn Iron Works anyway. But a joint plea would spare their feelings— and J.J. would only get a short sentence, one that would probably be commuted in a year or two. Besides, the cases were costing hundreds of thousands of dollars, most of it raised in the form of dimes and quarters from the salaries of working men and women who needed the money desperately. A guilty plea would let that hard-earned money be used where it was most needed, to buy bread and shelter for the children of their supporters.

Darrow then advanced a final and possibly even more powerful argument—one that would never be known or understood by the public. The district attorney was convinced that Johannsen, Tvietmoe, and Clancy were behind the dynamiting, and he was prepared to prove it in court. A trial and conviction of the San Francisco union leaders would be devastating to the effort to organize labor in the West. But in exchange for the guilty pleas, Darrow said, Fredericks would forgo any effort to indict those men. Johannsen, Tvietmoe, and Clancy would therefore remain free to devote their powerful voices to the cause of labor.

It is impossible to know just which argument finally brought Jim around. In all likelihood, even he didn't know for certain, though he later claimed to have been principally motivated by the desire to protect his friends in labor.

Joe Scott, who did not know of all of the arguments that had been made to Jim, offered a more romantic explanation. With Jim still undecided, Scott claimed, J.J. "finally settled the matter by saying that if it was not agreed that he was to plead guilty, and thus partially lessen the chances of his brother being sent to the gallows, he 'would scream out in the courtroom.' Unnerved and unstrung, James at last gave in."

Scott called it "the greatest exhibition of brotherly love that I have ever seen."

❋ ❋ ❋ ❋

By now everyone connected with the defense knew what was going on, as did the prosecutors, the leaders of the *Times,* the representatives of the National Erectors' Association, and most of the important businessmen and Good Government reformers in the city. But one important person had been kept in the dark—Job Harriman. Though he was the McNamaras' cocounsel, had represented them before Darrow arrived in Los Angeles, and had based his campaign largely on their innocence, he was not informed. Though Steffens was a staunch supporter, and had raised money for his mayoral campaign even before arriving in Los Angeles, he did not inform him. Though Darrow wanted him to win, and apparently had poured thousands of defense-fund dollars into his campaign, both in the belief that he should win and in the conviction that a Harriman victory on December 5 would be good for his clients, he also did not inform him. Though the settlement was certain to doom Harriman's chances of victory—and dash the hopes of Socialists everywhere that they could win an important election in Los Angeles—Harriman was not informed.

At first, Darrow explained that he "did not want to worry him with this problem, and he has practically been out of the case since the first week of the trial, on account of the campaign." Steffens simply reported that "nobody had the heart to tell him,"—a phrase also used by Darrow—knowing, of course, that it would crush Harriman personally as well as destroy his chances of victory. Perhaps Darrow was deterred by the understandable reluctance to deliver unwelcome news.

Or perhaps, as some people would later ungenerously claim, Darrow was afraid that Harriman would try to persuade the McNamaras to stay the course. That charge was given credence by Darrow himself in his autobiography some twenty-five years later. "I could not tell Mr. Harriman," he recalled. "It would place him in the position of either deserting his party or letting one client go to almost certain death, which we could not do." In short, Darrow was concerned that Harriman might be able to persuade the McNamaras not to confess.

❉ ❉ ❉ ❉

Ed Nockles, who had arrived from Chicago on Tuesday, was the only representative of labor that Darrow could consult. He had been with Darrow on the case from the start—from the first visit to Kankakee, to the first trip to the Coast, to the effort to keep some unfriendly witnesses from appearing at the trial. He had helped to twist Darrow's arm to persuade him to take the case.

After leaving the jail late Thursday afternoon, Darrow and Steffens went to Darrow's house, where they found Nockles waiting for them. Knowing that his friend wouldn't like it at first, Darrow explained what he had to do, going through his reasoning step by step. At first, Nockles was dead set against a guilty plea. All the leaders of labor were at that very moment in Atlanta passing resolutions reaffirming the brothers' innocence and looking for new ways to raise money for their defense. It would have been easy enough to accept a guilty plea by Jim in return for J.J.'s freedom. But a guilty plea by J.J., labor's new national martyr, was certain to produce a calamitous public relations setback for the AFL. Even if guilty, the brothers could best serve organized labor by maintaining their innocence, taking their chances at trial, and if convicted, claiming that they had been framed.

But as Darrow talked, Nockles realized that it was no use. Perhaps he was most persuaded by the need to save the pennies and dimes of working men and women. Perhaps he shared Darrow's passion to save a human life from the gallows. Perhaps he understood the importance of protecting Johannsen and Tvietmoe. Perhaps he believed that a guilty plea would make it less likely that Darrow would be indicted for bribing George Lockwood. Or maybe he just saw that his friend was bone tired; aged a decade since he last had seen him; beaten. Nockles couldn't give labor's consent. But he could and did give his own blessing to the settlement.

At eight-thirty P.M., Captain Fredericks was at home, awaiting the call that LeCompte Davis had promised to place at nine. The phone rang—but it wasn't Davis. It was Lincoln Steffens. Apparently Davis had given the muckraker Fredericks's home number. He wanted to know whether Fredericks had seen Harry Chandler, or had an appointment to meet him later that night. The call represented the last hope that J.J. could be spared without a guilty plea. But, unknown to Steffens, Harry Chandler had decided not to become directly involved.

No, the district attorney curtly reported, he had not seen Chandler, nor did he have an appointment to see him.

J.J. would have to confess.

The phone rang again at nine P.M. This time it was LeCompte Davis. The big man, Davis said, had given in. J.J. had agreed to plead guilty. They would meet Fredericks in his office early the next morning.

Friday, December 1, 1911

As soon as court convened on Friday morning, Fredericks requested "a continuance of the proceedings until after lunch." He said that he had "certain grave matters to be considered between now and the time for convening court this afternoon." Darrow, Scott, and Davis did not object to the request.

As he left the courtroom, Fredericks briskly told inquiring reporters that "everything is quiet as a millpond. There is absolutely nothing doing. My request for adjournment was one of the most ordinary matters."

The reporters assumed that the recess was connected with Franklin's bribery case. They followed him into the elevator, hoping for some other clue, but he refused further comment. "I couldn't even tell the court what requires the continuance," he said. "I certainly can't tell it to reporters."

❀ ❀ ❀ ❀

When court convened at two o'clock, the room was filled with newspaper correspondents, all anxiously asking each other "What's doing," and with the families of the prosecutors and detectives who had been specially summoned with the promise that something important was about to occur. The back of the room was filled with the workers with their old clothes, the socialists with their HARRIMAN FOR MAYOR campaign buttons, and the anarchists with their radical beliefs—the group that the San Francisco *Bulletin* said could have stepped out of a Dickens novel. Somewhat incongruously, the jurors were all wearing red carnations, courtesy of a Thanksgiving Day admirer.

To reporters, the faces at the defense table were already a portrait in pain. Darrow sat at the end, "nervously chewing a pencil which he was rolling around in his mouth as a child does a stick of candy, and his eyes were roving restlessly around the courtroom. His features were yellow and colorless and the lines about his mouth were twitching from nervousness. Scott looked like one who had been stricken. His face was ashen and tense. He sat staring at the table in front of him and blinking with slow, long, solemn winks of his eyes. LeCompte Davis seemed to be worn and very tired."

The hot sunlight that streamed into the room was somewhat shaded by a set of long brown curtains that were partially closed. Presently there was a stir outside the courtroom as Jim McNamara entered, escorted by two deputies. He crossed the room and took a seat next to Joe Scott, who warmly put an arm around the prisoner's shoulder. Then—to the audible astonishment of the press and spectators—J. J. McNamara entered the room. He had not been seen since October 11, the first day of the trial. He was as upright, powerful, and neatly dressed as ever. A reporter noted that "he was the same leonine leader of men to all appearances. He smiled pleasantly to some whom he recognized. His face was still of the ruddy color it had been when he was last in court. His brown, silvering hair, was combed back manelike as before. [Like his brother,] he, too, was chewing his gum."

Then Judge Bordwell entered the courtroom, and the climax to the drama began. LeCompte Davis rose to make the announcement.

"Your Honor," Davis began, "the defendant is in court. In this case, *People* versus *McNamara,* that is now on trial, may it please the court, after a long consideration of the matter and final consultation between counsel for the defendant, we have concluded to withdraw the plea of not guilty and have the defendant in this case enter a plea of guilty."

The room was totally silent. Everyone strained to hear, unsure what Davis's words meant. Some even sprang to their feet, prompting the bailiff to order them to "keep your seats!"

Davis continued. "And we intend to pursue a like course with reference to J. J. McNamara, in the case of the people against him, wherein he is charged with having placed dynamite at the Llewellyn Iron Works." Davis had not seen J.J., who was still sitting in the back of the room. "We have sent for him," he continued, "and he will probably be here."

Darrow, who had seen his client enter the room, interrupted. "He is here now," he said.

J.J. remained at the back of the room as Fredericks asked the younger brother, sitting at the defense table, to rise. "James B. McNamara," he began, "you have heretofore been arraigned on this indictment, Number 6930, and have entered your plea thereto of not guilty. Do you wish to withdraw that plea?"

"Yes, sir," Jim answered, almost inaudibly.

"The prisoner answers yes," Fredericks continued. "J. B. McNamara, you have withdrawn your plea of not guilty. Do you wish now to plead at this time?"

Davis could see that his client needed help. "At this time," he said, "yes, sir."

"To this indictment, charging you with the crime of murder, do you plead guilty or not guilty."

There was no turning back. "Guilty," Jim answered, without a quaver.

To the stunned courtroom, the people who had not quite understood Davis's opening remarks, there was still another piece to the drama. What of J. J. McNamara? What was to happen in his case?

After it was arranged that the younger brother would be sentenced on the following Tuesday, Fredericks asked J.J. to come forward. With the same winning smile that had won him so many admirers, J.J. stepped forward to the defense table. Since all of the seats were filled, Darrow rose slowly, offering J.J. the seat next to his brother, and stepped back as Fredericks continued.

"J. J. McNamara," he began, "you have heretofore been arraigned on indictment Number 6955, in which you are charged with the crime of exploding or attempting to explode dynamite, nitroglycerine, etcetera, in the buildings adjacent to the Llewellyn Iron works. You have been arraigned on that indictment and entered your plea of not guilty. Do you now wish to withdraw that plea of not guilty?"

"I do." His shoulders were squared and he held his hands behind his back, one resting easily in the palm of the other.

"J. J. McNamara, this is the time agreed upon for you to plead to the same. Do you want to plead guilty or not guilty?"

J.J. gave his answer in a voice as steady and distinct as any that had been heard in the courtroom. "Guilty," he said. As the audience gasped, somewhere in the back of the room a baby began to cry.

Sentencing was set for the following Tuesday. Election Day. As pandemonium spread through the room, observers could hear the click of the telegraph keys, muffled by their padded boxes, carrying the startling development to newspapers throughout the world. In a fit of hyperbole that captured the emotion of the moment, one reporter wrote that "the greatest mystery of the age is solved, the greatest criminal trial of the century is over, the most dramatic climax in the history of all trials has been reached."

❊ ❊ ❊ ❊

A throng of spectators rushed down to Darrow, tears in their eyes, wanting to know why it happened, *why?* Darrow's face was pale, the long wrinkles in his skin looked even deeper than usual. He looked twenty years older as he murmured that "it was a hard struggle to bring this about, but it was the best thing that could have happened." His voice was low, husky, exhausted. "I did the best I could. If I'd have seen any way out of it we would not have pleaded guilty."

"Do you think labor will suffer?" shouted a reporter. Workers who had believed so deeply in the case, in the boys' innocence, stood listening to every word.

"Oh, no," Darrow answered with a sigh. "It's just an incident in the evolution of things. Because one does wrong does not mean that all the others are wrong. James McNamara did not mean to kill anybody. They have told me the whole story. It was meant as a scare to the *Times*. But the crime is the same, no matter what the intent."

"Why didn't you wait until after Tuesday's election? Don't you know this will hurt Job Harriman's chances to be elected mayor?"

"I know, but we could not take any chances. Maybe the state would have backed out of their agreement. Lives were at stake, and I think we saved them."

An angry reporter asked Darrow a sharp, pointed question about the abandoned theory that the explosion was caused by gas. "Why, maybe it was gas, or—or ink or something," he said, looking wearily for a hole in the crowd. "I am very tired. I am worn out and very sorrowful."

❋ ❋ ❋ ❋

While Darrow, lonely and sad, found his way out of the courtroom and onto a street filled with angry Socialists and laborites, Captain Fredericks took an elevator to his tenth-floor offices where a celebration had been arranged for prosecutors, detectives, friends, and press. The tables were filled with exhibits planned for use at the trial, and everyone present had a story to tell about how the great case had been brought to a close. In Los Angeles, Fredericks was the man of the hour.

Around the country, there were those who were overjoyed by news of the McNamaras' confession. From New York, Theodore Roosevelt sent a wire to his friend William Burns. "All good American citizens feel that they owe you a debt of gratitude for your signal service to American citizenship." Burns received the telegram in Chicago, where he was already celebrating his triumph with attacks on Samuel Gompers—who "accused me of planting the dynamite" and "of trying to put over a great hoax."

"I have gained a great personal vindication," Burns told reporters.

He predicted that the case would ensnare other top union officials and that "the ultimate effect of the McNamara case will be the expulsion of the radical element from the labor union movement."

Walter Drew of the National Erectors' Association called the McNamara case a "side issue." He urged the government to grant clemency. "We, too, are fighting for a principle," he said, "just as they are. The big principle behind it all, on our part, is the prosecution of the men who paid the McNamaras and countenanced and instigated this outrage."

In Los Angeles, General Harrison Gray Otis called the guilty pleas "a great triumph for truth and law. As to me and mine, we stand vindicated in our quarter-of-a-century stand for industrial freedom."

❊ ❊ ❊ ❊

On the streets of Los Angeles, the McNamaras' supporters were first shocked, then distraught, then in a fighting mood, angry at everyone connected with the case. A leading national correspondent, in town to cover the trial, watched as a streetcar conductor learned the news at three o'clock, at his stop in front of the Hall of Records. "The McNamaras!" he asked, incredulous. "Go on. You're joshing." But he was assured that it was true, and "as he went through the car tears were rolling down his cheeks into his grizzled mustache. He could not repress them. No one laughed, no one sneered at him. All over the city that sunny, warm afternoon the eyes of men blinked and winked in vain efforts to repress the scalding tears that would well up. The shock was too great, the release of the pent up strain too sudden. So they wept, shaken by emotions beyond their control."

For Socialists, the confessions were especially devastating. Some Harriman loyalists tore off their campaign buttons in disillusionment. The *Times,* whose reporting was not always considered objective, claimed that street sweepers picked up as many as ten thousand buttons.

The San Francisco *Bulletin* described the scene at Harriman's Socialist Party headquarters, where hundreds of rank-and-file labor workers heard the news. "Strong working men threw themselves forward on the table and wept like children," the paper reported. "It's a plot to beat Harriman," others shouted. "The McNamaras have been paid by the capitalists from the beginning." "Labor should demand a hanging."

Harriman heard about the guilty pleas from newsboys while driving in his automobile. He knew at once that he had no chance of winning, that thousands of voters would desert him. He met with reporters later that afternoon.

"I would never have given my consent to any such a proceeding," he said, leaning against a wall in his campaign office. He was white and gaunt and hoarse. "I would have fought the case to the bitter end."

At the Labor Temple the mood was equally angry. "We ought to form a mob and go down to the jail and hang those dirty traitors to the nearest lamppost," shouted a worker who was wearing a tattered coat. "That's right," someone answered, "let's hang the men who have led us into this trap." A crowd began to gather as the first man yelled that "they have sold us out. They are Judas Iscariots and we have been betrayed for pieces of silver." Some of the workers blamed the lawyers. "We have been sold out. They had the confession for days and kept it back to hurt us in this election," shouted a man whose lapel was covered with Socialist buttons. "That's right," answered a voice in the crowd. "The lawyers and everybody else are trying to defeat us."

One of the most poignant comments came from a man with a Swedish accent, who told of a striker who had given his last dollar for the men in jail. "Why did they keep us in the dark?" he asked in broken English, tears in eyes. "They had no right to do it. They knew they were guilty."

❋ ❋ ❋ ❋

Reporters found Mary McNamara, a scarf around her neck, sitting in a stiff-backed chair at her home in Quarry Street, in Cumminsville, Ohio, just outside Cincinnati. She had learned the news when she saw the newspaper headlines while on a streetcar on her way home from a visit to friends in the city. But she didn't believe it.

"I know my boys are innocent," she said, holding back tears. "I am forced to believe that they pleaded guilty, but I know they are innocent and I never will believe it until I hear it from their own lips." Then she broke into tears as her daughter led her into the bedroom.

Her youngest son, Robert, continued the interview. He, too, held on to the certainty they were innocent. "I do not believe my brothers guilty of the crimes to which they have confessed," he said. "Our family received a letter from James, dated November twenty-fourth, just a few days ago, in which he wrote favorably of the proceedings in court."

❋❋❋❋

The announcement sent the labor world into turmoil. At its Atlanta convention, the AFL had been dominated by talk of the trial, reiterating its certainty that the brothers were innocent, seeking new ways to raise funds, calling on workers to devote a week's wages to the cause, deputizing Anton Johannsen to travel around the country seeking money from every source. When the leaders left Atlanta on Wednesday, November 29, trying to reach their homes, or other favorite destinations, in time for Thanksgiving dinner, they were filled with the righteousness of the cause.

Even the San Francisco labor leaders were unprepared for the announcement, which was made at five-thirty P.M. EST. Although Darrow's negotiated settlement was designed, in part, to protect Tvietmoe and Johannsen from further prosecutions by the Los Angeles authorities, neither man had expected or asked for such treatment, nor did they know that it was part of the arrangement. Indeed on Friday afternoon, when Tvietmoe—just arrived in New York City, where he was staying at the Victoria Hotel—saw the first news bulletins about the confessions, he had just posted a letter to Frank Morrison, head of the McNamara Ways and Means Committee, enclosing a check for $127—a week's wages for Anton Johannsen ($42) and a week's wages for himself ($85).

Anton Johannsen heard about the confession while visiting his friend and biographer, Hutchins Hapgood, in Dobbs Ferry, New York. Having just been named a special representative of the AFL's McNamara Defense Committee, Johannsen, the Laugh of Labor, was in high spirits, telling lusty stories and singing such songs as "He bumped her up against the wall," and "There's no use scratching the blind," when someone showed up with an Extra edition of the local paper. Stunned, Johannsen burst into tears and walked up and down the room, paper in hand, sobbing, tears running down his face, crying out, "That's the way they are, you fight for them and they turn on you—but I love them, the poor slaves."

As Johannsen said later, "the story of how the McNamaras were persuaded to plead guilty was the most pathetic and saddest story that I have heard for many days. Millions of men and women and children from all parts of the civilized world were depressed and sad when the news came over the wire on that fatal December 1, 1911. They could not understand and were bitterly disappointed and felt that the chain of industrial slavery would become by reason of this act still more binding."

❊ ❊ ❊ ❊

If the San Francisco labor leaders—along with millions of working men and women—felt depressed and sad, the AFL's national leaders felt exposed and betrayed. They had put their prestige, their money, their power on the line, all in the belief that that the brothers were innocent. Now this. Just back in his office at the AFL's national headquarters in Washington, D.C., after two weeks in Atlanta, Frank Morrison had stayed late working on Friday afternoon. Much of his time was devoted to his responsibilities as the sole AFL official with the power to deposit or expend funds from the McNamara Ways and Means Committee.

At five-fifteen P.M.—responding to the urgent request that Darrow had sent him two days earlier—Morrison sent Darrow a letter enclosing ten thousand dollars, more than depleting the defense committee's meager funds, drawing against checks that Morrison expected to receive and deposit during the next few days. Then, just twenty minutes later, Morrison learned that the McNamaras had confessed. He rushed off to the post office to try to have the letter recalled, but it was too late. The best the superintendent could offer was to wire the postal authorities in Los Angeles, to try to intercept the letter at the other end.

"I feel bitterly over Attorney Darrow wiring for check with the information he had at that time," Morrison wrote to the AFL's executive council the next day. Why, he wondered, had Darrow begged for money on Wednesday, when he planned to plead his clients guilty on Friday? Why would he ask for a fresh ten-thousand-dollar draft of money, when he knew that the funds would have to come from "checks that were not collected, and that under the circumstances there was the grave possibility of the payment of many checks being stopped"?

* * * *

Bitter as Morrison felt upon hearing the news, however, his feelings came nowhere near those of Samuel Gompers, who had staked his public reputation on the McNamara cause. Gompers was on his way from Washington to New York, comfortably dozing in a Pullman car on the Pennsylvania Railroad's *Congressional Limited,* when a young reporter from the Associated Press woke him up at a railroad station in northern New Jersey. Not believing what the reporter had to say, half imagining he was still in a dream, Gompers struggled up from his seat and found his way to the rear of the car, where the lights were brighter, to read the wire service dispatches from Los Angeles. Tears came into his eyes, and his hands shook as he read the typed pages.

"If this is all true, my credulity has been imposed upon," he told the young reporter. "I am astonished at this news. We have had the gravest assurances given to us by everyone connected with the trial, either directly or indirectly, that these men were innocent."

When he disembarked from the train at New York's Pennsylvania Station, Gompers tried to hide his emotions by pulling a slouch hat down over his eyes. But the New York press was there to meet him, and they, too, insisted on a comment. How would it affect labor and the AFL?

"I am utterly dumfounded," he said, his voice betraying his strong feelings. "The news that came to me was simply a bulletin from a press association and I have had no chance as yet to think on the subject and on what it will mean for the laboring men of this country. We have been imposed upon in that affair cruelly, for there has been no doubt in my mind that the accused boys were innocent of the charges. In this I was backed by their own assurances. I have letters from them telling of their innocence. When I was out West I went to see them. They begged me to convey this assurance to labor, which believed and had faith in them."

Gompers continued to talk to the press, at the station and then at the desk of the Hotel Victoria—where he, like Tvietmoe, was to stay for the next few days. He kept formulating and restating his belief in the men, his confidence that "the effect on labor will be depressing but it will not be lasting," his sense of betrayal. As he talked, there was one phrase that he kept repeating. "We have been imposed upon," he said again and again, with a mixture of pain and anger; "we have been cruelly deceived."

Indeed the news was so shocking that Gompers couldn't bring himself to believe it until the next day, when he received a telegram from Darrow. "There was no avoiding step taken today," Darrow's wire said. "When I see you I know you will be satisfied that all of us gave everything we had to accomplish the best. Hope you will believe we realize our responsibility and did the best that could be done." In fact, Darrow sent the telegram on Friday evening, addressed to the AFL national office in Washington. It arrived at ten-thirty P.M., long after the office had closed for the day, long after Gompers had left for New York, and long after he had been informed of the remarkable and devastating news.

* * * *

For Gompers's enemies, the McNamara confessions offered a golden chance to attack him and his leadership of the AFL. Powerful additional ammunition for such attacks also came from Los Angeles the next day, after Darrow, in a bylined story carried by the Hearst papers, said that "I have known for months that our fight was hopeless." If Darrow had known for months that their case was hopeless, Gompers's enemies reasoned, surely Gompers knew it, too.

Detective William Burns called Gompers a "discredited leader," and "a shifty, false-hearted demagogue" who had known of the McNamaras' guilt all along. Still seething over Gompers's claim that he had manufactured the evidence against the McNamaras, Burns reversed the charges, contending that Gompers, "like attorney Clarence Darrow, was convinced that the men were guilty before they were taken to California." Further, Burns maintained that Gompers was complicitous in the national dynamiting conspiracy. "The iron workers are not the only labor leaders implicated in the dynamiting," he asserted. "I dare Gompers to make an affidavit stating that he does not know who the dynamiters are."

✳ ✳ ✳ ✳

Other critics focused on another story that had started to emerge, the claim that the case had been settled in order to secure freedom for a few key labor leaders. When Darrow issued a statement on Saturday asserting that "organized labor was not hurt," and that "the leaders would not be so bitter if they knew the facts," some reporters suggested that the McNamaras had been pawns in a much larger game. *The New York Times* reported that "it is believed that the compromise was much more extensive than hitherto has been hinted, namely that the State of California had in its possession information that would have involved other prominent persons and that the agreement to get the McNamaras to plead guilty practically saves a score of indictments and prosecutions."

The attacks on Gompers and organized labor were widely repeated by newspaper editorial writers. Joseph Pulitzer's New York *World* called the McNamara confessions "the deadliest blow ever dealt to organized labor in the United States . . . because organized labor, through the incredible folly of its officers and spokesmen, made itself the champion, the defender, the very shield of this gang of cold-blooded scoundrels and murderers." Other papers across the country took a similar tone. "Will organized labor now do justice to itself by abjuring murder and criminal acts?" asked an editorial in *The New York Times*. "It is time for the unions and federations to take action effectively to free themselves of the odium which they must inevitably share if they do not promptly disclaim all sympathy with false leaders who have put themselves in the attitude of tacitly approving the use of dynamite and bludgeon and the knife in labor's strikes."

The AFL felt the need to issue an immediate statement. "The McNamaras have outraged the confidence that organized labor had in them and have deceived the thousands of workers who rallied to their support with financial assistance," it said. "The use of violence of any kind is contrary to the principles of unionism and is repulsive to the entire mass of our membership." But it was impossible to keep up with the criticisms. How could Gompers prove that he didn't know that the McNamaras were guilty?

To make matters worse, Darrow told reporters that "I never told Samuel Gompers or anyone else that J. B. McNamara was innocent." If Gompers knew that the men were guilty, or even that their fight was hopeless, he also had plenty to answer for with his own members—who had given their hearts and their pennies to the cause.

※ ※ ※

The attacks on Gompers came from his left as well as his right, provoked in part by Gompers's frantic effort to disassociate himself from the McNamaras. Socialist leader Eugene Debs, who was generally engaged in a pitched battle with Gompers, jumped at the opportunity to issue a blistering statement. "Samuel Gompers and his official associates should be the very last to join the labor-crushing magnates of the trusts and their swarms of mercenary hirelings in condemning the McNamara brothers and expressing satisfaction over their tragic fate. Rather should they weep in anguish that in their moral cravenness they not only deserted their own deluded followers, but joined their enemies in the cry to crucify them *to exculpate themselves.*"

Asked to comment on Debs's remarks, Gompers issued a terse reply. "I will not discuss the utterances of that man."

※ ※ ※

Darrow's motives, too, were immediately challenged by both allies and enemies. He stated that his central concern was to save his clients' lives, but others were convinced that he was principally motivated by a desire to save his own skin. C. P. Connolly, a reporter for *Collier's* magazine, who had also covered the Haywood trial, expressed his views candidly. "My own judgment is that Darrow turned the affair for his own salvation," he wrote. Although no one had yet publicly accused Darrow of complicity in the bribery, Connelly was certain that he must have been involved, that Franklin could not have gone around spending large sums of money without Darrow's knowledge. "No agent," he quipped, "would dare attempt to account for the disappearance of four thousand dollars to a man of the world like Darrow by saying he had fed it to the pigeons."

One of the bitterest attacks on Darrow came from O. N. Hilton, attorney for the Western Federation of Miners, who had handled part of the McNamara case before Darrow was formally hired. "Inside of a few days," Hilton told a reporter for the *Denver Post,* "the mystery of Darrow's course will confirm the old adage 'murder will out.' Mark my words, you will see that Darrow has not acted in good faith. There isn't a man who has once been associated with him in the profession of law that will not tell you the same thing. Not one of them cares to associate with him again."

Laughing, Hilton recalled that "when I first went into the case out there every one of the seven men associated with Darrow in the Haywood and Moyer trial sent me telegrams, which I have fortunately kept, putting me wise to him and saying that if I had a chance I'd better withdraw. No sir, there never was and there never will be a time when you can't find a yellow streak down Darrow's back."

There were those who condemned Darrow in even harsher terms, asserting that he had quite literally sold his clients out. No one was more vicious than J.J.'s friend Albert Detch, an Indianapolis minister and sporting goods store owner whose poetry and polemics often appeared in *Bridgeman's,* the iron workers' magazine.

"Capital whipped Darrow into capitulation," Detch wired J.J. on December 2. "What did Capital pay him to quit?" He then released a public letter that was even more specific. "The bribe case against Darrow was necessary to cover the real excuse for Darrow's withdrawal," he charged. "The day will come when somebody will let out what Capital paid and the Los Angeles politicians paid to Darrow to quit. Some men believe that he got $100,000 from the capital crowd."

No matter how unfair they may have been, such assertions and rumors were widespread—and, to Darrow, intensely painful.

❋❋❋❋

Within days, the changed circumstances had thrown the plans and emotions of Darrow's circle of friends into turmoil. Sara, in the courtroom when the guilty pleas were entered, rushed up to all of her friends in tears, holding on to them, wanting to know what had happened. The more she learned, the more depressed she became. She wired her husband that she had "full facts" of "crooked dealings," of "the truth which involves the reputation of trusted men." With the sudden end of the trial, she was obliged to return home immediately, return to the world where she lived with a man she did not love, and loved a man she was forbidden to see. To Erskine, she wrote that the "sudden ending of the McNamara case involving, as it has, such deceit, such shaken confidence, such ill will, such betrayed trusts and social disorder and disaster," along with "Mary's heart-rending situation, her loyal tho misplaced faith, her hopeless love [for Darrow] and most of all you, my darling, to whom I may not come except as a stranger—all this fills my heart with unutterable anguish."

But none of what happened really surprised Erskine Wood—except perhaps that Franklin had been caught—since he was sure such methods had been used more skillfully elsewhere, without being detected. He had predicted that there would be crooked tactics, including bribery; he had predicted that the tactics would ultimately misfire, damaging the cause of labor; he had predicted that the time would come when Darrow would reject and deny Mary.

"I think it was just a case of plain blundering," he wrote to Larry Sullivan. He concluded that it was the bribery charges that "did force the hand and settle the case."

Nevertheless, Wood still loved Darrow, especially the literary Darrow, and felt compassion for what the case had done to him. He sent a telegram offering solace and support and inviting his friend to come to Oregon to escape from the pressures he must be feeling.

"I wish I could come," Darrow wrote back, "but a lot is demanded of me. How I would like to get into the forests or the mountains and get some peace of mind, but I can't yet. I want to come to you and I will when I can. Anyhow, dear friend, thank you."

❊ ❊ ❊ ❊

For a moment, the episode seemed to be a heroic success for Lincoln Steffens, who had engineered the settlement, had created a world-renowned experiment in the application of the Golden Rule to problems of capital and labor, and who had a remarkable scoop to share with the world. As he told his sister, the immediate response was overwhelming. "Telegrams poured in; congratulations and offers of big money for statements, which I refused of course, and there was one wire asking me to write a play," he said. "It reminded me of the olden days when I began to expose cities. I'm famous again. I'll use it to make people think. They'll listen again now, and I can do something. . . ."

When they started to appear on December 2, 1911, his syndicated articles were front-page headlines around the world, with the compromise explained from his point of view, and with Steffens as hero. But his manic enthusiasm at being "famous again" quickly faded as the compromise, and his role in it, became the center of a controversy that pitted Steffens against Socialists who could not forgive him for defeating Harriman; against labor leaders of the conservative stripe who could not forgive him for embarrassing Gompers; against radical labor leaders who could not forgive him for encouraging the dynamiters to plead guilty; and against intellectuals, including his dear friend John Reed, who felt that he had been duped by the business establishment, and could not forgive him for dashing their illusions. Even E. W. Scripps, whom Steffens considered an inspiration, felt that Steffens had totally botched everything, playing into the hands of the forces of capital.

"The pleas of guilty were a great shock," Scripps told a top aide. "If they were to be entered, why was it not postponed until after next Tuesday? Did these murderers get special consideration because they would make their plea before next Tuesday's election and insure the defeat of Harriman? It appears that Steffens had been negotiating for some time. At this distance, it looks as if he had sold out his party, Union labor, and the Scripps newspapers."

Within a few days, Steffens was on his way back East, to face the most intense scorn and humiliation of his life.

❄ ❄ ❄

Sad and dejected, Darrow had little to say as he went through the motions at the McNamara sentencing hearing on Tuesday, December 5, a day that was one of the most painful in his life. As if to underline his dilemma, newspapers that morning carried the startling news that this top jury investigator, Bert Franklin, had bribed a second juror, Robert Bain, and that Bain was cooperating with the district attorney. An observer watched Darrow in the courtroom that morning, "the deep seams and the pallor of his face betraying the humiliation of desolation. Beside him, Lincoln Steffens, blanched and worried, suffering the fate of all unselfish mediators in that both sides were condemning him."

Outside the courthouse, more than fifteen thousand men and women, many whose hopes and ideals had been so deeply invested in the brothers' innocence, lined the streets and the plaza across from the courthouse, hoping to see the confessed dynamiters, waiting until they learned that the brothers had not recanted, that Jim had actually given the court a signed confession, and that the judge had sentenced Jim to life and J.J. to fifteen years.

Elsewhere in the city there was an election, but it must have seemed a charade, a foregone conclusion that Harriman would be trounced, as he was, by twenty thousand votes.

❄ ❄ ❄

Darrow had not slept well for days—certainly not in the week since Franklin had been caught at the corner of Third and Main—and he would not, as it developed, sleep well for months and months to come. On leaving the courtroom, Darrow announced that he had handled his last case.

"The public ought to be satisfied," Darrow told reporters, his voice breaking as he spoke. "I've fought my last fight and am through, beaten. I don't mean that I am through fighting for the principles that I believe are involved, but my active court work is done.

"It is hard to finish with everyone pointing their thumbs down. I hoped to be victor in the fight, but I've got to quit. I love the people for whom and with whom I have fought many a battle in this war, but new leaders must come and even those in the ranks such as I must retire for recruits."

He was, of course, wrong. His greatest cases remained well in the future. But first he would be forced to go through a kind of personal purgatory, starting with the most difficult case of his life: the case of *The People* versus *Clarence Darrow*.

****

****

INTERLUDE

I F THE MCNAMARA CASE came upon the world as a "thunderclap," to use Darrow's phrase, the confessions were an earthquake. Institutions were reformed or destroyed, lives were changed, and attitudes were profoundly revised. For the most part, the results damaged Socialists and the more radical elements in labor, while working to the benefit of the business community and of those labor leaders and progressive reformers who opposed violence.

The impact was most profound in Los Angeles, where the business leadership gained another generation of total control. Although Job Harriman ran for office again in 1913, he was defeated resoundingly, and neither the Socialists nor organized labor emerged as the powers that they might have become. As Carey McWilliams observed in *Southern California Country,* "the plea of guilty entered by the McNamaras aborted the labor movement in Los Angeles. It set back by twenty years a movement which, even in 1911, was dangerously retarded in relation to the growth of the community."

Nationally, the labor movement ultimately recovered, but only after a traumatic period. As George Creel put it, "The pleas of guilty sent organized labor into a tail spin." Building on events in Los Angeles, the federal government successfully prosecuted the entire leadership of the Structural Iron Workers' Union for its role in the national dynamiting conspiracy. In late 1912, after a lengthy trial in Indianapolis, thirty-eight of the fifty-four men who had been indicted, including union president Frank Ryan, were sent to jail. Olaf Tvietmoe was convicted in the Indianapolis case, but his sentence was reversed on appeal. The series of events became the defining experience of the era. Max Eastman recalled that "the McNamara trial, and the trials which flowed from it, formed the spearpoint of the labor struggle in the years when we were starting *The Masses.*" By the time the smoke cleared, the events in Los Angeles had helped to make the AFL a more conservative and mainstream organization.

The National Socialist Party was forced to change as well. With Harriman's backing—and over Bill Haywood's strong protest—the party adopted a provision at its May 1912 convention that banned the advocacy of violence as a means of achieving economic and social change. A few months later, Haywood was expelled from his position as a member of the party's National Executive Committee. *Appeal to Reason,* the party's once-powerful newspaper, began a sharp descent, thanks, in some measure, to the guilty pleas. Though the party had been growing rapidly for a decade, it soon began to stagnate and decline.

For progressive reformers, the episode did produce some salutary results. Theodore Roosevelt, who opposed labor excesses as much as business malfeasance, was vindicated for his aphorism that "Murder is Murder"; indeed, he wrote a second column for *Outlook* advancing that theme. But as much as they hated violence as a tactic, progressive reformers recognized that the bombing of the *Times* and of the Llewellyn Iron Works carried an important message. They felt more compelled than ever to search for constructive, nonrevolutionary ways to end the labor-capital war, or to ameliorate the conditions that had led the McNamaras—along with many other labor leaders—to use violence as an instrument of change.

In December, 1911, *The Survey* magazine devoted an entire issue to a discussion of the McNamara case and the conditions that had created it. Late that month, a group of reformers, led by Jane Addams and Rabbi Stephen S. Wise, delivered a petition to President Taft in the White House asking him to name a commission to study the problem. Taft agreed to do so, possibly with the assumption that he could choose commissioners who would put a conservative spin on their findings. He didn't announce his choices, however, until mid-December, 1912, a month after he lost the presidential election to Woodrow Wilson. "A hungry Democratic Party, out of office for sixteen years, felt in no mood to carry out the wishes of a lame-duck President," one historian explained. As a result, President Wilson was able to name the members of the Commission on Industrial Relations.

During the next two years the commission attracted continuing national attention with 154 days of eye-popping hearings featuring more than seven hundred witnesses. The witnesses ranged from John D. Rockefeller to Bill Haywood, from General Harrison Gray Otis to Anton Johannsen. One of the most effective presentations was by Clarence Darrow. Historian Page Smith observed that "If there is one 'document' (the hearings were published in eleven volumes) that tells what America did and thought in the era between 1901 and 1921, it is preeminently the Commission's Report."

The human impact of the confessions was at least as profound. Most directly, it affected Jim and J.J. McNamara, who entered San Quentin prison on December 10, 1911. In a curious sense, Jim found himself at San Quentin, relishing the role of a political martyr. Over the years he remained in touch with many of those who had helped with the trial, including Fremont Older, Lincoln Steffens, Mary Field, and both Darrows. Gradually he moved to the left politically, growing contemptuous of organized labor and ultimately joining ranks with the Communist Party. When he died on March 8, 1941, the most moving obituary was in *The Daily Worker,* which called him "Labor's Stoutest Heart."

Times were harder for J.J. in prison. He had been led to believe that he would be released within a year or two, but that was not to be. If there was an arrangement, it was one that the government felt free, or politically obliged, to reject. He remained in San Quentin until 1921. After his release, he was a pariah. The world and labor had changed. He briefly found a job as a business agent for the Structural Iron Workers but was dismissed when he was accused of treading close to the edge of the law. Broke and alone, he, too, died in 1941, just two months after his younger brother. No one felt moved to write him a stirring epitaph.

Part III

THE TRIAL OF CLARENCE DARROW

When the fight [for one's soul] is on, there is a call, not for an umpire, but a friend. That's why I'm here with Darrow. He is scared; the cynic is humbled; the man that laughed sees and is frightened, not at prison bars, but at his own soul. Well, then, what do I care if he is guilty as hell; what if his friends and attorneys turn away ashamed of him and of the soul of Man—Good God, I'll look with him, and if it's any comfort, I'll show him my soul, as black as his; not so naked, but—Sometimes all we humans have is a friend, somebody to represent God in the world.

Lincoln Steffens
Letter to Laura Steffens
Los Angeles, June 25, 1912

Chapter Eleven

DARROW AT THE DEPTHS

D ARROW'S PERSONAL AND PUBLIC trial, like the McNamara case, was about means and ends. It came at a time when America was at a crossroads, struggling to digest the ethical and social changes wrought by the move from an agricultural to an industrial world. In a way, Darrow was a part of both worlds—born in rural Ohio, trained as a small-town lawyer, he abruptly became a big-city success in Chicago. He had much in common with the people of Los Angeles, most of them recent arrivals from Iowa, still trying to find a moral compass in the urban maze. However they felt about capital and labor, they believed in—though did not always practice—the simple virtues of decency, integrity, family, and above all, religious charity and redemption. Disillusioned as he had become, Darrow understood the power of those moral precepts. But his pursuers understood it, too. In the months to come, Darrow's trial—and his life—became a canvas on which each side tried to write its version of the true meaning of justice in America.

After the confessions, Darrow was exiled to a form of purgatory. He was rejected and abandoned by his friends, most of whom believed that he had betrayed and deserted them. Socialists, intellectuals, and labor leaders accused him of the most vile personal motives. Some of the charges were fair; others were not. Whether true or not, they were everywhere. Anton Johannsen, for example, called him greedy and selfish, and insisted that as a result of the McNamara case Darrow had "something like two hundred thousand dollars socked away." Worse, Johannsen told friends that Darrow pleaded the brothers guilty, against their will, "to save his own skin in a deal with Fredericks." Other labor leaders, including Tvietmoe and Gompers, were even more unkind.

For almost two months, Darrow lived with fear of the unknown. Ruby desperately wanted to return to Chicago, but it was out of the question. He knew that it was only a matter of time until he would be charged with bribing Lockwood and Bain. His defense would cost a fortune, and it was money that he did not have. Despite Johannsen's suspicions, Darrow had less than $100,000 and it was the money that he hoped to use to retire. To save what they could, the Darrows moved out of their large house on Bonnie Brae and into a small apartment in Venice, near the Pacific Ocean.

He took long walks on the beach and visited with those friends who had not abandoned him. His talk was filled with self-pity, recriminations, and bitterness. He was particularly angry at Larry Sullivan, blaming him for telling the prosecutors about the bribery. Above all, he constantly repeated his terror of prison.

One of his visitors was W. W. Catlin, his old friend from the Sunset Club in Chicago, who was a neighbor at the beach. After spending time with Darrow, Catlin concluded that he was guilty. "I am assuming Darrow to be guilty," Catlin wrote, "because his course, not only here but elsewhere, and his talk, justifies the belief that he thinks such a course was right, under the conditions existing. . . . Darrow said no word to me of innocence, or regret that anyone had resorted to bribery. His whole talk was divided between intense and bitter attacks upon Larry [Sullivan], and a shuddering fear of the 'pen.' "

❋ ❋ ❋ ❋

Every day there was fresh evidence that he would be indicted for bribery. On Thursday, January 11, Bert Franklin, who had personally given the bribe money to both Bain and Lockwood, pleaded not guilty, but then spent an hour talking privately with Joe Ford, the deputy district attorney in charge of the case. Three days later, after spending part of the afternoon in conference with Darrow and LeCompte Davis, Franklin secretly took a Sunday afternoon drive with Ford, where he was observed by one of Darrow's friends. Surely they were discussing some kind of deal. The next morning, Franklin failed to show up for a grand jury hearing, fueling press speculation that he would be a prosecution witness. On Tuesday he hired a new lawyer, cutting ties with the legal team assembled by Darrow. On Wednesday, Franklin appeared in court and pleaded not guilty, but the *Times* predicted that he would change his mind and start cooperating with the government. That Friday he spent seven minutes in a secret session in front of the grand jury.

Darrow knew what the government was doing. It was using its overwhelming power to persuade Franklin to place the blame on him in exchange for a light fine. But his pursuers were doing more than that. The federal government was calling witnesses into the state, allegedly to aid in the investigation of the national dynamite conspiracy, but actually to provide further evidence against Darrow. Gradually the prosecutors were assembling a powerful case. With Bert Franklin's help, they were tracing the bribe money back to the ten-thousand-dollar check that Darrow had given to Olaf Tvietmoe on September 1, 1911. Equally important, they were working to secure the cooperation of a second key witness, John Harrington, Darrow's top investigator, the man he had brought with him from Chicago, and whose name was confusingly similar to that of Darrow's cocounsel, Job Harriman. The government continued to keep a lid on the fact that Darrow had been present at the scene of the crime. But that information, too, was sure to come to light.

On January 25, Franklin held a long meeting with Ford, representing the district attorney's office, and Oscar Lawler, who was in charge of the federal probe of the dynamiting conspiracy. Lawler then sent a letter to U.S. Attorney General Wickersham summarizing the evidence assembled to date. "Franklin confessed fully to Mr. Ford and myself, which confession, with the bank records at Washington and San Francisco and the Morrison check, makes a very complete case against [Darrow], the incidental corroboration being very satisfactory. There is another witness available [presumably

Harrington] who can give direct evidence as to Darrow's complicity in the bribery, and the following is a fairly conservative inventory of the corruption brought to surface to date:

"Two jurors bribed; two witnesses paid to get out of the country; two witnesses paid to testify falsely; a corrupt scheme to destroy certain physical evidence in the possession of the state authorities; the corruption of practically every employee of the Los Angeles County Jail who came in contact with the McNamaras; complicity in a scheme of Tvietmoe, Johannsen and others to get Mrs. Caplan out of the state (she being the wife of one of those indicted for the *Times* murder, and still being secreted); the hiring of George Behm, uncle of Ortie McManigal, to induce the latter to repudiate his confession, on the personal guarantee of Darrow that McManigal would be made a free man; and other minor irregularities almost too numerous to mention."

It was a powerful package of wrongdoing. "What a wave of crime you are unearthing!" Wickersham wrote to Lawler a few days later. "I sincerely hope that you will be able to bring some of the scoundrels to justice."

※ ※ ※ ※

As the case against him grew stronger, Darrow felt increasingly isolated. Mary had moved north, to a town near San Francisco, after Darrow announced that he could no longer see her romantically. She remained his loyal friend, but she no longer offered a comfort zone in the hostile city. A few friends like Erskine Wood sent money and good wishes, despite believing that Darrow was guilty of betrayal as well as bribery. But letters from such national leaders as Debs and Gompers regularly inflicted fresh wounds. Debs told Darrow that "the Socialists and others" had long since lost respect for him, "having concluded that you loved money too well to be trusted by the people." Gompers was equally cruel. The unions felt betrayed by his conduct in the McNamara cases, Gompers said. Any appeal by Darrow for labor union funds would "fall upon indifferent ears and elicit little, if any, response at this time." He would have to face the charges—and pay his bills—alone.

Darrow grew increasingly despondent. Ruby captured his mood

in a letter to Brand Whitlock, treating him as representative of a class of crusaders who had abandoned her husband, pleading with Darrow's old friend to send some message of encouragement. *"How can* you have remained silent so long!!" she thundered. "Are *you all* going to sit on the fence and see Mr. Darrow . . . marched *past* you *to prison?* Have you lost your *heart* as well as your *heads?* Are you not going to send him at least a word of encouragement and cheer—and once more assure him that you at least *you of all,* are still 'with him'? At least you men who tower above the laboring class will understand and *not* add *your blows* and forever *break* this *man's heart* past all healing!"

But during those long bitter winter months Whitlock, and most of Darrow's other old friends, remained painfully silent.

❊ ❊ ❊ ❊

"The intense strain on my mind and feelings was undermining my health," Darrow wrote later, "and I did not feel the strength and enthusiasm necessary for the fight." As a practical matter, he had two choices. He could play by the rules and accept the results, or get down in the mud and play rough and dirty.

One night during a visit at his Ocean Park apartment, Darrow asked his friend Dr. Perceval Gerson for advice. An important labor leader had just been in town urging Darrow to "fight back like hell." What did Gerson think of that advice?

"Do just the opposite, Darrow," Gerson pleaded. "State the facts of the case and take the consequences without resistance."

Darrow thought it over for a moment. It struck a chord. It was advice he had given to others on more than one occasion. But it was not a course that he could take with his own neck on the line.

"Gerson," he finally said, "you're right. But I can't do it."

Despite the odds and his mood, Darrow was still Darrow. He decided to "fight back like hell."

The best way to do that was to hire Earl Rogers.

❊ ❊ ❊ ❊

In the winter of 1911–1912, Earl Rogers was at the height of his powers, already a criminal lawyer of national note, well on his way to becoming the legendary creator of courtroom antics, tactics, and drama that novelists would try to capture and criminal lawyers would try to imitate. His reputation had already begun to emerge as the larger-than-life prototype of a defense counsel whose matinee idol following is only enhanced by his remarkable combination of wit, charm, intemperance, and deviousness, and his wide range of friendships with journalists, detectives, barkeepers, and prostitutes.

Earl Rogers was a comet on the horizon of criminal law, a blazing figure whose brief but remarkable career left an image that still remains. He was born in upstate New York, the son of the Reverend Lowell Rogers, an evangelist who came west to teach the gospel and then was swept up in the Southern California real estate mania of the 1880s. Rogers learned music from his mother, became fluent in several languages, including Latin and Greek, and was attending college at Syracuse University when the collapse of his father's real estate venture in Riverside County forced him to drop out of school. Not yet twenty, Rogers worked briefly as a reporter, but when he started to cover the courthouse he quickly became convinced that there was far more money and fame to be made by trying cases than by reporting them.

In that era when lawyers could earn admission to the bar through apprenticeship rather than law school study, Rogers managed to charm his way into the employ of U.S. senator Stephen M. White, widely regarded as "California's greatest lawyer and most brilliant statesman." By 1897, when Rogers was sworn into the bar and hung out his own shingle, some of the senator's magic had rubbed off: White's friends had become Rogers's friends; White's skills had become Rogers's skills. Perhaps as important in the long run, Rogers soon came to imitate White's greatest weakness—his propensity for exceptionally hard drinking.

Starting with his first case, Rogers established a reputation as a winner—brilliant, resourceful, innovative, and prepared to test the outer boundaries of legal propriety. The case began when "Doc" Crandall—better known as a pimp than as a veterinarian—was charged with murdering a client during a wild weekend party with two prostitutes. His case looked hopeless since Ruby Gaines, one of the prostitutes and an eyewitness to the murder, was scheduled to testify. But Crandall was acquitted when Ruby failed to appear in court. Though it couldn't be proved, the press was convinced that Rogers had arranged to have Ruby abducted and had fed her a steady diet of alcohol to keep her from the witness stand.

His reputation continued to build during the months that followed, but it didn't reach full flower until two years later, when he took on an unpopular and apparently hopeless case that pitted him against the best lawyer in the city—his mentor, Stephen White. As it happened, White was serving as a special prosecutor in the murder of Jay Hunter—a rich, handsome, and debonair attorney, the scion of Southern aristocrats, and a popular member of the city's plutocracy. Hunter had been murdered in the hallway of his office building by an obscure mechanic and odd-jobman named William Alford. Witnesses had seen Alford with the murder weapon and had heard Hunter, in his dying breath, say that he had been killed in cold blood.

To other defense lawyers, the case looked airtight, but to Rogers it looked like a once-in-a-lifetime opportunity to display the tactical skills he had been developing. Rogers's excuse was self-defense, the claim that Alford had been forced to shoot Hunter when the gentleman knocked him to the ground and began to beat him with his large walking stick. To diffuse the impact of the prosecution's damaging testimony, Rogers ridiculed it—causing laughter in the courtroom. He attacked and teased White's cocounsel, "General" Johnstone Jones, who was a bit too corpulent and pompous for the jury's taste; once—to the jury's delight—he even jabbed his finger into the general's paunch when the prosecutor asked a witness to describe the exact location of "the anterior superior spinous process of the ilium."

Rogers didn't have much evidence of his own, however, other than the testimony of his client, who was sure to be torn to pieces on cross-examination by Senator White. Knowing his mentor's habits, Rogers had lunch with White one day during the trial, making sure that the senator had so much to drink that he would, as was his custom on such occasions, take a brief nap before appearing in court. As soon as court began that afternoon, Rogers put Alford on the stand, out of turn, and raced through a recitation of how he had been knocked to the floor by Hunter and had used his gun in self-defense. After less than a half hour of questioning, Rogers turned the defendant over to the prosecution. Without White at his side, General Jones was left helpless. By the time the senator strolled into court that afternoon, Alford had left the witness stand, his testimony intact. White was furious, but there was nothing he could do.

Nor was White able to do anything but protest when Rogers, for corroboration, stunned the courtroom by producing a jar containing Hunter's bowels, which had been preserved in alcohol. Rogers had made himself an expert on human anatomy, so much so that he was able to tear apart the testimony of medical experts and was soon to become a lecturer at various medical colleges. Over White's strenuous protests, Rogers used a twenty-five-year-old physician named Dr. Edward Pallette to prove that the bullet had been fired from *below*—a direction that could only be explained if, as Rogers claimed, Alford had been lying on the ground when the shots were fired. White made no effort to recall the autopsy surgeon to offer a rebuttal.

Still, since the prosecution was entitled to make the final statement to the jury, Rogers was worried that White would win his case with the force of his closing argument. So he bought a small, schoolhouse blackboard, brought the blackboard into the courtroom, set it on an easel, and implored the jury to keep looking at it while White presents his "spellbinding oratory." Then he wrote a single, brief question on the blackboard:

> The Special Prosecutor did not recall Autopsy Surgeon Khurtz to the stand on rebuttal. Was this because he knew Dr. Khurtz agreed that the evidence of the dead man's own intestines and the testimony of Dr. Pallette proved before your own eyes that the bullet travelled UP from the floor, not DOWN?

To the astonishment and delight of the press, and most of the public, Alford was acquitted—and a star was born.

✳ ✳ ✳ ✳

Earl Rogers loved star status. In an era when movies were in their
infancy, and radio and television had yet to be developed, Rogers's
live performances made him a singular celebrity. Theatrical luminar-
ies such as Maude Adams and Ethel Barrymore passed through town
to perform for a week or two before traveling to the next city, but
Earl Rogers was on stage week in and week out, turning the courtroom into theater, his feats publicized by such friendly reporters as
Harry Carr of the *Los Angeles Times.* Noting that Rogers was "one of
the greatest criminal lawyers of all time," Carr later observed that he
"was one of the first to realize that a criminal lawsuit is a drama. And
the lawyer who puts up the best drama wins. Each of his criminal
trials was like a great play."

And as with stars of the theater, Rogers found his own style of
dress and his own forms of behavior. With his sultry, almost self-
satisfied look, his jet black hair that was parted in the middle and fell
lightly into distinctive locks on either side of his large forehead, and
his penetrating blue eyes that were the most compelling feature of
his perfectly shaped face, he was an impressive figure to behold. But
he soon improved on his natural good looks. Hugh Baillie, a young
reporter who was to become head of the United Press, later remembered the Earl Rogers of 1912 as "a sharp dresser—a howling swell,
as we said in those days. In an age when many men of some
distinction thought it no harm to go without a shave for a day or two,
Rogers was always neatly barbered, his face glowing, his black hair
well trimmed. At a time when it was no disgrace to be seen in baggy
pants, Rogers would appear in cutaway coat with braided edges,
fawn waistcoat, spats, boutonniere, lavish cravat, and bat-winged
collar." And his voice and his eyes were extraordinary instruments.
"Rogers played his voice the way a musician plays a church organ.
He could make it full-throated and menacing, or gentle and beguil-
ing. He had bright blue eyes spaced rather widely apart, and he
could use them as penetrating searchlights when he wished—or
dull them with counterfeit indifference."

One of his most unusual affectations was the use of the lorgnette, though Rogers used the lorgnette (and all of his other eccentricities) for a purpose as well as a pose. "He wore a lorgnette on a long ribbon," Baillie recalled, "and would hold it to his eyes and stare through it at a witness, leaning into the box to face the man down. When the lorgnette had served its purpose, he would twirl it on the ribbon and shoot it into the breast pocket of his coat. He never missed the pocket. As a feat of juggling, this was fascinating in itself, and frequently the jury paid more attention to the stunt than they did to the witness and what he was saying. Having restored the lorgnette to its resting place, Rogers might ask the next question from behind the witness stand, or turn his back on the witness and shout the question at the audience in the courtroom, or coo it at the members of the jury. He put on quite a show."

He was famous for representing pimps and gangsters, but was equally notorious as what Debs called an "all around capitalist retainer." Anton Johannsen labeled Rogers "the leading servant for privilege" in a "city of slaves." In 1910, he drafted the antipicketing ordinance that sealed the city's reputation as "the scabbiest city in America." When the *Times* was bombed, General Otis and the Merchants and Manufacturers Association naturally hired Rogers to oversee the investigation; after the McNamaras were located, no one was surprised that he was chosen to serve as the special prosecutor who presented the case to the grand jury; and there were those who expected and even urged the district attorney to hire Rogers to beef up the prosecution's team in the McNamara case itself—to give the prosecution someone of the stature and talent of the legal heavyweights who had been hired by the defendants. But there was no love lost between Rogers and Fredericks, and Fredericks was in no mood to share the glory.

❋ ❋ ❋ ❋

In many respects, Clarence Darrow and Earl Rogers were polar opposites. Darrow had a reputation as something of an idealist, a defender of righteous causes, the lawyer for the weak against the powerful, the poor against the rich. If not precisely accurate, that was how Darrow was best known. As a legal tactician, he was, of course, a realist, and apparently had, from time to time, felt obliged to find a way to get rid of unwelcome witnesses and to make sure that the jury contained some members who were committed to vote for his client; but his real forte was as a pleader, an eloquent spokesman for the righteousness of the cause and the understandable and praiseworthy, if perhaps misguided, passion of his clients. He played, at once, to the compassion of the jury and the passion of the public, building sympathy for his clients' cases and admiration for his own noble qualities. If an affair or two found their way into his personal life, the story never found its way into the press. Whatever his personal doubts about religion, no matter how often he debunked the excesses of the clergy, he was so repressed that he served as his own censor, avoiding written profanity; unlike many of his correspondents, who felt comfortable writing out the phrase "God damn," Darrow's handwritten letters invariably present the words as "G-- d---."

While the public Darrow was a candidate for a certain kind of secular saint, the public Rogers was a candidate, indeed a deliberate candidate, for sinner. He made no pretense about fighting for a cause or clients who were just. After winning an acquittal for Charlie Mootry, who was accused of killing his Bible-reading wife, his client tried to thank him. "Get away from me, you slimy pimp," Rogers shouted in disgust. "You're guilty as hell." It was a reputation he relished—and cultivated—despite the pleas of his father, the minister, who tried in vain to persuade his son to confine his cases to the defense of the innocent or, at worst, the *honest* defense of the guilty. He wasn't the attorney for the damned. He was the attorney for the guilty. "Close to one hundred slayers escaped the gallows" due to Rogers, his admiring biographers claimed, "though most of them were guilty."

Rogers's personal life was even more amoral, or at least out of step with social convention. In her adoring biography, Rogers's daughter, Adela, portrays a loveless home life with a woman who drove Rogers to bars and streets and hotels, to Pearl Morton's famous sporting house and to a young woman there named Dolly, a natural-born comic who played the piano and made Earl Rogers laugh. But however understandable his needs, and however admirable Dolly and Pearl Morton may have been, these were not the kinds of relationships that were accepted in polite society, particularly not in the kind of society that was important to Ruby Darrow.

❋❋❋❋

Ruby was reluctant to see her husband defended by such a man. Her husband's clients had, as she knew, gained stature from their association with him. Wouldn't Clarence be sure to lose stature through an association with a man known for his decadent life-style, his amoral and even antilabor views, and for winning cases for guilty men? Even if acquitted, wouldn't people say that this was just another example of a brilliant Rogers defense of a guilty man?

But Darrow knew that the state would have a powerful case against him, that they would present credible-sounding witnesses to attest to his guilt, and that it would be hard to explain away his presence at Third and Main when Franklin was arrested. There would be a lot of questions—and he would need to produce a lot of answers. As he began to sink into depression, he knew that he would need to do whatever it took to win his freedom. If it took Earl Rogers, then Darrow wanted him at his side.

❋❋❋❋

Rogers was not shocked by Darrow's depression. He was used to finding men at the bottom, their spirits dimmed and their minds paralyzed by fear. His clients had included the poor and the powerful. Helping the mighty with the process of personal and legal regeneration was nothing new to him.

Rogers immediately set forth a plan of action. Together, he and Darrow would be the greatest legal team ever fielded in Los Angeles, perhaps the greatest team ever to handle any case anywhere. They would decimate the opposition. They were far more clever and resourceful than Fredericks and Ford and, with a little work, they could make the prosecutors look foolish. After all, Darrow was one of the most respected lawyers in America; who could believe that he would bribe a juror? Was the court going to believe the word of Bert Franklin, a man who admitted that he had engaged in bribery himself, a man who—if he testified against Darrow—would be doing so

At a few minutes past one A.M. on October 1, 1910, the *Los Angeles Times* building was rocked by a deafening explosion followed by a fire that swept through the structure, destroying the building and leaving twenty men dead.

To no avail, fire fighters in horse-drawn wagons tried to get the blaze under control. LOS ANGELES TIMES HISTORY CENTER

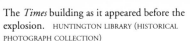

The *Times* building as it appeared before the explosion. HUNTINGTON LIBRARY (HISTORICAL PHOTOGRAPH COLLECTION)

The scene the following morning as thousands gathered to witness the wreckage. LOS ANGELES TIMES HISTORY CENTER

PER ANNUM, $9.00 | For Month, 70 Cents; By 1½ Cents a Copy.   SATURDAY MORNING, OCTOBER 1, 1910.   On All News Stands, Trains and Streets, 5 CENTS

UNIONIST BOMBS WRECK THE TIMES; MANY SERIOUSLY INJURED

Terrific Explosion at 1 o'Clock This Morning Starts Fire Which Engulfs Score of Employes in Great Newspaper Plant---Many Victims ---Great Property Loss.

Many lives were jeopardized and half a million dollars' worth of property was sacrificed on the altar of hatred of the labor unions at 1 o'clock this morning, when the plant of the Los Angeles Times was blown up and burned, following numerous threats by the laborites.

Not quite as many of the employes were on duty as would have been the case earlier in the night, when all departments were working in full blast, but even so, the murderous cowards knew that fully 100 people were in the building at the time.

With the suddenness of an earthquake, an explosion, of which the dry, snappy sound left no room to doubt of its origin in dynamite, tore down the whole first floor wall of the building on Broadway, just back of the entrance to the business offices. In as many seconds, four or five other explosions of lesser volume were heard.

In the time it took to run at full speed from the police station to the corner of First and Broadway, a distance of less than half a block, the entire building was in flames on three floors. Almost in the same instant flames and smoke filled the east stairway on First street, driving down in a frenzied panic those employes of the composing room who had been so fortunate as to reach the landing in time.

Elbowing past the last of these fugitives, men fought their way up to the first floor with flash lights and handkerchiefs over their faces. There efforts were unavailing, the blistering hot smoke and the lurid light of the flames almost upon them and licking down at them fiercely, drove the would-be rescuers back, hurriedly.

Although they could hear clearly the cries of distress, the groans and screams of the men and women who, mangled and crippled by flying debris from the explosion, lay imprisoned by the flames, about to be cremated alive.

Along the windows of the editorial and city rooms, on the south side of the building, through a choking volume of black smoke, could be seen men and women crowding each other about the windows of the third floor. The cries for ladders went up, frantic.

A fire wagon drove up at full speed. Groans greeted it when it was seen that it was but a hose wagon instead of the hook and ladder truck.

"Nets; get nets, nets!" was the yell.

A policeman came running up from headquarters, carrying a short ladder, pathetically inadequate. Some one called him a fool. But the ladder saved the live of Lovelace, the country editor, who jumped upon it and escaped with broken leg and some minor burns. Other fire apparatus thundered up. The nets were jerked out in less time than it takes to tell, but by that time the fire had surged through the building with such rapidity that it was impossible to ap-

A PLAIN STATEMENT

By the Managing Editor of The Times

The Times building was destroyed this morning by the enemies of industrial freedom by dynamite bombs and fire.

Numerous threats to do this dastardly deed had been received.

The Times itself cannot be destroyed. It will be issued every day and will fight its battles to the end.

The elements that conspired to perpetrate this horror must not be permitted to pursue their awful campaign of intimidation and terror. Never will the Times cease its warfare against them.

Gen. Otis, the principal owner of the Times, is on his way home from Mexico and will arrive here this afternoon.

The Times has a complete auxiliary plant from which this issue was printed on its own presses.

The management is under great obligations to The Herald for hearty assistance and to the Examiner for friendly offers.

The Times will soon be itself again. All business will be conducted at the Times Branch Office, 531 South Spring street.

A further statement cannot be made at this hour in the presence of frightful death and destruction.

Harry Chandler, assistant general manager of the Times, happened to be on the street when the explosion occurred and immediately took command of the situation.

They can kill our men and can wreck our buildings, but by the God above they cannot kill the Times.

HARRY E. ANDREWS,
Managing Editor of The Times.

INJURED

E. B. ASPINALL, linotype operator. Cut over left eye.

S. W. CRABILL, foreman composing room. Burned and cut with flying glass.

WILL LATTA, stereotyper. Burned arms and back.

U. S. G. PENTZ, linotype operator. Jumped from window; wrist broken.

G. RICHARD, cut.

M. WESTON, cut on shoulders.

RANDOLPH ROSS, lynotype operator. Jumped from second story window; abrasion left knee; ankle sprained.

CHARLES VON VELSEN, fireman. Cut on left hand.

MRS. J. B. ULRICH, fell down elevator.

CHARLES E. LOVELACE, editorial staff. Jumped from third floor window; injuries perhaps fatal.

AUGUST KOTSCH, compositor. Slightly burned.

J. F. LINK, glass cuts on head.

CHURCHILL HARVEY-ELDER, burned over body and head; broken right leg; will probably die.

RICHARD GOFF, slight burns and cuts.

MISSING

J. C. GALLIHER, 40, linotype operator, married and five children.

W. G. TUNSTALL, 45, linotype operator, married.

FRED LLEWELLYN, 36, operator, married.

JOHN HOWARD, 45, printer, married and one child.

GRANT MOORE, 42, machinist, married and three children.

ED WASSON, 35, printer, married.

ELMER FRINK, 25, operator, married.

EUGENE CARESS, 35, operator, married and one child.

DON E. JOHNSON, 36, operator, married.

ERNEST JORDAN, 32, operator, married and one child.

FRANK UNDERWOOD, 48, printer, married and one child.

J. WESLEY REAVER, stenographer.

R. L. SAWYER, 34, telegraph operator, married and two children.

HARRY L. CRANE, 38, assistant telegraph editor, married and one child.

CHARLES GULLIVER, 35, compositor, married.

proach the reddening walls of the great building, cooking the bound--not to be rescued and mus...

It is less than four minutes from the time the explosion was heard the entire building was ablaze.

The Work of Demons

It reeked little to the man who placed the bombs which wrecked a splendid newspaper plant that 100 men were at work on the various floors, busily engaged in getting out the great newspaper. That the instant that the bombs were exploded their lives were in peril that as a result of the hellish work lives were probably lost and other lives precious to wives, children and relatives were in death peril.

The bombs were planted by experienced hands. They did the work for which they were intended; at least temporarily, to cripple a great newspaper.

All o'clock the Times plant was humming in every department. Forms were being closed up, stereotyped and sent down to the pressroom. An hour later the great presses would run at lightning speed to print the many thousands of papers which carriers were waiting to serve to their customers.

So it had left but little hours. A deafening detonation, a sickening uplift of men's hearts and lungs, then vivid tongues of flames, dense stifling smoke which obscured the electric lights on every floor.

One instant busy occupation, lights, the whir of machinery, the next, black midnight, smoke that overpowers, flames that shot their wicked tongues from basement to roof.

Trapped on all floors, the men of the Times, picked men they were, preserved their coolness in the midst of this appalling scene.

But it would seem that there was no escape. The murderers had planned with hellish cunning. The broad stairways were filled with deadly smoke almost as soon as the echo of the dynamite bomb had died away. The building was on fire on every side. But three

CHIEF'S STATEMENT

CHIEF GALLOWAY, at 2 o'clock this morning, said:

"That the building was wrecked by dynamite seems certain from all we may can learn. There are, about six patrolmen on duty at the fire now, and they dodged dead for fear the murderers are not yet through with their hellish work."

All Business for
THE TIMES
Will be Transacted at Their Branch Office
531 SOUTH SPRING ST.

N. Y. DEMOCRATS SELECT DIX FOR STANDARD BEARER

State Chairman Finally Agrees to Run for Governor of the Empire State

FULL TICKET IS NOMINATED

When Independence League Is Mentioned It Is Greeted with a Storm of Hisses

ROCHESTER, N. Y. (by...

WINSLOW HOMER, NOTED ARTIST, DIES, AGED 74

PORTLAND, Me. Sept. 30 Winslow Homer, the famous artist, died at his home in Scarborough, yesterday, aged 74. He had been ill for some months...

When the explosion occurred, Otis was on a short trip to Mexico, serving as an envoy for President William Howard Taft. In his absence, the paper was run by his financially astute son-in-law, Harry Chandler (*right*). Chandler had left the building shortly before the blast, and his secretary was one of those killed by the fire.

SECURITY PACIFIC COLLECTION/ L.A. PUBLIC LIBRARY

As soon as he returned to town, Otis went to the site to observe the damage (*below*).

LOS ANGELES TIMES HISTORY CENTER

The city immediately hired the nation's most famous detective, William J. Burns, to search for the perpetrators. After a massive six-month manhunt, Burns obtained a confession from Ortie McManigal, a member of the Bridge and Structural Iron Workers' Union (*left*). McManigal claimed that the *Times* fire had been caused by an "infernal machine," or time bomb, set by James B. McNamara, brother of Iron Workers secretary-treasurer John J. (J.J.) McNamara. He said that, acting on J.J.'s instructions, he had set off the bomb at the Llewellyn Iron Works on Christmas Day, 1910.

In a highly publicized (and legally questionable) episode, Burns arrested J. J. McNamara at the union's headquarters in Indianapolis. He then put both brothers on a train and sent them across country to stand trial in Los Angeles (*below*).

Ortie McManigal explains the workings of a time bomb, also known as an "infernal machine."
LOS ANGELES TIMES HISTORY CENTER

A squad of men from the Burns detective agency and the Los Angeles Sheriff's office escort the McNamara brothers to court.
LOS ANGELES TIMES HISTORY CENTER

The McNamara case was immediately embraced by the forces of labor, who were convinced that the McNamara brothers (or at least J.J.) had been framed. Men like AFL president Samuel Gompers believed that the only lawyer who could save the McNamaras was Clarence Darrow, who had to be lured out of semiretirement.

For the moment, Darrow loved being back at the center of international attention.

Samuel Gompers put the full weight of the American Federation of Labor into the fight to win freedom for the McNamara brothers. This photograph shows J.J. in a typically forceful pose. (*Left to right:* Jim McNamara, Gompers, J. J. McNamara.) LOS ANGELES TIMES HISTORY CENTER

Back at the helm of a great case, Darrow was a commanding presence. (*Left to right:* cocounsel Joseph Scott, Jim McNamara, Darrow, cocounsel LeCompte Davis.) CLEVELAND PUBLIC LIBRARY

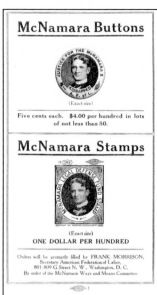

Labor halls were flooded with brochures asking for contributions; stamps and buttons with J.J.'s likeness were sold to workers to raise money for the case.
TAMIMENT LIBRARY, NEW YORK UNIVERSITY

At Darrow's suggestion, labor mounted a massive nationwide publicity campaign featuring J.J.'s face on stamps and buttons and even making him the hero of a movie called *A Martyr to His Cause.* All materials stressed that he had been "kidnapped" and unfairly charged. To finance the defense, workers were urged to contribute nickels and dimes from their meager earnings.

Meanwhile, in a major coup for the defense, Darrow brought Ortie McManigal's wife and children to Los Angeles to try to talk her husband out of testifying. But Burns's men and the district attorney's office tormented her, threatening her with criminal prosecution. Within weeks they broke her spirit and forced her to leave town.

Shortly after arriving in Los Angeles, Emma McManigal posed happily with her children and three members of the defense team. (Job Harriman is seated at left, Darrow is standing next to Emma McManigal, and Joseph Scott is seated at the right.)
LOS ANGELES TIMES HISTORY CENTER

Mary Field's bohemian circle of friends included sculptor Jo Davidson, who sent her this drawing of a nude in 1912. It is signed, "To Mary Field, with love." MARGARET PARTON PAPERS, ARTWORK 53/7, SPECIAL COLLECTIONS, KNIGHT LIBRARY, UNIVERSITY OF OREGON

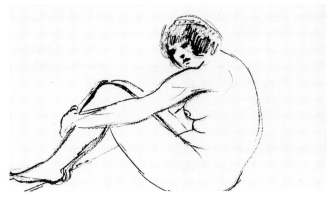

Darrow was attracted by Mary Field's spunk and humor, which don't quite shine through in this photograph taken about eight years later. MARGARET PARTON PAPERS, SPECIAL COLLECTIONS, KNIGHT LIBRARY, UNIVERSITY OF OREGON

Darrow was soon joined in Los Angeles by a group of allies that included his girlfriend, Mary Field. She was a radical journalist who moved to New York at Darrow's suggestion (and with Darrow's money) and quickly became a success. At first, Darrow urged her not to come to Los Angeles, afraid that they would be trailed by detectives. But she came anyway and they resumed a romance that became a source of intense pain and humiliation for Darrow's wife, Ruby.

Mary settled into a small flat near downtown Los Angeles, where she was joined by her sister Sara Field Ehrgott, a feminist poet from Portland, Oregon. Sara wrote daily letters to her boyfriend, Colonel Charles Erskine Scott Wood. Darrow wanted Wood to serve as his cocounsel in the McNamara case, but Wood declined, certain that Darrow would use improper tactics, including bribing jurors.

Sara Field Ehrgott signed this deliberately intellectual-looking picture with the words " literarily yours." HUNTINGTON LIBRARY

After being introduced by Darrow in late 1910, Sara Field Ehrgott and C.E.S. Wood began a passionate love affair. Since both of them were married, they had to keep their relationship a secret. Years later they established a wonderful home in Los Gatos, California, and maintained close friendships with scores of artists and intellectuals. (*Left to right:* Lincoln Steffens, Ella Winter, Colonel Wood, Sara Field.) HUNTINGTON LIBRARY

Juror Robert Bain, pictured here running after a photographer with a broom. LOS ANGELES TIMES HISTORY CENTER

Lincoln Steffens in 1911.
CULVER PICTURE COLLECTION

With facts turning against the McNamaras, members of the defense team decided to bribe one or two of the jurors, starting with Robert Bain.

In early November, Lincoln Steffens came to Los Angeles convinced of the McNamaras' guilt. He tried to persuade Darrow to work out a plea bargain. Then on November 28, Darrow's chief jury investigator, Bert Franklin, was apprehended while bribing a juror. Darrow, who was present at the time of the arrest, decided to plead both brothers guilty. On December 1, Jim admitted to bombing the *Times* and J.J. admitted complicity in the bombing of the Llewellyn Iron Works.

Upon learning of the confessions, thousands of people gathered at the court building to find out whether the brothers really had decided to plead guilty. LOS ANGELES TIMES HISTORY CENTER

News of the guilty pleas astonished the city and the nation. People reacted with disbelief. Job Harriman, a Socialist mayoral candidate who had run a strong campaign, was soundly defeated at the polls. Labor leaders and Socialists blamed Darrow.

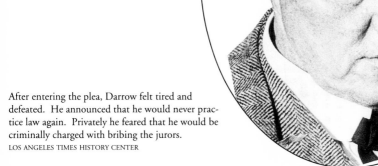

After entering the plea, Darrow felt tired and defeated. He announced that he would never practice law again. Privately he feared that he would be criminally charged with bribing the jurors.
LOS ANGELES TIMES HISTORY CENTER

The McNamara brothers were taken to San Quentin prison in mid-December.
(The photograph above shows Los Angeles sheriff Hammel pointing to the island where they were
about to land.) Jim spent his entire life in prison, ending his years as a Communist Party hero. J.J.
was released in 1923 but was treated as a pariah.

LOS ANGELES TIMES HISTORY CENTER

Labor leaders and Socialists blamed Darrow for
pleading the men guilty after leading the public
to believe in their innocence. Some, like
Samuel Gompers, never forgave him. But the
San Francisco labor leaders who were
responsible for bringing Jim McNamara to Los
Angeles soon came to Darrow's defense. The
most important of those leaders were Anton
Johannsen and Olaf Tvietmoe, known as "the
Viking." (Tvietmoe is pictured at left.)

THE BANCROFT LIBRARY

Earl Rogers was as famous for his drunken evenings as he was for the sartorial attire he wore into court.
KATHLEEN ST. JOHNS SLOAN

Darrow was indicted for bribery on January 29, 1912. As he sank into a deep, even suicidal depression, he knew that he had to hire the most resourceful criminal lawyer in the West. He chose Earl Rogers, the brilliant but unscrupulous attorney who, as general counsel of the city's Merchants and Manufacturers Association, had written the notorious "anti-picketing law."

One of Rogers's favorite props was a lorgnette that he used for emphasis, distraction, and, occasionally, for reading while in court. Here he tries the lorgnette out on his infant son, Thornwell.
KATHLEEN ST. JOHNS SLOAN

Darrow at a pretrial conference. Prosecutor Joseph Ford is to his right, cocounsel Jerry Geisler is to his left. Bailiff Martin Aguirre is behind Geisler, partially hidden from view. LOS ANGELES TIMES HISTORY CENTER

As the trial began, Ruby Darrow sat directly behind her husband, sharing his pain, often offering him a fresh flower or a comforting smile. The jury began to sympathize with her anguish, particularly when she was bedridden with nervous prostration. For many, by the end of the ten-week ordeal, she had become a heroine.
LOS ANGELES TIMES HISTORY CENTER

When the trial began, Darrow sat in the defendant's chair, filled with self-pity, an attitude that infuriated his chief counsel, Earl Rogers. But within a few weeks, Rogers's behavior became increasingly erratic, forcing Darrow to become his own chief counsel and to get back on his feet emotionally as well as physically.

As the old-line Republican district attorney, Captain John Fredericks seemed a surefire candidate for governor, but his erect bearing and self-righteous attitude made him the perfect symbol of government oppression to Darrow's followers.
THE SEAVER CENTER FOR WESTERN HISTORY RESEARCH, NATURAL HISTORY MUSEUM OF LOS ANGELES COUNTY

At the end of a trial filled with drama and pathos, Darrow took the witness stand. He later claimed that "I had no more trouble about answering every question put to me than I would have had reciting the multiplication table." In fact, a dizzying series of questions and revelations left him on the defensive, "sparring for time."

SECURITY PACIFIC COLLECTION/ L.A. PUBLIC LIBRARY

Darrow addresses his final emotional plea to the jury, his eyes swollen with tears, a lock of hair characteristically falling over his forehead, his pocket filled with handkerchiefs he has been using to wipe away his tears. Juror F. E. Golding sits in the center of the front row, watching intently. In the background is the huge chart prepared by Earl Rogers to list—and debunk—all of the testimony offered by witnesses for the prosecution.

LOS ANGELES TIMES HISTORY CENTER

On August 15, 1912, Darrow stood up to make a plea in his own defense. Many considered it the greatest speech he had ever delivered. Speaking to those inside and outside the jury room, to former friends who had abandoned him, he asked for understanding and forgiveness. Whatever his weaknesses and his sins, he was being punished, he said, for devoting his life to helping the poor and the powerless. He was often in tears, as were the men on the jury and the hundreds of people packed into the courtroom.

As soon as the trial ended, there was a spontaneous celebration in the courtroom. In this picture (which is probably a composite prepared by the Los Angeles *Herald*) the wife of jury foreman Manley Williams offers Darrow a bouquet as her husband watches (*right*) and Anton Johannsen (*left*) stands beaming.
SECURITY PACIFIC COLLECTION/ L.A. PUBLIC LIBRARY

The jury took less than forty minutes to reach its verdict. When they announced Darrow's acquittal, the room exploded with joy. The jurors rejoiced in the jury box, where they were joined by an emotionally overwhelmed Darrow.

The verdict had a profound effect on Darrow, helping him to become the man he once had been, the champion of the poor whom he had described in his final plea.

At a victory luncheon, Darrow studies the headlines in a newspaper extra. Fremont Older is at his right and Ruby Darrow at his left. Mary Field stands behind and between Clarence and Ruby Darrow, clasping the hand of Anton Johannsen, who is at her right, immediately behind her. LILA WEINBERG

as a result of a deal with the prosecution, a deal that had saved him from going to the penitentiary? Surely it could be proved that Bert Franklin had told any number of people that Darrow was innocent, a statement that was only slightly compromised by the fact that Darrow had paid for Franklin's bail and had arranged for his legal defense. Before the defense was through, the community would be convinced that Franklin was a part of a giant frame-up and, from the outset, had been in the employ of the government, the National Erectors' Association, and William J. Burns.

Besides, Rogers argued, reviewing the case that he would ultimately present to the press and the jury, what motive did Darrow have for bribing the jury? After all, as Lincoln Steffens had written, the case was already all but resolved at the time the alleged bribery took place.

There was, of course, the nettlesome fact that Darrow had been found at the scene of the crime, a fact that was not yet known but soon would be. The public and the jury would surely want to know what he was doing there, why he was present when the bribe took place if he knew nothing about it. But Rogers pointed out that his presence at the scene of the crime might work to their advantage. After all, who would believe that so sophisticated a lawyer would have arranged for a bribe to be given on a busy street in downtown Los Angeles, in broad daylight? And, to add stupidity to foolishness, who would believe that he would have himself appeared at the scene? Clearly it was a setup, a prosecution meant for one purpose only, to destroy Clarence Darrow, the great champion of labor— and, through him, to try to reach Samuel Gompers, the very soul of America's organized workers.

❋ ❋ ❋ ❋

Normally, arrests take place at the home of the accused, who is then taken downtown by the police. But on Monday morning, January 29, 1912, the district attorney's office called Darrow at his home in Venice and advised him that the indictments would be issued that afternoon. It was an act of courtesy to one of America's great men. When the court sent for him at three-thirty P.M., Darrow was standing by at Rogers's law offices, waiting with Rogers and Cyrus McNutt, the former Indiana judge who had served as a cocounsel in the McNamara case.

Entering the courtroom a few minutes later, Darrow "was white and plainly stirred to the depths of his being." He sat down just inside the bar and nervously waited for the proceedings to begin. The court session, to his great relief, was mercifully brief. The district attorney charged him with bribing juror Robert Bain and prospective juror George N. Lockwood. Together, the charges carried a maximum penalty of thirty years' imprisonment and twenty thousand dollars in fines. After two friends posted a bail of twenty thousand dollars, Darrow was released.

The roomful of reporters immediately flocked to the side of the famous attorney, asking for a comment.

"I can just say what I have from the first," he answered. "I know nothing of the bribery charge; know nothing of any attempt to approach one of the prospective jurors; and knew absolutely nothing of the thing until Franklin was arrested." For a few moments he managed to straighten up and smile, but he lost his composure again as a mass of cameras were aimed in his direction. He lit a cigarette and began to leave the room.

As he was on his way out, someone asked the question that he had been dreading since the day of his arrest. "It is said that part of the evidence that caused your indictment was the fact that you were within two hundred fifty feet of the alleged briber when he was passing money to a juror," a reporter began. Of course the evidence presented to the grand jury was still secret; no one could know for sure; but was it true? Had he been there at Third and Main?

At last the information was out. He had been present at the streetcorner bribe. Now he would have to explain what he had been doing there.

Cyrus McNutt politely intervened, nudging him gently. "Don't talk about anything like that," McNutt advised.

Darrow smiled grimly and followed his friend's advice. "I am not going to discuss the case or talk about it in any way," he told the reporter. But he knew that, sooner or later, he would have to answer the question.

❃ ❃ ❃ ❃

Stories around the country the next day made the case against him look credible, fortified by his presence at the scene of the bribe. A long article in the *Los Angeles Times* was particularly cruel.

> "Well, boys, is everything fixed?" This is the remark attributed to Clarence Darrow as he stepped between Bert H. Franklin and George N. Lockwood at the intersection of Third and Los Angeles streets on the morning of November 28. It is alleged that evidence went before the grand jury during the past few weeks that showed Darrow was standing close by when Franklin is said to have paid $500 to Lockwood.
>
> According to the theory of the prosecution, Darrow was on the spot to see that his confidential man, Franklin, paid over the agreed amount of money. There are at least ten or more detectives and attachés of the District Attorney who will swear that the scene took place and that Darrow placed his arms confidently on the shoulders of Franklin and Lockwood.

Was Rogers right in thinking that the incident could easily be dismissed, ridiculed as too unprofessional for a man with Darrow's experience? Or was it the irrefutable piece of evidence that would send him to San Quentin?

"This will be a real fight," Rogers told the press. "I believe Darrow to be an innocent man. There will be no milk and water methods in this trial."

That proved to be an understatement.

Chapter Twelve

"NO MILK AND WATER METHODS IN THIS TRIAL"

POWERFUL AS THE EVIDENCE was against Franklin, none of it pointed directly to Darrow. One might surmise that Franklin could not have acted on his own, but a surmise is not proof. That is what made Darrow's appearance at the scene of the bribe so troubling. It seemed to implicate him directly in the event. But if Darrow's appearance at Third and Main could somehow be explained away, shown to be a setup or a coincidence, then it could be argued that Franklin might have been acting on behalf of someone other than Darrow, such as Nockles, or Job Harriman, or the San Francisco labor leaders; or, that he might have been an agent for Burns or for General Otis or for Captain Fredericks. To convict Darrow, there would have to be either physical proof—such as a clear line of evidence linking him with the payoff money—or a credible witness. The best way for the defense to win the case was to make certain that there was no such witness—either real or manufactured.

With his trial set for mid-May, Clarence Darrow had three months to make sure that people with knowledge of the events would testify for him—or would stay away from the courtroom. In the weeks following his indictment, three of Darrow's former employees loomed as possible, dangerous witnesses. Larry Sullivan, John Harrington, and Bert Franklin all gave Darrow nightmares.

To Darrow's astonishment, Larry Sullivan proved totally loyal. When Captain Fredericks asked him to testify to the grand jury, Sullivan refused. Fredericks announced that he would send Sullivan to jail if he did not cooperate. Sullivan said that he would rather go to jail than take the stand against Darrow. But Fredericks was adamant, so Sullivan took the highly unusual step of leaving the country. He went to Mexico, where he hid out and used the name Malachi.

Writing in broken English, "Malachi" sent a candid assessment to Erskine Wood on March 1. "I had to get out of Los Angeles for a while," he explained. "They wanted me to be a witness against D. So I come to this country. . . . That fellow D. is in a bad way and he has nobody to blame but himself for it. . . . Colonel Wood, he is the lowest man I ever knew. I will tell you when I see you how low he is."

Within a few weeks, Sullivan was able to return to Los Angeles. He told Wood that he had made up with Darrow, although he still held the lawyer in total contempt. "I have never in my lifetime seen a man fall away as fast as has Darrow," he said. "I honestly think that Darrow will either plead guilty or commit suicide."

Sullivan did not turn against him, but a more important witness did. John Harrington, the man that Darrow had brought with him from Chicago, the man he had once called "the best evidence-gatherer I have ever seen," soon started to cooperate with Captain Fredericks.

❋ ❋ ❋ ❋

Two days after Darrow's indictment, the *Los Angeles Times* reported that Harrington "is expected to be another strong witness for the prosecution" and that he had "declared his readiness to give some startling facts about alleged jury-bribery and the intimidation of the state's witnesses." Two weeks later, the same paper reported that "Bert Franklin and attorney John Harrington of Chicago will be the star witnesses against Darrow."

Darrow hoped the *Time*'s reports were wrong. He had known Harrington for more than a decade and had shown the man plenty of kindnesses. Indeed, the Darrows had taken Harrington into their home during the Christmas season just passed. True, Harrington had often told Darrow that he felt underpaid for the McNamara case: He had been working on the case since late April and had only been paid five thousand dollars, whereas the other attorneys working for Darrow, who had started work in May or June, had each been paid fifteen thousand dollars. Maybe Darrow did owe him some more money. But to be fair, Harrington hadn't really been working as a lawyer; he had been hired as an investigator. Darrow was certain that the man had never been paid so well for his services. Besides, it would be suicidal to antagonize Darrow. After all, Harrington hoped to reestablish a law practice in Chicago, where no one had heard of Captain Fredericks but everyone knew Clarence Darrow. It would, as anyone with any wits must know, be better to have Darrow as a friend than as an enemy.

Unknown to Darrow, however, Harrington was already cooperating with the government. Oscar Lawler of the federal government and Joseph Ford of the district attorney's office both had possible cases against Harrington, but they promised to drop all such charges if he would cooperate with their efforts to trap and convict Darrow. Harrington accepted their offer.

Lawler and Ford devised a devious plan. They made an arrangement with Robert Foster, a Dublin-born detective from New York who had done most of the legwork for Walter Drew and the National Erectors' Association in Indianapolis. At the prosecutors' request, Foster arrived in Los Angeles on February 12 and went to organized labor's favorite downtown hotel, the Hayward, where he rented three connecting rooms on the fourth floor. He took Room 438 for himself; he reserved Room 437 in the name of James Gorman, who, he explained, would be arriving in a day or two. He saved room 436 for the use of two stenographers who would be able to hear conversations in the other rooms by listening to a dictagraph machine—a new and potentially frightening technological innovation.

The second phase of the plan began on February 14. By arrangement with Oscar Lawler, John Harrington arrived in Los Angeles in response to a federal subpoena. He went immediately to the Hayward Hotel, where he registered in Room 437 under the name of James Gorman. He then called Darrow at Earl Rogers's office and urgently asked for a meeting.

Darrow knew that Harrington might be cooperating with the prosecution. Before going to Harrington's hotel room, he met with Earl Rogers to lay out plans for the visit. At two twenty-five that afternoon, Darrow knocked on the door of Room 437 and walked into what Darrow's lawyers later called the "Dictograph Trap." Foster had placed a microphone behind the bureau in Harrington's room. As the two men talked in Room 437, the two stenographers sat at a desk in the room next door, wearing earphones that were attached to the microphone by means of a hidden wire. Their job was to transcribe every word that Darrow said.

The meeting that afternoon was the first of a series of visits that continued on February 15, 16, 18, and 19, lasting for what Darrow later estimated as a total of about ten to twelve hours. Coached by Oscar Lawler and Robert Foster, Harrington used the meetings to try to get Darrow to admit his guilt, to recognize the strength of the case against him, and to stay out of jail by helping the authorities locate Schmidt and Caplan—or, better, by agreeing to "open up about Gompers."

✻ ✻ ✻ ✻

At ten A.M. on February 19, Harrington got a formal summons ordering him to appear before the county grand jury to testify about the bribing of jurors. He immediately called Darrow at Earl Rogers's law office. They needed to talk. After consulting with Rogers about just what to say to Harrington, Darrow left for the Hayward Hotel for what turned out to be the last meeting in Room 437.

Darrow pleaded with Harrington not to cooperate with the district attorney. They discussed the five thousand dollars that Harrington claimed was still owed to him. Darrow said he would try to pay it the next day.

When Darrow returned to the office and described his latest conversation to Earl Rogers, his lawyer was alarmed. The suggestion that

Darrow might pay five thousand dollars to Harrington on the eve of his former associate's testimony could look like hush money.

Rogers told Darrow to call at once to say that he would not give Harrington any money. He put one of his secretaries on the line to transcribe the conversation.

"Say, John," Darrow began, "I am indicted and you are subpoenaed this morning, and we couldn't afford to have any financial transaction at this time. If I am owing you anything on the old deal, I will pay you when these matters are disposed of. Don't you think that is best?"

Harrington agreed that it was.

If Darrow had any lingering questions about Harrington's intentions, they were answered a few weeks later, when the press reported that Harrington had come to Los Angeles specifically to get Darrow into an incriminating conversation that could be reproduced by Dictograph. His motive, the story accurately said, was to gain immunity from prosecution.

The real bombshell hit on March 23, 1912, when the *Evening Herald* printed a large picture of Robert Foster and the two stenographers listening to the Dictograph in Room 436, while Harrington and Darrow were meeting in Room 437. The story claimed that "the evidence gleaned by the reporters while this picture was being taken is in itself sufficient to assure the state of victory in the Darrow prosecution."

❋ ❋ ❋ ❋

In the depths of his depression and desperation, Darrow considered entering into a plea bargain of his own. The case against him was beginning to look exceedingly powerful and his defense was going to be exceptionally expensive. With practically no one contributing to his defense fund, the case could wipe him out—even if he won. To lose was almost unthinkable. But by working with the authorities and talking about Gompers, he might be able to escape jail and negotiate a fine that would be far less than Rogers's proposed $25,000 fee.

In late February, Darrow started to talk with the government. Commissioner Walter Drew of the National Erectors' Association described the proposed settlement in a letter to one of his top associates. "Darrow has offered to plead guilty and tell all he knows if he is let off with a $10,000 fine," Drew wrote to James Badorf, his associate in Los Angeles. "I am in favor of this course."

Badorf was less inclined to be lenient. He was convinced that Darrow had committed some very serious crimes—and that the prosecution would be able to prove it. "Regarding Darrow's proposition," Badorf wrote back to Drew on March 2, "I think that Darrow is entitled to a jail sentence rather than that a compromise should be made with him, by which he could be let off with a fine. In speaking with other parties here in connection with the case, it may be a hard proposition to convict Gompers on Darrow's testimony alone."

Word of the proposed plea bargain briefly made its way into the press, where it was again rejected by prosecutors. "Friends of Darrow are trying to arrange some kind of compromise that will keep the enfeebled lawyer from standing trial," the *Los Angeles Times* reported on March 18. The story claimed that Darrow's friends, concerned about his failing health, were proposing "a possible fine of $10,000 for Darrow should he make a confession and supply the State and Federal officials with valuable information."

But the story said that the district attorney had rejected the proposed settlement. "The attitude of the prosecutors appears to be to accept nothing short of a plea of 'guilty' without conditions." Even if he wanted one, a guilty plea with no jail sentence seemed out of the question.

❀ ❀ ❀ ❀

Darrow decided to take one aspect of the case into his own hands. He wanted to eliminate John Harrington as a witness against him, and he thought Erskine Wood could help him do it.

In early April, Darrow sent a telegram to Wood asking for a meeting in San Francisco on Saturday, April 13. When Wood agreed to the meeting, Clarence and Ruby headed north by train.

After arriving in San Francisco on Saturday morning, Darrow met Wood for lunch. They were joined by Johannsen and Tvietmoe, who were still furious with Darrow, but had become convinced that his acquittal was imperative. "To have Darrow convicted or plead guilty on top of the McNamaras's plea," Johannsen told Wood, "would be ruinous to labor."

At lunch, without being very specific, Darrow informed Wood that he wanted "to get [Larry] Sullivan's aid" on something. He did not reveal just what aid was needed. Darrow and Wood then took an afternoon drive through the park with Mary Field and Fremont Older, but Darrow said nothing further about his reasons for summoning Wood to meet him in San Francisco.

Wood got an explanation later that afternoon, however, while relaxing in the cottage that Mary Field was renting in Corte Madera. Wood was sitting at a desk writing a letter to Sara when Anton Johannsen—Mary's next-door neighbor—stopped by for a visit. The details of the ensuing conversation are reliably preserved in the letter that Wood resumed writing to Sara perhaps a half hour later, as soon as Johannsen left Mary's house.

"I was interrupted a few lines back by Mr. Johannsen," Wood explained. "He wanted a letter to Sullivan from me which would stimulate Larry into doing for Darrow a great service—no other or less than kidnapping Harrington, the lawyer who has turned state's evidence against D."

So that was what Darrow wanted: to enlist Wood's aid in persuading Larry Sullivan to kidnap John Harrington, thus eliminating the strongest corroborating witness in the forthcoming trial. Was this suggestion made with Darrow's knowledge? Was this the mission that he had had in mind for Sullivan? Was this the reason Darrow had wanted to meet Wood in San Francisco? Wood answered all of those questions in the affirmative. "I am sure Darrow knows of it," Wood told Sara. "I am sure he set Johannsen on this, yet he talked with me so guardedly that he is perfectly safe in saying that 'I never thought of such a thing.'

"When I told Johannsen that I positively would not play Mephistopheles and push Larry back into his old gulf," Wood reported, "Johannsen said he respected me, that Darrow had all my philosophies but was too weak to abide by them."

Johannsen then launched into an astonishingly bitter attack on Darrow. He condemned Darrow for getting rich off of the McNamara case and for betraying the cause of labor by pleading the brothers guilty "to save his own skin." Nevertheless, because the case was of such symbolic importance to labor, Johannsen was committed to helping in the Darrow defense.

❋ ❋ ❋ ❋

As the trial approached, there seemed no way out. It looked like a replay of the McNamara case, with an overwhelming amount of evidence on the prosecution's side.

"I have known Darrow for thirty years," a mutual friend wrote to Samuel Gompers on April 28. "I saw him yesterday and I have never seen such a change for the worse in a human being as is apparent in him. I know him so well that it would not surprise me to know that he has committed suicide any day, for they surely have the goods on him and he knows it."

Chapter Thirteen

THE PROSECUTION'S CASE

WHEN THE TRIAL STARTED, Darrow's suicidal mood was his greatest enemy. He felt—and looked—like he wanted to crawl into a hole somewhere. His appearance was a constant source of friction with his chief counsel. Rogers insisted that Darrow had a role to play. The prosecution would try to show that Darrow was a desperate man, at the end of a long career, who had been caught in the act of corrupting justice. Darrow's best defense was to present himself as the distinguished and unfairly accused defender of labor, framed by a government that hated his good deeds and was determined to use this trial to destroy organized labor. The performance would only be credible, Rogers said, if Darrow appeared as a stately oak, not a weeping willow. But it wasn't easy, especially for a man who felt humiliated, abandoned, and old.

Darrow arrived at the courthouse at nine-thirty on Wednesday morning, May 15, 1912. He seemed to have aged ten more years since pleading the McNamaras guilty. His body was more slouched than ever. A reporter noted that his "face was haggard and the muscles of his cheeks twitched unceasingly, while the lines round his eyes and mouth told of nights of sleeplessness and worry." He was dressed in the same gray three-piece suit that he wore during the McNamara trial, a suit that was far too warm for a day where temperatures would run into the eighties. With him were Rogers's young assistant, Jerry Geisler; Horace Appel, one of the most colorful members of the bar, part Mexican, part Jew, known for his pugnacious oratory; and Rogers himself. Freshly shaved and manicured, dressed in a Prince Albert coat, straw hat, and patent leather shoes, and smoking an ever-present cigarette, Earl Rogers was every bit the matinee idol, the object of as much interest as his world-famous client.

The start of the trial had been postponed for a day in deference to a hotly contested California Republican presidential primary that pitted President William Howard Taft against former president Theodore Roosevelt. The results were just coming in as Darrow and Rogers left for court, and to the astonishment of many observers, Roosevelt was trouncing President Taft, despite the vigorous support of General Otis and the *Los Angeles Times*. To lift Darrow's spirits, Rogers confidently predicted a similar upset at the Darrow trial. It didn't work. Nothing worked. The defendant felt miserable.

Entering the Hall of Records, the lawyers pressed through the large crowd that had already gathered for what promised to be the greatest trial in the city's history. Most of the spectators were waiting outside, hoping to get seats, though their chances were slim. The prosecutors knew that Rogers and Darrow were both master performers, certain to use a large courtroom audience to their advantage. In a clever pretrial maneuver, Captain Fredericks had managed to have the case assigned to Department Twelve, a small courtroom with limited seating. Twenty-four seats were reserved for reporters, telegraphers, and photographers. Another block was set aside for thirty veniremen or potential jurors. At most, there was space for twenty to thirty spectators.

The crowd pulled back respectfully as the lawyers entered. Darrow walked down the aisle, past the railing, to the long counsel table at the front of the room. The brilliant May sunlight illuminated the words etched on a circular stained-glass skylight: TRUTH, PEACE, LAW, JUSTICE, and GOVERNMENT. Darrow took a seat directly below the word JUSTICE and slipped down in his chair, as if trying to hide from view.

❋ ❋ ❋ ❋

At a few minutes to ten, Ruby Darrow walked up the hill to the courthouse, forcing herself to maintain a cheerful smile. "I shall attend court constantly with my husband," she told reporters. "I believe it may help him to know that I am right there. I have but one thought—to help my husband in any way I can."

Her companion that morning, the press reported, was "Miss Mary Field of San Francisco, who is making a stay in this city and spends most of her time with Mrs. Darrow." In fact, Mary was in town to cover the trial for *Organized Labor,* Olaf Tvietmoe's newspaper. She was no longer Darrow's lover, nor did she admire him uncritically. Sara said Mary was " 'widowed,' the widowhood of the living death of all she held dear. Slowly her idol has crumbled into dust before her eyes." But she was still Darrow's friend, and she was there to support him.

A photographer snapped a picture of the two women as they entered the building. Ruby was beautifully outfitted. Tall and erect and handsome, she wore a tailored suit that flattered the contours of her corseted figure. Her broad-brimmed hat was stylishly trimmed by a green ribbon and a colorful flower. Mary's plain figure was gowned in a loose-fitting thrift-shop dress. Her hat looked like an inverted washbucket. But something of Mary's determination pierced through in the squint of her eyes and the fix of her mouth. Whatever their differences (and, in fact, they despised each other), here were two women prepared to join ranks to save their man.

Ruby seemed to shrink visibly as she entered the courtroom. As Mary found a place for herself in the section reserved for the press, Ruby made her way to the front, to a special seat inside the railing, just behind her husband. Then she saw him, sunk low in his chair, caught in a mood of self-pity. Ruby lost her composure and began to cry. When Clarence looked back at her, she wiped away the tears and tried to smile.

✳ ✳ ✳ ✳

Across the room, chatting with reporters, Captain John Fredericks was in great spirits, the man of the hour, the crusader who had forced the McNamaras to confess. He had just returned from a long vacation, capped by a highly publicized visit in Washington with President Taft. Fredericks's name was now often mentioned as the next gubernatorial candidate of the regular Republican party in California—and if he became governor, who could tell what might be next? This case was certain to seal his national as well as his local reputation. As it opened he was "supremely confident of victory."

Observers noted that Fredericks was "more erect and firm than at any time of his life." Admiring reporters had begun to compare his rather homely and austere visage to Abraham Lincoln. He was "chock full of ginger," in the words of Martin Aguirre, the court bailiff. At his side was the same man who had been with him in the McNamara case, Joseph Ford, the tough Irish intellectual who was an uncompromising prosecutor.

✳ ✳ ✳ ✳

At ten A.M., Judge George H. Hutton, the man who held so much of Darrow's fate in his hands, entered the room. Elected to office four years earlier, he was young and handsome, with a gentle smile and a kindly face. Unlike Judge Bordwell, who presided at the McNamara trial, he was not a member of the California Club establishment. His compassion for the poor was illustrated by his post as chairman of the city's Insanity Commission, a role that required him to limit court hours on Mondays. Whatever his personal leanings or attributes, he lacked the experience and temperament necessary to handle a complex and contentious criminal trial. Before long, he was at the mercy of the lawyers and their theatrics.

Judge Hutton began by welcoming the veniremen. The pressure of public interest in such a case is so great, he explained, that it is almost impossible for jurors to keep an open mind. To protect them, and to preserve the integrity of the process, the jurors would be sequestered for the duration of the trial. They would live at the

Trenton Hotel, under the care of court bailiff Martin Aguirre, and have minimal contact with family or friends. The newspapers would be clipped each morning to remove any references to the trial. It was an inconvenience, to be sure, but they also had a chance to be part of what might be the most important case in the city's history.

While jury selection in the McNamara case had lasted for two months, it took less than ten days to select the jury that would try Clarence Darrow. Earl Rogers asked each juror a series of questions designed to underline the major themes of his case. This was a sham, his questions implied. Bert Franklin was lying in order to save his own hide, and it was a lie that no one else could or would corroborate.

"Suppose that Bert H. Franklin did approach a juror in the McNamara case, but Mr. Darrow knew nothing of it," Rogers asked each of the veniremen. "Then suppose that Franklin, to save himself from being sent to the penitentiary, accused Mr. Darrow of having authorized the giving of the bribe to which he has confessed. Would you require additional evidence of Darrow's guilt before you voted for conviction on Franklin's testimony?"

There were a few fights. A young rancher named E. H. Kidd said he had read Darrow's writings and had made up his mind that Darrow was innocent. Fredericks asked that Kidd be excused and, over Rogers's objections, Judge Hutton agreed. To Darrow's friends, the process seemed unfair. It was one more example of the way in which the courts were controlled by the forces of capital. Rich and respectable men were accepted for jury service, Mary Field told the readers of *Organized Labor*. "But then there comes into the box a tailor, a rooming-house owner, an expressman, a carpenter. He perhaps owns a little dot of the earth. His eyes have seen trouble." And he is sure to be rejected.

The most important interrogation involved an opinionated young business executive named Fred E. Golding. As treasurer and part owner of the Patten and Davies Lumber Company, Golding admitted to a strong prejudice against "unscrupulous labor leaders." As Joseph Timmons noted in the *Examiner,* "on account of his business affiliations and his social relations, judged by the usual standards, he would fall before a peremptory challenge of the defense." But there was no such challenge.

Golding's views proved to be a surprise. The streetcorner bribe, he said, looked like a frame-up. It didn't seem plausible that anyone in his right mind, let alone Clarence Darrow, would arrange for a bribe to take place on a busy intersection, in broad daylight.

"The arrest of Franklin appears like a stage play, doesn't it," Rogers observed with a smile. "A case of the stage set, the lights all turned up and the orchestra playing?" It was a metaphor that Rogers liked and would often repeat.

"Well, I reasoned that a man like Darrow would not carry out any such affair in the daytime," Golding commented.

But Fredericks liked Golding, too. He was, after all, a capitalist. "If we convince you by the evidence," Fredericks said, "I presume it doesn't make any difference whether Franklin tried to bribe a man in the open or in a cellar?" Golding said that he would be guided by the evidence. He was deemed fit by both sides.

By Friday, May 24, the selection of the jury was complete—twelve jurors and a thirteenth man who would sit as an alternate. On its face, the jury did not look ideal for Darrow. The twelve regular jurors included seven ranchers, two contractors, and business executive Fred Golding. Almost all were Republicans. None had supported or voted for Job Harriman in the recent election.

"Over and over I asked myself this question," Mary said that weekend. "Whose justice is it? And as if in answer, I thought I could see on the shoulder of Fredericks, the heavy dominant hand of the Lawgiver of Los Angeles—General Otis." While there is no evidence that Otis was involved in the Darrow trial, Mary's metaphor was still apt. His spirit was everywhere.

❊ ❊ ❊ ❊

The prosecutors knew that it would be exceedingly difficult to persuade the jury to send Clarence Darrow to jail for his involvement, if any, in such a badly botched scheme. Something else would be needed. To win, they would have to show that he was a misguided and even evil genius, a once good man gone wrong. They would have to prove that the attempted bribe was part of a much broader pattern of misconduct. To Darrow's astonishment, they started to attack his character as soon as the trial began.

In criminal cases, the prosecutor was entitled to make an opening statement to outline what he intends to prove during the course of the trial. Unlike modern criminal procedure, the defense was not permitted to make a rebuttal. Under the circumstances, Darrow and Rogers knew that Fredericks would score the first blow. But they were not prepared for what they got.

Fredericks started out his presentation speaking in the same calm and reserved manner that had characterized all of his other performances to date. "May it please the court and gentlemen of the jury," he began. "It is sometimes customary, before beginning a trial which may take a number of days, for a prosecutor to make a statement to the jury as to what he expects to prove. In brief, the charge against this defendant is that he gave a bribe to George N. Lockwood on or about November twenty-eighth, 1911.

"We will show you that beginning on the eleventh of October last year, there was a trial in the case of *The People* versus *McNamara*. We will show you that Clarence Darrow, the defendant in this case, was in sole charge of the defense of that case. We will show you that Clarence Darrow, the defendant in this case, employed detectives and other attorneys to assist him. We will show you that among the detectives employed by the defense was Bert Franklin. We will show you that Bert Franklin was in the employ of Clarence Darrow and was not in the employ of anyone else during his work on that case. We will show you that a man by the name of Hammerstrom . . ."

Ruby winced at the name of Hammerstrom, her maiden name, the name of her brother. Why was he being dragged into this case? At most, he had been a minor figure in the defense. Now Fredericks was making him seem second in importance to Bert Franklin. The answer was simple, of course. Fredericks wanted his blows to land. If he could shake Darrow's composure, he could score important points with the jury. Ruby listened intently as Fredericks continued.

". . . a man by the name of Hammerstrom, Bert Hammerstrom, was also working under the orders of Clarence Darrow in that case, and that Mr. Darrow also employed a man by the name of John Harrington, a detective from Chicago.

"We will show you that the name of Mr. Lockwood was in the main jury box. We will show you that in mid-November, about two weeks before the bribe, Bert Franklin went to Mr. Lockwood, whom he knew, and offered him a certain sum of money. We will show you that Bert Franklin was acting at the request and under the direction of this defendant, of Clarence Darrow. We will show you that Mr. Lockwood immediately reported this conversation to the district attorney's office. We will show you that Mr. Lockwood's name was drawn from the box on November twenty-fifth and that Bert Franklin went to his house again and renewed his offer of a bribe.

"We will show you that they made an appointment to meet on the morning of November twenty-eighth, on the Tuesday before Thanksgiving. They agreed that Franklin would give him the bribe that morning, on the corner of Third and Los Angeles Street, and that a mutual friend named C. E. White would be there and that Mr. White would hold the thirty-five hundred dollars until Mr. Lockwood had fulfilled the conditions of the contract.

"We will show that this transaction, exactly as arranged, came off and that they were then arrested. We will show you that when Franklin and White were arrested, they were found with the money on them. We will produce that money here in court and we will show you that the money was the money of Clarence Darrow, that Clarence Darrow gave it to Franklin that morning. We will show you that the money was part of the money that was raised in the East for the purpose of defending the McNamaras. We will trace that fund into Mr. Darrow's hands."

The defense had anticipated all of the arguments up to that point. They had not expected what happened next. It was, as one reporter noted, "a bolt out of the blue into the defense camp."

Fredericks, the righteous avenger of legal ethics, pointed his long arm toward the defendant. "We will next show you, that that act on the part of Mr. Darrow was one of a series of efforts to pervert justice in that case by paying money to other jurors and to witnesses who were scheduled to testify for the People against the defendant McNamara."

Rogers jumped to his feet. "Just a moment," he shouted. "I take exception to the statement of counsel. The rules of evidence do not permit the introduction of any such evidence. This man is in court to answer to the allegation of one offense. He is not presumed to be ready to meet the proof of other offenses."

But Judge Hutton allowed Fredericks to continue.

Fredericks's tone was more righteous than ever. "We will show you gentlemen that this defendant endeavored to defeat and obstruct justice in this case by offering and paying money to other jurors." Horace Appel started to shout an objection, but Judge Hutton waved him down. "In the same case for the same purpose that he paid money to Lockwood," Fredericks continued, "Clarence Darrow paid money to witnesses to leave the state so that they would not be available to testify. He brought agents here for the purpose of corruptly influencing our witnesses, particularly to persuade Ortie McManigal not to testify to the truth."

All the lawyers were on their feet, talking at once, offering or rebutting objections. Once again, Judge Hutton told Fredericks to proceed.

"We will show that he paid large sums of money to bring people here to Los Angeles to work upon McManigal by offering him inducements and bribes to change his testimony or to refuse to testify for the state."

As the withering attack continued, Darrow seemed stunned. He fumbled with a piece of cigarette paper, his face flushed, his eyes on the floor. Ruby leaned over, stroked her husband's hair, and whispered something in his ear. He turned and smiled at her, a smile that struck one friendly observer as "at once winning and pathetic."

Shaking with emotion, Rogers objected again, protesting that Fredericks's statement was filled with claims that he could not, and in any event should not be permitted to prove. But Fredericks confidently concluded his opening remarks with a promise.

"Before the trial closes, the jurors will be satisfied that we have proved every charge that I have made."

❋ ❋ ❋ ❋

The prosecution's first important witness was George Lockwood. With his gray beard, erect bearing, and Grand Army of the Republic lapel button, the Civil War veteran made a powerful impression on the jury and the court. He described Franklin's visits to his ranch in mid-November and on November 26, the bribe offers, and his own indignant reaction. He was so outraged, Lockwood said, that he agreed to help the district attorney observe the bribe and arrest the perpetrators.

Originally the payment—and the arrest—was to take place at Lockwood's ranch on Monday evening, November 27. It was Franklin's third visit to the ranch. By the time Bert arrived, detectives were hidden everywhere. But the bribe had to be postponed until the next morning. Bert didn't have the money. Nor did he have the "Big One" with him.

By the Big One, Bert meant Captain White, the burly ex-jailer who was supposed to act as the stakeholder. But Lockwood assumed the Big One was Darrow.

"I asked him where Mr. Darrow was," Lockwood testified. " 'Why?' Bert says. 'Did you think Darrow was coming out here?' I says, 'I sure did.' 'What made you think Darrow was coming out?' Bert asks. 'Well,' I says, 'you asked me if you should bring the Big One out.' And he remarks that he had reference to Captain White. I asked him where Captain White was and he said that he had a bad cold and couldn't come out that night." The meeting was rescheduled for the next morning at nine o'clock at the corner of Third and Los Angeles. Lockwood described meeting Captain White and then Bert Franklin on the corner and then walking north on Third, toward Main.

This was the testimony that the press and spectators had been waiting for. As one, the people in the courtroom leaned forward to listen more carefully as Fredericks asked Lockwood to describe Darrow's appearance at the scene of the famous streetcorner bribe.

"As we approached the corner of Third and Main," Lockwood said, "I saw a man coming across the intersection, and Bert said to me, 'Wait a minute. I want to speak to this man.' "

"And who was the man that came there and met Franklin?" Fredericks asked.

"I have since learned that it was Clarence Darrow."

"The defendant in this case?"

"Yes, sir."

"What happened next?"

"Detective Browne [the district attorney's head detective] arrived on the scene and put his hands out, just like this, and separated them." Lockwood demonstrated the gesture. "He then placed Mr. Franklin under arrest."

"And what did Mr. Darrow do?"

"Well, really, I lost sight of Mr. Darrow right there. I saw no more of Mr. Darrow."

❋ ❋ ❋ ❋

Lockwood had been an effective witness for the prosecution, but he was also the kind of witness that Earl Rogers loved to taunt. On cross-examination, he hoped to damage Lockwood's veneer as a humble farmer, an occupation that would have given him something in common with most of the jurors. By Rogers's reckoning, Lockwood wasn't a rancher at all; he was nothing more than a former sheriff's office employee who was willing to lay a dastardly trap.

With very little preliminary banter, Rogers launched into what one observer called "one of the bitterest and most scathing cross-examinations ever heard in a Los Angeles courtroom." He began by showing that Lockwood was not really a disinterested citizen, a salt-of-the-earth, homespun idealist. His career had been spent in law enforcement, not ranching. He had never earned a living by raising or selling fruit and alfalfa.

"You are trying to pose as a farmer here, aren't you?" Rogers finally asked. The district attorney objected to the question as insulting. But it left its mark.

Then Rogers asked a series of questions calculated to show that the entire episode had been staged by the government to entrap Darrow. Like a musical refrain, Rogers intended to introduce it time and again, each time with a variation, but always with the same tune. The entire episode was a trap, and Darrow had been framed. If

Rogers's plan worked, the jury would be humming his refrain, not the prosecutors', by the time the case was over.

"You deliberately tried to trap Darrow, didn't you?" Rogers asked.

"No, sir."

"Did not the district attorney say, 'We will get Darrow tonight?' "

"He may have expressed himself along that line."

"When you got those detectives out there at the ranch and the district attorney out there at your ranch you thought the Big Fellow was coming out."

"I sure did."

"You thought it was Darrow?"

"I sure did."

"And you got the whole thing up for that purpose, didn't you?"

"No, I couldn't say as I did."

"Well, the whole *play* was postponed until next morning because Darrow was not there?"

"Not on that account by any means."

"Wasn't the whole thing put over until the next morning at Third and Los Angeles so that Darrow could be caught there?"

"No, sir, not so far as I know."

"Now Mr. Lockwood," Rogers said with an acid tone of satire. "What direction did Franklin come from while on his way to join you and White at the place of that *performance,* that *frame-up?*"

The word "frame-up" hit the mark. It was aimed at the prosecution, not at the witness. Fredericks hopped out of his chair as though he had sat on a pin. The very insinuation drove him wild—as Rogers knew it would. The suggestion that he, the district attorney, the avenging angel of judicial ethics, had been party to a fraud, was more than he could bear.

"Now see here," Fredericks shouted, pointing his long arm and index finger toward the bench. "That language has no place here. I want him punished for contempt of court for that statement. If the prosecution has any right in the world in endeavoring to keep the courts pure and decent and to punish and prosecute those who try to corrupt them, if they have got any right under God's heaven, certainly they have a right to be protected from a man who comes in here and makes a statement such as that."

Rogers was delighted at this development. He had gotten under Fredericks's skin—and the trial was only beginning.

"Your Honor," Rogers yelled, crouching in front of the bench as though ready to spring forward. "I say it again and I say it in the presence of the Court. I contend that this meeting at Third and Los Angeles was a fake. I contend it was a frame-up. I contend it was a trap. And I will prove it before I get through."

When Lockwood left the witness stand, most observers felt that his testimony had survived under fire. But Rogers had accomplished his purpose. He had planted a seed that was sure to grow.

※ ※ ※ ※

Sooner than expected, the prosecution brought on its star witness, Bert Franklin. Nattily attired in a dark suit, his hair and mustache neatly trimmed, Franklin looked jaunty and self-confident as he entered the courtroom. For the press and public, this was the first opportunity to hear Franklin's story. Darrow gave his former aide a scornful look as he sat down on the witness stand and swore to tell the truth and the whole truth.

This time the questions were asked by Joe Ford, the fiery deputy prosecutor. He quickly led Franklin through a series of questions designed to implicate Darrow in the bribery.

"When was the first occasion you discussed the question of bribing jurors?" Ford asked.

"The first time Mr. Darrow and I had a conversation—direct conversation—in regard to bribing jurors, was on the fifth day of October, 1911."

"Who was present?"

"Nobody but himself and myself."

"Just tell the jury what was said at that time with reference to that matter."

"I met Mr. Darrow, Mr. Davis, and Judge McNutt on the corner of Second and Spring. Mr. Darrow and I walked away by ourselves, the others following leisurely behind. Mr. Darrow made the remark it was time for us now to get busy with the jury and that he wanted me to talk over the matter in regard to Mr. Bain."

Franklin said that Darrow returned to the subject of bribery the following morning, October 6. The men were in Darrow's Higgins Building office. "Mr. Darrow said that 'we have been talking the matter over and have decided that five thousand dollars would be a proper amount to pay to the jury, for jurymen.' Four thousand to go to the juror and one thousand to myself."

The judge overruled an objection by Horace Appel, and Franklin continued.

"He then asked me what I thought about Mr. Bain. I told him that Mr. Bain was the kind of man if he didn't want to go in that way he would come out and tell me so and that would be all there would be to it. He said, 'All right. I will give you a check for one thousand dollars.' He turned to his desk and wrote the check and handed it to me and I left the office."

There was a quick conference at the defense table. Was it true that Darrow had written a check to Franklin on October 6? If so, the check would corroborate Franklin's testimony. It could be an extremely damaging piece of evidence.

❋ ❋ ❋ ❋

Franklin resumed his testimony at nine-thirty the next morning. The crowd inside and outside of the packed courtroom listened intently as he described the visit to Bain's house on the evening of October 6. Bert recounted his conversation with Mrs. Bain and her promise to persuade her husband to cooperate. Later that night, he said, he returned to the Bains' home and left four hundred dollars with Mr. Bain as a down payment on the promise to vote for acquittal.

"Did you report this matter to Mr. Darrow?" Ford asked.

"I did."

"Where and when?"

"The next day, at his office."

"Please state what was said there at that time between you and Mr. Darrow."

"I can only repeat it in substance. I reported to him that I had seen

Mr. Bain, that I had paid him the money and that he had promised to vote for an acquittal. Mr. Darrow asked me if I thought he would stand and I told him yes. I didn't think there was any question about that at all."

"What if anything did Mr. Darrow say in reply to that?"

"He said that was good."

Finally Ford asked if Franklin knew George Lockwood.

"Yes, sir."

"How long have you known him?"

"About twelve years."

"Had you had any conversations with Mr. Darrow in reference to Mr. Lockwood before the twenty-fifth of November?"

"Upon numerous occasions. He asked me if I thought Mr. Lockwood was a man to be trusted and I told him emphatically that I thought he could. I thought he would at least listen to me patiently and, on account of our friendship, repeat nothing that was said."

It was nearing time for adjournment, and Judge Hutton cut the session short so that he could attend a special meeting of the Insanity Commission. Since Thursday was Memorial Day, the court adjourned until nine-thirty on Friday morning.

❋❋❋❋

That night, according to his daughter, Earl Rogers disappeared on an alcoholic binge. He may have been led to it by frustration with Darrow or, as Adela concludes, with Ruby, but it could as easily have been the lure of the liquor itself, or a bout with his private demons. Whatever the explanation, Adela says that Clarence and Ruby Darrow came to her house the next day in a panic. It was a holiday, but the defense team was hard at work—and Rogers was nowhere to be found.

"Where is your father?" Darrow asked urgently.

"He's taking a rest," Adela lied. "He hasn't had much sleep lately."

"Do you know where he is?" Darrow persisted.

"I always know where he is," she said, continuing the lie.

"Is he drunk?" Darrow asked.

Adela reports she could have smacked him. Instead, she hit him verbally. "If he is, you're enough to drive anyone to it."

Then Ruby, whom Adela hated, got into the act. "I knew it," Ruby said. "He drinks secretly all the time. I can smell it on him."

"I'm surprised he ever lets you close enough," Adela jabbed back. (If she didn't land that punch in 1912, she landed it fifty years later when she recreated the scene.)

"He'd better be here tomorrow morning," Darrow insisted.

Young Adela, who was just eighteen but well hardened to her father's haunts and the underside of the city, spent Wednesday night with Frank Dominguez, her father's friend and officemate, searching for Rogers. They went to Pearl Morton's, the house of pleasure owned by their dear friend, but he wasn't there. Finally, Adela remembered, they found him at another favorite outpost of pleasure, "sitting in a stately teakwood chair, shrunk into the rich embroidered silk. He seemed *small* and his face was gray white and his *eyes* . . . I couldn't do anything but run and put my arms around him and hide his face for him against my breast and hold and hold him and feel his hands hold onto me."

❋ ❋ ❋ ❋

One of Earl Rogers's most remarkable skills was his power of recuperation. He could spend an entire night in a drunken daze, make an early visit to a Turkish bath, and appear in court early the next day as the most elegant and presentable man in the room. His appearance on Friday morning was no exception. When court opened at nine-thirty, Rogers was there with a long formal black coat, a silk tie, a white vest, a fresh haircut, and a beautiful manicure.

Ford began the morning session by asking Franklin if he had talked to Darrow after visiting Lockwood's ranch on Sunday, November 26.

"I made a report to Mr. Darrow at about nine o'clock in the morning of Monday, November twenty-seventh, in his office in the Higgins Building."

"What was the conversation?"

"I informed Mr. Darrow that I thought Mr. Lockwood would act as a juror and follow my request as to the way he would vote." Bert explained that the bribe was scheduled to take place that night at Lockwood's ranch. As a result, he would need four thousand dollars in cash that same afternoon. "Mr. Darrow's answer was, 'I will try to get the money, if I have time.'"

Darrow was unable to get the money in time for the Monday night meeting at Lockwood's ranch, Franklin continued, but promised to "have the money at his office in the Higgins Building the next morning some time before nine o'clock."

Franklin remembered arriving at Darrow's office Tuesday morning at eight-forty A.M. "I asked Mr. Darrow if he had gotten the money. He said that he had not at that time received the money but that he would ring up Job and find out what time he would be at the office with the money."

"Ring up *who*?" Rogers interrupted. This was the first public suggestion that Job Harriman, the mayoral candidate and McNamara case cocounsel, had been involved in the bribe.

"Job," Franklin repeated. "I said, 'It is almost time for me to meet Captain White.' He then called someone on the phone. When he hung up he said, 'Job will be here in about ten minutes.'"

"What occurred next?" Ford asked, trying to get the full story without leading the witness.

"In about five minutes Mr. Harriman came into Mr. Darrow's office with his overcoat over his left arm. He said, 'Good morning, Franklin; good morning, Mr. Darrow,' and he walked with Mr. Darrow to the room immediately adjoining on the north."

"How long did they remain in there?"

"In about ten seconds Mr. Darrow came out and handed me a roll of bills, a small roll. I don't think he made any remark. He just handed me the money, is my recollection."

"What did you do?"

"I immediately left the office, walked to the elevator and looked to see how much money was in the roll in my hand. Then I went down in the elevator."

"Do you remember the denominations?"

"One thousand-dollar bill and six five-hundred-dollar bills, to the best of my recollection."

As Franklin continued, Darrow seemed nervous. He began to chew on a long slip of yellow paper.

Franklin described giving the money to Captain White, going to the saloon, then returning to the streetcorner, where he met White and Lockwood. Then, he said, he noticed a police officer and started to walk north. As he neared Main Street, he said, he saw Clarence Darrow hurrying toward him across the street, through the traffic.

"What did Darrow say?" Ford asked.

"I think he said, 'Bert, they are on to you.' I made no reply."

Just at that moment, Franklin testified, Sam Browne of the district attorney's office placed him under arrest and took him down to the police station to be booked. He was released later that day, when Darrow arranged for LeCompte Davis to put up a ten-thousand-dollar cash bail.

❋ ❋ ❋ ❋

Ford ended his examination by asking Franklin to describe his conversations with Darrow in the weeks after his arrest. His answer did not reveal a man of sterling character.

On one occasion, he said, "I told Mr. Darrow that if he had not happened to be at that particular place at that particular time that I thought I could have turned the tables on Mr. Lockwood and charged him with taking and accepting a bribe. I said, 'If you had not happened to be at that particular place, my arrest would not have taken place until after I could have pulled off my stunt at Third and Main.' "

Stunt. The circus equivalent of a performance or a play. It was the kind of word Rogers loved. He could hardly wait to get Franklin into the clutches of his cross-examination.

❋ ❋ ❋ ❋

After one day of direct examination by Joe Ford, Bert Franklin was forced to endure more than a week of cross-examination by Earl Rogers. Since Bert was the prosecution's principal witness, it was essential for the defense to destroy his credibility. As Rogers told friends, he was determined to prove that Franklin was a liar—and "to cast the baneful garb of the informer and traitor over his whole nature and being," to boot. The ordeal lasted longer than many important trials.

Franklin had been an unimpressive witness for the prosecution.

Writing in the *Examiner,* Joe Timmons called Franklin's answers "so unsatisfactory that the suspicion arose in the courtroom at times that he was failing deliberately to 'deliver the goods' to the prosecution." But Rogers's clever and often vicious cross-examination brought the detective to life.

"Franklin had been a cowering rabbit with his foot in the trap," Timmons wrote. "He had been uncertain and halting, a wretched witness in the hands of a friendly counsel. But when he saw a bull-dog charging down upon him, with teeth bared and eyes red with anger, the rabbit shook himself and puffed out, and lo, the charging bull-dog found himself confronted by another bull-dog, with foot entrapped still to be sure, but able and willing to give a fair account of himself in the melee that ensued.

"Rogers's voice was like the yell of a band of painted Comanches," Timmons continued, "as terrifying as the famous 'rebel yell' of a bristling battalion. Every word was a blow in the face, every tone a scornful insult. But the miracle had happened. The change in Franklin was so instant that spectators wondered if he had been shamming, to lead Rogers into ambush. He pitched his voice in the same Rogers key and shot back his answers with the same word-by-word emphasis with which Rogers catapulted the questions at him."

❋ ❋ ❋ ❋

With his first set of questions, Rogers managed to show that Franklin was a pretty despicable fellow, a man who would lie and even sell out his friends if it were the only way to save himself. And if he would lie about his friends, why would he not also lie about his former employer?

"You have known Mr. Lockwood how many years?" Rogers began.

"About twelve years."

"He has been a friend of yours?"

"Yes, sir. I always considered him so."

"Yet you told Mr. Darrow that if he had not showed up on the scene at that unfortunate moment that you would have pulled off your stunt of turning Lockwood over to the police and charging him with extortion, did you not?"

Less than a minute into the cross-examination, Franklin had already been accused of betraying a friend. Instead of trying to redeem his character, he foolishly reacted to Rogers's stinging use of the word *stunt*.

"I did not say that," Franklin objected.

"What did you say?"

"I didn't say anything about a stunt."

Rogers asked his aide, Jerry Geisler, to give him the record of Franklin's earlier testimony. Then, to Franklin: "You didn't say anything about a stunt?"

"No, sir."

"What did you say, then?"

"I told Mr. Darrow that if he had not appeared upon the scene at that time, that particular moment—that inopportune moment, if you please—that I would have turned Lockwood over to the police at the corner of Third and Main, and charged him with accepting a bribe in the McNamara case."

"So that was your *first* attempt to get out of your crime by charging somebody else, was it?" Everyone knew what Rogers believed the second attempt had been.

"Yes, sir. That was my first and *only* attempt."

✳ ✳ ✳ ✳

Rogers allowed Franklin to make mistakes in his testimony and then came back a day or two later to show that his memory was faulty—or that he was prepared to lie under oath. He took particular satisfaction in returning to the word *"stunt,"* highlighting Franklin's denial that he had used it, and then quoting from the official transcript in which he referred to "my stunt at Third and Main." Before leaving the subject, Rogers managed to claim that by the word *stunt,* Franklin "meant a trick, a fraud, a deceit."

Rogers kept pounding away at Franklin's character and motives. Though Franklin tried to deny it, Rogers showed that the former detective had, in effect, been granted immunity in return for agreeing to testify for the prosecution. He implied that Franklin had been or was now working with the district attorney, that he was part of a frame-up. Rogers tried to underline his charges by asking a series of questions concerning Franklin's long employment with the county law enforcement authorities, where he had been on the sheriff's payroll and had worked with Captain Fredericks. If Franklin wasn't *trying* to get caught, why had he been so careless, arranging a meeting in broad daylight on a busy street corner?

"Well, now, Mr. Franklin, will you tell the jury which it was. Tell them whether you was careless and was incompetent and was lacking in judgement," Rogers asked ungrammatically, "was lacking in good sense, leaving a trail painted right down the center of the street behind you on every occasion, meeting on a prominent street in daytime where people are all around you—or, whether, as a matter of fact, you were trying to get caught under an arrangement. Which of these is true?"

When Franklin offered a series of unresponsive answers, Rogers persisted. "Why don't you answer my question?"

"I don't know what you mean by *trail,*" he said at last.

"I thought you had been in the business of trailing."

"Trailing and leaving a trail is a different proposition," Franklin said. "I evidently left one."

He also left a trail of witnesses who were prepared to swear that Franklin had said that Darrow was innocent. Laying the groundwork for witnesses that the defense intended to introduce later, Rogers asked about statements that Franklin allegedly had made to allies, friends, and reporters—starting with LeCompte Davis.

"Did you tell Mr. Davis that Mr. Darrow never gave you one five-cent piece for a dishonest purpose?"

"No, Mr. Rogers," Franklin answered. "I didn't have to. I was saying I was innocent myself."

"At the time of your preliminary examination on the charge of bribery, did you see Mr. Timmons of the *Examiner,* who sits there?" Rogers pointed to Timmons, who was sitting in a prominent position in the reporters' section.

"I did."

"Did you see Mr. White of the *Express,* Mr. Dunn of the *Herald,* Mr. Jones of the *Tribune,* and Mr. Pearson of the Associated Press?"

"I think so."

"When Mr. Lockwood testified at the preliminary examination, he claimed that you mentioned Mr. Darrow's name when you went out to visit him at his ranch. Did you not then and there get up from your place in that room and go over to these men sitting here and voluntarily make this statement—" Rogers pulled his famous lorgnette out of his breast pocket, took a scrap of paper from the desk, and began to read. "Didn't you say, 'Any man who says I mentioned Darrow's name at the time is a damned liar. I might be guilty of all I am charged with, but I am not a damned fool. I certainly am not going to drag an innocent man into this.' "

"I said all of it except the last part."

"You did not tell them, 'I am certainly not going to drag an innocent man into this thing?' "

"I did not," Franklin insisted. "I was maintaining my own innocence at the time."

In similar fashion, Rogers asked Franklin about conversations with a series of other friends and associates. In each instance, Franklin denied that he had told them that Darrow was innocent. Since he was maintaining his *own* innocence, he said, and claiming that he never bribed Bain or Lockwood, it was never necessary to say that Darrow was innocent as well.

Franklin did admit to telling a couple of friends that the money had come from someone in Chicago or the East, someone other than Darrow. But he had a plausible explanation for those conversations. They occurred, he said, during a three-day period in mid-January. They were the result of a January 14, 1912, conversation with LeCompte Davis, who advised Franklin that he was certain to be convicted and sent to jail. But, Davis said, Franklin's family would be well cared for if he claimed that he was acting on the instructions of someone other than Darrow. For three days, Franklin said, he followed that advice and misled his friends by admitting his own guilt, denying Darrow's involvement, and claiming that the money had come from someone else. But on January 17, at his wife's insistence, he decided that the best course for him and for his family was to tell the truth. As a result, Franklin testified, he dropped the pretense and testified truthfully to the grand jury two days later.

❋❋❋❋

Although Rogers's cross-examination had been forceful, Franklin's answers had been remarkably resourceful and, quite possibly, persuasive to the jury. Joe Timmons, whose name had been invoked by Rogers, was impressed. "Frequently during the day's proceedings, Franklin looked unflinchingly into the eyes of Darrow," he noted. "To the end, Franklin retained his composure and most of the time seemed to enjoy the contest of intellectual jujitsu with Rogers."

Franklin had been a stronger witness than Rogers had expected. He knew that he would need something more to discredit him, something not yet in his possession.

"I will have to recall this witness for further cross-examination a little later," Rogers told the court toward the end of his sixth day of cross-examination. "Certain materials have not yet arrived, and I will ask leave to put them to him when they do arrive."

"When will you be ready to finish?" the judge asked.

"Tomorrow morning," Rogers promised.

❋ ❋ ❋ ❋

In fact, it took Rogers two days to find what he was looking for. In all likelihood, the information came from one of Rogers's friends and former clients in the Merchants and Manufacturers Association. Rogers had learned about a meeting that Franklin attended in late January, shortly after testifying to the grand jury. It was a meeting with several leaders of the Merchants and Manufacturers Association— including ironworks owners Fred Baker and Reese Llewellyn.

Without revealing what he knew, Rogers crept up on the subject softly.

"Do you know where the Merchants and Manufacturers office is?" Rogers began.

"I think I do, yes, sir."

"Have you ever been there?"

"Yes, sir."

"When?"

Franklin didn't want to volunteer too much. "Oh, I was in the M and M Association numerous times on lodge work they were interested in—land shows, things like that. I don't remember the dates."

"Any time since your arrest have you ever been there?"

"I have, yes, sir."

"When were you at the office?"

"I can only tell you approximately. The latter part of January or the first of February."

"At whose invitation were you there?"

Fredericks and Ford posed a series of objections, but Judge Hutton instructed Franklin to answer.

Bert knew there was no way out. "I will very frankly tell you how I happened to go there and what occurred there, if you wish it," he said.

"Who told you that you were to go to the Merchants and Manufacturers Association, if anyone?"

"J. A. Crook, a contractor." Franklin related how he had told Crook that he was having difficulty finding work.

"What did he tell you?"

"He said there would be some of my friends there that I could talk to about it."

Rogers asked who was present at the meeting. Franklin named Felix Zeehandelaar, secretary of the Merchants and Manufacturers Association; Stoddard Jess of the First National Bank; Fred Baker of the Baker Iron Works; and Reese Llewellyn of the Llewellyn Iron Works. In addition, there were two men he didn't know and a few others he was meeting for the first time.

"These men were friends of yours?" asked Rogers, his voice rich with sarcasm.

"Yes, sir, friends of mine. That is what I said."

"Two of them you don't remember, and others you had seen for the first time. Do you call these men friends?"

"Yes, sir, I do."

"Had you ever been in the house of any one of this committee in your life?"

"Not to my knowledge."

"Had they ever been in your house, any one of the committee?"

"Not to my knowledge."

"Did you ever do any business for any one of them—before that time?"

"Not to my recollection."

Rogers had made his point. "All right," he asked. "Who opened the conversation?"

"I think Mr. Zeehandelaar did."

"What did he say?"

"At the time I went into the room, Mr. Zeehandelaar said to me, 'Do you wish to make a statement to the gentlemen present?' And I said, 'Yes.' I told them I had made a statement to the district attorney of the county as to the facts in relation to my arrest, and that my future in the city was going to be a very difficult one. I felt that those men, being friends of mine, would assist me to try to build me up in the community, being business men."

"And assist you by giving you business particularly."

"That is what I meant, yes, sir."

One more time. "Assist you by giving you business."

"Yes, sir. That is what I meant."

❊ ❊ ❊ ❊

When it was over, Franklin was bloodied, his character largely destroyed. But most observers felt that his testimony remained almost entirely untouched. "Despite the grilling handed out by Rogers," the *Herald* reported, "Franklin's testimony remains intact." Joe Timmons reached a similar conclusion in his articles for the *Examiner*. The defense had succeeded in "holding the witness up to contempt and distrust as a confessed bribe-giver, a man willing to turn on his friends to save himself and a man with alleged connections with opponents of the defendant," he said. But "Franklin went through the ordeal without any but trivial contradictions."

To Adela Rogers, watching her father in court every day, Franklin's performance proved that he was telling the truth. "Rogers had created a despicable creature out of this witness," she wrote fifty years later, but "it was the coldest, hardest fought, eye-for-an-eye-and-tooth-for-a-tooth battle I ever saw any witness give my father in any court. I thought then, I think now, that Bert Franklin could have done this against Rogers *only* if he was telling the truth."

Chapter Fourteen

"GIVE ME THE HEART OF A MAN"

A s THE DAYS TURNED to weeks and the weather grew hotter, Darrow began to doubt Earl Rogers's skill and loyalty. There were plenty of fireworks and theatrics, but witness after witness scored points with powerful testimony. Sitting in front of the small courtroom as a defendant, the object of the action but curiously out of the action, was an unfamiliar and humiliating role. But as the trial continued to take its toll on him and, even more so, on Ruby, Darrow found a new and vital source of strength.

The San Francisco labor leaders, led by Anton Johannsen and Olaf Tvietmoe, came to his aid in full force. Unlike Gompers and the other national leaders of labor, they felt that it was essential for Darrow to win. His conviction or acquittal might not be of national importance to labor, but following on the heels of the McNamara confessions, it would have a profound effect in California. Though they would never admit it, they may have been influenced, as well, by the fact that the McNamaras' confessions had been designed, in large measure, to prevent either of them from being prosecuted for the *Times* bombing. In any case, they swallowed their anger and came to Darrow's aid.

Their first assignment was to change the entire tone of the proceedings. Somehow they would have to lift Darrow's spirits, provide him with a cheering section, make him feel loved, while showing the jury what a remarkable man he was—and beginning to undermine the prosecutors' self-confidence. In mid-June, Darrow and his allies found two surprisingly obvious ways to do just that. First, the defense finally persuaded Judge Hutton to move the proceedings to a larger room that they could pack with Darrow's friends. More important, they encouraged Darrow to take over his own defense.

They were motivated, in part, by the sense that Rogers couldn't or wouldn't put a break on the damaging testimony. C. E. White, for example, confirmed aspects of Lockwood's account, as did several detectives. More important, two bank tellers testified that Darrow gave Tvietmoe a ten-thousand-dollar check from the McNamara defense fund—that Tvietmoe immediately converted to cash. Fredericks promised that one of his witnesses would prove that Tvietmoe gave the cash to Darrow, who used it to bribe the jurors.

❊ ❊ ❊

One of the most damaging witnesses was Detective Sam Browne. He confirmed that Darrow was present at the scene of the bribe and left the scene without comment immediately after the arrest. To an astonished courtroom, Browne then reported that Darrow had approached him, a few minutes later, as Browne entered the Hall of Records.

Rogers made no objection when Browne read from a contemporaneous memorandum describing the conversation.

"Darrow said, 'My God, Browne, what is all this?' " Browne began, reading from the memo.

"I answered, 'You ought to know what it is, it is bribery.'

"Darrow then said, 'My God, I wouldn't have had this happen for the world; if I had known that this was going to happen this way I never would have allowed it to be done. Isn't there anything that you can do? This is terrible.'

"I said, 'You will have to talk to Captain Fredericks.'

"Darrow then said, 'Browne, this is terrible, for God's sake can't you do anything for us?'

"I answered, 'You ought to have known better than to employ a man like Franklin, as he is always drunk. I don't know what I can do for you.'

"Darrow then said, 'He came to me highly recommended from Mr. McCormick and others. Browne, do the best you can and I will take care of you.' "

The prosecution then put the memorandum itself into evidence.

❋ ❋ ❋ ❋

"If I had known that this was going to happen *this way* I never would have allowed it to be done." The statement seemed to confirm that Darrow had "allowed it to be done," but didn't expect it to happen "this way." What else could it mean? Equally damaging, Darrow's statement that "I will take care of you" if you "do the best you can" sounded like another offer to corrupt the judicial process. What innocent meaning could it possibly have?

Rogers chose to deal with Browne's powerful testimony by using an approach that humiliated his client. He began by showering Browne, an old friend and ally, with compliments. Heralding his role as "the man who ran down the perpetrators of the *Times* horror," Rogers said that Browne, not William J. Burns, was entitled to the reward money for capturing the McNamaras. There was glee in his voice as he scored a double hit—promoting the success of his friend, Browne, who had been working for Rogers at the time that the McNamaras were captured; and embarrassing Rogers's old enemy, Detective Burns.

Rogers never attacked Browne's testimony directly. Instead, he argued that Darrow couldn't have been dumb enough to make such a foolish statement to the county's top cop.

Rogers's total response to what some observers called a "sensational development" was as follows: "Darrow knew all the time, when he made his statement to Mr. Browne, when he did all the talking that he did to Mr. Browne, that he was talking to that very man. So it would be most unlikely, knowing as he did that this was the chief detective, that he would say anything corrupt to him, that he would attempt to say to him, 'I will take care of you, Mr. Browne.' "

To Darrow, who *had* made the statement, and who assumed that everyone else would believe that he had made the statement, Rogers's words were nothing less than a public humiliation. It was as though Rogers was asking: How *could* you be so stupid?

❊❊❊❊

In her biography of her father, Adela Rogers St. Johns remembers a break between the two men that started that same night, after Rogers embarrassed Darrow in court.

"A fine fool you made me look," Darrow told Rogers bitterly as they were leaving the courtroom. "So it began," Adela reported, "on the street and in the elevators and crossing the reception room and on into my father's private office."

"I cannot sit there day after day and hear you make a fool of me," Darrow complained. Adela said he was "quivering all over."

"Nuts," Rogers answered. "We must insist that if you, Clarence Darrow, had taken to a life of crime you would have been as good as Caesar, Borgia, or Moriarty. You couldn't have left such a trail."

It was getting harder and harder for Darrow to accept Rogers's strategy, arrogance—or glee. His counsel was advancing his own career, enhancing his own reputation, helping his own friends and settling his own scores—all at Darrow's expense. Who needed such treatment at the hands of an egomaniacal alcoholic who, after all, had written the antipicketing ordinance that symbolized all that was most oppressive and corrupt in the place that Darrow now called the "City of the Dreadful Night"?

It was time for Darrow to take control of his own case.

❊❊❊❊

The opportunity arose in mid-June. The prosecution wanted to show that bribery was typical of Darrow's mode of operation—that it was part of Darrow's larger conspiracy to corrupt the system of justice. As proof, Fredericks intended to call such witnesses as Kurt Diekelman, the hotel clerk whom Darrow had lured to Chicago; George Behm, who had come to Los Angeles in order to persuade Ortie McManigal to change sides; Guy Biddinger, the Burns detective whom Darrow had paid for confidential information about the prosecution's case; and John Harrington, who could describe Darrow's methods from the inside.

On Thursday, June 13, Earl Rogers made his first serious and obvious legal error, offering the opening that Darrow's allies needed. The afternoon started with the testimony of a Los Angeles police detective named Eula Hitchcock. She described driving out to a remote location in the mountains near Redwood City and delivering a subpoena to Flora Caplan, wife of suspected bomber David Caplan. Detective Hitchcock said she had told Mrs. Caplan to remain available as a possible witness in the McNamara trial.

Then the prosecution brought on a San Francisco taxi driver named Malcomb Loughead to testify about his role in driving Flora Caplan out of the state a day or two later—in the company of Anton Johannsen and with the assistance of Olaf Tvietmoe. As soon as Loughead took the stand, Rogers began to object. There was no justification for introducing such collateral evidence into the case. This testimony was too far afield. "They don't prove *any* connection between Mr. Johannsen and Mr. Darrow," he complained.

"Don't worry," said Ford. "We will connect it."

Johannsen and Olaf Tvietmoe—in town for a federal court appearance—were both in the courtroom, along with several of their friends from the building trades unions.

Rogers pointed to the gallery. "Here is Mr. Johannsen right here," said Rogers. "I venture to say you will never connect it."

Ford admitted that it would take time to make the connection to Darrow, but he promised that the nexus would ultimately become clear. "A conspiracy is not something that is entered into the way an agreement is entered into," he argued. "Conspirators do not meet out in public. They meet in secret."

Judge Hutton sided with the defense. He said that he would not allow Loughead to testify. That should have ended the matter. But for some reason Rogers couldn't let well enough alone; he had to get in one last point. And in so doing, he admitted, inadvertently, that Tvietmoe and Johannsen had had "some connection with the defense of the McNamara case."

Based on that statement, Hutton reversed himself and allowed Loughead to testify. "The situation is somewhat changed by Mr.

Rogers's remarks," he announced. "He now states that those gentlemen were connected with the defense in the McNamara case." Amazingly, Rogers had managed to seize defeat from the jaws of victory.

On the witness stand, the driver then told an adventure story in a manner that was both frank and credible. In late July, 1911, he said, he met Johannsen in Tvietmoe's office at the Asiatic Exclusion League in San Francisco, drove Johannsen off in a seven-passenger Pierce-Arrow touring car, first to a remote hideaway near Redwood City, where they picked up Flora Caplan and her two children, and then across the state and over the border to Reno, Nevada. Once there, Johannsen and the Caplans registered at the Golden Hotel and prepared to take the *Overland Limited* for Chicago. Finally, Loughead returned to San Francisco with a letter from Johannsen to Tvietmoe, who paid him twenty-five dollars for his services.

None of the testimony would have been allowed but for Rogers's misstep, and his error did not go unnoticed. "Earl Rogers made one speech too many in the Darrow case yesterday," his friend Joseph Timmons said at the top of his story the next morning, noting that it was potentially a costly error, since "young Loughead proved one of the best witnesses the State has put on the stand."

In a bit of hyperbole, Timmons added that "the reversal of ruling by the court changed the whole complexion of the case in the twinkling of an eye." It was an overstatement. But it was an overstatement that both Clarence and Ruby Darrow—already disillusioned with Rogers—were inclined to believe.

That night, there was another storm in the Darrow camp, but this time Tvietmoe and Johannsen were part of it. They convinced Darrow to let them help him regain control of the case.

In some respects, Tvietmoe and Johannsen had reason to be at least as depressed as Darrow. During the past few months they had lived through the McNamara confessions, the death of Anton Johannsen's young daughter, the defeat of Mayor McCarthy in San Francisco, the loss of their investment in Tvietmoe's Sunset National Oil Company, and the federal criminal indictments against them in Indianapolis and Los Angeles. Yet after spending several months reacting to the forces arrayed against them, the labor leaders had snapped back to life; they were, once again, feeling powerful and angry—and on the offensive. And they were determined to use their own passion, their own fire and spirit, to re-energize Darrow.

For all of their resentment against him for pleading the McNamaras guilty, Johannsen and Tvietmoe were now determined to make sure that Darrow was acquitted. Darrow remained one of the great symbols of labor, a symbol that had now become particularly powerful on the Coast. He was also still the greatest labor lawyer in America, and despite his announced plan to retire, they may have hoped that he would agree to represent them in the trial in Indianapolis, assuming that he was acquitted. In any case, with Gompers remaining detached, the Socialists still disillusioned, and the political left as a whole unsure what to believe, Tvietmoe and Johannsen were quickly emerging as Darrow's strongest supporters, the only ones supplying him with money, with allies, or with political support. But in return, they insisted on taking control of the case.

As Tvietmoe explained it a few months later, he decided that he had to take Darrow's case into his own hands. He proceeded to treat Darrow as a schoolteacher would an unruly student. "I didn't use any sop with him, either," Tvietmoe said. "I went at him with a club. I told him this was labor's game and labor's money. I *made* him take direction and recognize leadership and authority."

※ ※ ※ ※

In her diary, Mary describes a powerful scene that probably took place that same night. Mary and Darrow and the labor leaders had dinner at the Turner and then returned to one of the rooms at the Hayward Hotel. Tvietmoe, Mary wrote, "loomed the biggest among us—'The Viking' they call him, and such he is. You feel he could open his mouth and roar his commands across angry waves and they would be still.

"Johannsen. He has been called 'The Spirit of Labor.' He *is* spirit! His laugh, big uproarious, contagious, is ever spilling from him as the foam runs over the edge of a schooner of beer."

There were others in the room that night, including Tvietmoe's friend Eric Morton, an editor of *Organized Labor,* the man who had provided the hideout for Flora Caplan; and Abraham Yoell, who worked for Tvietmoe at the Asiatic Exclusion League.

"And then," Mary wrote, there was "Darrow, poor broken Darrow, with the great marks of suffering on his face—looking like an oak that has been cleft by a lightning bolt. For a time he forgot his pain, his sense of failure in the contagion of brave men's presence."

Pacing the room, his big thumbs looped in the armholes of his vest, "something of the elephant in his stride, something of the panther in his big eyes," Tvietmoe stirred his friends by quoting a poem that applied to them all, could inspire them all. It was a poem from the American plains, John G. Neihardt's "Battle-Cry."

> *More than half beaten, but fearless,*
> *Facing the storm and the night;*
> *Breathless and reeling, but tearless,*
> *Here in the lull of the fight,*
> *I who bow not but before Thee,*
> *God of the fighting clan,*
> *Lifting my fists I implore Thee,*
> *Give me the heart of a man!*

"Give me the heart of a man!" It applied to them all; and it was the perfect message for Darrow.

"A thrill ran through us all," Mary wrote. "We were caught, and our hearts beat to the tonic vibrations of his deep bass tones. We felt the bravery, the defiance, the sheer purpose of the man.

" 'God!' said Johannsen, breaking the strain. 'That's a God damn son of a bitch of a poem! Say it again!' "

So Tvietmoe said it again, calling on the God of the fighting clan, imploring Him to "Give me the heart of a man!" And as he recited the poem this time, some of the others joined in, as if in prayer.

When Tvietmoe had finished, they passed around a bottle of whiskey. "Even Darrow drank," Mary said. "His great brave spirit somewhat revived, though it was only, I knew, a reflection of the spirit of these warriors.

"Then they read." Usually it was Darrow who read on such occasions, who read to anyone who would listen, to his friends or to a public audience. But this time it was he who was listening as Tvietmoe, translator of Bjornstjerne Bjornson's plays, sat at a small table next to Eric Morton, who read from Bjornsen's *Beyond Human Power*. As he read, "dramatically gesticulating," Morton's voice "thundered the protest of the strikers in the play, wheedled the part of the ministers and boasted the replies of the mill owners. And Tvietmoe's face, usually a blank wall of emotional control, played the passions of the play—sympathy for the dead striker, his wife, his little children; hatred of the masters; appreciation of the noble lines of the leaders.

" 'It's great,' he would mutter.

" 'God damn it,' would echo Jo. And Darrow's eyes, those wise, sad eyes within which was the wounded look of the child, would grow moist.

"Till after midnight we read," Mary reported. "The streets were empty when we left.

" 'Fighting the fight is all,' said Tvietmoe," quoting a stirring passage from "Battle-Cry." " 'Goodnight!'

"Jo's laugh echoed through the cool night air. Jo's laugh and Tvietmoe's last words sounded in my ears," Mary wrote. " 'Fighting the fight is all.' "

And for them, the fight for Darrow's acquittal would become a crusade. They would give *him* the heart of a man.

❋ ❋ ❋ ❋

The courtroom the next morning was even more chaotic than usual. A film crew had asked for permission to take moving pictures of a courtroom scene and the lawyers and judge had agreed to engage in a mock argument for the benefit of the photographers. It didn't much matter what was said, of course, since the movies were silent. But in fact, the legal struggle inside the courtroom was as unusual and intense as any in the trial to date. For the defense had hit upon a strange and bold tactic that was procedurally unorthodox, was totally unanticipated by the prosecution, and was calculated to place Darrow—along with Tvietmoe and Johannsen—back at center stage.

Darrow's supporters came into court that Friday morning knowing that Timmons's assessment in the *Examiner* might well be correct. Loughead's exceptionally credible testimony on Thursday
afternoon might, indeed, have "changed the whole complexion of
the present state of the case." At the very least, it had set a dangerous
precedent. Unless stopped at once, the prosecutors were certain to
put on other witnesses who—though they knew nothing about the
bribery and had no connection with Darrow—would make colorful
and damaging statements.

Normally, the defense is not allowed to introduce any witnesses
until the prosecution completes its case. In fact, no one in Los
Angeles had ever heard of an exception to that rule. Yet Johannsen
and Tvietmoe, who were unintimidated by legal niceties, demanded
a chance to rebut Loughead's testimony immediately, to show the
judge and jury that Darrow had had nothing to do with Flora Caplan's escape from California. It was the sort of unorthodox move that
also appealed to Earl Rogers.

Rogers presented the unusual request to the Judge Hutton, first in
chambers, and then in open court.

"Counsel is undoubtedly planning to put in incident after incident
which the defendant had nothing to do with," Rogers argued. "We
have a right to show that there is no foundation for that testimony.
We therefore demand the right at this time to produce witnesses on
our behalf on this issue raised by this testimony, to show that Mr.
Darrow had not the slightest thing to do with this, and we demand
the right to be heard at once."

The proposal was unusual under any circumstances, but in this
instance it also posed another problem. If Judge Hutton allowed
Johannsen to testify, at once and out of order, Earl Rogers would
have to withdraw from the case, because Johannsen intended to
claim that it was Earl Rogers's conduct as the special prosecutor in
the *Times* bombing case—and not any improper motive of the
McNamara defense team—that had forced Flora Caplan to leave the
state.

"I find myself in an absolutely intolerable position," Rogers explained. "I request that you permit me to withdraw from this room
and allow the defendant himself to put Mr. Johannsen and Mr.

Tvietmoe on the stand to show that this matter has no business in this case. Mr. Johannsen stands ready to go on the stand to tell this court that Mr. Darrow had nothing whatever to do with this matter."

In a ruling that attorneys for both sides agreed was wholly unprecedented in English and American jurisprudence, Judge Hutton agreed to interrupt the prosecution's case so that Johannsen could take the witness stand. It was fast becoming clear that the judge was not controlled by the forces of Capital. In an almost equally unusual gesture, he also allowed Rogers temporarily to resign from the case, to remove himself as the counsel of record, leaving Darrow—for the first time—as his own lead attorney.

As court adjourned on Friday, it was generally agreed that Rogers and Darrow had scored a procedural coup. "From the standpoint of the defense," the *Times* noted, "it was a clever move and one that was unexpected by either Fredericks or Ford." Some people thought it would cause Captain Fredericks to move for the dismissal of the case.

But after spending all night considering his options, Fredericks decided not to seek a dismissal; indeed, he came up with a plan designed to turn Johannsen's testimony to his own advantage.

❀ ❀ ❀ ❀

With his bright red tie and dark three-piece suit, Johannsen happily settled into the witness stand on Saturday morning. Short, stocky, powerful, direct, and still full of fun despite the loss of his daughter and the federal indictment against him, Anton Johannsen could not wait to tell his story. And there, sitting in the lead counsel's chair for the first time in the trial, was Clarence Darrow, who had not previously played an active role in his own defense. He had Horace Appel at his side, but Rogers was temporarily out of the case.

As Darrow rose, a lock of his sandy hair falling casually over his forehead, his tall frame slightly hunched, he felt pleased to be back on his feet, in control of the courtroom, no longer simply another defendant sitting by his lawyer's side. At first his questions were awkwardly stated and it seemed that he lacked "his old spirit," but as the day wore on, his voice grew stronger and his questions sharper as he regained a measure of self-confidence, settling back into the profession that he had pursued for so long and with such brilliance.

How was Flora Caplan treated by the Burns people and others, Darrow asked.

"The detectives were at the doorsteps all the time she was in Los Angeles, watching every move and following her every place she went."

"When she went back to San Francisco, did she say anything to you about the way she was treated and threatened and humiliated by the Burns men up there?"

"She told me that detectives were following her every place she went, and had actually went so far as to grab hold of her on the street, and on one particular occasion she had found it necessary to slap one of them in the face. I wouldn't believe they went that far, so I went home with her, and seen with my own eyes, seen the detectives. They got on the streetcars and off the cars, into the restaurant, any place she went. They hounded her and followed her, threatened and bulldozed her."

"What did you say to her?" Darrow asked. By now he was moving around the room as he posed questions, or standing with one foot on his chair, arms resting on a bent knee, listening with keen intensity.

"I advised her to leave the state and told her that I would go with her."

"Did you consult with anybody before you went, any lawyers?"

"I should say not," Johannsen laughed. "I never consult lawyers on those matters."

"Did you consult with *me* about it?" Darrow asked.

"I did not."

"Or anybody connected with the defense of the McNamara case?"

"Not with any of the attorneys."

"Did you ever give me or any attorney connected with the defense any information you were going to do it?"

"No, sir."

Darrow rephrased the question twelve different ways to drive home his point and close any possible loophole. Johannsen was emphatic. Darrow didn't know about it, no one connected with the defense knew about it, and there was no way Darrow could have known about it. Finally, Darrow ended the questioning by showing that he had not in any way helped to finance the expedition, either.

"Did you get any money from me or from any of the attorneys for the defense?"

"I did not. You were too stingy."

"What is that?" Darrow asked.

"I said you were too stingy."

On that pungent note, Darrow ended his questioning.

Johannsen had been effective and persuasive—"an ideal witness for the defense while Darrow had him in his hand," Timmons reported.

But Johannsen had also provided an extraordinary opening for Fredericks to pursue on cross.

※ ※ ※ ※

Fredericks could not wait to get at the witness. As the *Times* reported the next day, "attorneys who have followed Captain Fredericks's upward career declared they never saw him so eager to interrogate a witness." He was, the paper said, "in fighting trim."

"Mr. Johannsen," Fredericks asked, "was there anybody in the defense that knew you were going to take Mrs. Caplan away; anybody that was working with Mr. Darrow?"

"No."

"No?" Fredericks repeated. "You never talked to anybody in the defense and told them that you were going to take her away before you took her, did you?"

"No."

"Never told anybody for the defense after you took her away, that you had taken her away?"

"No, I don't know that I did."

"Do you know whether you did or not?"

"I said *no.*"

"Did you ever report to Mr. Darrow that you had taken this woman out of the state?"

"No."

"Did you ever report to Job Harriman that you had taken her out of the state?"

"No."

"Did you ever report to John Harrington that you had taken her out of the state?"

"No."

"Did you ever report to—let's see. There are two names. Job Harriman and John Harrington. You understand that they are two different people?"

"I know that John Harrington is not Harriman and Harriman is not Harrington."

"What was John R. Harrington's position with the defense, if you know?"

"He was the investigator for the defense, I presume."

"You so accepted and so talked to him and so understood him, is that correct?"

"Yes."

"Now when you got off the train in Reno, did you telegraph anybody telling them that you got there, or anything of that kind?"

"I might possibly have telegraphed Tvietmoe."

"But you didn't telegraph to Darrow, did you?"

"No."

"Didn't telegraph to John R. Harrington, did you?"

"No."

"You are sure of that?"

"I am not certain."

"You may have telegraphed to Harrington?"

"I don't remember whether I did or not." Though still game, Johannsen was starting to look worried.

"Well, Harrington didn't know you were going East with this woman, did he?"

"Nobody knew but Tvietmoe."

A reporter for the *Record* glanced over at Tvietmoe. He was chewing anxiously on an unlighted cigar.

"You would know if you told anybody connected with the defense, wouldn't you, that you took Mrs. Caplan out of the state. You would remember that, wouldn't you?"

"I don't think I would telegraph something like that."

"You don't think you did," Fredericks persisted. "Are you sure you didn't?"

"I am not sure. I am reasonably certain. I don't remember telegraphing."

"You don't!" Fredericks exclaimed. Now he was ready to attack Johannsen with his whip. "Well, Mr. Johannsen, didn't you send Mr. Harrington a telegram from Reno, telling him that you were all right, that you had crossed the state line?"

"I don't remember telegraphing."

"You don't? Well you and Mr. Harrington and the other members of the defense had a secret code by which you could telegraph in secret, didn't you?"

Judge Hutton overruled an exception by Appel.

"Yes, we had a code."

"And the code was in a little dictionary?"

"I guess you know," Johannsen replied with contempt.

"Wasn't it?"

"I guess they told you about it all right." Johannsen directed his answer and his anger to Fredericks. "They," of course, were the spies or turncoats who were helping the prosecution.

"Mr. Johannsen, permit me to show you a document," he said. To his supporters, his attack was thrilling, but to Darrow's friends Fredericks's tone was despicable. "With a hiss of joy," Mary Field wrote, "he sprang forward like a snake uncoiling and about to fasten its fangs on the flesh of its victim." After showing it to Darrow and Appel, Fredericks gave Johannsen a sheet of paper. "Now I exhibit to you a document which appears to be a telegram, and ask you if you ever saw it before and if that is not your handwriting."

"That is my handwriting."

The court instructed the clerk to mark the document as an exhibit for the prosecution.

"Now I will read to the jury the document which has been offered in evidence." Fredericks proceeded to read from the telegram.

" 'Postal Telegraph and Cable Company. Night Letter. C 7 P.M. Check 27, Paid 40, John R. Harrington, Hotel Argonaut, San Francisco, California. 10-43-129-49 A is 54-40- all on 156-38,' signed 'C.'

"Now, Mr. Witness, let's see if we can find out what that means. I would like to show you a little red dictionary and ask you if you ever saw such a dictionary before, and if that is not the dictionary which is the key to the code which you used in that telegram. Do you have one of these books, or one like it, in your pocket?"

"No," Johannsen answered, but he was losing some of his self-composure and assurance. A reporter from the *Record* watched his movements as he "ran his hands through his hair and looked vaguely around the room. He crossed and uncrossed his legs and appeared very nervous."

"You have not. Did you ever have one?"

"I don't remember. Let's see the book."

Before showing Johannsen the book, Fredericks showed him the telegram and asked, "Do you know what this *ten* means?" Then, sharing the book, Fredericks told the witness to "Turn to page ten and find the forty-third word in the second column."

"I don't know whether that is the book or not."

"Is it similar to the one you used in making that telegram?"

"Looks like it."

Then, writing the letters and words on a blackboard, Fredericks proceeded to decode the telegram. As he did so, Darrow tore off long sheets of yellow paper and began to chew them nervously. Reporters noted that atmosphere in the room was tense with excitement as jurors and spectators leaned forward eagerly to hear his presentation.

The first number referred to a page in the dictionary, Fredericks explained. The second number referred to a word on that page, the third number referred to another page, and the fourth number to a word. For example, the forty-third word on page 10 was "all;" the forty-ninth word on page 129 was "right." The letters corresponded to a code written in the back of the book. Flora Caplan was "A." Johannsen was "C."

When he had completed his explanation, Fredericks read the decoded message. The telegram said: ALL RIGHT. FLORA CAPLAN IS FINE.

ALL ON TRAIN. It was signed JOHANNSEN. There was no denying it. Johannsen had kept Darrow's top investigator informed of his efforts.

"Having refreshed your memory with the telegram," Fredericks asked, "what have you to say as to whether or not the defense had anything to do with the getting of Flora Caplan out of the state of California the next day after she was subpoenaed?"

"I would like to explain the matter if I am permitted," Johannsen said. "I had no reason to apprehend that the defense could in any way be interfered with. I told Flora Caplan to wire John D. Fredericks as soon as the jury in the McNamara trial would be completed, to tell him her whereabouts and her willingness to come and testify if they wanted her."

"What did you mean by telling John Harrington, the chief of detectives for the defense, that it was 'all right?' "

"I meant that Burns was outwitted," Johannsen said.

But to observers in the courtroom that Saturday morning, it seemed that the ones who had been outwitted were Clarence Darrow and his friends in organized labor.

❉ ❉ ❉ ❉

For the moment, Fredericks had won a remarkable victory. He had, as Joe Timmons observed in the *Examiner,* "led the defense into an ambush. He had seemed to be in full retreat, with forces in confusion, and the defense, hastening to make the rout complete, fell squarely into the trap." In a highly theatrical session, Fredericks had demonstrated Darrow's link to at least one troubling if collateral matter. As a result, the prosecution would be allowed to bring in other examples of Darrow's efforts to "corrupt justice" in the McNamara case. Equally important, the episode seemed to prove that some important defense witnesses were willing to deceive the jury.

But something else was happening, something that neither Rogers nor Fredericks had anticipated. The jury was getting to know and like Clarence Darrow.

❉ ❉ ❉ ❉

Over the weekend, there was widespread gossip that Earl Rogers was planning to withdraw from the case. The stories gained greater credibility on Monday when Appel persuaded the court to grant a one-day postponement after explaining that he was suffering from lung congestion and that Rogers was "sick in bed." That afternoon, a banner headline in the *Record* announced that DARROW MAY TAKE FULL CHARGE. Although the stories were "vehemently denied" by Rogers, they told volumes about the changing dynamics of the defense.

On Tuesday morning the new, large courtroom was once again packed with Darrow's friends and allies, including a large number of women who sat in the front rows, wearing magnificent bonnets, giving the trial the feeling of a matinee. Old friends from Chicago had begun to arrive, such as labor leader Ed Nockles (Darrow's one remaining staunch friend from the national labor movement) and society leader Mrs. Robert Grotte. They took seats on the new steel benches alongside the West Coast labor leaders, the core of radical sympathizers, and the wives of such Darrow supporters as Earl Rogers and Socialist Party leader Frank Wolfe.

The spectators were braced for a sizzling examination of Tvietmoe, when Horace Appel began with a surprising announcement.

Tvietmoe, he said, would not be called to the stand after all.

With the Johannsen-Tvietmoe interlude over, Rogers returned to the room and resumed his seat at the counsel table. But, still showing signs of his recent "indisposition," he left the courtroom for long stretches of time. As the prosecution called its next witness to the stand, Darrow remained fully in charge of the defense.

※ ※ ※ ※

The next prosecution witness was George Behm, Ortie McManigal's well-meaning but somewhat addled old uncle. Speaking slowly and thoughtfully, in a voice so low that the jury could hardly hear his words, the old railroad engineer told how Darrow had persuaded him to come to Los Angeles in June to try to talk his nephew into changing sides. "Mr. Darrow told me to do all I could to get Ortie to come across," Behm related. "He said if Ortie took back his confession, he would see that he got a good job in Chicago; that he wouldn't be climbing around on buildings to make a living. Darrow gave me a hundred dollars to come to California and said he would give me some more when I got there." As proof, the prosecution introduced a letter from Darrow to Behm.

Once in Los Angeles, Behm said, Darrow sent him on repeated missions to see his nephew in jail, always with the same result: He couldn't get Ortie to repudiate his confession. But on each occasion, Darrow asked him to go back again, always suggesting that Behm use some new form of pressure to persuade Ortie to "come across." Finally, Behm said, Darrow threatened to have Ortie prosecuted for murder in Chicago if he testified against the McNamaras.

Behm was not a particularly effective witness for the prosecution, since his voice was barely audible and his memory vague. When Darrow began his cross-examination, he knew that he could tear the weak-minded old fellow to bits, but he knew, too, that there is a risk when you have a mental lightweight on the witness stand, at least when he is elderly and reasonably sympathetic. The trick is to negate his testimony without appearing to be unkind. In this case, that concern was especially profound, since Darrow hoped to use the cross-examination to present himself to the jury, to begin to establish himself in their minds as a man of decency, substance, intelligence, and integrity. The last thing Darrow wanted was to alienate the jury.

Darrow's questions were so rapid and penetrating that within less than ten minutes, Behm was asking him to slow down. He couldn't remember which meeting was which, or just what instructions he had been given by Darrow. "Take your own time," Darrow said kindly. It was just the right tone, a mixture of toughness and kindness, and his intelligence and style immediately impressed those in the room. "The defendant showed his old-time skill as a keen examiner," the *Times* observed, "and put the questions so fast that the witness said more than once: 'Wait a minute until I can answer. I can't think so fast.' "

Watching what one reporter called the "amazing density of the witness," it was easy to forgive Darrow for an occasional display of anger. As Behm continued to confuse times and dates, even Judge Hutton became exasperated. After admonishing the lawyer for one of his pithier comments, the judge noted that Darrow was being "very patient."

When Behm left the stand, deflated and humiliated, Darrow had succeeded in presenting himself in a new light to the jurors. "By turns he was patient, vehement, sarcastic, and at all times intensely in earnest," Joe Timmons reported. "The famous lawyer's keen intellect and power of incisive interrogation profoundly impressed the spectators and probably the jurors as well."

❊❊❊❊

In some respects, the prosecution's most dangerous witness was John Harrington. The defense had long been afraid of his testimony—so much so that Anton Johannsen, presumably with Darrow's knowledge, had tried to have him kidnapped. A roly-poly Irishman with a musical brogue and a delightful, unflappable manner, Harrington was the man Darrow considered a great "evidence-gatherer." According to Mary, he had been "an intimate personal friend of Darrow's" for fifteen years. Harrington had worked on the McNamara case with Darrow from April 27, 1911, when Darrow first agreed to take the case, to December 5, 1911, when the McNamaras were sentenced to prison. As the chief investigator for the McNamara defense team, Harrington was extremely knowledgeable about almost all aspects of Darrow's strategy in that case.

Worst of all, he had held the series of meetings with Darrow in February, 1912. Darrow had consulted with his lawyers before each meeting and had debriefed them afterward; he had tried to be cautious when talking to Harrington, knowing that the state was doing everything in its power to get his former investigator to testify. Nevertheless, there was a risk that Darrow had made some foolish remarks; he might even have made some damaging admissions; and any such missteps would be particularly dangerous since the sessions apparently had been transcribed by means of a Dictograph machine, and Fredericks presumably intended to introduce the transcripts as evidence.

There was also a somewhat technical reason why Harrington was an essential witness for the prosecution and worrisome for the defense. Under California law, it would be exceedingly difficult, and perhaps even impossible, to convict Darrow on the uncorroborated testimony of Bert Franklin, since Franklin was a coconspirator. The prosecution needed at least one other live witness to confirm his story. While testimony about other efforts to corrupt justice might be interesting, and might help convince a jury that bribery was simply a part of Darrow's style of operation, it did not provide any direct proof that Darrow had told Franklin to bribe Lockwood. Evidence that Darrow had given a check to Tvietmoe, and that Tvietmoe might have converted the check into cash that Darrow used as the bribe money, was significant, but it still left room for doubt. Darrow's presence when Franklin was arrested by Sam Browne was an extremely powerful bit of evidence for the prosecution, as was the testimony that Darrow, moments later, told Browne to "do the best you can and I will take care of you." But Darrow's comment to Browne was subject to various interpretations, as was Darrow's appearance at Third and Main at the time of the bribe. In short, it was possible that, without Harrington's testimony, the prosecution's case could totally collapse.

Knowing his importance to the prosecution, Mary called Harrington "the star witness."

❋ ❋ ❋ ❋

When Harrington took the stand on Friday, June 21, the court was filled with Darrow's friends. At a few minutes after ten A.M., Ed Nockles entered the room with Olaf Tvietmoe, walked down to Darrow, and exchanged warm greetings. The mood was too friendly for Joe Ford, who had observed how Darrow's spirits improved when his allies were around. He asked the judge to enforce the state law that required that all potential witnesses—including Johannsen, Tvietmoe and LeCompte Davis—be excluded from the room. But Judge Hutton again demonstrated that he was unusually sympathetic to the defense. After admitting that he was "straining the rule a little bit," the judge said that the three men could stay.

Harrington quickly impressed observers as the state's most effective witness, answering questions crisply, comfortably, and with a touch of humor. Never looking at Rogers or Darrow, he directed all of his comments to the jury. Harrington quickly confirmed Behm's account of the way that he was brought to Los Angeles and asked to persuade Ortie to recant his testimony; reaffirmed the claim that Darrow and Johannsen had devised a secret code that had been used in Johannsen's telegram about the escape of Flora Caplan; and provided support for Diekelman's account of the way in which he was induced to move from Albuquerque to Chicago in order to avoid testifying in the McNamara case.

Then Harrington revealed two fresh and startling pieces of evidence connecting Darrow with the effort to bribe Lockwood. First, Harrington described a conversation with Darrow in late September, in which Darrow allegedly showed him ten thousand dollars in cash and suggested that it could be used to bribe jurors.

"After Mr. Darrow returned from San Francisco to Los Angeles in early September, state whether you had a conversation with him in regard to a roll of bank bills," Fredericks asked.

"I did."

"And where and when did you have that conversation?"

"Between the twentieth and thirtieth of September, 1911, on the porch of Mr. Darrow's house on Bonnie Brae."

"What time of day or night?"

"It was in the evening."

"State that conversation, insofar as it relates to the subject I have inquired about."

"Mr. Darrow showed me a roll of bills there in which he stated there was ten thousand dollars and that if he could arrange to reach a couple of jurymen, that J.B. would never be convicted."

"What was the rest of that conversation, so far as it relates to that matter?"

"I told Mr. Darrow not to attempt such a thing. It would be his ruin; be the ruin of the case; ruin everybody connected with the case; that his conduct would be repudiated by labor leaders all through the country."

"What, if anything, did he say?"

"He then says, 'I guess you are right. I won't do it.' "

"Did Mr. Darrow say anything about where he got that money and how?"

"He told me that he got it from Tvietmoe's bank in San Francisco.

He said that he had the check cashed in San Francisco so that the money could not be traced through the Los Angeles banks."

"Now, coming down to the twenty-eighth of November, you remember the day on which Bert Franklin was arrested," Fredericks began. "State whether or not, on that morning, at a time an hour or so after Bert Franklin was arrested, you had a conversation with Mr. Darrow in his office."

"Yes, sir."

"Relate the entire conversation."

"I was sitting in my office when Mr. Darrow came in and called me into his office. It was about ten o'clock. He told me Bert Franklin was arrested. I asked him what for. He says, 'jury bribing.' "

"What was his appearance?" Fredericks asked.

"Mr. Darrow seemed to be very nervous," Harrington continued. "I then asked him if Mr. Franklin could involve him in the matter in any way. He says, 'My God, if he speaks I am ruined.' "

With that, Fredericks turned Harrington over to the defense for cross-examination.

❈ ❈ ❈ ❈

Darrow knew that the cross-examination of Harrington would have to be brutal. It was not a task for a man who wanted to appear likable. It was a job for Earl Rogers, if Rogers could perform at his peak.

Rogers was more than up to the task. He immediately lit into the witness, using every trick at his disposal, issuing what Joe Timmons described as "broadsides of invective, poisoned barbs of sarcasm, and interrogations loaded with contempt and loathing."

As he had done with Franklin and Lockwood, Rogers began by trying to show that the witness was a contemptible creature who would turn in his own mother for a mess of pottage or a grant of immunity.

"You are testifying for immunity, aren't you?" Rogers asked.

"No, sir."

"You are testifying to get yourself out of a hole, aren't you?"

"No, sir."

Rogers spent the rest of the day exploring other subjects, but he returned to the matter of immunity on Saturday morning, wanting to show that Harrington was testifying to save his own skin.

"Now yesterday, Mr. Harrington, you denied that you are testifying for immunity or to get yourself out of a hole, didn't you?" Rogers began.

"Yes, sir."

Rogers walked back to the table and picked up a copy of the *Evening Herald* newspaper dated March 11, 1912.

"Now, I will ask you if you didn't know of Mr. Fredericks saying this," Rogers began. Lifting his lorgnette to his eyes and squinting slightly, Rogers started to read from the paper. "Mr. Harrington will be a state witness in the Darrow case without doubt, and he'd better tell all and the truth. If he don't, it will go hard with him. We know absolutely all he knows, and if he veers from the truth it may be he will be called upon to face a serious charge."

Fredericks was on his feet at once, complaining that the quotation was incompetent, irrelevant, and immaterial, that it was not cross-examination. "I suppose counsel is reading from some newspaper account of something the district attorney is supposed to have said," Fredericks stated.

"Makes no difference where I got it," Rogers answered.

"I will say I never said it," Fredericks insisted.

"Possibly," Rogers said knowingly. "It is in quotation marks." He had already elevated Fredericks's temper to the boiling point, just where he wanted it.

"Oh, yes," Fredericks said. "We have all been quoted world without end."

Rogers began to read again. "Here is what Mr. Fredericks is said to have said: 'District Attorney Fredericks said Harrington will be a state witness in the Darrow case, without doubt, and he'd better tell the truth'—Isn't it true that your fear of prosecution induced you to be a witness in this case against Mr. Darrow?"

"No sir, it is not."

"Were you here on March 11, 1912?"

"Yes, sir."

"Did you read the *Evening Herald* on March 11?"

"I don't remember."

"You do not remember?" Rogers held up his copy of the *Evening Herald* of that date. He showed it to Harrington, the judge, and the jury. A large front-page headline announced J. R. HARRINGTON MUST TESTIFY IN BRIBERY CASE OR TAKE THE CONSEQUENCES. "You do not deny reading this paper on March 11, do you?"

"I deny I ever saw that article that you read now."

"Do you recognize that article is on the front page with a very large headline?"

"I never saw that article before."

"Did any of your friends call your attention to this fact, that in very large, black type, the statement was made that you must testify or face the consequences?"

"No, sir."

Unlike Fredericks, who seldom attempted to underline testimony for the jury's benefit, Rogers restated the question several different times, asking if Harrington read newspapers, if he ever read the *Herald,* if his friends read the *Herald,* if Harrington hadn't said, after his attention was called to the article, that "I had better get under the tent," or "I do not want any trouble." Each time, Harrington denied it.

"Did you have any idea that they were after you or trying to get you in trouble at that time or afterwards?"

"No, sir."

Rogers had managed to spring another trap. He went back to the counsel table, retrieved a document, and approached the witness with the document in his hand. The document was a letter that Harrington had written to Darrow on January 20, 1912. "Is this your handwriting?" he asked, handing the letter to Harrington.

"Yes, sir," Harrington answered, "it is." He was still looking at the jury rather than at Rogers.

"I offer this letter in evidence," Rogers said, after showing it to Fredericks and Judge Hutton.

"It does not impeach anything the witness had said," Fredericks stated. "We would like to have it read to the jury."

Rogers again took out his lorgnette and started to read. "Dear Darrow," he began. "I have been shadowed since my return and one evening the fellow called on my house and tried to get some information from me. I let him do all the talking. Burns men are making great cracks here that they are going to get you, and some of your friends are worrying and quite a few lawyers spoke to me and expressed sympathy for you. You are, according to the enemy, in their grasp. This Burns fellow also mentioned about Hammerstrom and it seems they are after him, too. I do not like to put too much in this letter as it may be tampered with. They know a good deal and are certainly after us." After *us.*

Still holding the letter, Rogers approached Harrington. "Now, in this letter you say here, 'They know a good deal and are certainly after *us.*' Do you desire to change your testimony that you gave just before I showed you this letter?"

"No, sir," Harrington replied, still unflappable, still looking at the jury.

"When you wrote to Darrow and said 'they are after us,' and you signed it 'Harrington,' you kind of meant that they were after you, Harrington, and Darrow, too, didn't you?"

"I meant they were after the defense."

"Of which you were a component part."

❊❊❊❊

As he had with Franklin, Rogers then asked Harrington about a series of statements that he allegedly had made denying that he had any information connecting Darrow with the bribery. One statement was to a reporter at the *Herald* named Dunne; another was to a steelworker from Seattle named W. H. Pohlman (who happened to be in the courtroom, observing the proceedings with his young son); another was with Sara Ehrgott.

"Did you not say to this lady that Darrow had always told everyone in connection with the case that it must be run honestly and on the square?" Rogers asked. Sara, of course, would have been skeptical of any such assertion since it would have flatly contradicted everything that she and Erskine Wood believed about Darrow's tactics.

"No, sir, I did not make any such statement," Harrington said.

Rogers then asked about an alleged conversation between Harrington and Billy Cavenaugh, the Venice police sergeant and longtime Darrow friend, whose house served as Darrow's secret mail-drop.

"Did you not tell Mr. Cavenaugh that the idea that he knew of any corrupt work was absurd?"

"No, sir, I did not."

"Nor anything like it?"

"Oh, no. Nothing at all like it."

"Did you ever make the same statement to Mr. Cavenaugh at his home in Venice?"

"I did not," Harrington stated, his eyes still fixed on the jury. Then he added a surprise of his own. "Both Cavenaugh and I agreed to it that Darrow was guilty."

"What is that?" Rogers asked. He and the attorneys at the defense table were stunned. This was not an answer that they had expected. Rogers started moving around the room aggressively, trying harder than ever to make Harrington look at him, but Harrington kept looking at the jury.

"Both Cavenaugh and I said down there that Darrow was guilty," Harrington repeated.

"Tell me what Cavenaugh said."

"Cavenaugh said that Darrow was guilty."

This was damaging testimony, all the more so because Darrow knew that it was probably true. On at least one occasion during the past few months Cavenaugh—sympathetically, supportively, lovingly—had expressed the wish that Darrow had used him, rather than Franklin, to pass the bribe.

Rogers had been hopping around the room all day, trying to force Harrington to look at him. Now he moved over so far that he was almost sitting in the jury box. "Was anybody else present?" he asked.

Despite Rogers's most inventive efforts, Harrington remained impassive, his eyes fixed on the jury, refusing to look at either Rogers or Darrow. "Earl Rogers was struggling in the effort to confuse, expose and overwhelm Harrington," Joe Timmons reported. "His play of facial expression, the scorn, loathing and taunting triumph that would do credit to any actor in the 'legitimate,' were as completely lost as is the face that one boy makes at another when his back is turned. Rogers sat down, he stood up, he padded about the courtroom with the stealthy tread of a panther, trying to slip up on Harrington's eyes and surprise them. He got over close to the jury and even leaned over farther still in that direction, as if he meant to reach out some tendrils of vision and kidnap the gaze Harrington was bestowing on the jurors."

As Rogers continued his inquiries, Darrow was also on his feet moving restlessly around the room.

"Was anybody else present?" Rogers asked again.

"His wife," Harrington replied, still managing to avoid looking at Rogers.

Darrow walked over to Rogers and whispered something in his ear. He reminded his lead counsel that Harrington had been a guest in the Darrow home at about that time.

"When did you have that conversation with Billy Cavenaugh?" Rogers asked.

Then he turned back to Darrow, who had started to return to his seat. "Make him look you in the eye," Rogers said in a voice just loud enough to be audible.

Fredericks heard Rogers's comment to Darrow. "May it please the court," he interrupted, "we would like to have Mr. Darrow keep his seat. I do not want to say why."

Appel opposed the motion. "We do not propose to have him sit down," he said. "Mr. Darrow is an attorney."

"Then I will say why," Fredericks replied. It sounded like a threat.

But Rogers knew that it was better to keep the initiative. "If counsel does not want to say why, then I will say why."

"All right," Fredericks said.

"I have been trying to get this man to look at me for two days now, ever since he has been on the stand." Rogers began, moving around the courtroom for emphasis. "I have walked over there, I stood here, I sat here, and I walked around yonder, with the hope and purpose of seeing if I could not get him to look me in the eye or look Mr. Darrow in the eye, and he has never done it." As he spoke, Harrington continued to look at the jury rather than at Darrow or Rogers.

"We have no objection to his looking counsel in the eye," Fredericks answered, leaping to his feet. "But counsel said, right here in back of me, when Mr. Darrow came over, counsel said to Mr. Darrow, 'Make him look you in the eye.' "

Then, due to stupidity or exhaustion or anger, Fredericks made one of the most startling and damaging statements of the trial. "We maintain that Mr. Darrow is attempting to use hypnotism on this witness."

With that, the room exploded. *Hypnotism!* It was the release that Darrow's friends in the room needed. Led by Johannsen, they started to laugh. And the jury started to laugh. And even the judge found it hard not to laugh. The bailiffs called for order, but to no avail. Mary Field called it "a hearty, splendid, intelligent laugh; the laugh of the people."

Angry and humiliated, quivering with rage, Fredericks kept on going. "Yes, and they—the fact is right here, he did it right here when he had Behm on the stand." His face was beet red. "Let Mr. Darrow keep his eyes to himself. We know something about this case. This is for the jury. I know what I am talking about."

With every sentence, there was another roar of laughter. By now even Darrow was chuckling, his eyes brimming with laughter.

Appel tried to interrupt. "This is the most childish—" he began, but Fredericks was still talking.

"I absolutely know what I am talking about," Fredericks repeated.

"This is the most childish statement made by—"

Finally Judge Hutton tried to take control. "Now gentlemen," he began. "Mr. Rogers is interrogating the witness and Mr. Darrow approached him and spoke to him. I can see no serious impropriety in that."

Fredericks wouldn't let it alone. "And Mr. Rogers said to Mr. Darrow—that is the point I am getting at, Mr. Darrow had no business over here."

"Gentlemen," Judge Hutton said, "so far as this question of hypnotism is concerned, it is not a science that this court will recognize."

"Before we get through, perhaps the court will," Fredericks insisted.

Again the spectators broke into jeering, derisive laughter. It was genuine, but it was also a deliberate device. As the *Times* noted,

"Court attachés who have served for a score of years declared the laughter and applause for the defense exceeded anything they had ever heard in any court. It is alleged that the same tactics would have been attempted in the McNamara trial if the case had not been brought to an abrupt conclusion." Finally Judge Hutton felt compelled to announce a five-minute recess so that the crowd could finish laughing and return to order.

For Fredericks, with his pride and his intense need to assert his manhood, few things were so painful as humiliation. Only a week earlier, he had been in "fighting trim" and on the offensive, embarrassing Johannsen and the forces of labor. Now he was the subject of ridicule, laughed at by the very men he had so recently thrashed.

To Rogers, who focused on the theatrics and human dynamics of the criminal process, it felt like a turning point in the long, important, and increasingly emotional proceeding. The prosecutors were feeling the pressure and beginning to look foolish. It was only a matter of time before they would begin to make mistakes and begin to look sinister.

❊ ❊ ❊ ❊

On Monday, June 24, the San Francisco labor leaders had some good news for Darrow. They sent him a telegram, formally inviting him to be their featured speaker on September 2, Labor Day. Only a year earlier, the speaker had been Samuel Gompers. Expressing admiration for "your magnificent past services to the Labor Movement and the workers of our country, and reposing the utmost confidence in your integrity," the leaders promised that the demonstration would be "the largest and most epoch-making in the history of the trade union movement of California."

When Harrington resumed the witness stand that afternoon, Rogers was not feeling well. His throat was still troubling him and he had spent a sleepless weekend, working and drinking. Moreover, the atmosphere in the courtroom was stifling due to a lack of ventilation. But Rogers jumped on the witness with the brilliance and intensity that made him such a joy to watch. Dressed in a swallow-tailed coat, a standup collar, and a tie fastened by a glittering diamond stickpin, he was dynamic, impressive, and dominant. It was the kind of afternoon that led Jerry Geisler to recall that "when I was in the same courtroom with him, I couldn't pull my eyes away."

Rogers had a plan. He would discredit Harrington by leading the jury to believe that he had actually planned the jury bribery in the first place, that he had been Franklin's secret accomplice. It was not a claim that Darrow would ever make, nor was it a tactic that he would have been likely to use. But for Rogers, who was able to use the courtroom in exceedingly creative ways, it was an irresistible strategy. Though he had no evidence of Harrington's complicity in the bribery plan, there were ways to plant suspicion in the minds of the jurors. After all, Harrington had worked with the government in an effort to trap Darrow into making an admission at the Hotel Haywood; why not assume that he had also worked with the government to set him up in the first place?

"Rogers prodded and poked at that pudgy gentleman, holding him up, constantly, as an object for contempt," Joe Timmons observed, enjoying the "gentle sport of torturing Harrington." But Rogers had also discovered an even more satisfying pastime. Torturing Captain John Fredericks.

Some people have claimed that Earl Rogers invented the technique of putting the prosecutors, rather than the defendant, on trial. In fact, probably most great lawyers have always known that the outcome of a case depends in large measure on the jury's impression of counsel for both sides. Clarence Darrow once noted that "a jury watches every movement of a lawyer, and the verdict depends to a considerable extent on what the jury thinks of him." But Rogers perfected the technique of putting opposing counsel on trial, rather than simply attempting to make a good impression himself; and he had one particularly important talent. He had a profound understanding of psychology, of what would affect witnesses, impress juries, and provoke other lawyers. Never did he use those skills to greater effect than in the Darrow trial, where he was aided immeasurably by the brilliant, accented nagging of Horace Appel.

Over a two-day period, Rogers repeatedly asked for a copy of the Dictograph transcript of the conversations in the Hayward Hotel. The prosecution denied his request and Judge Hutton upheld their refusal. But Rogers persisted. He may have wanted the transcript to prevent his client from being surprised if the transcript was introduced during the cross-examination of Darrow himself, to try to impeach his testimony on the witness stand. Or, he may have hoped that the transcript would contain some useful data for the defense. But there is another explanation that seems even more likely. With his contacts in government, Rogers had probably learned that there really were no transcripts at all. The Dictograph trap had not worked. The technology was too primitive. The conversations had been almost impossible to hear and the stenographers' transcripts were virtually unintelligible.

In any case, Joe Ford opened the prosecution up to criticism when, at one point, he declined to turn the transcript over because, he said, "the public interest would suffer by disclosure of it at this time." The statement was as pretentious as it was disingenuous.

On his feet in an instant, Appel saw a new chance for a brawl. "There is no such thing in a criminal case, Your Honor," he began, walking around the counsel table, toward the judge, speaking with a thick Mexican accent. "The public interest will suffer, Your Honor, if an innocent man is convicted by suppression of the evidence."

That was too much for Fredericks, the self-appointed champion of legal ethics. "There won't be any innocent man convicted," he insisted. "It will come out at the right time."

"Yes," Appel continued, getting extremely personal, accusing Fredericks of suppressing evidence and of making false and misleading statements. He was now standing directly in front of the judge, and he directed his comments to the court, without looking back at Fredericks, who was still seated at the counsel table.

"It will come out as *you* are coming out," he said, referring to Fredericks. "Your conduct of the case here is the most prominent part. 'The suppression of the evidence for public interests,' " he said, parodying Ford. "Just think what sort of a misnomer it is, just think how they interpret the law like chewing gum." The barb was aimed at Ford, who often chewed gum in court, but it was Fredericks who took offense.

"I am done, Your Honor," Fredericks announced. "That has got to stop! That has got to stop!" He asked the court to intervene, to point out that the request for documents had already been denied after a lengthy debate. But Judge Hutton was silent as tempers in the courtroom rose.

Appel continued his assault. " 'Public interest' demands that the papers be given to us."

It was too much for Fredericks. "Now stop it!" he shouted, heading around the counsel table toward Appel. "I have stood this thing just as long as I am going to stand it and I will stand it no longer."

The courtroom was in pandemonium. "Captain Fredericks!" Judge Hutton yelled. "Sit down!" Rushing to the aisle, Rogers put his hands on Fredericks's shoulders and Fredericks appeared about to head back for his seat. But his temper got the better of him.

"I have stood this thing until I have gotten sick and tired of it," he shouted, standing up again. "If this is going to be a court of justice, let us have a court of justice, and if it is going to be a fight—then I will have a fight." With that he picked up a heavy glass inkwell and appeared about to throw it at Appel. Rogers, Ford, and bailiff Martin Aguirre all rushed over and struggled to stop him.

"Captain! Be seated!" Judge Hutton screamed. Finally Fredericks sat down, but Rogers's wrist was badly gashed in the encounter.

"I want to know, Your Honor, how much longer have I got to endure the insults of the other side?" Fredericks asked.

"Do you include me in that?" Rogers asked.

"Sometimes I do, Mr. Rogers," said Fredericks.

"Captain Fredericks!" the judge shouted again.

"I have just saved Captain Fredericks from committing a crime," Rogers proclaimed, proudly displaying his fresh wound, "and I don't deserve it."

As the lawyers began to regain their composure, Judge Hutton finally spoke up. He pointed out, at last, that he had already denied the application for the transcript. While he was speaking, bailiff Aguirre tied a handkerchief around Rogers's still-bleeding wrist.

"Now," the judge said, "I want to say something else. There is no necessity, absolutely no occasion for this outburst on either side. If counsel on either side are so overworked and nervously exhausted as to become hysterical, they can say so and the court will adjourn and give them a reasonable opportunity to get over it. But the hysterical outbursts are entirely out of place.

"Counsel on either side are not on trial here," he added. "Mr. Appel's personal attack upon Captain Fredericks was entirely out of order, and Captain Fredericks's reply was shockingly out of order. The court is amazed. Gentlemen that have presented the brilliant and scholarly arguments that have been presented here, that they should so far forget themselves." He paused. "Let us drop the incident and proceed."

It was a nice sentiment, an effort to serve as peacemaker after a battle among friends. But it was not entirely accurate. In fact, counsel on both sides *were* being judged—but, amazingly, the one counsel who seemed above the fray, who was not the subject of any of the blistering attacks, was the one man who was, in fact, on trial.

❊ ❊ ❊

Observing Darrow day after day in the courtroom, one fact was becoming clear. Whether guilty or innocent of attempting to bribe Lockwood, Darrow was far and away the most decent and educated man in the room. He was also the most sympathetic.

All of the other lawyers were exploding under the pressure of the trial. The day after Fredericks tried to throw the inkwell at Horace Appel, Rogers behaved so badly that he was forced to apologize to the court by explaining that he had been worn thin by a series of demanding cases. "After seven months being steadily in a courtroom under the hardest possible circumstances, and with my nerves not as calm as I would like to have them, I am pretty well worn out," he told Judge Hutton. "At times I do go beyond what I ought to go, beyond what I would go if I had a little time to rest, a little time to recover my nervous condition."

But for Fredericks and Rogers—and for Ford and Appel, whose demeanor was only slightly less explosive—the only thing at stake, the only thing to be gained or lost through the trial, was a promotion or a new trophy to display on the shelf. For Darrow, the stakes were ever so much higher.

❊ ❊ ❊

Though he worked hard at disguising his feelings while in the courtroom, trying to follow Rogers's advice, Darrow was never free from anguish. He never threw an inkwell or a temper tantrum, but it was impossible to hide the all-consuming pain. His private demons continued to haunt him even when the trial was going reasonably well—even, for example, when he was able to spend a moment chuckling along with the crowd as Fredericks insisted that he was a hypnotist.

One of Darrow's favorite reporters was young Hugh Baillie, who was twenty-one years old and was covering the trial for Scripps's prolabor *Record*. They met regularly to talk about the case. Baillie later claimed that Darrow "never made an optimistic statement about the results of the trial. He was increasingly glum and grim; he felt mortified and resentful, heartbroken and trapped."

It was not just the fear of conviction that haunted him; it was the continuing rejection of friends he held dear, the sight of himself as reflected in their eyes. He had the support of Ed Nockles and the San Francisco labor chiefs—but not of Sam Gompers, Frank Morrison, or the other national labor leaders; he had been joined by a few longtime friends like Jim Griffes and Fay Lewis—but Eugene Debs, one of Darrow's true heroes, had concluded that Darrow loved money too much; he had Erskine Wood in his corner and Lincoln Steffens at his side, but they believed in him, not in his innocence; and such friends as Brand Whitlock—the man Darrow had always deemed "one of his bravest and strongest fellow-soldiers"—had only offered the most tepid words of encouragement.

Darrow "believed that his friends had joined his foes," Baillie recalled; "that they seemed ashamed of knowing him, that they had turned against him because he had thrown in the towel in the McNamara case. Darrow burned when he sensed that some of those whom he regarded as associates felt privately that he was guilty as charged. He told me that he thought that even Rogers believed him guilty."

Writing to his sister while Harrington was on the witness stand, Lincoln Steffens described the mood that Darrow was projecting to his friends as well as to the public. "He is scared; the cynic is humbled; the man that laughed sees and is frightened, not at prison bars, but at his own soul. Well, then, what do I care if he is guilty as hell; what if his friends and attorneys turn away ashamed of him and of the soul of Man—Good God, I'll look with him, and if it's any comfort, I'll show him my soul, as black as his [but] not so naked."

It was a noble sentiment, but it seemed to suggest that not only "his friends and attorneys" but even Steffens—the man who would become Darrow's most important defense witness, a friend he deemed "clever and kindly and understanding"—even Steffens thought he might be "guilty as hell."

❋ ❋ ❋

The trial, combined with Darrow's dark moodiness, was taking a toll on Ruby. During the past several weeks, she had emerged as a kind of silent heroine. Sympathetic dispatches described her as "an anxious little woman, dressed in blue, who sits behind Darrow in the crowded courtroom;" they said that she "sits at his side as if wishing to get her portion of the barbed arrows that may enter his heart." With her articles in *Organized Labor,* Mary was using her pen as a spear. But Ruby was performing an even more noble role, serving as Darrow's human shield.

Time and again, the papers reported, Darrow would sink down in his chair, "until only his fighting, wrinkled face and shaggy head, drawn in between his shoulders, is visible." But then Ruby would pat him on the shoulder or whisper something in his ear, and "he will straighten up suddenly as the old fighting look sweeps his face."

Observers commented on her every motion. In the hot and stuffy courtroom, they watched as she cooled herself with a fan and then used the fan to bring some relief to her husband. Every now and then they saw her offer Darrow a chance to smell a bright red rose, bringing the scent of summer into the room. If it was painful to watch the brave smile and occasional tears that followed a bitter attack by Fredericks or Ford, her reactions to Rogers's counterthrusts were a joy to behold. Whatever private contempt she felt for the famous lawyer's personal habits and beliefs evaporated as she watched him spar with the prosecutors. "When the thundering Rogers, brows drawn down and pugnacious jaw thrust aggressively forward, springs to his feet and startles the quiet courtroom with a noisy denunciation of some question asked by the district attorney, she really gets into the swing of the trial," one admirer reported.

"Her eyes flash and her head nods slightly but decisively as Rogers makes his points, and at the final peroration her fan closes with a snap and she hearkens with tense face until he ends the speech and drops into a seat."

But as the prosecution's case drew toward a close, Ruby looked nervous, pale, and ill. Rumors quickly spread that she had not been able to sleep for weeks. On July 3, she was confined to bed under the care of her physician.

The press, the public, and the jurors were watching a soap opera. They were getting to know and like Clarence Darrow—and to feel immense sympathy for the brave woman at his side.

Chapter Fifteen

THE DEFENSE BEGINS

B Y THE TIME THE state finished presenting its case, Darrow and Rogers had decided not to ask Judge Hutton to issue a directed verdict. A court can issue a directed verdict for the defense if it finds that no jury could find the defendant guilty on the basis of the prosecution's evidence. But here, there was plenty of evidence. Even ignoring all of the information concerning collateral crimes, the case against Darrow included the testimony of Franklin and Harrington, the bank checks, Darrow's presence in the vicinity of the bribery, and his statement to Detective Browne later that morning. The jurors might well find that the evidence lacked credibility, that the bribe had been orchestrated by someone from San Francisco or from the East, or that Darrow had been framed by the prosecution, Burns, or the NEA. But in ruling on a directed verdict, the court is required to construe all evidence in the light most favorable to the prosecution. Under the circumstances, Judge Hutton was certain to reject a call for a directed verdict and such a decision would be a psychological setback for the defense.

While there was no way of knowing for certain, many people who had been close to the defense or to Darrow had concluded that the jury was leaning his way. Even Larry Sullivan, who was certain that

Darrow was guilty, was convinced that he would be acquitted. Darrow's old friend W. W. Catlin was less certain of acquittal, but was confident that his old friend would not be convicted, either. Juror Golding seemed to be firmly in Darrow's corner, and there might well be others. "I think he will be able to carry part of the jury with him anyway—and he may be able to carry 'em all," he wrote to Erskine Wood in late June.

Nevertheless, it did not seem prudent to take the case directly to the jury without putting on a defense. That high-risk strategy sometimes works. It implies that the prosecution's case is weak and worthless and it provides an excellent method of keeping the defendant from testifying. It also prevents the prosecution from introducing any evidence that it may have been holding back for its rebuttal. For example, it still seemed possible that the prosecution would use its rebuttal time to introduce the dictaphone transcripts of Darrow's conversations with Harrington. But the transcripts no longer seemed so ominous, the jury now seemed to be listening attentively, and the defense had prepared an excellent case, which Darrow wanted to present.

Darrow's lawyers had organized a brilliant defense, with credible witnesses prepared to swear to at least five important propositions. First, they would offer a series of depositions by prominent men, vouching for Darrow's excellent reputation and character, offering a powerful rejoinder to the suggestion that jury tampering was consistent with Darrow's style of operation. Second, several of Darrow's associates would provide an alibi, disputing Franklin's claim that he had received any bribe money from Darrow on the morning of November 28—and explaining, at last, the reason that Darrow had been in the vicinity of the bribe on the morning that it occurred. Third, they would attack the credibility of Franklin and Harrington by offering proof that those gentlemen had told journalists, friends, and associates that Darrow was innocent. Fourth, Lincoln Steffens, Fremont Older, and LeCompte Davis would attest that Darrow had no motive for bribing Lockwood on November 28, since the case had already been settled. Finally, Darrow would testify in his own defense. His testimony could, they knew, be a disaster; but it could also represent a high point of his career.

✳ ✳ ✳ ✳

On Monday afternoon, Earl Rogers launched the defense with a remarkable array of depositions by leading citizens of Chicago, fifty-five statements by former mayors, former United States senators, and a large share of the judges residing in Cook County. With the exception of two religious leaders and the president of a coal company, all of them were lawyers. Each witness asserted that Darrow had a good or excellent reputation for truthfulness, honesty, and integrity.

All fifty-five depositions were prepared by Edger Lee Masters, Darrow's former law partner. Working feverishly for several weeks in May, Masters had called on every community leader in Chicago, and most of them were only too happy to help. Darrow was a fellow townsman in trouble far from home. They traipsed into Masters's new office in the Marquette Building; answered a few quick questions about their background, their acquaintance with Darrow, and their view of his reputation; and then left. Arthur Keetch of the district attorney's office was present at each deposition and asked a few questions, most of which simply offered a new chance for the witness to say something nice about Darrow.

✳ ✳ ✳ ✳

The reading of depositions can be a boring affair, but not when they are read by the master of courtroom theatrics. Using a variety of voices and poses, Rogers kept the jury's attention, though each deponent simply repeated the assurance that Darrow had a good or excellent reputation for truth, honesty, and integrity. Meanwhile, the prosecution sat by, helplessly listening to a waterfall of praise.

Rogers's readings were only interrupted once for live testimony. On Tuesday morning, Darrow noticed a former congressman from Chicago named Charles McGavin sitting among the spectators. When Rogers had finished reading the deposition of an attorney named John S. Miller, he called McGavin to the stand to underline Miller's importance. McGavin, who was now living in Los Angeles, testified that John Miller was the most prominent corporate lawyer in Chicago, lead counsel for John D. Rockefeller and Standard Oil.

That said, McGavin left the stand. But the point was made. Darrow was admired by the most respectable men in the city, by Republicans as well as Democrats, by judges as well as lawyers. He was even admired by the men who represented the most powerful corporations in America.

Fredericks wanted desperately to find a Chicago community leader to rebut those claims. While in Chicago for the taking of the depositions, Deputy District Attorney Keetch had done his best to find someone, anyone, to attack Darrow's character, to place a scratch in the Darrow veneer. His efforts bore no fruit. He finally sent word to Captain Fredericks "as to the impossibility of obtaining testimony against Darrow from proper witnesses."

To Darrow's good fortune, Keetch never guessed that the people who were most critical of Darrow were not the leaders of the community, the church, and the bar. They regarded him as an engaging and thoughtful critic; sometimes an ally and sometimes an adversary; sometimes idealistic and sometimes practical; but always honest and responsible. No, Darrow's critics were not the lawyers for Standard Oil. They were, instead, representatives of the poor and the dispossessed, such as Eugene Debs, Jane Addams, and Emma Goldman; labor leaders such as Samuel Gompers; and such longtime friends as Brand Whitlock and Erskine Wood.

Even some of Darrow's uncritical admirers thought him more than capable of the crime. Based on his deeply held philosophy, as expressed in countless conversations, they doubted that Darrow was committed to truth, honesty, and integrity—the qualities addressed by the depositions. Or at least they doubted that Darrow viewed such basic moral concepts in the same way as the leaders of the Chicago bar. Friends such as Billy Cavenaugh and Dr. Perceval Gerson thought him guilty.

The view was best articulated publicly by Hutchins Hapgood, the radical columnist and the biographer and friend of Anton Johannsen. "Some of his sympathizers had a 'hunch' that he had tried to bribe the jury," Hapgood explained in a column published shortly after the trial. Their view, he said, was based on Darrow's fundamental "moral cynicism." Hapgood explained that Darrow "is, or was, inclined to make light of the deep, custom-moralities of the race. He sees that sometimes political and industrial injustice has pressed into its service religion, art, and morality. He therefore says that all art, religion, and morality, except the art and morality of definite revolt, are bad and on the side of injustice." Darrow's contempt for morality—or for the morals of society—was what troubled men like Hapgood. "The general cynicism of his mental bearing on the side of morality," Hapgood concluded, "would lead many people to think him capable of it."

But Fredericks had no way of knowing what men like Debs and Hapgood thought of Darrow. Nor would such radicals ever have testified for the prosecution. So the character witnesses marched on for two days, a dazzling array of Chicago's political and legal establishment, attesting to Darrow's unblemished reputation for truth, honesty, and integrity.

❊ ❊ ❊ ❊

While Rogers read the depositions, another drama was unfolding that was to have an even greater impact on the jury. On Sunday night, while the jurors were asleep in their rooms at the Trenton Hotel, their sanctity was invaded by an unknown intruder. The intruder lifted a mirror up over the transom of one of the dormitory-style rooms and moved it back and forth in an evident effort to determine whether the jurors were asleep in their beds. But the mirror reflected a light which woke up one of the jurors, Fred Golding. Startled, he quickly slipped into his trousers and went to find Martin Aguirre, the chief bailiff, the man who took care of all of the jurors' needs during the course of the trial. Aguirre joined Golding in a midnight search for the culprit, but he was nowhere to be found.

Before court convened on Monday morning, Golding met privately with Judge Hutton to register a complaint. The only plausible explanation, he said, was that Burns's men were spying on the jury. Judge Hutton asked the bailiff and the district attorney to join him in his chambers. Aguirre confirmed Golding's account. Captain Fredericks, however, was furious at the suggestion that the spies were working for him or for Burns rather than for the defense; he promised to conduct an inquiry of his own.

The incident added fuel to a simmering dispute between Aguirre and Fredericks, who was convinced that the bailiff was too close to the defense team and that he might be making disparaging remarks about the prosecution to the jurors. But if he was troubled by the meeting in Hutton's office, Fredericks's fears seemed confirmed the next day when the *Herald* quoted Aguirre as saying that the spies must be working for Burns or for the district attorney.

During a short recess in the trial on Tuesday afternoon, Aguirre and Horace Appel held a brief conversation in Spanish. They were within earshot of Joe Ford. The incident provoked a new rumor. An article in the *Examiner,* written without a byline, claimed that Aguirre and Appel were related.

Early the next morning, before court convened, Fredericks made a formal complaint to Judge Hutton about Aguirre's bias. To clear matters up, Judge Hutton marched down to the jury room and interviewed each of the jurors, including the alternate juror. All thirteen men denied unequivocally that Aguirre had tried to influence them directly or indirectly, or that he had made any remarks that could be construed as favorable or unfavorable to either side. Nevertheless, under the circumstances, Aguirre asked to be relieved of his duties. He told Judge Hutton that it would be too uncomfortable and embarrassing for him to continue.

After the morning recess, the judge made a public announcement, briefly describing the circumstances and explaining that Bailiff Aguirre had asked to be relieved from the case. Since the jurors were extremely fond of Aguirre, Judge Hutton was very careful not to say who had raised questions about Aguirre's fairness, whether the complaints had come from the prosecution or from the defense.

Rogers was on his feet at once with an objection. "There are circumstances which lead me to think there is more to it," he began.

Judge Hutton tried to interrupt, suggesting that the jury be excused for any further discussion of the matter. He was afraid that the discussion would reflect unfavorably on the prosecution. That, of course, was just what Rogers hoped it would do.

"No, sir," Rogers said. "This statement has been made to the jury and I think that they ought to know the full circumstances."

Rogers then charged that the district attorney had planted the story in the *Examiner* in order to force Aguirre to resign. "I openly charge," he shouted, "that there was caused to be published a criticism of Martin Aguirre for the sole purpose of offending his well-known sense of justice and pride in order to replace him and disgrace him. I have known Mr. Aguirre since I was a little fellow so big." Rogers placed his hand at the level of a young boy's head. "All of us have loved him and trusted him and believed in him and do now, and I say it is a shame and an outrage that the object of that article, which is a scandalous and scoundrelly thing, should be accomplished simply by offending Mr. Aguirre's well-known sense of justice."

Seldom had Rogers been more eloquent, and he knew that the jurors, who also loved Aguirre, shared his sense of outrage. "I say it was a scheme from the start," he continued, "and I stand ready to prove it. It was written by a man who has been in the employ of the district attorney's office, and published for the sole purpose of offending Mr. Aguirre, in order that he might be driven from his position—and Mr. Appel, mentioned in that article because he belongs to the same race, stamps this as a scandal, a shame, and it ought to cease, and I don't intend to stand here and let Mr. Aguirre be stamped in such fashion.

"I call for the production of the author of that article," he announced. "I would like to cross-examine him for about two minutes. I will show who he is and where he got it from."

That request went too far for Judge Hutton, who had not even read the article. "The newspaper article is not the governing factor in this matter," he said.

But the colloquy was having its effect. In a dramatic gesture, juror Golding stood up to register his objection. "You have found out what each and every one of us think about Mr. Aguirre and his honesty and integrity," he said to Judge Hutton. "We don't want him to leave. We have tried him and we know him and have been practically sleeping with him. We can see a man when we rub against him like that. We have every confidence in him. Why should we change now? For myself—I don't know about the rest of them; I think they are of the same mind, though—we don't care to change.

We want an honest square deal here and he certainly is giving it to us, and to the court and everybody."

His moving statement seemed to speak for all of them. "I am of the same mind as Mr. Golding, Your Honor," juror Moore announced.

Foolishly, Fredericks did not sense the mood of the moment. He was alienating the jury. Even if he was right about Aguirre's sympathies, he was making a mistake. The jury didn't know Darrow personally, though they had been watching him every day and were impressed with what they saw. But they did know Martin Aguirre. He was honest and kind, a man of integrity. They liked him so well that they had bought him a birthday cake. While living at the Hotel Trenton, he was their family, their friend, and their benevolent jailor. From their experience, he had all of the qualities that Darrow was said to have. Now he was being removed—and removed unfairly. It was not exactly a frame-up, but it had many of the worst qualities that Rogers, Appel, and Darrow had been attributing to the government. It seemed that people were spying on the jury—very likely Burns agents or men working for the district attorney's office—and now Aguirre had been set up or unfairly accused. As an object lesson in justice, the significance of the episode was not lost on the jury.

But it was lost on Captain Fredericks. Rather than acknowledging the heartfelt statements of Golding and Moore, Fredericks stood up to assert that Aguirre was right to resign. "It seems to me," he said, "that the only person in this matter who has exhibited good judgment is Martin Aguirre. Mr. Aguirre has taken the only manly ground."

The court turned to Aguirre and asked him how he wanted it handled. "I would rather go," Aguirre said. "I think that is the best for both sides."

Fredericks, the warrior, had won the battle. After lunch, there was a new chief bailiff, George Van Vliet, who had worked directly under Aguirre. But the battle had been won at an incredible cost.

And Darrow's defense was just beginning.

✳ ✳ ✳ ✳

The first witness for Darrow was Job Harriman. Thin, almost cadaverous, he filled only half the witness chair; his jet black hair, rugged, dark complexion, high collar, and formal attire made him a striking figure, a cross between a Native American and a churchman arriving to preside at a wedding. Even for those who had opposed his candidacy, he had gained a special niche of respectability. He was a martyr. Many believed that he would have become mayor but for Darrow's decision to plead the McNamaras guilty on the eve of the election. There were thousands who would never find it in their hearts to excuse Darrow for that. But simply by being there, by standing at Darrow's side, Harriman conferred a benediction of Christian forgiveness.

Harriman had a single assignment: to contradict Bert Franklin's sensational claim that on the morning of November 28, just minutes before the bribe took place, he had come down to the Higgins Building office in order to give the bribe money to Darrow and Franklin. Before the case was over, Rogers announced to some of his friends in the press, he planned to show that the bribe money was actually provided by the turncoat John Harrington.

Harriman was an exceedingly effective witness for the defense. Both friends and foes had long admired his rigorous logic. On the witness stand he was concise and clear, offering brisk, rapid and emphatic answers. He admitted that he had been in the Higgins Building early that Tuesday morning, but said that he had only been there for a few minutes. He and Darrow had separate suites of offices on the ninth floor. Though his law office was directly across the hall, he did not set foot in Darrow's office that morning. Nor did he go through his own reception room. Wanting to make his visit as brief as possible, he said, he slipped into his own office by a side door, avoiding any visitors who might be hoping to see him. After spending a few minutes gathering up his mail, he remembered, he left the building to return to his campaign headquarters, which were about four blocks away.

It was a plausible, if convenient, account. The prosecution might have been able to find a witness to testify that Harriman had not been in his own office that morning. Such testimony would have given great credence to Franklin's claim that Harriman had been in

Darrow's office, not his own. But by testifying that he had deliberately gone into his own office through a side door, and had avoided seeing anyone in his own office, Harriman was able to explain his presence in the building that morning without fear of contradiction.

After his first day of testimony, reporters noted that Harriman had "flatly contradicted the sensational testimony of Bert Franklin." As one headline put it, HARRIMAN SCORES FOR THE DEFENSE. Even the *Times* noted that "several of the jurors seemed greatly impressed with Harriman's recitation."

❊ ❊ ❊ ❊

To reinforce Harriman's testimony, the defense then invited veteran journalist Frank Wolfe to come to the stand. During the McNamara trial, Wolfe had been a Socialist candidate for the city council and a member of the defense team, paid to run Darrow's "clipping bureau." He swore that he had been with Darrow from eight A.M. to nine A.M. on the morning of November 28, 1911. During that time, he had not seen either Franklin or Harriman. Darrow left at about nine A.M., he said, when someone called on the phone and asked him to come over to the Socialist Party offices. Wolfe's testimony, combined with Harriman's, provided a powerful alibi, although their affiliation with the McNamara defense made them something less than objective witnesses.

❊ ❊ ❊ ❊

A crucial piece of the puzzle was still missing. What had drawn Darrow to the vicinity of the bribe that morning? His alibi would not be credible unless he could explain what he had been doing at Third and Main, what unlucky coincidence had brought him there just as the bribe was taking place.

Darrow intended to offer a perfectly simple explanation. At nine o'clock, he was called by someone who wanted him to hurry over to the offices of the Socialist Party in the Canadian Building on South Main Street. He promptly took an elevator down to the lobby of the Higgins Building and started walking south on Main Street, toward the party's headquarters, a route that took him past Third and Main.

Wolfe's testimony provided support for that claim. But a central question remained: Who had placed the call? For months Darrow's friends and lawyers, led by Earl Rogers, had fueled speculation that Darrow had walked into a trap, that he had been called down to the street by an enemy, most likely an operative of Burns or Otis, or of the NEA or the district attorney, someone hoping to lure him to the scene of the crime. It was an allegation that Rogers had already advanced during the trial while cross-examining Bert Franklin. It was a centerpiece of the assertion that the events at Third and Main were a stage play, a performance, a frame-up designed to snare Darrow.

Now, as the final slice of his alibi, Darrow surprised observers—and the district attorney—by calling on a witness named Charles O. Hawley. An insurance broker and former Los Angeles fire commissioner, Hawley had known Harriman for more than two decades. He had moved to San Francisco, but during the fall of 1911 spent time in Los Angeles helping with his friend's mayoral campaign. On the morning of November 28, Hawley testified, he read a troubling editorial in the Los Angeles *Tribune*. It seemed to confirm the rumor that the city's liquor interests had formed an unholy alliance with *Tribune* publisher E. T. Earl and the Good Government Organization to help Mayor Alexander's reelection campaign.

By his account, Hawley ran into Harriman on the street at about eight-thirty that morning. When Hawley told the candidate about the editorial, Harriman suggested that he call Darrow. "He said that if there was any truth in it, Darrow would likely know it or could find out," Hawley testified. After all, Darrow had long represented the liquor interests in their campaign against prohibition. So Hawley called Darrow and told him that "Harriman wanted to see him down at the Socialist headquarters" to talk about the editorial.

During cross-examination, Ford pointed out that Mayor Alexander had thrown Hawley off the fire commission, that Hawley had been in a hot dispute with the *Los Angeles Times* and had helped Harriman organize a lawsuit against the paper by victims of the fire who claimed that the explosion had not been caused by dynamite, but rather by gas, faulty construction, and lack of careful maintenance. Ford then emphasized that Hawley's testimony contradicted the theory that the phone call had been designed to lure Darrow into a trap, a theory advanced by no less a Darrow partisan that Earl Rogers. After all, how could the Burns people be accused of staging a "frame-up" at Third and Main if Hawley—and not Burns—was responsible for his being in the vicinity?

But despite Ford's jabs, Hawley was an effective witness. The *Record*'s assessment was especially positive. "Concrete, compact testimony, each bit dovetailing into the next," it said, "is being introduced by the lawyers defending Clarence S. Darrow in building up an apparently ironclad defense."

❋ ❋ ❋ ❋

The trial was continuing to take a toll on the participants. Juror Manley Williams later likened it to "ninety-two days in jail." Juror L. A. Leavitt started to complain of pains in his abdomen. After a week's absence, Ruby Darrow had managed to return to the courtroom, but she looked thin and pale.

Confounded by the combination of alcohol, drugs, sleepless nights, and the pressure of the long trial, Earl Rogers's health remained on a downward spiral. He told friends he was on the verge of a nervous breakdown. For days at a time he was absent from court entirely, and when he did appear he spent much of his time reclining in a small anteroom next to the court that Judge Hutton made available for his use. Darrow and Appel took over the bulk of the trial work, although Rogers remained in touch with the proceedings and briskly emerged into the courtroom when the arguments became particularly heated.

The weather didn't help. After weeks of mild temperatures, a high pressure front from the northwest sent mid-July thermometers into the nineties. People began to complain of excessive heat in the badly ventilated courtroom.

❋ ❋ ❋ ❋

With the heat rising and Rogers on the sidelines, the defense quickly put on a series of witnesses who contradicted bits and pieces of the prosecution's testimony. DARROW TO DISCREDIT ACCUSERS, the San Francisco *Bulletin* announced. "The chief object of the assault" would be Franklin and Harrington, it said, and "about fifteen witnesses will be called to impeach the testimony of each of the two."

Some of the witnesses were friends of Bert Franklin, like haberdasher Joseph Musgrove, who said that Franklin had promised to put someone else in jail to save his own skin, and dairyman George Hood, who said that Franklin had told him that the money came from someone he had never seen before. Some were former employees of the McNamara defense team. Franklin and Harrington had testified that they only met occasionally, but secretaries in the office said that they saw the two men together almost daily, lending credibility to the theory that Franklin and Harrington had been part of a plot to destroy their employer.

For several days a stream of witnesses recounted meetings with Franklin where he had denied Darrow's guilt. Four reporters quoted statements made to them by Franklin at the time of his own grand jury hearing. J. L. Barnard and Carl White of the *Evening Express,* D. M. Willard of the Associated Press, and Harry Jones of the Los Angeles *Tribune* all testified that Franklin had walked over to the press section and announced that "anyone who says that Clarence Darrow gave me a cent to bribe a juror is a goddamn liar." Another journalist, Fletcher Bowron of the *Examiner,* who later became mayor of Los Angeles, quoted a statement by John Harrington. On the eve of his own grand jury testimony, Harrington asserted that "he knew absolutely nothing against Mr. Darrow and couldn't tell anything against him of any kind."

Fredericks and Ford tried to preserve the credibility of their chief witnesses. In some cases they were able to contest the memory of a witness who had attacked Franklin or Harrington; in others they showed that the witness's testimony had been different six months earlier, when speaking to the grand jury. For example, a former secretary who claimed that she had seen Harrington and Franklin together on a regular basis had told the grand jury six months earlier that she did not know who Franklin was.

Still other testimony could be largely discounted because it came from someone closely allied with the defendant, or it only dealt with a trivial aspect of the prosecution's case, or it could be explained away. It was only natural for Franklin to assure the press of Darrow's innocence, for example, at a time when he was proclaiming his own. Indeed, Joe Ford objected to testimony about Franklin's statement to the four reporters since, he argued, "Franklin did not deny having made that statement." Similarly, it was natural for Harrington to try to deceive the press about what he knew, and what he would say, at the time that he was pretending to remain Darrow's friend and trying to lead him into making a confession in front of the Dictograph machine.

Nevertheless, the cumulative impact was impressive. At the very least, the credibility of Franklin and Harrington was significantly diminished.

❋❋❋❋

In criminal cases, the prosecution's best proof is a credible witness backed by contemporary documentation or physical evidence that links the defendant with the crime. Absent such proof, the state can still win if it has sufficient circumstantial evidence and can convince the jury that the defendant had both motive and opportunity. After two weeks of defense testimony, Darrow and his colleagues had succeeded in raising serious questions about the credibility of Franklin and Harrington, the state's strongest witnesses. Equally important, they had managed to offer an innocent explanation for the most important bit of circumstantial evidence—Darrow's presence at the scene of the crime.

Now they faced what might well be their most important task: to show that Darrow lacked a motive for bribing Lockwood. For as Darrow noted, "it is almost impossible to prove a crime without proving the motive which caused it." Their theory was that Darrow had no motive to bribe Lockwood since, thanks to Lincoln Steffens's efforts, he had already decided to plead both brothers guilty.

For the remainder of the trial, that became the key issue of fact. Had Darrow definitely concluded that he would and could plead both brothers guilty prior to Tuesday, November 28, 1911?

Indeed, Fredericks had taken an important risk by choosing to prosecute Darrow for bribing Lockwood on November 28. He could, instead, have charged him with bribing Bain on October

6—on the eve of jury selection. Though by that date Darrow had already concluded that the case would be exceptionally difficult to win, no serious effort to settle the case had commenced. But by the time Franklin tried to bribe Lockwood, on November 28, 1911, Lincoln Steffens was working feverishly to arrange some sort of compromise. The question thus naturally occurs: Why did Fredericks choose to prosecute Darrow for bribing Lockwood, not Bain?

There are several possible explanations for Fredericks's decision. The most obvious is the fact that when Lockwood was arrested, Darrow was at the scene of the crime. It was an important piece of circumstantial evidence. Fredericks may also have felt that the jury would be swayed by Darrow's apparent effort, minutes later, to bribe Detective Browne, in a conversation that Browne transcribed immediately.

But there is something else that should be taken into account. There is every reason to believe that Fredericks had total contempt for Lincoln Steffens, the man he called Stinken Leffens, and never took his settlement efforts seriously. As soon as Steffens's first article appeared, Fredericks gave out interviews disputing the muckraker's version of events. The district attorney said that his office had always been willing to settle the case if both men would plead guilty, that he had offered such a settlement as early as July, but that Darrow had consistently refused to enter into any agreement that included a guilty plea by J.J.—that is, he had refused to plead J.J. guilty until Franklin was arrested for attempting to bribe Lockwood.

Moreover, Fredericks knew that his view of events would be supported by the men who had been acting as Steffens's intermediaries. If necessary, Fredericks could call those men—including Harry Chandler, Oscar Brant, Tom Gibbon, and Meyer Lissner—as witnesses. They would testify, accurately, that the defense had remained inflexibly opposed to a guilty plea for J.J. until the day after the arrest. Similarly, Steffens's own newspaper accounts of the settlement stated that J. J. McNamara did not agree to plead guilty until the crucial meeting that took place in the county jail on Thanksgiving Day, November 30, 1911, two days after Franklin's arrest.

Fredericks's perspective was also bolstered by an unusual statement issued by Judge Bordwell on December 5, 1911, just after imposing sentence on the two brothers. Bordwell released the statement, he explained, "in the hope of correcting, if possible, some of the misconceptions due to [an article] over the signature of Lincoln Steffens. The claim of Steffens that the termination of the cases was due to himself and other outsiders, is without justification in fact. I also wish to denounce the claim of that gentleman and of other persons for him that the change of pleas from 'not guilty' to 'guilty' was due to his efforts as groundless and untrue. . . . There is no ground for any claim that he induced the prosecution to come to an agreement in the matter. The district attorney acted entirely without regard to Mr. Steffens and on lines decided upon before the latter arrived on the scene."

Indeed, Bordwell contended, the capture of Franklin on November 28 was the reason for the guilty plea. "The public can rely on it," Bordwell said, "that the developments of last week as to the bribery and attempted bribery of jurors were the efficient causes of the change of pleas which suddenly brought these cases to an end." According to Bordwell, the defense had been prepared for some time to plead Jim McNamara guilty "on the condition that he should not be sentenced to death, and that his brother should go free." The district attorney resisted those overtures consistently, always insisting that J. J. McNamara plead guilty as well. But the defense continued to refuse to enter into a settlement on those lines, Bordwell reported, "until the bribery development revealed the desperation of the defense and paralyzed the effort to save John J. McNamara by sacrificing his brother. Then it was that the pleas of these men was forthcoming."

The most important and presumably credible witness on Darrow's lack of motive was Steffens himself. Not having taken Steffens seriously, Fredericks may have assumed that he would not be taken seriously by the jury. If so, it was a serious miscalculation.

❋ ❋ ❋ ❋

It was another scorchingly hot day, with temperatures in the high eighties, when Lincoln Steffens took the stand. Elegantly dressed, with his tight-fitting vest and orange tie, he was, as the *Times* commented, "sartorially perfect." His testimony would be of immeasur-

able importance to Darrow; but it would be almost equally important to Steffens himself. After months of ridicule from such friends as
John Reed and Anton Johannsen, who labeled him Golden Rule for
his role in arranging the guilty plea, Steffens finally had a public
forum in which to exonerate himself.

The crowded courtroom was "hushed to breathless stillness" as
Earl Rogers led Steffens through the fascinating story of his secret
negotiations with the city's business and political leadership. At the
end of the first week of negotiations, Steffens said, the National
Erectors' Association sent a telegram to General Otis objecting to any
settlement that did not require *both* brothers to plead guilty. "I went
instantly and reported that to Darrow," he said, "and Darrow's
answer was that if it were absolutely necessary of course he would
consent to that."

"To what?" Rogers asked.

"To having the two men plead guilty."

"The two McNamaras?"

"The two McNamaras instead of one."

Somewhat impetuously, Captain Fredericks jumped in with a
question, asking when that conversation had taken place.

"This was in the end of the week," Steffens answered. "I will fix
the date before Sunday, because we were to meet with the
McNamara boys on Sunday. Darrow told that to me, and he told no
one else. He instructed me to go back and make as hard a fight as
I could the rest of the week, to have only one man go. As he kept
putting it, 'I only want one man punished.' "

Fredericks must have realized that Steffens was creating a virtually
unrebuttable claim: Darrow had decided to plead J.J. guilty, but,
Steffens claimed, *"Darrow told that to me, and he told no one else."*
Indeed, as a negotiating ploy, Steffens added, Darrow told him to
pretend that he was *not* willing to plead J.J. guilty. So much for
rebuttal testimony by Chandler, Brant, Gibbon, Lissner, or the other
members of the Citizens Committee. No doubt they would testify
that they had been told that Darrow would never agree to let J.J.
serve jail time. But that could be said to prove that Steffens had
played his hand well, put on a good bluff, knowing all along that
Darrow was willing to do what had to be done to settle the case.

On Sunday, Steffens testified, he visited the jail with Darrow and Cyrus McNutt, Darrow's cocounsel, now deceased. Jim "was willing to take a sentence for himself, but he didn't want his brother to take a sentence. Since Jim was only willing to plead guilty in order to protect his brother and organized labor, Steffens said, "we had our understanding with J.J. separately." J.J. told them that he would be willing to plead guilty and serve time in jail if it was the only way to save his brother from hanging.

A reporter glanced over at Darrow. He was in tears, listening to Steffens's description of the daylong session with the McNamaras.

"When we left the jail," Steffens continued, "there was a feeling of elation that the thing had been consented to and agreed upon, dampened somewhat by the fear that we would have to let the two men go to jail instead of one, and that we had led those two boys to hope that we could still save J.J."

Rogers gave Steffens's testimony a moment to sink in. Then he continued. "So on that Sunday, it was agreed that both should go?"

"If necessary."

"What understanding did you have with Mr. Darrow after having reached this agreement that J. J. McNamara should plead guilty if necessary on this Sunday?"

"That it was all up to me to go back to see Mr. Chandler, Mr. Gibbon, and Mr. Lissner and make a plea to have them stand for the one man going to jail." Steffens's role, he said, was to pretend that Darrow was still insisting that J.J. go free. "I was doing my best to give everybody, intentionally, the impression that there could be no settlement unless J.J. were allowed to go."

In fact, Steffens said, he and Darrow did not even tell their other cocounsel that they were prepared to plead J.J. guilty. LeCompte Davis was conducting negotiations directly with Captain Fredericks, but was being kept in the dark. "Mr. Davis didn't know all the plans," Steffens said. "Mr. Davis didn't know that Darrow was willing to consent yet, to have J.J. go, too."

On Monday, November 27, Davis told Darrow that Captain Fredericks would not agree to a settlement that did not include both brothers.

"What did Mr. Darrow say when Mr. Davis reported what the district attorney had said to him on that Monday?" Rogers asked.

"As I remember it, he told Davis that he would *not* let J.J. go, and he told me to tell everybody that J.J. could not go. At any rate, the rest of the week I was telling everybody it would be impossible to settle if J.J. were asked for, too."

So on Monday, November 27, Darrow and Steffens were telling everybody—business leaders, prosecutors, defense counsel, and Jim McNamara—that they would never agree to a settlement that required J.J. to plead guilty. And everyone also knew that the district attorney was insisting that he would not agree to end the case on that basis.

As Captain Fredericks put it, "there is no controversy over the fact that the defense was willing to let J. B. McNamara plead guilty, but there is a controversy over the claim that they were ever willing to let J. J. McNamara plead guilty until after Franklin was detected in this bribery."

But Steffens had pretty well cut off any lines of rebuttal. He and Darrow were the only men living who had known of Darrow's plan. Judge McNutt had died, and everyone else had been intentionally deceived. Yet, as Darrow had said, he was the only person whose knowledge mattered. "The question is what I thought about it and that is the only question: the question of motive. It is the condition of my mind that counts."

By the end of his direct testimony, Lincoln Steffens had effectively argued that Darrow had no motive for bribing Lockwood, that he had already, albeit secretly, decided to end the case. As the *San Francisco Chronicle* explained, "The story of Steffens accentuated what appears now to be the crucial issue in the case—whether the agreement to have the McNamara brothers plead guilty was sanctioned by Darrow more than a week previous to the alleged bribery of juror Lockwood, as claimed by the defense, or that the negotiations virtually had been declared off because of the unwillingness of Darrow to allow John J. McNamara to plead guilty, as contended by the prosecution."

❊ ❊ ❊

For Fredericks, there were several ways to treat Steffens's testimony. He could have accepted it as fact but said that Darrow still had a motive for bribing Lockwood. Darrow might have worried that labor would veto the proposed plea bargain. As of Tuesday, no one representing Gompers and the AFL had yet arrived on the scene, and it seemed more than likely that they would disapprove of the deal. More important, Darrow's clients had not yet agreed to the arrangement. By Steffens's own testimony, Jim was only willing to plead guilty if it would allow his brother to escape unscathed. He did not agree to a joint plea until Thanksgiving Day, November 30, two days after the bribe, as the result of a series of emotional pleas, including a visit from Father Brady. Alternatively, Fredericks could have tried to call Steffens's memory into question by a brief cross-examination showing, for example, some of the inconsistencies between Steffens's testimony and the version of events set forth six months earlier in his dispatches.

Instead, the district attorney chose a riskier course of action. Having personal contempt for Steffens, and probably convinced that the muckraker was lying in order to protect a friend while puffing up his own role, Fredericks chose to try to discredit the testimony by discrediting the witness. He underestimated his adversary.

When court opened the next morning, the *Record* reported, "Society was out in force to hear the verbal duel." The room was packed to overflowing, with more than fifty spectators sitting inside the rail. Many of them had brought fans for relief from the continuing heat wave.

After asking Steffens about a few preliminary matters, Fredericks rose from his chair and stepped back to the rail. "Now, Mr. Steffens, I want to ask you a few questions which I think are a little personal, but they are to get at your views." He started walking slowly and forcefully toward Steffens, his hand high in the air. "As I understand it," he charged, "you are an avowed anarchist." With that he thrust his finger into Steffens's face, exclaiming, "Is that correct or not?!"

Rogers registered a quick objection. The witness sat quiet for a moment, amused by what he later called Fredericks's "playacting." As judge, jury, and spectators leaned forward, waiting for his response, Steffens smiled his deliberate, thin smile. Never mind Rogers's objection. He wanted to respond.

"No," he answered slowly. "that is not true. I am a good deal worse than an avowed anarchist."

Fredericks stepped back, surprised. What could be worse than an anarchist?

"You are a good deal worse than an avowed anarchist?" Fredericks asked.

"Yes, sir," Steffens smiled. "I believe in Christianity."

Without knowing it, Fredericks had given Steffens a chance to play his favorite verbal sport, to exercise what Max Eastman called his "kittenish delight in paradox." Eastman may have been correct in dismissing the practice as "a way to be happy without hard thinking," but for that moment, in that setting, with the world's press watching, Darrow's freedom in the balance, and a humorless prosecutor for a foil, it was a dazzlingly effective retort.

More important, it set the tone for the rest of Fredericks's cross-examination. Steffens was in control. When asked a hard question, he would come back with a quick response or a bit of biting sarcasm. On other occasions, he would cover his answers with a cloak of apparent deferential courtesy. But most of the time, he would raise the level of debate to a higher level of abstraction, to a field where he was comfortable and Fredericks was lost, to an arena where he was the teacher and Fredericks the confused pupil.

The audience loved it—and no one loved it more than Mary, who called "his manner of exposition so rare, so subtle. His purpose so elusive, yet as real as the odor of lilacs." Steffens "makes such a profound impression on me—emotional and intellectual," she told a friend. "I feel as if my mind had been set in more rapid vibration and as if I experienced an actual rise in temperature."

When Fredericks asked why he would want to free a man like J.J., whom he knew to be guilty of a crime, Steffens asked the court for a chance to give a complete answer. Judge Hutton agreed to give the witness considerable latitude. "If the crime is not an individual crime," he began, "but what I would call a social crime, a crime that is the result of the feelings of a large part of the people, of resentment against certain conditions, I would call it a revolutionary crime, not a legal crime."

"And you believe that such a crime is a crime of warfare?"

"Yes."

"And you believe, do you not, that you or anybody else would be justified in doing anything to assist and protect them in that warfare?"

Steffens saw where Fredericks was going. Would he condone murder or bribery to assist them? Would he lie to protect someone charged with bribery? Again the court let him give his answer in depth. "In all my talks with the McNamara brothers day after day, we had arguments, I urging on them my belief that they and labor were going at this in an entirely wrong way, just as capital was; that force was wrong from them just as it was from everybody else, even from the state, and I believed that."

He had a national audience for his view, bankers and workers, politicians and judges, lawyers and journalists, a seminar interested in his theories. Fredericks tried to interrupt, but Rogers noted that "it's not often that we have a chance like this to hear a lecture on Christianity. It may do us some good." Fredericks rubbed his chin, at a loss for words. Observers noted the "gasp that ran around the room as the intense little man warmed up to the subject."

Much as he was enjoying himself, Steffens was beginning to perspire profusely as the room grew warmer. After a while the judge took pity and handed Steffens his huge, palm leaf fan. Steffens wafted himself cool, then handed the fan back to the judge, starting a gentle ceremony between the judge and the witness that continued for the rest of the day, as they continued to pass the fan back and forth.

"But after the McNamaras had committed this crime," Steffens continued, "after understanding that they had been bred up into this, that they had had experiences that made them want, individually, to commit these crimes, and that they represented a great mass of American citizens who feel that there is no other way to get justice in the United States except by crime, thinking that, I could see that these two men, no matter how you punish them, would not solve the problem that produced them. All my efforts were to get them both, both capital and labor, to see that there is a problem that cannot be solved in courtrooms, but that can be solved with reason."

Fredericks was not about to let go of his central thesis: that Steffens was an anarchist who would lie to protect a friend who had committed bribery in a just cause. "Under the circumstances of warfare, which you believe exist, Mr. Steffens, do you not believe it would be perfectly justifiable even to bribe jurors if it were necessary to save these men?"

"No," Steffens replied, drawing on his moral authority as the man who had gained fame by exposing political corruption and legislative bribery throughout the country. "My feeling about bribery is exactly like my feeling about murder or the bribery of legislators. Is that clear?" He was trying to explain his point to a slow pupil. Fredericks, not Steffens, was being interrogated.

It wasn't clear, so Steffens continued. "I think these crimes are not justifiable, but I think they are understandable."

❉ ❉ ❉ ❉

Fredericks did score some blows when he finally asked about the stories that Steffens had originally written about the trial. He called the writer's attention to the article that he wrote on the day after the guilty plea, the article published on December 3, 1911.

He read Steffens a passage stating that "Thanksgiving Day was the crucial day. The terms had been negotiated down to a point where there were only two differences. Harry Chandler went to see the district attorney to ask him to concede one point and counsel for the McNamara boys went to the jail. I went with the latter group. The story of what happened there, I shall tell later. All that need be said now is that Jim—who had consented four or five days before to plead guilty himself—objected to having his brother Joe do the same. Joe was willing. He gave his consent after five or ten minutes' talk."

"Now, having refreshed your memory," Fredericks continued, "was that statement correct?"

"Yes, that is correct."

"Well, then, how can it be a fact that J.J. had consented four or five days before? What matters is whether or not J.J. had agreed to plead guilty on Sunday, or whether he agreed to plead guilty later, on Thanksgiving Day," Fredericks said. "That is the point I am making."

In fact, of course, the date on which J.J. agreed to plead guilty was crucial. But by then virtually everyone in the courtroom was in a trance. Like Mary Field, they were finding Steffens's impact both emotional and intellectual, with his call for peace and justice and compassion, and his invocation of the names of the most prominent men in the community, the tough-minded, hard-driving leaders of business, who for the first time in memory had tried to bring about a period of labor peace.

It was hard to ignore what Steffens had said, truthfully, at the outset. He believed in Christianity. So it was easy to believe what this man of God, or this man who believed in the teaching of Christ, said about his agreement with Darrow. When Fredericks finally asked about all of the meetings Steffens held on November 26–29, meetings in which Steffens consistently insisted that Darrow would never let J.J. go to prison, Steffens had a simple answer. He had been engaging in a "bluff," trying to get a better deal, doing everything he could to spare the man from prison, while knowing all along that Darrow was prepared to plead him guilty.

Many in the courtroom thought that Fredericks had engaged in "the best cross-examining of his career." Even Mary Field expressed admiration as he "skillfully sought to lead the witness" into one trap after another. But it didn't work. Steffens was too cool, too witty, too philosophical. "I had his goat," Steffens later remembered, "and he could not get mine."

Naturally Darrow's friends in the press all loved Steffens. The *Record* said "he proved a star witness for the defense." Writing for Fremont Older's *Bulletin,* Mary said "a great human story had been told by a man who had followed a vision and had the courage of his ideals." But he impressed other reporters as well. Joe Timmons felt that his direct testimony had "scored heavily for the defense" and if anything, his cross-examination was even better. It was, Timmons observed, "a day of evangelism in court, removed from the sordid tales usually recounted there"; and all of Fredericks's efforts had "failed to shake the testimony."

Steffens was delighted with his performance. He told his sister that "everybody thinks that, if it isn't denied (and I don't see how it can be) by Charles or somebody, my testimony will have freed Darrow."

After court, Steffens went up to Fredericks and asked whether it would be all right for him to leave town.

Fredericks laughed. "I wish you had gone two or three days ago," he said.

* * * *

The testimony was going well, but there was still a wild card. Juror Leavitt seemed increasingly hostile. At the end of Steffens's testimony, he asked the old muckraker a single question. "Do you believe in direct action?" Steffens handled the query with aplomb, saying that he wanted to stick with the Golden Rule a little longer. But Darrow and Rogers were beginning to think that they smelled a capitalist rat.

Over the weekend, they did some research. Before he was selected for jury service, they learned, Leavitt had told friends that he suspected Darrow was guilty, that he should be hanged, that Darrow had bribed jurors in the Idaho cases. What's more, the defense team ferreted out rumors that one of Fredericks's aides, a man named Robert Hicks, was a close friend of the juror's and had visited his house during the trial. If the stories were true, and if they had been known at the time of jury selection, Leavitt would surely have been disqualified from service. Under the penal code, however, it was far from clear that the court could consider such newly discovered evidence about a juror.

While the defense was checking out rumors of bias, Leavitt was suffering from an intense abdominal ailment. Although only in his mid-forties, Leavitt had been an invalid for years. Judge Hutton sent him home to spend the weekend resting under the care of his personal physician—and the supervision of a deputy sheriff. There were rumors that he would have to leave the jury, that he would be replaced by the thirteenth juror.

Prosecutors, however, quickly produced letters from his doctor, assuring the court that Leavitt would soon be well. A court-appointed physician reported that the juror had only suffered from three or four acute attacks, that he was fine otherwise, and that "a return of his attacks might take place [but] on the other hand, he might go for a number of weeks without any trouble whatever."

After delaying the trial for two days, Judge Hutton drove out to El Monte to visit the patient, who was resting in bed at home with an ice pack on his abdomen. The judge returned to town convinced that Leavitt would recover swiftly, that he was suffering from a form of appendicitis that could be controlled by a special diet. He would be back in court on Thursday morning.

Leavitt was back in court all right, but the defense team was ready for a fight. Earl Rogers had been out to El Monte himself during the week, interviewing several of the juror's acquaintances, including his brother-in-law. Rogers told the press that he had subpoenaed eight or ten men to fortify his argument. On Thursday morning, in the presence of spectators and the press, but not the jury, Rogers rose to ask the court to remove Leavitt from the case. He pointed to Leavitt's health, but he based his strongest complaint on Leavitt's bias against Darrow.

"I have been informed by friends and relatives of juror Leavitt that he is bitterly prejudiced against Darrow," Rogers began. "This defendant must be acquitted or convicted by a jury of fair-minded men, so I ask your honor to replace him with A. M. Blakesley, the thirteenth juror."

Blakesley, as it happened, had medical problems of his own. Well past seventy years of age, he had been spending nights at home under the care of a private nurse and a deputy sheriff. Still, he would have to do; the alternative would be to declare a mistrial and start the ordeal over from scratch.

The argument went on for hours. Rogers pleaded with Judge Hutton to let him introduce witnesses who would swear to Leavitt's bias. Ford and Fredericks angrily charged that Rogers was making up a series of false claims in an effort to intimidate juror Leavitt. As they shouted at one another, Darrow sat quietly, his head buried in his arms. Was it possible that the best he could hope for was a hung jury? Surely there must be some way to remove the man.

Judge Hutton was sympathetic to the issues Rogers was raising, but he was convinced that his hands were tied. The law would not allow him to interrupt the case to examine new information about a juror's qualifications. Leavitt could be removed for ill health, he said, but not for prejudice.

❋❋❋❋

Leavitt spent the luncheon recess resting, but by two P.M. he was ready to join the other jurors in court. Already delayed by almost a week, the defense called LeCompte Davis to the stand to reinforce Steffens's testimony.

A headline in the *San Francisco Chronicle* called Davis "a strong witness for Darrow defense." Like Steffens, he offered support for the claim that Darrow had decided to plead both men guilty by Tuesday, November 28.

The best news for Darrow occurred outside of the courtroom. Over the weekend, juror Leavitt experienced a fresh flash of pain in his abdomen. His family doctor concluded that he would need to have an operation after all. He could not be back in court for another six weeks, at the earliest. Consequently, the thirteenth juror was called into service.

The stage was set for Clarence Darrow, star witness.

Chapter Sixteen

DARROW TAKES THE STAND

DICTATING HIS MEMOIRS SOME twenty years later, Clarence Darrow remembered his ordeal as a criminal defendant. The whole episode was unspeakably painful, filled, he said, with "old ghosts" out of his past that "dance around me as if in glee, and I am anxious to drive them back and lock them up where I cannot see their haunting faces or hear their mocking jeers." But he had more pleasant memories of his own testimony. "I told my own story," he recalled, "denying any knowledge of or connection with an attempt to bribe any juror, and was cross-examined for four days. I had no more trouble about answering every question put to me than I would have in reciting the multiplication tables."

If so, Darrow must have had a devil of a time with math.

It started easily enough. Expecting to see the great man testify, a throng of spectators came to court early on the morning of Monday, July 29, hoping to watch Darrow's testimony. More than one thousand hopeful spectators were turned away, but hundreds found space in the corridor, some standing, some squatting or sitting on the cold floor, hoping to see or hear fragments of the trial, or to gain access to the proceedings after the noon break.

Inside, the courtroom was packed. During the previous weeks a score of Darrow supporters, primarily women, had become courtroom regulars, entering the room with a special ticket of admission, bending the court's rules by sitting in front of the rail, near the lawyers, providing moral support for their friend and jeering the dreary men who were trying to send him to prison. Alongside dozens of fascinated observers who had been admitted by the bailiff on a first-come, first-served basis, Darrow's friends were ushered into the room early that morning, outfitted with snacks and lunch bags, planning to stay for the full day. Joe Timmons called them Darrow's "partisan claque." Their number was swelled for Darrow's own testimony. Margaret Johannsen, for example, had come down from Corte Madera. For this sensational session, and the days to follow, the bailiff insisted that Darrow's partisans move in back of the rail, to specially reserved seats in the front row.

Dressed entirely in white, Ruby Darrow was still the only woman seated next to the counsel table, her clothes a stark contrast with the lawyers' dark suits. Looking tired and frail, she used a fan to shield her tearful face from curious spectators, the martyred heroine of a great drama.

As he began a week on the stand, Darrow looked tired, his face drawn and flushed. But his demeanor was calm and confident. The case was running his way and now, at last, he had a chance to do the thing he loved best, to talk, to deliver a lecture that would last for days and would be heard by foes and friends alike. Most important, this was his opportunity to reclaim his good name.

Darrow's slow, deep voice, his thoughtful answers, and his quiet, clear testimony, made an immediate impact. Once again, he was above the fray, larger and more thoughtful than the lawyers swarming around him. Sometimes, when Rogers or Appel started to argue with the prosecutors, Darrow would wave them off, conceding some point of law or of evidentiary privilege, suggesting that there was nothing that he was afraid to answer. Even the *Times* reporter was impressed. "This attitude, whether natural or the result of studied art, is not without effect," the paper noted after his first day on the stand. Sitting sideways in the witness chair, his hands clasped over his right knee, he talked directly to the jury: composed, concise, and convincing. In his hands he held his gold-rimmed glasses. Every now and then he would use them for emphasis, waving them as a baton or slapping them against his knees. His tone and his demeanor were Darrow's most powerful defense, more important than the words he spoke.

But the words were important, too, and no one spun a tale better than Clarence Darrow. As Rogers led him through his personal autobiography, Darrow put his work for labor and unpopular causes into a perspective that was designed to appeal to a jury composed of ranchers, political moderates, men of means. He presented himself as a man whom everyone could trust, a lawyer for corporations as well as unions, much sought after as an arbitrator and mediator, known for compassion and fairness, not radicalism or ideology. He listed his work for the Chicago and North Western Railway, as Chicago city attorney, as counsel to the city's elevated railroads, as lawyer for the coal miners before President Roosevelt's Commission on the Anthracite Coal dispute (mentioning Roosevelt's name four times in less than a printed page of testimony), as arbitrator in disputes involving newspapers, clothiers, railroads, and the National Brick Company.

At Rogers's insistence, Darrow downplayed his role as the defender of the damned. In six pages of testimony on his work as a lawyer, he spent less than a sentence on his criminal and labor cases, briefly listing Haywood, Debs, and Kidd. "I suppose nine tenths of my practice has been civil practice," he emphasized, "and perhaps one tenth of it criminal and about one third of it for charity."

Turning to his work on the McNamara case, Darrow explained that he had tried to persuade the labor unions to find someone else, someone younger and healthier. When they continued to insist that he take the case, he said, he hired John Harrington "to take hold of it, come out here and prepare the evidence for the case, take charge of it, and to hire whom he pleased." If there was any wrongdoing by the people in his employ, Darrow suggested, Harrington was to blame.

❋❋❋❋

Then Rogers and Darrow dropped their first bombshell. One fact, one provable, irrefutable fact, can win a case. To be successful, the fact need not establish the defendant's innocence. It will achieve its goal if it casts a lingering shadow over the prosecution's case. It will, then, serve as a thirteenth chime, discrediting all the rest.

And Rogers had found just such a fact. He had found the check for a thousand dollars, the check that Darrow had given to Franklin. According to Franklin, Darrow gave him the check on October 6, 1911, and told him to use the money to bribe Robert Bain. Franklin said he cashed the check and held his first meeting with Bain later that same day.

"Did you hear Mr. Franklin testify that the first time you ever spoke to him about bribing jurors was on the fifth day of October, 1911?" Rogers asked.

"I did."

"Did you have such a conversation with him?"

"I had no such conversation with him on the fifth."

"You heard him say, did you, also, that on the sixth day of October, the succeeding morning, you gave him one thousand dollars by check?" Rogers continued. "Did you give him a check on the sixth?"

"I gave him no check of any sort on the sixth of October."

Darrow directed his answer to the jury, hardly looking at Rogers. The room was silent. Juror Golding leaned forward, transfixed.

"When did you next give him a check after the fifth?"

"Not before, I suppose, about the fifteenth."

"Did you give him a check before the fifth?" Rogers continued.

"I gave him a check on the fourth for a thousand dollars."

"On October fourth. Why did you give him a check on that date?"

"Well, I gave him a check on the fourth exactly as I had given him checks before—and exactly as I gave him checks after that date."

Rogers handed a slip of paper to the witness. It was a check from Darrow to Franklin, endorsed on the back by Franklin, bearing the deposit date of October 6. But on the front, the check was dated October 4.

"Is that the check?" he asked.

"That is the check," Darrow said, handing it back to Rogers.

"What is the date on that check?"

"October fourth."

"For what purpose did you give it to him?"

"Whenever he needed money for himself and his men and his expenses, he asked me for it," Darrow calmly explained. "I gave him money, sums from two hundred to one thousand dollars, by check. I presume that he asked me for a check on that date."

It was a powerful point. It seemed to discredit the sequence of events that had been so carefully established by the prosecution. The testimony by the employees of the First National Bank, backed by deposit slips, confirmed Franklin's claim that he had deposited Darrow's check on October 6 and that he had withdrawn five hundred dollars in cash the same day. The testimony by Dora and Robert Bain confirmed Franklin's account of his visit to the Bain home that same afternoon and his efforts to bribe the aging carpenter. But tantalizing questions were beginning to emerge. First there was the fact that the bribe money consisted of a stack of twenty-dollar bills, whereas the bank teller claimed that the cash that he gave to Franklin consisted of fifties and perhaps hundreds. Now there was the fact that Darrow's check was dated October 4, not October 6. It was dated one day prior to their first alleged conversation about bribing jurors.

Perhaps there was a reasonable explanation. Darrow might have written the wrong date on the check or he might have deliberately tried to leave a confusing trail of evidence in the event that the bribery ever came to light. Or Franklin might have gotten the date wrong; he might have been off by a day or two in his memory of the date on which Darrow first discussed bribery or the date on which he gave him the check to use in bribing Bain. Perhaps. But there was, at last, the glimmerings of reasonable doubt. Or, to be less charitable, there was the possibility that Franklin's whole story was a fabrication.

In case there might still seem to be a loophole in Darrow's testimony, Rogers put the question as broadly as possible. "Did you give him this check or any other check for the purpose of paying Bain or any other juror any money whatsoever?"

"I never did." Darrow's voice was steady and firm.

✳ ✳ ✳ ✳

It had been a triumphant first day, capped by a dramatic incident of the kind that Rogers loved. The check was a piece of physical evidence that seemed to discredit Franklin's case. CHECK PROVES BRIBE STORY FALSE, SAYS DARROW ON THE STAND, the headline in the *Herald* announced.

By the next morning, the crowds were even larger, and Darrow was in a bright mood as he denied every important detail of Franklin's story, asserted that he knew neither Bain nor Lockwood, and attacked Harrington and his story about the roll of bills. If I was going to show him so much cash, Darrow said, it would not be on a lighted porch that could be seen by people up and down the street.

Rogers asked him to explain the episodes that the prosecution had labeled a "conspiracy to defeat the ends of justice." The abduction of Flora Caplan, he said, was designed to help a poor, defenseless woman who had been hounded by Burns's detectives; it was carried out at her request, by her friends. He was not involved, he said, but "if I was consulted, I would have advised her to go." After all, her disappearance could not affect the prosecution's case since, as the wife of a defendant, she could not be compelled to testify. Darrow offered an equally simple explanation for his efforts to hire Guy Biddinger, the Burns agent, to serve as a spy for the defense. Burns had planted a bunch of his spies in the unions and in the McNamara defense team, he explained, and "it was a case of dog eat dog." Under the circumstances, it seemed only fair to try to even the odds a bit by hiring one of Burns's men to do some work for his side.

Sitting among the reporters, Mary watched Darrow's answers with love and admiration. "Many of the circumstances introduced by the prosecution as acts 'done to defeat the ends of justice' in the McNamara case," she reported, "became perfectly legal steps" when explained by Darrow, "their alleged illegality disappearing as goblins and ghosts before the sun."

Darrow even had a deft explanation for the ten-thousand-dollar check that he had given to Tvietmoe in San Francisco in early September—the check that the prosecutors claimed had been converted into cash used to bribe Lockwood. He gave the check to Tvietmoe, he explained, to reimburse him for expenses incurred by labor during the grand jury inquiry.

"Tvietmoe told me he had spent some twenty-five or thirty thousand dollars over that matter. He asked me to reimburse him for it. I told him I couldn't do it at that time, for I hadn't the money, but I said I would do what I could later if funds came in to warrant it. Every time I went to San Francisco, he asked me about it, and about the second of September I was in San Francisco and gave him one of those checks for ten thousand dollars."

Darrow's testimony on this point is hard to reconcile with the records of the McNamara Defense Fund, which show that there was never enough money to reimburse Tvietmoe. There was certainly no such surplus on September 2, 1911. Just one day earlier, before leaving for San Francisco, Darrow sent an urgent appeal to Frank Morrison calling it "absolutely essential that a substantial amount be forwarded at once." It seems doubtful that Darrow *ever* had ten thousand dollars to spare. He certainly had no surplus in early September. Fortunately for Darrow, this information was not in the hands of the prosecutors.

❈ ❈ ❈

Unable to contain her tears, Ruby sat in front of the rail, weeping silently, as Darrow spoke slowly to the jurors, without a nerve tremor. Darrow's manner, according to the *Herald,* "had a most peculiar effect upon the jury. Each member kept his eyes riveted upon the witness. They followed his every facial movement. Not a syllable was lost to them."

By afternoon, Darrow was prepared to present his core defense—"to show a lack of motive," as Rogers repeatedly told the jury. Darrow's efforts to settle the case, the defense insisted, had succeeded *prior* to Tuesday, November 28. Therefore, Darrow would never have ordered, condoned, or paid for a bribe offer that week.

Slowly, patiently, emotionally, Darrow repeated the story that the jury had already heard from Steffens. But in some respects, he told it better, because his deeply felt emotions had a dramatic impact on the audience. "At times," Joe Timmons observed, Darrow "seemed to forget he was on trial for jury bribery and remember only that labor had bitterly condemned him for the settlement he made; his testimony was directed not so much to the jury as to the world of labor"—a world personified in the courtroom by men like Anton Johannsen, but a world that was listening to his words from around the country—"to workingmen who misunderstood and who he hopes will now understand."

The most powerful and heart-rending moment was his tearful claim that he had decided to plead the brothers guilty even though LeCompte Davis and others warned him that "it would ruin me with labor." Speaking to his friends in labor, more than to the jury, Darrow explained his reaction. "I told Davis that while the money had been furnished largely by labor, organized labor was not our client and was not on trial. These two men were our clients and nobody could possibly give us money that could in any way influence us in an action that was due to our clients. So far as I was concerned I had no right to consider myself. All I had to consider was these two men."

These words brought forth more tears, Timmons wrote, "as he gave his justification of the decision for which labor did condemn him, a decision which caused hundreds of thousands of men who had looked upon him as one of their greatest champions to turn on him in rage and declare he had done this thing to save himself from prison for jury bribery. His hour had come to defend himself at one and the same time against labor's charge and the State's charge."

It was a powerful story. It had a profound impact on the spectators, the jury—and the men in organized labor, whose doubts were beginning to melt away.

❀ ❀ ❀

After reading glowing accounts in the press (the *Herald* called him "an excellent witness for himself;" the *Times* said he told his story "in his own impressive, gripping way"), Darrow arrived in court Wednesday morning in a good humor. The courtroom was overflowing once again, and Darrow bowed to friends as he moved down the aisle on his way to the rail. There he consulted briefly with his counsel and moved back into his accustomed place on the witness stand, ready to face Joe Ford.

Put simply, the two men had grown to hate each other. As Joe Timmons noted, Darrow had come to regard Joe Ford "as his special bête noire," partly because of Ford's role in kidnapping and prosecuting the McNamaras and then relentlessly seeking Darrow's indictment, but partly, too, because of Ford's increasingly hostile and even cruel approach to the case.

For all of his brilliance, Ford was still a young man, eager to make his mark against a great lawyer and, perhaps, to convict a man who seemed to have so little regard for legal ethics. Although he could not use them at the trial, Ford may well have believed the reports of skulduggery in the Idaho cases.

There was something else as well, something more personal. Ford was convinced that Darrow had tried to put him into a compromising position with a woman, perhaps in order to embarrass or even blackmail him. The episode occurred in the fall of 1911, while Ford was still mourning the death of his wife. Just after church one Sunday, Ford's friend Father Hegarty called him over and warned him not to go to an Irish picnic that was scheduled to be held that afternoon. Hegarty explained that during confessional that week, one of his parishioners, a switchboard operator in Darrow's office, had stated that the McNamara defense forces planned to try to get Joe Ford drunk at the picnic and then to arrange for an attractive young woman to get him in a compromising position. Ford chose not to attend the picnic—but he became more convinced than ever that Darrow was using every imaginable device to corrupt the ends of justice.

During the defendant's two days of direct examination, a battle had been brewing between Fredericks and Ford on how best to interrogate Darrow. Knowing his adversary's brilliance, and respecting if not fearing his eloquence, Fredericks wanted the cross-examination to be brief. Score some points and get out of there. But Ford wanted a full chance to stalk his prey, to match wits, to break him down, to prove his guilt.

Most important, Ford hoped to show that Darrow had only settled the case *after* the November 28 bribe, when convinced that there was no remaining alternative for him or for his clients. As proof, Ford was prepared to introduce a series of telegrams that would be as sensational as Darrow's discovery of the check that was dated October 4, rather than October 6.

❋ ❋ ❋ ❋

Peering closely from behind his thick glasses, Ford began by noting that the authorities in Indianapolis had assembled a large amount of evidence that the Los Angeles authorities desperately needed in order to go forward with a case against J. J. McNamara. Indeed, without the evidence from Indianapolis, the case against J.J. was hardly worth pursuing. At Darrow's instructions, therefore, Indianapolis attorney Leo Rappaport was using every possible device to keep the material away from Los Angeles.

"Now, you understand, Mr. Darrow, that the Los Angeles authorities were trying to get possession of that evidence for use in the case of *The People* versus *J. J. and J. B. McNamara*," Ford asked.

"I think I heard it somewhere," Darrow answered somewhat sarcastically.

"Well, as a matter of fact, wasn't Mr. Rappaport instructed by you to use all legal means possible to prevent the Los Angeles authorities from getting possession of the evidence that was back there?"

"I think Mr. Rappaport wrote me about the proceedings there and I think I sent him word to take charge of that himself and to keep it there if he could." Darrow's answers were deliberately vague. No point offering any information that Ford did not know.

"Did you not instruct Mr. Rappaport to take all possible legal means to regain that evidence?

"I don't recall." Darrow crossed his legs and threw one arm over the back of the chair. He spoke slowly, watching Ford through half-closed eyes. "I might or might not have."

Ford glared at Darrow. "Did you not instruct Mr. Rappaport that he could spend one thousand dollars to regain possession of all those articles for you?"

"I don't remember. I have a recollection of sending a telegram, but no recollection of its having contained that. It may have."

"The McNamaras pleaded guilty at two o'clock on the afternoon of December 1st," Ford said. "Did you not immediately after that realize that there was no further necessity of regaining the evidence consisting of the alleged bombs and clocks and dynamite?"

For the first time the defense recognized that Ford must have some evidence in his possession. Appel offered strenuous objections, but the court ordered Darrow to answer.

Ford repeated his question. Didn't Darrow continue to seek the evidence from Indianapolis up until December 1—three days after the streetcorner bribe?

Darrow denied it. "A good many days before that I realized that it was of no further use in the McNamara case and not to be feared by us," he said. "I didn't want to spend a thousand dollars because I didn't need it."

This was the answer Ford wanted. "So after you decided that the McNamaras should plead guilty, you had no further need for that evidence," he asked.

"Yes."

"As soon as you made up your mind that the McNamaras were to plead guilty and end the cases, you had no further desire to spend a thousand dollars and so revoked Rappaport's authority to spend one thousand dollars in that behalf. That is the point I want to get at, Mr. Darrow."

"At the time that telegram was sent, on December 1st, I didn't want to spend any more money."

Ford could hardly contain himself. He had laid his trap. He began to pace the floor, hands deep in his pockets, almost hyperactive.

"When did you tell Mr. Rappaport that he could spend a thousand dollars to regain that evidence?"

"I do not recall," Darrow stammered. "I do not recall that I ever did, but I think I did."

"You have testified already, Mr. Darrow, that on Sunday, November twenty-sixth, you had determined that the McNamaras should plead guilty, if necessary."

"Yes."

"The both of them."

"Yes. I said before that, too, but I had on Sunday."

"On Sunday."

"Yes."

"The matter was settled. Now, was it before or after that date that you authorized Mr. Rappaport to regain that Indianapolis evidence and spend one thousand dollars in doing so?" If he had authorized the expenditure after that Sunday, it would seem to prove that the case was not yet settled. More important, it would seem to show that Darrow didn't think it was settled—that he had a motive for the bribe.

The court overruled another objection by Horace Appel.

"I couldn't tell you."

"Isn't it a fact, Mr. Darrow, that on Tuesday, the day of Franklin's arrest, that you did not intend to have both of the McNamaras plead guilty?"

"It is not," Darrow said.

Now for the bombshell.

"Isn't it a fact that on Wednesday, *the day after Franklin's arrest,* you instructed Rappaport to spend one thousand dollars to regain that evidence?"

Darrow was scrambling for an answer. "Might be, I don't know," he said.

"Didn't you endeavor, after Franklin's arrest, to prevent the Indianapolis evidence from coming to Los Angeles?" Ford persisted.

Something was clearly afoot. It was becoming obvious that Ford had some letter or telegram in his possession.

"If there is a letter or telegram, I have a right to see it," Darrow said.

Ford was undeterred. "I have a right to an answer to my question."

Rogers was on his feet. "I instruct you not to answer," he shouted at Darrow.

"Have you such a document, Mr. Ford?" Judge Hutton asked.

"To save time," Ford said, "I will ask the witness a different question. Did you receive a telegram from Leo M. Rappaport on November twenty-ninth, 1911?"

"Let's see it," Darrow and Rogers shouted simultaneously.

Ford showed a copy of the telegram to Rogers and then handed it to Darrow. It was written in code.

"I now exhibit to the witness a document which purports to be a telegram dated November twenty-ninth, 1911, from Mr. Leo M. Rappaport at Indianapolis to Clarence Darrow at the Higgins Building."

Appel interrupted. "How did they get it?" he gasped. "They said they had no telegrams from Mr. Darrow's office."

"We never had any telegrams from Mr. Darrow's office," Ford

explained. "This is the handwritten copy that Mr. Rappaport gave to the telegraph office in Indianapolis."

Darrow looked at the telegram for a moment, knowing that he could never decipher the code. "Will you translate it?" he asked.

"It says, 'May I spend a thousand dollars?' " Ford said.

Appel shouted another objection. "The telegram's not in English. What do you know about it?"

"He asked me to translate it," Ford answered smugly.

For once Judge Hutton was aggressive. "Let him go ahead and translate it," he said. "The witness asked him to."

Ford asked the bailiff to bring over a blackboard. Then he wrote down the words of the telegram along with the code. The words, as he deciphered them, said: "May I spend a thousand to regain Indianapolis evidence."

"Now," Ford asked, "did you not, on November twenty-nine, receive a telegram from Mr. Rappaport in substance and in code, saying 'May I spend thousand dollars to regain Indianapolis evidence?' "

As one reporter noted, Darrow seemed surprised and flustered and he began "sparring for time, trying to find a breathing space."

"Well, now, I refuse to answer it for this reason," Darrow began. "My remembrance is that there was a series of these telegrams, copies of which we have, some of them, at least, and I want to translate them first."

"What is your independent recollection?" Ford persisted.

"As I said, Mr. Ford, I should refuse to answer until we could translate the series so as to know just what it meant."

But Ford wasn't through. "In response to that telegram," he persisted, "did you not send a telegram to Mr. Rappaport on the same day, November twenty-nine, in which you said, 'May spend thousand dollars if necessary'?"

"Now, I will give you my remembrance and version of it, subject to a correction in the morning after I see the rest of the telegrams," Darrow answered.

"All right, go ahead."

"I don't want to commit myself, because I am not certain."

"Did you send that telegram saying 'May spend thousand if necessary?' "

"You say what day?"

"November twenty-nine. Isn't it a fact that on November twenty-nine you sent a telegram to Rappaport saying, 'May spend thousand if it is necessary'?"

"Mr. Ford, I have the impression that I instructed them to tell Mr. Rappaport that I would stand good for a thousand dollars, but that correspondence began a week or two earlier—"

"But did you—"

"It is one of a series."

"But did you send a telegram on November twenty-nine saying, 'May spend thousand dollars if necessary'?"

Of course Darrow had sent the telegram. It did tend to prove that as of that date, one day following the streetcorner bribe—and three days after the date on which he claimed to have decided to plead both men guilty—he still expected the case to go to trial. If Darrow had a motive to send $1,000 to Rappaport, he also had a motive to try to bribe a prospective juror.

It was nearing five o'clock, and the court agreed to postpone further questioning until the following morning. The recess came just in time, with Darrow struggling for answers and, as reporters observed, "on the defensive." It gave him time to work with Rogers to prepare for what was certain to be another grueling day of cross-examination.

❊ ❊ ❊ ❊

For the next two days, Ford kept hammering away at Darrow, trying to chip away at his armor. As further proof that Darrow did not think that the case had been settled before his visit to the jail on Thursday, Ford got Darrow to admit that he had continued fighting hard for favorable jurors on the days after the case was allegedly settled. And as evidence that Darrow knew about the bribe in advance, he suggested that an innocent man would have wanted to know why Detective Browne was arresting his chief jury investigator. Yet Darrow never asked.

"You were near Franklin when he was arrested?" Ford inquired, after taking a drink of water.

"I was, yes."

"Did you ask Mr. Browne at that time why he was arresting Mr. Franklin?"

"I think not."

"Why not?"

"Probably didn't think of it."

"The arrest of Franklin was not important enough for you to inquire right there when he was arrested, why he was arrested?"

"It probably was important enough, but I didn't. He went right on and I went right on."

"You didn't make any attempt at that time to see where Browne was taking Franklin?"

"I did not."

"Did you ask *anybody* why he was arrested?"

"Not until I saw Browne near the courthouse."

Darrow ran into Browne at the Hall of Records a few minutes later, of course, by coincidence, while going into the courtroom to participate in jury selection.

"You considered the drawing of the jury of more importance than to inquire into the arrest of Franklin?" Ford asked.

"I did at that time."

Why, Ford wondered, would the drawing of the jury be more important than the arrest of Franklin if, as Darrow claimed, he had made a definite decision to plead his clients guilty later that week?

❋ ❋ ❋ ❋

Later that day, Ford asked Darrow whether he had asked Franklin where the bribe money came from.

"I did not," Darrow answered.

"Did you ever ask Franklin yourself, at any time, where he got that money?"

"I don't think I ever did."

"Wasn't the reason that you did not ask him because you know of your own knowledge where he got it?"

"It was not," Darrow answered angrily. "No such reason."

❋ ❋ ❋ ❋

Even the *Record* was impressed by Ford's efforts. The paper noted that Ford had "secured a number of admissions that will probably be used in arguments by the state. The points 'rung up' by the prosecution," the paper reported, "seem to be that Darrow didn't ask Detective Sam Browne why he was arresting Franklin, never asked Franklin where he got the $4,000 for bribery, failed to inquire for him after the arrest, fought hard for favorable McNamara jurors after the case was apparently settled, and authorized Leo M. Rappaport to spend $1,000 after Franklin's arrest."

* * * *

Hard as he attacked him on the evidence, though, Ford must have realized that Darrow was coming across as a man of extraordinary qualities; of compassion, intelligence, dignity, and legal skill. Although Darrow "appeared dogged" by the end of the week, showing the strain "in the deeper lines on his face and a bored and irritable manner," the jury could not help sympathizing with his predicament. If he occasionally spoke with bitter sarcasm, showing "scorn, contempt, defiance and rage in his face," if he "flushed scarlet time and time again and fidgeted uneasily in the witness chair," who could blame him? Through it all, his statements were remarkably effective and dignified.

"The calmest person in the room was the defendant himself," Mary wrote that weekend in a somewhat overstated article for the San Francisco *Bulletin*. "After the heat and passion of the lawyers for the defense, after the bitterness and malice of the lawyers for the state, Darrow's gentle answers came in strong contrast. The old Darrow, the great Darrow, the philosopher, the poet, the dreamer of days when courts and jails shall be no more, the life long exponent of non-resistance, answered his enemies. He spoke quietly, without vindictiveness or anger, a certain weary sadness pitching his voice in somewhat lower tones than usual and running like a minor chord through his testimony."

If it was not quite true that he had answered every question with no more difficulty than he would have had in reciting the multiplication tables, Darrow had, at least, survived. At last he allowed himself to believe that his chances of winning were excellent. From a life spent studying juries, he knew that he had made as many as a dozen new friends. Counting heads, he knew that juror Golding and several of the others were on his side. They seemed to share his suffering and his pain.

They seemed drawn, too, to the woman who had been with him through thick and thin, watching him so lovingly, trying to smile through eyes filled with tears, her body shaking uncontrollably. As his testimony ended, the press reported that Ruby looked worn and frail, showing the effects of several illnesses. They speculated that she was, once again, on the edge of a nervous breakdown. Surely she—and her husband—had suffered enough.

✼ ✼ ✼ ✼

To celebrate the end of his ordeal on the witness stand, Darrow spent Sunday driving through the countryside with Mary Field and his old friends Fay Lewis and Jim Griffes. "Darrow sang all day, sang and talked to himself his speech—and joked all day," Mary told Erskine Wood. "So you can see his mood." No doubt it defied superstition, but the defense team had even begun to plan a victory celebration.

By Tuesday, as the prosecution began putting its rebuttal witnesses on the stand, Darrow was working on his next presentation, the closing argument. The case was to last for another week, but Darrow was already spending all of his waking hours working on his final statement. "Darrow is working on his speech now—he walks up and down muttering to himself—rehearsing its essential features," Mary observed in a letter written in court one afternoon.

It was becoming clear that this would be the most important speech he had ever delivered: a speech to the jury, proclaiming his innocence; a speech to his friends in labor and on the left, asking for understanding and forgiveness. In anticipation, the *Record* predicted "one of the greatest pieces of oratory ever heard in a courtroom . . . the supreme effort of Darrow's life."

For once, the predictions were on target.

Chapter Seventeen

SUMMING UP

B Y THE TIME THE jury summations started, both sides knew that the facts of the case were secondary. The crucial question, the center of the argument, the issue that would determine Darrow's guilt or innocence, was not what he had said to Harrington or Franklin, not whether he had given money to Tvietmoe or offered to "take care" of Sam Browne. Those facts would be important, of course. But what would seal Darrow's fate—as it had from the start—was character. The jury would have to decide whether this was a man who could orchestrate a scheme to defeat the ends of justice, a scheme that culminated in the bribing of jurors. More profoundly, the jury would have to decide whether Darrow, whatever he had or had not done for his clients, should be treated as a sinner or a saint.

For Darrow, the summation offered one last great chance to vindicate his life, his career, his values—for it was they that were on trial. This was the opportunity of a lifetime, a chance to sum up his own life, to give *himself* a eulogy even greater than the one he had offered a decade earlier to his mentor, John P. Altgeld. He had called Altgeld "the most devoted lover, the most abject slave, the fondest, wildest, dreamiest victim that ever gave his life to liberty's immortal cause," and he had observed that "the fierce bitterness and hatred that sought to destroy this great, grand soul had but one cause—the fact that he really loved his fellow man." That was how Darrow saw himself and how he wanted others to see him.

In his greatest criminal cases—defending Debs and Kidd and Haywood—he had spoken for men who, whatever their transgressions, had been fighting for the poor and the defenseless, fighting against great odds, rich corporations, evil detectives, and merciless prosecutors, men who were on trial because they were on labor's side in the great battle of the age. This speech offered Darrow the chance to define himself as he pleased, to do for himself what he had done for many others, to put the facts into order, and to use the prosecution—the forces that had kidnapped the McNamaras and now were trying to destroy *him*—as a foil to prove his case for mercy, if not canonization.

The prosecution's task was more delicate. Clearly the jurors were impressed with the man they had been watching for three months. They had observed his intelligence, his wit, his compassion, his demeanor, his restraint. They had witnessed a tragedy and a love story, watching a great man in tears and his wife in ruins. Had the Darrows not already suffered enough? Whatever Darrow might have done, how could the prosecution persuade the jurors to send him to prison? Somehow, Fredericks and Ford would have to present their case in a way that justified the destruction of one of America's greatest lawyers.

❈ ❈ ❈ ❈

A crowd was on hand early Monday morning, but few seats were available for spectators. All of the chairs inside the rail had been set aside for the attorneys' wives and law partners; the first four rows had been reserved for the press, photographers, and jurors' families; the next five rows had been allotted to Darrow's friends, who came equipped with tickets signed by the defendant. The judge's chambers were reserved for special guests who could hear the trial through the open doors. That left only one row of seats for other spectators. In deference to the intense interest shown by the public,

Judge Hutton ordered that the doors at the back of the room be left open, so that the arguments could be heard by as many as one thousand spectators who remained crammed in the outside corridor.

Since the prosecution has the burden of proof, the courts give them the better position in the closing order of battle: the chance to open and to close the summation. Joe Ford opened for the state. Ironically, his passionate statement set the perfect tone for the defense to rebut.

Ford started with a stunning personal attack on Darrow. He compared him to other once-great men who had turned sour, men like Francis Bacon, Judas Iscariot, and Benedict Arnold. "History," he said, "is filled with the examples of men whose minds are brilliant, whose sentiments are noble, but whose practices are ignoble." He narrated the story of Lord Bacon, who was stripped of his office when he pleaded guilty to the crime of receiving bribes; he reminded the jurors that Judas's integrity and honesty were so great "that Christ made him the treasurer of that little band"; and he described Benedict Arnold's courage, valor, and "great reputation for truth, for honesty, for integrity." Yet all of these men had committed crimes. "Previous good reputation," he said, "is no guaranty against the commission of an offense."

Not only did Ford compare Darrow to Judas Iscariot and Benedict Arnold. He said that his crime was even *more* despicable. "The act of the defendant in this case," he argued, "the act of the jury briber, is worse than all of these, for it strikes at the very foundation of government. For without courts of justice to maintain the relation between the individual and the commonwealth, there is no government."

The invidious comparison to Judas and Benedict Arnold was only the beginning. Moments later, Ford argued that Darrow was the true cause of the Crime of the Century. Darrow, he claimed, had been "preaching to the criminal classes of this country that there is no such thing as crime, as the word is generally understood"; that "there are no courts of justice; that criminals have the right to do anything necessary to defeat and obstruct justice; and that there is no difference between the people in jail and those out of jail, except this: that if you are in jail, it is better if you have a smart lawyer like Clarence Darrow."

Horace Appel screamed an objection. "Wait a minute, wait a minute, wait a minute," he shouted. "I object to his telling the jury anything like that. I assign it as error." Judge Hutton instructed the jury to disregard any arguments that were not based on the evidence produced in court. Then he told Ford to proceed.

"It was the example of men like Darrow that caused the poor deluded wretch, J. B. McNamara, to believe that he could commit the crimes he did with safety to himself."

Ford stood with his arms folded, glaring fiercely at the defendant. He peered out through thick glasses that "made his eyes look big and black and gave him a disconcerting stare." Then he turned to face the jury and continued.

"Picture in your mind, if you can, gentlemen of the jury, the agonized faces of the mothers and wives and children, as they stood at the fire-lines on that fateful October morning, watching the fiery furnace at First and Broadway, hoping against hope that their loved ones might be saved; hoping against hope that at least the bodies of their loved ones might be recovered for identification and burial. Picture, if you can, the poor fathers of a family, caught like a rat in a trap, praying upon his scorched knees for the safety of his little children who would be deprived of a father's care during the years they needed his guidance most."

Ford started to move over toward the defendant. "Ah, well and truly may the widowed mother turn to the defendant and say, 'Give me back my boy.' " With that, Ford dramatically stretched out his arms toward Darrow.

For Darrow, that theatrical gesture was the final straw. "Is it the ruling of this court that counsel may say *anything*?" he asked incredulously.

"No, it is not," Judge Hutton answered. He instructed the jury that it should disregard any arguments that "go beyond a rational discussion of the evidence." But he let Ford proceed.

Ford's summation lasted for several more hours, covering the testimony in the case in detail. Nothing matched the power of the opening salvo—until he reached an equally venomous and startling closing. He surprised the defense, and everyone else in the court-room, by claiming that Darrow's own defense, the case on trial, had been rife with criminality.

"This case reeks with perjury," he told the jury. Suggesting that the jurors had been locked up for the past three months in order to protect them from criminal conduct by the defense, he proclaimed that "this case reeks with rottenness and crime as presented to you gentlemen by this very defendant. It will be the duty of the district attorney to investigate every angle of *this* case as he did the McNamara case."

Ford must have known that he was taking a risk. Either his speech would persuade the jurors that they had a duty to convict the admit-tedly brilliant and appealing man with whom they had spent almost every waking hour for three full months—or it would further con-vince them that the prosecutors were a bunch of overzealous, labor-baiting politicians who would stop at nothing to emasculate the labor movement and imprison its greatest lawyer.

"In between frequent drinks of ice water and more frequent pec-torations into a handy spittoon, Ford made his venomous speech against Darrow," Mary told the readers of *Organized Labor*. The speech showed "the real reason for Clarence Darrow's indictment and disclosed to every listener the fact, long known to Labor, that Fredericks and Ford of the District Attorney's office are but carrying out the hatreds of the M & M and the National Erectors' Association. Darrow was damned to the jury not so much because he was a 'jury briber,' but because he had been for years the champion of labor."

That was precisely the theme that Darrow intended to present when he had his chance to address the jury.

❊ ❊ ❊ ❊

Late Tuesday afternoon, Earl Rogers stepped into the spotlight. News reports had already announced that he planned to introduce "a novelty in the presentation of an argument in a criminal case." He intended to use a dramatic diagram to illustrate and highlight certain aspects of the witnesses' testimony.

Wearing a long Prince Albert coat, a spotless white waistcoat, choker collar, high cravat, and light trousers, Rogers was a sight to behold. One reporter likened his attire to "the classic garb of a southern gentleman of the antebellum period." Some of the women in the audience observed that he resembled portraits of Patrick Henry. As promised, he set up a huge chart to illustrate his points. It was strung from the judge's bench to a courtroom wall. On it were the names of all thirty-eight of the witnesses who had testified for the prosecution. Each was classified by the subject he or she had covered. Rogers dismissed them all as "the vomiting of turkey buzzards."

Starting in a suave, soft voice that was in sharp contrast to Ford's vehement exhortation, Rogers told the jurors that the only thing they were called upon to decide was whether Darrow had arranged for the bribery of Lockwood. He then turned to the huge chart. Using a large wooden pointer to indicate names, he showed that only Franklin and Harrington had implicated Darrow directly.

If you are going to convict Darrow of bribing Lockwood, Rogers argued, "you have to do it on the testimony of Franklin and Harrington. There are but these two witnesses." And neither of them could be trusted.

Harrington only offered two pieces of relevant information: the claim that Darrow showed him a roll of bills from Tvietmoe's bank and said that he planned to use the money to "fix jurors"; and the assertion that, after Franklin's arrest, Darrow said, "My God, if he opens his mouth I am ruined."

"Now what does that consist of?" Rogers asked. "Statements made on two different occasions where no one else was present."

Franklin's statements were even more suspect, Rogers argued. He was an accomplice who had been given either immunity or an exceptionally light fine. "According to law, an accomplice must be corroborated," Rogers correctly explained. But there was no real corroboration.

Continuing with his argument on Wednesday morning, Rogers produced a huge new poster listing the names of eleven witnesses who had challenged Franklin on the facts and sixteen witnesses who had contradicted Franklin's memory concerning statements he had made. "Gentlemen, all these men gave Franklin the lie," Rogers said, pointing to some of the names on the poster. "Look at these men.

Willard, Jones, Barnard, Musgrove, White, Warner, Pirotte, Hood, Drain, Stineman, Nicholson, Watt. Newspaper men, friends of Franklin, fellow lodge members. They all contradicted him. Who will you believe? Franklin, a self-confessed felon, testifying for immunity, or all of these disinterested witnesses?"

Moreover, Rogers argued, there was no reason for Darrow to corrupt the jurors. "Did Darrow have a *motive* to bribe Lockwood?" he asked. "We have shown by testimony, that no one has seen to contradict, that Darrow, eight days before the bribery, had laid plans to dispose of the case.

"Do you think Darrow would throw four thousand dollars to the birds when he had the McNamara case practically settled? No! When he lets go of a dollar it squeals! It's a mental, moral, physical impossibility for him to do it."

Finally, speaking in hushed tones, Rogers concluded with a moving tribute to Darrow.

"Go into the mines of Pennsylvania today and ask the man there with the lamp on his cap who gave him his education. He'll tell you he was a breaker boy, working fourteen hours a day, picking slate from coal on the breaker, and that the strike came—and Clarence Darrow got him his rights, shortened his hours, lightened his labor, raised his wages.

"Ask the firemen on the railroads or the clerks in the Chicago department stores. Ask them who arbitrated their strikes, lightened their lives, and they'll tell you—Clarence Darrow.

"And who carried the fight of the City of Chicago against the street railways to the Supreme Court? And who won it? Clarence Darrow. They say he corrupts everybody he comes in contact with. Did he corrupt the Supreme Court?

"And now they say he blew up the *Times*. I saw those charred bodies taken out of there, no bigger, some times, than the buckets in which they carried them. I saw the weeping women and children. And the man who would assassinate Darrow's character by telling you he had anything to do with that would assassinate something else besides character." Rogers spoke quietly, his arms folded. Sobs could be heard in the courtroom.

"I tell you, when all men in this country get their rights, when all men have work, when all are equal, there will be no dynamiting. But so long as there are hungry babies while others are living on the fat of the land, there will be violence.

"I do not favor violence. I have fought the labor unions all my life. I drew up the famous antipicketing ordinance. Yet, if I had walked the streets all day long, offering to sell my hands or head to feed my hungry, crying baby, and couldn't get work, and knew there were others living on bee's knees and hummingbirds' tongues, and giving monkey dinners, I'd commit violence. I'd tear the front off the First National Bank with my fingernails.

"In this country of ours there are many things that must be settled and settled quick. We can't go on like this. We can't do it. So Darrow, through all these years, with all his heart and mind and conscience, has been doing what he can to help those who can't help themselves."

Rogers finished just in time for the noon recess. The emotions of all those in the courtroom were spent. A reporter observed that Rogers had "moved his audience to tears and to laughter at will." It had been a masterly performance.

And Clarence Darrow was scheduled to begin his summation at two P.M.

* * * *

During the lunch break, there was a mad rush for seats in the courtroom, or even places in the outside corridor. The word was out. Darrow was about to begin. According to the *Record,* two thousand spectators "fought and struggled with bailiffs in the narrow corridor for two hours." Half of them had to be turned away. By two o'clock, when court was ready to start again, "hundreds of people were crowded into a space 10 feet wide and a thousand pressed in on them in a wild effort to gain entrance to the courtroom. The bailiffs shut the doors in the faces of the crowd to keep the courtroom from being taken by storm. Women fainted and men gasped for breath. Mrs. Earl Rogers and her daughter [Adela] were caught in the crush and attorneys for both sides were imprisoned. Reserves were called in from the sheriff's office to quell the crowd and clubs had to be drawn before it could be handled. Finally, when the doors were opened, the mob surged into the room and filled all of the standing space."

At least one woman fainted, and others were knocked down, as people scrambled to get near the open doors, to find positions from which they could hear Darrow's self-defense. The bailiffs had to erect a wooden bar to block entrance from those without tickets. The men and women who did have tickets had to struggle through the mob, arriving in the courtroom with their hair and clothes awry. It took Earl Rogers ninety minutes just to force his way through the hallway crowd and into the courtroom.

❉❉❉❉

At precisely two twenty-two P.M., with the commotion still continuing in the hallway, Clarence Darrow rose to speak. He walked forward slowly, wearing the same gray suit that he had worn in the McNamara case. His hair was unkempt; an unruly lock fell down over his forehead.

He began in a low voice, hands thrust in his pockets. "Gentlemen of the jury, it is not easy to argue a case of importance, even when you are talking about someone else." Darrow looked from juror to juror as he spoke. The pandemonium in the hallway ceased. The room was silent.

"An experience like this never came to me before. Of course, I cannot say how I will get along with it. But I have felt, gentlemen, by the patience you have given this case for all these weeks, that you would be willing to listen to me. I might not argue it as well as I would some other case, but I felt that I ought to say something to you twelve men besides what I said on the witness stand.

"In the first place, I am a defendant, charged with a serious crime. I have been looking into the penitentiary for six or seven months, waiting for you twelve men to say whether I shall go or not. In the next place, I am a stranger in a strange land, two thousand miles away from home and friends, although I am proud to say here, so far away, there have gathered around me as good and loyal and faithful friends as any man could ever have upon the face of the earth. Still, I am unknown to you.

"I think I can say that no one in my native town would have made to any jury any such statement as was made of me by the assistant district attorney in opening his summation. I will venture to say he could not afterward have found a companion except among detectives and crooks and sneaks in the city where I live if he had dared to open his mouth in the infamous way that he did in this case. But here I am in his hands. Think of it! In a position where he can call me a coward."

Warming to his attack, Darrow's low voice began to rise. "In all my life, I never saw or heard so cowardly, sneaky, and brutal an attack, as this *thing* here perpetrated upon me." He pointed at Ford as he continued with restrained anger. "Was any courage displayed by him? It was only brutal and low, and every man knows it. This attack of Ford's was cowardly and malicious in the extreme. It was not worthy of a man and it did not come from a man.

"What am I on trial for, gentlemen of the jury?" Darrow's tone was again quiet, moderate, almost intimate. "You have been listening here for three months. If you don't know, then you are not as intelligent as I believe. I am not on trial for having sought to bribe a man named Lockwood. There may be and doubtless are many people who think I did seek to bribe him, but I am not on trial for that. I am on trial because I have been a lover of the poor, a friend of the oppressed, because I have stood by labor for all these years, and have brought down upon my head the wrath of the criminal interests in this country. Whether guilty or innocent of the crime charged in the indictment, that is the reason I am here, and that is the reason that I have been pursued by as cruel a gang as ever followed a man.

"Will you tell me, gentlemen of the jury, why the Erectors' Association of Indianapolis should have put up as vicious and cruel a plot to catch me as was ever used against any American citizen? Are these people interested in bribery? Why, almost every dollar of their ill-gotten gains has come from bribery.

"It is not that any of these men care about bribery, but there never was a chance before, since the world began, to claim that bribery had been committed for the poor.

"Suppose I am guilty of bribery. Is that why I am prosecuted in this court? Is that why, by the most infamous methods known to the law, these man, the real enemies of society, are trying to get me inside the penitentiary?

"No, that isn't it, and you twelve know it. These men are interested in getting me. They have concocted all sorts of schemes for the sake of getting me out of the way. Do you suppose they care what laws I might have broken? I have committed one crime, one crime which is like that against the Holy Ghost, which cannot be forgiven. I have stood for the weak and the poor. I have stood for the men who toil. And therefore I have stood against them, and now this is their chance. All right, gentlemen, I am in your hands, not theirs, just yet.

"I am tried here because I have given a large part of my life and my services to the cause of the poor and the weak, and because I am in the way of the interests. These interests would stop my voice— and they have hired many vipers to help them do it. They would stop my voice—my voice, which from the time I was a prattling babe my father and mother taught me to raise for justice and freedom, and in the cause of the weak and the poor."

The speech was having a decided effect on the jury. A *Herald* reporter watched in fascination as "tears from the jurors' eyes [began] to trickle down their worn and care laden faces."

"They would stop my voice with the penitentiary!" Darrow thundered. Then, lowering his voice, he continued with sudden solemnity. "Oh, you wild, insane members of the Steel Trust and Erectors' Association! Oh, you mad hounds of detectives who are willing to do your master's will! Oh, you district attorneys! You know not what you do. Let me say to you, that if you send me to prison, within the gray, dim walls of San Quentin there will brood a silence more ominous and eloquent than any words that my poor lips could ever frame. And do you think that you would destroy the hopes of the poor and the oppressed if you did silence me? Don't you know that upon my persecution and destruction would arise ten thousand men, abler than I have been, more devoted than I have been, and ready to give more than I have given in a righteous cause?

"I have been, perhaps, interested in more cases for the weak and poor than any other lawyer in America, but I am pretty nearly done, anyhow. If they had taken me twenty years ago, it might have been worth their while. But there are younger men than I, and there are men who will not be awed by prison bars, by district attorneys, by detectives, who will do this work when I am done."

Darrow suddenly stopped and stood for a moment, silently looking at the jurors. They, in turn, leaned forward, waiting for him to continue.

"Gentlemen," he finally went on, "I say this is not a case of bribery at all. I could tell you that I did this bribery, and you would still turn me loose. I have been thirty-five or thirty-six years in this profession and I tell you I never saw or heard of a case where any American jury convicted anybody, even the humblest, upon such testimony as that of Franklin and Harrington. There are other things in the world besides bribery. There are other crimes that are worse. It is a fouler crime to bear false witness against your fellow man, whether you do it from a witness chair, or in a cowardly way in an address to a jury—infinitely fouler.

"Suppose you thought I was guilty? Suppose you thought so. Would you dare, as honest men protecting society, would you dare to say by your verdict that scoundrels like Franklin and Harrington should be saved from their own sins by charging those sins to someone else? If so, gentlemen, when you go back to your homes, you had better kiss your wives a fond good-bye, and take your little children more tenderly in your arms than ever before, because, though today it is my turn, tomorrow it may be yours.

"Now gentlemen, I am going to be honest with you in this matter. The McNamara case was a hard fight. Here was the district attorney with his sleuths. Here was Burns with his hounds. Here was the Erectors' Association with its gold. A man could not stir in his home or go out of his office without being attacked by these men ready to commit all sorts of deeds. Besides, they had the grand jury; we didn't. They had the police force; we didn't. They had organized government; we didn't. We had to work fast and hard. We had to work the best we could. I would like to compare notes with them. I wish some grand jury could be impaneled to inquire into their misdeeds. But no, we cannot. They send out their subpoenas and they get two or three hundred telegrams, public and private, that had been sent from our office. What did they get?

"They had detectives in our office. They had us surrounded by gumshoe and keyhole men at every step; and what did they secure? Nothing. Nothing. I am surprised, gentlemen, that we were so peaceful in fighting the district attorney and Burns. What did they get, with all their grand juries and all their powers, gentlemen? They got conclusive evidence, it seems to me, that everything was regular, that nothing illegal was done.

"I am about as fitted for jury bribing as a Methodist preacher. If you twelve men think that I would pick out a place a block from my office—and send a man with money in his hand in broad daylight to go down on the streetcorner to pass four thousand dollars—why, find me guilty. I certainly belong in some state institution.

"Gentlemen, I have been human. I have done both good and evil. But I hope that when the last reckoning is made the good will overbalance the evil, and if it does, then I have done well. I hope it will so overbalance it that you jurors will believe it is not to the interest of the state to have me spend the rest of my life in prison."

✤ ✤ ✤ ✤

Darrow had spent almost two hours putting the case in context, in his context, winning the jury's sympathy for him as a man and as a crusader for justice, presenting himself as the victim of a conspiracy aimed at him for his past deeds on behalf of labor and the poor, denigrating the prosecutors and witnesses against him. He only discussed the facts, or asserted his innocence, in a few tangential asides. He wanted the jury to choose between them—and him. He was, in effect, putting the prosecution on trial. If the jury found him guilty, it would be finding them innocent; if it found him innocent, it would find them guilty.

✤ ✤ ✤ ✤

As the day drew to a close, Darrow turned to a line of argument that Rogers had warned against. He began to defend James McNamara, and to defend him in terms that almost seemed to condone his crime.

"I defy any living man to say where, either by speech or word of pen, I have advised anything cruel in my life," he began. "I would have walked from Chicago across the Rocky Mountains and over the long dreary desert to lay my hand upon the shoulder of J. B. McNamara and tell him not to place dynamite in the *Times* building. All my life I have counseled gentleness, kindness, and forgiveness to every human being. At the same time, gentlemen, even speaking for my own liberty, I do not retreat one inch or one iota from what I really believe as to this.

"You were told about the horrors of the *Times* explosion by Mr. Ford. Why? So that some of the horrors of that terrible accident might be reflected upon me to get me into the penitentiary. It hasn't anything to do with this case, excepting as they dragged it in here to prejudice the minds of this jury and to argue that this man should not have been defended by me.

"Let me tell you something, gentlemen, something which I know District Attorney Fredericks will use in his closing argument against me, and which I have no reason to feel will meet with favor in the minds of you twelve men. But it is what I believe and I will just take a chance.

"Lincoln Steffens was right in saying that this was a social crime. That does not mean that it should have been committed, but it means this: It grew out of a condition of society for which McNamara was in no wise responsible. There was a fierce conflict in this city, exciting the minds of thousands of people, some poor, some weak, some irresponsible, some doing wrong on the side of the powerful as well as upon the side of the poor. It inflamed their minds—and this thing happened. Let me tell you, gentlemen, and I will tell you the truth. You may hang these men to the highest tree; you may hang everybody suspected; you may send me to the penitentiary if you will; you may convict the fifty-four men indicted in Indianapolis; but until you go down to fundamental causes, these things will happen over and over again. They will come as the earthquake comes. They will come as the hurricane that uproots the trees. They will come as the lightning comes to destroy the poisonous miasmas that fill the air. We as a people are responsible for these conditions, and we must look results squarely in the face.

"And I want to say another thing in justice to that young man who was my client, and whom I risked my life, my liberty, and my reputation to save. He had nothing on earth to gain. His act was not inspired by love of money. He couldn't even gain fame, for if he succeeded he could never have told any human being so long as he lived. He believed in a cause and he risked his life in that cause. Whether rightly or wrongly, it makes no difference with the motives of the man. I would not have done it. You would not have done it. But judged in the light of his motives, which is the only way that man can be judged—and for that reason only the infinite God can judge a human being—judged in the light of his motives, I cannot condemn the man, and I will not.

"Gentlemen, do you think for a moment that I do not feel sorry at the destruction of those lives, and for the wives and the children and the friends that were left behind? I tell you today, there will come a time when crime will disappear. But that time will never come or be hastened by the building of jails and penitentiaries and scaffolds. It will only come by changing the conditions of life under which men live and suffer and die."

With that, Judge Hutton closed the session. He instructed Darrow to continue his summation the next morning.

❈ ❈ ❈ ❈

All afternoon there had been tears and sobs throughout the courtroom. Anton Johannsen wept at Darrow's discussion of the cause of labor. One newspaper reported that "the jurors must have read on the scales an overwhelming balance for good in the heart and the deed of the man who stood before them."

For all of his eloquence, however, Darrow had not spent much time claiming to be innocent. In fact, some listeners thought he had asked to be acquitted *in spite* of his guilt. That was the claim advanced by Mary Field in a newspaper dispatch that afternoon.

"Clarence Darrow has shaken his clenched fist in the faces of the Los Angeles persecutors," she wrote in a special article for Fremont Older's San Francisco *Bulletin*. "He has asked the jury to take his guilt for granted and then dare to convict him in the face of the showing that the Steel Trust and Merchants and Manufacturers Association, past masters at bribery and deception, had singled him out for punishment, not because he bribed jurors, but because he has been a life-long champion of labor."

It was a bit of an overstatement. Darrow had, in fact, proclaimed his innocence. But those assurances were almost pro forma. His greatest passion had been reserved for the argument that the jury should vote for an acquittal even if it believed him guilty, a plea based on the centuries-old doctrine of jury nullification, which has allowed juries, as a matter of collective conscience—and in the interest of a higher sense of justice—to free such defendants as William Penn and John Peter Zenger.

❋ ❋ ❋ ❋

Court opened at eight-thirty the next morning, Thursday, August 15. Again the room and the outside hallway were jammed. By some accounts the crowd was even larger than on the day before, but it was better organized, standing in two lines to gain admission. The *Times* reported that "hysterical women grasped at Darrow's hand as he passed into the interior" of the courtroom.

With the aid of a huge stack of papers, Darrow continued his argument, spending several hours reviewing the facts of the case, attacking the testimony of Franklin and Harrington. He spent much of his time, as had Rogers, reiterating his claim that he had no motive for the bribe since "the McNamara case was disposed of several days before November 28, so far as I was concerned"; and asking, "With this condition of affairs, when I had no thought whatever that the McNamara case would be tried, is it likely that I would use four thousand dollars of money that was sorely needed?"

In his concluding—and most powerful—statement, he returned to a plea for compassion: compassion for his former clients, and compassion for himself.

It was, above all, a plea for the return of his friends. "The settlement of the McNamara case cost me many friends, friends that have been coming back slowly, very slowly, as more and more this matter is understood. I am not a fool. I knew I was losing friends. With the eyes of the world upon me, knowing that my actions would call down the doubt and, in many cases, the condemnation of my friends, I never hesitated for the fraction of a second. Was it wise or unwise? Was it right or wrong? You might have done differently. I don't know. . . . I heard these men talk of their brothers, of their mothers, of the dead; I saw the human side; I wanted to save them, and I did what I could to save them—"

"I have been a busy man. I have never had to look for clients. They have come to me. I have been a general attorney of a big railroad. I have been the general counsel, as it were, for the great city of Chicago. I have represented the strong and the weak—but never the strong against the weak.

"I could have tried the McNamara case, and a large class of the working people of America would honestly have believed, if these men had been hanged, that they were not guilty. I could have done this and saved myself. But I knew that if you hanged these men you would have settled in the hearts of a great mass of men a hatred so deep, so profound, that it would never die away.

"And I took the responsibility, gentlemen. Maybe I did wrong. But I took it. Here and there I got praise for what was called a heroic act, but where I got one word of praise, I got a thousand words of blame! And I have stood that for nearly a year. But I have gone on about my way as I always have regardless of this, without explanation, without begging, without asking anything of anybody who lived, and I will go on that way to the end."

A reporter described the scene in the courtroom. "The court and jury and hundreds of spectators who filled the seats and stood jammed together against the walls in the aisles and in the corridors without the courtroom listened as though transfixed. There was not the move of an eyelash during the address, a rustle of a skirt to break the steady flow of beautiful words. It was one of the most wonderful scenes that has been presented in a local court or in the whole world, according to a score of lawyers who were present."

Dozens of people in the audience were sobbing. Tears were streaming from Darrow's eyes as he spoke; he turned to Ruby for a handkerchief, and then for another. He paused to regain control of his voice. Then he continued.

"I know the mob. In one way I love it. In another way, I despise it. I know the unreasoning, unthinking mass. I have lived with men and worked with them. I have been their idol and I have been cast down and trampled beneath their feet. I have stood on the pinnacle and I have heard the cheering mob sound my praises; and I have gone down to the depths of the valley, where I have heard them hiss my name—this same mob. But I have summoned such devotion and such courage as God has given me, and I have gone on—gone on my path unmoved by their hisses or their cheers.

"I have tried to live my life and to live it as I see it, regarding neither praise nor blame, both of which are unjust. No man is judged rightly by his fellow men. Some look upon him as an idol and forget his feet are clay, as are the feet of every man. Others look upon him as a devil and can see no good in him at all. Neither is true. I have known this, and I have tried to follow my conscience and my duty the best I could and to do it faithfully, and here I am today in the hands of you twelve men who will one day say to your children, and they will say it to their children, that you passed on my fate.

"Gentlemen, there is not much more to say. You may or may not agree with my philosophy. I believe we are all in the hands of destiny, and if it is written in the book of destiny that I shall go to the penitentiary, that you twelve men before me shall send me there, I will go. If it is written that I am now down to the depths and that you twelve men shall liberate me, so it will be.

"As one poet has expressed it:

Life is a game of whist. From unknown sources
The cards are shuffled and the hands are dealt.
Blind are our efforts to control the forces
That though unseen are no less strongly felt.
I do not like the way the cards are shuffled,
But still I like the game and want to play,
And through the long, long night, I play unruffled
The cards I get until the break of day.

"I have taken the cards as they came: I have played the best I could. I have tried to play them honestly, manfully, doing for myself and for my fellow man the best I could, and I will play the game to the end, whatever that end may be.

"Gentlemen, I came to this city a stranger. Misfortune has beset me, but I never saw a place in my life with greater warmth and kindness and love than Los Angeles. Here to a stranger have come hands to help me, hearts to beat with mine, words of sympathy to encourage and cheer, and though a stranger to you twelve men and a stranger to this city, I am willing to leave my case with you. I know my life. I know what I have done. My life has not been perfect. It has been human; too human. I have felt the heartbeats of every man who lived. I have tried to be the friend of every man who lived. I have tried to help in the world. I have not had malice in my heart. I have had love for my fellow men. I have done the best I could. There are some people who know it. There are some who do not believe it. There are people who regard my name as a byword and a reproach, more for the good I have done than for the evil.

Darrow was in tears and so were dozens of his supporters. "Sobs were audible during his dramatic pauses," the *Record* reported. "Men and women wept unashamedly." Even the court stenographer was crying.

"There are people who would destroy me. There are people who would lift up their hands to crush me down. I have enemies powerful and strong. There are honest men who misunderstand me and doubt me; and still I have lived a long time on earth, and I have friends—I have friends in my old home who have gathered around to tell you as best they could of the life I have lived. I have friends who have come to me here to help me in my sore distress. I have friends throughout the length and breadth of the land, and these are the poor and the weak and the helpless, to whose cause I have given voice. If you should convict me, there will be people to applaud the act. But if in your judgment and your wisdom and your humanity, you believe me innocent, and return a verdict of not guilty in this case, I know that from thousands and tens of thousands and yea, perhaps millions of the weak and the poor and the helpless throughout the world, will come thanks to this jury for saving my liberty and my name."

As Darrow ended his plea, with the clock nearing noon, the chimes in St. Vibiana's Cathedral, a block away, began to play. "His face was streaming with tears and the jury was weeping like children," the *Record* reported, "with not a dry eye in the crowded courtroom."

Observers called it "the greatest oratorical effort of his long career."

⁂

It was not an easy argument for Fredericks to rebut. The district attorney had neither the temperament nor the skill to break the trance that Darrow had created. When court resumed after lunch, Fredericks sensibly began by acknowledging the sentiment that the jury felt. Before they were chosen, all of the jurors had promised not to let their verdict be determined by the force of Darrow's oratory. Now the prosecutor used that promise to try to acknowledge the mood that hung in the courtroom.

"When you said at the beginning of this trial that you would not permit the oratory or personal appeal of the defendant to influence your verdict," he began, "you did not mean, and I did not mean, that your hearts would not be touched, and that perhaps a tear would not dim your eye when you were confronted with the unfortunate predicament in which the defendant finds himself." But, Fredericks said, "I expected that like true American citizens, you would write your verdict, even though you would have to wipe a tear from your eye."

Standing tall and lanky, in a lightweight three-piece suit and bow tie, Fredericks started in a low voice and a quiet manner as he tried to turn some of Darrow's own rhetoric to the prosecution's benefit. "Clarence Darrow told you yesterday, that he would have walked from the East to the West in his bare feet to have prevented the commission of that crime," he recalled. "Well, gentlemen, that is not the way to prevent the commission of that crime and of other similar crimes. That would be idle, sentimental, and useless. The experience of the ages has taught us, yea, the handiwork of God Almighty teaches us the way to prevent wrong and crime is by punishment. Punishment."

Throughout the afternoon, and well into Friday morning, Fredericks worked mightily to rehabilitate his witnesses and to reestablish contact with a jury that had been so powerfully affected by Darrow's words, but in the end he appealed to the jurors' patriotism and sense of duty, hoping that it would overcome their sense of compassion.

"You have listened to one of the most marvelous addresses ever delivered in any courtroom," he said. "But that only reflects upon the ability of the man; it has mighty little to do with his guilt and innocence.

"This is your affair from now on. If you want to make jury bribery a safe industry, then acquit this man on his testimony. If your sympathy for Clarence Darrow weighs more with you than the desire to blot out this damnable thing, then let him go. But let me call your attention to the fact that history tells us that George Washington wept when he signed the death warrant for Major Andre. But he signed it nonetheless."

Fredericks's presentation had been superb. Friends called it "a beautiful oratorical effort," and "one of the most effective addresses ever heard in a local courtroom," and even critics reported that "Fredericks called all of his oratorical powers into play today in a last supreme effort to send Darrow to the penitentiary."

Some people predicted that the jury would be "locked up for some days." Darrow hardly slept on Friday night, waiting for the day of judgment.

* * * *

Court opened early on Saturday morning. Everyone was exhausted, but Judge Hutton was determined to end the trial in time for the jurors to have a chance to spend Sunday at home with their families, if possible. Darrow entered the courtroom at a few minutes after eight A.M. He was ill at ease. A sympathetic reporter called him "hunted, nervous," and described the spectators who watched him "in pity, pity for a brave man making the fight of his life; pity for a hunted human, guilty or not guilty, they cared not which."

At eight-twenty A.M., Judge Hutton mounted the bench. He was almost as tired as Darrow. His face was white, and he had dark circles under his eyes. He had spent the night preparing lengthy jury instructions that were certain to have a profound impact on the deliberations. He blamed the length of his charge on the "seriously impaired condition" of his health. "This trial has exhausted my strength and sapped my vitality," he said apologetically.

All of the lawyers knew just how important the judge's words could be. By his explanation of the laws of evidence, the judge could effectively tell the jurors to assign little or no weight to certain testimony.

Judge Hutton's instructions were exceptionally favorable to Darrow. He explained that a conviction could not be based on the uncorroborated testimony of an accomplice, such as Franklin. Nor could the testimony of one accomplice be corroborated by the testimony of a second accomplice. If there was any doubt about whether Harrington was an accomplice, Hutton said, the jury should resolve the issue in favor of Darrow. So Darrow could not be convicted on the testimony of Franklin and Harrington unless there were some other form of corroboration. How about Darrow's presence at the scene, or the claim that the cash used to bribe Lockwood had come from Tvietmoe's bank? "Circumstantial evidence," Hutton said, could only be relied on if it was "absolutely incompatible" with any other "reasonable hypothesis."

Moreover, Hutton virtually told the jury that it would have to acquit Darrow if it concluded that he had already settled the case, or decided to settle it, at the time of the bribe. "The court instructs the jury that seldom, if at all, is any offense or crime committed without an express motive to commit it. When the evidence fails to show any motive to commit the crime charged, on the part of the accused, that is a substantial circumstance in favor of his innocence."

It took Judge Hutton almost an hour to finish reading the instructions. At nine-twenty A.M., he concluded with this admonition. "May God give you the wisdom to see the right and the courage to do the right."

❋ ❋ ❋ ❋

As the twelve jurors retired from the room in silence to decide her husband's fate, Ruby broke down and started to cry hysterically.

Since almost everyone agreed that the jury would take several hours to decide the case, most of the spectators started to exit, expecting to come back at noon. Only about two hundred people, including most of Darrow's strongest supporters, remained. Captain Fredericks and the members of his staff took the elevator up to the D.A.'s offices. The clerk left the room, as did Earl Rogers, who went out into the hall to smoke a cigarette. In a nearby anteroom, a group of reporters set up a card table and started a game of poker, prepared for a long vigil.

Darrow paced up and down the courtroom, hands deep in his coat pockets. From time to time he stopped at the counsel table for a drink of water. Ruby sank deeper into her chair, laughing and crying by turns.

At nine-fifty A.M., an electric rumor started to run through the room. The jury was ready with its verdict. They had been gone for less than forty minutes.

Bailiff Van Vliet was the first to arrive. He held up his hand and asked for quiet. "Remember, there shall be no demonstrations of any kind, no matter what the verdict shall be," he announced.

As the jurors filed into the jury box, spectators rushed to their seats and Judge Hutton took his place on the bench. Darrow chewed on a pencil. Ruby, "trembling like a leaf," held a handkerchief to her mouth.

There was a tense delay for a few moments while the court waited for the clerk and a representative of the district attorney's office to arrive. At last, Joe Ford appeared, looking nervous and abstracted. There was no sign of Captain Fredericks.

"Gentlemen of the jury, have you agreed on a verdict?" Judge Hutton asked.

"We have, your honor," said M. R. Williams, the jury foreman.

"You may read it."

The foreman hesitated for a moment and then shouted his answer.

"Not guilty!"

Anton Johannsen jumped up from his seat with a thunderous clap of his hands and an electrifying whoop of victory. Ruby stood up and threw her arms around her husband. They stood holding each other, half laughing, half crying, as the room exploded with excitement and their friends rushed down the aisle to share in the joy.

Elsewhere in the courtroom, supporters rushed to Earl Rogers, slapping him on the back and pressing toward him until he was backed up against a wall. Another emotional group formed around Job Harriman. A few well-wishers mistakenly offered a congratulatory word to Joe Ford, who exited the room quickly.

Fremont Older forced his way down the aisle, seized Darrow by the shoulders, and shoved him through the throng to the jury box. Darrow kept Ruby at his side. His face lit up as jurors Golding and Dunbar threw their arms around him and patted him on the back.

"Oh, Mr. Darrow, this is the happiest moment of my life," juror Dunbar exclaimed, with tears streaming down his cheeks.

Standing in the box, the jurors held a reception. Each of them grasped Darrow's hand with a word of joy. "You old bully fellow, you," the foreman said. "We are Americans and the world has moved," said another. Many of the jurors embraced Ruby who, for the first time in months, looked radiant.

Spectators fought their way into the box, slapping Darrow's back. "Behind Darrow came society women, business men, labor leaders, a negro, an Indian, members of the underworld, many crying with joy. They shook the hands of the jurors, while the boom of flashlight powders resounded as half a dozen photographers snapped the most remarkable scene ever witnessed in a local courtroom."

Finally Judge Hutton made his way to Darrow. "There will be hallelujahs from millions of voices through the length and breadth of this land," he said as he grasped Darrow's hand. Echoing a phrase from Darrow's closing argument, he said that workers around the country would rejoice that Darrow was once again free to come to their aid.

Darrow said that he would like to visit the judge at his residence.

"I will be most honored to have you as my guest, Mr. Darrow," Judge Hutton replied. "Good-bye and God bless you."

The rejoicing lasted for over two hours, until it was time for lunch. At noon, the Darrows and many of their strongest supporters went off to a reception at the Café Martan, where Darrow held court, reading telegrams that flooded in from around the country from such friends as Lincoln Steffens, Ed Nockles, and Edgar Lee Masters.

Mary Field had planned to skip the reception. "I don't want the crowds," she told Erskine Wood, "the palms and Hosannas are for the multitudes." Nor did she want to be anywhere near Ruby. "When it's all over, I skiddoo—Ruby's too much for me. . . . I shall all my life avoid her. . . . I hate to lose Darrow's presence, but I hate more to be out of harmony with my environment." But in the excitement of the verdict she joined the celebration anyway, walking over with her friend Anton Johannsen. A photo taken at the lunch shows her standing just behind the table, directly between Clarence and Ruby Darrow.

While the celebration was underway, a delegation representing all of the city's trade unions arrived to pay their respects. After offering their congratulations, the men gave Darrow a large bouquet of flowers. Attached to it was a note that Darrow must have treasured.

"Organized labor sends you this," it said, "feeling it is typical, with the stems for our organization and the flowers for the thousands of hands reaching out to you today. We want you to feel that each petal represents the voice of the humble laborer going up to you in grateful thanks for your loyal devotion to their cause."

It was more than an acquittal. After eight months of torment, Darrow felt vindicated and loved.

He also felt that his life had regained its purpose. A year earlier, when he reluctantly agreed to represent the McNamaras, he longed to leave the law, to write and edit works of fiction and philosophy. Eight months earlier, after pleading the brothers guilty, he had announced that he planned to retire, that he had fought his last case. But the battle for his freedom and redemption provided him with a new sense of mission and purpose. The man who had described himself on the witness stand as a corporate lawyer and arbitrator now thought of himself as "a lover of the poor, a friend of the oppressed," who had "stood by labor all these years" and had handled "more cases for the weak and the poor than any other lawyer in America."

The trial had served to redefine his future as well as his past. After his victory, he released a public statement that he undoubtedly believed was true. "I shall spend the rest of my life as I have that which has passed, in doing the best I can to serve the cause of the poor."

And, to a remarkably large extent, he was true to his word.

Chapter Eighteen

FINAL VERDICT

I N THE EYES OF history, the jury in the Lockwood case acquitted Darrow of bribing the McNamara trial jurors. The facts are not so simple. The jurors held three ballots, polling 8–4, 10–2, and finally 12–0. In late January 1913, Darrow was tried for bribing Robert Bain. Since Bain had been bribed in early October, 1911, long before Steffens began his efforts to settle the McNamara case, Darrow could not use lack of motive as a defense. Nor did he have Earl Rogers at his side. Rogers spent most of the winter in a sanatorium suffering from "nervous prostration" and only appeared in court on rare occasions. Darrow handled his own defense with the aid of O. W. Powers, a former judge from Salt Lake City, and young Jerry Geisler. The prosecution's case was presented by a special prosecutor named Wheaton Gray. In the second trial, the jury couldn't decide on a verdict. On March 8, 1913, after deliberating for forty hours, it divided 8–4—for conviction.

By early spring, Captain Fredericks had tired of the case. A shoo-in as the regular Republican candidate for governor, he had no desire for a further trial, though the hung jury allowed him to file charges once again. In mid-April, he allowed Darrow to return to Chicago. Some people claimed that Darrow had promised Fredericks that he would never again set foot in Los Angeles.

This book involves a series of mysteries that have survived for eighty years. Did Darrow bribe the jury—or was he framed? What impact, if any, did the arrest of Franklin while bribing Lockwood at Third and Main have on Darrow's decision to plead the McNamaras guilty? If guilty, why did he engage in such reprehensible and illegal conduct and how did he carry it out; and, finally, how should that affect our view of one of America's greatest lawyers?

❋ ❋ ❋ ❋

Criminal law requires prosecutors to prove guilt beyond a reasonable doubt, and arguably some doubt still remains. Historians, however, can't be held to such a stringent standard of proof. On the basis, then, of all of the available evidence, it is fair to conclude that Darrow bribed both Lockwood and Bain.

Over the course of this century, the power of Darrow's myth has obscured the fact that this was a widely held opinion at the time. Most reporters who covered the trial, for example, were convinced of Darrow's guilt. Even Hugh Baillie, the *Record*'s sympathetic young reporter, later admitted that "I never had any doubts on the subject. In my opinion Darrow was guilty—on the evidence, which included his presence across the street, as a spectator, while Franklin was passing the money to Lockwood; on his attitudes and appearance during the trials; and on the basis of my private conversations with him." But the reporters, like the men on the first jury, were glad to see him set free.

All of the evidence gleaned from dozens of personal memoirs, private papers, and government files adds further reason to believe Darrow guilty. Neither the press nor the court knew the extent to which Darrow's own circle of friends thought him capable of the crime—and, indeed, believed he had bribed juries before. Some of the most damning evidence appears in the letters of Erskine Wood, who predicted what Darrow would do and was then convinced that he had done it. W. W. Catlin came to the same conclusion, after several long conversations with Darrow in February 1912, "because of his course, not only here but elsewhere, and his talk [which] justifies the belief that he thinks such a course right, under the circumstances existing." Moreover, his lead counsel reportedly thought he was directly responsible for the bribery. According to Adela Rogers St. Johns, her father was convinced of Darrow's culpability. Despite his exceptionally effective testimony, Lincoln Steffens, too, apparently believed Darrow guilty. "What do I care if he is guilty as Hell," Steffens told his sister during the trial; "what if his friends and attorneys turn away ashamed of him . . ." Darrow needed a friend, and Steffens would be there at his side.

Furthermore, there is no evidence that the case against Darrow was manufactured by the forces of government and capital. The private papers of Walter Drew demonstrate that the National Erectors' Association believed Darrow guilty. Documents available from the National Archives show that Oscar Lawler, the government's special prosecutor, was genuinely indignant when he sent Attorney General Wickersham a series of coded letters listing Darrow's pattern of misconduct and explaining how Tvietmoe and Darrow had conspired to generate the cash used to bribe the jury. It is highly unlikely that anyone associated with the government or private industry could have set Darrow up without the knowledge of Drew or Lawler. A bribe could, perhaps, have been arranged without Darrow's knowledge by one of the McNamaras' supporters—by Tvietmoe or Johannsen or one of the other labor leaders—but no evidence points to them, either.

❋ ❋ ❋ ❋

While they condemned his cynicism, greed, and vanity, most of Darrow's friends were not shocked or even particularly angry at the thought of his bribing the jury. "At the very worst most people believe that you possibly took a long chance for your clients," one prominent friend wrote in a letter to him. "If by any chance you did so, I am certain that you did nothing that any other lawyer would not have done placed in the same position in such an important case." They were much more upset by his decision to plead the brothers guilty—for that decision, after so many months of intense commitment to their defense, seemed a betrayal of his clients and their cause, rather than a betrayal of some abstract theory of justice.

Darrow's reasons for entering the guilty pleas were the subject of an intense and unresolved debate. Judge Bordwell was almost certainly correct when he insisted that Franklin's arrest for "the bribery and attempted bribery of jurors" led directly to the change of pleas. But that still left much to be said about Darrow's motivation.

Ten weeks after Darrow's indictment, Johannsen said that he would "always believe that Darrow did it to save his own skin in a deal with Fredericks." It is not clear how such a deal would have worked, or why Johannsen still believed it after charges against Darrow were filed; did he think that Fredericks double-crossed the lawyer after getting him to plead his clients guilty? It is easier to give credence to the theory that he pled the brothers guilty to establish lack of motive as a defense to use if he were ever charged with bribing Lockwood; that argument makes particularly good sense if one assumes that Darrow did not yet know that the government was aware of his efforts to bribe Bain.

There may also have been financial considerations involved. One major incentive in Darrow's decision to represent the McNamaras, to undertake such grueling work in a city far from his comfortable home, was the promise of a very large fee; a law partner, Francis Wilson, said Darrow was lured by "the chance of winning that $50,000 fee quickly, in a few months." Since he had collected his full fee by late summer, there was an economic incentive to end the case as expeditiously as possible. (After returning to Chicago in the spring of 1913, Darrow told Hamlin Garland that he had earned "forty-four thousand dollars out of the McNamara case.")

But Darrow also had purer motives. He wanted to protect Clancy, Johannsen, and Tvietmoe from further prosecutions; he did not want to continue wasting the hard-earned nickels and dimes of workers around America; and, after Franklin's arrest, Darrow knew that there was no longer any hope of a hung jury, much less an acquittal, for the McNamaras.

Remembering the episode some twenty years later, recalling the "profound sensation" and pain the pleas caused him, Darrow said that his duty was "perfectly plain." He pled the boys guilty, he said, "to save the lives" of his clients. If so, that was not the chief interest of the man whose life was at stake. Jim McNamara *wanted* to go to trial; he was prepared to die for the cause. "The young fellow [Jim] wept and begged to be allowed to go on," Johannsen claimed, "saying that they would not hang him anyway and that if they did he was willing to hang for them all." The argument that won Jim over was the need to save leaders of the labor movement. Shortly after the confessions, Johannsen insisted Jim was "forced into it" to protect "Darrow himself"; years later, Jim said he had been motivated by the importance of helping Clancy, Johannsen, and Tvietmoe. "We were forced to plead guilty," he told a friend in the labor movement, "or take the San Francisco crowd with us."

In a sense, both Darrow and McNamara were remembering their most noble and magnanimous sentiments. The truth probably lies somewhere in between, in a mixture of self-interest and high purpose. Johannsen was probably correct in decrying his friend's motives. But no doubt Darrow, who had always hated capital punishment, cared deeply about his clients' welfare, and was capable of persuading himself, as well of others, of almost anything, was convinced of his own virtue and believed that he was telling the truth.

❊❊❊❊

Some details of Darrow's role in the bribery scheme remain unclear, but it was a direct result of his decision to manipulate the process; once started, there was no clear place to stop. The case against the McNamaras was exceptionally strong, and Darrow and his colleagues used devices that students don't learn at Ivy League law schools. They began by intimidating and manipulating witnesses and planting spies in the opposition camp; the goal, as Fred Moore told Wood early that summer, was "to frame up or carry out a plan looking to the defense and acquittal of the accused men regardless of the facts." But when those tactics seemed to be failing, Darrow decided that he had to become even more aggressive. On September 2, 1911, at a time when the defense team was in desperate need of funds, Darrow gave a ten thousand dollar check to Olaf Tvietmoe, who converted it into cash used for a variety of unusual purposes, probably including jury bribery. It seems clear that Darrow told Bert Franklin to reach a few prospective jurors who could be trusted not to divulge the plan. Acting on Darrow's orders, Franklin first secured the cooperation of Robert Bain and, six weeks later, began to work on George Lockwood.

As of Tuesday, November 28, 1911, at nine A.M., when Franklin met Lockwood on the streetcorner, Darrow still wanted the jurors bribed because, notwithstanding Steffens's efforts, he expected the case to go to trial. Fredericks had made it clear that he would not accept any arrangement that did not include confessions from both brothers—and Darrow was unwilling to let J.J. go to jail. No agreement was possible, or so it seemed until Franklin was arrested at Third and Main.

❈ ❈ ❈

To his detractors, the bribery showed that Darrow was immoral or, at best, amoral. Even some friends who "had a 'hunch' that he had tried to bribe the jury" found an explanation, Hutchins Hapgood reported, in Darrow's "moral cynicism" and his inclination "to make light of the deep, custom-moralities of the race." Erskine Wood offered a different explanation, arguing that Darrow's vanity and ego led him to use any tactic necessary to win. But there is another way to view his actions. Darrow may actually have believed that, under some circumstances, bribery was the right course, the moral course of action.

The sweeping phrases that Darrow used to defend men accused of defying injunctions, organizing boycotts, and even committing murder, the argument that they were engaged in a great battle for human liberty where industry had the power of tyrants and workers were forced to use the tools of the revolutionary, all of that was more than rhetoric to Darrow. He believed it.

"The high motive of the revolutionist is one side," he had written; "the strength of the government to protect itself is the other." Twenty-five years earlier he had concluded that "society is organized injustice, that business is a legal fraud," and he had determined to use what power he had "to *destroy* the system." For all of the success that he had found in the intervening quarter-century, for all of the compromises he had made, Darrow retained a revolutionary streak. He agreed with the thrust of E. W. Scripps's disquisition on the parallels between the McNamaras, who sometimes resorted to violence to win industrial justice, and John Brown, whose bloody abolitionist tactics had been sainted by the righteousness of the Civil

War. The illegal and sometimes violent acts of his clients were justified by the importance of their cause, the purity of their purpose, and the power of their oppressors; by analogy, his unorthodox legal strategies were given legitimacy by the abusive power of industry and government.

With considerable justification, and a bit of paranoia, Darrow felt that the judicial system was rigged against his clients. The prosecutors controlled the police and the grand jury, and they were backed by Burns detectives, by the Erectors' Association's money, and by a generally hostile press led by a *Times* that was bent on revenge. His clients had been illegally kidnapped, dragged across state lines, and forced to face criminal charges. Their friends were harassed, their witnesses intimidated. The judge was a member of the most elite club in the city, and no one would be allowed on the jury who did not own property and was not acceptable to the prosecution. The jurors all knew that they would be rewarded for voting to convict the McNamaras and punished if they voted for acquittal. In voting to set Darrow free, juror Golding once noted, he acted "contrary to my best interests (from a mercenary standpoint)." The forces of capital bribed jurors, too, but the approach was a bit more subtle.

Darrow could respect the notion of legal ethics in a state where justice was blindfolded and the scales were balanced, but with his client facing the death penalty, he felt a moral responsibility to be more resourceful in Los Angeles, where justice wore the face of General Otis and the scales were weighted by money from the coffers of the National Erectors' Association and the Merchants and Manufacturers Association. "Darrow believed in saving lives," Mary Field explained to her daughter many years later. "I think that if he thought bribery was the only way to keep the boys from being killed, he would have felt justified in using it."

Those committed to the integrity of the legal system will agree with Erskine Wood, who deemed the judiciary the highest evolution of rational debate, the best means of achieving personal, political, and economic justice. But to understand Darrow's view, it is worth asking what measures would have been justified to help free the Scottsboro Boys, who were framed and railroaded to justice in the racist courts of Alabama in the 1930s; and what tactics would ethicists disallow for those seeking to free Jews facing punishment in Nazi Germany? Of course, Darrow's clients had not been framed; he knew that they were "guilty as hell"; and America in 1911 was not Germany in 1940. But Darrow regarded the McNamaras as selfless revolutionaries whose violent crime was an accident, who "never morally committed murder"; heroic if misguided participants in the battle for industrial justice who could never be fairly tried or punished in Los Angeles. If extreme measures would be justified in other places, or in other eras, then perhaps Darrow should be faulted—or forgiven—for his cynical analysis of American society in the early years of the century rather than simply for the tactics he employed.

Those concerned with Darrow's reputation as a lawyer may be troubled, too, by his conduct during his own trial. There is evidence that, while at the depths, he tried to arrange for the kidnapping of John Harrington, a key prosecution witness. Arguably worse, from the standpoint of his clients and friends in labor, apparently Darrow made a secret effort to win a lighter sentence for himself by offering to testify against Samuel Gompers. Such misdeeds are perhaps understandable coming from a man filled with panic and dread, but they cannot be lightly excused.

❋ ❋ ❋

It took years for most leaders of the AFL to forgive Darrow for the way that he had handled the McNamara case—stringing them along, allowing them to raise huge sums from their members, and then pleading the men guilty. Samuel Gompers barely mentions the great crusader in his memoirs. Union leaders never again called on his services in a major case.

But Darrow was sustained by the love of his friends, starting with those in the San Francisco unions. On September 2, 1912, less than three weeks after winning the acquittal in the Lockwood case, he journeyed north to give the Labor Day oration at Shellmound Park. "I have been through many dark days in the past year, but this reception makes it almost worthwhile," he drawled. The crowd was the largest in San Francisco history, but so many people were turned away that Darrow agreed to give another speech a few nights later at the Dreamland Rink on the topic of "Industrial Conspiracies." It was a speech that he would give to audiences around the West.

His thesis was unrepentant. Hundreds of labor leaders had been sent to jail for "conspiring" to strike against oppressive working conditions in the decades since the government first perverted the Sherman Anti-Trust Act by charging Eugene Debs with a "conspiracy in restraint of trade." But the real conspirators, Darrow argued, were the monopolists, aided and abetted by the courts. Judges have the power to make the laws, since they have to power to interpret them. The forces of capital are content to let the people adopt all the laws they wish, he said, so long as the forces of industry own the courts.

"The country is filled with cripples and orphans because the courts have twisted the law so that the poor man couldn't possibly recover damages when hurt. The judges say if a man is foolish enough to go down and work in a railroad yard, he ought to lose an arm.

"Laws are passed, judges elected, sheriffs created, and jails built to protect the few in the ownership of the earth," Darrow charged. "That is the real industrial conspiracy."

❋ ❋ ❋ ❋

From San Francisco, Darrow took a train to Portland, Oregon, to deliver his Industrial Conspiracies lecture. Mary Field, now celebrated in the labor world for a series of tough-minded articles in *Organized Labor,* served as his advance agent, meeting with political activists and journalists, accompanied by Sara who "watched, as one might watch a scene on the stage, Mary's wonderful love at work for the man she has given her soul to."

Darrow spent the night at the Ehrgotts' home. (Erskine Wood was in the countryside, composing a long verse called "Poet in the Desert.") Mary, Sara, and Darrow had dinner together at the Oregon Grill and then went off to the lecture hall, where Sara was, once again, impressed almost equally by Darrow's humor, his sophistry, and the force of his ideas. At an early breakfast and quiet walk the next morning, they spoke of politics, his second trial, and Mary. As always, Sara found Darrow an impossible mixture of the base and the noble. "At the very moment I recall some small act or word, I can think of a big fine one, too."

Sara's heart ached for Darrow, she told Erskine, "even more because he deserves it" than if he didn't. "The penalty for self-inflicted wrong is rather more painful than that drawn upon us by others.

"I don't forgive Mr. D.'s wrong [in bribing the jurors]," she said, "but I can forgive the man of which it came because from him, from his composite, has come his great good."

"Darrow," Mary asked a few weeks later, after stops in Bakersfield, Fresno, Stockton, Sacramento, San Jose, and Salt Lake City. "What do you think of the tour as a whole?"

"I'm glad the labor people are my friends again," he answered a bit hoarsely. He had caught a cold during the trip, but refused to slow down. "I think they are beginning to understand. Of course I don't care about all this clapping for *me*. That can change overnight. But I do care that people clap for what I say, for it shows that Labor is waking up, and once Labor wakes up, even I don't know where things will stop.

"I'm part fanatic, part philosopher," he continued. "The part of me that's fanatic is glad when I hear the cheering. It is the oncoming of the people. The part of me that's a philosopher knows that the struggle of mankind for a richer, fuller, happier life will go on and on, in some form, forever and forever."

Though he was enigmatic as ever, the trial had rekindled a spark of idealism. Maybe there was some hope for the future, something worth living for, after all.

❄❄❄❄

As the years passed, Darrow's grand pronouncements and noble deeds washed over wounds that he had inflicted on himself and on others. Many friends on the left were outraged when he promoted America's involvement in World War I. While Eugene Debs and others went to jail in defense of the pacifist principles that Darrow had long espoused, Darrow traveled around the country championing America's military commitment. "When Germany invaded Belgium," he explained, "I recovered from my pacifism in the twinkling of an eye."

His friends on the left were furious. "Too bad, too bad that old General Otis is dead not to sit on the platform with Darrow!" Mary Field wrote in anger. Yet Darrow always managed to win his friends back to him. When the war ended, he told Mary that "all through the war he felt most keenly our intellectual separation." He told her that whenever he lectured on the war he would pretend that she was in the audience, hoping to make her understand how they could differ on an issue so profound. She was now living in Chicago, too, married to Lemuel Parton, a thoughtful reporter for the Associated Press. As the years passed, she coauthored Mother Jones's autobiography—Darrow wrote the introduction—and had a child, Margaret Parton, who became a journalist herself. Eventually Mary forgave Darrow—for what he had done to her and for where he had stood on the war.

Slowly, he won back Debs's affection, too, after visiting his old friend at the federal penitentiary in Atlanta and offering to help free the men who had been incarcerated by the government in its foolish wartime zeal. Somehow Darrow had that effect on his followers. They wanted to forgive him and to love him. It was a phenomenon that fascinated and appalled Darrow's dear friend Charles Edward Russell, the journalist and Socialist leader who had joined Darrow in supporting the war. "As soon as the war was over, Parlor Pinkdom pardoned all of [Darrow's] offense but declined the least amnesty for mine, which only (and humbly) duplicated his," Russell wrote in his memoirs.

In the 1920s, as America lost its innocence, Darrow's philosophy found an even larger audience. No longer known for his work on behalf of organized labor, he became a powerful critic of the death penalty, organized religion, and racial discrimination. During an era of belief, his views had seemed out of sync. Writing in 1911, Hamlin Garland had called Darrow "bitter, bitter and essentially hopeless," noting that his philosophy was "essentially destructive." But in the aftermath of World War I, in the age of Palmer raids and speakeasies and H. L. Mencken, his voice found new acceptance. When he humiliated William Jennings Bryan, his old hero, in the Scopes "monkey trial," attacking fundamentalism as a "fool religion," the story dominated the national news and won the support of Eastern sophisticates. Few of them stopped to think about the rights and feelings of the believers whom Darrow chose to ridicule. Later he attacked the death penalty on behalf of Leopold and Loeb, the schoolboys who had elaborately murdered one of their schoolmates in an effort to commit the perfect crime. Darrow's spellbinding plea for human tolerance in that case overcame those people who (somewhat unfairly) charged that Darrow had made a pact with the devil in order to receive a massive fee.

There was something else, too. Darrow had changed; he was fundamentally chastened by his experience in Los Angeles. As Steffens observed, "the cynic is humbled, the man that laughed sees and is frightened, not at prison bars, but at his own soul." Where he had once had the capacity to feel the suffering of others, now he had experienced it, profoundly, for himself. And his freedom had been secured through the kindness and understanding of a few good men who had held his fate in their hands. After that, he was less self-centered, less arrogant, less rapacious—and, at the same time, just a smidgen more optimistic about the human race.

In his most introspective moments, Darrow recognized the change. "What we are is the result of all the past which molds and modifies the being," he wrote in his autobiography. "I know that the sad, hard experience made me kindlier and more understanding and less critical of all who live. I am sure that it gave me a point of view that nothing else could bring."

※ ※ ※ ※

Darrow died on March 13, 1938. He was eighty years old. For two days, mourners filed past his casket at the funeral parlor on Sixty-third Street in South Chicago. His funeral was held at the Bond Chapel at the University of Chicago. As an overflow crowd of admirers stood outside in a torrential rainstorm, listening to the service, one of Darrow's former law partners, Judge William Holly, delivered the main address.

"Clarence Darrow was always and at all times a lover of his fellow man," Judge Holly said. "Those who reviled him have tried to teach the world that he was bitter and relentless, that he hated more than he loved. We who know the man, we who had clasped his hand and heard his voice and looked into his smiling face; we who knew his life of kindness, of charity, of infinite pity to the outcast and the weak; we who knew his human heart, could never be deceived.

"A truer, greater, kindlier soul has never lived and died; and the fierce bitterness and hatred that sought to destroy this great, grand soul had but one cause—the fact that he really loved his fellow man."

Darrow could not have delivered a more moving oration himself. And, in fact, the words were his. They were from the text of his address at the funeral of his great friend and mentor, John Peter Altgeld, the man he had called "the most devoted leader, the most abject slave, the fondest, wildest, dreamiest victim that ever gave his life to liberty's immortal cause." In a tribute to Darrow's eloquence as well as his compassion, Judge Holly explained, he had simply changed the names.

And everyone in the crowd seemed to agree that Darrow—some twenty-five years after his second trial in Los Angeles—was worthy of that lavish and inspiring tribute.

NOTES

ABBREVIATIONS

AFLP	AFL Papers
Autobiog.aphy	*The Story of My Life*
BWP	Brand Whitlock Papers
CDP	Clarence Darrow Papers, Library of Congress
CESWP-B	Charles Erskine Scott Wood Papers, Bancroft Library (University of California, Berkeley)
CESWP-H	Charles Erskine Scott Wood Papers, Huntington Library
EWSP	E. W. Scripps Papers
Farmington	Book by Clarence Darrow
FMP	Frank Morrison Papers
ISP	Irving Stone Papers
LSL	*Letters of Lincoln Steffens*
LSP	Lincoln Steffens Papers
McNP	McNamara Papers
MPP	Mary Field Parton Papers
Testimony	Testimony in *The People* v. *Clarence Darrow*
WDP	Walter Drew Papers

Except where there are two or more works by the same author, books are given by the name of the author. For their titles, see the bibliography.

PROLOGUE

p. 3 Opening scene: The opening scene in the prologue is drawn from Margaret Parton's draft biography of her mother, Mary Field Parton, pages 80–81. MPP.

pp. 3–4 She knew only what she read: "I never appeared in any private sessions in our home, excepting when C.D. sometimes summoned me to serve drinks, and perhaps cheese and crackers. I respected his right to manage his life, his affairs, even his enjoyment without having to include me in everything. We both realized that even married people need some degree of freedom from the other half." Ruby to Irving Stone. ISP. (Reading this passage in an early draft of *Clarence Darrow for the Defense,* Stone's editor wrote "Ouch!" in the margin. Stone omitted it from the final manuscript.)

p. 4 "hot water bag": Erskine Wood to Sara Ehrgott, October 16, 1911. CESWP-H.

p. 6 Irving Stone's agreement with Ruby Darrow: Ruby Darrow's letters to Irving Stone. CDP.

p. 6 "Aren't we a pair": Ruby to Stone, undated. CDP.

p. 6 "a clever and talented woman": Stone, p. 365.

pp. 6–7 Darrow quipped: *Organized Labor,* September 14, 1912.

p. 7 Judges regularly invalidated: See *Final Report of the Commission on Industrial Relations,* vol. 1, Government Printing Office, 1916.

p. 7 Roosevelt quote: *Theodore Roosevelt: An Autobiography,* p. 478.

p. 7 "awful compulsion of the age": Brand Whitlock, August 1898, *Letters and Journals of Brand Whitlock,* p. 18.

p. 7 "moral cynic": Hapgood column, August 29, 1912. Beinecke Library, Yale University.

p. 7 Old friends commented: *Hamlin Garland's Diaries,* March 19, 1911.

PART I: THE EDUCATION OF CLARENCE DARROW

The best sources for Darrow's early years are his autobiography, *The Story of My Life,* which he wrote in 1932, and *Farmington,* the autobiographical novel that he wrote thirty years earlier. He also sent an exceptionally revealing letter to Ellen Gates Starr in about 1897. Although I often differ from their conclusions, I am indebted to the insights and information offered by Darrow's many excellent biographers, notably Irving Stone in *Clarence Darrow for the Defense,* Kevin Tierney in *Darrow: A Biography,* Abe Ravitz in *Clarence Darrow and the American Literary Tradition,* and Arthur and Lila Weinberg in *Clarence Darrow: A Sentimental Rebel.* The Weinbergs also collected many of Darrow's writings in *Verdicts Out of Court,* and Arthur Weinberg assembled Darrow's greatest courtroom speeches in *Attorney for the Damned.* Ray Ginger's "Clarence Seward Darrow, 1857–1938," published in *The Antioch Review,* is a little gem.

There are countless revealing, if often critical appraisals of Darrow in the private correspondence of men and women such as Eugene Debs, Mary Field, Sara Bard Field, Samuel Gompers, Edgar Lee Masters, E. W. Scripps, Lincoln Steffens, Brand Whitlock, and Charles Erskine Scott Wood as well as in the published works of reformers and radicals such as Max Eastman, Hamlin Garland, Emma Goldman, Hutchins Hapgood, Frederick Howe, Moses Koenigsberg, and Steffens. There are also a number of extremely useful contemporaneous articles and news stories.

Darrow's profound relationship with John Peter Altgeld is described in his own writings as well as in Harry Barnard's *Eagle Forgotten, Altgeld's America* by Ray Ginger, and Altgeld's own writings, many of which are collected in Henry Christman's *The Mind and Spirit of John Peter Altgeld.* There are a number of excellent descriptions of Chicago in the late nineteenth century, including the writings of Theodore Dreiser, James Gilbert's *Perfect Cities* and *Chicago: The History of Its Reputation, Part One* by Lloyd Lewis. The classic study of the Haymarket Affair is Henry David's *The History of the Haymarket Affair.* There are countless descriptions of the battles between capital and labor; I particularly like Philip Foner's *History of the Labor Movement in the United States* and Page Smith's discussion in *The Rise of Industrial America.* The best existing account of the Haywood-Moyer-Pettibone trial is David Grover's *Debaters and Dynamiters,* though the forthcoming book by Anthony Lukas should be extremely revealing.

The relationship between Darrow and Mary Field is drawn primarily from Darrow's letters to Mary, Mary's letters to her sister, Sara, the correspondence between Sara and Erskine Wood, and Mary's taped interviews with her daughter, Margaret Parton.

CHAPTER ONE

p. 11 Darrow's feelings about his name: Autobiography, p. 11.

p. 11 "expurgated story of a life": *Farmington,* p. 11.

p. 11 "neither fact nor fiction": Preface to 1932 edition of *Farmington.*

p. 11 virtually all . . . details and observations are accurate: In *The Story of My Life,* written thirty years after *Farmington,* he noted that "autobiography is never entirely true. . . . Every fact is colored by imagination and dream." Autobiography, p. 6.

p. 12 "feeling of closeness": *Farmington,* p. 33–34.

p. 12 "went to bed to toss and turn": Ibid, p. 177.

p. 12 Not allowed to believe in Santa Claus: Ibid, p. 182.

p. 12 "not a single word": Ibid, p. 78.

p. 12 "could never write a book": Ibid, p. 15

p. 12 "very cruel father": Ibid, p. 41.

p. 12 No "great affection": Ibid, p. 34.

p. 13 "endless regret": Ibid, p. 35.

p. 13 Looked for "companionship . . . somewhere else": *Ibid,* p. 36.

p. 14 Father's influence: Quoted in Weinberg, *Sentimental Rebel,* p. 19.

p. 14 Education of Amirus Darrow: Much of the material is from Tierney, p. 5–6.

p. 14 "out on the open sea": Autobiography, p. 11.

p. 15 "stubborn little town": *Farmington,* p. 246–47.

p. 15 "the village infidel": Autobiography, p. 14.
   "strangers in a": Ibid, p. 15.

p. 15 "Frederick Douglass . . . and the rest": *Farmington,* p. 247.

p. 15 "I could never be thankful enough": Ibid, p. 29.

p. 16 "My sympathies always went out": Autobiography, p. 32.

p. 17 On Darrow's law school experience: Tierney, p. 14.

p. 17 Story about Darrow's reasons for moving to Chicago: Autobiography, p. 39.

p. 19 "a constant war of races": Boyer and Morais, p. 66, quoting from *John Swinton's Paper,* December 30, 1883.

p. 19 "I can hire one half the working class": Boyer and Morais, p. 65.

p. 20 "horse trades" . . . "to the factory": Autobiography, p. 34.

p. 21 "I lived in a small town": Darrow to "My Dear Miss S." CDP. Probably written in 1897. Miss S. was Ellen Gates Starr, cofounder of Hull House.

p. 22 *Chicago Mail* article: Quoted in David, p. 185.

pp. 22–23 Neebe's speech: Boyer and Morais, pp. 98–99.

p. 23 Spies' speech: Quoted in Foner, *May Day,* p. 35.

p. 23 Page Smith quote: Smith, p. 255.

p. 24 Analysis of strikes in 1886: David, p. 92.

p. 24 "spread the idea": David p. 65

p. 24 Statistics: David, p. 112

pp. 24–25 Dreiser's description: Dreiser, *Dawn,* pp. 159–60; 297–98.

p. 25 "Chicago had that wonderful power": From a Darrow short story manuscript, quoted in Stone, p. 25.

p. 25 On Darrow's earnings: Autobiography, p. 42.

p. 26 Darrow's pronunciation of Ashtabula: Margaret Parton interview with Mary Field. MPP.

p. 26 "I was in gloom": Autobiography, p. 45.

p. 26 "name all over the front page": Autobiography, p. 47.

pp. 26–27 Actual newspaper coverage of the speech: Chicago newspapers on February 21, 1889.

p. 27 "rather dull": Hunsberger, p. 7.

p. 27 "This book": Autobiography, p. 41.

p. 27 Visit to Altgeld: Autobiography, p. 96.

pp. 27–28 Description of Altgeld: Whitlock, *Forty Years of It,* p. 65.

p. 28 Role of Sunset Club in Darrow's intellectual development: Tierney, p. 48.

p. 28 "What ought to be done now": Barnard, p. 121.

p. 29 "swift, noiseless weapon": Barnard, pp. 135–43.

p. 29 Offer to Darrow: Barnard, p. 145.

p. 29 "He would do whatever would serve his purpose": Interview in Illinois Historical Survey, November 9–10, 1918. Italics in original.

p. 30 The surviving Haymarket anarchists: The fourth man had committed suicide, or possibly been killed, in prison.

p. 30 Darrow's March 1893 visit to Altgeld: Interview with Darrow, Illinois Historical Survey, November 9–10, 1918.

p. 30 "Don't deceive yourself": Autobiography, p. 101.

p. 31 "The great building": Autobiography, p. 103.

p. 32 "tired, with the expression": Whitlock, *Forty Years of It,* p. 84.

p. 33 "We are born in a Pullman house": Quoted in Ginger, *The Bending Cross,* p. 110.

p. 34 Relying, in part, on the Sherman Anti-Trust Law: Darrow was outraged by the use of the law against unions. Its "clear purpose," he said, was "to apply to combinations in the shape of trusts and pools . . . In no place is there any mention of any labor organization or strike or boycott." In upholding Debs's conviction, the Court of Appeals relied heavily on the antitrust law, but the Supreme Court affirmed the decision on other grounds. *United States* v. *Debs,* 64 F. 724 (1894); *In Re Debs,* 158 U.S. 565 (1895).

p. 35 "If the government does not": Quoted in Stone, p. 58.

p. 35 "It is not strange": Quoted in Stone, p. 63.

p. 36 "A storm has been gathering": From an address on "The Rights and Wrongs of Ireland," delivered in Chicago in November, 1895. Reprinted in Darrow, *Verdicts Out of Court.*

p. 37 "In the last days of the campaign": Autobiography, p. 92.

p. 37 "would connive": Barnard, p. 385.

p. 37 The final humiliation: Christman, p. 175.

CHAPTER TWO

p. 39 "household God": Quoted in Weinberg, *Sentimental Rebel,* p. 73.

p. 40 "exclusively to the law": Letter to Miss S. CDP.

p. 40 "so many of my good friends": Ibid.

p. 42 Darrow's speech in Kidd case: Reprinted in Weinberg, *Attorney for the Damned.*

pp. 44–45 Darrow's speech to the arbitration commission: Ibid.

p. 45 "brilliant": *Philadelphia North American,* quoted in Weinberg, *Attorney for the Damned.*

p. 45 Gompers quote: Tierney, p. 191.

p. 45 "young lawyers": Autobiography, p. 105.

p. 46 "sat in his office": Autobiography, p. 108.

p. 46 "had never been a good lawyer": Darrow's interview in *Illinois Historical Survey.*

p. 46 "I have gone to work": Letter to Henry Demarast Lloyd, quoted in Barnard, p. 426. Question mark in original.

p. 48 On Leckie's work for Hearst's *Chicago American*: Goldman, p. 302.

p. 48 Irving Stone's description of Leckie: Stone, p. 83.

p. 48 their affair flew apart: In the notes for his book, Stone reports that Darrow almost married Leckie in 1904 but didn't because of her jealousies. It can't have been 1904, since he married Ruby in 1903. Stone called Leckie *X* in his biography and omitted the facts about their wedding plan. ISP.

p. 49 "Clarence Darrow, on this day of carnage and devastation": Ginger, *Altgeld's America,* pp. 231–33.

p. 49 his partner, Edgar Lee Masters: As the years passed, Masters grew to hate Darrow and later wanted to destroy his ex-partner's reputation. But while the men were still at least ostensibly friendly, Masters wrote a poem in which he offered his own form of speculation about what had happened to Darrow:

> He lived on his own thought
> As starving men may live on stored fat
> And so in time he starved
> So by analysis he turned on everything he once believed.

Masters, *The Excluded Middle.* For a more extended discussion of the Darrow-Masters relationship, see notes for page 366.

p. 49 dirty fingernails: Gertrude Barnum to Stone. ISP.

p. 49 manicure and pedicure: Ruby Darrow to Stone. CDP.

p. 50 Iroquois Theater fire: In a spirit of full disclosure, it should be noted that two of the author's mother's cousins, Helen and Hazel Regensburg, who were young children, were killed in the blaze. For a list of the victims, see Marshall Everett, *The Great Chicago Theater Disaster.* Chicago: Publishers Union of America, 1904.

pp. 50–51 "It is not just": Lewis, p. 283.

p. 51 "nature and effect": Tierney, p. 187.

p. 51 "defending men": Ginger, p. 269.

p. 52 hired Cyrus Simon: Ginger, pp. 262–63.

p. 52 of the courts: *The Mirror,* June, 1912.

p. 52 of reformers: Autobiography, p. 112.

p. 52 of socialism: Autobiography, p. 53.

p. 52 of anarchism: Autobiography, p. 53.

p. 52 "in harmony with": Darrow, "Why Men Fight for the Closed Shop," *American Magazine,* September 1911, pp. 545–56.

p. 52 "were not advisable": Quoted in *Kankakee Journal,* April 26, 1911.

p. 52 Darrow had no confidence: Darrow, "The Late Election," *The Mirror,* November, 1910.

p. 53 Garland's journal entry: Garland, *Companions on the Trail,* pp. 321–23.

p. 53 "Darrow has no principles whatever": Austin Willard Wright to Wood, January 12, 1904. CESWP-B.

p. 54 Howe's memories of Darrow: Howe, pp. 190–92.

p. 54 Interview with Steffens: *The Autobiography of Lincoln Steffens,* p. 424.

p. 55 forty-two men were killed: Stone, pp. 186–87.

p. 55 As the battle intensified: Grover, pp. 52–53.

p. 55 Steunenberg. Although no longer in the spotlight, Governor Steunenberg had earned the miners' hatred a few years earlier when, after winning office with labor's support, he called upon federal troops to end the miners' general strike against mine operators in the Coeur d'Alene mining district. The troops made wholesale arrests of mine workers, holding them in insufferable conditions in bullpens built for the occasion, and Steunenberg established a "permit system" that required laborers to use permits issued by military authorities. After that, Steunenberg's life was repeatedly threatened, and he was denounced by every labor organization in the West.

p. 55 McParland's tactics: McParland's reports to Idaho governor Gooding can be found in the Hawley and Borah Manuscript Collections, Idaho Historical Society. They were first reprinted in Philip Foner's *History of the Labor Movement in the United States, Volume IV.*

p. 56 Labor leaders' arrests: Grover, pp. 65–68.

p. 57 At dinner with Darrow: Garland, *Companions on the Trail,* pp. 322–23.

p. 57 Darrow's tactics: Haywood, p. 213.

pp. 58–59 The Haywood Trial: There are many useful accounts of this trial including: *Debaters and Dynamiters,* by David H. Grover; *The Rocky Mountain Revolution,* by Stewart H. Holbrook; *Prisoners at the Bar,* by Francis X. Bush; Stone's *Darrow for the Defense;* and Darrow's *Story of My Life.* Also see *Current Literature* articles from the period.

pp. 59–60 Darrow's speech to the jury in the Haywood case: Darrow, *Verdicts Out of Court;* Grover, p. 218.

p. 60 Richardson's comments: Tierney; Grover, p. 271, quoting from the *Capital News,* August 6, 1907.

p. 60 "Haywood was not shown": Stone, p. 241

p. 61 "I think we should take and enjoy the good": Catlin to Wood, August 5, 1907. CESWP-H.

p. 61 Rumors of jury bribery: Stone, p. 241.

p. 61 "The newspaper grape vine": Masters to Harrison, March 21, 1938. Harrison Papers, Newberry Library.

p. 62 Problems with mastoiditis: Autobiography, pp. 157–71.

p. 62 "Do you realize": Stone, p. 247.

pp. 62–63 "as though life were a mere mechanical going on": *Hamlin Garland's Diaries,* entry dated March 19, 1911.

p. 63 Description of Mary: Author's interview with her niece, Katherine Caldwell.

pp. 63–64 "those who have loved": Mary to Sara, August 1910. CESWP-H.

p. 64 "Mary could say the funniest things": Johannsen statement, Darrow Papers, University of Chicago.

p. 64 She tried to tease him: For many years Darrow maintained that only Mary Field could write the biography he would want. He was still thinking of it in 1918, after she was married and had had a baby. "I keep thinking of that biography which I would only want you to write," he said. "No one else would magnify the good and forget the bad as you my dear friend." Darrow to Mary Field Parton, Darrow Papers, Newberry Library. A few years later, Mary Field Parton was the editor-author of the *Autobiography of Mother Jones,* for which Darrow wrote the introduction.

p. 64 Scenes with Mary and Darrow in Chicago: Mary's taped interviews with her daughter, Margaret Parton. MPP.

**p. 65 *The Delineator:* ** *Reader's Encyclopedia of American Literature,* p. 248.

p. 65 "That piece of yours": Phillips to Mary Field. MPP.

p. 66 On Davidson's relationship with Mary: Davidson, p. 76.

p. 66 "You have gone so far": Darrow to Mary Field, Darrow Papers, Newberry Library.

p. 66 Darrow's plans to move to New York: Darrow to Mary Field, Darrow Papers, Newberry Library. Darrow also told other friends of his intention to leave Chicago and to move to New York. In a July 14, 1910, letter to Brand Whitlock, he wrote: "I am strongly thinking of leaving here [Chicago] before long and probably going to New York. Would have done it long before if I had not lost all my money a few years ago and did not care to risk it, but I can do it very soon." BWP.

p. 66 "I miss you all the time": Darrow to Mary Field, March 15, 1910, Darrow Papers, Newberry Library.

PART II: THE MCNAMARA CASE

For more than a year—from the night of the *Times* bombing until the dramatic end of the McNamara case—the story made great copy in newspapers and magazines around the country. The contemporary publications listed in the bibliography were of great assistance in reconstructing the night of the bombing, the capture of J. J. McNamara, Darrow's actions in Chicago, San Francisco and Los Angeles, the jury selection process, the negotiations over the plea bargain, and the reactions to the guilty pleas. Letters, diaries, memoirs, and court records offered more intimate details about the private motives and machinations of the participants.

The most remarkable insights about Darrow come from the correspondence contained in two collections of the papers of Charles Erskine Scott Wood and Sara Bard Field (who was Sara Field Ehrgott at the time of the trial). One collection is at the Huntington Library and the other is at the Bancroft Library at the University of California. But there were scores of other exceptionally useful sources, including the papers of those on the McNamara's side—including Mary Field, the McNamara family, E. W. Scripps, Lincoln Steffens, and various labor leaders—and those on the side of the prosecution, including Walter Drew and the Justice Department files at the National Archive. There are also several wonderful memoirs—some unpublished, including autobiographies of Jim McNamara and Robert Foster and oral histories of Sara Bard Field and Helen Valeska Bary—and some published, including those of William J. Burns, Ortie McManigal, Lincoln Steffens, and of course, Clarence Darrow.

Many details of the bombing scheme were spelled out in court proceedings—in the cases against Caplan and Schmidt, who were prosecuted a few years later, and in *U.S.* v. *Ryan,* the national dynamite conspiracy case against the leadership of the Bridge and Structural Iron Workers' union. The tactics used by the prosecution and defense were presented in riveting detail in the case of *The People* v. *Clarence Darrow,* and the background of the bombing was explored in the extensive hearings and reports of the Commission on Industrial Relations.

In addition to primary sources, the McNamara case has been of intense interest to both popular and professional historians, ranging from those interested in labor issues, like Louis Adamic, Graham Adams, Philip S. Foner, and Grace Stimson, to those interested in socialism, the *Los Angeles Times,* Los Angeles history, and California history. It has also been treated in biographies of such participants as Darrow and Steffens. The episode fascinated at least two great novelists, Theodore Dreiser and Sinclair Lewis. Each planned to make it the basis of a major work. Apparently neither of them ultimately followed through on the project, though there is a draft manuscript that may be a fragment of Lewis's projected labor novel.

CHAPTER THREE

p. 71 The description of the Meyerhoff case: *Kankakee Daily Republican,* May 2–19, 1911.

p. 72 "the bloodiest arena": Mayo, p. 139.

p. 73 Background on Otis: Gottlieb and Wolt were a very useful source as were files obtained from the history section of the *Los Angeles Times.*

p. 73 "Go ahead": Palmer, "Otistown of the Open Shop."

p. 73 ITU buttons: Stimson, p. 250.

p. 74 Stories about Bishop's Pills: Mayo, p. 147.

p. 74 *Times* Circulation for 1912: Meyer Lissner Papers, Stanford University, notes from the collection catalogue.

p. 74 *Times* profits: Otis, "Milestones," *Times* collection.

p. 74 Pope story: Pope memoirs, UCLA.

p. 74 "a tyranny": Quoted in Gottlieb and Wolt, p. 44.

p. 75 *Bulletin* quote: Mayo, p. 148.

p. 75 Otistown: Palmer, "Otistown of the Open Shop."

p. 75 "the most unfair": Foner, vol. 5, p. 9.

p. 75 "not a hammer": David Warren Ryder in the *American Mercury,* quoted in Mayo, p. 150.

p. 76 San Francisco became the first and only closed-shop city: See Foner, vol. 3, pp. 287–96.

p. 76 "The contracts": Stimson, pp. 334–35.

p. 76 "The ultimatum": Stimson, pp. 334–35.

p. 76 full-scale attempt: Stimson, p. 340.

p. 76 Letter in trash basket: Stimson, p. 340.

p. 77 Clancy letters: *People* v. *David Caplan,* Brief of Facts, at Los Angeles County Law Library.

p. 78 The violence worked: Luke Grant, *Report of the US Commission on Industrial Relations,* (1915).

p. 79 Jim McNamara's background and early life as a dynamiter: Jim McNamara's unpublished biography, Robert Cantwell papers at the University of Oregon.

p. 80 Sunset National Oil Company: See the 1911 bankruptcy records of the Sunset National Oil Company. Record Group: 21; Subgroup: U.S. Dist. Ct. Bkcy, No. Dist. Cal; Series: Bankruptcies Case Files, 1867–1945; Box 151; Case 6850; FRC location number: between 1,1257,689—1,258,557; Association number: 61-AG650.

p. 80 "a man of power": This quote, along with some of the facts, comes from Helen Valeska Bary's oral history. Other facts are from "O. A. Tvietmoe:

Labor Leader" by Lloyd Hustvedt, published in *Norwegian-American Studies,* vol. 30, 1985.

p. 81 "the powerful body": Hapgood, *The Spirit of Labor,* pp. 16–17, p. 25.

p. 81 "He laughed like the Olympians": Hapgood, *Victorian in the Modern World,* pp. 188–89.

p. 82 Antipicketing ordinance: Graham Adams, Jr., p. 5.

p. 82 Clancy telegram: evidence in Caplan case.

p. 82 Description of Schmidt: McManigal, p. 75.

p. 82 McNamara and Schmidt in San Francisco: evidence in Caplan case.

p. 83 Dynamitings in Oakland and Seattle: list of dynamite jobs in Ryan evidence; letters in Ryan evidence; Burns, *Masked War,* p. 39, McManigal, p. 75.

p. 83 "the scabbiest town": letter to *Bridgeman's Magazine,* September 1911.

p. 84 Clancy speech: *Bridgeman's Magazine,* October 1910.

p. 86 Libel case against Otis and Chandler: *Los Angeles Times,* May 23, 1911; *San Francisco Call,* September 4, 1910.

p. 87 Jim McNamara's setting of the bombs: His confession. An original copy is in the files of LeCompte Davis at UCLA.

p. 87 McNamara's actions later that night: summary of evidence of witnesses in the Caplan case; McManigal.

p. 87 Tony's Spanish Kitchen: Carr, p. 102.

p. 88 "Their half-ashamed pleasure": *Los Angeles Times,* October 2, 1910.

p. 89 Description of destruction of *Times* building, Cy Sawyer, deaths of Elder and the engravers, etc: Reports in *Los Angeles Times* and *The New York Times;* letter to the *Los Angeles Times* from Ernest Rhoads, ex-battalion chief, LAFD, July 8, 1957, *Times* Archives. *Destruction of the* Times *Building,* Special Report, *Times* Archives.

p. 89 Eddie King story: James Pope to Schippers, June 29, 1964. Pope Papers, UCLA.

p. 90 Chandler and surviving employees: *Among Ourselves* (*Times* in-house publication), December 1931.

p. 91 Jim McNamara's return to San Francisco: evidence in Caplan case.

p. 91 "Everything is OK": evidence in Ryan case.

p. 92 Eckhoff story: Eckhoff in Ryan evidence.

p. 93 Jim McNamara's trip to Wisconsin: McManigal's accounts in his autobiography and legal testimony.

p. 94 Bombing of Llewellyn Iron Works in December 1910 and bombings in March 1911: evidence in Ryan case.

CHAPTER FOUR

p. 95 Hearst cartoonists' treatment of Burns: Hichborn, p. 252.

p. 95 "William Burns is without doubt": *Indianapolis News,* April 23, 1911.

p. 96 Burns and Oregon land fraud: William Boly, "How They Stole the Oregon Land," in McCormack and Pintarich.

p. 97 Calhoun almost elected senator: *The Graphic,* December 2, 1911.

p. 97 "I believe him guilty": Quoted in Mowry, *The California Progressives,* p. 34.

p. 97 Description of Heney: *Autobiography of Lincoln Steffens,* pp. 545–56.

pp. 97–98 Kidnapping of Fremont Older: Wells, pp. 190–95.

p. 98 San Francisco graft trials: For Steffens's account of these events see his autobiography. See also Mowry, Cleland, and Hitchborn. For a somewhat different view, see St. Johns's *Final Verdict.*

p. 98 For more on the *Times*'s role in the San Francisco graft cases: Gottlieb and Wolt pp. 70–71.

p. 98 Mayor George B. Alexander: Gottlieb and Wolt, p. 75.

p. 99 Burns had reasons for suspecting the Iron Workers: His suspicions were confirmed when he managed to find a secret source on the inside of the union. His informer was union executive Herbert Hockin.

p. 99 Burns-Alexander meeting: Burns, "My Greatest Cases—No. 10."

p. 100 The California State Federation of Labor panel's report: Quotes are from *Report on the Los Angeles Times Disaster* by the Committee of the California State Federation of Labor, reprinted in *The Pattern Makers' Journal,* January 1911.

p. 100 Bombs at homes of Otis and Zeehandelaar: The fifteen sticks of dynamite planted at Zeehandelaar's home failed to ignite because the clock was wound too tight. The bomb planted at Otis's home was in a suitcase that a caretaker discovered. He called the police, who barely escaped injury when the bomb exploded a few minutes after they arrived.

p. 100 Debs's statements: Ford, *The Darrow Bribery Trial.*

p. 101 Alexander . . . stopped paying: Burns, "My Greatest Cases—No. 10."

pp. 101–102 Scene at union headquarters: This description comes from several sources, including the *Indianapolis News* and *Indianapolis Star* for April 23–24, 1911; *The Masked War* by Burns; and Burns's "My Greatest Cases—No. 10."

p. 102 Scene with Judge Collins: *Indianapolis Star,* April 23, 1911, p. 1.

p. 104 Description of Walter Drew: Field, *Organized Labor,* November 2, 1912.

p. 105 Burns opens the safe: *Los Angeles Examiner,* April 24, 1911, p. 2.

p. 106 "an arrangement had been made": President Ryan's report to the union membership on May 2, 1911; *Bridgeman's Magazine,* May 1911.

p. 107 "Being hard pressed": Burns, p. 135.

p. 108 McNamara arrived in Holsington: Los Angeles *Herald,* April 23, 1911.

p. 108 They boarded the *California Limited*: *Los Angeles Times,* April 27, 1911.

p. 108 A brochure boasted: Duke and Ristler, p. 60.

pp. 110–11 Description of J.J.: John Gray in the *Los Angeles Examiner,* April 26, 1911, p. 1.

p. 111 J.J.'s reaction: *The New York Times,* April 27, 1911.

p. 113 Mrs. Ingersoll's report: *The New York Times,* April 24, 1911.

p. 113 Ride to Hotel Chapman: *Los Angeles Examiner,* April 26, 1911.

p. 114 Reporter John Gray's description: *Los Angeles Examiner,* April 27, p. 1.

p. 114 J.J.'s reaction on seeing his brother: *The New York Times,* April 27, 1911.

CHAPTER FIVE

p. 115 "the capitalistic interests": *Indianapolis News,* April 24, 1911.

p. 115 "when we recall": *Indiana Labor Bulletin,* April 28, 1911.

p. 116–117 Similarities to Haywood case: When the McNamaras were arrested, many felt that this was simply a replay of an outrage that they had already witnessed. The president of the Indiana Federation of Labor, for example, immediately announced that "the capitalistic interests are behind this, just as they were behind the fight on Haywood, Moyer, and Pettibone." A group of labor leaders issued a statement noting that "when we recall that the detectives were as cocksure of the conviction of Haywood, Moyer, and Pettibone as Burns now is of convicting the three men he has arrested, we have a right to doubt their guilt."

Analogies between the cases were obvious at once. Both began with "kidnappings" of union officials, arrested by private detectives, transported from one state to another by train. Both hinged on the confessions of an accomplice whose testimony seemed highly suspect. Indeed, the labor press began to refer to McManigal as "Harry Orchard." Haywood quickly wrote an article for the *International Socialist Review* underlining the similarities between the cases.

The parallels were so strong that Frank Wolfe, a leading Los Angeles journalist and socialist leader, published a pamphlet entitled *Capitalism's Conspiracy in California: Parallel of the Kidnapping of Labor Leaders in Colorado and California.*

p. 117 *Charles Meyerhoff* v. *The Kankakee Manufacturing Company*: The judge ultimately ruled for Meyerhoff, after telling Darrow and his clients that "the defendants would have done well to have paid a little attention to the Golden Rule." *Kankakee Daily Republican,* May 20, 1911.

p. 118 Darrow in Indianapolis: AFLP.

p. 119 "Little children with old-young faces": Gompers, vol. 1, p. 188.

p. 120 "They preferred to see evils continue": Ibid, p. 191.

p. 120 "I want to tell you Socialists": Livesay, p. 71.

p. 120 Gompers's own legal problems: When he learned of J. J. McNamara's arrest, Gompers himself, as it happened, was facing a possible—and highly celebrated—criminal conviction. The case had its origin in the battle between the Buck's Stove & Range Company of St. Louis and the Metal Polishers' union. In 1907, after Buck's Stove & Range fired its union employees in the course of a labor dispute, the AFL placed the company's name on the "We Don't Patronize" list published each month in the *American Federationist.* That provided a unique opportunity for James W. Van Cleave, who, in addition to serving as president of Buck's Stove & Range, was also president of the National Association of Manufacturers and a leading member of the Anti-Boycott Association. At Van Cleave's request, a court issued an injunction against any action by the AFL or its employees designed to further the boycott or damage the company's business.

After consulting Alton B. Parker, former chief justice of the New York State Court of Appeals and one-time Democratic Party presidential nominee, Gompers decided to remove the company's name from the "We Don't Patronize" list, but to continue to discuss the boycott in AFL speeches and editorials. On December 23, 1908, Judge Daniel T. Wright found Gompers, along with union leaders John Mitchell and Frank Morrison, guilty of contempt of court for refusing to abide by the earlier injunction. He sentenced Gompers to twelve months in jail. Gompers appealed, and he was expecting the U.S. Supreme Court to hand down its decision on Monday, April 24, 1911.

The court issued its decision on May 15, 1911, sending the case back to Judge Wright's court for a further hearing.

During the next two years, the Buck's Stove & Range case continued to intersect with the McNamara case and, later, Darrow's own trial. On June 24, 1912, after a twenty-five day hearing, Judge Wright reaffirmed his original prison sentence, and Gompers once again appealed. Meanwhile, new leadership emerged at Buck's Stove & Range that was sympathetic to labor. Van Cleave died and was replaced by Frederick W. Gardner, who desperately wanted the company to earn its way back into Gompers's good graces. Under Gardner's management, the company agreed to end the celebrated dispute, and Gompers agreed to do everything that he could to encourage workers to begin to patronize Buck's Stove & Range once again.

In March 1913, at the conclusion of Clarence Darrow's second trial, Gardner sent him a check for one thousand dollars. In his autobiography, Darrow reported that "the name was totally unknown to me. This came from a total stranger. My eyes filled with tears" (Autobiography, pp. 190–91). If Darrow was, in fact, unfamiliar with the name of the new president of Buck's Stove & Range, who had helped Gompers stay out of jail, it demonstrates just how far he had drifted away from the world of organized labor.

(See Gompers' autobiography; Buck's Stove & Range letters in the San Francisco Labor Council files at the Bancroft Library, University of California at

Berkeley; Pettigrew Papers at the Siouxland Heritage Museum; files of the AFL; American Federation of Labor, *History and Encyclopedia and Reference Book.*)

p. 121 "Feel confident": Gompers to Ryan, AFLP.

p. 121 "There is no other advocate": April 27, 1911, news story in McNamara file clips, McNP.

p. 122 "You will go down in history": Stone, p. 263; oral history of J. P. Frey.

p. 122 Leave the law, to write: One of Darrow's law partners, Francis Wilson, told Irving Stone that Darrow felt "there was always the chance of winning that fifty thousand dollars quickly, in a few months, so that he could retire and write his novel." Stone, pp. 263–64.

p. 122 start some kind of magazine: Darrow told Scripps that he had saved $100,000, which presumably included his $50,000 fee, and that he planned to use it to leave the law and start a magazine. EWSP.

p. 122 Darrow's conditions for taking the case: J. P. Frey, oral history, p. 252.

p. 123 "I would have much preferred": McNamara clips, McNP.

p. 123 He was convinced they would be hanged: After pleading the McNamaras guilty the following December, Darrow told the press, "When I took the case last [May] I could look ahead to this very moment and see just what was before us." Widely published comment, e.g. *Miners Journal,* December 14, 1911.

p. 123 "would not defend the McNamaras": Roy Howard to Porterfield, April 27, 1911. EWSP. Parentheses in original.

p. 123 "I go at it with fear and foreboding": BWP.

p. 124 "The things they said": John Barry to Brand Whitlock, June 3, 1911. BWP.

p. 124 Meetings with labor leaders: Los Angeles *Herald,* May 25, 1911.

p. 124 "I did not want to take this case": *Los Angeles Examiner,* May 25, 1911.

p. 125 "It is a lawyer's business": Los Angeles *Herald,* May 24, 1911.

p. 125 Description of J.J.: Barry to Whitlock. BWP.

p. 125 Twelve straight hours: Los Angeles *Herald,* May 26, 1911.

p. 126 "Li Hung-chang": *San Francisco Examiner,* May 26, 1911. Li Hung-chang was a Chinese statesman under the Manchu dynasty (1644–1912) who for many years was in charge of relations with the West.

p. 126 "I will think about socialism": Los Angeles *Record,* May 25, 1911.

p. 126 The Burr Harris case: Harris was charged and convicted of a second murder some years later. *Los Angeles Times,* October 6, 1913.

p. 126 The most brilliant defense: *Los Angeles Examiner,* May 27, 1911.

p. 126 Extension of time: Los Angeles *Herald,* May 28, 1911.

p. 126 "I always believe": *Los Angeles Examiner,* May 26, 1911.

p. 127 "the public is all we have": Darrow to Gallagher, July 10, 1911. San Francisco Labor Council Papers, Bancroft Library, University of California at Berkeley.

p. 127 "I am very deeply interested": Older to Whitlock, June 2, 1911. BWP.

p. 127 Shoaf's reports from Los Angeles: *Talkin' Socialism,* pp. 206–10, and sources cited.

p. 128 "we are absolutely innocent": Wire in McNamara clips, April 28, 1911. McNP.

p. 128 "I have known John J. . . . personally: Clarence Mullholland to Gompers, McNamara clips, early May 1911. McNP.

p. 128 Comments by Gompers's friends in San Francisco: Gallagher to Gompers, May 9, 1911. AFLP. See also Gompers, vol. 2, pp. 185–88.

p. 128 "We all feel confident": Gompers to J.J., May 8, 1911. AFLP.

p. 128 Messages to AFL Executive Board: AFLP.

p. 128 Messages to Tveitmoe: Gompers to Tvietmoe, May 19, 1911. AFLP.

p. 128 "these men have been arrested": Mayo, pp. 165–66.

p. 129 "The day will come": *Indianapolis News,* May 10, 1911.

p. 129 "Our solicitors": Chandler to Otis, May 30, 1911. Taft Papers.

CHAPTER SIX

p. 132 Darrow had asked Wood to be his cocounsel: Four years later, when Schmidt and Caplan were tried for their role in the *Times* bombing, they tried to get Wood to act as chief counsel in their case. Darrow, among others, asked Wood to accept. Wood ultimately refused, partly because the defendants would not agree to give him full charge of the conduct of the case and he feared that improper tactics would again be used. Correspondence in CESWP-B and CESWP-H.

p. 132 One of the great men of the era: Mary Field to Erskine Wood, January 1913, quoting Darrow. CESWP-H.

p. 132 The relationship between Wood and Corinne Robinson: Bits and pieces of their correspondence can be found in the Oregon Historical Society Library, the Bancroft Library, and at the Houghton Library at Harvard.

p. 132 Darrow and Wood were working together on behalf of a rich bank executive: In 1908 or 1909, Louis J. Wilde left a post at the Oregon Trust and Savings bank to become president of the American National Bank of San Diego, California. When the Oregon bank changed hands and the new bank failed, the new owners brought charges against Wilde. Wilde and his supporters claimed that the new owners were trying to blackmail him.

In the spring of 1910, the banker retained Wood as one of his attorneys, and Wood suggested that they involve Darrow as a cocounsel. When it seemed that an indictment had been avoided, Wilde gave Darrow two checks for five hundred dollars—one as payment to Darrow, one to be forwarded to Wood. Unfortunately, Darrow kept both checks, leading Wilde to tell Wood that "Mr. Darrow was a trifle greedy, and you and I were the victims." (Wilde to Wood, July 29, 1910. CESWP-B.) In response, Wood said that he was sure that there had simply been "a misunderstanding." (Wood to Wilde, August 1, 1910. CESWP-B.)

As it turned out, the case was not dropped. Wilde was indicted on July 3, 1911. Wood and Darrow continued to serve on his legal team throughout the following year. (News clips and correspondence in CESWP-B.)

p. 133 Description of Darrow's first introduction of Erskine Wood and Sara Field Ehrgott: This whole account is from Sara's oral history.

p. 135 Galsworthy's new play, *Justice*: *Encyclopaedia Britannica,* entry on Galsworthy.

p. 136 "It would be fun": Erskine to Sara, October 17, 1911. CESWP-H.

p. 136 "The jurors in Boise": Erskine to Sara, October 16, 1911. CESWP-H.

p. 136 "The more I have thought": Wood to Catlin, July 18, 1911. CESWP-B.

p. 137 Jack Simpson disappeared: According to the Thiele Detective Agency, Darrow met with Simpkins in Spokane, after his disappearance: Grover, p. 69.

p. 137 "one of the most important witnesses": *Los Angeles Examiner,* May 1, 1911.

pp. 138–39 Description of permissive life of Padres and Dons in early Los Angeles: Cohn and Chisholm, pp. 7–10, 186–90.

p. 139 "fandangos and fiestas": Starr, *Inventing the Dream,* p. 18.

pp. 139–40 Story of Juan Bandini and Abel Sterns: Hart, *Companion to California;* Nadeau, *City-Makers.*

p. 140 Trip to Los Angeles before the railroad: Nadeau.

p. 140 Dangerous trip to Los Angeles from St. Louis: Clark, *Los Angeles,* p. 62.

p. 140 "America's one unpronounceable city": Wright, "Los Angeles—The Chemically Pure." In the spring of 1911, one journal noted that Teddy Roosevelt had been criticized "for his barbarous pronunciation of Los Angeles, which he rendered as if spelled 'Loss An-gee-lees.' I winced myself when I heard him, but the colonel is no worse in this respect than hundreds of citizens who have lived here for many years. At a recent banquet, I noted that of ten speakers who referred to their home city, nine grossly and lamentably twisted the beautiful Spanish name out of all semblance to the true rendering." *The Graphic,* April 1, 1911.

p. 141 Number of building permits: Guinn, p. 375.

p. 141 Miles of new dwellings: Woehlke, "Los Angeles—Homeland."

p. 141 Picnic for former Iowans: Steele, "The Little Red Car of Empire."

p. 141 "The Iowa invasion": Carr, p. 125.

p. 142 Conversation with Iowa native at the Mason theater: Steele, "The Little Red Car of Empire."

p. 143 "In the mind of the average Way Down Easterner": Woehlke, "Angels in Overalls."

p. 143 Description of Madam Van: Carr, p. 160.

p. 143 Description of Pearl Morton's: St. Johns, pp. 133 ff.

pp. 143–44 "athletic clubs: Carr, pp. 178–79.

p. 144 Description of Edwin T. Earl: Profile of Earl in Dickson Papers, UCLA; also see St. Johns and Gottlieb and Wolt.

p. 146 "if we follow up": Lissner to LaFollette, November 15, 1909. Lissner Papers, Stanford.

p. 146 Feud between the *Los Angeles Times* and Hiram Johnson: Mowry, *The California Progressives.*

p. 147 1910 census data: Johnson, "Socialism in Los Angeles: The Municipal Election of 1911." Unpublished monograph.

p. 148 Capital-labor war in Los Angeles. "From 1907 to 1910, a state of war existed in Los Angeles, with the community being torn apart by industrial strife." McWilliams, p. 279.

p. 148 "from the workers' standpoint": *The Agitator,* July 1, 1911. Quoted in Johnson.

p. 148 "the progressives' bias": Mowry, *The California Progressives,* p. 92.

p. 148 "Two years ago": *Mother Earth.*

pp. 148–49 "fascinating and handsome": Adamic, *My America,* p. 16.

p. 149 Harriman's investments: Harriman letters to Morris Hillquit, Hillquit Papers, State Historical Society of Wisconsin.

p. 149 "My position is": Harriman to Hillquit, April 5, 1909. Hillquit Papers.

p. 149 "whenever there is a labor movement": Harriman to Hillquit, December 21, 1909. Hillquit Papers.

p. 149 Local leaders remained "bitterly opposed" to Harriman: Harriman to Hillquit, December 21, 1909. Hillquit Papers.

p. 149 Socialists convinced Harriman was "intriguing": Report in Socialist Party of America File, headed "Harriman, Job—and his tactics in California." See also Adamic, *My America,* p. 7ff.

p. 149 "we will have to use war measures": Harriman to Hillquit, July 7, 1910. Hillquit Papers.

pp. 150–51 Meetings between Ortie and Emma McManigal: contemporaneous newspaper accounts.

p. 151 Episode involving the trunk: *Los Angeles Times,* June 27, 1911.

p. 152 Fredericks's education: Author's interview with John Fort, a grandson. November 19, 1987.

p. 152 "One thing his troop was famous for": Carr, "This is another Checkerboard," *Los Angeles Times,* November 1, 1914.

p. 152 "reads like a romance": From *Faithful as a Clock,* a pamphlet printed by the Anti-Saloon League. UCLA Special Collections.

p. 154 "Darrow, my friend": *Los Angeles Times,* June 29, 1911.

p. 154 Darrow and Behm: Testimony, p. 2476.

p. 155 "serious injuries": quoted in *Miners Journal,* August 3, 1911

p. 155 "Everywhere she turned": *The New York Times,* July 22, 1911; *Organized Labor,* July 29, 1911.

p. 155 "public sympathy took such a decided swing": quoted in *Miners Journal,* August 3, 1911

pp. 155–56 Behm's preparation for and testimony at the grand jury: Testimony, pp. 2087–89.

p. 157 "We are having a fierce time": Darrow to Gompers, July 8, 1911. AFLP.

p. 157 "You may count upon": Gompers to Darrow, July 15, 1911. AFLP.

p. 157 "There is no way to try this case": Darrow to Gompers, July 15, 1911. AFLP.

p. 158 Sullivan's colorful past: Morgan Robertson, the short-story writer, incorporated some of Sullivan's exploits in his celebrated sea stories.

p. 158 Sullivan's background: For more on Sullivan, see C. B. Glasscock; *Los Angeles Times,* "Another Earl Crony Sought," March 7, 1914; *Los Angeles Times,* May 22, 1915, "History: Yellow Streak in the North: Was Picturesque Characters in Many Ways"; Los Angeles *Record,* March 29, 1915, "Former 'Pirate' Attacks Chief". There is extensive correspondence with and about Sullivan in CESWP-B and CESWP-H.

pp. 158–59 "I believe those McNamara men are getting jobbed": Moore to Wood, May 10, 1911. CESWP-B.

p. 159 "a certain unscrupulous temperment": Wood to Catlin, July 19, 1911. CESWP-B.

p. 159 Fred H. Moore: Moore later represented the "free speech" forces in San Diego, the "bread and roses" strikers at Lawrence, Mass., and much later, Sacco and Vanzetti. See Lyons, *Assignment in Utopia,* and Russell, *The Unresolved Case of Sacco and Vanzetti.*

p. 159 Moore and LeCompte Davis: Davis, too, had been hired at Wood's suggestion. "Mr. Darrow arrived in the city yesterday morning, and through the assistance of your good word, together with the good word of Mr. Catlin, arrangements were perfected yesterday evening whereby Mr. LeCompte Davis of this firm is taken into the case as associate counsel with Mr. Darrow." Moore to Wood, May 26, 1911. CESWP-H.

p. 159 Moore's visit to Wood, and Wood's reaction: Wood to Catlin, July 19, 1911. CESWP-B. Catlin had been friendly with Darrow for more than twenty years. They had served together on the Steering Committee of the Sunset Club in Chicago in the 1890s (Sunset Club Records, Chicago Historical Society). Nevertheless, it is not clear whether Catlin showed Wood's letter to Darrow.

p. 160 Sullivan's work in San Francisco: Burns, *Masked War;* Harrington statement, February 19, 1912.

p. 161 Attempt to pay Ingersoll: *Los Angeles Examiner,* September 19, 1911; Harrington statement, February 19, 1911.

p. 161–62 Diekelman story: The Diekelman story is all taken from testimony.

pp. 162–63 The Darrow-Biddinger relationship: This account is drawn from testimony, volumes 42, 43, and 73.

p. 164 Darrow note to Older: Darrow to Older, August 17, 1911. Older files, Bancroft Library, University of California at Berkeley.

p. 166 The checks had stopped coming: Correspondence and records in FMP.

p. 166 Darrow's September 1, 1911, letter to Morrison: Morrison to Darrow, September 7, 1911. Morrison to Rappaport, September 7, 1911. FMP.

p. 166 Morrison and Darrow: Darrow had agreed that he would give Morrison an accounting of every dollar spent in excess of his fifty-thousand-dollar fee. He was to use the first fifty thousand dollars as an advance, and then send the AFL an itemized bill for further expenses as they were incurred. But as of September, Morrison had yet to receive a single itemized record from his chief counsel. Morrison to Gompers, September 7, 1911. FMP.

pp. 166–67 The visit to the bank by Darrow and Tvietmoe: This account is drawn from testimony of Hunt, Ledeme, and Darrow. Also, see oral history of Oscar Lawler, p. 126.

p. 167 "a day of protest against the outrage": Gompers letter, July 29, 1911. New York University.

p. 168 Description of parade and celebration: Los Angeles *Herald,* Sept. 5, 1911; *California Social Democrat,* September 9, 1911.

pp. 168–69 Gompers's Labor Day speech in San Francisco: *Organized Labor,* September 9, 1911.

p. 169 Gompers's speech in Los Angeles: *California Social Democrat,* September 10, 1911.

p. 169 "I went to see big John": Los Angeles *Herald,* September 12, 1911; *The New York Times,* December 3, 1911, and December 4, 1911; Gompers's autobiography.

p. 170 "After talking to them": *Bridgeman's Magazine,* October 1911.

CHAPTER SEVEN

p. 171 Mary's work for *American Magazine:* Sara to Erskine, September, 1911. CESWP-H.

p. 171 "expose or divert" him: Quotes are from Sara to Erskine, October 12, 1911. CESWP-H.

p. 172 Sara's letters to Erskine: From Los Angeles, Sara wrote at least one letter a day to Erskine Wood in Oregon.

pp. 172–73 Description of events of October 10, 1911: Sara to Erskine, Mid-October 1911. CESWP-H.

p. 173 Darrow's view of women's suffrage: Margaret Parton interview with Mary Field Parton. Tape 21, MPP.

p. 174 Darrow's advances toward Sara: Sara to Erskine, letter dated "Wednesday night," probably October 25, 1911. Emphasis in original. CESWP-H.

p. 175 A wound that remained raw: Stone, p. 365; Ruby's letters to Stone. CDP.

p. 175 Darrow promised to prove: *The New York Times,* Oct 10, 1911.

p. 175 "a miniature business block": *The New York Times,* October 10, 1911.

p. 175 The cost of the miniature: To add to his problems, Darrow's defense fund owed $4,750 to J. H. Levering, who had prepared plans and blueprints and had constructed the model, and it was money that Darrow did not have on hand. Los Angeles *Herald,* December 8, 1911.

p. 176 "guilty as hell": Sara to Erskine, mid-October 1911. CESWP-H.

p. 176 Darrow's consideration of insanity defense: Helen Valeska Bary's oral history.

p. 177 "I myself think": Wood to Catlin, July 19, 1911. CESWP-B.

p. 178 Darrow tired of criticism: He called any critic "a damn fool" or "a damn idiot." Sara to Erskine, October, 1911. CESWP-H.

p. 178 Roosevelt aphorism: "Murder is Murder," editorial by Theodore Roosevelt in *The Outlook,* May 6, 1911.

p. 178 "It is difficult for me": Older to Whitlock, October 23, 1911, BWP.

p. 178 Plan to name Nockles as police chief: Helen Valeska Bary's oral history.

p. 179 "The old venire contains": *Organized Labor,* October 14, 1911.

p. 179 Date of hiring Bert Franklin: Testimony, p. 356.

p. 180 List of those who urged that Franklin be hired: Stone's notes for chapter 8, ISP. Also Testimony, vol. 5.

p. 182 Franklin's meetings with Dora and Robert Bain: Testimony; also interview in the *Los Angeles Examiner,* Dec 5, 1911.

p. 183 "the greatest trial of the century": e.g. *Los Angeles Examiner,* Oct 10, 1911 and Los Angeles *Herald,* October 12, 1911.

p. 183 "mild café au lait": Hamilton in *San Francisco Examiner,* October 12, 1911.

p. 184 "ruddy and Oregon apple-like": Sara's Oct 17, 1911, letter to *Oregon Daily Journal.* CESWP-H.

p. 184 "How many see in this trial": Sara's report in *Oregon Daily Journal,* October 17, 1911. CESWP-H.

p. 185 Description of McNamara brothers entering the courtroom: *San Francisco Chronicle,* Oct 12, 1911.

p. 185 Headline: *Los Angeles Examiner,* October 12, 1911.

p. 185 J.J.'s statement to the press: *Los Angeles Examiner,* October 13, 1911. Los Angeles *Herald,* same date.

p. 185 Prediction of a six-month jury selection: *The Graphic.*

p. 186 "Clarence Darrow, whose slightest act or play": Joseph Timmons, *Los Angeles Examiner,* October 14, 1911.

p. 186 "the activity of a jumpingjack": Hamilton in *San Francisco Examiner,* Oct 14, 1911.

p. 186 Darrow pacing the floor: Sara in *Oregon Daily Journal,* October 17, 1911. CESWP-H.

p. 186 "He drills with the ruthlessness of the dentist": Mary Field, unpublished manuscript on McNamara case. MPP.

p. 187 "The smile that is as winning as a child's": San Francisco *Bulletin,* November 11, 1911.

p. 188 Judge Bordwell: Interestingly, the prosecution also distrusted Bordwell. Unknown to Darrow, perhaps, District Attorney Fredericks asked Bordwell to let another judge handle the case. Bordwell Papers, Stanford University.

p. 188 California Club: San Francisco *Bulletin,* November 15, 1911.

p. 188 Fight over seating of Winter and Frampton: *San Francisco Examiner,* October 27–28, 1911.

p. 189 Hamilton's views: Ibid. Also, Sara to Erskine, November 5, 1911. CESWP-H.

p. 189 The questioning of Bain: *The New York Times,* October 21, 1911.

p. 189 Judge Bordwell's notes: Bordwell files, Stanford University.

p. 190 Description of people in the courtroom: Sara's November 1, 1911, *Oregon Daily Journal* article. CESWP-H.

p. 190 "detachment of society's outcasts: San Francisco *Bulletin,* November 15, 1911,

p. 191 Description of Jim McNamara in court: The *New York Times* and *Los Angeles Examiner,* October 14, 1911.

p. 191 Jim McNamara grew paler: Ibid.

p. 192 "a story that I was telling him": *Current Literature,* January 1912, p. 8; The *New York Times,* December 6, 1911.

p. 192 "a demonstration ordered by Darrow": Erskine to Sara, October 13, 1911. CESWP-H.

p. 192 Plans for release of movie: Morrison to Nockles, September 23, 1911. FMP; Hockin to J. J. McNamara, October 10, 1911. McNP; Foner, vol. 5, p. 19.

p. 193 "The scenario has been favorably": Morrison to Darrow, September 22, 1911. FMP.

p. 193 Script of *A Martyr to His Cause*:
> Scene 1.—Upper Story of Skyscraper.
> > McNamara at work with riveting gang. Foreman arrives and tells him he is wanted below. He leaves the job and exits.
> Scene 2.—On the Street Below.
> > The Executive Committee arrive and ask for McNamara. One of the men looks up toward roof and calls to him.
> Scene 3.—On Edge of Roof.
> > McNamara appears, looks over and waves to men below. Then gets on chain of Derrick and waves to Engineer to lower away.
> Scene 4.—McNamara's Descent from the Roof.
> Scene 5.—Street.
> > McNamara comes down and is received by committee who hand him: ("letter of appointment") He reads it and receives the congratulations of his friends.
> > > [Silent film title says:]
> > "McNamara hastens to tell his Mother the good news."
> Scene 6.—Porch of McNamara's Home.
> > Mother on porch reading as Mac arrives. He shows her his letter of appointment. She is proud of her boy and gives him a kiss of congratulations as they enter house.
> > > [Silent film title says:]
> > "He departs to assume his new duties."
> Scene 7.—Porch of Home.
> > Mac and mother come out of house. She tells him to always be upright and trust in God. He says that he will. Kisses her and departs while she waves a smiling good-bye.

The film then portrays the arrest on April 22, 1911, shows how "The Executive Board are kept prisoners while McNamara is served with illegal extradition papers and hurried out of town," depicts "The Wild Ride to Terre Haute" and the train ride to Los Angeles, and winds up in McNamara's prison cell.
> Scene 23.—Prison Cell.
> > McNamara seated writing. He finishes his task and reads. As he finishes, flash on screen the following message to organized labor.
> > > TO THE BROTHERHOOD OF ORGANIZED LABOR
> > > In this second attempt to crush and discredit the cause we represent I realize fully the desperation of the enemies of labor arrayed against us, but I am of good heart, for it will fail. That I am innocent of any infraction of the law in word or act needs no emphasis from me, for the truth is mighty and will prevail right speedily; and for it I shall contently wait.
> > >
> > > I send to all brothers and friends of union labor the world over my earnest and affectionate greetings, with the assurance there

is no villainy of which we are afraid. I am also confident that it
is not asking too much of the public to suspend judgment in
these matters until opportunity for a full and fair defense has
been afforded.

J. J. Mc

Scene 24.—Porch of McNamara Home.

Mother is watching and waiting for her boy. He does not come. Her
head gradually sinks on her arms and her aged form is shaken by
sobs.

The script is reproduced from *A Martyr to His Cause,* which is in the National
Civic Foundation Collection, New York Public Library. The message to
organized labor is quoted from Foner, page 19, who relies on a slightly different
version of the script.

p. 193 Darrow's strategy in urging public protests: The campaign was
designed to raise the stakes for the prosecutors and, hopefully, make a
conviction politically impossible, a campaign Darrow had helped to inspire by
telling labor leaders that "it would be a good thing to have all the meetings in
the way of protests, etc, that it is possible to hold. In fact, the public is all we
have to rely on in this case." Darrow to Gallagher, July 10, 1911. San Francisco
Labor Council Files, Bancroft Library, University of California, Berkeley.

pp. 193–94 Debs's speech: The *New York Times,* October 27, 1911, p. 7.

p. 194 "To the dispossessed in the rear": San Francisco *Bulletin,* November
15, 1911.

p. 194 "He would have faith in the morning": Statement of Anton
Johannsen, Darrow Papers, University of Chicago. Lincoln Steffens offered a
similar observation. "When people ask me what sort of man Darrow is, I ask
them the apparently irrelative question: When? And my answer is that at three
o'clock he is a hero for courage, nerve, and calm judgement, but at 3:15 he may
be a coward for fear, collapse, and panicky mentality." *The Autobiography of
Lincoln Steffens,* p. 664.

p. 194 Darrow "was so horrid tonight": Sara to Erskine, Oct 25, 1911.
CESWP-H.

p. 195 a "glorious spin": Sara to Erskine, October 29, 1911. CESWP-H.

p. 195 "Ed will explain something": Darrow to Tvietmoe. Only dated
"Sunday." Probably October 29, 1911. AFLP.

p. 196 "I know there is some talk": Gompers to Tvietmoe, November 8,
1911. AFLP.

p. 197 Walter Drew and the NEA had a different goal: From the
perspective of the National Erectors' Association, the Los Angeles cases were
essentially a sideshow. "Our people have nothing to do with the *Los Angeles
Times,* or with the Llewellyn Iron Works," Drew said. "Neither of them is
connected with us in any way. It is the series of over eighty explosions
throughout the country, preceding and following the Los Angeles troubles, with
which we are concerned." However, the NEA did hope that the Los Angeles
case would go well, since "a failure there would largely take the props from any
prosecution elsewhere." Drew to NEA executive board. WDP.

p. 197 Evidence in Indianapolis would "bury J.J.M.": July 20, 1911, Badorf to Drew. WDP.

p. 197 "About the only hope": Drew to Badorf, July 19, 1911. WDP.

p. 197 Drew trailed by seven men: Drew to his mother, May 6, 1911. WDP.

p. 197 Badorf followed by eight union representatives: Badorf to Drew, May 13, 1911, WDP.

p. 197 "There is no coup that they would not undertake": Drew to Badorf, July 22, 1911. WDP.

p. 197 Warnings of physical danger: Herbert Hockin of the Iron Workers warned Drew that union president Frank Ryan and Chicago labor organizer Ed Nockles wanted bloodshed. Drew believed the warnings at the time, but later concluded that they might have been invented by Hockin or by William Burns. Foster to Drew, October, 1912. WDP.

p. 197 a "scheme maturing": Burns to Drew, October 9, 1911. WDP.

p. 198 "Take care of yourself personally": Drew to Badorf, Oct 11, 1911. WDP.

p. 198 Unions owned Baker "Body and Soul": Foster to Drew. WDP, October 5, 1911.

p. 198 "The need for federal action": Drew to Wickersham, October 6, 1911. National Archives.

p. 199 Political challenges to President Taft in 1912: In the end, of course, Taft faced a general election challenge from Theodore Roosevelt, running as a third party candidate with California Governor Hiram Johnson as his running mate; from Woodrow Wilson on the Democratic ticket with Indiana Governor Thomas Marshall as his vice president; and from Debs on the Socialist ticket. All of those men, except Wilson, played a significant role in the McNamara case.

p. 199 "In view of the public feeling": Harr to Wickersham, September 28, 1911. National Archives.

p. 199 "swing around the circle": Cohn and Chisholm, p. 199.

p. 200 "a first class man": Taft to Interior Secretary Walter L. Fisher, March 9, 1911. Quoted in Shapiro, "The McNamara Case: A Window on Class Antagonism in the Progressive Era."

p. 200 Efforts to use Taft to involve the federal government: There are several major sources for this account, including Cohn and Chisholm, the articles by Herbert Shapiro, Oscar Lawler's oral history, Walter Drew's papers, and material available in the National Archives.

p. 201 Start of Federal Criminal Grand Jury Investigation: *The New York Times,* October 28, 1911.

p. 201 Conflicting theories on the source of the dynamite affixed to the bridge: For an interesting account speculating that agents of capital were the real culprits, see Shapiro, "The McNamara Case: A Crisis of the Progressive Era." However, a confidential letter from Oscar Lawler to Attorney General Wickersham supports a contrary view, since it indicates a genuine belief that the bomb was set by labor radicals. "Railroad Secret Service men are convinced, from the character of the explosive and the methods employed, that it was engineered by certain of the persons connected with the conspiracy, having their headquarters on the Pacific Coast," he reported. Lawler to Wickersham, October 23, 1911. National Archives.

p. 201 "The recent attempt to dynamite": Drew to Harr, October 17, 1911. National Archives.

p. 202 Eckhoff left Cincinnati: *San Francisco Examiner,* November 15, 1911.

p. 202 Comment by Eckhoff's wife: November 11, 1911, clipping. McNP.

p. 202 Press reported he went willingly: evidence in *U.S.* v. *Ryan;* Letter from Hockin to J.J., November 13, 1911. McNP.

p. 202 Eckhoff "knows nothing": Robert McNamara, quoted in *The New York Times,* December 2, 1911.

p. 202 Burns's comments: *The New York Times,* December 3, 1911.

p. 203 "The Socialists were equipped": Connolly, "The Saving of Clarence Darrow." Connolly had also reported on the Haywood trial in Idaho, where he felt that similar tactics had been used.

p. 203 One expert predicted: *The Graphic,* October 21, 1911.

p. 204 "My Socialist blood is running high"" Sara to Erskine, October 31–November 1, 1911. CESWP-H.

p. 204 Sara's conversation with Edward Hamilton: Sara to Erskine, November 5, 1911. CESWP-H.

p. 205 "Now there's a great man for you!": Sara to Erskine, November 6, 1911. CESWP-H.

p. 205 "If you get a key to a person's nature": Erskine to Sara, October 16, 1911. CESWP-H.

p. 207 "Truth is inseparable from the cause": Erskine to Catlin, July 19, 1911. CESWP-B.

p. 207 Darrow viewed Jim McNamara as a pawn: Darrow's closing argument in his second trial, *Organized Labor,* March 15, 1913.

p. 208 Proposed debate on "What is Truth?": Sara to Erskine, November 7, 1911. CESWP-H.

CHAPTER EIGHT

p. 209 "He was a delicately built little man": Luhan, p. 66.

p. 209 "Steffens learned to be happy without hard thinking": Eastman, *Enjoyment of Living,* p. 426.

p. 210 "My observation was that none of the creed-bound radicals": *Autobiography of Lincoln Steffens,* p. 634.

p. 210 Only previous encounter: Testimony, p. 5427.

p. 210 He had grown wary of reformers: In 1907, his first wife wrote that he had become "increasingly radical, practically a socialist." He expressed similar sentiments to Teddy Roosevelt. Kaplan, p. 160.

p. 210 "the people are a jury": Steffens to Heney, June 1, 1908. Heney Papers, Bancroft Library, University of California, Berkeley.

p. 210 Belief in "strong men": Lasch, pp. 266–68; Kaplan, p. 172.

p. 211 Everyone confided in him: Steffens, introduction, p. xiii. LSL.

p. 211 He knew that he could be bribed: Lasch, p. 270.

p. 211 "help bring about an essential change": Steffens to Laura, 1908, quoted in Kaplan, p. 164.

p. 211 "a little heaven for friends": As he wrote to Brand Whitlock, "My idea is to seek out some beautiful wild spot in California, plan it out, and, while we are able, make it ready for us: build little bungalows, make paths and roads, put up a common club-house for our meetings—all simply; and then one by one, as we fail and are done up, retire there to exchange experiences and try to find out how much we really know." Steffens to Whitlock, January 21, 1911. LSL, p. 260.

p. 211 Steffens's dinner with Burns: Date and details of dinner are in Steffens to the Suggetts, July 3, 1911. LSL, p. 270.

p. 211 He had long heard rumors: *Autobiography of Lincoln Steffens,* p. 657.

p. 211 Conversation with Kier Hardie: As Kier Hardie saw it, the English labor movement had been a terrible failure during recent years. Labor, he felt, had made great strides for workers in the middle of the nineteenth century, at a time when labor was well organized and businesses were still small, individually owned, and fragmented. But since 1897, when companies had become far larger and employers had begun to organize effectively, the tide had turned. "The bosses had won," Kier Hardie argued, and "the economic position of the worker was getting worse," with wages declining or remaining stagnant while the cost of living went up dramatically. It was an analysis that could have applied equally well to the steel industry, where the National Erectors Association and United States Steel had pretty well crushed the union movement.

p. 211 "Why don't you as a journalist": *Autobiography of Lincoln Steffens,* p. 659.

p. 212 Steffens's contrast with radical friends: *Autobiography of Lincoln Steffens,* p. 660.

p. 212 "Not the trial itself": Steffens to his father, November 3, 1911. LSL, p. 278.

p. 212 "It's a delicate job": Ibid.

p. 212 Horton's questioning of Morton: *San Francisco Examiner,* November 7, 1911.

p. 212 "Old men are not the only garrulous ones": San Francisco *Bulletin,* November 7, 1911.

p. 213 The drunken evening with Steffens and Johannsen: *Hearings of Commission on Industrial Relations,* vol. 11, p. 10,690; author's interview with Irving Klass.

p. 215 "I want to assume": Steffens to Laura Steffens, November 17, 1911. LSL, p. 280.

p. 215 "Irwin": probably Alexander Irvine, Job Harriman's campaign manager.

p. 215 His ace reporter in Chicago had informed him: Howard to Porterfield, April 24, 1911. EWSP.

p. 216 "old crank": Scripps welcomed the title "old crank," as he explained in an essay collected in *Damned Old Crank.*

p. 216 The Darrow-Steffens visit to Scripps: Descriptions of the day are from the Darrow and Steffens autobiographies, Steffens's December 2, 1911, article, and Scripps's lengthy November 20, 1911, letter to Negley Cochran in EWSP. Descriptions of Scripps and the ranch are also drawn from Eastman, *Great Companions,* McCabe's *Damned Old Crank,* and Knight's *I Protest.* The portrait of Scripps is also based on the frontpiece of Knight's book.

p. 216 "rather odd . . . the boy will be hanged": Steffens's dispatch dated December 2, 1911; Steffens autobiography; testimony by Steffens and Darrow.

p. 217 Disquisition on "Belligerent Rights": Scripps had drafted the disquisition on May 1, before Darrow formally entered the case.

pp. 217–18 Text of disquisition: EWSP.

p. 218 Darrow's reaction to the article: Testimony by Darrow and Steffens.

p. 220 He would not agree to let Jim be hanged: Steffens's testimony.

p. 220 Endorsement by owners of *Times:* Darrow's testimony.

p. 220 Steffens would have to pretend he had not discussed the proposal with Darrow: *Autobiography of Lincoln Steffens,* p. 672. If accurate, the admission that both Darrow and Steffens would be willing to lie about their arrangement is extremely revealing. Steffens claims that they agreed to lie in order to help the McNamaras. Presumably they would have been be at least equally willing to lie about their arrangement in order to save Darrow from going to prison. Interestingly, neither one mentioned the plan to lie while on the witness stand, though both discussed the conversation and said that it would be important to keep their conversation secret.

p. 220 "Dear Joe": The original of this note is in McNP.

p. 221 Sketch of Robert Bain: Besides his other attainments, Wood was an amateur artist of some note. The sketch is in CESWP-H.

p. 221 Sara's comments on Bain: Sara to Albert, November 17, 18, and 20, 1911; Sara to little Albert, November 20, 1911. CESWP-H.

p. 221 "the only face in the jury box": Sara Ehrgott, "McNamara Jurors All Approaching Evening of Life," November 24, 1911. CESWP-H.

p. 221 "a sort of political boss": *Autobiography of Lincoln Steffens,* p. 672.

p. 221 Lissner told Governor Johnson: Mowry, *The California Progressives,* p. 93, quoting Lissner to Johnson, March 23, 1911, Lissner Papers, Stanford University.

p. 221 Coaxed on by a broad coalition: Governor Johnson felt it urgent that Lissner help Mayor Alexander. "I am hoping against hope that you're placed in charge of the local situation in Los Angeles," he told Lissner. "If Lissner again takes command of the local situation," the governor wrote to a mutual ally, "it would help us throughout the state, help in every conceivable fashion and generally be of vast benefit to our movement." Johnson to Lissner, November 9, 1911; Johnson to Charles Willard, November 9, 1911; Johnson Papers, Bancroft.

p. 222 "Anyway, labor is licked here": *San Francisco Examiner,* December 2, 1911.

p. 222 Steffens's proposed deal with "big men": Steffens's December 1, 1911 dispatch.

p. 222 Lissner's motives: See statement by Lissner in Lissner Papers, Stanford University; interview in Los Angeles *Express,* December 6, 1911; and Lissner to Older, December 13, 1911. Older Papers.

p. 223 Steffens's memo regarding "Party on trial": introduced in evidence during Steffens's testimony at Darrow trial.

p. 223 Brant's role as front man for Otis's purchase of the *Herald:* Gottlieb and Wolt, p. 30.

pp. 223–24 San Fernando Valley and the Aqueduct: The first major sections of the San Fernando Valley were annexed to Los Angeles in 1915. Along with the addition of Palms, the annexation more than doubled the size of the city, from 108 to 285 square miles. Kahrl, p. 226.

p. 224 Socialists' battle over the Aqueduct: Irvine, *Revolution in Los Angeles,* pp. 22–29.

pp. 224–25 Moses Sherman's note: Sherman to Brant, November 20, 1911. Sherman Library.

p. 225 "I was aware": Autobiography, p. 184.

p. 225 "if they did not plead": Stone, p. 294.

p. 225 Hiram Johnson's prediction: Johnson to Lissner and Johnson to Willard, both November 9, 1911. Johnson Papers.

p. 225 "Alexander is going to win": Harriman to Morris Hillquit, November 6, 1911. Hillquit Papers.

p. 225 Encouraging reports to Older and J.J.: Older to J.J., November 16, 1911. McNP.

p. 225 Meeting between Fredericks and Brant: Los Angeles *Herald,* December 4, 1911; *San Francisco Examiner,* December 3, 1911.

p. 226 "I tell you they have the money": *The New York Times,* November 24, 1911.

p. 226 "furnished by liars": Los Angeles *Herald,* November 23, 1911.

pp. 227–28 Conversation between Darrow and Fredericks: Sullivan to Wood, December 10, 1911, CESWP-H; testimony of Darrow and Steffens.

p. 228 Understandably, Steffens brimmed over with enthusiasm: Older's testimony.

p. 228 Discussions between Chandler, Brant, and Fredericks: Brant's deposition, July 19, 1912, Sherman Library; Frederick's statement to the *San Francisco Examiner,* December 2, 1911; Steffens's dispatches, autobiography, and trial testimony, including Fredericks's "testimony" during cross-examination of Steffens.

p. 229 "furnished by liars": *The New York Times,* November 24, 1911.

p. 229 "Have Tvietmoe, Nockles": AFLP.

p. 230 Gompers simply gave the telegram to Tvietmoe: *The New York Times,* December 5, 1911.

p. 230 Jim "is willing to plead guilty": Drew to Hunter, November 25, 1911. WDP.

p. 230 "I hardly believe that J.J. intended to kill": Drew to Fredericks, November 25, 1911. WDP. Anything less than a full confession by J.J. would be foolhardy, Drew said in another note that same day, since "if J.B. is permitted to suffer and J.J. is released without such confessions, it will always be said that J.B. was a martyr and sacrificed himself for his older brother, and that both were innocent." Drew to Hunter, November 25, 1911. WDP.

p. 230 "I believe that attorneys for the defense are more dominated": Drew to Fredericks, November 26, 1911. WDP.

p. 231 On Friday, Fredericks announced: *San Francisco Examiner,* November 24, 1911.

p. 231 Fredericks's strategy: Fredericks interview in *San Francisco Examiner,* December 3, 1911.

p. 232 Darrow's cold: *Los Angeles Times,* November 26, 1911.

p. 232 Clerk entered the courtroom and: Testimony.

p. 232 Meeting between Franklin and Lockwood: Testimony of Lockwood and Franklin.

p. 233 Description of room in jail: Sara's November 28, 1911, unpublished interview with J.J. CESWP-H.

p. 234 Contents of meetings with McNamaras: Darrow and Steffens testimony.

CHAPTER NINE

p. 235 The events at Third and Los Angeles: Testimony of the various participants.

p. 236 Six yellow bills: San Francisco *Bulletin,* November 30, 1911.

p. 236 Franklin emerged from the saloon: Testimony of Officer Home.

p. 237 Description of traffic on the street: Testimony of Lockwood and White.

p. 237 Description of Detective Browne's approach: Lockwood's testimony.

p. 238 Darrow's arrangements with Franklin and Gage: *The New York Times,* November 30, 1911.

p. 238 "Can't you send us": Darrow to Morrison, November 29, 1911. AFLP.

p. 239 Darrow's conversation with Steffens: Testimony of Darrow and Steffens.

p. 239 Large banquet: *Collier's,* December 23, 1911.

p. 239 Steffens invited Mary and Sara: Perhaps the highlight of the evening was Sara's speech on "The Woman's Sphere in Journalism," given in response to a last-minute invitation from the chairman of the event. With some grace and gusto, she told the assemblage that there was "no department of life to which women did not have something to contribute."
After describing the evening in a letter to Erskine Wood, who was now back in Oregon, Sara touched on Franklin's arrest. "I am sick about the bribery business here. It has hurt the defense fearfully—I guess it's true—but how brainless." Sara to Erskine, November 29, 1911. CESWP-H. See also Sara to Albert, November 29, 1911. CESWP-H.

p. 239 "I have read of the Franklin bribery": Erskine to Sara, November 30, 1911. CESWP-H.

p. 240 "Fredericks admits that no more arrests": San Francisco *Bulletin,* November 30, 1911.

p. 240 "names of lawyers for the defense are mentioned freely": *The New York Times,* November 30, 1911.

p. 241 "The only way out": Autobiography, p. 180–81.

p. 241 "you could see him age": Steffens dispatches and testimony.

p. 241 Darrow seemed to have grown twenty years older: Los Angeles *Herald,* December 1, 1911.

p. 241 "Any statement": *The New York Times,* November 30, 1911.

p. 241 Questioning of A. W. Stewart: *Los Angeles Times,* November 30, 1911.

p. 242 "Presumably the District Attorney": *Los Angeles Examiner,* November 30, 1911.

p. 242 Meeting in Lissner's office: The assemblage included Stoddard Jess, a leading financier; J. O. Koepfli, former president of the Municipal League and a large employer of labor; R. W. Burnham, local manager for R. G. Dun & Company; Edwin T. Earl, proprietor of two newspapers, including the Los Angeles *Express,* which was to publish Steffens's account of the trial; Fred Baker of the Baker Iron Works; M. T. Snyder, banker and former mayor of Los Angeles; T. E. Gibbon, the lawyer and Harbor Commission member; Paul Shoup, vice-president and general manager of the Southern Pacific Electric lines in Southern California; James Slauson, president of the chamber of commerce;

H. W. Frank, a prominent merchant; former U.S. senator Frank P. Flint; and W. J. Washburn, a prominent banker and member of the city council.

p. 242 Steffens's plan for a new relationship between capital and labor: Under his plan, the confessions were to be followed by a series of high-level meetings at which the leaders of both groups would jointly seek to understand each other's needs and problems, meetings that he hoped would end the warfare and lead to a new set of arrangements between the contending forces.

p. 242 Steffens's pitch: Steffens's testimony.

p. 242 Comments of business leaders: Steffens's dispatch, December 2, 1911.

p. 243 Discussions between Davis and Fredericks: Fredericks's account in the *San Francisco Examiner,* December 3, 1911. It is especially credible since Steffens, who had a different version of some events, had this to say in an article that he wrote later that day, after reading Fredericks's version of events: "Capt. Fredericks has told his story and it differs from mine. Both accounts are correct, I believe, and it takes both to give the truth" (Steffens's dispatch, December 4, 1911). Steffens, of course, never spoke to Fredericks directly during the negotiations. Evidently he decided, after reading Fredericks's comments, that the district attorney's version was accurate.

CHAPTER TEN

p. 244 Activities of jurors on Thanksgiving Day: *Los Angeles Examiner,* December 1, 1911.

p. 244 "to spend the day" Steffens to Dot Hollister, November 28, 1911. LSL.

p. 244 Mary and Sara on Thanksgiving: Sara to Erskine, December 4, 1911. CESWP-H.

p. 244 Wood's Thanksgiving: Sara to Erskine, December 4, 1911. CESWP-H.

p. 245 Prisoners' menu: Los Angeles *Herald,* November 30, 1911.

p. 245 List of prisoners: *Los Angeles Examiner,* December 1, 1911.

p. 245 Button on J.J.'s lapel: Picture in *Los Angeles Examiner,* December 2, 1911.

p. 245 J.J.'s speech: *Los Angeles Examiner,* December 1, 1911.

p. 245 "I'll go the limit for you, Joe": Los Angeles *Herald,* December 1, 1911.

p. 245 "Altogether, the prisoners spent the best day": *Los Angeles Times,* December 1, 1911.

p. 246 Explosion of miniature model: *The New York Times,* December 2, 1911.

p. 246 Sequence of events: Steffens's testimony.

p. 246 Jim's position—and lawyers' reaction: Los Angeles *Herald,* December 1, 1911.

p. 247 "J.B. is weakening": WDP.

p. 247 Exchange between Jim and J.J.—and Scott's reaction: Los Angeles *Herald*, December 1, 1911.

p. 247 It would be unfair to his brother: Darrow's testimony.

p. 247 Dialogue between Jim and Scott: *Los Angeles Examiner,* December 2, 1911.

p. 248 The search for Father Edward Brady: Joe Scott to C. J. Bryans, September 6, 1950. *Los Angeles Times* History Center.

p. 248 Conversation between Fredericks and Davis: *San Francisco Examiner,* December 3, 1911.

p. 249 Darrow argued that a guilty plea would allow Tvietmoe and Johannsen to remain free: "In 1910 the Metal Trades Strike Committee sent for me and paid me for everything I did while in California. . . . We were forced to plead guilty or take the San Francisco crowd with us." Jim McNamara to Paul Sharrenberg, December 23, 1928, Scharrenberg Collection, Bancroft Library, University of California–Berkeley; quoted in Burki, p. 96.

p. 249 He later claimed to have been principally motivated: Ibid.

p. 250 Darrow "did not want to worry him": *San Francisco Examiner,* December 2, 1911

p. 250 "nobody had the heart to tell him": Steffens's first dispatch, December 2, 1911.

p. 250 Darrow's use of the phrase: Darrow to Harriman and Irvine the next day as quoted in Irvine, *Revolution in Los Angeles,* p. 63.

p. 251 "I could not tell Mr. Harriman": Autobiography, p. 184.

p. 251 Nockles realized that it was no use: Steffens's first dispatch and Steffens's testimony.

p. 253 "What's doing": *Los Angeles Times,* December 2, 1911.

p. 253 Darrow was "nervously chewing a pencil": *Los Angeles Times,* December 2, 1911.

p. 253 J.J. "was the same leonine leader": *Los Angeles Examiner,* December 2, 1911.

p. 254 The McNamara confessions: This account is drawn from reports in the *San Francisco Examiner,* the *Los Angeles Examiner,* the *Los Angeles Times,* the Los Angeles *Herald,* and *The New York Times.*

p. 255 "the greatest mystery of the age is solved": Los Angeles *Herald,* December 1, 1911.

p. 255 "it was a hard struggle": *The New York Times,* December 2, 1911.

p. 256 "Why, maybe it was gas": *Los Angeles Times,* December 2, 1911.

p. 256 Roosevelt's wire to Burns: Los Angeles *Herald,* December 2, 1911.

p. 256 "I have gained a great personal vindication": Los Angeles *Herald,* December 2, 1911; *Los Angeles Times,* December 2, 1911.

p. 257 "a great triumph for truth": *Los Angeles Times,* December 2, 1911.

p. 257 Account by leading national correspondent: Woehlke, "The End of the Dynamite Case—Guilty".

p. 257 Ten thousand buttons: *Los Angeles Times,* December 3, 1911.

pp. 257–58 "Strong working men threw themselves forward": San Francisco *Bulletin,* December 2, 1911.

p. 258 Harriman knew he had no chance: "I of course knew that we had no chance of election as soon as the plea of guilty was entered, but we would have been elected had this not happened. Twenty or twenty-five thousand votes were changed by that act." Harriman to Hillquit, December 19, 1911. Hillquit Papers.

p. 258 I would never have given my consent": *San Francisco Examiner,* December 2, 1911; *Los Angeles Examiner,* December 2, 1911; *Los Angeles Times,* December 2, 1911.

p. 258 "We ought to form a mob": *Los Angeles Times,* December 2, 1911.

p. 258 "Why did they keep us in the dark": San Francisco *Bulletin,* December 2, 1911.

p. 258 Scene with Mrs. McNamara: *The New York Times,* December 2, 1911; *Los Angeles Times,* December 2, 1911.

p. 259 Tvietmoe letter to Morrison: FMP.

p. 259 Johannsen had just been named a special representative: AFLP.

p. 259 Johannsen was in high spirits: Hapgood, *A Victorian in the Modern World,* pp. 287–88.

p. 260 "the story of how the McNamaras were persuaded": Johannsen's report to the carpenters' union, September 25–26, 1912, as quoted in *Bridgemen's Magazine,* November 1912.

p. 260 Morrison's reaction on learning of the confessions: Morrison to Executive Council, December 2, 1911, John Mitchell Papers, Catholic University.

p. 261 "If this is all true": AP report in *Los Angeles Times,* December 2, 1911.

p. 261 "I am utterly dumfounded": *The New York Times,* December 2, 1911.

p. 262 Gompers couldn't bring himself to believe it: Gompers's note to himself, December 2, 1911. AFLP.

p. 262 "There was no avoiding step taken": Darrow to Gompers, December 1, 1911, 10:22 P.M. AFLP.

p. 262 "I have known for months": Darrow article in the *San Francisco Examiner,* December 2, 1911.

p. 262 A "discredited leader": *The New York Times,* December 3, 1911.

p. 263 "The iron workers are not the only": *Current Literature,* January 1912; *The New York Times,* December 7, 1911.

p. 263 "it is believed": *The New York Times,* December 3, 1911.

p. 263 "the deadliest blow ever dealt": *Current Literature,* January 1912.

p. 263 "Will organized labor now do justice": *The New York Times,* December 2, 1911.

p. 263 AFL statement: issued December 2, 1911, it was quoted in the *The New York Times* on December 3, 1911.

p. 264 "I never told Samuel Gompers": *The New York Times,* December 3, 1911.

p. 264 Debs's statement: Debs, "The McNamara Case and the Labor Movement," *International Socialist Review,* February 1912. Italics in original.

p. 264 "I will not discuss the utterances of that man": *The New York Times,* December 2, 1911.

p. 265 "Inside of a few days, the mystery": *Western Federation of Miners Magazine,* December 14, 1911.

p. 265 Wire from Albert Detch: Detch to J.J., December 2, 1911. McNP.

p. 265 "Capital whipped Darrow into capitulation": Detch circular. McNP.

p. 266 Sara, in the courtroom: Sullivan to Wood, December 10, 1911. CESWP-H.

p. 266 "Full facts" of "crooked dealings": Sara to Albert, December 2, 1911. CESWP-H.

p. 266 "sudden ending of the McNamara case": Sara to Wood, December 4, 1911. CESWP-H.

p. 266 "I think it was just a case of plain blundering": Wood to Sullivan, December 19, 1911. CESWP-H.

p. 266 "I wish I could come": C.D. to Wood, December 14, 1911. CESWP-H.

p. 267 "Telegrams poured in" to Steffens: Steffens to Dot Steffens Hollister, misdated as November 1911. LSL. The letter was actually written on December 3 or 4.

p. 267 "The pleas of guilty were a great shock": Scripps to Porterfield, December 2, 1911. EWSP.

p. 268 "the deep seams and the pallor of his face": Connolly, *Collier's,* December 23, 1911.

p. 268 Jim's signed confession: Jim McNamara's confession is in the LeCompte Davis Papers at UCLA.

p. 268 The judge had sentenced them: They both went to confession the night before and took Holy Communion from Father Brady on the morning of sentencing. Scott to A. R. (Robert) McNamara, January 2, 1912. McNP.

p. 268 "The public ought to be satisfied": New York *World,* December 6, 1911.

INTERLUDE

p. 273 "thunderclap": Summation to jury in *People* v. *Darrow*.

p. 273 "the plea of guilty . . . aborted the labor movement in Los Angeles": McWilliams, p. 283.

p. 273 "The pleas of guilty sent organized labor": Creel, p. 98.

p. 273 "the McNamara trial . . . formed the spearpoint of the labor struggle": Eastman, *Enjoyment of Living,* p. 427.

p. 274 The events . . . helped make the AFL . . . more conservative: "More than any other one factor," according to one recent study, "the McNamara case marked the turning point for the AFL, which rejected confrontation and sought to make unions an accepted pillar of society." Shore, p. 214.

p. 274 The National Socialist Party banned the advocacy of violence: The amendment stated: "Any member of the party who opposes political action or advocates crime, sabotage or other methods of violence as a weapon of the working class to aid in its emancipation shall be expelled from membership in the party." Haywood was expelled from the party a few months later. Haywood, p. 258; Foner, vol. 4; Weinstein, p. 15.

p. 274 It soon began to stagnate and decline: "Socialists in every part of the nation felt the effects of the Los Angeles trial. . . . After 1912, the Socialists split into factions and their power disintegrated." Graham Adams, Jr., p. 18.

p. 274 Roosevelt's second column: Roosevelt, "Murder is Murder," the *Outlook,* December 16, 1911.

p. 274 Issue of *The Survey* magazine: "The Larger Aspects of the McNamara Case." *The Survey,* December 30, 1911.

p. 275 "A hungry Democratic Party": Graham Adams, Jr., p. 48.

p. 275 "If there is one 'document' ": Smith, *America Enters the World,* p. 359. Parenthesis in original. For an excellent study of the Commission on Industrial Relations and its work, see Graham Adams, Jr., *Age of Industrial Violence, 1910–1915.*

p. 275 "Labor's Stoutest Heart": *Daily Worker,* March 9, 1941.
     He was a pariah: People quickly forgot the achievements that Anton Johannsen set forth passionately in 1915. "When J. J. McNamara was elected general secretary of the Iron Workers International Union eleven years ago, the Iron Workers had less than six thousand members [and] an average wage of $2.30 a day," Johannsen told workers at a union rally that also featured Clarence Darrow and Mother Jones. "When J. J. McNamara and his colleagues went to prison, the Iron Workers had a membership of over fourteen thousand . . . an average wage of $4.30, and it wasn't done by ice cream, or by the Salvation Army; don't you forget it." Johannsen, p. 8.

p. 275 J.J. was accused of treading close to the edge of the law: JOHN J. MCNAMARA ARRESTED AT HIS OLD GAME IN INDIANA, *Los Angeles Times,* January 1, 1924.

p. 275 Just two months after his younger brother: J.J. died on May 7, 1941, in Butte, Montana, *San Francisco Chronicle,* May 8, 1941.

p. 275 No one felt moved to write him a stirring epitaph: History played a foul trick on J. J. McNamara. He had not been connected with, or even known about, the plans to dynamite the *Times*. He had commissioned scores of dynamiting jobs in an attempt to improve the wages and working conditions of the union's members, but no one was ever killed as the result of his efforts. When he pleaded guilty on the same day as his brother, it was to save Jim's life and to forestall the prosecution of Eugene Clancy, Olaf Tvietmoe, and Anton Johannsen. He pleaded guilty to bombing the Llewellyn Iron Works, not the *Times*. To make the limited extent of his plea indelibly clear, he executed a hand-written statement on December 5, 1911, the day of his sentencing. In it he said, "I hereby certify that I have never at any time made any confession or statement of any kind whatever about these cases, or any offenses that I might have been charged with." (The original statement is in the Lecompte Davis Papers at UCLA.)

Nevertheless, history has charged J. J. McNamara with the murder of twenty men. In virtually every book or article or play that mentions the case, it is claimed that J. J. confessed to bombing the *Times*. That confusion ultimately worked greatly to Clarence Darrow's benefit. But it is an unfair scar on the memory of J. J. McNamara.

PART III: THE TRIAL OF CLARENCE DARROW

Much of the courtroom drama in these pages is drawn from the actual trial transcript of *The People* v. *Clarence Darrow*. The explosive trial lasted for more than three months; the transcript is more than eight thousand pages long. Unless otherwise identified, courtroom dialogue is taken from those transcripts. Though the narrative seeks to present the highlights of the case, it proved necessary to leave many of the most colorful scenes and characters on the cutting room floor.

For each day of the months leading up to the trial, as well as of the trial itself, I read news accounts in at least a dozen diverse publications. "Newspapers are, and have ever been, against Labor," Mary Field claimed in assessing reporting of the trial. " 'The Morning Lie' should be the name of most morning newspapers; 'The Evening Cheat' the cognommen of the evening editions." Her own reporting, she said, was no less biased. When a reporter asked her why she didn't "see both sides," she had a ready answer. "There aren't both sides," she told him. "There's only one side, and that's the right side, and that's the Labor side" (*Organized Labor,* August 3, 1912).

To compensate for the possible slant of the daily journals in Los

Angeles (where only the *Record* was openly on Darrow's side), I read several pro-Darrow publications, notably Fremont Older's San Francisco *Bulletin* and Olaf Tvietmoe's *Organized Labor* (with its powerful reports by Mary Field). Probably the best reportage, however, was by Joe Timmons of the *Los Angeles Examiner.* Lincoln Steffens called Timmons's accounts "the best from all points of view" (Steffens to Dot and Jim Hollister, July 21, 1912, Steffens Papers, Columbia University). Timmons's voice, along with Mary Field's, offers important commentary.

One of Timmons's friends and sources was Darrow's chief counsel—and occasional chief nemesis—Earl Rogers. Over the years Rogers has attracted a loyal core of admirers, smaller perhaps, but no less intense, that Darrow's. The two men could not have been more different. "In the legal profession," Irving Stone observed, "Earl Rogers was at the polar extremity from Clarence Darrow"—venal, amoral, lawyer for the Merchants and Manufacturers' Association, author of the city's notorious antipicketing law, special prosecutor in the grand jury investigation of the *Times* bombing: in short, capital's most trusted advocate in its war against organized labor (Stone, p. 313; Debs to Darrow, February 19, 1912, Debs Papers). Yet fate brought Rogers and Darrow together in the highly charged courtroom arena that each man thought he owned.

Rogers's biographers have served him well, if not quite accurately, and I have profited immensely from Cohn and Chisholm's *Take the Witness* and Adela Rogers St. Johns's *Final Verdict.* Both are often wrong, albeit colorfully so, about large and small facts that can be verified, as is explained in a few of the notes that follow. As Adela accurately observed, "the lies that [Ruby Darrow] told afterwards for her husband are probably somewhat like the ones I probably tell here for my father" (St. Johns, *Final Verdict,* p. 390).

Several books describe parts of the trial. Most notable are the biographies of Rogers and the biographies and autobiographies of Darrow and Lincoln Steffens. Though often skewed, the accounts are filled with fascinating insights and details.

Once again, many of the richest aspects of the story—particularly the pain and the intrigue of the months leading up to the trial—are drawn from unpublished accounts, including the unpublished biography of Robert Foster and the secret interview with John Harrington; from previously classified government records, including those of the justice department, which are now in the National Archives; and from private letters and diaries, particularly those in the Drew Papers at the University of Michigan, the Parton Papers at the University of Oregon, the Steffens Papers at Columbia, and the Wood Papers at the Huntington Library and at the Bancroft Library at the University of California at Berkeley.

CHAPTER ELEVEN

p. 280 Johannsen said Darrow pleaded the brothers guilty "to save his own skin": Wood to Sara, April 12, 1912. CESWP-H.

p. 280 Others were even more unkind: For example, comments in Helen Valeska Bary's oral history.

p. 280 "I am assuming Darrow to be guilty": Catlin to Wood, February 14, 1912. CESWP-B.

p. 280 Franklin spent an hour talking privately with Joe Ford: *Los Angeles Times,* January 12, 1912.

p. 281 Franklin's secret Sunday afternoon drive with Ford: *San Francisco Examiner,* January 30, 1912.

p. 281 Lawler's letter to Attorney General Wickersham: Lawler to Wickersham, February 24, 1912. National Archives.

p. 282 "What a wave of crime you are unearthing": Wickersham to Lawler, March 3, 1912. National Archives.

p. 282 A few friends like Erskine Wood sent money: On December 21, 1911, Darrow asked Wood to come to Los Angeles. "I wish you could come down," he said, "I need you if you can. Still, I presume you are busy" (Darrow to Wood, December 21, 1912, CESWP-H). Wood was pretty certain that Darrow was guilty (Wood to Sullivan, December 19, 1911, CESWP-H). Nevertheless, as much as he despised the act of bribery, he felt sorry for his old friend and asked mutual friends to help out in his defense (Wood to Sullivan, January 30, 1912, CESWP-H). Somewhat sheepishly, Darrow asked Wood for money (Darrow to Wood, February 20, 1912, CESWP-H), then, embarrassed, withdrew the request (Darrow to Wood, February 23, 1912, CESWP-H). But Wood did send money, prompting Darrow to say that "I feel as if I ought to return your generous check. I need it so badly I will keep it. I hope you will get the money back. I believe you will." (Darrow to Wood, March 1, 1912, CESWP-H).

p. 282 Debs told Darrow that "the Socialists and others" had "concluded that you loved money too well": Debs to Darrow, February 19, 1912. Debs Papers.

p. 282 Gompers told Darrow that any appeal would "fall upon indifferent ears": Gompers to Darrow, March 16, 1912. AFLP.

p. 283 "*How can* you have remained silent so long!!": Ruby Darrow to Whitlock, February 14, 1912. BWP.

p. 283 "The intense strain on my mind": Autobiography, p. 187.

p. 283 Conversation with Dr. Gerson: Gerson to Darrow, January 17, 1918, Gerson Papers, UCLA.

p. 284 Stephen M. White was "California's greatest lawyer": This quote and much of the account is from Cohn and Chisholm, p. 6.

p. 285 Rogers's representation of William Alford: This account is drawn from Cohn and Chisholm and from St. Johns.

p. 287 "was one of the first to realize that a criminal lawsuit is a drama": Carr, p. 165.

p. 287 Hugh Baillie's description of Rogers: Baillie, pp. 15–16.

p. 288 "all around capitalist retainer": Debs to Darrow, February 19, 1912. Debs Papers.

p. 288 "leading servant for privilege": Johannsen, et al., pp. 2–3.

p. 289 "Get away from me, you slimy pimp": St. Johns, p. 97.

p. 289 Rogers's father's request: St. Johns, pp. 102–6.

p. 289 "Close to one hundred slayers escaped the gallows": Cohn and Chisholm, p. 1.

p. 289 Pearl Morton and Dolly: St. Johns, pp. 133–46.

p. 290 Rogers's plan of action: These are the arguments that Rogers used either in the press during the next few weeks or later in court.

p. 292 Darrow "was white and plainly stirred to the depths of his being": *San Francisco Examiner,* January 30, 1912.

p. 292 "I can just say what I have from the first": *Los Angeles Times,* January 30–31, 1912.

p. 292 Darrow lit a cigarette and tried to leave: *Los Angeles Times,* January 30, 1912.

p. 293 "Well, boys, is everything fixed?": *Los Angeles Times,* January 30, 1912.

p. 293 "This will be a real fight": *Los Angeles Examiner,* January 30, 1912.

CHAPTER TWELVE

p. 295 Sullivan went to Mexico and used the name Malachi: Catlin to Wood, February 23, 1912. CESWP-B.

p. 295 "I had to get out of Los Angeles for a while": "Malachi" (Sullivan) to Wood, March 1, 1912. CESWP-H.

p. 295 "I have never in my lifetime": Sullivan to Wood, March 21, 1912. CESWP-H.

p. 295 "The best evidence-gatherer": Darrow to Gompers. AFLP.

p. 295 Harrington "is expected to be another strong witness": *Los Angeles Times,* February 1, 1912.

p. 295 "Bert Franklin and attorney John Harrington": *Los Angeles Times,* February 15, 1912.

p. 296 Lawler and Ford devised a devious plan: Foster, unpublished autobiography, p. 127. WDP.

p. 297 Meetings between Darrow and Harrington: The information in this section is from Darrow and Harrington's testimony, from news accounts from several papers, and from Harrington's transcribed statements to Lawler on February 19 and 29, which are in WDP.

p. 297 Darrow's consultation with Rogers: Darrow testimony.

p. 298 "Say, John," Darrow began: Transcript of phone conversation, introduced during Harrington's testimony.

p. 298 The press reported that Harrington had come to Los Angeles: Los Angeles *Herald,* March 15, 1912.

p. 298 The real bombshell hit on March 23: Los Angeles *Herald,* March 23, 1912.

p. 299 "Darrow has offered to plead guilty and tell all": Drew to Badorf, February 29, 1912. WDP.

p. 299 "Regarding Darrow's proposition": Badorf to Drew, March 2, 1912. WDP.

p. 299 "The attitude of the prosecutors": *Los Angeles Times,* March 18, 1912. On April 26, 1912, Captain Fredericks made this statement: "While no one representing this office has ever approached Darrow or any of his counsel with offers of compromise or immunity, it is true that certain persons have come to me, representing that they came from Darrow. They offered compromise. I have given every one of them the same statement—that under no circumstances would I consider anything from Darrow but an unconditional plea of guilty," *Los Angeles Times,* April 27, 1912.

pp. 299–300 "To have Darrow convicted or plead guilty": Wood to Sara, April 12, 1912. CESWP-H.

p. 300 Wood conversations with Darrow and Johannsen on April 12, 1912: Wood to Sara, April 12, 1912. CESWP-H.

p. 301 "I have known Darrow for thirty years": Memo to Gompers dated April 28, 1912. AFLP.

CHAPTER THIRTEEN

p. 302 "face was haggard": Los Angeles *Herald,* May 15, 1912.

p. 303 Description of Rogers: Los Angeles *Record,* July 6, 1912, article by Hugh Baillie.

p. 304 The words etched on the skylight: *Town Talk,* June 1, 1912; *Organized Labor,* May 25, 1912, article by Mary Field.

p. 304 "Miss Mary Field of San Francisco, who is making a stay in this city": Los Angeles *Herald,* May 15, 1912.

p. 304 " 'widowed', the widowhood of the living death": Sara to Erskine, April 17, 1912. CESWP-H.

p. 304 Description of Ruby and Clarence Darrow at front of courtroom: Los Angeles *Herald,* May 15, 1912.

p. 305 Fredericks was "supremely confident of victory": *Los Angeles Examiner,* May 16, 1912.

p. 305 "chock full of ginger": Los Angeles *Herald,* May 15, 1912.

p. 305 Judge Hutton's gentle smile: Stone, p. 315.

p. 305 Judge Hutton's kindly face: *Organized Labor,* May 25, 1912, Mary Field called him "a kind-faced man."

p. 306 "Suppose that Bert H. Franklin did approach": Los Angeles *Record,* May 17, 1912.

p. 306 "But then there comes into the box a tailor": *Organized Labor,* June 1, 1912.

p. 307 "If we convince you by the evidence": *Los Angeles Examiner,* May 18, 1912; *Los Angeles Times,* May 19, 1912.

p. 307 "Over and over I asked myself this question": *Organized Labor,* June 1, 1912.

p. 308 "May it please the court": The trial dialogue throughout the remainder of the book is taken from the eight-thousand-page transcript. Since the court stenographer seems to have missed or misstated some passages, the dialogue is occasionally supplemented by news accounts of what was said.

p. 309 "a bolt out of the blue": *Los Angeles Times,* May 25, 1912.

p. 310 Darrow fumbled with a piece of cigarette paper: *Los Angeles Times,* May 25, 1912.

p. 310 "at once winning and pathetic": *Town Talk,* June 1, 1912.

p. 310 "Before the trial closes": *Los Angeles Times,* May 25, 1912.

p. 311 Description of Lockwood: Los Angeles *Herald,* May 27, 1912; *San Francisco Chronicle,* May 26, 1912.

p. 312 "one of the bitterest and most scathing": Los Angeles *Herald,* May 28, 1912.

p. 313 Description of Fredericks shouting: *Los Angeles Examiner,* May 29, 1912.

p. 314 Description of Rogers yelling and crouching: *Los Angeles Examiner,* May 29, 1912.

p. 314 "it was a frame-up": Contrary to Adela Rogers St. Johns's account, there is no reference to Darrow waving a hat. Compare for example, the transcript, pages 311–12, with *Final Verdict,* pages 414–15.

p. 314 His testimony had survived under fire: The *Herald* reported that "the witness bore the ordeal well." *The New York Times* stated that Rogers's "grueling" cross-examination had "failed to shake the witness's original story." Lockwood himself quipped that it was "harder work than irrigating." *Los Angeles Examiner,* May 29, 1912.

p. 314 Description of Bert Franklin: *Los Angeles Times,* May 29, 1912.

p. 314 Darrow gave his former aide a scornful look: *Los Angeles Times,* May 29, 1912.

p. 315 The crowd inside and outside: Los Angeles *Record,* May 28, 1912.

p. 316 Earl Rogers's disappearance and Adela's search for him: St. Johns, *Final Verdict,* p. 416–21,

p. 317 Rogers's appearance and attire in court: Ibid; *Los Angeles Examiner,* June 1, 1912, description and photograph.

p. 318 Darrow started to chew on a long slip of yellow paper: *Los Angeles Times,* June 1, 1912.

p. 319 "to cast the baneful garb of the informer": Los Angeles *Herald,* May 29, 1912.

pp. 319–20 "so unsatisfactory that the suspicion arose": *Los Angeles Examiner,* May 30, 1912.

p. 320 "Franklin had been a cowering rabbit": *Los Angeles Examiner,* June 1, 1912.

p. 322 "Tell them whether you was careless": Grammatical errors are in the transcript.

p. 324 "To the end, Franklin retained his composure": *Los Angeles Examiner,* June 5, 1912.

p. 326 "Franklin's testimony remains intact": Los Angeles *Herald,* June 7, 1912.

p. 326 "holding the witness up to contempt": *Los Angeles Examiner,* June 7, 1912.

p. 326 "Rogers had created a despicable creature": St. Johns, *Final Verdict,* pp. 421, 428.

CHAPTER FOURTEEN

p. 330 "Nuts," Rogers answered. "We must insist that if you": St. Johns, *Final Verdict,* p. 415.

p. 330 "City of the Dreadful Night": Mary Field, writing in *Organized Labor,* September 28, 1912.

p. 332 "the reversal of ruling": *Los Angeles Examiner,* June 14, 1912.

p. 332 Tvietmoe's Sunset National Oil Company: Tvietmoe was president of the Sunset National Oil Company, which owned an oil well in Kern County. The company issued capital stock with a face value of $1 million. Tvietmoe and Johannsen were two of the largest shareholders, with more than ten thousand shares each. Although other shareholders did invest money, Tvietmoe, Johannsen, Mayor P. N. McCarthy, and a few other labor leaders got their stock for free. Tvietmoe, however, loaned $2,714 to the company. The company was adjudged bankrupt on January 25, 1911. Apparently Tvietmoe's loan was never repaid. Bankruptcy case files of the National Archives and Records Administration office in San Bruno, California.

p. 333 "I didn't use any sop with him": Sara to Wood, September 7, 1912, describing a conversation earlier that same evening with Tvietmoe. CESWP-H.

p. 334 " 'God!' said Johannsen. "That's a God damn son of a bitch of a poem": Johannsen and the others loved "Battle-Cry" so much that they made it their poem, the poem of the movement that sustained them through the battles in Los Angeles and Indianapolis. So much so that they appended the entire poem to a pamphlet called "The True History of the Famous McNamara Case," a collection of speeches by Johannsen, Darrow and Mother Jones, given at the Labor Temple in Kansas City on August 7, 1915, and published as a booklet by Carpenters Local No. 61.

p. 335 "Fighting the fight is all": The poem concludes:

> *What though I live with the winners*
> *Or perish with those who fall?*
> *Only the cowards are sinners,*
> *Fighting the fight is all.*

p. 335 Mary Field's diary entry on the scene in the Hayward Hotel: The scene is quoted in Margaret Parton's letter to Arthur and Lila Weinberg, Newberry Library. The original is in her diary. MPP.

p. 335 A tactic that was . . . totally unanticipated by the prosecution: *Los Angeles Times,* June 15, 1912.

p. 337 A tactic that both sides agreed was unprecedented: *Los Angeles Examiner,* June 16, 1912.

p. 337 "From the standpoint of the defense": *Los Angeles Times,* June 15, 1912.

p. 337 Some people thought it would even cause Captain Fredericks to move for the dismissal: Los Angeles *Herald,* June 15, 1912; *San Francisco Examiner,* June 15, 1912.

p. 337 At first his questions were awkwardly stated: Quotes are from Los Angeles *Herald*, June 15, 1912, and Los Angeles *Record*, June 15, 1912.

p. 339 "an ideal witness for the defense": *Los Angeles Examiner*, June 16, 1912.

p. 340 starting to look worried: *Los Angeles Examiner*, June 16, 1912.

p. 340 Tvietmoe chewing cigar: Los Angeles *Record*, June 15, 1912.

p. 341 "With a hiss of joy": *Organized Labor*, June 22, 1912.

p. 342 Johannsen "ran his hands through his hair": Los Angeles *Record*, June 15, 1912.

p. 342 Darrow began to chew strips of yellow paper: *Los Angeles Times*, June 16, 1912.

p. 342 Jurors leaned forward eagerly: Los Angeles *Record*, June 15, 1912.

p. 343 Fredericks had "led the defense into an ambush": *Los Angeles Examiner*, June 16, 1912.

p. 344 Gossip that Rogers was planning to withdraw: *Los Angeles Examiner*, June 18, 1912.

p. 344 DARROW MAY TAKE FULL CHARGE: Los Angeles *Record*, June 17, 1912.

p. 344 Stories were "vehemently denied": *The Los Angeles Examiner*, June 18, 1912.

p. 344 Large number of women in bonnets: The *Los Angeles Times* commented on the presence of "many ladies" starting on June 18 (*Los Angeles Times*, June 19, 1912). For a description of the bonnets, see the Los Angeles *Herald*, July 3, 1912, photo with caption "Matinee at Real Life Drama."

p. 345 Behm was barely audible: *Los Angeles Examiner*, June 19, 1912.

p. 345 "The defendant showed his old-time skill": *Los Angeles Times*, June 19, 1912.

p. 345 "amazing density of the witness": *Los Angeles Examiner*, June 20, 1912.

p. 346 "By turns he was patient": *Los Angeles Examiner*, June 20, 1912.

p. 346 Attempts to have Harrington kidnapped: Erskine to Sara, April 12, 1912. CESWP-H.

p. 346 roly-poly Irishman: *Los Angeles Examiner*, June 20, 1912.

p. 346 "intimate personal friend of Darrow's": *Organized Labor*, June 29, 1912.

p. 347 "the star witness": *Organized Labor*, June 29, 1912.

p. 353 Cavenaugh . . . had expressed the wish that Darrow had used him: Stone, p. 322.

p. 353 "Earl Rogers was struggling in the effort to confuse": *Los Angeles Examiner*, June 23, 1912.

p. 355 "a hearty, splendid, intelligent laugh": *Organized Labor*, June 29, 1912.

p. 355 even Darrow was chuckling: *Organized Labor,* June 29, 1912.

pp. 355–56 Laughter was a deliberate device: Johannsen statement, Darrow Papers, University of Chicago.

p. 356 "Court attachés who have served for a score of years": *Los Angeles Times,* June 23, 1912.

p. 356 admiration for "your magnificent past services": The telegram was reprinted in *Organized Labor,* June 29, 1912.

p. 357 "when I was in the same courtroom with him": Geisler, p. 270.

p. 357 "a jury watches every movement of a lawyer": Autobiography, p. 427.

p. 358 Ford, who often chewed gum in court: Baillie, p. 17.

p. 361 Darrow had the support of a few longtime friends: Autobiography, p. 187.

p. 361 "one of his bravest and strongest fellow-soldiers": Ruby Darrow to Brand Whitlock, February 14, 1912. BWP.

p. 361 Darrow "believed that his friends had joined his foes": Baillie, p. 21.

p. 361 "He is scared": Lincoln Steffens to Laura Steffens, June 25, 1912. LSL.

p. 362 "clever and kindly and understanding" Autobiography, p. 187.

p. 362 "When the thundering Rogers, brows drawn down": Hugh Baillie's portrait in the Los Angeles *Record,* June 1, 1912.

p. 363 But as the prosecution's case drew toward a close: The prosecution presented two other witnesses who produced fireworks and publicity. William J. Burns testified that none of the prosecution witnesses was on his payroll. Still bearing a grudge from their years as adversaries in the San Francisco graft trial, and as leaders of the manhunt for the men who had blown up the *Times,* Rogers wanted to tear Burns to bits. During Burns's first day on the stand, the men glared at each other and exchanged threats. The press predicted that Rogers's cross-examination the next day would be fierce.

But to everyone's astonishment, Rogers treated Burns with kid gloves. As Joe Timmons wrote, "Two men have never anywhere been more courteous to each other. They were cooing doves. . . . The lawyer and detective now have a joint claim on the Nobel Peace Prize" (*Los Angeles Examiner,* July 3, 1912). Colorfully but inaccurately, one Rogers biography claimed that "it is doubtful if any witness of the prominence of Burns ever underwent the manhandling that Rogers subjected him to. Sparks flew almost continuously and both men were frequently on the verge of physical encounter" (Cohn and Chisholm, p. 217).

The other witness was Burns's employee, Guy Biddinger, the detective who captured Jim McNamara and escorted J.J. across the country. As part of the effort to show Darrow's scheme to corrupt justice, Biddinger told of Darrow's efforts to bribe him. His testimony was accurate and sensational, but Darrow managed to take all the sting from it during cross-examination by getting Biddinger to admit that the Burns agency had been paying spies planted in the McNamara defense team. Under the circumstances, Darrow argued, it was only fair for the McNamara defense forces to try to pay someone on the Burns team to spy for them.

p. 363 Ruby looked ill; rumors quickly spread: *Los Angeles Examiner,* July 4, 1912.

CHAPTER FIFTEEN

p. 364 Larry Sullivan was certain Darrow was guilty: Catlin to Wood, June 22, 1912. CESWP-B.

p. 365 "I think he will be able to carry": Catlin to Wood, June 22, 1912. CESWP-H.

p. 366 Depositions prepared by Edgar Lee Masters: One of those who would not have spoken so kindly of the defendant was Masters himself. He considered Darrow greedy, unprincipled, cowardly, and dishonest. Like many others, he was convinced that Darrow had won the Idaho cases by bribing the jury and that "having watched his methods, they caught him in the McNamara case." Moreover, Masters interpreted letters from Darrow to mean that "he was promised immunity for pleading his clients guilty" (Masters to Carter Harrison, March 21, 1938. Carter Harrison Papers, Newberry Library).

Masters described his feelings a quarter of a century later in a letter to Carter Harrison, who had served five terms as mayor of Chicago. As it happened, Harrison was one of the civic leaders who gave Masters a deposition swearing to Darrow's good reputation. Whatever he felt about Darrow in 1912, however, Harrison later agreed with Masters's view that "he was as crooked as a snake's tail" (Masters to Harrison, July 29, 1944; Harrison to Masters, August 7, 1944. In Harrison Papers, Newberry Library). In 1938, just after Darrow's death, Masters filled the former mayor in on some of the background facts. "He was completely broke and in disgrace," Masters recalled. "I got him one thousand dollars and sent it to him. Then he wrote me that he needed depositions as to his good reputation in Chicago, and I got those for him."

Not everyone wanted to help. "I went to see [Kenesaw Mountain] Landis about testifying," Masters remembered. Landis was a federal judge, appointed to the bench a few years earlier by Theodore Roosevelt. Known as a man of uncompromising integrity, he became the first commissioner of baseball in 1920, following the famous Black Sox Scandal. "Landis said he would do anything he could for me, but nothing for Darrow, who was a crook who had been caught at last, for which he was glad."

Nevertheless, Masters assembled the depositions. "These depositions were read there in court," Masters said, "and he told me they saved him. I have his letter here where he wrote me that he could never forget the kindness and that he would love me forever. Well, he changed his mind" (Masters to Harrison, March 21, 1938).

In fairness, it should be noted that Masters's contempt for Darrow matured over the years and may not have been so firmly held in 1912. In 1915, shortly after the publication of his celebrated *Spoon River Anthology,* Masters picked away at Darrow in a poem called "On a Bust." Six years later, Darrow got even by representing Masters's wife in an exceptionally bitter divorce action. At the time of the divorce, Masters told a friend that Darrow "is revenging himself for the poems I wrote on him—'On a Bust' in *Songs and Satires;* and 'Excluded Middle' in *Toward the Gulf.* But these are just Sunday School persiflage compared to what he will get as I go along. I'll make that son of a bitch the most detestable figure in American history. The material is so abundantly at hand" (Masters to Eunice Tietjens, July 26, 1921. Tietjens Papers. Newberry Library). Masters also attacked Darrow in "Louis Raguse," which appeared in *The New Spoon River* (Masters to Harrington, July 29, 1944). Masters failed miserably in that goal, of course, but not for want of trying.

p. 367 "as to the impossibility of obtaining testimony against Darrow": Badorf to Drew, May 13, 1912. WDP.

p. 367 Cavenaugh and Gerson thought him guilty: Stone, pp. 322, 323.

p. 367 "Some of his sympathizers had a 'hunch' ": Hapgood column, August 29, 1912. Hapgood Papers, Beinecke Library, Yale University.

p. 372 Rogers announced to some of his friends in the press: *Los Angeles Examiner,* July 10, 1912. "The defense will try to establish at least a strong suspicion that Harrington unlocked the safe and gave Franklin $4,000 which he had stowed away there in a box which he kept in the safe."

p. 372 Harriman's rigorous logic: Harold H. Story, oral history, pp. 145–46.

p. 372 He was concise and clear: Los Angeles *Record,* July 10, 1912.

p. 373 HARRIMAN SCORES FOR THE DEFENSE: *San Francisco Chronicle,* July 10, 1912.

p. 373 "several of the jurors seemed greatly impressed": During cross-examination, Fredericks tried to prove that Harriman had been involved with the dynamiters. His evidence came from Edward Cantrell, a socialist leader, who ran for secretary of state in 1910 (when Harriman was running for governor) and ran for city council in 1911 (when Harriman ran for mayor). Cantrell claimed to have been with Harriman on the morning after the blast and to have heard him admit his involvement. His report was colored by the fact that he and Harriman had been involved in a bitter feud in the two years between the bombing and the trial.

Charles Edward Russell was quoted by the San Francisco *Bulletin* as saying that Harriman could not have been involved in the bombing since he was part of the conservative faction of the party, at the extreme wing of those who believed in the ballot box rather than in direct action. This makes sense superficially, but fails to note the alliance that Job had formed with the San Francisco labor leaders. They had promised to rally to his campaign in return for his support of their efforts. That support included his work as their lawyer, of course. But since they were behind the dynamiting, it could also have included support—if not endorsement—of dynamiting. As a scare tactic only, of course.

This view of Harriman's role is strongly reinforced by a July, 1910, letter that Harriman sent to Morris Hillquit, who was a leader of the conservative faction of the Socialist Party. Harriman said that "we will have to use a war measure. I trust you boys will not take too close notice of it, and if you will let us alone we will have a great movement here. . . ."

It is also worth noting that Louis Adamic, whose *Dynamite* became one of the most important accounts of the *Times* bombing, was a friend of Cantrell's. He accepted Cantrell's version of events uncritically. See Adamic's *My America* for a more complete discussion of his relationship with Cantrell—and a description of his reasons for believing Cantrell's account.

In any case, Harriman had strong personal reasons for coming to Darrow's defense in the bribery trial. Franklin had testified that Job Harriman opened the office safe and gave the bribe money to Darrow on the morning of November 28, 1911. If true, that made Harriman an accessory to the crime. During the *Darrow* trial, Fredericks made it clear that if Darrow were convicted, he intended to indict Harriman for his role in the episode. But Harriman could not be prosecuted, of course, if Darrow were acquitted.

p. 375 "Concrete, compact testimony": Los Angeles *Record,* July 11, 1912. Many observers agreed that Hawley was an effective witness. Some felt, in the words of the *Chicago Tribune,* that Hawley had "cleared up the mystery of the telephone message which called Darrow to the vicinity of the arrest" (*Chicago Tribune,* July 12, 1912). Moreover, his testimony, when combined with that of Harriman and Wolfe, "served the double purpose of accounting for the whereabouts of Darrow on the morning of the alleged bribery exposé and of tending to impeach Franklin's veracity" (*Chicago Tribune,* July 12).

p. 375 "ninety-two days in jail": Irving Stone interview with juror Williams. CDP.

p. 375 Ruby Darrow looked thin and pale: *Los Angeles Times,* July 10, 1912.

p. 375 Rogers spent much of his time in an anteroom: *Los Angeles Times,* July 12, 1912.

p. 375 DARROW TO DISCREDIT ACCUSERS: San Francisco *Bulletin,* July 11, 1912.

p. 377 "Franklin did not deny having made that statement": Franklin had admitted making the statement to Joe Timmons, but the judge allowed the testimony since he had not admitted making it to the other reporters.

p. 377 Stinken Leffens: Testimony, p. 5611.

p. 378 Bordwell statement: Quoted in Robinson, *Lawyers of Los Angeles,* p. 137, and in Steffens's fourth dispatch, dated December 6, 1912. Also, see Bordwell Papers, Stanford University.

p. 380 "hushed to breathless stillness": San Francisco *Bulletin,* July 19, 1912.

p. 381 Darrow in tears: Los Angeles *Record,* July 20, 1912.

p. 382 "The question is what I thought about it": Joe Timmons reported that the members of the Citizens Committee had been subpoenaed to testify that, up until Thanksgiving Day, Darrow had insisted that J.J. be set free. "But as Steffens admitted that fact in his own testimony, the District Attorney may not be able to use these witnesses in rebuttal." *San Francisco Examiner,* July 23, 1912.

p. 382 "The story of Steffens accentuated": *San Francisco Chronicle,* July 19, 1912.

p. 383 As of Tuesday, no one representing Gompers: Ed Nockles did not arrive until after the bribe on Tuesday—and did not agree to the plan until Thursday.

p. 383 Fredericks thrust his finger into Steffens's face: *Autobiography of Lincoln Steffens,* p. 700.

p. 384 "kittenish delight in paradoxes": Eastman, *Enjoyment of Living,* p. 426.

p. 384 "I feel as if my mind had been set": Mary Field to Lem Parton, February 1913. MPP. This is one of several letters from Mary to Lem that she wrote during the second Darrow trial. Many are misdated.

p. 385 "gasp that ran around the room": Los Angeles *Record,* July 20, 1912.

p. 385 The judge and Steffens passed the fan back and forth: Los Angeles *Record,* July 20, 1912; *The Autobiography of Lincoln Steffens,* p. 701.

p. 387 "the best cross-examining of his career": Los Angeles *Record,* July 20, 1912.

p. 387 "skillfully sought": *Organized Labor,* July 27, 1912.

p. 387 "I had his goat": The *Autobiography of Lincoln Steffens,* p. 701.

p. 388 "everybody thinks that, if it isn't denied": Lincoln Steffens to Laura Steffens, July 20, 1912. LSL. "Charles" was probably Charles D. Willard, who was present during at least one of Steffens's meetings that week. Steffens considered Willard "the man who, more than any other, represented the public spirit and ideals of Los Angeles." *Autobiography of Lincoln Steffens,* p. 683.

p. 388 "I wish you had gone": Lincoln Steffens to Laura Steffens, July 20, 1912. LSL.

p. 388 Rumors Leavitt would be replaced: *Los Angeles Examiner,* July 23, 1912.

p. 388 Letters from his doctor: Los Angeles *Herald,* July 23, 1912.

p. 389 Judge Hutton drove to Leavitt's home: *Los Angeles Examiner,* July 24, 1912.

p. 389 Rogers told the press that he had subpoenaed: *Los Angeles Examiner,* July 25, 1912.

p. 389 Blakesley had medical problems of his own: *Los Angeles Examiner,* July 25, 1912.

p. 389 Darrow's head buried in his arms: Los Angeles *Record,* July 25, 1912.

p. 390 "strong witness for Darrow defense": *San Francisco Chronicle,* July 27, 1912.

p. 390 Leavitt's doctor concluded he needed an operation: San Francisco *Bulletin,* July 29, 1912.

CHAPTER SIXTEEN

p. 391 "I told my own story": Autobiography, pp. 188–189

p. 392 Darrow's "partisan claque" in the courtroom: Photograph and caption in Los Angeles *Herald,* July 29, 1912.

p. 392 Looking frail and tired: Los Angeles *Record,* July 30, 1912.

p. 392 "This attitude, whether natural or the result": *Los Angeles Times,* July 30, 1912.

p. 394 The room was silent: *Los Angeles Examiner,* July 30, 1912.

p. 396 CHECK PROVES BRIBE STORY FALSE: Los Angeles *Herald,* July 29, 1912.

p. 396 Porch that could be seen: In fact, as a visit to 804 Bonnie Bray would have demonstrated, the house sits on a hill and cannot be seen by others on the street or by those in neighboring houses.

p. 396 "Many of the circumstances introduced": San Francisco *Bulletin,* August 3, 1912.

p. 397 "absolutely essential that a substantial amount": Morrison to Rappaport, September 7, 1911. FMP.

p. 397 Doubtful that Darrow ever had ten thousand dollars to spare: The defense fund was consistently strapped for cash. On September 2, 1911, Frank Morrison wrote to a colleague that "We have got some money in, but not near so much as Attorney Darrow believes we should have, and it is going to be very difficult to raise the smallest amount" (Morrison to Rappaport, September 2, 1911, FMP). Two weeks later, Morrison again reported that "urgent demands for money continue to come from Los Angeles" (Morrison to Rappaport, September 16, 1911, FMP). On September 26, 1911, Morrison wrote J. J. McNamara that "I have had several telegrams and letters from Attorney Darrow, in which he shows he is disappointed in the amount raised so far" (Morrison to McNamara, September 26, 1911, FMP). Moreover, Darrow wrote to Tvietmoe in October pleading for money. "I am not going to bore you any more," he said, suggesting that he had solicited money before, "but I am going to have to have assurance of the next money that is needed or finish up Jim's case without putting any more money in it and then quit the game. I am simply not going to kill myself with this case and then worry over money and not know what to do" (Darrow to Tvietmoe, October 29, 1911, AFLP).

p. 397 Darrow's manner "had a most peculiar effect": Los Angeles *Herald,* July 31, 1912.

p. 397 core defense—"to show a lack of motive": *Los Angeles Times,* July 31, 1912.

p. 397 dramatic impact on the audience: *Los Angeles Times,* July 31, 1912.

p. 397 "At times Darrow seemed to forget": *Los Angeles Examiner,* July 31, 1912.

p. 398 These words brought forth more tears: *Los Angeles Examiner,* July 31, 1912.

pp. 398–99 Darrow regarded Ford "as his special bête noire": *Los Angeles Examiner,* July 31, 1912.

p. 399 Story about Ford and Father Hegarty: Author's interview with Moira Ford.

p. 400 Darrow spoke slowly, watching Ford through half-closed eyes: Los Angeles *Record,* July 31, 1912.

p. 403 Darrow was "sparring for time": Los Angeles *Herald,* July 31, 1912.

p. 404 Darrow "on the defensive": Los Angeles *Herald,* July 31, 1912; *Los Angeles Times,* August 1, 1912.

p. 406 Ford had "secured a number of admissions": Los Angeles *Record,* August 1, 1912.

p. 406 Darrow "appeared dogged" by the end of the week: Los Angeles *Record,* August 1, 1912.

p. 406 "The calmest person in the room was the defendant himself": San Francisco *Bulletin,* August 3, 1912.

p. 407 eyes filled with tears, shaking uncontrollably: *Los Angeles Examiner,* July 30, 1912.

p. 407 Speculation that Ruby was again on the verge of breakdown: *Los Angeles Times,* August 4, 1912.

p. 407 "Darrow sang all day": Mary to Erskine, August 6, 1912. CESWP-H.

p. 407 The defense team had begun to plan a victory celebration: Ibid.

p. 407 "Darrow is working on his speech now": Ibid.

p. 407 Prediction of "one of greatest pieces of oratory": Los Angeles *Record,* August 10, 1912.

CHAPTER SEVENTEEN

p. 408 Darrow's address at Altgeld's funeral: Delivered on March 14, 1902, it is printed as an appendix to Darrow's autobiography.

p. 411 Ford stood . . . glaring fiercely: Los Angeles *Record,* August 12, 1912.

p. 411 Ford's glasses "made his eyes look big and black": Baillie, p. 21.

p. 412 "In between frequent drinks of ice water": *Organized Labor,* August 17, 1912.

p. 412 Rogers planned to introduce "a novelty": Los Angeles *Herald,* August 12, 1912.

p. 413 "the classic garb of a southern gentleman": Los Angeles *Record,* August 13, 1912.

p. 415 Rogers had "moved his audience": Los Angeles *Record,* August 13, 1912.

p. 415 Two thousand spectators "fought and struggled": Los Angeles *Record,* August 13, 1912.

p. 417 Darrow's low voice began to rise: Los Angeles *Herald,* August 14, 1912.

p. 418 "tears from the jurors' eyes": Los Angeles *Herald,* August 14, 1912.

p. 418 lowering his voice: Los Angeles *Record,* August 15, 1912.

p. 419 Darrow stopped and stood for a moment: Los Angeles *Record,* August 15, 1912.

p. 422 tears and sobs . . . Johannsen wept: *Los Angeles Times,* August 15, 1912.

p. 422 "the jurors must have read on the scales": San Francisco *Bulletin,* August 15, 1912.

pp. 422–23 "Clarence Darrow has shaken his clenched fist": San Francisco *Bulletin,* August 15, 1912.

p. 423 Jury nullification: The concept of jury nullification was first established in England in 1670, when a jury acquitted William Penn of charges of seditious libel. Since the acquittals directly defied the trial judge's instructions, the judge jailed the jury for contempt. In releasing the jury, Chief Justice Vaughan held that juries could never be punished for their verdicts. Sixty years later, an American jury refused to convict printer John Peter Zenger of libel after his lawyer, Andrew Hamilton, argued that he should be freed in "the cause of liberty"—not because he was innocent of the charges. As one court noted, "the cases of William Penn and John Peter Zenger illustrate how well our society's interests have been served by acquittals resulting from application by the jurors of their collective conscience and sense of justice," *United States* v. *Simpson,* 460 F.2d 515 (9th Cir., 1972).

Although disapproving of such conduct by juries, in 1895 the U.S. Supreme Court held that the government cannot usurp the jury's power to nullify. *Sparf and Hanson* v. *United States,* 156 U.S. 51 (1895). In the 1920s, juries regularly refused to convict defendants in prohibition cases. In the 1960s, defense counsel asked juries to use their power to acquit men and women who had used illegal methods to resist the draft or to protest the war in Vietnam. More recently, antiabortion protesters have asked juries to use the power of jury nullification to acquit members charged with criminal trespass (ABORTION PROTEST JURIES TOLD TO IGNORE NULLIFICATION AD, *Los Angeles Times,* January 27, 1990, San Diego edition).

The concept of jury nullification has been discussed in several excellent law review articles, including "Jury Nullification and Jury-Control Procedures," 65 NYU Law Review 825 (June 1990).

p. 423 "hysterical women grasped at Darrow's hand": *Los Angeles Times,* August 16, 1912.

p. 424 "The court and jury and hundreds of spectators": Los Angeles *Herald,* August 15, 1912.

p. 424 Dozens of people . . . were sobbing: The Los Angeles *Herald* said that "Darrow, with tears streaming from his eyes, sought to justify the crime of Jim McNamara." In *Final Verdict,* St. Johns reported that Darrow "wept each handkerchief into a sodden ball, cast it from him, and Ruby Darrow supplied another, which soon suffered a like fate. At last he began to wipe away the floods on his sleeves" (p. 451).

p. 425 "Life is a game of whist": "Whist," by Eugene Fitch Ware. See discussion in Ravitz, pp. 18–20.

p. 426 "Sobs were audible during his dramatic pauses": Los Angeles *Record,* August 15, 1912.
  "Even the court stenographer was crying": Baillie, p. 22.

p. 426 the chimes in St. Vibiana's Cathedral: Los Angeles *Record,* August 15, 1912.

p. 426 "the greatest oratorical effort": Los Angeles *Record,* August 15, 1912. "It was a good argument," Darrow wrote two decades later. "I have listened to great arguments and have made many arguments myself, and consider that my judgement on this subject is sound." Autobiography, p. 189.

p. 427 Fredericks's oration was "a beautiful oratorical effort": Los Angeles *Herald,* August 16, 1912.

p. 428 "one of the most effective addresses": *Los Angeles Times,* August 16, 1912.

p. 428 "Fredericks called all of his oratorical powers": San Francisco *Bulletin,* August 16, 1912.

p. 428 Predictions that the jury would be "locked up for some days": *Los Angeles Examiner,* August 17, 1912.

p. 428 Darrow was "hunted, nervous": Los Angeles *Record,* August 17, 1912.

p. 428 Judge Hutton had dark circles under his eyes: San Francisco *Bulletin,* August 17, 1912.

p. 429 Ruby started to cry hysterically: Los Angeles *Record,* August 17, 1912.

p. 430 Ruby, "trembling like a leaf": Los Angeles *Record,* August 17, 1912.

p. 431 "Behind Darrow came society women": San Francisco *Bulletin,* August 18, 1912.

p. 431 reception at the Café Martan: The victory party included Earl Rogers, Fremont Older, Anton Johannsen, Mary Field, and Darrow's old friends Jim Griffes and Fay Lewis.

p. 431 "I don't want the crowds": Mary to Erskine, August 6, 1912. CESWP-H.

p. 432 "Organized labor sends you this": Los Angeles *Record,* August 17, 1912.

p. 432 "I shall spend the rest of my life": Los Angeles *Herald,* August 17, 1912.

CHAPTER EIGHTEEN

p. 433 Rogers spent most of the winter in a sanatorium: *Los Angeles Times,* January 4, 1913.

p. 434 "I never had any doubts": Baillie, p. 27.

p. 434 Darrow's own circle of friends thought him capable of the crime: Those who considered Darrow guilty included W. W. Catlin, Austin Willard Wright, Edgar Lee Masters, Sara Field Ehrgott, Erskine Wood, and many friends of journalists Hutchins Hapgood and William Marion Reedy. According to Irving Stone, Billy Cavenaugh and Dr. Perceval Gerson also assumed that Darrow was responsible for the bribe.

p. 434 W. W. Catlin came to the same conclusion: Catlin to Wood, February 14, 1912. CESWP-H.

p. 435 "What do I care if he is guilty as Hell": Lincoln Steffens to Laura Steffens, June 25, 1912. LSL.

p. 435 "At the very worst most people": William Marion Reedy to Darrow, February 15, 1912. CDP.

p. 435 Judge Bordwell's statement: Issued on December 5, 1912. Quoted in W. W. Robinson, *Lawyers of Los Angeles,* p. 137.

p. 436 Johannsen said he would "always believe that Darrow did it to save his own skin": Erskine to Sara, April 12, 1912. CESWP-H.

p. 436 "the chance of winning": Stone, p. 264.

p. 436 Darrow told Garland he had earned "forty-four thousand dollars": Garland, *Hamlin Garland's Diaries,* p. 122. Darrow added that "his own trial had cost him twenty thousand so that for two years' work and all his worry he had only twenty-odd thousand dollars."

p. 436 Darrow said he pled the boys guilty "to save the lives": Autobiography, p. 180.

p. 436 "The young fellow [Jim] wept and begged to be allowed to go on": Erskine to Sara, April 12, 1912, quoting Johannsen. CESWP-H.

p. 437 Jim was "forced into it": Ibid.

p. 437 "We were forced to plead guilty": Jim McNamara to Paul Scharrenberg, December 23, 1928. Quoted in Burki, *Paul Scharrenberg: White Shirt Sailor,* p. 96. Jim also wrote a letter to a Communist party leader saying: "did not J.J. and I plead guilty to save Dave [Caplan] and Matt [Schmidt] and the twenty-six on the Metal Trades Strike Committee of 1910. . . . I wanted the trial to show up the class struggle on the industrial field, but I was overwhelmed by a two-hundred-thousand-dollar defense, with a constant nightmarish fear that there was great danger in taking the San Francisco 'labor leaders' with me." Jim McNamara to William Z. Foster, February 1, 1935. Southern California Research Library.

Clancy and Tvietmoe were indicted and convicted in the federal case in Indianapolis, but since the federal government only had the power to prosecute interstate transportation of dynamite it did not deal with the *Times* bombing, where the dynamite was transported within the state of California. Although the Los Angeles district attorney later successfully prosecuted Schmidt and Caplan for their role in the *Times* bombing, he never brought charges against Clancy, Johannsen, Tvietmoe, or any of the other San Francisco labor leaders who were on the Metal Trades Strike Committee of 1910.

Tvietmoe's conviction in the federal case was reversed on appeal.

p. 437 the goal was "to frame up or carry out a plan": Wood to Catlin, July 19, 1911. CESWP-B.

p. 438 "had a 'hunch' that he": Hapgood, "Clarence Darrow as a Radical," August 20, 1912. The column can be found in the Hapgood Papers, Beinecke Library, Yale University.

p. 438 "The high motive of the revolutionist": Darrow, "The Right of Revolution," collected in *Verdicts out of Court,* p. 59.

p. 438 "society is organized injustice": Letter to Miss S. CDP. Underlining in original.

p. 439 Golding acted "contrary to my best interests": Golding to Darrow, November 22, 1913. CDP.

p. 439 "Darrow believed in saving lives": Margaret Parton's unpublished biography of Mary Field, p. 81. MPP.

  The McNamaras "never morally committed murder": Darrow to jury in second bribery trial, *Organized Labor,* March 15, 1913.

p. 440 Darrow tried to arrange the kidnapping of Harrington: Erskine to Sara, April 12, 1912. CESWP-H.

p. 440 offering to testify against Samuel Gompers: On February 29, 1912, Walter Drew told one of his colleagues that "it will interest you to know that Darrow has offered to plead guilty and tell all he knows if he is let off with a $10,000 fine. I am in favor of this course" (Drew to Badorf, WDP). Two days later, Badorf argued for "a jail sentence rather than a compromise," noting that "it may be a hard proposition to convict Gompers on Darrow's testimony alone. . . . It would be wise to know just what evidence could be procured against Gompers before any promises are made" (Badorf to Drew, WDP).

p. 441 "Laws are passed, judges elected": *Organized Labor,* September 14, 1912.

p. 441 Description of Darrow in Portland: Sara to Erskine, September 1 and 11, 1912. CESWP-H.

p. 441 Mary Field's conversation with Darrow about the tour: *Organized Labor,* October 5, 1912.

p. 442 "When Germany invaded Belgium": Autobiography, p. 210.

p. 443 "Too bad, too bad that old General Otis": Mary to Sara, September, 1917. CESWP-H.

p. 443 "all through the war he felt": Mary to Sara, 1918. CESWP-H.

p. 443 "As soon as the war was over": Russell, p. 295.

p. 443 "bitter, bitter and essentially hopeless": Garland, *Hamlin Garland's Diaries,* entry dated March 19, 1911.

p. 444 "the cynic is humbled": Lincoln Steffens to Laura Steffens, June 25, 1912, LSL.

p. 444 "What we are is the result": Autobiography, p. 207. The change in Darrow was captured in a letter from Marcet Haldeman-Julius, who became a friend of Darrow's in the 1920s. Haldeman-Julius's aunt, Jane Addams, once told her that "we knew two different Darrows." The letter continued:

> "You, my dear," she said, "know him as he is now, mellowed by life and more than ever interested in advocating causes—in defending victims—than in the years when he was also interested very much in advancing his own career in his profession—and in the financial side of it, too." CDP.

p. 444 871. Judge William Holly's eulogy: Memorial Service. Darrow Papers, University of Chicago Library.

SELECTED BIBLIOGRAPHY

I N LARGE PART, THIS book is based on primary research in manuscript collections, government archives, memoirs, oral histories, periodicals, newspapers, government hearings, and court records. The most important materials appear in letters—including those by Darrow and the group of friends that included Mary Field Parton, Sara Field Ehrgott, Erskine Wood, Lincoln Steffens, E. W. Scripps, and the leaders of the American Federation of Labor; in the letters of such industry representatives as Walter Drew and Oscar Lawler; in the court transcript of Darrow's first trial; and in thousands of contemporaneous news accounts. Since newspapers and periodicals of the era were notoriously biased, I read daily and weekly accounts in several publications that were sympathetic to labor, the McNamaras and to Darrow, as well as the more numerous stories that appeared in journals that were generally on the side of capital, the *Los Angeles Times,* and the prosecution.

Though less reliable, the oral histories and memoirs of participants were also extremely helpful, as were countless books—particularly biographies of participants—that covered some aspect of the story. Finally, the book was enriched enormously by works of social, legal, labor, and intellectual history, by studies of Chicago, Los Angeles, California, and the press, and by novels of the era, especially those written by women and men who knew the participants well.

MANUSCRIPT COLLECTIONS

Bancroft Library, University of California–Berkeley.
> Erskine Wood and Sara Field; Francis J. Heney; Hiram Johnson; Cora and Fremont Older; the San Francisco Labor Council.

Beinecke Library, Yale University.
> Mable Dodge Luhan; Hutchins Hapgood.

Boston Public Library.
> Fred H. Moore.

Butler Library, Columbia University.
> Lincoln Steffens; Charles Yale Harrison.

Chicago Historical Society.
> Chicago Commons Papers; Chicago Teachers Federation Archival Records; Sunset Club Records.

Circle Campus, University of Illinois.
> Jane Addams; Haldeman-Julius; Hull House; Ben Reitman.

Cunningham Library, Indiana State University.
> Eugene V. Debs.

Dartmouth College.
> Ramon Guthrie Papers (Sections of a labor novel based on events in Los Angeles, possibly written by Sinclair Lewis).

Duke University.
> Frank Morrison Letterbooks.

Houghton Library, Harvard University.
> Lincoln Steffens; Corinne Roosevelt Robinson.

Huntington Library.
> Mary Austin; Erskine Wood and Sara Bard Field (Erghott Wood).

Library of Congress.
> Clarence Darrow; Charles Edward Russell; Theodore Roosevelt; William Howard Taft; Brand Whitlock.

Los Angeles Times History Center.
Newberry Library.
> Edgar Lee Masters; Margaret Parton (including letters from Clarence Darrow to Mary Field); Carter H. Harrison.

New York Public Library.
> Emma Goldman; Samuel Gompers; National Civic Federation; Frank Walsh.

Ohio University Libraries.
> E. W. Scripps Papers.

Oregon Historical Society.
> Corinne Roosevelt Robinson (letters to Erskine Wood).

San Francisco State Labor Archives and Research Center.
> P. N. McCarthy (including his unpublished autobiography).

Schlesinger Library, Radcliffe College.
> Francis Perkins.

Sherman Library.
> Otto Brant; Moses Sherman.

Siouxland Heritage Museum.
> Senator Richard F. Pettigrew.

Smith College.
> Jane Addams.

Southern California Library for Social Studies and Research.
> Leo Gallagher Papers.

Stanford University.
> Walter Bordwell; Meyer Lissner.

State Historical Society of Wisconsin.
> Adolf Germer; Morris Hillquit; American Federation of Labor Records: the Samuel Gompers Era.

Taniment Institute, New York University.
> Emma Goldman; McNamara Defense Conference of Greater New York.

University of California, Los Angeles.
> LeCompte Davis; E. A. Dickson; Katherine Edson; Perceval Gerson; J. R. Haynes; Franklin Hichborn; Frances Noel; James Pope; W. W. Robinson; Irving Stone.

University of Chicago.
> Clarence Darrow; Charles Merriam.

University of Cincinnati.
> J. B. McNamara; J. J. McNamara.

University of Michigan.
> Bentley Historical Library: Walter Drew Papers; transcribed interviews with John Harrington; Robert Foster's unpublished autobiography.
> Labadie Collection: Austin Willard Wright.

University of Oregon–Eugene.
> Parton Papers (including Mary Field); Robert Cantwell Papers (including the unpublished autobiography of J. B. McNamara).

University of Pennsylvania.
> Theodore Dreiser.

University of Southern California.
> Hamlin Garland.

University of Texas, Austin.
> Edgar Lee Masters.

Yale University Library.
> William Kent.

ORAL HISTORIES

Helen Valeska Bary—Bancroft Library.

Seth Brown—UCLA Institute of Industrial Relations (in *Los Angeles Times* History Collection).

Clarence Darrow—Illinois State Historical Society.

Sara Field Ehrgott, with an afterward by Katherine Field Caldwell—Bancroft Library

John Frey—Columbia University.

Oscar Lawler—University of California–Los Angeles; Claremont College.

Walter Millsap—University of California–Los Angeles.

Mary Field Parton—interviews with Margaret Parton, Parton Papers, University of Oregon.

James Pope—University of California–Los Angeles.

Paul Scharrenberg—Bancroft.

Harold Story—University of California–Los Angeles.

COURT PROCEEDINGS AND DOCUMENTS

J. H. Bullard v. *Clarence Darrow, et al.,* deposition of Job Harriman, Bordwell Collection, Stanford University Library.

People v. *David Caplan,* Brief of Facts, Los Angeles County Law Library.

People v. *Clarence Darrow,* first case trial transcript, Los Angeles County Law Library.

People v. *M. A. Schmidt,* brief of evidence, Los Angeles County Law Library.

United States v. *Ryan, et al.,* Huntington Library.

Frank M. Ryan et al. v. *The United States of America,* brief in support of petition for rehearing, October Term, 1913, National Archives.

GOVERNMENT HEARINGS, FILES, DOCUMENTS, AND REPORTS

California State Archives.
    U. S. Webb.

Committee of the California State Federation of Labor.
    "Report on the *Los Angeles Times* Disaster," published in *Pattern Makers' Journal,* January, 1911.

Federal Bureau of Investigation.
    William J. Burns; LeCompte Davis; Job Harriman; Anton Johannsen; Edward Nockels; Lincoln Steffens; J. J. McNamara; J. B. McNamara; Sara Field Ehrgott.

Los Angeles City Archives.

National Archives, Washington, D.C.
    Justice Department coded messages, correspondence and documents in preparation for *People* v. *McNamara, People* v. *Darrow,* and *People* v. *Ryan.* Also, records of appeal of Olaf Tvietmoe, parole and pardon proceedings for Frank Ryan, etc., and a file relating to Anton Johannsen's service for the War Labor Board in World War I.

National Archives and Records Administration, San Francisco Branch.
    Bankruptcy records of Sunset National Oil Company (president: Olaf Tvietmoe).

U.S. Bankruptcy Court.

U.S. Commission on Industrial Relations. hearings and final report. Washington, D.C., 1915.

ORAL INTERVIEWS

Katherine Caldwell (daughter of Sara Field Ehrgott)—March 16, 1988.

Moira Ford (daughter of Joseph Ford)—August 26, 1987.

Elmer Gertz—April 1992.

Irwin Klass—March 3, 1988.

Clarence Mullholland—October 25, 1988.

Ralph Poyer—January 25, 1988.

Judge Lester Roth—July 19, 1989.

Irving Stone—summer 1987.

PRIVATE COLLECTIONS

Moira Ford

Merchants and Manufacturers Association

Pinkerton Detective Agency

MASTER'S AND PH.D. THESES

Baker, Robert Munson. "Why the McNamaras Pleaded Guilty to the Bombing of the *Los Angeles Times*." University of California–Berkeley, Master's dissertation, 1949.

Burki, Mary Ann Mason. "Paul Scharrenberg: White Shirt Sailor." University of Rochester, Ph.D. dissertation, 1971.

Johnson, Daniel J. "Socialism in Los Angeles: The Municipal Elections of 1911." University of California–Los Angeles, Master's dissertation, 1987.

Searing, Richard Cole. "The McNamara Cases: Its Causes and Results." University of California–Berkeley, Master's dissertation, 1947.

Weintraub, Hyman. "The I.W.W. in California: 1905–1931." University of California–Los Angeles, Ph.D. dissertation, 1947.

SELECTED BOOKS AND PAMPHLETS

Adamic, Louis. *Dynamite: The Story of Class Violence in America (Revised Edition)*. New York: Viking, 1934.

———. *My America, 1928–1938*. New York: Harper & Brothers, 1938.

Adams, Brooks. *The Theory of Social Revolutions*. New York: The MacMillan Company, 1913.

Adams, Graham, Jr. *Age of Industrial Violence, 1910–1915*. New York: Columbia University Press, 1966.

Addams, Jane. *Twenty Years at Hull-House: with Autobiographical Notes.* Chautauqua, N.Y.: The Chautauqua Press, 1911.

Allen, Frederick Lewis. *Only Yesterday: An Informal History of the 1920's.* New York: Harper & Brothers, 1931.

Altgeld, John Peter. *Live Questions: Including Our Penal Machinery and Its Victims.* Chicago: Donohue & Henneberry, 1890.

————. *The Mind and Spirit of John Peter Altgeld: Selected Writings and Addresses.* Edited with a preface by Henry M. Christman. Urbana, Ill.: University of Illinois, 1960.

Atkinson, Linda. *Mother Jones: The Most Dangerous Woman In America.* New York: Crown Publishers, 1978.

Austin, Mary. *Love and the Soul Maker.* New York and London: D. Appleton and Company, 1914.

Baillie, Hugh. *High Tension: The Recollections of Hugh Baillie.* New York: Harper & Brothers, 1959.

Barnard, Harry. *Eagle Forgotten: The Life of John Peter Altgeld.* Indianapolis: Bobbs-Merrill, 1938.

Bean, Walton. *Boss Ruef's San Francisco: The Story of the Union Labor Party, Big Business, and the Graft Prosecution.* Berkeley and Los Angeles: University of California Press, 1968.

Berger, Meyer. *The Life and* Times *of Los Angeles: A Newspaper, A Family and A City.* New York: Athenaeum, 1984.

Bingham, Edwin R. *Charles F. Lummis: Editor of the Southwest.* San Marino, California: The Huntington Library, 1955.

Bonelli, William G. *Billion Dollar Blackjack: The Story of Corruption and the Los Angeles Times.* Beverly Hills, California: Civic Research Press, 1954.

Boyer, Richard O., and Herbert M. Morias. *Labor's Untold Story: The Adventure Story of the Battles, Betrayals and Victories of American Working Men and Women.* New York: Cameron Associates, 1955.

Brecher, Jeremy. *Strike: The True History of Mass Insurgence in America from 1877 to the Present*. San Francisco: Straight Arrow Books, 1972.

Brody, David. *Steelworkers in America: The Nonunion Era*. Cambridge, Mass: Harvard University Press, 1960.

Browning, Frank, and John Gerassi. *The American Way of Crime*. New York: G. P. Putnam's Sons, 1980.

Bruns, Roger A. *The Damndest Radical: The Life and World of Ben Reitman, Chicago's Celebrated Social Reformer, Hobo King, and Whorehouse Physician*. Urbana and Chicago, Ill.: University of Illinois Press, 1987.

Burns, William J. *The Masked War*. New York: George H. Doran Company, 1913.

Bush, Francis X. *Eagle Forgotten: The Life of John Peter Altgeld*. Indianapolis: Bobbs-Merrill, 1938.

Caesar, Gene. *Incredible Detective: The Biography of William J. Burns*. Englewood Cliffs, N.J.: Prentice-Hall, 1968.

Campbell, John B. *Rose of Los Angeles: Love Story of a City*. Los Angeles: Tribune Press, 1924.

Carr, Harry. *Los Angeles: City of Dreams*. New York: Grosset and Dunlap, 1935.

Cather, Willa. *Alexander's Bridge*. New York: New American Library, 1988.

Caughey, John, and LeRee Caughey, eds. *Los Angeles: Biography of a City*. Berkeley and Los Angeles: University of California Press, 1977.

Chaplin, Ralph. *Wobbly: The Rough and Tumble Story of An American Radical*. Chicago: University of Chicago Press, 1948

Cleland, Robert Glass. *California in Our Time: 1900–1940*. New York: Alfred A. Knopf, 1947.

Cochran, Thomas C., and William Miller. *The Age of Enterprise: A Social History of Industrial America.* New York and Evanston: Harper & Row, 1961.

Cohn, Alfred and Joe Chisholm. *"Take the Witness".* New York: Frederick A. Stokes Company, 1934.

Conkin, Paul K. *Two Paths to Utopia: The Hutterites and Llano Colony.* Lincoln, Nebraska: University of Nebraska Press, 1964.

Creel, George. *Rebel at Large: Recollections of Fifty Crowded Years.* New York: G. P. Putnam's Sons, 1947.

Crouch, Winston W. and Beatrice Dinerman. *Southern California Metropolis: A Study in Development of Government for a Metropolitan Area.* Berkeley and Los Angeles: University of California Press, 1963.

Crunden, Robert M. *A Hero In Spite of Himself: Brand Whitlock in Art, Politics, & War.* New York: Alfred A. Knopf, 1969.

Darrow, Clarence. *Attorney for the Damned.* Edited and with notes by Arthur Weinberg. New York: Simon and Schuster, 1957.

———. *Farmington.* New York: Charles Scribner's Sons, 1904.

———. *The Story of My Life.* New York: Charles Scribner's Sons, 1932.

———. *Verdicts Out of Court.* Edited with an introduction by Arthur and Lila Weinberg. Chicago: Elephant Paperback Edition, 1989.

Darrow, Clarence, and Edgar Lee Masters. *United States ex rel. John Turner* v. *William Williams, Commissioner of Immigration,* Brief and Argument of Appellant in the Supreme Court of the United States, October term, 1903.

Darrow, Clarence, and Wallace Rice. *Infidels and Heretics: An Agnostic's Anthology.* Boston: The Stratford Company, 1929.

David, Henry. *The History of the Haymarket Affair.* New York: Farrar & Rinehart, 1936.

Davidson, Jo. *Between Sittings: An Informal Autobiography of Jo Davidson*. New York: The Dial Press, 1951.

Degler, Carl N. *Out of Our Past: The Forces that Shaped Modern America*. New York and Evanston: Harper Colophon Books, 1959.

Dester, Chester McArthur. *Henry Demarest Lloyd and the Empire of Reform*. Philadelphia: University of Pennsylvania Press, 1963

Dreiser, Theodore. *Dawn*. New York: Horace Liveright, 1931.

———. *The Titan*. New York: New American Library edition, 1984.

Duke, Donald, and Stan Ristler. *Santa Fe: Steel Rails through California*. San Marino, California: Golden West Books, 1963.

Dumke, Glenn S. *The Boom of the Eighties in Southern California*. San Marino, California: Huntington Library, 1966.

Eastman, Crystal. *Work-Accidents and The Law: The Pittsburgh Survey*. New York: The Russell Sage Foundation, 1910.

Eastman, Max. *Enjoyment of Living*. New York: Harper & Brothers, 1948.

———. *Great Companions: Critical Memoirs of Some Famous Friends*. New York: Farrar, Straus and Cudahy, 1959.

Falk, Candace. *Love, Anarchy, and Emma Goldman*. New York: Holt, Rinehart and Winston, 1984.

Fink, Augusta. *I-Mary: A Biography of Mary Austin*. Tucson: The University of Arizona Press, 1983.

Flynn, Elizabeth Gurley. *I Speak My Own Piece*. New York: Masses and Mainstream, 1955.

Fogelson, Robert M., *The Fragmented Metropolis*. Cambridge, Mass.: Harvard University Press, 1967.

Foner, Philip S. *History of the Labor Movement in the United States, Volume III: The Policies and Practices of the American Federation of Labor, 1900–1909*. New York: International Publishers, 1964.

―――――. *History of the Labor Movement in the United States, Volume IV: The Industrial Workers of the World, 1905–1917.* New York: International Publishers, 1965.

―――――, *History of the Labor Movement in the United States, Volume V: The AFL in the Progressive Era, 1910–1915.* New York: International Publishers, 1980.

―――――. *History of the Labor Movement in the United States, Volume VII: Labor and World War I, 1914–1918.* New York: International Publishers, 1987.

―――――. *May Day: A Short History of the International Workers' Holiday, 1886–1986.* New York: International Publishers, 1986.

Ford, Patrick H., ed. *The Darrow Bribery Trial,* Whittier, California: Western Printing Company, 1956.

Garland, Hamlin. *Companions on the Trail: A Literary Chronicle.* New York: The Macmillan Company, 1931.

―――――. *Hamlin Garland's Diaries.* Donald Pizer, ed. San Marino, California: The Huntington Library, 1968.

―――――. *My Friendly Contemporaries: A Literary Log.* New York: The Macmillan Company, 1932.

Giesler, Jerry. *The Jerry Giesler Story: As Told to Pete Martin.* New York: Simon and Schuster, 1960.

Gilbert, James Burkhart. *Perfect Cities: Chicago's Utopias of 1893.* Chicago: The University of Chicago Press, 1991.

Ginger, Ray. *Altgeld's America: The Lincoln Ideal Versus Changing Realities.* New York: Funk & Wagnalls, 1958.

―――――. *The Bending Cross: A Biography of Eugene Victor Debs.* New Brunswick, N.J.: Rutgers University Press, 1949.

Glasscock, C. B.. *Gold in Them Hills: The Story of the West's Last Wild Mining Days,* Indianapolis: Bobbs-Merrill, 193–.

Goldman, Emma. *Living My Life*. New York: Alfred A. Knopf, 1931.

Gompers, Sam. *Seventy Years of Life and Labor: An Autobiography*. New York: E. P. Dutton & Company, 1925.

Gottlieb, Robert, and Irene Wolt. *Thinking Big: The Story of the* Los Angeles Times, *Its Publishers and Their Influence on Southern California*. New York: G. P. Putnam's Sons, 1977.

Grant, Luke. *The National Erectors Association and The International Association of Bridge and Structural Iron Workers*. A Report of the United States Commission on Industrial Relations. Washington, D.C. 1915.

Green, Martin. *New York, 1913: The Armory Show and the Paterson Strike Pageant*. New York: Charles Scribner's Sons, 1988.

Grover, David H. *Debaters and Dynamiters: The Story of the Haywood Trial*. Corvallis, Oregon: Oregon State University Press, 1964.

Guinn, J. M. *A History of California and an Extended History of Los Angeles and Environs*. Los Angeles: Historic Record Company, 1915.

Gutman, Herbert G. *Work, Culture, and Society in Industrializing America: Essays in American Working-Class and Social History*. New York: Alfred A. Knopf, 1976.

Halberstam, David. *The Powers That Be*. New York: Alfred A. Knopf, 1979.

Haldeman-Julius, E. *My First 25 Years*. Girard, Kansas: Haldeman-Julius Publications, 1949.

————. *My Second 25 Years*. Girard, Kansas: Haldeman-Julius Publications, 1949.

Haldeman-Julius, Marcet. *Famous and Interesting Guests at a Kansas Farm*. Girard, Kansas: Haldeman-Julius Company, 1936.

Hancock, Ralph. *Fabulous Boulevard*. New York: Funk & Wagnalls, 1949.

Hangerford, Edward. *The Modern Railroad.* Chicago: McClung and Co., 1911.

Hapgood, Hutchins. *A Victorian in the Modern World.* New York: Harcourt, Brace and Company, 1939.

————. *The Spirit of Labor.* New York: Duffield & Company, 1907.

Harrison, Carter H. *Growing Up with Chicago.* Chicago: Ralph Fletcher Seymour, 1944.

————. *Stormy Years: The Autobiography of Carter H. Harrison, Five Times Mayor of Chicago.* Indianapolis: The Bobbs-Merrill Company, 1935.

Harrison, Charles Yale. *Clarence Darrow.* New York: Jonathan Cape & Harrison Smith, 1931.

Haywood, William D. *Bill Haywood's Book: The Autobiography of William D. Haywood.* New York: International Publishers, 1929.

Hichborn, Franklin. *"The System" as Uncovered by the San Francisco Graft Prosecution.* San Francisco: The James H. Barry Company, 1915.

Higgins, C. A. *To California over the Sante Fe Trail.* Chicago: Passenger Department, Santa Fe, 1914.

Hofstadter, Richard. *The Age of Reform: From Bryan to F.D.R.* New York: Vintage Books, 1955.

Holbrook, Stewart H. *Dreamers of the American Dream.* Garden City, New York: Doubleday & Company, 1957.

————. *The Rocky Mountain Revolution.* New York: Henry Holt and Company, 1956.

Holloway, Jean. *Hamlin Garland: A Biography.* Austin, Texas: University of Texas Press, 1960.

Howe, Frederick C. *Confessions of a Reformer.* New York: Charles Scribner's Sons, 1925.

Howe, Irving. *World of Our Fathers: The Journey of the East European Jews to America and the Life They Found and Made.* New York and London: Harcourt Brace Jovanovich, 1976.

————. *Socialism and America.* San Diego, New York and London: Harcourt Brace Jovanovich, 1985.

Hunsberger, Willard D. *Clarence Darrow: A Bibliography.* Metuchen, N.J.: The Scarecrow Press, 1981.

Hunter, Robert. *Violence and the Labor Movement.* New York: The Macmillan Company, 1914.

Irvine, Alexander. *A Fighting Parson: The Autobiography of Alexander Irvine.* Boston: Little Brown and Company, 1930.

————. *Revolution in Los Angeles (1911).* Los Angeles: The Citizen Print Shop, 1912.

Johannsen, Anton, Clarence Darrow and Mother Jones. *The True History of the Famous McNamara Case.* Kansas City, Mo.: Carpenters Local No. 61, 1915.

Jones, Mary Harris. *The Correspondence of Mother Jones.* Edited with an introduction by Edward M. Steel. Pittsburgh: University of Pittsburgh Press, 1985.

Josephson, Matthew. *Sidney Hillman: Statesman of American Labor.* Garden City, N.Y.: Doubleday & Company, 1952.

Kahrl, William. Water and Power: The Conflict over Los Angeles' Water Supply in the Owens Valley. Berkeley and Los Angeles: University of California Press, 1982.

Kaplan, Justin. *Lincoln Steffens: A Biography.* New York: Simon and Schuster, 1974.

Kazin, Michael. *Barons of Labor: The San Francisco Building Trades and Union Power in the Progressive Era.* Urbana and Chicago: University of Illinois Press, 1987.

Knight, Robert Edward Lee. *Industrial Relations in the San Francisco Bay Area, 1900–1918.* Berkeley and Los Angeles: University of California Press, 1960.

Koenigsberg, Moses. *King News—An Autobiography.* Philadelphia: A. Stokes Company, 1941.

La Follette, Robert M. *La Follette's Autobiography: A Personal Narrative of Political Experiences.* With a forward by Allan Nevins. Madison, Wisconsin: The University of Wisconsin Press, 1913. Reprint 1968.

Lasch, Christopher. *The New Radicalism in America, 1889–1963: The Intellectual as a Social Type.* New York: W. W. Norton, 1965.

Lee, W. Storrs, ed. *California: A Literary Chronicle.* New York: Funk & Wagnalls, 1968.

Lens, Sidney. *The Labor Wars: From the Molly Maguires to the Sit-downs.* Garden City, N.Y.: Doubleday & Company, 1973.

Lewis, Lloyd. *Chicago: The History of Its Reputation, Part I.* New York: Harcourt, Brace and Company, 1929.

Lingeman, Richard. *Theodore Dreiser: At the Gates of the City, 1871–1907.* New York: G. P. Putnam's Sons, 1986.

————. *Theodore Dreiser: An American Journey, 1908–1945.* New York: G. P. Putnam's Sons, 1990.

Livesay, Harold C. *Samuel Gompers and Organized Labor in America.* Boston and Toronto: Little Brown and Company, 1978.

Longstreet, Stephen. *Chicago, 1860–1919.* New York: David McKay Company, 1973.

Lord, Walter. *The Good Years: From 1900 to the First World War.* New York: Harper & Brothers, 1960.

Luhan, Mabel Dodge. *Movers and Shakers.* New York: Harcourt, Brace and Company, 1936.

Lyons, Eugene. *Assignment in Utopia.* New York: Harcourt, Brace and Company, 1937.

McCormack, Win and Dick Pintarich, eds. *Great Moments in Oregon History.* Portland, Oregon: New Oregon Publishers, 1987.

McManigal, Ortie. *The National Dynamite Plot,* Los Angeles: The Neal Company, 1913.

McWilliams, Cary. *Southern California Country: An Island on the Land.* New York: Duell, Sloan & Pearce, 1946.

Mandel, Bernard. *Samuel Gompers: A Biography.* Yellow Springs, Ohio: The Antioch Press, 1963.

Marcaccio, Michael D. *The Hapgoods: Three Earnest Brothers.* Charlottesville, Va: University Press of Virginia, 1977.

Markham, Edwin. *California the Wonderful.* New York: Edwin Markham Press, 1922.

Masters, Edgar Lee. *The Tale of Chicago,* New York: G. P. Putnam's Sons, 1933.

————. *Doomsday Book.* New York: The Macmillan Company, 1920.

May, Henry F. *The End of American Innocence: A Study of the First Years of Our Own Time, 1912–1917.* New York: Alfred A. Knopf, 1959.

Mayo, Morrow. *Los Angeles.* New York: Alfred A. Knopf, 1933.

Meltzer, Milton. *Bread and Roses: The Struggle of American Labor, 1865–1915.* New York: New American Library, 1967.

Merriam, Charles Edward. *Chicago: A More Intimate View of Urban Politics.* New York: The MacMillan Company, 1929.

Morris, Lloyd. *Not So Long Ago.* New York: Random House, 1949.

Mowry, George. *The California Progressives.* Berkeley, California: University of California Press, 1951.

————. *Theodore Roosevelt and the Progressive Movement.* Madison, Wisconsin. The University of Wisconsin Press, 1946.

Nadeau, Remi A. *City-Makers: The Men Who Transformed Los Angeles From Village to Metropolis During the First Great Boom, 1868–76.* Garden City, N.Y.: Doubleday & Company, 1948.

Nathan, George Jean. *The Intimate Notebooks of George Jean Nathan.* New York: Alfred A. Knopf, 1932.

Newmark, Harris. *Sixty Years in Southern California, 1853–1913.* Edited by Maurice and Marco R. Newmark. Fourth edition, revised and augmented with an introduction and notes by W. W. Robinson. Los Angeles: Dawson's Book Shop, 1984.

Noel, James W. *Some Sketches of a Great Struggle,* Indianapolis: 1916.

Otis, Harrison Gray. "Special Report" to stockholders of the *Los Angeles Times,* October 31, 1910.

Parton, Margaret. *Journey Through a Lighted Room.* New York: The Viking Press, 1973.

Parton, Mary Field, ed. *The Autobiography of Mother Jones.* Chicago: Charles H. Kerr, 1925.

Perry, Louis B., and Richard S. Perry. *A History of the Los Angeles Labor Movement, 1911–1941.* Los Angeles: University of California Press, 1963.

Pitt, Leonard. *The Decline of the Californios: A Social History of the Spanish-Speaking Californians, 1846–1890.* Berkeley and Los Angeles: University of California Press, 1970.

Preston, William, Jr. *Aliens and Dissenters: Federal Suppression of Radicals, 1903–1933.* Cambridge, Mass.: Harvard University Press, 1963.

Pringle, Henry F. *Theodore Roosevelt: A Biography.* New York: Harcourt Brace Jovanovich, 1955.

Putzel, Max. *The Man in the Mirror: William Marion Reedy and His Magazine.* Westport, Conn.: Greenwood Press, 1963.

Ravitz, Abe C. *Clarence Darrow and the American Literary Tradition.* Cleveland: The Press of Western Reserve University, 1962.

Renshaw, Patrick. *The Wobblies: The Story of Syndicalism in the United States.* Garden City, N.Y.: Doubleday & Company, 1967.

Robinson, W. W. *Bombs and Bribery*. Los Angeles: Dawson's Book Shop, 1969.

————. *Lawyers of Los Angeles: A History of the Los Angeles Bar Association and of the Bar of Los Angeles County*. Los Angeles: Los Angeles Bar Association, 1959.

Rolle, Andrew. *Los Angeles: From Pueblo to City of the Future*. San Francisco: Boyd and Fraser Publishing Company, 1981.

Roosevelt, Theodore. *Theodore Roosevelt: A Biography*. New York: Charles Scribner's Sons, 1913.

Rosenstone, Robert A. *Romantic Revolutionary: A Biography of John Reed*. Cambridge, Mass., and London: Harvard University Press, 1975.

Rudnick, Lois Palken. *Mable Dodge Luhan: New Woman, New Worlds*. Albuquerque, N.M.: University of Mexico Press, 1984.

Russell, Charles Edward. *Bare Hands and Stone Walls: Some Recollections of a Side-Line Reformer*. New York: Charles Scribner's Sons, 1933.

Russell, Francis. *The Unresolved Case of Sacco & Vanzetti*. New York: Harper and Row, 1986.

St. Johns, Adela Rogers. *Final Verdict*. Garden City, N.Y.: Doubleday & Company, 1962.

————. *The Honeycomb*. Garden City, N.Y.: Doubleday and Company, 1969.

Schore, Elliot. *Talkin' Socialism: J. A. Wayland and the Role of the Press in American Radicalism, 1890–1912.* University Press of Kansas, 1988.

Scripps, E. W.. *Damned Old Crank: A Self-Portrait of E. W. Scripps*. Charles R. McCabe, ed. New York: Harper & Brothers, 1951.

————. *I Protest: Selected Disquisitions of E. W. Scripps*. Edited with a biographical introduction by Oliver Knight. Madison, Wisconsin: The University of Wisconsin Press, 1966.

Shoaf, George. *Fighting for Freedom*. Kansas City, Mo.: Simplified Economics, 1953.

Smith, Page. *The Rise of Industrial America: A People's History of the Post-Reconstruction Era, Volume Six*. New York: McGraw-Hill Book Company, 1984.

———. *America Enters the World: A People's History of the Progressive Era and World War I, Volume Seven*. New York: McGraw-Hill Book Company, 1985.

Starr, Kevin. *Americans and the California Dream, 1850–1915*. New York and Oxford: Oxford University Press, 1973.

———. *Inventing the Dream: California Through the Progressive Era*. New York and Oxford: Oxford University Press, 1985.

———. *Material Dreams: Southern California through the 1920's*. New York and Oxford: Oxford University Press, 1990.

Steel, Ronald. *Walter Lippman and the American Century*. Boston: Atlantic Monthly Press/Little Brown and Company, 1980.

Steffens, Lincoln. *The Autobiography of Lincoln Steffens*. New York: Harcourt, Brace and Company, 1931.

———. *Lincoln Steffens Speaking*. New York: Harcourt, Brace and Company, 1936.

———. *The Letters of Lincoln Steffens*. Edited with introductory notes by Ella Winter and Granville Hicks. New York: Harcourt, Brace & Company, 1938.

———. *The World of Lincoln Steffens*. Ella Winter and Herbert Shapiro, eds. New York: Hill and Wang, 1962.

Stein, Leon. *The Triangle Fire*. New York: Carrol and Graft/Quicksilver, 1985.

Stimson, Grace Heilman. *Rise of the Labor Movement in Los Angeles*. Berkeley and Los Angeles: University of California Press, 1955.

Stone, Irving. *Clarence Darrow for the Defense*. Garden City, New York: Doubleday, Doran & Company, 1941.

Sullivan, Mark. *Our Times in the United States (1900–1925) II: America Finding Herself.* New York and London: Charles Scribner's Sons, 1927.

————. *Our Times in the United States (1900–1925) III: Pre-War America.* New York and London: Charles Scribner's Sons, 1930.

————. *Our Times in the United States (1900–1925) IV: The War Begins (1909–1914).* New York and London: Charles Scribner's Sons, 1932.

Swanberg, W. A.. *Citizen Hearst: A Biography of William Randolph Hearst.* New York: Charles Scribner's Sons, 1961.

Tichenor, Henry M. *A Wave of Horror: A Comparative Picture of the Los Angeles Tragedy.* St. Louis: Rip Saw Publishing, 1911.

Tierney, Kevin. *Darrow: A Biography.* New York: Thomas Y. Crowell, 1979.

Turner, Ethel Duffy. *Revolution in Baja California: Ricardo Flores Magnon's High Noon.* Detroit: Blaine Ethridge Books, 1981.

Watkins, T. H. *Righteous Pilgrim: The Life and Times of Harold Ickes, 1874–1952.* New York: Henry Holt and Company, 1990.

Weaver, John. *L.A. El Pueblo Grande: Los Angeles From the Brush Huts of Yangna to the Skyscrapers of the Modern Megalopolis.* Pasadena, California: The Ward Ritchie Press, 1973.

Weinberg, Arthur, and Lila Weinberg. *Clarence Darrow: A Sentimental Rebel.* New York: G.P. Putnam's Sons, 1980.

Weinstein, James. *The Decline of Socialism in America, 1912–1925.* New Brunswick, N.J.: Rutgers University Press, 1984.

Weintraub, Hyman. *Andrew Furuseth: Emancipator of the Seamen.* Berkeley and Los Angeles: University of California Press, 1959.

Wertheim, Arthur Frank. *The New York Little Renaissance: Iconoclasm, Modernism, and Nationalism in American Culture, 1908–1917.* New York: New York University Press, 1976.

Wexler, Alice. *Emma Goldman in America.* Boston: Beacon Press, 1984.

White, John H. *The American Railroad Passenger Car.* Baltimore: John Hopkins University Press, 1978.

White, William Allen. *The Autobiography of William Allen White.* New York: The Macmillan Company, 1946.

Whitlock, Brand. *The Letters and Journals of Brand Whitlock: The Letters.* Chosen and edited with a biographical introduction by Allan Nevins. New York and London: D. Appleton-Century, 1936.

—————. *Forty Years of It.* New York: D. Appleton and Company, 1914.

Wiebe, Robert H. *The Search for Order, 1877–1920.* New York: Hill and Wang, 1967.

Wood, Charles Erskine Scott. *Earthly Discourse,* New York: Vanguard Press, 1937.

—————. *The Poet in the Desert.* Portland, Oregon: Press of F. W. Baltes and Company, 1918.

Wright, Theon. *Rape in Paradise.* Honolulu: Mutual Publishing, 1966.

Yarrow, Victor S. *My 11 Years with Clarence Darrow.* Girard, Kansas. Haldeman-Julius Publications, 1950.

Yeslah, M. D. *A Tenderfoot in Southern California.* New York: J. J. Little and Ives Co., 1908.

SELECTED ARTICLES

Burns, William J. "My Greatest Cases—No. 10: Solving the *Los Angeles Times* Holocaust." *True Detective Magazine* (October 1931, January 1932).

Burns, William J., and Samuel Gompers (interviews). "Gompers and Burns on Unionism and Dynamite." *McClures's Magazine* (February 1912).

Connolly, C. P. "The Saving of Clarence Darrow." *Collier's* (December 23, 1911).

———. "The Trial at Los Angeles." *Collier's* (October 14, 1911).

Darrow, Clarence. "If Men Had Opportunity" (a reprint of Darrow's speech on Labor Day, 1912). *Everyman* (January–February 1915).

———. "The Late Election." *The Mirror* (November 17, 1910).

———. "Second Plea of Clarence Darrow." *Everyman* (May 1913).

———. "Why Men Fight for the Closed Shop." *American Magazine* (September 11, 1911).

Debs, Eugene. "The McNamara Case and the Labor Movement." International Socialist Review (February 1912).

Deering, Mabel Craft. "The Women's Demonstration." *Collier's* (January 1912).

"E. T. Earl: The Real Leader." *Out West* (February 1911).

Field, Mary. "On Strike." The American Magazine (1911).

Fine, Sidney. "The National Erectors Association and the Dynamiters." *Labor History* (Winter 1991).

Freebey, M.P. "How and Why We Won Our Freedom." *Among Ourselves* (December 1931).

Ginger, Ray. "Clarence Seward Darrow, 1857–1938." *Antioch Review* (spring 1953).

Groff, Frances A. "A Philosopher at Large—Charles Erskine Scott Wood." *Sunset* (January 1912).

Holt, Henry. "A Foreign Tour At Home—Los Angeles." *Putnam's Monthly* (May 1908).

Hoffman, Abraham. "The Los Angeles Aqueduct Investigation Board of 1912: A Reappraisal." *Southern California Quarterly* (Winter 1980).

Hustvedt, Lloyd. "O. A. Tvietmoe: Labor Leader." *Norwegian-American Studies* 30 (1985).

Huxley, Aldous. "Ozymandias: The Utopia that Failed." *Fortnight* (April 27, 1953).

James, George Whartron. "Los Angeles, A Moral City." *Out West* (March–April 1913).

Kraft, James P. "The Fall of Job Harriman's Socialist Party: Violence, Gender and Politics in Los Angeles, 1911." *Southern California Quarterly* (spring 1988).

Langlois, Karen S. "Mary Austin and Lincoln Steffens." *Huntington Library Quarterly,* 49: 357–384 (1986).

Lawler, Oscar. "The Bombing of the *Los Angeles Times:* A Personal Reminiscence." *Claremont Quarterly* (winter 1959).

Lowell, Esther. "California Prefers Hanging." *New Masses* (May 1931).

McCarthy, Michael P. "Prelude to Armageddon: Charles E. Merriam and the Chicago Mayoral Election of 1911." *Journal of the Illinois State Historical Society* (November 1974).

MacFarlane, Peter Clark. "What is the Matter with Los Angeles." *Collier's* (December 2, 1911).

"A Militant Editor-General, Harrison Gray Otis." *Sunset* (June 1911).

Mosk, Edward. "Darrow on Trial." *California Lawyer* (March 1983).

O'Day, Edward F. "Clarence Darrow." *Town Talk* (June 1, 1912).

Otis, Harrison Gray. "Los Angeles—A Sketch." *Sunset* (January 1909).

Palmer, Frederick. "Otistown of the Open Shop." *Hampton's Magazine* (January 1911).

Parker, Jacqueline K. "Clarence Seward Darrow, 1857–1938." collected in Robert Muccigross, ed., *Research Guides in American History,* Beacham, 1988.

Russell, Phillips. "The Class Struggle on the Pacific Coast—An Interview with O. A. Tvietmoe." *International Socialist Review* (September 1912).

Shapiro, Herbert. "The McNamara Case: A Crisis of the Progressive Era." *Southern California Quarterly* (fall 1977).

————. "The McNamara Case: A Window on Class Antagonism in the Progressive Era." *Southern California Quarterly* (spring 1988).

Sherwin, Louis. "The Walrus of Moron-Land." *The American Mercury* (February 1928).

Shoaf, George. "Clarence Darrow and the McNamara Case." *American Socialist* (December 1957).

Steele, Rufus. "The Little Red Car of Empire." *Sunset* (October 1913).

Steffens, Lincoln. "Attorney for the Damned." [Review of Darrow's *Story of My Life.*] *Saturday Review of Literature* (February 27, 1932).

————. "Explosion of the McNamara Cases." Reprint of newspaper dispatches dated December 2, December 4, December 5, December 6, December 7, and December 27, 1911. (Available through Lissner Collection, Stanford University Library.)

Survey Symposium. "Many Viewpoints on the McNamara Case." *Survey* (December 9, 1911).

Unionist. "The Los Angeles Conspiracy Against Organized Labor." *International Socialist Review* (November 1910).

Weyer, Sister M. Anita. "Joseph Scott: A Life of Service." *Southern California Quarterly* (September 1966).

Woehlke, Walter. "The End of the Dynamite Case—'Guilty.' " *The Outlook* (December 16, 1911).

————. "Los Angeles—Homeland." *Sunset* (January 1911).

————. "Angels in Overalls." *Sunset* (January 1912).

Works, John D. "The Political Regeneration of California." *Twentieth Century Magazine* (August 1911).

Wright, Willard Huntington. "Los Angeles—The Chemically Pure." *Smart Set* (1913).

NEWSPAPERS AND PERIODICALS

American Federationist

Appeal to Reason

The *Bridgeman's Magazine*

The Carpenter

Current Literature, June, 1907; July, 1907; August, 1907.

Chicago Tribune

The Graphic

Hanford, California, *Journal,* November 1911–May 1912

Indianapolis Labor Bulletin, April–May 1911

Indianapolis Star, April–May 1911

Indianapolis Union, April–May 1911

Kankakee Journal, April–May 1911

Kankakee Republican, April–May 1911

Los Angeles Examiner, 1910–1913

Los Angeles *Express,* 1910–1913

Los Angeles *Herald,* 1910–1913

Los Angeles *Tribune,* 1910–1913

Miners Journal

Mother Earth

The New York Times, 1910–1913

New York World

Organized Labor

The Outlook

The Progressive Woman

San Francisco *Bulletin*

San Francisco Chronicle

San Francisco Examiner

The Typographical Journal

INDEX